Group
1:30 Wednesdays
1:30 - 3:00
come @ 1:00 tomorrow
" Tayo's group
1st

www.wadsworth.com

wadsworth.com **is the World Wide Web site for Wadsworth and is your direct source to dozens of online resources.**

At *wadsworth.com* you can find out about supplements, demonstration software, and student resources. You can also send e-mail to many of our authors and preview new publications and exciting new technologies.

wadsworth.com

Changing the way the world learns®

Chapter 1
due the 17th

Gerontological Social Work
Knowledge, Service Settings, and Special Populations

Second Edition

Robert L. Schneider
Virginia Commonwealth University

Nancy P. Kropf
University of Georgia

Anne J. Kisor
Virginia Commonwealth University

Brooks/Cole
Thomson Learning™

Australia • Canada • Mexico • Singapore • Spain • United Kingdom • United States

Executive Editor: Lisa Gebo
Assistant Editor: Susan Wilson
Editorial Assistant: Joanne von Zastrow
Marketing Manager: Caroline Concilla
Marketing Assistant: Jessica McFadden
Project Editor: Pam Suwinsky
Print Buyer: Barbara Britton
Permissions Editor: Bob Kauser

Production Service: Graphic World
    Publishing Services
Copy Editor: Dorothy Anderson
Cover Designer: Bill Stanton
Cover Image: Photodisc
Cover Printer: Webcom
Printer: Webcom

Printed in Canada
2 3 4 5 6 7 03 02 01

For permission to use material from this text, contact us by
Web: http://www.thomsonrights.com
Fax: 1-800-730-2215
Phone: 1-800-730-2214

Library of Congress Cataloging-in-Publication Data

Gerontological social work / [edited by] Robert L.
Schneider, Nancy P. Kropf, Anne J. Kisor.—2nd ed.
p. cm.

Includes bibliographical references and index.

ISBN 0-534-57807-1

1. Social work with the aged—United States. 2. Gerontology—United States. I. Schneider, Robert L. (Robert
Lawrence), 1941-II. Kropf, Nancy P. III. Kisor, Anne J.

HV1461.G465 2000

362.6—dc21   99-059307

 This book is printed on acid-free recycled paper.

For more information, contact

Wadsworth/Thomson Learning
10 Davis Drive
Belmont, CA 94002-3098
USA http://www.wadsworth.com

International Headquarters
Thomson Learning
International Division
290 Harbor Drive, 2nd Floor
Stamford, CT 06902-7477
USA

UK/Europe/Middle East/South Africa
Thomson Learning
Berkshire House
168-173 High Holborn
London WC1V 7AA
United Kingdom

Asia
Thomson Learning
60 Albert Street, #15-01
Albert Complex
Singapore 189969

Canada
Nelson Thomson Learning
1120 Birchmount Road
Toronto, Ontario M1K 5G4
Canada

Contents

Contributors

Chrystal C. Ramirez Barranti, Ph.D.
Director of Continuing Education and Outreach,
School of Social Work,
University of Georgia

Joyce O. Beckett, Ph.D.
Professor, School of Social Work,
Virginia Commonwealth University

Harriet L. Cohen, LCSW
Instructor, School of Social Work,
University of Georgia

Sherry M. Cummings, Ph.D.
Assistant Professor, School of Social Work,
University of Tennessee—Nashville

Delores Dungee-Anderson, D.S.W.
Associate Professor, School of Social Work,
Virginia Commonwealth University

Rosemary L. Farmer, Ph.D.
Assistant Professor, School of Social Work,
Virginia Commonwealth University

Stephen French Gilson, Ph.D.
Associate Professor, School of Social Work,
Virginia Commonwealth University

Marcia P. Harrigan, Ph.D.
Associate Professor and Director, MSW Program,
School of Social Work,
Virginia Commonwealth University

Elizabeth D. Hutchison, Ph.D.
Associate Professor, School of Social Work,
Virginia Commonwealth University

Deborah R. Jackson
Director of Planning and Research,
Randolph Community College

Anne J. Kisor, Ph.D.
Curriculum Development Specialist
and Adjunct Faculty,
School of Social Work,
Virginia Commonwealth University

Nancy P. Kropf, Ph.D.
Associate Professor and Associate Dean,
School of Social Work,
University of Georgia

Edward A. McSweeney, Ph.D.
Associate Professor, School of Social Work,
Virginia Commonwealth University
(deceased)

Margaret M. Robinson, Ph.D.
Assistant Professor, School of Social Work,
University of Georgia

Robert L. Schneider, D.S.W.
Professor, School of Social Work,
Virginia Commonwealth University

Michael J. Sheridan, Ph.D.
Associate Professor, School of Social Work,
Virginia Commonwealth University

Stephen D. Stahlman
Professor and Director,
Department of Social Work
Indiana Wesleyan University

Ellen J. Stevens, MSW
Doctoral Candidate, School of Social Work,
Virginia Commonwealth University

Etty Vandsburger, MSW
Doctoral Candidate, School of Social Work,
Virginia Commonwealth University

Introduction

The demand for social work services in the field of aging will increase through the year 2020 (Klein 1998, p. 220). The editors used similar prophetic words in the first edition (1992) of *Gerontological Social Work: Knowledge, Service Settings, and Special Populations*, hoping that programs of social work education would respond by adding and integrating content on aging into curricula and coursework for all social work students. Repeating this premonition in this second edition, we believe that there is still a considerable gap between providing sufficient gerontological education and producing knowledgeable social workers trained to deliver services to a growing population of older persons.

Of utmost importance are the demographics of the population in the United States. In 1999 there are more than 30 million Americans in the sixty-five and older cohort, with a projection to increase to 54 million by the year 2025 (Klein 1998). This is a percentage change from approximately 12 percent to 20 percent of the U.S. population (Taeuber 1993). Remarkably, there are contradictory findings among practicing social workers in light of these data. While only 4.2 percent of the National Association of Social Workers (NASW) members identify aging as their primary practice area (Gibelman and Schervish 1993), Peterson and Wendt (1990) identified 62 percent of NASW members stating the need for gerontological knowledge in their current practice. Linked to these developments is evidence that gerontological social work is alleged to be one of the fastest growing job markets in the United States (*U.S. News and World Report* 1995).

Nevertheless, Damron-Rodriguez, Villa, Tseng, & Lubben (1996) found that only 10 percent of social work students had taken even a single course in aging. Dawson and Santos (1996) found that social work educators asserted more strongly than other professions (medicine, nursing, and psychology) that there was a lack of institutional and departmental support for aging curricula. Seventy-five percent of the schools reported that they had no gerontological field faculty (Damron-Rodriguez et al. 1996). Lubben, Damron-Rodriguez, and Beck (1992) found that 80 percent of BSW programs provided no course work in aging.

While there has been a very modest increase in the MSW programs (39 percent offering specialized concentrations in aging (Damron-Rodriguez & Lubben 1994), only 5 percent of graduating MSW students have taken a course in gerontological social work (Klein 1998). The inescapable conclusion is that schools are still not "adequately preparing the numbers of professionals needed to serve the current and future aging population," and much work remains to be done (Damron-Rodriguez and Lubben 1997; Klein 1998).

But, the landscape is not without its sunrises, and we believe that there is a blueprint for social work educators to follow for the next ten years. Three resources are readily available: (1) the Association for Gerontological Education in Social Work (AGE-SW), a group of educators who since 1981 have committed themselves to leading the development of gerontological courses and curricula in programs across the country; (2) emphases about geriatric education and training from the 1995 White House Conference on Aging; and (3) a report called A National Agenda for Geriatric Education: White Papers, published by the USDHHS Health Resources and Services Administration in 1998. These resources can serve as guideposts to the profession in the new millennium. In brief, here is a sampling of issues raised recently that address the concerns mentioned earlier.

From the 1995 White House Conference on Aging, we point to the following emphases:

■ Social work education should include study of policy issues, including Medicare/Medicaid and the Older Americans Act.
■ The knowledge base of social workers should include the service continuum from home/community-based services to long-term care, financing, eligibility, and accessibility issues.
■ A focus on empowering older persons should be a part of education and training (Damron-Rodriquez and Lubben 1997; Saltz, 1997).

In the report, A National Agenda for Geriatric Education: White Papers, Klein (1998) suggests promoting the following:

■ Integration of aging content into all accredited programs of social work.
■ Preparation of social workers to practice in interdisciplinary settings.
■ Provision of post-graduation education in gerontology for social workers.
■ Establishment of leadership and research "centers of excellence" at key universities with geriatric resources.

All social work educators who are involved in gerontological social work education are urged to become members of the AGE-SW. This association publishes a newsletter, coordinates presentations at national conferences, provides leadership at planning meetings, and has a national e-mail network to keep members informed on news about opportunities in gerontology in social work. We encourage readers to use these resources steadfastly and consistently, because our energies should be spent on implementation, not on developing new plans, at least not for the next several years. With the vision provided by these resources, social work educators can advance the profession's mission and the goal of providing a well-prepared work force of gerontological social workers. This revised edition will complement the resources by providing a balanced coverage of important gerontological social work content and perspectives.

In 1998, the John A. Hartford Foundation committed $5.4 million for four years to the professional education of gerontological social workers. There are three components: (1) a geriatric field practicum development program which aims at strengthening the comprehensive training of MSW students; (2) a geriatric social work faculty scholars program that will identify ten outstanding young social work faculty committed to teaching, research, and leadership in the area of geriatric care; and (3) the development of standards and best practices for geriatric social work undergraduate and graduate education. This initiative is unprecedented in gerontological social work education and its impact in the next decade should be felt by students, faculty, field agencies, and practitioners alike.

This text is divided into three parts. Chapters 1 through 4 provide an overview of gerontological social work practice and complement the traditional structure of the social work curriculum. Principles of practice, application of research, and formulations of policies are discussed from a gerontological perspective. Chapters 5 through 8 focus on specific functions and on settings where social workers practice. The case management chapter has been completely revised. Along with the chapters on discharge planning and nursing home practice, these three chapters provide an emphasis on the *role* of the social worker. Chapters 9 through 12 provide insight into "special populations" that are identified as especially vulnerable: aging women, aging persons of color, the disabled elderly, and gay and lesbian aged. The latter two chapters are new additions to the book, written in recognition of diversity in the experience of aging.

Each chapter has a variety of suggestions and special aids for the faculty and students. There is an introduction, discussion questions, learning activities, and an annotated bibliography. In order to promote a practice-learning experience, each chapter has case vignettes which can be used to illustrate practice principles and the role of the social worker. Appendix B contains a guide to using the case vignettes.

We owe thanks to a number of persons:

■ Dean Frank Baskind of Virginia Commonwealth University School of Social Work and Dean Bonnie L. Yegidis of The University of Georgia School of Social Work, who supported the editors in many ways and provided resources required to complete the new edition.

■ The authors of each chapter who achieved their revisions with hard work and new ideas, and who accepted the editors' requests or suggestions with goodwill and humor.

■ Our publisher, Wadsworth, for their confidence in republishing our book in an increasingly competitive market for gerontological texts.

We hope that students will use these twelve chapters as a resource in their education in gerontological social work practice as the profession enters a period of uncharted waters. We know for certain that there will be great growth in the next decade and thereafter. If our book advances the capacity of social workers to serve the elderly, we believe that we will have contributed to the quality of life and care of older persons.

Robert L. Schneider
Nancy P. Kropf
Anne J. Kisor

References

Damron-Rodriguez, J. A., & Lubben, J. E. (1994). Multidisciplinary factors in gerontological curriculum adoption in schools of social work. *Gerontology and Geriatrics Education, 14*, 39–52.

Damron-Rodriguez, J. A. & Lubben, J. E. (1997). The 1995 WHCoA: an agenda for social education and training. *Journal of Gerontological Social Work, 27*, 65–71.

Damron-Rodriguez, J. A., Villa, V., Tseng, H. F., & Lubben, J. E. (1996). Demographic and organizational influences on the development of gerontological social work curriculum. *Gerontology & Geriatrics Education, 17*, 3–8.

Dawson, G. D., & Santos, J. F. (1996). National survey: Funding for geriatric health and mental health care trainers. Presentation at the Annual Meeting of the Association for Gerontology in Higher Education in Philadelphia, PA.

Gibelman, M., & Schervish, P. H. (1994). *Who we are: The social work labor force as reflected in NASW membership*. Washington, DC: NASW Press.

Klein, S. M. (1998). *A national agenda for geriatric education: White papers (Vol. 1)*. Health Resources and Services Administration, Bureau of Health Professions. Washington, DC: U.S. Government Printing Office.

Lubben, J. E., Damron-Rodriguez, J. A., & Beck, J. C. (1992). A national survey of aging curriculum in schools of social work. In Mellor, J. & Solomon, R., *Geriatric social work education*. Binghamton, NY: Haworth Press.

Peterson, D. A. & Wendt, P. F. (1990). Employment in the field of aging: A survey of professionals in four fields. *The Gerontologist, 30,* 679–685.

Saltz, C. C. (1997). *Social work response to the White House Conference on Aging: from issues to actions*. NY: Haworth Press.

Taeuber, C. M. (1993). *Sixty-five plus in America*. (U. S Bureau of the Census, Current Population Reports, Special Studies, P23-178 RV). Washington, DC: U.S. Government Printing Office.

U.S. News and World Report. (1995). Twenty hot job tracks. October 98, p. 108.

I Knowledge

1 Effective Practice with Elderly Clients

■■■■■■■■■■■■■■■

Nancy P. Kropf and Elizabeth D. Hutchison

Social workers are serving more elderly clients than ever before. Elderly adults are a diverse population, presenting a wide range of practice needs and social issues. Social workers encounter two general types of elderly clients. One group, older people with developmental disabilities, have used social services at earlier life stages and continue to use services into their later life. The second type of elderly client seeks a practitioner's help for conditions associated with the aging process. An example is the older person who requires assistance with household maintenance because of physical disabilities associated with aging. Both types of clients have similarities to younger clients. However, the unique aspects of aging must be understood if social work practice with older clients is to be effective.

Elderly clients have the same rights as any other clients. They have the right to participate in decisions affecting themselves and their families. These elderly clients also have the right to sensitive and ethical practice that preserves the greatest autonomy. Older clients also have the right to receive treatment that has been supported by empirical research such as evaluation of programs and practice outcomes (Saltz & Kropf 1998). Practitioners should be aware that they will encounter older clients requiring different levels of assistance, and that interventions with the well older adult, for example, are different from those practiced with the more frail. Social workers assisting older adults at any level of impairment can take measures to ensure that older clients and their families remain as healthy and functional as long as possible.

In an article celebrating 1999, the International Year of Older Persons, Galambos and Rosen (1999) stress that the five principles of independence, participation, care, self-fulfillment, and dignity need to guide practice in health care for older adults. As a gentle reminder that we all have a stake in effective practice with older adults, these authors aptly titled their article, "The aging are coming and they are us."

Levels of Intervention

Elderly people are possibly the most diverse group of clients with whom social workers will practice. Due to unique experiences and lifestyle patterns, older people differ more widely from one another than do younger cohorts (Zarit 1980). Since people bring into their later years a wealth of experiences, varying health conditions, and differing attitudes, behavior and levels of functioning are different between people of similar ages. In addition to these individual variations in lifestyle patterns, older adults demonstrate great variability in their levels of functional impairment associated with the process of aging.

Many older people benefit from involvement in some type of social program. Healthy older adults may need assistance in maintaining their health, such as making sure they eat well-balanced meals, exercise, and comply with drug prescriptions. The more impaired older adults may require assistance in containing any problematic condition. This may entail modifying dietary habits after being diagnosed as diabetic. Severely impaired older adults and their caregivers also may benefit from social work services, such as an Alzheimer's support group. These different needs form a continuum for social work practice with elderly clients, and three levels of interventions are proposed: primary, secondary and tertiary (Beaver & Miller 1985).

Primary

Many older people lead active and enriching lives. They derive satisfaction from their activities and interactions with others. Although these people maintain high levels of functioning, social work interventions can frequently benefit them. Practice with clients in this group constitutes primary intervention.

The goal of primary intervention is to prevent problems from occurring. Practice at this level attempts to keep older people as physically, socially, and emotionally healthy as possible. Primary prevention includes different activities which promote the health and wellness of older adults. One type of activity is a health promotion campaign. These programs are directed to older adults in general and seek to increase the overall health of this group. A second type of activity is a specific protection plan aimed at a particular high-risk group (Beaver & Miller 1985). The goal of both types of activities is to decrease the probability that older adults will experience a health-threatening event.

Health promotion campaigns can take two forms. One type attempts to keep people well by increasing good health habits. For example, such programs will help older people prepare low-budget nutritional meals or teach aerobic exercises. Programs also address the social needs of older people by sponsoring outings or gatherings. A second health promotion strategy attempts to decrease the threat of a problem occurring. An example of this strategy is teaching persons how to accident-proof a house. For example, the SAFE (Study of Accidental Falls in the Elderly) project was designed to prevent in-home falls by providing older adults with information, physical conditioning programs, and in-home risk assessments (Hornbrook, Stevens, Wingfield, Hollis, Greenlick, & Ory 1994). Home visits were conducted to assess hazards and participants were involved in fall prevention classes for four weeks. Results indicated that participants in this program decreased their odds of falling, compared to another group of older adults who were not part of this program. A well-rounded health promotion campaign covers both increasing good health habits and minimizing risk behaviors in order to promote healthy living.

The second type of primary intervention is specific protection for a particular group. Certain segments of the older population are at risk of problematic conditions, and protection strategies are aimed at those people who are particularly susceptible. For example, alcoholics are a high-risk group for many health and social problems. Unfortunately, awareness of alcohol abuse in the older population is low. An alcohol awareness program was offered to service providers, older adults, and their families to educate and to increase understanding of this problem (Coogle, Osgood, Pyles, & Wood 1995). Each session lasted two hours and presented specific content on alcohol and older adults. In an evaluation study, 1036 individuals attended one of these sessions, and demonstrated an increased awareness of addiction and alcohol abuse in the older population. Besides physiological problems, certain social problems are preventable. For example, one study on crime and older adults reports that older people have a greater fear of victimization when living in high crime neighborhoods (Ryder & Janson 1983). These fears echo realistic, not paranoid, concerns of victimization. Specific protection strategies for this group may include education about neighborhood areas to avoid, methods for crime-proofing a home and supplying phone numbers for emergency services.

Secondary

Secondary intervention begins with the onset of a problem. These interventions target early diagnosis and prompt treatment of a condition (Beaver & Miller 1985). This level of practice is aimed toward older persons who have started to manifest a problematic condition. An attempt is made to keep an acute problem from becoming chronic. The major emphasis of secondary intervention is to resolve problems to the greatest extent possible or to prevent more serious functional impairment from occurring (Beaver & Miller 1985).

Some problems facing older people are physical health concerns. Older adults tend to have lower rates of *acute* (temporary) health conditions (such as the common cold) than younger cohorts. Although these ailments are contracted by fewer older adults, those who are infected may experience more severe symptoms and outcomes than younger adults (Wacker, Roberto, & Piper 1998). For example, Hooyman & Kiyak (1996) report that death rates from respiratory problems are 30 percent in the elderly. In addition, *chronic* (longer term or permanent) conditions are higher in the older population. The National Center for Health Statistics (1990) reports that more than 80 percent of the population over age sixty-five has at least one chronic condition. Some of the more frequent ones are arthritis, hypertension, osteoporosis, incontinence, and visual/auditory impairments. Although chronic conditions do not necessarily lead to functional impairments, they can worsen without proper attention and treatment. An example of a secondary health intervention is an arthritis self-management program (Lorig, Laurin, & Holman 1984). This program teaches people afflicted with arthritis about the disease process, pain management, and community services which may be helpful.

During the aging process, a person often experiences losses without adequate chance for substitution. Multiple and cumulative losses can lead to depression, the most common mental health problem of older adults (Zarit 1980). Untreated depression can lead to numerous life-threatening problems, such as malnutrition, alcohol abuse, or suicide attempts. Relocation to a nursing home is a traumatic event for both the older adult and his or her family. Without support, a new resident can be disoriented, angry, confused, and depressed. This situation can lead to withdrawal and social isolation, possibly leading to other serious illnesses and death. In addition, families often experience guilt and depression that accompanies the decision to have the older person move to a long-term care facility. Both individual and group interventions have been found to help decrease anxiety and stress in nursing home residents (Dhooper, Green, Huff, & Austin-Murphy 1993; Rapp, Mayo, Cole, Shires, Williams, Fowler, & Steen 1989). In addition, support groups for care providers can be beneficial in helping families make these decisions and adjust after the relocation to the nursing home (Chiverton & Caine 1989; Mittelman, Ferris, Shulman, Steinberg, Ambinder, Mackell, & Cohen 1995).

Elderly people also encounter social problems. Loneliness and isolation affect older adults as social opportunities and resources decrease. While many older adults value their privacy, a lack of satisfying interactions can lead to serious physical and psychological problems.

Retirement is an event which many people joyfully anticipate. However, successful retirement requires economic and social planning to fill areas once covered through employment. When people retire without plans for leisure time, feeling of purposelessness and unconnectedness can develop. Effective planning and developing of leisure activities help people make a transition into new and satisfying roles (MacNeil & Teague 1992; Osgood 1982). Another area where older adults may struggle with social transitions is with relocation or immigration. These changes include a loss of cultural connections, disruption of social networks, and a feeling of isolation (Kropf, Nackerud, & Gorokhousky 1999). With these levels of transitions, social workers can help facilitate adjustment of both the family as a system, and the older adults.

Tertiary

The tertiary level of practice is targeted toward older adults. Tertiary interventions include both disability limitations and rehabilitation activities. Practice at this level assumes that severe functional or behavioral problems are present. The problems that clients experience are more severe than those at a secondary intervention level.

The goal of tertiary intervention is to ameliorate the effects of dysfunctional conditions and help clients regain as much functioning as possible (Beaver & Miller 1985). Social work at this level involves both the older individuals and their caregivers. The majority of functionally impaired older adults receive support from their families. We know that many families continue to provide care for a disabled member even when the person is greatly impaired (Shanas 1979; Virginia Long-Term Care Council 1985). Friends, neighbors, and formal agencies also supplement care provided by the family (Cantor 1985). However, some functionally impaired older adults live in long-term care facilities. Tertiary social work practice involves work with older adults in the community as well as in institutions.

When a severe functional impairment is present, tertiary interventions are required. For example, dementia is a type of organic brain syndrome, the most common type being Alzheimer's disease. Accompanying symptoms include memory loss, disorientation, speech difficulties and inability to perform activities of daily living. Providing care to someone with dementia is a stressful task. Support groups are effective methods of helping caregivers deal with the consequences of this illness. Groups have been used to assist caregivers with information about the disease process, linkage to other services and an opportunity for venting frustration about the caregiving role (Chiverton & Caine 1989). Although there are currently no cures for Alzheimer's disease, support services can assist both clients and caregivers.

Elderly people who have severe behavioral deficits or dysfunctions are also found in institutional settings such as hospitals, psychiatric facilities, or nursing homes. Clients residing in these facilities require interventions to enable them to maintain as much autonomy as possible. One strategy for nursing home residents is to encourage participation in a council which represents all residents and acts to assure that their opinions about facility operation are heard. Resident councils provide several basic functions for older adults who live in long-term care facilities (Meyer 1991). These include: making modest changes in care or the facility (e.g., menus, length of visitation), providing services to other residents or the community (e.g., making handcrafted items to sell), providing social outlets for residents (e.g., planning ethnic celebrations), and interacting with resident councils from other long-term care facilities. Tertiary interventions also include work with families of residents of long-term care facilities. Four crisis points have been identified for families with a member in a nursing home: considering admission, actual entry, movement to a more intensive level of care, and death (Solomon 1982). Social workers often help families cope with the emotional issues at each of these transition points.

In summary, social work practice with older adults encompasses many different individuals, groups, and practice settings. Helping older adults maintain healthy lifestyles entails different interventions from those strategies used to assist families of frail older adults. Social work practice can be viewed as a continuum that includes primary, secondary, and tertiary intervention strategies which enable practitioners to choose from a wide range of practice methods in working with older clients.

Interventive Roles

The social work practice literature includes concepts from role theory that are often used to focus attention on the nature of the professional–client relationship and to guide decisions about appropriate interventive strategies (Davis 1986). In one practice textbook, Connaway and Gentry (1988) define social work practice as "a constellation of social worker role sets" (p. 3) and use interventive roles as a framework for organizing practice.

Compton and Galaway (1994) define an interventive role as a set of behaviors which both client and practitioner expect the practitioner to perform in an effort to fulfill the goals of the service contract. The interventive roles help practitioners decide what specific actions to take in assisting clients. The interventive roles are defined in a general way and are applicable to work with various client systems. These roles are performed in practice with individuals, families, groups, and communities.

The essence of the interventive roles lies in the relationship between client and practitioner. With older clients, as with clients of all ages, the professional relationship is purposeful, client oriented, and guided by self-awareness of the practitioner (Pincus & Minahan 1973). The purpose of engaging in a relationship is to assist clients in reaching service goals, not in furthering the practitioner's personal or professional gain. While undertaking interventive roles, practitioners will also interact with systems external to the client, such as the client's family, agency colleagues, and staff of other community agencies. Keeping in mind the purpose of assuming different interventive roles helps practitioners with the decision about which roles to use with a particular client.

Compton and Galaway (1994) define five different interventive roles: broker, enabler, teacher, mediator and advocate. Each role has different purposes with a client. All five roles can be used with any size client system from individual work to community practice. Similarly, these roles can be undertaken at any practice level from primary to tertiary. The following section defines each of the interventive roles, and gives examples of social work on all practice levels and with all types of client systems.

Broker

When performing as a broker, a practitioner assesses both client needs and environmental resources. The goal of the broker is to link clients to existing resources which can best meet their needs. Effective performance of this role requires an understanding of client needs and resources as well as a thorough knowledge of existing community resources. The referral process, a basic activity of a broker, includes locating appropriate resources, gathering information about receiving services, and assisting clients with service entry tasks, such as application processes. Listed below are examples of broker roles.

- *Primary:* Linking elders in a rural town to a local high school so that the community members can participate in open swim sessions or use other appropriate facilities.
- *Secondary:* Locating a nutritionist with expertise in low salt meal preparation to give a lecture series to a group of people recently diagnosed with high blood pressure.
- *Tertiary:* Matching an older caregiver of an adult with severe mental retardation to a respite service so he or she can attend weekly church services.

Enabler

In the enabler role, a social worker helps to empower clients. When performing this role, the practitioner assists a client in finding internal strengths and coping mechanisms to meet service goals. The major distinguishing element of the enabler role is that change derives from the client's efforts. The responsibility of the practitioner is to facilitate client progress toward meeting established goals. Practitioner activities include supporting clients in efforts toward change, discussing with clients the consequences of their decisions, and offering information within the clients' decision-making process. Examples of enabling roles follow.

- *Primary:* Discussing with a recently widowed woman her fears about household management, such as paying bills or basic home maintenance, and expressing confidence in her ability to assume this responsibility once she learns the necessary procedures.
- *Secondary:* Helping members of a senior citizens apartment complex located in a high crime neighborhood make decisions about how to prevent crime in their building.
- *Tertiary:* Helping a group of nursing home residents decide on strategies to approach the administrator with a proposal to lengthen visiting hours.

Advocate

Similar to the legal professional, the advocate initiates action on behalf of a client. In essence, the practitioner takes the client's side and becomes a partisan spokesperson for an individual, group, or community. Advocacy may come from within a system. For example, the nursing home social worker may advocate for a resident's right to prompt medical attention. Another type of advocacy is external to a system, such as when a social worker negotiates with a landlord about a client's eviction notice. Both types of advocacy involve assertive action on behalf of a client. Listed below are examples of an advocate role at three levels of intervention.

- *Primary:* Negotiating with the senior center staff to have better lighting installed outside a senior center to decrease possibility of an accident.

- *Secondary:* Helping an older man on Medicaid receive services needed through an alcohol treatment program.
- *Tertiary:* Meeting with elected officials about possible changes in benefits to increase coverage for home health care services for patients with Alzheimer's disease.

Teacher

Teaching involves helping people learn new knowledge or skills. The goal of the teacher is to help clients build additional skills and other resources. To help clients learn, practitioners may use various techniques, such as modeling or role playing. Teaching involves imparting information, not necessarily advice or opinions of the social worker. As with any type of learning, clients will need practice, support, and feedback in using new skills and behaviors. Three teaching roles are outlined below.

- *Primary:* Drafting a brochure on winter safety tips for distribution at a community senior center.
- *Secondary:* Instructing a group of volunteers on how to staff a telephone reassurance system for homebound older adults.
- *Tertiary:* Demonstrating basic sign language techniques for a woman with language impairments due to a stroke.

Mediator

In the role of mediator, the social work practitioner attempts to resolve conflict between a client and another system. Unlike the advocate role, a mediator remains a neutral third party and does not solely argue the case of the client. A mediator helps clarify issues and attempts to find a common ground between the parties in dispute. Important to the mediating process are certain techniques, such as keeping the focus on issues, helping identify solutions acceptable to both parties, and helping determine unrealistic demands. The following examples illustrate the mediator role.

- *Primary:* Meeting with an employer and older worker who has been threatened with losing his or her job due to personality conflicts with younger workers.
- *Secondary:* Discussing menu complaints with staff and participants of a meal delivery program.
- *Tertiary:* Meeting with two factions of a family to discuss which long-term care facility would be the best residence for their ill mother.

Practice Skills Clusters

Interventive roles provide a framework for conceptualizing strategies for practice, but the competent practitioner must be able to transform role prescriptions into action (Hepworth & Larsen 1993). Specific practice skills, sometimes referred to as competencies, must be mastered and applied appropriately to the particular client situation. Roles are explicated by specified behaviors or practice skills of social workers to assist clients with accomplishing practice goals.

The following section organizes practice skills into five clusters. These clusters are referred to as skills of engagement, assessment skills, communication skills, interviewing skills, and documentation skills. Each cluster is discussed briefly, and guidelines are presented for specialized use with older clients.

Skills of Engagement

The planned engagement of the client in a working relationship with the social worker is basic to all of social work practice. Compton and Galaway (1994) describe a professional relationship as one demonstrating concern for the client's need, commitment to the relationship, and anticipation that practitioner–client collaboration will produce some problem resolution. The practitioner also must convey respect and acceptance of the clients and empathy for their unique needs. The working relationship is enhanced by the practitioner's interested exploration of the client's view of the problem while providing legitimate support, facilitating venting, highlighting strengths, and instilling hope.

Demonstrating respect is critical for engaging older clients in a working relationship. Older people may be infantilized or addressed in a demeaning fashion by a particular tone of voice, verbal messages, or nonverbal communication. Examples of condescending behavior to older clients are abundant, for example, the nursing home activity coordinator who tries to engage a resident by asking, "Mary, of course you want to do arts and crafts. Be a dear and come join the rest of the girls." There are ways that the staff member could have demonstrated respect for the dignity of the resident. Using older clients' surnames is one strategy to convey respect for them. For example, an older client would be addressed as "Mrs. Jones" instead of "Mary." Another sign of respect is to acknowledge the life space of older clients, especially those who live in nursing homes. Making appointments with these residents, knocking on room doors before entry, and allowing as much choice as possible are nonthreatening methods of engaging older clients.

Assessment Skills

Along with building a relationship with the client, the practitioner begins to assess the client's situation. The purpose of an assessment is to understand and individualize the client's situation and to identify and analyze relevant factors within this particular situation. A thorough assessment is the foundation for making decisions about interventions with the particular client. The components of a thorough assessment include:

1. Establishing the need for which the client is seeking service,
2. Finding out the client's perception of that problem,
3. Knowing the other people involved in this situation, and
4. Having a good knowledge of the resources available within the agency and surrounding community to assist with this problem.

Assessment with older clients includes information about functioning on a variety of levels. Although social work assessment always involves physical, social, and psychological functioning, the interaction of these factors takes on special meaning when assessing elderly clients. In many situations, biophysical functioning and its interaction with psychological and social processes needs special attention.

Another important part of the assessment with older adults is the type of support that is available to the client system. Silverstone and Burack-Weiss (1983) have developed an auxiliary function model for work with frail older adults. The foundation of this model is assessing existing strengths and resources and identifying unfilled needs of the client. The role of the social worker is to provide services or referrals to fill these gaps. For example, after assessing a homebound man, a social worker establishes that the wife, neighbors and adult-children provide him with assistance in dressing, meals, and social interaction. Due to time and physical limitations, no one is able to assist the man with certain hygiene concerns, such as bathing and shaving. The social worker has the responsibility to link the client with a resource such as a home health aide to fill these needs. A thorough assessment of this man's situation guides the worker's interventions in a way to preserve the informal support system yet attend to the client's need for service.

Communication Skills

Through all phases of work with elderly clients, social work practitioners attempt to adapt communication skills to the special needs of older people. Compton and Galaway (1994) define communication as an interactive process which includes transmission of a message, reception of that message, and interpretation of content between two or more persons. Social workers, aware that you "cannot not communicate," are sensitive to the content of the messages they deliver, the symbols that receivers attach to messages, and the need to clarify messages received. As sender and as receiver, they concentrate on both verbal and nonverbal content.

When communicating verbally, the practitioner must be aware of language use with older clients. Jargon or technical words and phrases should be avoided, since these terms make many older clients uncomfortable and unresponsive. Uncomplicated and straightforward language is the most effective method of verbal communication.

Attention to nonverbal communication is equally important when working with clients. Since older people are often deprived of physical contact with others, a handshake or touch can add warmth to the communication process. Seating arrangements are another form of communication. Sitting in close proximity to an older client both aids understanding of what is being said and is a gesture of acceptance. While many people do not think of listening as part of communication, it is a crucial component. Using active listening strategies, such as reflecting back, giving feedback, and maintaining eye contact, demonstrates to the client that the social worker is invested in what is being said.

Hearing and visual impairments are conditions which increase with age. Both of these sensory changes can inhibit effective communication. Figure 1.1 illustrates some strategies in communicating with clients who experience hearing impairments. While these strategies are important with people having difficulty hearing, they make good sense when communicating with any older client. Strategies which compensate for visual loss include enlarging printed or written material, using well-lighted and brightly colored rooms for conversations, sitting close enough so the client can see faces, and using clients' names so they know when they are being addressed.

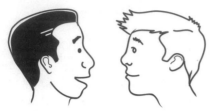

Face the hard-of-hearing person directly, and on the same level with him, whenever possible.

If you are eating, chewing, smoking, etc., while talking, your speech will be more difficult to understand.

Never talk from another room. Be sure to get the person's attention before you start speaking to him.

Keep your hands away from your face while talking.

Speak in a normal fashion without shouting. See that the light is not shining in the eyes of the hard-of-hearing person.

If a person has difficulty understanding something, find a different way of saying the same thing, rather than repeating the original words over and over.

Recognize that hard-of-hearing people hear and understand less well when they are tired or ill.

Reduce background noise when carrying on conversations—turn off the radio or TV.

■ **Figure 1.1** Communicating with Hearing Impaired Clients (Schnieder and Kroft 1987)

Interviewing Skills

Interviewing is a special form of communication used when information is needed about a specific issue or question. The practitioner uses an established relationship with the client to elicit information and to engage the client in problem-solving activities. Interviews are purposeful communication exchanges and are contrasted with casual exchanges of information or informal conversations (Compton & Galaway 1994).

To support the purposeful nature of the professional relationship, the practitioner gives direction to the helping process by developing and maintaining a focus of work. Clients are encouraged to move from abstract descriptions of situations to highly specific discussions of the current problematic situation and alternative solutions. Open-ended questions, both structured and unstructured, are used extensively to assist the client in exploration of the problem situation, and closed-ended questions to gather necessary factual information are employed sparingly near the close of the interview.

The first step in effective interviewing is preparation. Three components need attention when preparing an interview. These are:

1. Identify the problem.
   a. Know the goal of the interview.
   b. Know the basic questions to ask.
2. Know background information about the problem.
3. Plan time and setting of the interview.
   a. Consider time allotments. Will the interview be rushed?
   b. Consider setting. Is the setting quiet and private?
   c. Consider timing. Will there be interruptions?

Although some interviews will not allow for adequate preparation, practice in preparing interviews will facilitate the organization of on-the-spot, impromptu ones (Schneider & Kropf 1987).

Additional issues are important to remember when interviewing older clients. First, employ the strategies of communication with older clients, including speaking clearly and in a loud enough voice. Do not try to rush through an interview, as clients may need time to process questions and think through their responses. Second, watch for nonverbal clues, such as signs of fatigue. Since older clients may tire more easily than younger ones, the reliability of their responses may be reduced if they are fatigued. Third, be aware of consequences of a client's answers. For example, nursing home residents may be reluctant to discuss staff abuses since they will fear the consequences of disclosing this information. Fourth, use summarizing techniques, especially when terminating an interview. This strategy puts the total interview in perspective for the client. After the person has listened to the synopsis, ask if any information has been misrepresented or omitted. After all the information has been presented, let the client know how the information will be used (Schneider & Kropf 1987).

Documentation Skills

Social service agencies increasingly are being held accountable for delivering services to clients. Documentation is an important, yet dreaded, component of working with clients.

The majority of work with older clients is of an interdisciplinary nature, meaning social work is one of a number of professions involved with the case. Accurate and timely documentation is necessary to assure quality of services with clients. Social work documents must simultaneously meet the goals of accountability, efficiency, and confidentiality.

Documentation forms and procedures vary by agency. Some agencies have standardized forms, such as check lists. Other agencies require narrative summaries or histories about clients. With any documentation format, an important point is that time with clients is not the appropriate time for the writing of records. Taking time away from client issues adds to the reluctance and fear of services felt by many older clients. Older people may be particularly uncomfortable with rapid assessment instruments as they may have less experience with these protocols than younger cohorts. When working with clients, practitioners can take notes which can promptly be translated into a documentation format after the interaction is complete. Documentation has multiple purposes for clients and agencies, such as augmenting the memory of the worker, allowing collaboration with the other professionals involved with the case, and presenting data for program evaluation.

In summary, social work practice with older clients employs the basic skills of practice with any client population. However, the biopsychosocial effects of aging may necessitate modifying or adapting certain practices. The following section summarizes some barriers in providing services to older people.

Barriers to Services for the Elderly

Although many older people need mental health and social services, this group is under-represented in receiving services. Older adults comprise about 11 percent of the population, but only 3 percent of clinical psychological services are provided to people over sixty-five. Community mental health centers similarly serve few older persons, rendering about 4 percent of their services to this group (Gatz, Popkin, Pino & VandenBos 1984). Older adults are also under-represented in receiving various social services. A study on participation in a food stamp program reported that less than one-half of the eligible older adults receive benefits (Hollenbeck & Ohls 1984). Older adults from social or ethnic minorities experience even greater difficulties in accessing services (Biegel, Farkas, & Song 1997). For example, Burnette (1999) examined patterns of service use among Latino grandparents who are raising their grandchildren. Although the entire sample was connected to formal services, several barriers to services were reported, including lack of knowledge about services, high levels of stress, low education, and poor health status. An analysis of factors that produce barriers to service can be undertaken by examining the elderly clients themselves, social work practitioners, and the service delivery system.

Clients

One barrier to the use of services lies within the elderly clients themselves. The current cohort of older adults were raised during a time period when receiving social or mental health services was stigmatizing. This cohort is distrustful of any bureaucratic system and attaches a negative stigma to receiving services (Gatz et al. 1984).

A second barrier to services is the fear older adults have of losing their independence. Social programs can reinforce this fear if services are not delivered in a sensitive way. For example, a woman who has spent her entire life raising a family and managing the household may resent the intrusion of a homemaker even though help is needed. Older clients are frequently hesitant to give up tasks they have accomplished independently in the past.

The age difference between practitioner and client may also add to the older person's reluctance to use services. Most practitioners are younger than their clients. Older clients may feel that the younger service providers cannot possibly understand their problems and will not be effective helpers. Transference issues may be important with this set of clients. Older people may view the younger practitioner as a child or grandchild. These feelings often make an older person reluctant to use services, even if they are greatly needed.

Practitioner

Another set of barriers to practice with elderly clients is presented by practitioners. Social workers, like other professionals, are members of an ageist society. Practitioners are often unaware of the subtle ways society discriminates against and stereotypes older persons. A major problem in social work education is the lack of training in gerontology. Although many B.S.W. level practitioners are hired in agencies that serve older clients, 80 percent of baccalaureate social work programs do *not* offer aging courses (Klein 1995). Students who are not trained to work with older adults may hold ageist biases against older clients (Kosberg & Harris 1979). In a study of B.S.W./M.S.W. students' interest in working with older adults with dementia, Kane (1999) reported that only 2.9 percent identified an interest in this area of practice. In addition, the knowledge about Alzheimer's disease among this group of students was very low. One study of health care providers, physicians, nurses, and social workers reported that older people who presented problems occurring as a consequence of normal aging were judged to be undesirable clients (Baker 1984). These health care professionals stated a preference to work with older clients who had a disease process rather than those whose problems were associated with normal aging. Problems due to the aging process, such as hearing or sight difficulties, are seen as unglamorous by health care providers.

In addition to having negative stereotypes about older people, practitioners working with older adults may elicit uncomfortable feelings within themselves. Working with an older client may evoke fears of the aging process in one's parents or oneself. Corresponding to these fears are death anxieties or unresolved feelings surrounding death and dying (Greene 1986). Many practitioners work with older persons who are ill, and death is always present. Working only with frail older people causes practitioners to face their own mortality and reinforces negative stereotypes about the health of elderly people.

Service Delivery System

For older people, a major barrier to using services is the fragmentation of the service delivery system. People will not receive services if they are unaware of what is available or find limited access to what is needed. Many older people rely on family, friends, or media to find information about services (Silverstein 1984). However, most people are unaware of the services that are available. Using established sources, such as referral programs and formal agencies, is a more effective strategy to link older people to needed resources.

When older clients initially seek out professional services, they usually begin with the family physician. One study about service utilization by older adults reported that general practitioners were overwhelmingly the most common professionals used by older people (Waxman, Carner, & Klein 1984). This situation highlights the importance of establishing linkages between health and social service providers. However, these systems commonly have no established methods of referral. Physicians are frequently unaware of community agencies and their services, and therefore, they are unable to refer older clients to appropriate programs.

A second major system barrier is the method of payment for services. Medicare is the governmental health insurance used by older adults. This program is structured to provide acute, not long-term treatment. If a client requires continuous services, Medicare will not cover them. For example, Medicare will pay for diagnostic evaluations for a person with Alzheimer's disease but will not cover treatment services (Gatz et al. 1984). Similarly, in-home social work services are covered only if ordered by a physician, and insurance will not cover costs for psychosocial services, such as help in adjusting to an amputation. Older individuals who require on-going services, such as nursing home care, are forced to carry private insurance plans, pay privately for services themselves, or spend their resources down until they qualify for Medicaid coverage.

Discussion Questions

1. Discuss differences between primary, secondary, and tertiary interventions with elderly clients. What are typical problems experienced by clients in each of these levels of social work practice?
2. What are the five intervention roles of social workers? Give examples of each role.
3. How does social work interviewing differ from other types of communication? What modifications are required in order to interview older clients?
4. Discuss the importance of accountability and documenting work with an older client.
5. What are barriers to social work practice with older clients? What problems exist?

Experiential Learning

Activity: Old Age Portrait

Look at figure 1.2, the Portrait Form. It is a standard two vision picture. When you look at it one way, you see an old person; another way, a young woman. *Try to guess the age of the person in the portrait.* Then imagine what the young woman in the portrait believes old age to be like. Identify the age of the young woman and then guess her feelings about old age. This is a five minute exercise, and you should write down your own opinion.

After five minutes, share your opinions with other students. Statements may be similar to the following:

> This person is *forty-five* years *old*, thinks old is *ninety-five*, and when she is *ninety-five*, she'll probably value most of her *friends*.
> This person is thirty-two years old, thinks *old* is sixty-five, and when she is *sixty-five*, her financial situation will probably be bleak.

 **Figure 1.2**   Portrait Form

After this exercise, complete the form below about your own old age. Write down your first thought for each question, and try to write how you think you *will be*, not what you *prefer* to be.

After completing the form, read your answers and discuss with other students. Few "old age portraits" will view getting old in the same way. Each student is a unique person who will be equally unique when he or she is *old*. Remember: Old people are not alike and should not be categorized as such!

An Old Age Portrait of Me

When I'm _____ (write an age you think is *old*):

I'll probably value most my _____

I'll have the worst problems with my _____

My best friend will be _____

My spouse will probably _____

When I look in the mirror I'll probably see _____

My favorite activity will be _____

My relationships with my family will _____

_____

Source: Schneider and Kropf 1987.

Case Studies

See Appendix B for guidelines in analyzing gerontological social work practice.

Case 1: Primary Intervention: Mrs. C.

Mrs. C., a seventy-four-year-old retired schoolteacher, was lively, talkative, and alert. She was neatly and stylishly dressed, and the colors in her outfit were obviously selected with care. When she was standing or sitting, her posture was erect, and there were no signs of psychomotor retardation. When interviewed she spoke in a calm and relaxed manner about her achievements and exhibited no sign of an appreciable intellectual decline. No memory impairments were found on the mental status examination. Some general forgetfulness was noted, however, in her medical history.

Mrs. C. was born in Paris into a family of modest means. She was the third of five children. Mrs. C. said that her parents got along reasonably well although she sensed at times that her mother had ambitions to be other than a housewife. Her mother apparently had a strong influence on her life. As far back as Mrs. C. could remember, her mother had stressed the idea of getting ahead through a good education. Mrs. C. finished college at age twenty. She met her husband-to-be while in her junior year. At age twenty-two she married, and shortly afterward she and her husband emigrated to the United States.

She still describes herself as being in love with her husband, whose health is reported as being very good. Mrs. C. went through menopause at age forty-nine. She still has sexual relations with her husband on a regular basis.

Mrs. C. enjoys talking about her three children, all of whom live away from home with their own families and are obviously doing well. Mrs. C. has five grandchildren and seems especially fond of them. She sees each of her children (who live in different states) at least once a year, and maintains frequent telephone contact with them throughout the year.

Mrs. C. began teaching at the age of thirty-two, two years after her last child was born. She and her husband especially enjoyed having the children at home during their late teenage years when their peers came to visit them. Somehow, they were reminded of their own teenage years and they realized how much they had changed since that time in their own lives.

Since she retired nine years ago, Mrs. C. and her husband have enjoyed a satisfying emotional and social life. They have managed their financial resources well and look forward to the future. Mrs. C. is aware that life cannot go for them this way forever, despite the fact that she and her husband planned for and anticipated many of the changes they have experienced. Mrs. C. enjoys her present life, her participation in community and church affairs, and hopes these activities and interests will persist for some time. She and her husband have talked about death, but try not to actively dwell on it. They have made out a will and arranged for a burial site.

Mrs. C. is aware of certain changes in her functional capacity and has apparently accepted them. She knows she no longer walks as rapidly as she used to. She is also a bit more forgetful, but there is no evidence of psychopathology as she ages. She still has friends but entertains less frequently now that some of her old circle of friends have moved away or died. It is deemed likely that Mrs. C. will function well and adapt satisfactorily to further life changes as she continues to age.

Source: Beaver and Miller 1985.

Case 2: Secondary Intervention: Mrs. Jones

Mrs. Jones is unmarried, seventy-five-years-old, and lives alone. She draws a small pension and has a low-paying, part-time job in a local bakery. She has lived by herself in the family home for the last ten years since her mother passed away. It has become more and more difficult for her to bear the ever-increasing cost of home maintenance. If it were not for her part-time job she would have lost the house some years ago.

Although Mrs. Jones is in relatively good health (considering her advanced age and hard work), she has recently been more and more troubled with arthritic pains in her legs, chronic tiredness, and depressed moods. Over the last year, her doctor has urged her to give up her employment. The house is in need of repair, but she cannot afford to have the work done. Over the last year she has found it increasingly difficult to keep up with the minor repairs and daily routines of home management. It greatly taxes her to do such chores as mow the grass, put up storm windows, clean the furnace, and shovel snow. She cannot afford to pay someone to do these things without taking money away from other pressing areas. Her greatest fear at this time is that she will not be able to pay the real estate taxes, which were increased again this year while her income remained the same.

Mrs. Jones is aware that the cost is constantly rising for almost everything she needs: medicine, food, clothing, transportation, household supplies, and so on. She has pared the budget to the bone, cannot cut expenditures any further, and sees no new financial resources that might be available to her. Over the last six months she has become worried and apprehensive about her future in general. For the first time in her life she finds herself feeling depressed and agitated most of the time. More and more often she feels like staying in bed instead of going to work.

Being a rational and intelligent person, Mrs. Jones has frequently thought about the possibility of giving up the house and moving to smaller and cheaper quarters. This would mean moving to a small apartment, a prospect that is quite distressing to her given the fact that Mrs. Jones has lived for seventy-five years in a spacious house in a quiet, residential neighborhood. She knows, however, that she has to do something soon about her difficult situation, but she continues to put off making a decision. Very recently she has come to realize that her nervousness and depression may cause her to lose her job, and that the income reduction would make her situation critical. Mrs. Jones was persuaded by a co-worker to talk to a social caseworker at the local senior citizen center. After a few days of resistance, Mrs. Jones "got up her nerve" and made an appointment at the center.

It took several sessions for the caseworker to hear Mrs. Jones' complete story and to arrive at a general assessment of her psychosocial situation. Although the caseworker recognized the client's depression and anxiety, she viewed the distress as a reaction to Mrs. Jones' perceived inability to resolve a problem situation that was rapidly approaching a critical state. Because Mrs. Jones had many psychological strengths, including a strong motivation to help herself, the worker decided to use a problem-solving and task-oriented treatment strategy.

The worker began by teaching the client the sequential steps of a problem-solving approach. This was acceptable to Mrs. Jones and they contracted for brief, task-oriented counseling in which approximately eight weeks would be devoted to searching for a possible solution to the client's problem. They agreed to terminate counseling when Mrs. Jones had in hand a definite plan of action including the specific problem-solving tasks she had contracted to complete.

During counseling at least six different possible and feasible problem-solving alternatives were identified, designed, evaluated, and analyzed. The alternative selected for Mrs. Jones was to look for a live-in companion of similar age with a similar lifestyle and interests; and one who could pay enough room and board allowance to permit Mrs. Jones to hold onto her home. The plan also included Mrs. Jones' securing a position as a paid volunteer with a senior companion program. The money she would earn from such a job would allow her to give up the taxing job at the bakery. The worker informed Mrs. Jones of several income-augmenting programs for which she was eligible. Mrs. Jones took the responsibility for applying for food stamps, fuel supplement payments, and real estate tax rebates.

Mrs. Jones was successful in resolving her problem. The caseworker's timely and structured brief intervention helped to prevent a psychosocial crisis that could have resulted in chronic depression and an overall decline in functioning.

Source: Beaver and Miller 1985.

Case 3: Tertiary Interventions: The Walkers

Mr. and Mrs. Walker have been married for sixty years: He is ninety years old and she is eighty-five. They have lived in the same town since birth. They have outlived their siblings and most of their long-time friends. Their three married sons and grandchildren live a considerable distance away. One son lives two hours away, and the other two have a five-hour drive to get to their parents' home. All three children frequently telephone their parents and visit them fairly regularly on weekends.

Mr. and Mrs. Walker are both suffering from chronic hypertension. They have been taking medication for many years. Over the last five years their conditions have worsened, and more and more medication has been prescribed in an attempt to control the illness. In recent years the illness has slowed them down. Both must avoid heavy work, physical exertion, and emotional excitement in order to minimize the chance of stroke and heart failure. On several occasions during the past five years, each has blacked out from physical exertion.

Although their physical functioning has been quite limited for a number of years and has continued to decline gradually, they have been able to live on their own. Mrs. Walker is hard of hearing. This condition has gradually worsened over a seven-year period. They both take medicine for mild diabetic conditions.

They live in a mobile home that requires only minimal maintenance. Mrs. Walker has been preparing meals and doing the house cleaning. For two years neighbors and relatives have been doing the shopping. When the weather permits, Mr. and Mrs. Walker sit on the porch swing and take short walks in the yard. When medical attention is needed, a neighbor or one of their sons drives them to the doctor's office. Mr. Walker has been contented for years watching television. Mrs. Walker watches some television and reads a little. She enjoys company better than anything.

Mrs. Walker greatly misses the things she used to be able to do outside of the house before the reduction in her mobility. She has been discontented with the home-bound situation but has not become depressed or agitated. Both Mr. and Mrs. Walker have been able, over the years of declining physical mobility, to maintain a positive attitude.

Mr. and Mrs. Walker's retirement income is limited but sufficient to finance their rather simple lifestyle. They own their home and are free of debts. They have savings sufficient to cover their funeral expenses. Their home is comfortable, and when new furnishing or appliances are needed, they can afford to make the purchases. A catastrophic illness requiring extended hospitalization and/or nursing home care would, in a short period of time, wipe out their savings and make them eligible for SSI and Medicaid benefits.

Over a two-week period, neighbors and relatives became aware of a change in Mrs. Walker's mental functioning. During telephone and face-to-face conversations Mrs. Walker revealed very marked short-term memory loss and time disorientation. Her mood seemed to be mildly depressed and her affect was somewhat flat. Her hearing capacity seemed to be worse, but she was not wearing her hearing aid.

Close inspection revealed some disorder in the previously very tidy home. Mr. Walker, when pressed by his children, admitted that he was worried about his wife. He said she was forgetful lately and confused about the days of the month and the month of the year. He said she was able to prepare the meals and clean up a little each day, but that she seemed weak and was spending a lot of time in bed. He was worried that her blood pressure was out of control and that she might have a stroke.

Upon further questioning Mr. Walker reluctantly told one of his sons that several weeks ago Mrs. Walker had been too weak to get out of the bathtub. When he tried to help her, he passed out. He said it took him four hours to get up enough strength to eventually drag her out of the tub. On that occasion they had both crawled to bed.

Upon learning these facts and observing Mrs. Walker's obvious mental confusion and forgetfulness, the son took her to the family doctor, the only physician who had cared for the Walkers during the last twenty years. The physician confirmed an elevation in blood pressure. When asked if Mrs. Walker had experienced a small stroke, the physician was evasive. He preferred to believe that Mrs. Walker's mental symptoms were caused by her failure to take all prescribed medication.

The doctor believed that Mrs. Walker should continue on the same medication. Mrs. Walker was on five different medicines, each taken three or four times a day. No one could be certain that Mrs. Walker was taking the medicine properly. Even Mr. Walker could not be sure because he was not in the habit of watching her closely. Mrs. Walker appeared confused about the medicine but said she did not need any help. She was not aware of the extent of her confusion and memory loss.

The children could visit only on weekends. They coordinated their visiting, so that thereafter one of them would be with their parents each weekend. Whoever was home for the weekend prepared Mrs. Walker's weekly medication. Each separate dosage was placed in an envelope properly labeled for day and time of day.

Over a three-week period Mrs. Walker's condition neither worsened nor improved. The family became increasingly concerned about Mrs. Walker. They realized that their parents needed some sort of assistance if they were to remain in their home and sought advice from the adult services agency, which was located in a neighboring town, the county seat.

Source: Beaver and Miller 1985.

Annotated Bibliography

Biegel, D. E., Farkas, K. J., & Song, L. (1997). Barriers to the use of mental health services by African-American and Hispanic elderly persons. *Journal of Gerontological Social Work, 29,* 23–44.

Although mental health service use is low for all older adults, this study specifically looked at older adults of color. The research identified key barriers to using services and poses strategies to promote a more comprehensive mental health service model for these groups of older adults.

Gutheil, I. A. (Ed.). (1994). *Work with older people: challenges and opportunities.* New York: Fordham University Press.

This edited volume overviews various dimensions of working with older adults. Of specific interest to social workers is the section on practice and service delivery. Chapters include cultural diversity in practice, elder abuse, ethical issues in long-term care, interdisciplinary teams in geriatric settings, community-based case management, and issues facing the future of aging.

Kropf, N. P. & Pugh, K. L. (1995). Beyond life expectancy: Social work with centenarians. *Journal of Gerontological Social Work, 23*(3/4), 121–137.

This article explores social work practice issues with centenarians, those people one hundred years or older. Into the next century, this group of elderly adults will experience the greatest increase in numbers, yet often their practice needs have been neglected. Specific interventions related to health, psychosocial, and financial issues are outlined.

Perkins, K. & Tice, C. (1995). A strengths perspective in practice: Older people and mental health challenges. *Journal of Gerontological Social Work, 23*(3/4), 83–97.

This article provides a perspective on how to move from a deficit to a strength model in assessment with older adults. The key concepts are the older person's method of survivorship, examining how people live and cope in an oppressive environment. In addition, a case example is provided to illustrate this type of assessment.

Saltz, C. & Kropf, N. P. (Eds). (1998). Empirical research on gerontological social work. Special issue of *Research on Social Work Practice,* 8(1).

This special issue contains seven studies of treatment for older adults. These include articles on practice and programs, such as grandparents raising grandchildren, evaluating elders at risk for suicide, and task centered case management. In addition, other articles address measurement issues, such as defining adequacy of care, satisfaction with long term care, and a needs inventory for hospitalized elders.

Wagner, D. L. & Neal, M. B. (1994). Caregiving and work: Consequences, correlates, and workplace responses. *Educational Gerontology, 20,* 645–663.

This article reports on a study about the multiple demands of elder care and employment. The impact of care provision on employed caregivers is extensive and includes financial, social, and personal health consequences. In addition, the discussion suggests work-place programs that can support employed care providers.

General Bibliography

Crose, R. (1995). Assessment of strengths and coping skills of frail elders. *Clinical Gerontologist, 15*(4), 49–52.

Dhooper, S. S., Green, S. M., Huff, M. B., & Austin-Murphy, J. (1993). Efficacy of a group approach to reducing depression in nursing home elderly residents. *Journal of Gerontological Social Work, 20,* 87–100.

Diwan, S. & Moriarty, D. (1995). A conceptual framework for identifying unmet health care needs of community dwelling elderly. *The Journal of Applied Gerontology, 14,* 47–63.

Haight, B. K. (1992). Long-term effects of a structured life review process. *Journals of Gerontology, 47,* P312–P315.

Hepburn, K. W., Caron, W., Luptak, M., Ostwald, S., Grant, L., & Keenan, J. M. (1997). The family stories workshop: stories for those who cannot remember. *The Gerontologist, 37,* 827–832.

Hornbrook, C. M., Stevens, J. V., Wingfield, J. D., Hollis, F. J., Greenlick, R. M., & Ory, G. M. (1994). Preventing falls among community-dwelling older persons: Results from a randomized trial. *The Gerontologist, 34,* 16–23.

Kropf, N. P., Cummings, S., & Sukumar, B. (1998). Practice with older clients. In J. S. Wodarski & B. A. Thyer (Eds.), *Handbook of Empirical Social Work Practice: Social Problems and Practice Issues* (vol. 2). New York: Wiley.

Lopez, M. A. & Silber, S. (1991). Stress management for the elderly: A preventive approach. *Clinical Gerontologist, 10*(4), 73–76.

Lustbader, W. & Hooyman, N. (1994). *Taking care of aging family members: A practical guide* (2nd ed.). New York: Free Press.

Mittelman, M. S., Ferris, S. H., Shulman, E., Steinberg, G., Ambinder, A., Mackell, J. A>, & Cohen, J. (1995). A comprehensive support program: Effect on depression in spouse-caregivers of Alzheimer's disease patients. *The Gerontologist, 35,* 792–802.

Pugh, K. L., Kropf, N. P., & Greene, R. R. (1994). Planning health education for older adults: The use of a health model and interview data. *Gerontology & Geriatrics Education, 15*(2), 3–17.

Reis, M. & Nahmiash, D. (1995). When seniors are abused: An intervention model. *The Gerontologist, 35,* 666–671.

Rife, C. J. & Belcher, F. J. (1994). Assisting unemployed older workers to become reemployed: An experimental evaluation. *Research on Social Work Practice, 4,* 3–13.

Schneider, R. L., & Kropf, N. P. (1996). The admission process in nursing homes: A clinical model for ethical decision making. *Journal of Long Term Home Health Care, 15*(3), 39–46.

References

Baker, R. R. (1984). Attitudes of health care providers toward elderly patients with normal aging and disease-related symptoms. *Gerontologist, 24*(5), 543–545.

Beaver, M. L. & Miller, D. (1985). *Clinical social work practice with elderly: Primary, secondary and tertiary interventions.* Homewood, IL: Dorsey Press.

Biegel, D. E., Farkas, K. J., & Song, L. (1997). Barriers to the use of mental health services by African-American and Hispanic elderly persons. *Journal of Gerontological Social Work, 29,* 23–44.

Burnette, D. (1999). Custodial grandparents in Latino families: Patterns of service use and predictors of unmet needs. *Social Work, 44*(1), 22–34.

Chiverton, P. & Caine, E. D. (1989). Education to assist spouses in coping with Alzheimer's disease. *Journal of the American Geriatrics Society, 37,* 593–598.

Compton, B. R. & Galaway, B. (1994). *Social work processes* (5th ed.). Homewood, IL: Dorsey Press.

Connaway, R. & Gentry, M. (1988). *Social work practice.* Englewood Cliffs, NJ: Prentice-Hall.

Coogle, L. C., Osgood, N. J., Pyles, M. A., & Wood, H. E. (1995). The impact of alcoholism education on service providers, elders, and their family members. *Journal of Applied Gerontology, 14,* 321–332.

Davis, L. (1986). Role theory. In F. Turner (Ed.), *Social work treatment* (pp. 541–563). New York: Free Press.

Dhooper, S. S., Green, S. M., Huff, M. B., & Austin-Murphy, J. (1993). Efficacy of a group approach to reducing depression in nursing home elderly residents. *Journal of Gerontological Social Work, 20,* 87–100.

Gambos, C. & Rosen, A. (1999). The aging are coming and they are us. *Health and Social Work, 24*(1), 73–77.

Gatz, M., Popkin, S. J., Pinco, C. D., & VandenBos, G. R. (1984). Psychological interventions with older adults. In J. E. Birren and K. W. Schaie (Eds.), *Handbook of the psychology of aging* (2nd ed.). New York: Van Nostrand Reinhold.

Greene, R. R. (1986). Countertransferance issues in social work with the aged. *Journal of Gerontological Social Work, 9*(3).

Hepworth, D. & Larsen, J. (1993). *Direct social work practice: Theory and skills* (4th ed.). Pacific Grove: Brooks/Cole.

Hollenbeck, D. & Ohls, J. C. (1984). Participation among the elderly in the food stamp program. *The Gerontologist, 24*(6).

Hooyman, N. & Kiyak, H. A. (1996). *Social gerontology: A multidisciplinary perspective.* Needham Heights, MA: Simon & Schuster.

Hornbrook, C. M., Stevens, J. V., Wingfield, J. D., Hollis, F. J., Greenlick, R. M., & Ory, G. M. (1994). Preventing falls among community-dwelling older persons: Results from a randomized trial. *The Gerontologist, 34,* 16–23.

Kane, M. (1999). Factors affecting social work students' willingness to work with elders with Alzheimer's disease. *Journal of Social Work Education, 35*(1), 71–85.

Klein, S. (1995) (Ed). *A national agenda for geriatric education: White papers,* Rockville, MD: U.S. Department of Health and Human Services.

Kosberg, J. I. & Harris, A. P. (1979). Attitudes towards elderly clients. In J. I. Kosberg (Ed.), *Working with and for the aged.* Silver Spring, MD: National Association of Social Workers.

Kropf, N. P., Nackerud, L., & Gorokhovsky, I. (1999). Social work practice with older Soviet immigrants. *Journal of Multicultural Social Work, 7*(1/2) 111–126.

Lorig, K., Laurin, J., & Holman, H. R. (1984). Arthritis self-management: A study of patient education for the elderly. *The Gerontologist, 24*(5).

MacNeil, R. D. & Teague, M. L. (1992). *Aging and leisure: Vitality in later life.* (2nd ed.). Dubuque, IA: Brown and Benchmark.

Meyer, M. D. (1991). Assuring quality of care: Nursing home resident councils. *Journal of Applied Gerontology, 10*(1), 103–116.

Mittelman, M. S., Ferris, S. H., Shulman, E., Steinberg, G., Ambinder, A., Mackell, J. A., & Cohen, J. (1995). A comprehensive support program: Effect on depression in spouse-caregivers of Alzheimer's disease patients. *The Gerontologist 35,* 792–802.

National Center for Health Statistics. (1990). *Current estimates from the National Health Interview Survey: 1989.* Washington, DC: U.S. Government Printing Office.

Osgood, N. (1982). *Life after work: Retirement, leisure, recreation and the elderly.* New York: Praeger.

Pincus, A. & Minahan, A. (1973). *Social work practice: Model and method.* Itasca, IL: Peacock.

Rapp, S. R., Mayo, L. L., Cole, P., Shires, C. L., Williams, R., Fowler, C. D., & Steen, C. (1989). Interdisciplinary behavioral geriatrics in long-term care: A controlled study. *Clinical Gerontologist, 8*(2), 35–42.

Ryder, L. K., & Janson, P. (1983). Crime and the elderly: The relationship between risk and fear. *The Gerontologist, 23*(2).

Saltz, C., & Kropf, N. P. (Eds.). (1998). Empirical Research on Gerontological Social Work. Special issue of *Research on Social Work Practice, 8*(1).

Schneider, R. L., & Kropf, N. P. (1996). The admission process in nursing homes: A clinical model for ethical decision making. *Journal of Long Term Home Health Care, 15*(3), 39–46.

Schneider, R. L., & Kropf, N. P. (1987). *Virginia ombudsman program: Professional certification curriculum.* Richmond: Virginia Department for the Aging.

Shanas, E. (1979). The family as a social support in old age. *The Gerontologist, 23*(2).

Silverman, P. (1978). *Mutual help-groups: A guide for mental health workers.* Rockville, MD: National Institute of Mental Health.

Silverstein, N. M. (1984). Informing the elderly about public services: the relationship between sources of knowledge and service utilization. *The Gerontologist, 24*(1).

Silverstone, B., & Burack-Weiss, A. (1983). *Social work practice with the frail elderly and their families: The auxiliary function model.* Springfield, IL: Charles C. Thomas

Solomon, R. (1982). Serving families of the institutionalized aged: The four crises. *Journal of Gerontological Social Work, 5*(1/2).

Virginia Long-Term Care Council. (1985). *Study of the public and private cost of institutional and community based long-term care:* Richmond, VA.

Washington State Long-Term Care Ombudsman Program Manual. (1978). Washington, DC: National Council of Senior Citizens.

Wacker, R. R., Roberto, K. A., Piper, L. E. (1998). *Community resources for older adults: Programs and services in an era of change.* Thousand Oaks, CA: Pine Forge.

Waxman, H. M., Carner, E. M., & Klein, M. (1984). Underutilization of mental health professionals by community elderly. *The Gerontologist, 24*(1), 23–30.

Zarit, S. H. (1980). *Aging and mental disorders.* New York: Macmillan.

2 The Myths and Facts of Aging

Marcia P. Harrigan and Rosemary L. Farmer

This chapter provides descriptive information about the biological, psychological, social, and spiritual dimensions of old age. Such information can be used to understand the behavior of older persons in relation to their environment. Knowledge about human behavior, such as how and why people do what they do, is basic to an understanding of the individual and his/her problems. This type of information includes both individual and environment factors.

The general term "environment" covers such things as the mother-infant interactions in utero, a person's relationship with other family members, school, and the adults' interactions with friends, employers, neighborhood, community, economy, and country. An understanding of human behavior is prerequisite to an accurate assessment of life and planning social work interventions with older clients. The information included in this chapter provides a foundation upon which social workers can begin to build a professional understanding of the older person, the problem situation, and the kind of assistance required.

Definition and Theories of Aging

What Is "Aging"?

Biologically speaking, aging is a process that begins at birth, continues throughout life, and marks the passage of years. However, the term "aging" commonly refers to people over a given age, such as sixty or sixty-five. There are several different age categories that are used to define the aged population (Neugarten & Neugarten 1987). Many writers believe that age alone is an insufficient indicator of behavior, but it seems necessary to provide some chronological parameters. One classification describes the young-old (age fifty-five to sixty-four), the old (ages sixty-five to seventy-four), older old (ages seventy-five to eighty-four), and the very old (ages eighty-five and older) (National Association of Social Workers 1995). Recently, gerontologists subdivide old age into only three periods: The "young-old" are those persons between the ages of fifty-five and seventy-five; the "old-old" are between seventy-five and eighty-four; and the "oldest-old" are over eighty-five years of age. Old age classification can also be based on public policy, such as eligibility for Social Security and Medicare.

Definitions have changed over time and reflect changing demographics. Between 1960 and 1994 the oldest-old population increased by 274 percent compared to a 100 percent increase for all persons sixty-five and older, and a 45 percent increase for all persons. Centenarians have more than doubled since 1980. In addition to those who study and write about older people, there are social practices that help define older people. In American culture, the official designation of aging is now determined to be sixty years, the age at which establishments such as movie theaters or restaurants give Senior Citizen discounts.

Theoretical Perspectives

Several theories have been proposed to assist with the understanding and prediction of the behavior of the elderly, as well as to guide research on older people. This section summarizes nine theories and one model which have been developed to predict and explain human behavior of the elderly.

The theories included in this overview are not an exhaustive list of existing perspectives, nor are they all equally developed to meet the criteria to be called a "theory." They were selected based upon current usage and potential usefulness. For each theory presented, the name of a major developer, the central assumption, and an example of behavior that represents the theory are given.

Disengagement theory was initially presented by Elaine Cumming and William Henry (1961). The major premise is that as one ages, there is a gradual decrease of activity and social involvement. This withdrawal can be initiated by the person or by others in the social environment to prepare the older person for death. A major assumption of this theory is that the disengagement process is mutually beneficial for the older person and society. Although ample evidence has supported the reciprocal influence of the aged and society, there is little or no evidence to support the benefits of disengaging for either elderly or society. Consequently, this theory provokes considerable debate. Mandatory retirement exemplifies this theory, as the elderly give up their role of worker while other roles also decrease in scope and number. Consequently, "room is made" in the workplace for younger and more able workers.

Activity theory is in direct opposition to disengagement theory. Developed initially by Robert Havighurst (1968), the major premise is that active involvement in relationships and social roles is critical to successful aging. The activities of old age must be qualitatively similar to those of middle age. This theory does not explain the adaptation of elderly who are unable to maintain the middle-age activity level and yet report high levels of life satisfaction. An example of activity theory is pre-retirement programs. These programs encourage participants to identify roles which will be lost or significantly reduced with retirement and to replace relationships and roles to maintain a comparable quality of activity level in the post-retirement stage.

Substitution theory (Baum & Baum 1980) attempts to extend activity theory, by stating that as roles and/or the capacity to perform a role is lost, substitutes can be found. Although adaptive, this process can occur only if roles are available to meet the needs of the elderly. The roles which replace lost ones do not exactly substitute for the type and intensity of the last role. An example of this theory is the community programs which capitalize on expertise of the older person. The Foster Grandparent Program, for example, gives older men and women an opportunity to substitute previous caregiving experience with surrogate grandparenting. This program matches a grandparent with a high risk child who could benefit from additional interaction with an adult. Furthermore, volunteer experience substitutes for employment which was lost through retirement.

Continuity theory incorporates theory from the disciplines of psychology and sociology (Cox 1984). Psychological theory contributes assumptions that life is a continuous process which utilizes experiences before old age in order to adapt to the demands of aging. Sociological theory focuses on the roles that have been assumed and those roles which will be assumed as people age. The major assumption of continuity theory is that the experiences of previously held roles prepare a person to meet the demands of future roles. Continuity theory states that the behavior of the elderly can only be understood by examining the interrelatedness of the biological, social, and psychological dimensions and previous behavior in earlier life stages. By identifying life habits, goals, preferences, and lifestyles, one is able to predict behavior and adaptation in later life. An example of this theory is leisure-time planning with a retired person. Information about past enjoyments and hobbies can help predict what activities the older person will find satisfying post-retirement.

Age stratification theory is credited primarily to Matilda Riley (Riley, Johnson, & Foner 1972). This perspective is based on the low status assigned to the elderly in an age-stratified and industrialized society. The status, power, roles, and social position of the elderly as a group are in direct relationship to those held by other age groups. In contemporary society, older people have fewer skills, information, and resources which are considered valuable. Younger people will have a higher degree of valued resources, such as high levels of education, and hold more powerful positions in society than the elderly. For example, white middle-aged men are afforded the highest power and status when compared to other age and sex stratified groups. This group has access to the most powerful resources of society. All other groups, such as blacks, women, and the elderly, have less power and status.

The *subculture of aging theory*, as advanced by Arnold Rose (Rose & Peterson 1965), presents the elderly as a minority group. Thus, behavior is predicted when minority status propositions are applied. Due to the shared biological characteristic of age, the elderly have an affinity towards each other and are simultaneously excluded by other groups based on age alone. However, this perspective does not always account for the high degree of heterogeneity within the aged population. Although samples of age discrimination, particularly in employment can be found, one can also find employment practices which value the aged, such as in the appointees to the U.S. Supreme Court.

Exchange theory, initially proposed by Peter Blau (1964) and applied to the elderly by James Dowd (1975), is based on the notion that the balance of rewards and costs of behavior to the individual and society predicts the overall behavior of the elderly. This theoretical perspective has been developed to understand both the larger society along with individuals and families. In families, for example, satisfying relationships will continue between the generations as long as the individuals involved perceive a balance between the rewards and the costs of the relationship. More specifically, families are predicted to meet the needs of elderly members only as long as the older person can contribute to other members.

Labeling theory is derived from symbolic interactionism of George Mead (Kuypers & Bengtsen 1973; Mead 1934). The major assumption is that one's self-concept is derived from interactions with others in society. The definition of self, as reflected by another person's attitude, language, and other behavior, is critical in identity development. For example, the negative stereotyping of the elderly as incapable of learning or producing goods and services becomes part of the belief system of the elderly. More specifically, individuals may be labeled dependent within a family system and cease to do tasks such as writing checks, cooking, and dressing even though they still have the ability to perform these tasks. Older people come to accept the dependency label and their independent behavior decreases.

Transpersonal theories focus on developmental processes and other life experiences that account for the part of human existence beyond the biological, psychological, and social dimensions. These theories explain the spiritual dimension and incorporate concepts such as life meaning, creativity, communion, and self-transcendence. Some of the several transpersonal theories which can be applied to the elderly include: humanistic; existentialism; and Jungian (Robbins et al. 1998). Transpersonal theories can help to explain an elderly person's acceptance of mortality and death. For example, the elderly person who is terminally ill may find comfort through individual and group prayer as well as holding the belief of spiritual existence beyond the life of the body.

The *transition model*, developed by N. K. Schlossberg (1981) (figure 2.1, p. 35), can be applied across the lifespan, but is especially helpful in understanding adaptation to old age. According to Schlossberg's model, transition occurs "if an event or non-event results in a change in assumptions about one-self and the world and thus requires a corresponding change in one's behavior and relationships" (Schlossberg 1982, p.5). The transition from middle adulthood to old age has an impact on the quality of one's later years. Adaptation to retirement can be used to exemplify the transition model. Adaptation outcome is influenced by a person's *perception* of the event (retirement) in relation to timing and choice. Thus, one's ability to adapt may be different if retirement is chosen at age seventy versus forced at age sixty. The pre- and post-*transition environments* also influence adaptation. A person who focused on the work setting to meet much more than vocational needs will adapt differently from another person whose work was a smaller part of the total life experience. Finally, *individual characteristics* impact adaptation to retirement. Research has clearly shown that one's state of health is a primary predictor of retirement adjustment. The model indicates that the perception, environmental changes and individual characteristics need to be viewed simultaneously from a resource/deficit perspective. If all three areas contribute only deficits, the predicted adaptation would be problematic.

The information in the rest of the chapter is organized around the Myths of Aging. A myth can be defined as a belief that encourages a stereotyped response. Our society has developed many ideas about older people that are fictitious. With the help of factual information, the power of these myths can be diminished. Armed with knowledge about the normative process of aging, the reader will be less likely to make generalized assumptions about old people, and more apt to see the uniqueness that each person presents.

Myths of Aging

Biological Myths

Biological myths address the physical changes associated with the aging process. While the body does change over time, most older people are fairly healthy. This section discusses some common myths about the biological changes of the aging process.

Illness: Getting older means a life fraught with physical complaints and illness.

The interrelatedness of the biological, social, psychological, and spiritual dimensions of behavior across the lifespan as well as cultural, ethnic, and gender differences is critical in assessing the biological dimension of behavior of an elderly person. However, most people equate aging with a decline in biological functioning. As much variation exists in the type, rate, quantity, and impact of biological changes for the elderly as for younger age cohorts. Chronological age is a poor indicator of health or vigor. Most of the changes typically associated with the elderly begin to occur long before the later years, sometimes as early as the twenties. In 1992, three out of four of all noninstitutionalized elderly reported their health to be good to excellent compared to two out of three for those aged seventy-five and older. However, older people become increasingly aware of biological changes as they age and these changes occur more rapidly after the age of eighty.

Primarily due to preventive health practices, longevity continues to increase as more and more people reach adulthood. Life expectancy has also extended, from 48 years in 1900 to 75.8 years in 1995 (Kaplan & Saddock 1998). In 1990, a sixty-five-year-old female could expect to live another 18.9 years, and a sixty-five-year-old male, 15.1 years. Gender differences in life expectancy at birth continue to favor females by 7.1 years, but the gap is narrowing as the life expectancy for men has risen at a more rapid rate than for women (U.S. Bureau of the Census 1996). For persons of color and those living in poverty, there is a lower life expectancy compared to whites who are not poor. For those persons of color who do reach the age of sixty-five, the racial and ethnic differences in life expectancy rapidly diminish to the point of reversal over the age of eighty-five years (Clark et al. 1993). As more people reach old age and remain in good health, more people will realize the lifespan of the species, estimated to be 110 to 112 years by Bee (1996) and about 85 years by Fries and Crapo (1981). Those people whose lives are stimulating, complex, and highly organized experience longer lifespans (Newman & Newman 1987).

About 80 percent of people over the age of sixty-five have at least one chronic condition, such as arthritis, hypertension, or diabetes. However, over 80 percent of the noninstitutionalized elderly aged eight-five and older independently manage the tasks of basic living (Newman & Newman 1987). Only 5 percent of the elderly are in a nursing home facility at any given time and only 25 percent of the elderly are estimated to ever need nursing home care (Silverstone & Hyman 1982). Many of the biological changes associated with age are impacted by earlier lifestyle choices. For example, the amount of sun exposure throughout life is related to the onset and quantity of facial skin wrinkling in aging.

Memory changes are related to biological, learned, and motivational causes (Newman & Newman 1987). From the biological dimension, there is a gradual slowing of neural firing in certain brain areas, possibly resulting in slower response rates. There is also a loss of nerve cells resulting in a decrease in actual brain size with the connections between nerve cells becoming less numerous (Bee 1996). The impact of these biological changes is seen in cognitive processing.

> **Unattractiveness:** Old people are not attractive people. They smell, have no teeth, can hardly see or hear, and are underweight.

The aging process does not necessarily detract from a person's desire to remain physically attractive. Some change in appearances is due to such factors as preferences in clothing style and functional abilities. Older women, for example, may stop using cosmetics because they cannot afford these products or cannot apply them correctly. However, this fact does not imply that older people do not care how they look. For example, about 50 percent of people over the age of sixty-five have lost their teeth (Bee 1996). People of younger cohorts may have a lower rate of dentures since more emphasis is currently placed on preventive dental care. The older generation had lived in the time period where dentures were expected in old age.

Older people do begin to experience sensory changes. Most sensory changes begin to occur in early adulthood but may not be particularly noticeable until old age. Hearing changes include a decreased sensitivity to both high frequency and low intensity sounds, usually beginning around the age of fifty. As the decline increases, the aging person increasingly has difficulty hearing lowered voices, and loud noises become problematic. Men experience greater hearing loss than do women, perhaps due to environmental factors, such as exposure to loud machinery. In 1989, 48 percent of men and 37 percent of women reported having hearing problems (Guralnik et al. 1989). One estimate is that 15 to 30 percent of people age seventy-five and older have impaired functioning due to hearing loss. Only 5.7 percent of the young-old use hearing aids compared to 19 percent of the oldest-old (U.S. Bureau of the Census 1996). The social implications of hearing loss are profound, making it the most disabling of the sensory losses, although recent research indicates that, for most people, hearing loss is not related to life satisfaction or psychological health. Those with a severe loss, however, report greater levels of depression (Scheibel 1992). For example, older people may stop attending worship services since they cannot hear the sermons. Cohort variation is expected, as the younger people today are expected to have greater hearing impairment when they are older due to acoustic trauma (loud music). Adaptation to hearing loss is assisted by hearing aids and sensitivity of those around the hearing impaired person. Such sensitivity results in slower and louder speech and conversations limited to one speaker at a time (Bee 1996; Hooyman & Lustbader 1986).

Vision changes are another sensory change found in older people. Vision changes are typically seen around the age of forty when many people begin to wear glasses or bifocals for the first time. Many older people require increased illumination to compensate for a decrease in pupil size and the amount of light which can reach the retina. Increased sensitivity to glare is common, particularly when cataracts (yellowing of the lens) are present. Due to a loss of muscle elasticity and flexibility, the elderly may experience difficulty focusing on close objects and require greater time to adjust to light level changes, particularly after the age of sixty. The size of the visual field and depth perception decreases as well.

Since vision changes are common for the elderly, it is important that more serious disorders such as glaucoma not be mistaken for less serious changes. Glaucoma is a buildup of eye fluid which can cause blindness. Although not all vision impairments can be prevented, many can be treated if found in the early stages. Overall, vision changes may impact the person's ability to function as independently or fully as before. There are numerous adaptive strategies such as the use of appropriate corrective lenses, the use of night lights, coded clothing when colors are no longer discriminated, large print media, changing activities from night to day, and greater reliance on the other senses such as hearing (Hooyman & Lustbader 1986; Silverstone & Hyman 1982).

Another sensory change accompanying the aging process is in taste and smell. The ability to taste and smell starts to decline in the twenties. By age seventy, about two-thirds of the taste buds in a person's mouth have died as well as many of the cell receptors in the nose. The salivary glands secrete less, and dry mouth is a common complaint of the old-old. Doty, Sharman and Dann (1984) found that 60 percent of people ages sixty-five to eighty had a severe smell loss and 25 percent had a total loss. From a preventive perspective, smoking exacerbates both the incidence and intensity of decline in taste and smell perception.

Nutritional problems may be a result of changes in taste and smell. This fact is particularly related to the social meanings of foods, which may be lost as the social dimension changes. For example, some elderly may "forget" to eat after the death of a spouse. The social implication of cooking and eating alone may deter the older person from fixing an adequate meal. The threat of malnutrition is further increased, as there is reduced absorption of nutrients, increased excretion, and nutrient-drug interactions which can occur particularly in the frail elderly (Ludman & Newman 1986). The elderly experience a slower metabolic rate which requires a reduced caloric intake. Care must be taken that important nutrients are not lost as certain foods are eliminated from the diet due to these changes (Newman & Newman 1987).

The need for reduced caloric intake is accompanied by the other changes in body shape and height. Up to two inches in height is lost after the age of forty. Aging results in fat tissue being lost in the face, legs, and lower arms but gained in the upper arms, buttocks, and belly. Cohort variations may occur as the current weight and shape conscious middle-age adults reach later life, but some changes are inevitable. Expectations and body image issues become important considerations in predicting adaptation to these changes.

The last sensory change relates to pain and touch. Although the evidence is inconclusive, as high as 25 percent of the elderly lose some sensitivity in these two areas (Kenshalo 1977). These senses signal us to change potentially harmful behaviors, and the implications are important to consider. For example, an elderly person may experience a more severe burn without the early signal of heat or pain.

> **Exertion:** Old people should not exert themselves; they may have a heart attack or fall and break a bone.

The elderly can and do participate in aerobic activities without necessarily jeopardizing their health. However, due to the physiological changes of aging, exercise should be started and structured in consultation with a physician. Some of the physical changes are described below.

Cardiovascular and respiratory changes are prevalent with aging. The ability to take in and transport oxygen declines about 1 percent per year starting in young adulthood. Cardiac flow decreases 30 to 40 percent between ages twenty-five and sixty-five (Bee 1996). Breathing capacity decreases and the recovery time for strenuous activity increases with age. Related behavioral changes which are adaptive may include slower-paced walking and movement. This adaptive behavior should not be interpreted or equated with impaired cognitive abilities. After age fifty, a significant amount of muscle tissue is lost. All muscles are affected, which has implications for lung and heart functioning and physical strength. Recent research indicates that muscular and strength decline can be slowed significantly, or regained, through regular weight bearing exercise (Pyka et al. 1994). Heart disease remains the major killer of all elderly, but there has been a marked decline in death due to heart disease for all persons aged sixty-five to seventy-four and for Caucasians regardless of age (U.S. Bureau of the Census 1996).

The occurrence of incontinence is increasingly being recognized. Both urinary and fecal control are affected by this diminished muscular capacity and control. An estimate is that up to 25 percent of males and 42 percent of females over the age of sixty-five experience some degree of incontinence, the majority experiencing urinary incontinence (Hooyman & Lustbader 1986). Because of the loss of self-esteem and social embarrassment of the problem, it is difficult to ascertain the prevalence. Incontinence tends to be progressive, typically starting with slight losses of urine, particularly when sneezing or laughing. Since urinary control may also be related to other physical problems, such as tract infections, it is important to medically rule out more serious problems. Preventive and adaptive strategies include the use of protective undergarments, muscular development through specific exercise, fluid intake regulation, and social changes such as ensuring quick access to a toilet.

Bone changes in later years start before a person is elderly. Osteoporosis is a condition of calcium loss experienced primarily by post-menopausal women and typically begins in midlife with the crippling effects seen in the later years. This condition is preventable with calcium replacement and exercise, and for women, hormone replacement diminishes bone loss. Today's middle-aged women who are informed of the disease and who regularly engage in exercise may not experience osteoporosis in the same proportions as today's elderly. Other risk factors of osteoporosis include caucasian race, having a light weight body type, having a family history of the disease, being early menopausal or having surgically induced menopause, having sedentary lifestyles, and having borne children (Bee 1996).

The most prevalent change in the bones and connective tissues is arthritis, comprised of over one hundred different types. Arthritis affects one in seven Americans of all ages, but primarily the elderly. Ninety-seven percent of people over the age of sixty show evidence of joint deterioration by X-ray, yet *many* report no symptoms (Fallcreek & Mettler 1983). For noninstitutionalized elderly over the age of seventy-five, more than three of five men and one of three women report having arthritis (U.S. Bureau of the Census 1996). Rheumatoid arthritis causes inflammation of the membranes which line joints and tendons. Osteoarthritis affects the actual bone through wearing away joints, particularly those which are heavily used. Although many people report "good" days, the "bad" days may include aching, pain, swelling, and stiffness in joints or connective tissues. Ways to slow this chronic disease, decrease the pain, and prevent crippling of the limbs include medication, exercise and rest, weight reduction and heat. Remediation for selected joints involves surgery, joint replacement, and rehabilitation. The interrelatedness of arthritic conditions and the social and psychological dimensions are important to assess. One's attitudes toward exercise and pain, the perception of significant others of the invisible pain associated with arthritis, and the impact on social participation are a few examples of interrelated factors (Hooyman & Lustbader 1986; Silverstone & Hyman 1982).

Sleep: Old people sleep all the time.

Sleep patterns typically change as aging occurs. Older people do not necessarily sleep more, but may begin sleeping at different times of the day and experience fewer total hours of "deep sleep." Over one-third of all people over age sixty do report problems with sleeping, with females experiencing more disturbance than males (Woodruff 1985). A normal, healthy eighty-year-old can expect to spend about 20 percent of the night awake (Fallcreek & Mettler 1983). For most elderly persons, REM (dream) sleep and deep sleep decrease with age with an increase in the number of awakenings during the night (Woodruff 1985). More important is the fact that most elderly adapt well to these changes.

The older person may begin napping at certain times, such as noon or dinner time. While this pattern may give the impression that older people are sleeping more, they may nap to compensate for lost hours at night. Napping may also be due to boredom. Older people who participate in fulfilling activities will not use naps as a way to pass time.

Sexuality: Sex ends at sixty.

Sexuality is another area affected by biological changes of aging. Since functioning is heavily influenced by both the psychological and social dimensions, assessment becomes more complex when sexual dysfunction is found. There are certain changes which occur for all people but need not lead to dysfunction. Most elderly continue to engage in sexual activity, although the frequency and type may change with age. For heterosexual women, partner availability impacts sexuality more than does biological change.

Changes in men begin in middle age with a decrease in testosterone level. About 18 to 40 percent experience impotence between the ages sixty and sixty-five. With hormonal decline, there is a diminished production of sperm, some shrinkage of the testes, reduced volume of seminal fluid, the need for more time to achieve ejaculation, and a longer wait between ejaculations (Bee 1996; Hooyman & Lustbader 1986).

Female changes begin at menopause with little change thereafter regardless of age. These changes include some loss of tissue in the genitalia and breasts, reduced size of the ovaries and uterus, and loss of elasticity in the vaginal walls which also thin and produce less lubrication during intercourse (Bee 1996; Hooyman & Lustbader 1986). Most heterosexual women have reduced sexual activity due to their status as widows. Lack of an available partner is a major issue in discussing sexuality in older women.

Medical problems also affect sexuality of older people. For example, heart disease, cancer, stroke, prostatitis, and arthritis can cause fear and anxiety around sexual functioning. These worries exist for both the patient and his or her partner. If surgery is required to treat any of these illnesses, especially the more traumatic forms such as hysterectomy, mastectomy, or prostatectomy, apprehensions related to self-concept and capacity for intimacy may increase (Edinberg 1985). Finally, decreased sexual desire and impotency can result from some medications such as antihypertensives and antidepressants.

In summary, successful adaptation to the biological changes of aging is affected to a large degree by the perception of the particular change (see figure 2.1, A Model for Analyzing Human Adaptation to Transition). An older person can be helped to view some age-related changes as part of the normal aging process. Although a person has little control over hereditary factors and certain environmental factors, the impact of social class, income, and living arrangements on adaptation to biological changes can be profound. Finally, personal characteristics such as attitude toward exercise and personality type impact adaptation (Bee 1987).

Although biological change is inevitable, the impact is greatly influenced by personal health habits which are under one's control. Belloc (1973) found the following practices to be positively related to health and longevity: seven to eight hours of sleep per night, daily breakfast, little-to-no between meal eating, weight control not more than 5 percent under or 20 percent over desired weight for males and 10 percent over for females, involvement in regular exercise, moderate use of alcohol, and no smoking. Overall, there is considerable evidence that more people born today will reach the end of their lives having remained relatively healthy and active (Fries & Crapo 1981).

The statistics on causes of death support this fact. For example, for the young-old, fifty-five to sixty-four, cancer and heart dysfunction comprise the major causes of death. As age increases, the probability of death due to cancer decreases whereas death due to heart dysfunction increases. (Over the age of eighty-five, death by cancer compared to heart dys-

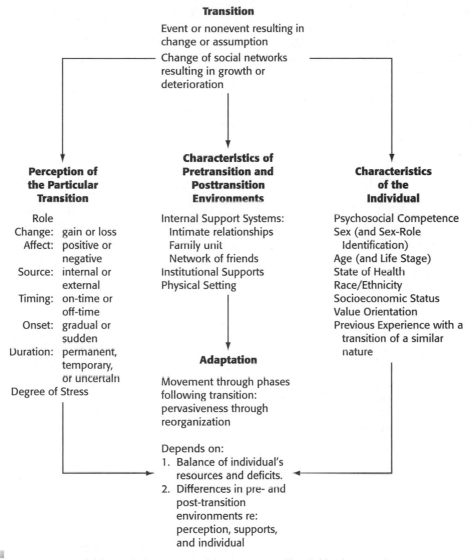

Transition

Event or nonevent resulting in change or assumption

Change of social networks resulting in growth or deterioration

Perception of the Particular Transition

Role
Change: gain or loss
Affect: positive or
negative
Source: internal or
external
Timing: on-time or
off-time
Onset: gradual or
sudden
Duration: permanent,
temporary,
or uncertain
Degree of Stress

Characteristics of Pretransition and Posttransition Environments

Internal Support Systems:
Intimate relationships
Family unit
Network of friends
Institutional Supports
Physical Setting

Characteristics of the Individual

Psychosocial Competence
Sex (and Sex-Role
Identification)
Age (and Life Stage)
State of Health
Race/Ethnicity
Socioeconomic Status
Value Orientation
Previous Experience with a
transition of a similar
nature

Adaptation

Movement through phases following transition: pervasiveness through reorganization

Depends on:
1. Balance of individual's resources and deficits.
2. Differences in pre- and post-transition environments re: perception, supports, and individual

■ **Figure 2.1**   A Model for Analyzing Human Adaptation to Transition (Schlossberg 1981)

function is 1:2). Although gender differences have declined somewhat relative to longevity and causes of death, females experience more acute illnesses whereas men experience more chronic illnesses (Bee 1996).

As the elderly become increasingly better educated, possess higher economic status, and practice life-long preventive health care, the clinical presentation of such changes as arthritis will decline. Today 80 to 90 percent of the people over sixty-five function without major restriction due to health problems (Hartford 1985). Adaptation to changes in sleep patterns, cardiovascular and sensory decline, nutritional requirements, and decreased muscular elasticity affecting vision and other bodily functioning will continue. There will continue to be great variability in the onset and impact of change.

Psychological Myths

A common stereotype of an older person is a confused, depressed or contrary woman or man. However, research does not support this type of profile. The following section discusses some common myths about psychological aging.

Rigidity: Most old people are set in their ways and unable to change.

Contrary to this myth of aging, the years after age sixty are seen as a period of continued psychological growth and adaptation (Newman & Newman 1987). This growth and change varies from person to person and within each individual and is related to an individual's personality. Personality is defined as "the total combination of relatively permanent tendencies to act, think, or feel in specific ways" (Jackel 1975, p. 287). Since personality is unique for all individuals, people's life-long personality traits will have a direct bearing on the kind of older person they become. For example, a woman who is assertive, confident and positive as she approaches new experiences will probably view old age as one more new and exciting adventure. Someone who approaches life from a pessimistic, complaining viewpoint no doubt will behave similarly as an aged person.

Within this diversity of personality types, a general agreement exists that there are some normative changes in personality that correlate with age. Carl Jung spoke of an "introverted type" that becomes especially noticeable in later life. This type is characterized by an attitude of withdrawal, a concentration on subjective factors, and a preference for reflection over activity (Fordham 1953). Neugarten (1979) refers to this change from outer-world directedness to inner-world directedness as "interiority." Regardless of the term used for this phenomenon, for some people there does appear to be a definite turning inward of the psyche toward the later years of life. But studies by others have found no age differences on measures of "interiority" (Ryff 1984; Ryff & Heincke 1983). An added dimension is the role played by other people and society, which may reinforce or encourage this tendency to turn inward (Botwinick 1978).

Another personality change is related to the traditional sex-role orientation of men and women. Men are seen as moving from an active to a more passive mode, while women move toward increased instrumentality and assertiveness. Gutmann (1987) has found this pattern to occur in a number of different cultures, and explained it as a possible way for older adults to reconnect with parts of their personality that had to be suppressed in earlier years. During early adulthood, women must suppress their aggressive impulses in order to provide appropriate parenting, while men must suppress their affiliative impulses in order to provide adequate financial resources for the family (Gilligan 1982; Gutmann 1987). When these roles are no longer important for the older person, he and she are "freed" to re-experience other components of their personality.

Tranquility: Old age is a time of relative peace and tranquility.

Much of the research on older adults has found that old people frequently report fewer worries about who they are and how they look to others. Their self-esteem is higher and many of the stresses of the middle adulthood years are no longer in evidence. However, some stress is always present in life. For older adults, there are some specific anxieties, fears, and depression that relate to their stage of development. Although always a part of living, losses are more pervasive in later life. Physiological losses, such as hearing, hair, and muscle tone, begin at about age thirty and become much more pronounced with age. There are the losses of spouses, friends, and relationships. There is the loss of some vigor and strength, work and status. For older persons with less income, there is the loss of financial security. The losses which older people face are present in multiple aspects of functioning.

Older people respond to losses in various ways. Some old people react to these losses with fear, anxiety, and depression while others maintain a more positive attitude. Considering the quantity and quality of the losses inevitably experienced by the aged, some form of reaction is normal. Anticipatory anxiety may be present with older people posing questions such as "What will happen if my spouse dies before I do?" and "Will I be able to continue living in my own apartment for the rest of my life?" Fear and anxiety can be related to health problems, anticipated helplessness, loneliness, and being vulnerable to crime.

Reactions to these losses appear to account for much of the normal depression seen among older people. Physical loss and the death of friends and loved ones can result in feelings of sadness, of having been cheated, and lowered self-esteem. Life circumstances, such as living in poverty or moving into a nursing home, can also cause feelings of depression and negativism. It is frequently difficult to distinguish between these feeling states and more severe clinical depression. Often the aged are not evaluated and treated for depression because symptoms are seen as being typical for old age and frequently are related to somatic complaints. Considering that depression, but not diagnosable depressive disorders, is more common in older people (and the incidence of suicide among the aged is high), lack of treatment may reflect a form of ageism (Kaplan & Sadock 1998).

Unresponsiveness: Older people are unresponsive to psychosocial interventions.

This myth addresses the ageist idea that older people cannot be helped by mental health interventions. For example, complaints about fatigue or lack of appetite are viewed as a natural consequence of aging. However, these symptoms may indicate depression.

While later-life depression is sometimes the ongoing manifestation of a chronic and life-long depressive disorder, frequently it is a reaction to the stresses and losses of later life. Events such as retirement, bereavement, and a move to a new residence can precipitate depression, especially since many of these events often cluster together. In old age, people experience more losses and have fewer ways of coping with them. A younger person may deal with low periods by vigorous exercise, being with friends, and other active pursuits, while health limitations may prevent these ways of coping in later life.

While there are conflicting findings from studies on depression and other emotional problems, depending on who was interviewed and how problems were measured, a very large study conducted at five sites in the United States sampled 18,571 adults from rural and urban environments. The researchers found that depression and other emotional disturbances (i.e., substance abuse disorders, affective disorders, and anxiety disorders) are lower in the over sixty-five age group and decline in frequency from early adulthood through old age

(Regier et al. 1988). However, another study found that there is an increase in the number of persons over the age of seventy who report sad, lonely, or blue feelings (Kessler et al. 1992). These studies may represent the difference between mental disorders that are diagnosed by a mental health professional—dysthymia, major depression, bipolar disorder, anxiety disorder (APA 1994)—and feelings of depression.

Whether emotional problems are officially diagnosed or not, as our knowledge of older adults increases we are becoming more aware of the fact that older persons are not doomed to depression as a function of age, but that there are interventions that help to alleviate these problems. Older persons are increasingly being treated for emotional difficulties through group and individual psychosocial interventions, often provided by social workers.

In addition, the use of psychotropic medications is now well accepted in the treatment of depression and anxiety among the aged population. There are special considerations to be taken into account when psychotropic medication is administered that are important for social workers to understand. Due to the physiological changes of aging, absorption of a medication into the bloodstream is slowed, and drugs do not take effect as quickly. Generally, less medication is required for the same effect, and toxic amounts of a drug build quicker in the bloodstream. Based on other physical problems the older person may be experiencing, kidney and liver function may be slowed, and this too can affect drug metabolism. Substance use/abuse among older persons, misuse of over-the-counter drugs, and the possibility that psychological symptoms may be the result of medical illness all must be carefully evaluated when psychotropics are prescribed (Bentley & Walsh 1996).

Since all antidepressant medications are equally effective, the choice of which one to use is usually made based on the side-effect profile (Kaplan & Sadock 1998). The newest antidepressants, the selective serotonin re-uptake inhibitors (SSRIs), have fewer side effects and are well-tolerated by older persons. Benzodiazepines are the most widely used drugs for treatment of anxiety among the elderly, but their long term use is controversial based on their potential for abuse (Kaplan & Sadock 1998).

Senility: Senility is inevitable in old age.

This myth stems from the antiquated idea that confusion and loss of one's mental faculties are a natural part of the aging process. Only a small percentage of the aged develop an irreversible brain disorder. An important part of social work practice with the elderly is to be able to identify the symptoms of a brain disorder, to know something about the etiology, and have an understanding about the progression of this illness.

In addition to depression and anxiety, the most common mental disorder of old age is dementia, which is a deterioration of intellectual abilities as reflected by significant impairment in memory, judgment, social functioning, and control of emotions (Bee 1996). Dementia is diagnosed when the loss of cognitive and intellectual abilities is severe enough to impair social or occupational performance. Impairments occur in short- and long-term memory, abstract thinking and judgment, and personality change. About 5 percent of the over-age sixty-five population in the United States have a significant degree of dementia and are unable to care for themselves. Another 15 percent of the aged population have mild dementia. Among persons over the age of eighty, about 20 percent have severe dementia. However, dementia is not always irreversible, and approximately 10 to 15 percent of those with symptoms of dementia have conditions that are potentially treatable

(Kaplan & Sadock 1998). Some of these illnesses are heart disease, renal disease, congestive heart failure, endocrine disorders, vitamin deficiency, medication misuse, and depressive disorders.

Fifty to sixty percent of persons with dementia have dementia of the Alzheimer's type, commonly referred to as Alzheimer's disease (Kaplan & Sadock 1998). The course of this illness is generally progressive and marked by deterioration, with an average time span of eight years from onset to death. In the last stages of the illness, the person is usually totally incapable of self-care. Due to the level and severity of impairments, many people are in nursing homes at this stage of the disease. The other major type of dementia is vascular dementia, which is due to cerebrovascular disease, or multiple strokes. This is most common in men. The course is much more erratic, and early treatment of hypertension and vascular disease may prevent further progression.

Delirium is also a syndrome commonly found in older adults, and advanced age is a major risk factor in its development. This condition is reversible if the underlying cause is diagnosed and treated in a timely manner. In older adults, delirium can be caused by congestive heart failure, malnutrition and anemia, strokes, alcoholism, drug toxicity, and the stress of surgery. Delirium is usually of brief duration and marked by confusion, disorientation, and an inability to test reality. Since some of the symptoms of delirium are similar to dementia, it is extremely important that a careful history and medical team assessment be conducted in order to differentiate the two disorders.

As mentioned earlier, drug toxicity can lead to delirium. This problem has become serious among people over age sixty-five, who are estimated to consume at least twice the amount of prescription drugs as younger adults. In an effort to self medicate, some elderly people collect prescriptions from several physicians and combine these with over-the-counter preparations. Sedatives, digitalis drugs, diuretics, antihypertensives, antidepressants, and anti-anxiety medications are some of the prescription drugs that are most likely to be misused.

> **Intelligence:** Older people cannot learn anything new; intelligence declines with advancing age.

It is difficult to make any definite statements about the cognitive functioning of the aged, as there seems to be much variability among different people. Cohort factors reflect environmental influences based on the period of time during which one was raised and the opportunities available. For example, the current cohort lived during the Great Depression. This event may have a major impact upon saving and investment patterns. "Hoarding behavior" demonstrated by some older people may be a response to the major financial and social changes associated with the Depression era and not be a sign of decreased ineffectual functioning. A cohort factor accounts for much of the differences in performance among people of different ages.

The use of intelligence tests with the elderly presents some of the same problems as with other subgroups. Test results can be affected by education and familiarity with testing procedures, or the test questions may not be relevant to older people. In addition, the type of research methodology employed when making comparisons between groups of people can alter results. For example, a cross-sectional design often compares intelligence among groups of different aged people. If people in the oldest age group score lower than younger people,

less years
formal education

a frequent interpretation is that intelligence declines with age. However, differences between scores of older and younger people could be the result of the cohort effect. In our society, older people have had fewer years of education than their children or grandchildren. Low scores on intelligence tests may reflect educational achievements and not declining intelligence. Most gerontologists would agree that there is a general decline in intellectual ability as one ages, but that this decline is quite small until late in life, probably the seventies and eighties (Bee 1996). Verbal skills show almost no decline until the advanced years of old age, but performance requiring psychomotor skills generally diminishes with increasing age, especially when speed is involved.

Horn (cited in Newman & Newman 1987) distinguished two kinds of intelligence. Crystallized intelligence is the ability to apply past learning to new situations, and fluid intelligence is the ability to impose organization on information and to generate new hypotheses. Crystallized intelligence increases with age, experience, and physical maturation. Fluid intelligence does decline with age (Newman & Newman 1987). This dichotomy of intelligence parallels what is referred to as the "classic aging pattern"; with increased age, verbal abilities are maintained while performance skills decline (Botwinick 1978).

Memory: Memory loss in old age is inevitable.

Few clear answers exist about how memory is affected by age. More commonly people contrast short-term and long-term memory, with short-term referring to a few seconds to several weeks, and long-term referring to memories beyond several weeks. Using this model, short-term memory is found to be more adversely affected by aging than is long-term memory. A more refined definition distinguishes between primary memory (PM) or secondary memory (SM). Primary memory is temporary and immediate. For example, remembering what just took place does not require any processing. Secondary memory involves anything longer than a few seconds and requires processing of the information. Studies have shown that there is little, if any, difference between young and old people on primary memory capacity. However, there does seem to be an age effect when a memory task is more demanding. For example, when subjects are asked to remember information and then rearrange it in backward order, older persons perform less well than younger persons (West & Crook 1990). Younger people perform better on tasks related to secondary, or long-term, memory. While the reasons for this are not certain, they are probably related to greater retrieval problems as we age and a decreased ability to encode information (i.e., how material is organized in our memory) (Poon 1985).

Problem-Solving: Old people can't solve day-to-day problems.

Problem-solving ability is another cognitive process. Studies show that from age twenty-one to thirty-five years problem-solving ability is high. After age thirty-five, this ability begins to decline, with increasing amounts of decline after age fifty (Botwinick 1978). Several longitudinal studies, for example, the Baltimore Longitudinal Study of Aging (Costa & McRae 1988), have found that the ability to problem solve does not significantly decline until age seventy. Some of the decline in problem-solving ability seen among the aged may be related to a memory deficit. When one attempts to solve a problem, information about the situation has to be learned and remembered in order to be related or integrated with what is learned next. This process requires a higher degree of fluid intelligence. Problem solving may be inhibited by the older person's changes in memory systems.

Some evidence exists that the elderly have more difficulty than younger people in solving certain problems that require abstract thought. Older adults frequently have a preference for more concrete thought processes and tasks. Educational level could be a cohort factor on this dimension, since it has been found that the higher the education level, the lower the preference for thinking in concrete terms. If a cohort effect does exist, a prediction is that the current middle-age cohort, which is highly educated, would not evidence this preference for concrete thoughts and tasks.

Rigidity or inflexibility of thought could also be a factor in the problem-solving ability of older persons. For example, if people are inclined to consider only true and false as absolute in viewing a problem, they might be prevented from looking at other possibilities. The research on rigidity and the relationship to age demonstrates inconclusive results. Cross-sectional studies showed increased rigidity with age while longitudinal studies showed a mixture of age-decreases and age-increases (Botwinick 1978). The degree of rigidity is probably determined more by culture and experiential factors than by the normal changes of aging. With increasing opportunities for the aged to continue their intellectual growth, a concomitant decrease in rigidity may result (Botwinick 1978).

Sexual Interest: Older persons are asexual, have no interest in sex and are unable to function as sexual beings.

Prevalent in our society are two common myths about sexuality and the aged. First is the myth that sexuality is characteristic for the young but not typical or even normal after a certain age. The second myth is that if sexuality does exist in later life, it is unusual, wrong, and even sinful. These stereotypes of decreased sexual interest as one ages may adversely affect the elderly. Older people might feel guilty and uncomfortable with their sexuality, since our society creates an expectation that sexual intimacy and sensuality are only acceptable for younger people. A person's self-concept and sense of personal identity are closely connected to one's sexual identity. If sexual identity must be denied, either due to societal restraints or lack of available partners, the elderly person's image of self can be negatively affected. This situation would be especially relevant for an older person who had experienced sexual and intimate relationships throughout young and middle adulthood. While studies show that the frequency of sexual activity declines with increasing age, approximately 70 percent of men and 20 percent of women over the age of sixty are sexually active (Kaplan & Sadock 1998). The gender difference may be a function of partner availability, since women live longer than men. Though biological changes of aging and the duration of marriages and partnerships can have adverse effects, it is clear that the sex drive for men and women does not decrease with age.

Dependency: Old people are dependent and need someone to take care of them.

Independence, dependence, and interdependence are terms heard frequently in talking about older adults. Independence is defined as "self-perceived and actual behavioral and psychological individuality" (Quinn & Hughston 1984, p. 244). This concept does not imply social or physical distancing. An elderly person who is able to perform basic self-maintenance functions, such as dressing, cooking, shopping, and handling finances, would be seen as independent. Another definition of independence is the ability to master one's environment, to continue a lifestyle that is familiar, and to have some control over one's life, friends, actions, and self-esteem. American society strongly values independence. From the toddler stage of development through adolescence and into young adulthood, success is measured by the amount of independence or autonomy the person has achieved. Older adults do not lose their desire for independence.

Independence is closely related to self-esteem. Aged people who are able to maintain control over life decisions and to provide their own self-care will feel a sense of pride in these accomplishments. This ability will enhance their feeling of positive self-regard. These reasons explain why the elderly who live in institutions frequently experience low self-esteem. Dependent behavior is sometimes required and subtlely encouraged in institutions for the aged.

While independence is highly valued, normal aging processes lead to increased dependencies among the elderly. Economic dependency can result from loss of a job or career, and be due to loss of wages as a result of retirement. As physical changes such as hearing and sight loss occur, the older person may become dependent on someone else for transportation, home repairs, and housework. If chronic medical conditions exist, such as arthritis or diabetes, the aged person may be dependent upon others for the basics of daily living. Social dependencies can also increase. As aging processes make a person less mobile, especially after retirement from a job or career, there tend to be fewer people in one's environment for social support. Loss of contact with others because of mobility impairments, death or lack of resources such as transportation may make an older person more dependent on certain people. Family members and neighbors may become an older person's only source of social contacts.

Rather than viewing the elderly as either independent or dependent, this group may be viewed as interdependent. Quinn and Hughston (1984) believe that healthy independence requires an interconnectedness or relationship with other people. For example, older adults can maintain independence via interdependence with their adult children. These relationships are frequently a two-way flow, in which parents give to their children and children give to their parents. This reciprocal exchange can benefit the older and the younger person. An example of this relationship exists when grandparents watch the grandchildren in exchange for adult children making repairs on the parents' home. Everyone feels they are making a contribution, and all can feel needed. Such exchange situations can also occur between nonrelatives, for instance where younger and older people live on the same block, and help each other with mutually beneficial tasks. These interdependent relationships can enhance the older person's sense of usefulness, competence, and importance, while contributing to a sense of belonging for the elderly.

Bertram Cohler (1983) questions our society's placing such great importance on psychological independence. He believes that the dynamics of the early infant-mother relationship, referring to dependency, separation, and individuation are not always an appropriate paradigm for understanding interdependence across the lifespan. The supreme value placed on autonomy is in conflict with the simultaneous need for interdependence in adulthood. Cohler (1983) believes that an older person requires a balance in the autonomy which provides the time and energy to prepare for death and a need for interdependence. With persons now living longer and longer, it is much more likely that two or more generations of adults will be able to continue long-standing relationships and both benefit from the greater depth and meaning of this interdependence (Cohler & Altergott 1995).

This need for autonomy is related to the developmental tasks of old age and the attitude one adopts about life in the later years. Several developmental tasks have been identified for the elderly: to clarify, deepen, and find use for what one has already obtained in a lifetime of learning and adapting; to adjust to those changes and losses that occur as part of the aging experience; to learn not to think in terms of the future, because this is the only period of life that has no future (Butler 1985). Erik Erikson (cited in Newman & Newman 1987) characterizes old age as the period in life when one struggles with the psychosocial crisis of ego integrity versus despair. Integrity is the ability to accept one's life and to face death without great fear. This acceptance can only be achieved after considerable thought about the meaning of one's life, being honest with oneself about one's life, and being able to integrate one's past and present to feel content with the outcome. The opposite pole is despair, which is a feeling of regret about one's past and a nagging desire to be able to do things differently. Despair involves thinking and wondering about how things might have been. If one's life results in despair, it is impossible to calmly accept death. Integrity can be achieved by engaging in deliberate self-evaluation and private thought and by reminiscing to recapture some memorable events in one's life history. Through this process of introspection, aged people hopefully reach an attitude of self-acceptance, of feeling content and worthwhile (Newman & Newman 1987).

The life review can be a normal process of old age, though it is not always seen as having beneficial effects (Bee 1996). This review brings into consciousness many past experiences and unresolved conflicts which are reconsidered and can then be integrated. A review of one's life, from the vantage point of being able to look back over the entire life cycle, is important for self-acceptance, life planning for the remaining years, and deciding upon material and emotional legacies (Butler 1985). The life review process can also help to reduce fear and anxiety as one approaches death (Silverstone & Hyman 1982).

Social Myths

Older people are victimized by stereotypes about their social functioning. The elderly are frequently viewed as being alone without social contacts. While loneliness and isolation are a consequence of aging for some people, most older people have contact with family, friends, and neighbors. The following section addresses the social myths associated with the elderly.

> **Withdrawal:** Older people inevitably withdraw from the mainstream of society as they grow older.

Role changes and transitions continue in the later years but with qualitative and quantitative differences from earlier periods of life. Young adults frequently feel role overload which is a sense of being pulled by multiple responsibilities. For example, a woman may feel role overload from tasks of simultaneously being a wife, mother, and paid worker. Many roles may continue, such as that of parent, but these roles become qualitatively and quantitatively different as age increases. Generally, there are fewer expectations associated with roles that continue into old age. Whether such changes are positive or negative appears to be a matter of personal perspective. Some elderly shed roles with regret, but others enjoy fewer roles resulting in a less hectic lifestyle or activities that may reflect more personal interests and choice. Yet, maintaining social roles is important to all dimensions of human behavior. Considerable research has supported the strong interrelationships among social integration, health, and well-being for the elderly (Lubben & Gironda 1996).

In recent years, however, research has shown that the elderly are also acquiring new roles. The vast majority adapt, oftentimes in creative ways, to the social changes. For many people, the later years offer new opportunities for social growth and a sense of integrity. Over the last thirty years, volunteerism has increased from only one-third of all elderly to almost half of the elderly engaging in a volunteer activity (Chambre 1993). For others, however, the lack of education, income, community resources, life experiences, and health may lead to a life of loss, isolation, and little hope.

Fanaticism: The elderly become preoccupied with religion as they age.

The elderly do in fact report increasing levels of religious participation and spiritual meaning compared to younger cohorts (U.S. Bureau of the Census 1993). However, evidence points to this participation reflecting possible changes in life meaning and increased self-acceptance versus a preoccupation with religion or a desire to proselytize generally associated with fanaticism (Veroff, Douvan, & Kulka, 1993).

Religion and the accompanying rituals offer social support and involvement, and aid in the adaptation to death and dying. More frequent church attenders (versus less frequent or nonattenders) have shown higher levels of life satisfaction (Doff & Hong 1982). Blacks evidence a particularly high life-satisfaction rate when regularly attending church (Neighbors, Jacobson, Bowman, & Gurin 1983). Taylor (1986) reported that blacks were not only more likely to indicate a higher degree of importance of religion, but that women were more religious than men. One exception is in relation to church attendance where rural women and urban men were the most frequent attenders. The old-old tend to decrease church attendance due to poor health and difficulty in getting around, but engage in solitary religious rituals such as prayer or scripture reading.

Isolation: The elderly are dependent but socially isolated and neglected by their families.

Most older people remain connected to their family. Many people continue to live with a family member all their lives. Until the age of seventy-five, most elderly live in family households, mostly as married couples. About 70 percent of elderly men are married and live with their spouses. This figure compares to 23 percent of females who live with husbands. Twenty-two percent of men and 68 percent of females are widowed. In addition to being marital partners, the elderly form other relationship patterns. Homosexual relationships between the elderly are predicted to have less social stigma for future cohorts as social norms have changed for younger people. Lesbian partners report a high incidence of monogamous, long-term relationships, a situation much less common among gay men (Blumstein & Schwartz 1983). In a large study of gay males, Gray and Dressel (1985) report findings that challenge the common beliefs that the aged homosexual is lonely, secretive, and stigmatized. Subcultural support of the aging gay male was found to exist to a far greater degree than previous research had indicated.

In addition to marriage, two other household patterns are common for older people. One living arrangement is the one person household. Forty percent of all one-person households are age sixty-five and over, with widowed people being the largest group. In 1980, for all persons aged eighty-five and over, 39 percent lived alone, but this figure rose to 48 percent by 1993 (U.S. Bureau of the Census 1993). In 1993, 18 percent of men over age sixty-five lived alone, a 2 percent increase since 1970. For women, 76 percent lived alone in 1993 compared to 75 percent in 1970. Two times more females than males live alone after the age of eighty-five, 59 and 28 percent, respectively. This proportion of elderly women living alone has risen continually over the last twenty years. In addition to there being more women than men, both social stereotypes and economic disincentives negatively impact the remarriage rate for the elderly, particularly women (Bee 1996). A second household pattern is living with a relative who is not a spouse. About 18 percent of elderly females, versus 7 percent of elderly males, live in this type of arrangement. If the elderly do live with a relative, it is considerably more likely that it will be an elderly female living with a daughter. For elderly living with a middle-aged child, co-residence averages about four years (Beck & Beck 1984). Nonfrail elderly living with an adult child report more advantages than disadvantages to co-residence (Harrigan 1992). Considerable documentation over time indicates that both adult children and their elderly parents prefer to live independently of each other (Sussman 1976). In fact, for the oldest old, the rate of co-residence with a relative other than a spouse declined from 36 to 25 percent between 1980 and 1993 (U.S. Bureau of the Census 1996).

Even when a parent does not live in the same household as an adult child, interaction between the generations remains high. About 75 percent of all elderly have at least one surviving child. Furthermore, the vast majority (75 percent) of these elderly live within a thirty minute travel time of at least one adult child in both urban and rural areas (Sussman 1989). An extensive national study revealed that 53 percent of the elderly surveyed had visited with an adult child on the day of the survey or the previous day (Shanas, 1979). Research does not support the belief that adult children do not stay in contact with older parents who live in a different household.

Migration and housing also impact the social dimension of aging. Sunbelt state migration has increased considerably in the last thirty years. However, the vast majority of the elderly do not move but "age in place." Between 1975 and 1979, only 6 percent of the elderly moved with 64 percent of the moves being in the same county. Only 17 percent of the moves were interstate (Lawton 1980).

Even when housing accommodations are substandard, older people resist moving. Elderly also tend to overrate the condition of their housing. In fact, 83 percent of the elderly rate their housing as excellent or good despite evidence by housing experts to the contrary (Lawton 1980). For those who do move, there does not seem to be much difference in housing quality, housing satisfaction, and neighborhood satisfaction when compared to those who do not move. A house, even if not reflective of the standards set by "experts," is a symbol and touchstone for reminiscence, past effects, and prior relationships for many older people (Rowles 1980). While most elderly people adapt both socially and psychologically to a new environment, recent research on those in nursing homes indicates that adaptation was predicted by the match between the degree of choice and control offered by a facility and the level of self-determination of the person (O'Conner & Vallerand 1994).

Not all elderly live in their own home/apartment or with relatives. While only 5 percent of all elderly reside in a nursing home at any given time, the probability of institutionalized living increases with age and is related to several factors, such as marital status, health, income, and the presence and gender of adult children (Naleppa 1996). For the vast majority of families, institutional placement of an elderly family member is done only after exhausting other alternatives. Consequently, this event is considered to be a family crises due to the emotional stress it encumbers (Schneewind 1990).

After an elderly person is placed in an institution, interactions with his or her family members change but continue (Palmer 1991; Zarit & Whitlach 1992). Influenced by the distance involved as well as the flexibility of the institution in allowing visitors, most elderly receive visitors, and a little more than half reported satisfaction with visitation they receive (Bitzan & Kruzich 1990). Caregiving also continues for nursing home residents, although the tasks involved become shared with the staff and the degree to which family involvement is delineated and encouraged (Riddick et al. 1992; Safford 1980).

Social Services: Social services provided to the elderly by organizations usurp the family's traditional care and interpersonal functions.

Abuse and Neglect: Most elderly are abused and neglected.

Although the vast majority of elderly live independently and require minimal assistance, the prevalence of family caregiving is at the highest level ever. From an historic perspective, the frequency of elderly living with adult children was never as prevalent as people tend to believe, and the demographics of the past do not support this arrangement (Cherlin 1979; Hareven 1995). It is speculated that, as current political and social philosophies lead to a decrease in federal investment in human service programs, families will be asked to provide more caregiving with fewer resources. This is further impacted by decreasing family size, increased longevity, and the aging of the baby boomers, thus resulting in fewer adult children per elderly person. Consequently, family stress will become even greater (Brody 1985; Sussman 1985). The important role of governmental services in family caregiving has been documented. Researchers indicate that governmental support of families strengthens family bonds by decreasing anxiety about the ability to provide for one's parents (Cicarelli 1981; Treas 1977).

Elder abuse and neglect occurs at all socioeconomic levels of society and for all racial and ethnic groups. Although definitions of elder abuse vary across the country, the National Aging Resource Center on Elder Abuse (NARCEA) provides a definition that parallels those of most states as well as the definition proposed by the Older American's Act. The NARCEA lists seven types of maltreatment: physical abuse; sexual abuse; emotional or psychological abuse; neglect; financial or material exploitation; self-abuse and neglect; and all others not included the first six categories.

More elusive than a definition is the incidence and prevalence of elder abuse. While far from conclusive, researchers estimate that at least 1.5 to 3 percent of all elderly suffer abuse other than self-neglect (Pillemer & Finkelhor 1988; Tatara 1992). Tatara's data from thirty states indicated that neglect accounts for almost half of all elder abuse, followed by physical abuse in almost 20 percent of cases; exploitation, 17 percent; psychological/emotional, 14 percent; and sexual abuse, less than 1 percent of cases. Women suffer more abuse than do men, most often at the hands of a man. Similar to child abuse, the contributing factors reflect personal, contextual, and abuser characteristics. Although research is sparse, abuse occurs due to caregiver stress (Bendik 1992; Pillemer & Finkelhor 1989; Tatara 1993), inter-generational transmission of abuse in response to conflict (Fulmer & O'Mallery 1987), personal problems of the abuser such as substance abuse or financial (Anetzberger 1987; Greenberg, McKibban, & Raymond 1990; Tatara 1993), and impairment of dependent elderly (George 1986; Pillemer & Moore 1989).

The profile of the elderly who are abused, particularly the females, indicates that they have greater needs than the unabused but that they lack alternatives to meet these needs. In addition, they have at least two physical disabilities (Hancock, 1987). Several other factors perpetuate both abuse and neglect. Increased numbers of the frail elderly are living longer without adequate community resources to assist with family care giving. Prejudice and discrimination which devalue the elderly contribute to abuse and neglect as well. Society's acceptance of violence further encourages abuse and neglect (Hancock 1987).

All care giving situations are not detrimental to the elderly and their families. The vast majority of family care to an elderly member is provided by a female, regardless of consanguinty or blood relationship. Exchange theory has guided some of the research on caregiving. The elderly are care recipients but also providers in such areas as companionship, child care, and family income (Harrigan 1992). Imbalance in the exchange is more likely to occur with the declining health and need for increasing care of the older person. The impact of caregiving on all family members can be profound without additional family supports when care giving demands increase (Hooyman & Lustbader 1986; Silverstone & Hyman 1982).

After considerable hardship, most families ask for help in caring for the elderly (Brody 1978). Only about 5 percent of the elderly are institutionalized at any given time. The probability of ever needing a nursing home is estimated to be 25 to 30 percent (Newman & Newman 1987). This fact reveals that even frail people continue to reside within the community. Families continue to provide care even when an older person is impaired.

Alienation: Generation gaps lead to alienation of the elderly.

Older people do not appear to be alienated by younger family members. Intergenerational relations research has documented the perceptions of satisfying relationships within families. An extensive national panel study of three generations (Black & Bengtson 1973; Glass, Bengtson & Dunham 1986) found that close and meaningful relationships were reported by the vast majority of people. Another national study found that four out of five adults reported an emotionally close relationship with parents (Lawton, Silverstone, & Bengtson 1994). These relationships were reported to improve over time.

Extremely high intergenerational solidarity is found within minority groups. This situation is attributed to both the cultural heritage patterns of the groups and economic adaptation. Yet within ethnic elderly groups there is considerable variation which has implications for the design and use of social services. Some groups use social services more readily, seemingly aware that the family is already too stressed economically to provide any type of care. Other groups will provide for the elderly despite devastating economic and psychosocial impacts (Sussmann 1976, 1985).

Although conflicts between the generations exist, the desire to maintain family relationships continue to override the destructive potentials of such conflict (Quinn & Hughston 1984). In fact, middle-aged people perceive themselves as not having "generational gaps" with their own parents and/or children. However, these people report that generation gaps do exist in other families (Black & Bengtson 1973).

Grandparenthood appears to have taken on new meanings as more people age and social roles change. While this role is typically acquired before a person becomes elderly, most elderly will become great and even great-great grandparents (Cherlin & Furstenberg 1986). In fact, in the United States more than 90 percent of older adults are grandparents (Kornhaber 1996). Although there are several "types" of grandparent/child relationships, most grandparents enjoy a rewarding relationship with grandchildren (Cherlin & Furstenberg 1986). These relationships are characterized by free expression, warmth, and support and are qualitatively different from the relationships that many older people had with their own grandparents. In fact, some grandparents have more satisfying relationships with grandchildren than with their own children. These different relationships are due to decreased pressures, a less hectic lifestyle, and a perspective that spans the life cycle (Cherlin & Furstenberg 1986). The grandparent role contributes to a sense of self-worth and purpose in life (Kivnick 1983).

Grandparents also are contributing increasingly to the lives of their grandchildren as surrogate parents in the absence of the biological parent due to substance abuse, child abuse, neglect or abandonment, death, divorce, joblessness, HIV-AIDS, poverty, and incarceration. In 1995, 2.5 million grandparents provided care to grandchildren and almost 1 million of these were the primary caretakers (Minkler 1994). With most of these major social problems continuing to rise, it is anticipated that more frequently grandparents will return to parenting (Minkler & Rose 1993). The assumption of this role for most is in sharp contrast to the expected and is further challenged by economic and legal issues (Flint & Perez-Porter 1997; Robertson 1995).

Stress: Old age is a time of relative peace and tranquility when people can relax and enjoy the fruits of their labor after the stresses of life have passed.

Although older people may not experience the exact problems and worries as younger people, the elderly are faced with stressful issues. One area which may become problematic is the marital situation of an older couple. Marital satisfaction in previous family life stages obviously impacts the degree of satisfaction as the couple age. However, life events such as retirement impact marital satisfaction, as both people must renegotiate the type and amount of time they spend together. For the current aging cohort, women may find the increased presence of their spouses to be disruptive to their household routines of many years. Furthermore, the more loneliness a man feels post-retirement, the more pressure he may put on his spouse for togetherness. As a result, wives tend to report a loss of privacy and too much demand for their time, thereby decreasing other leisure and work activities. Ultimately, a decrease in marital satisfaction may occur. However, a more flexible pattern of carrying out household tasks may also evolve among retired couples when compared to earlier patterns (Palmore, Fillenbaum, & George 1984). In spite of early relationship adjustments to retirement, overall marriage for elderly persons becomes a resource by contributing a better quality of life for both people as individuals and as a couple.

The high divorce rate in our society has had an effect upon older couples. Each year about ten thousand Americans over the age of sixty-five are divorced. Although only one-fourth of all divorces occur after the age of forty (Uhlenberg, Cooney, & Boyd 1990), the elderly continue to adjust less well to divorce compared to younger adults (Kitson 1992). This event may become more prevalent as younger cohorts age (Uhlenberg & Myers 1981). As of the year 2000, over half of those entering old age have been divorced a least once. A divorce has an impact upon more than just the marital status. Other roles, such as grand-parent, are affected. The resulting economic changes are another area worthy of considera-tion (Hagestad 1982).

Another change in marital status—the death of a spouse—is a stressful event for older people. Widowhood is considered to be one of the most disruptive of all social changes. To-day, over 50 percent of women and only 12 percent of men over sixty-five are widowed (Bee 1996). The average widow is age fifty-six with a life expectancy set at age seventy-five. This role status can be expected to exist for another twenty years for the majority of widows. Adaptation to the death of a spouse is facilitated by social support, resilience, creative prob-lem solving, and a strong commitment to a belief in one's personal worth. For today's widow, however, this role change is accompanied by a sharp decrease in income and few marketable skills. Future cohorts are expected to have both higher income and skills level which may better facilitate adaptation to this role change.

Retirement: The elderly are unable to work or do not want to work. Old people are poor people.

Retirement is frequently perceived as one of the most profound social adjustments, al-though there is increasing normative acceptance. The average age of retirement is increas-ing, particularly for men and those individuals with a college education. As with other social changes, good health and adequate income predict better adjustment to retirement. When retirement is coupled with the recent death of a spouse, the adjustment process is especially problematic. Retirement adjustment is further related to the ability to engage in a socially active life yielding more social support in general (Antonucci 1985). Variation in post-retirement lifestyles occurs with a tendency to maintain lifestyle patterns of pre-retirement. For example, a person who led a complex and active life prior to retirement will tend to seek out, find and engage in substitute activities (Baum & Baum 1980).

Adjustment to retirement may vary by gender. Recent findings indicate that women take longer to adjust to retirement than do men. One reason for this difference is that com-pared to men, women have larger social networks, which include co-workers. Kahn and An-tonucci (1983) report an average network size of 9.3 members for women compared to 7.6 for men. Women may expect to have fewer interactions with network members after a re-tirement which inhibits the adjustment to this event. A second explanation of a gender dif-ference is due to the reasons for retirement. There is some belief that women may retire against their will in order to provide caregiving (Szinovacz 1986–87) or retire later to en-sure income if a spouse is in poor health and not employed (O'Rand, Henretta, & Krecker 1992). A caregiver role is not supported by the midlife developmental changes of women who tend to become less family oriented as men become more family oriented (Gilligan 1982). More research is needed to explain gender differences in retirement patterns.

An aspect of the retirement myth is that older people do not want to work. In 1981 there was reported an increase in both the desire to work and the incidence of part-time work after the age of sixty-five. This preference was as high as 79 percent for workers age fifty-five to sixty-four and 73 percent for those over age sixty-five (National Council on

Aging 1981). Yet, Schiller (1998) reported that today, for all elderly, only one out of ten works, which includes one out of six elderly men. Demographic changes and economic cut backs do not favor employment of the elderly. In fact, one-third of all retired elderly reported that they were forced out of their jobs, and almost half of the poor elderly reported forced retirements (Schiller 1998). Older people are exemplary employees. They are less prone to accidents and absenteeism and demonstrate more commitment and loyalty to employers (Hartford 1985).

The economic status of the elderly has improved considerably in the past thirty years. By 1992 the median income for all elderly had doubled since 1957, and the poverty rate for all elderly had declined to 12.9 percent from 24.6 percent in 1970. Most elderly today can expect retirement income to drop by 25 percent of preretirement income, yet for most, expenses do not decrease in the same proportion. In contrast, Smeeding (1990) found that the average retired U.S. adult has 85 to 100 percent of preretirement income.

Despite these changes, income for some elderly continues to be a major concern. As the elderly become the old-old group, inflation further devalues their postretirement income, which is typically fixed. Minorities in particular experience the greatest decline in income. For African-American elderly, 25 percent experience poverty compared to 24 percent of Hispanics and only 10 percent of Anglos. Due in part to the fact that minorities die earlier than do Caucasians, Caucasians account for eight out of ten old poor. One out of four widows over 85 is poor compared to only 4 percent of married couples age sixty-five to sixty-nine (Schiller 1998).

Most people continue to believe that Social Security will adequately provide for retirement, although economists adamantly state the need for private pension plans and savings to provide supplemental income after retirement. Today, 90 percent of all elderly receive Social Security, which is the primary source of income for 63 percent of recipients. Social Security is the sole source of income for 14 percent of recipients. And, again, women and minorities are the most likely to rely on Social Security as the primary or sole income source.

Several other income sources support the elderly. Savings provide some income for almost 80 percent of the aged nonpoor in the form of dividends and interest. This compares to only 33 percent of the aged poor who receive any income from stocks, saving accounts, and bonds. About 50 percent of nonpoor retirees receive private pensions compared to 8 percent of poor retirees. Families are another source of income for the elderly. Of the less than one-third of all elderly residing with families, only 3 percent receive any income support from them. Less than 25 percent of poor elderly receive welfare benefits (cash, food stamps, and housing assistance) compared to less than 5 percent of the nonpoor. Finally, almost 9 percent of the nonpoor compared to 5 percent of the poor receive unemployment, disability, or veterans benefits (Schiller 1998). While the elderly as a whole have acquired a more favorable economic base over the last few years, women, minorities, and particularly those who are old and in poor health have significantly higher levels of poverty.

Leisure Time: The elderly desire to be left alone and spend most of their time watching television.

Leisure activities do change as age increases, with the old-old and oldest-old preferring more sedentary activities, particularly if done in the home with a family focus. What does not appear to change is the need, desire, and meaning/reasons for engaging in leisure activities, including enjoyment of nature; appreciation for peace, quiet, and solitude; affection for those with whom the activity is done; and attraction to novel events. Changes in leisure activities for the elderly are most related to accessibility, which reflects changes in health, income, and mobility (Mancini & Sandifer 1995). Four interrelated lenses are needed to examine how the elderly pursue leisure: time, activities, preference, and competence. Time encompasses a person's perception of availability and control of time. Activity conveys the degree and type of interaction with others. Preference refers to the degree to which there is a match between what a person prefers to do and what is actually done. This also includes accessibility factors noted earlier and the perception of the motivation of others to be involved with the elderly person. Finally, competence relates to a person's ability either to do a previously mastered activity or to learn a new one (Mancini & Sandifer 1995).

Leisure activities have increased for the elderly as well as for other age groups in the past few years. For many elderly, leisure involvement becomes a new role due to increased free time after retirement. Most leisure activities have psychosocial benefits to the elderly which vary by type of activity (Tinsley, Teaff, Colbs, & Kaufman 1985). For example, dancing and bowling primarily offer companionship whereas reading and gardening offer solitude and security. Other activities contribute to self-esteem, stimulation, self-expression and biological functioning. For younger cohorts who have engaged in leisure activities across the lifespan, future elderly lifestyles may include even more leisure time involvement.

Volunteerism also has become a form of leisure for the elderly. In the past, this role was typically discarded with old age. Today almost one in three people over the age of seventy-five volunteers, a statistic that compares favorably to persons in their late teens and early twenties (Chambre 1993). As attitudes about aging have changed, and the elderly have experienced more education, better health, and more migration, social policies also have fostered volunteerism in both the public and private sectors.

Conclusion

Health, income, and social support are extremely important in adapting to the social changes of aging. Adaptation to the social changes of old age is largely related to available social support, which acts as a buffer of stress (Antonucci 1985). For example, health factors are most likely to place an elderly person in a less independent living arrangement, thereby decreasing social activity and contacts. Personal attitudes and the environmental context continue to impact adaptation. Some elderly manage to present a positive attitude and always look toward those who are "worse off," thereby placing their own circumstances in a favorable light. This attitude may then help them in the formation of new social relationships.

The interrelatedness of the biological, psychological, and social dimensions across the life span provide the basis for understanding the behavior of the elderly. The elderly display more uniqueness and variation in these dimensions than do young age groups. This fact is largely due to the elderly having had more years of development and a greater number of life experiences.

Demographic changes foretell a more favorable future for tomorrow's elderly. Increased educational levels of baby-boomers relate to predicted better health, greater independence of living, improved income, particularly for women who were in the labor market, and later widowhood (U.S. Bureau of the Census 1996).

Discussion Questions

1. How might the bio-psycho-social-spiritual model enhance assessment and broaden the interventive roles of the social worker?
2. What facts of aging are the most challenging to your beliefs about the aging process?
3. What adaptive processes and skills that you have already used in your own life might be of use to you as you age? Be specific in identifying the anticipated adaptations related to your own aging.
4. In what ways does the comparison between old age and childhood hamper our understanding of the elderly and contribute to commonly held myths of aging?
5. What bio-psycho-social variations would you predict, based on cultural and ethnic diversity, to impact the aging process? Consider groups such as Native Americans, Latin Americans, African Americans, and other groups with which you are familiar.

Experiential Learning

Activity: Experiencing the Biological Changes

This activity will help you become more sensitized to the biological processes of aging. You will have an opportunity to "try on" an impairing condition that simulates age-related changes. By participating in this exercise, you will also gain awareness of how biological changes impact psychological and social functioning.

The materials needed for this activity are: waxed paper, cotton balls, several pairs of gloves (surgical gloves work well), two elastic bandages, a yardstick, 1- to 2-inch wide strips of any type of material (to fasten yardstick to leg), cellophane tape, clear glass goggles or glasses, food items such as peanuts, raisins, apples, bread, or crackers, large handkerchiefs, clothespins (spring-type), ping-pong balls (2), and index cards (5).

PROCESS

Form groups of five members. Each group needs a set of the materials listed above. Copy each of the five impairing conditions described below on index cards. One set of cards will contain all five conditions. Each group member draws a card to select his or her impairment. In the context of your small group "try on" the condition described on your card. After everyone has finished this process, discuss the questions presented at the end of this activity.

Vision Impairment. Put tape on your eyeglass lenses, use a pair of taped goggles, or hold a sheet of waxed paper in front of the eyes. Talk to your group members, walk around the room, try to read.

Arthritis and Other Bone and Joint Changes. Wear gloves and wrap your knee, elbow, and other joints tightly. Then try to complete simple tasks such as buttoning a button, tying shoelaces, walking, bending, and dressing.

Hearing Loss. Use ear muffs or put cotton in your ears. Engage in a conversation with a group member. Gradually increase the size of the group of people talking and the background noise.

Stroke or Paralysis. Fasten the yardstick to your leg and try to walk, sit, climb stairs, or stand up. Try to write names or take class notes using the hand you don't normally use. Finally, place a marble or a ping-pong ball in your mouth and try to carry on a conversation.

Smell and Taste. Taste (1) similar and (2) contrasting foods while you are blindfolded and you hold your nose. A clothespin may work if it is not too tight.

DISCUSSION QUESTIONS

After students share their initial reactions to these experiences, continue the discussion by asking:

1. How could "limitation" affect behavior in the psychological and social dimensions?
2. If students have known an elderly person with a similar impairment, what did they observe in his or her behavior?
3. What might be some ways to adapt to the change or limitation? What resources would be needed? Examples are an appliance such as a hearing aid, money, assistance of a professional (physical therapist), a particular psychological disposition, support and/or adaptation of family or friends, etc.

Case Studies

See Appendix B for guidelines in analyzing gerontological social work practice.

Case 1: Identifying Nutritional Needs

A social worker from protective services visits the apartment of Mr. and Mrs. James, a frail-appearing couple in their eighties who have been referred by a neighbor. The neighbor is concerned about the apartment being a "fire trap" and causing the entire building to burn down.

The social worker finds a number of newspapers and cardboard boxes, but no other fire hazards. He also notices that there is almost nothing in the kitchen to eat. As he talks with the couple, he learns that they are receiving a noon meal from a Meals on Wheels service, and nothing at all on weekends. They order pizzas on weekends and sometimes during the week, as they can have them delivered, but the result is gastric distress for both of them.

The social worker learns that neither of them is able to shop for groceries, although they have money to pay for whatever food they need. Mr. James receives a pension which is more than ample to meet their needs. Mrs. James has crippling arthritis in her hands, wrists, and ankles. Mr. James has congestive heart disease and has been advised not to try to shop for or carry groceries.

The social worker suggests they pay a neighbor to do the shopping. Mrs. James nods, but her husband stridently objects to "forking out money" for this service. The social worker discusses the possibility of one or both of them becoming ill from lack of proper nutrients and the additional costs that would ensue. Finally, with some reluctance, the husband agrees. Mrs. James delightedly announces that she knows the person who will shop for them.

They immediately start making a grocery list, and the social worker realizes that the items do not comprise the elements of a balanced, nutritious diet. Thinking quickly, the social worker comments that he or she knows a way for the Jameses to have assistance in deciding what to buy and possibly save some money by making use of a dietitian service offered by the health department to older people.

Mrs. James agrees to this suggestion. The social worker leaves the apartment with a feeling of relief.

Source: Hancock 1987.

Case 2: Sexuality and Age

Mrs. Jarvis is a sixty-five year-old widow who is attending an outpatient hypertensive clinic at City Hospital, which serves the indigent. There is an open-ended patient education group meeting every week for hypertensive patients. The group is led once monthly by the same outpatient social worker.

Other group meetings are led by a dietitian, clinical nursing specialist, physical therapist, or physician. Each of these leaders presents patient education in regard to diet, medication, and exercise in relation to hypertension. The social worker discusses the effects of stress and tension and acts as facilitator in the group interaction that takes place in regard to patients' feelings and concerns about their illness. The social worker always stops by after meetings held by the other leaders and lets it be known that her time is available for anyone who may need social work service.

The social worker receives a referral from one of the city hospital internists in regard to arranging transportation for Mrs. Jarvis to attend group meetings. Mrs. Jarvis' blood pressure is elevated, and the internist doubts that she is taking her prescribed medication on a regular basis.

The social worker is surprised about the referral, for Mrs. Jarvis is one of the group's most faithful members. She has been attending the group for four months, and the social worker doubts that she has missed more than one or two meetings. The social worker recalls that Mrs. Jarvis told the group that she has been widowed for less than a year and that her husband had cancer and died after a long, bedridden illness. She remembers too, that Mrs. Jarvis lives with an arthritic son and his wife and children. The son is frequently hospitalized. Mrs. Jarvis receives Social Security and Supplemental Security Income.

It is difficult for the social worker to believe that Mrs. Jarvis would be careless about her medication or unwilling to follow the physician's directions. She is one of the most attentive members of the group and seems to have a good understanding of the patient role in the management of hypertension. During the group meeting, the social worker pays special attention to Mrs. Jarvis. She has the same interested expression she usually has. She is sitting next to a large man who appears to be about her age. The social worker recalls that this man is another of the regulars who nearly always attends the meetings. Mr. Franklin has been coming for about eight or nine weeks. He is a newly diagnosed hypertensive patient who suffered a light stroke which cleared in two weeks. The social worker remembers that he, too, is recently bereaved.

After the meeting, the social worker asks those who would like to see her afterward, to stop by her office. Mrs. Jarvis is waiting in her office when she arrives a few minutes later. She tells the social worker that her doctor has told her to talk to her, but she doesn't know why. The social worker explains the physician's concern. The patient appears uncomfortable and speaks so softly that the social worker can hardly hear her. She is apologetic about not taking her medication. She comments that she doesn't know why, but she simply cannot remember to take the medication. She thinks her forgetfulness may be due to her worries about her son.

Mrs. Jarvis then hesitantly tells the social worker that she is having some problems with her son and his family. There is a man she would like to be with, but she knows her children "would have a fit." She wishes now that she had not moved into her son's crowded home when her husband died. She would like to move and have her own place to live, but her son and daughter-in-law "won't hear of it." She is afraid her son will find out that she has a "beau." Mrs. Jarvis worries that the social worker will think she is terrible to think about a beau, since her husband is deceased for less than a year. The social worker says it is natural for Mrs. Jarvis to seek companionship as she is probably lonely. Also, older men and women have a need for intimacy just as younger people do.

Mrs. Jarvis and Mr. Franklin met at the hypertensive group meeting and immediately found they had much in common. He wants to get married right away, but she prefers to wait a while and live in her own place while she thinks about it. She seems to be feeling guilty about her new relationship. She also seems fearful about arousing her children's anger and ill will and depriving her arthritic son of the extra money that her Social Security checks bring into the home, if she should move.

The social worker believes that the client's feelings of guilt stem not only from the fact that the affair is extramarital, but from lying about her meeting with Mr. Franklin and deceiving her son. She suspects that Mrs. Jarvis's "forgetfulness" about taking her medication is an unconscious self-punishment for lying, or perhaps an unconscious desire to remain "sick" so that there is a valid reason for attending every group meeting. The social worker helps Mrs. Jarvis to explore the reasons for the feeling of anxiety she expresses. In a sense, she gives Mrs. Jarvis "permission" to continue the sexual relationship with Mr. Franklin and assures her that she is not "bad." The social worker supports the client's wish to find her own apartment and to think through a possible remarriage. She provides concrete suggestions for the client to relay to her son regarding rent, food, and transportation resources and arranges for a dietitian to help the client and her family.

The social worker continues to see Mrs. Jarvis weekly and learns that she continues to be troubled about something from her past. At age fifteen, Mrs. Jarvis became pregnant and was sent to live with an aunt until the baby was born. However, she had a miscarriage. She had tried to forget this incident and later told her husband what had occurred. Lately she kept thinking about this incident and the shame she brought to her parents. The social worker helps Mrs. Jarvis to realize that the present relationship with Mr. Franklin is probably reminding her of the earlier event. The fear of her son's learning about it is a repetition of the fears she experienced in relation to her mother. She helps Mrs. Jarvis to differentiate between the two experiences. In future meetings, they talk more of the unwed pregnancy and its effects on Mrs. Jarvis. As she begins to experience some relief from talking over this experience from her past, Mrs. Jarvis reports that she is remembering to take her blood pressure medication.

In the ensuing weeks Mrs. Jarvis and Mr. Franklin meet with the social worker to discuss their plans. Mrs. Jarvis moves into her own apartment and tells her son about her relationship with Mr. Franklin. Mrs. Jarvis's physician advises that her blood pressure is going down.

Source: Adapted from Hancock 1987.

Case 3: Correcting Misinformation—Arthritis

Agnes Barton comes to the attention of a social worker at a senior citizens center when she comes into his office seeking help in regard to transportation to the center. While there, she complains at some length about the painful arthritis in the joints of her hands and wrists. She supplements Social Security by doing domestic work. When she has jobs that require rubbing and polishing furniture, silver, and brass, the joints in her hands become swollen and red. She was advised by a physician at the city hospital to avoid using her hands in the same activity for long periods of time. A large dosage of aspirin was prescribed, but nothing else. She was disappointed because they did not give her any "real" medication. She does not bother to take the aspirin. She is taking " some pills" she ordered from an advertisement. They are expensive and aren't helping now, but she thinks they eventually will.

The social worker suggests that Mrs. Barton comply with the physician's recommendations in regard to aspirin. If it does not help her condition, she can return to the clinic physician and seek further help. He warns her that the medication she ordered from the advertisement may be harmful. He reminds her that a public health nurse attends the senior citizens center once a week and suggests she make an effort to come that day and talk with the nurse.

The social worker makes a mental note to suggest at the next staff meeting an informational program at the center on arthritis. Mrs. Barton has been the third person in the past few days to mention buying a "wonder drug" for arthritis from an advertisement of some kind.

Source: Hancock 1987.

Case 4: Responding to Depression

Julia Phillips had lived in the same house for fifty-seven years, a home where she and her husband had raised four children. Widowed for almost twenty years, Julia had taken pride in her ability to live alone and maintain the house. It was a place where her adult children, their spouses, and their children could stay when they "came home." But the joy of these visits from family and friends began to fade as the house aged and even routine chores seemed monumental. When she began to experience short-term memory lapses, utility bills were misplaced, food items were left to spoil, and minor decisions preoccupied her thoughts.

Perhaps her recent dizzy spells were a consequence of these changes, but the doctor was unable to find a cause. Julia had enjoyed a lifetime of good health; she remembered being ill only once and then only for a week; her four hospital stays related to childbirth. She had always felt safeguarded by her life-long adherence to sound nutrition and other preventive practices. Paradoxically, she now felt ill-prepared emotionally to accept an unknown health problem that seemed to foretell that she no longer could live alone.

Julia had several options, including an invitation to live with her daughter, a move that would take her over five hundred miles from her community. She had a son and three sisters in town whom she saw frequently. For a brief time one of the adult grandchildren lived with her, but she realized that her lifestyle differed to the point that this was not the solution. Julia still drove to church and attended several monthly functions to play the piano. This provided social contacts, a creative outlet, self-expression of her spirituality, and even some extra "pocket money." Increasingly, the invitations to play the piano exceeded what she felt able to do. The control she felt over her life was eroding.

Her annual visit to the ophthalmologist changed her life forever. The early stage of glaucoma was diagnosed, but even more critical, she was unable to pass a peripheral visual exam. Her driver's license was revoked, her life-line cut. Her calm and satisfying life seemed to come to an abrupt halt and was replaced with anxiety, confusion, and a rising feeling of sadness. When her children visited, her mood elevated temporarily, but it was apparent that the responsibilities of living alone outweighed the satisfactions. Her son increasingly oversaw Julia's daily activities and handled most of her financial affairs.

Exploring housing options was not hard, as Julia had entertained residents in several of the retirement communities—she knew them all. Ironically, she could not envision her eighty-seven-year-old self living in "one of those places," but neither could she accept any of the other options available to her. Her world became more constricted and her mood more sullen as her pride hid the tears from those who cared the most—her children. The house where she had welcomed the daily sunshine became her prison. Her four children spent hours on the phone with her and each other, sharing the ambivalence of moving yet knowing it was imminent. Against her will but not her judgment, a plan was made for an assisted living apartment in a nearby life-care community.

Unable to accept the inevitable, Julia played the piano as her children, their spouses, and some of the grandchildren packed her belongings, sorting through the years of accumulated memories that would accompany her to the life care community. Julia sang, joked, and smiled, but these feelings were fleeting, attached only to the temporary joy of having all four children with her at the same time. After Julia moved into "the new apartment," the anxiety increased and was accompanied by new fears of the elevator, entering the dining room, getting lost, and not being socially accepted. Her memory became more fragmented, her thoughts unfocused. Was this the beginning of a downward spiral leading to even more restricted living arrangements? The staff commented to her son on the marked contrast of her behavior in relation to what they had seen only a few months earlier when Julia had visited and played the piano. Where had the joy of living gone? How could this spry, healthy, happy woman change so suddenly? Why couldn't the doctor find a reason? Could Alzheimer's disease strike so rapidly? What other illnesses created these symptoms? The questions seemed endless, the answers elusive.

Depression can be insidious. While some suffer with it over a lifetime, others encounter it only later in life. It takes many forms, and different personalities express it in unique ways. For Julia it was shrouded in shame, interpreted by her as a characterological weakness. A life-long pattern of rapid adaptation and coping with life events did not insulate her from this new experience. Her daughter, a social worker, recognized that this behavior was an understandable response to the myriad changes imposed on her mother, changes that impacted all dimensions of living: biological, psychological, social, and spiritual. Fortunately, the vast majority of elderly who encounter depression can be helped.

Julia's daughter called Julia and questioned her specifically about the major symptoms of depression, then telephoned Julia's sister to take her to the family doctor. The doctor listened as the list of symptoms were read and diagnosed Adjustment Disorder with Depressed Mood (Kaplan & Sadock 1998). Fortuitously, this physician also was the geriatric consultant to the life care community and understood the pharmacological responses that are unique to the elderly. One of the new SSRIs, Paxil, was prescribed. Within a few days the anxiety abated; a few weeks later the depression was replaced with the motivation to meet the challenges of a new living arrangement. Within a few months Julia began to talk about her new friends and her daily piano playing in her "new home."

Annotated Bibliography

Binstock, R. H. & George, L. K. (1995). *Handbook of aging and the social sciences*. New York: Academic Press.
    Elaborates on much of the content presented in this chapter. Written by various experts in specific areas of gerontology, the chapters identify key content areas, issues, current research, and future directions for gerontologists.
Hooyman, N. R. & Kiyak, H. A. (1998) *Social gerontology* (5th ed.). Boston: Allyn & Bacon.
    A comprehensive text covering multiple dimensions of aging in the United States.
Lustbader, W. & Hooyman, N. R. (1993). *Taking care of aging family member: A practical guide*. Thousand Oaks, CA: Sage.
    Written for families with elderly members to promote development of life skills. Provides an excellent overview of human behavior of the elderly from a family systems perspective. Additional readings, self-help organizations, and practical suggestions are provided.
Merriam, S. B. (1993). Butler's Life Review: How universal is it? *International Journal of Aging and Human Development*, 37(3), 163–175.
    Describes Butler's concept of Life Review, which has been widely accepted in the field of gerontology. Commonly held assumptions that underlie the Life Review are discussed, and previous literature is reviewed. A recent study is described, and its conclusions further question some aspects of the Life Review.
Padgett, D. (1995). *Handbook on ethnicity, aging and mental health*. Westport, CT: Greenwood Press.
    Presents the life course of aging, service needs and utilization of special populations, and caregiving issues that acknowledge race as a significant influence on the social and psychological dimensions of aging.
Silverstone, B. & Hyman, H. K. (1990). *You and your aging parent* (3rd ed.) New York: Pantheon.
    Provides an overview of the needs of the elderly. The authors offer practical advice from a family systems perspective in order to plan for the care of an elderly family member.
Strawbridge, W. J., Camacho, T. C., Cohen, R. D., & Kapplan, G. A. (1993). Gender differences in factors associated with change in physical functioning in old age: A six-year longitudinal study. *The Gerontologist*, 33(5), 603–609.
    Gender differences are highlighted in this report of a longitudinal study which explored what variables might predict physical functioning among women and men over age sixty-five. Internal health locus of control was found to be stronger for women. Findings support the value of preventative interventions.
Wacker, R., Roberto, K., & Piper, L. E. (1998). *Community resources for older adults: Programs and services in an era of change*. Thousand Oaks, CA: Pine Forge.
    Provides comprehensive review of a broad range of resources to meet the biopsychosocial needs of people as they age.
Williams, M. (1995). *Complete guide to aging and health*. New York: Harmony Books.
    Written for elderly persons and their families as a comprehensive reference guide to promote healthy lifestyles and respond to medical problems associated with aging.

General Bibliography

Adams, R. G. (1985). People would talk: Normative barriers to cross-sex friendships for elderly women. *The Gerontologist, 25*, 605–611.

Altman, I., Lawton, M. P., & Wohlwill, J. F. (1984). *Elderly people and the environment*. New York: Plenum Press

Bee, H. L. (1996). *The journey of adulthood* (2nd ed.). New York: Macmillan.

Bengtson, V. L. & Roberston, J. (Eds.). (1985). *Grandparenthood*. Beverly Hills: Sage.

Bengtson, V. L., Schaie, K. W., & Burton, L. M. (Eds.). (1995). *Adult intergenerational relations: Effects of societal change*. New York: Springer.

Binstock, R. H. & Shanas, E. (Eds.). *Handbook of aging and the Social sciences* (4th ed.). New York: Van Nostrand Reinhold.

Birren, J. & Schaie, K. W. (Eds.). (1996). *Handbook of the psychology of aging*. San Diego, CA: Academic Press.

Butler, R. N., Lewis, M. I., & Sunderland, T. (1998). *Aging and mental health* (5th ed.). Needham Heights, MA: Allyn & Bacon.

Cantor, M. H. (1979). Neighbors and friends: An overlooked resource in the informal support system. *Research on Aging, 4*, 434–463.

Cohen, F., Bearison, D. J., & Muller, C. (1987). Interpersonal understanding in the elderly: The influence of age-integrated and age-segregated housing. *Research on aging, 9*(1), 79–100.

Coward, R. T. & Lee, G. R. (Eds.). (1985). *The elderly in rural society: Every fourth elder*. New York: Springer.

Florian, V. & Kravetz, S. (1983). Fear of personal death: Attribution structure, and relation to religious belief. *Journal of Personality and Social Psychology, 44*, 600–607.

Flynn, C. B., Longino, C. F., Jr., Wiseman, R. F., & Biggar, J. C. (1985). The redistribution of America's older population: Major national migration patterns for three census decades, 1960–1980. *The Gerontologist, 25*, 292–296.

Hanson, S. L., Sauer, W., & Seelbach, W. (1983). Racial and cohort variations in filial responsibility norms. *The Gerontologist, 23*(6), 626–631.

Hays, J. A. (1984). Aging and family resources: Availability and proximity of kind. *The Gerontologist, 24*, 149–153.

Hooyman, N. & Kayak, H. (1996). *Social gerontology* (4th ed.). Needham Heights, MA: Allyn & Bacon.

Klemmack, D. L. & Roffy, L. L. (1984). Fear of personal aging and subjective well-being in after life. *Journal of Gerontology, 39*, 756–758.

Mindel, C. & Wright, R. (1982). Satisfaction in multigenerational households. *Journal of Gerontology, 37*(4), 483–489.

Morris, R. & Bass, S. (1988). *Retirement reconsidered: Economic and social roles of older people*. New York: Springer.

Neugarten, B. L. (1985). Time, age, and the life cycle, In M. Bloom (Ed.), *Life span development* (pp. 360–369). New York: Macmillan.

Padgett, D. (1995). *Handbook on ethnicity, aging and mental health*. Westport, CT: Greenwood Press.

Strom, R. & Strom, S. (1990). *Becoming a better grandparent: A guidebook for strengthening the family*. Newbury Park, CA: Sage.

Tilson, D. (1990). *Aging in place: Supporting the frail elderly in residential environments*. Glenview, IL: Scott Foresman.

Wentowski, G. J. (1985). Older women's perceptions of great-grandmotherhood: A research note. *The Gerontologist, 25*, 593–596.

References

American Psychiatric Association. (1994). *Diagnostic and statistical manual of mental disorders* (4th ed.). Washington, DC: APA.

Anetzberger, G. J. (1987). *The etiology of elder abuse by adult offspring*. Springfield, IL: Charles C. Thomas.

Antonucci, T. (1985). Personal characteristics, social support and social behavior. In B.H. Binstock & E. Shanas (Eds.), *Handbook of aging and the social sciences* (pp. 94–128). New York: Van Nostrand Reinhold.

Baum, M., & Baum, R. C. (1980). *Growing old: A societal perspective*. Englewood Cliffs, NJ: Prentice-Hall.

Beck, S., & Beck, R. (1984). The formation of extended households during middle age. *Journal of Marriage and the Family, 46*(2), 277–287.

Bee, H. L. (1996). *The Journey of Adulthood* (3rd ed.). Upper Saddle River, NJ: Prentice-Hall.

Belloc, N. B. (1973). Relationship of health priorities and mortality. *Preventive Medicine, 2*, 67–81.

Bendik, M. F. (1992). Reaching the breaking point: Dangers of mistreatment in elder caregiving situations. *Journal of Elder Abuse and Neglect, 4*, 39–59.

Bennett, W. L. (1987, December 13). Monitoring drugs for the aged. *New York Times Magazine*, pp. 73–74.

Bentley, K. J., & Walsh, J. (1996). *The social worker and psychotropic medication*. Pacific Grove, CA: Brooks/Cole.

Bitzan, J. E., & Kruzich, J. M. (1990). Interpersonal relationships of nursing home residents. *The Gerontologist, 30*, 385–390.

Black, K. D., & Bengtson V. L. (1973, August). *The measurement of family solidarity: An intergenerational analysis*. Paper presented at the annual meeting of American Psychological Association, Montreal, Canada.

Blau, P. M. (1964). *Exchange and power in social life*. New York: Wiley.

Blumstein, P., & Schwartz, P. (1983). *American Couples*. New York: William Morrow.

Botwinick, J. (1978). *Aging and behavior*. New York: Springer.

Brody, E. M. (1978). The aging of the family. *Annals of the American Academy of Political and Social Science, 438*, 13–27.

Brody, E. M. (1985). Parent care as a normative family stress. *The Gerontologist, 25*(1), 19–29.

Butler, R. N. (1985). Successful aging. In M. Bloom (Ed.), *Life span development* (pp. 370–377). New York: Macmillan.

Chambre, S. M. (1993). Volunteerism by elders: Past trends and future prospects. *The Gerontologist, 33*, 221–28.

Cherlin, A. (1979, April). *Extended family households in the early years of marriage*. Paper presented at the Annual Meeting of the Population Association of America, Philadelphia.

Cherlin, A. J., & Furstenberg, F. F. (1986). *The new American grandparent: A place in the family, a life apart*. New York: Basic Books.

Cicarelli, V. (1981). *Helping elderly parents: The role of adult children*. Boston: Auburn House.

Clark, D. O., Maddox, G. L., & Steinhauser, K. (1993). Race, aging, and functional health. *Journal of Aging and Health, 5*, 536–53.

Cohler, B. J. (1983). Autonomy and interdependence in the family of adulthood. *The Gerontologist, 23*(1), 33–39.

Cohler, B. J., & Altergott, K. (1995). The family of the second half of life: Connecting theories and findings. In R. Blieszner & Victoria H. Bedford (Eds.), *Handbook of aging and the family* (pp. 59–94). Westport, CT: Greenwood Press.

Costa, P. T., & McCrae, R. R. (1988). Personality in adulthood: A six-year longitudinal study of self-reports and spouse ratings on the NEO personality inventory. *Journal of Personality and Social Psychology, 54*, 853–863.

Cox, H. (1984). *Later life: The realities of aging*. Englewood Cliffs, NJ: Prentice-Hall.

Cumming, E., & Henry, W. E. (1961). *Growing old: The process of disengagement*. New York: Basic Books.

Doff, R. W., & Hong, L. K. (1982). Quality and quantity of social interactions in the life satisfaction of older Americans. *Sociology and Social Research, 66*(4), 418–434.

Doty, R. L., Sharman, P., & Dann, M. (1984). Development of the University of Pennsylvania smell identification test: A standardized microencapsulated test of olfactory function. *Physiology and Behavior, 32,* 489–502.

Dowd, J. J. (1975). Aging as exchange: A preface to theory. *Journal of Gerontology, 30,* 584–594.

Edinberg, M. A. (1985). *Mental health practice with the elderly.* Englewood Cliffs, NJ: Prentice-Hall.

Fallcreek, S. & Mettler, M. (1983). A healthy old age: A sourcebook for health promotion with older adults. *Journal of Gerontological Social Work,* 6(2/3), 267–307.

Flint, M. M. & Perez-Porter, M. (1997). Grandparent caregivers: Legal and economic issues. *Journal of Gerontological Social Work, 28,* 63–76.

Fordham, F. (1953). *An introduction to Jung's psychology.* New York: Penguin.

Fries, J. F. & Crapo, L. M. (1981). *Vitality and aging.* San Francisco: W. H. Freeman.

Fulmer, T. & O'Mallery, T. (1987). *Inadequate care of the elderly: A health perspective on abuse and neglect.* New York: Springer.

George, L. G. (1986). Caregiver burden: Conflict between norms of reciprocity and solidarity. In K. Pillemer & R. Wolf (Eds.), *Elder abuse: Conflict in the family* (pp. 67–92). Dover, MA: Auburn House.

Gilligan, C. (1982). *In a different voice.* Cambridge, MA: Harvard University Press.

Glass, J., Bengtson, V. L., & Dunham, C. C. (1986). Attitude similarity in three generation-families: Socialization, status inheritance, or reciprocal influence? *American Sociological Review,* 51(5), 685–698.

Gray, H. & Dressel, P. (1985). Alternative interpretations of aging among gay males. *The Gerontologist,* 25(1), 83–87.

Greenberg, J. R., McKibben, M., & Raymond, J. A. (1990). Dependent adult children and elder abuse. *Journal of Elder Abuse and Neglect, 2,* 73–86.

Guralnik, J. M., Lacroix, A. Z., Everett, D. F., & Kovar, M. G. (1989). *Aging in the Eighties: The prevalence of co-morbidity and its association with disability, advance data.* National Center for Health Statistics, No. 170. Washington, D.C.: U.S. Government Printing Office.

Gutmann, D. G. (1975). Parenthood: A key to the comparative study fo the life cycle. In N. Datan & L. Ginsberg (Eds.), *Life-span developmental psychology.* New York: Academic Press.

Guttman, D. G. (1987). *Reclaimed powers: Toward a new psychology of men and women in later life.* New York: Basic Books.

Hagestad, G. O. (1982). Divorce: The family ripple effect. *Generations, 6,* 24–25.

Hancock, B. L. (1987). *Social work with older people.* Englewood Cliffs, NJ: Prentice-Hall.

Hareven, T. (1995). Historical perspectives on the family and aging. In R. Blieszner & V. H. Bedford (Eds.), *Handbook of aging and the family* (pp. 13–31). Westport, CT: Greenwood Press.

Harrigan, M. P. (1992). Multigenerational family households: Advantages and Disadvantages. *Journal of Applied Gerontology, 11,* 457–474.

Hartford, M. E. (1985). Understanding normative growth and development in aging: Working with strengths. *Journal of Gerontological Social Work,* 8(3/4), 37–54.

Havighurst, R. J., Neugarten, B. L., & Tobin, S. S. (1968). Disengagement and patterns of aging. In B. L. Neugarten (Ed.), *Middle age and aging.* Chicago: University of Chicago Press.

Hooyman, N. R. & Lustbader, W. (1986). *Taking care: Supporting older people and their families.* New York: Free Press.

Jackel, M. M. (1975). Personality disorders. In G. Wiedeman (Ed.), *Personality development and deviation* (pp. 286–320). Madison, WI: International Universities Press.

Kahn, R. L. & Antonucci, T. C. (1983). *Social support with the elderly: Family/friend/professional.* Final report to the National Institute on Aging.

Kaplan, H. I. & Sadock, B. J. (1998). *Synopsis of psychiatry* (8th ed.). Baltimore, MD: Williams & Wilkins.

Kenshalo, D. R. (1977). Age changes in touch, vibration, temperature, kinesthesis, and pain sensitivity. In J. E. Birren & K. W. Schaie (Eds.), *Handbook of the psychology of aging.* New York: Van Nostrand Reinhold.

Kessler, R. C., Foster, C., Webster, P. S., & House, J. S. (1992). The relationship between age and depressive symptoms in two national surveys. *Psychology and Aging, 7,* 119–126.

Kitson, G. C. (1992). *Portrait of divorce: Adjustment to marital breakdown.* New York: Guilford Press.

Kivnick, H. Q. (1983). Dimensions of grandparenthood meaning; Deductive conceptualization and empirical derivation. *Journal of Personality and Social Psychology, 44,* 1056–1068.

Kornhaber, A. (1996). *Contemporary grandparenting.* Thousand Oaks, CA: Sage.

Kuypers, J. A. & Bengtson, V. L. (1973). Competence and social breakdown: A social-psychological view of aging. *Human Development, 16*(2), 37–49.

Lawton, M. P. (1980). Residential quality and residential satisfaction among the elderly. *Research on Aging, 2,* 309–328.

Lawton, L., Silverstone, M., & Bengtson, V. (1994). Affection, social contact, and geographic distance between adult children and their parents. *Journal of Marriage and the Family, 56,* 57–88.

Lubben, J. & Gironda, M. (1996). Assessing social support networks among older people in the United States. In N. Litwin (Ed.), *Networks of older people: A cross national analysis* (pp. 143–161). Westport, CT: Praeger.

Ludman, E. K. & Newman, J. M. (1986). Frail elderly: Assessment of nutritional needs. *The Gerontologist, 26*(2), 199–202.

Mancini, J. & Sandifer, D. M. (1995) Family dynamics and the leisure experiences of older adults: Theoretical viewpoints. In R. Blieszner & V. H. Bedford (Eds.), *Handbook of aging and the family* (pp. 132–147). Westport, CT: Greenwood Press.

Marshall, W. A. (1973). The body. In R. R. Sears & S. Feldman (Eds.), *The seven ages of man.* Los Altos, CA: William Kaufman.

McAdoo, H. P. (1982). Stress absorbing systems in black families. *Family Relations, 31,* 479–488.

McCracken, A. (1987). Emotional impact of possession loss. *Journal of Gerontological Nursing, 13*(2), 14–19.

Mead, G. G. (Ed.), (1934). *Mind, self, and society.* Chicago: University of Chicago Press.

Miletich, J. J. (1986). *Retirement: An annotated bibliography.* New York: Greenwood Press.

Miller, D. (1980). The sandwich generation. *Social Work, 26*(5), 419–423.

Minkler, M. (1994). Grandparents as parents: The American experience. *Aging International, 21*(1), 24–28.

Minkler, M. & Rose, K. (1993). *Grandmothers as caregivers: raising children in the crack cocaine epidemic.* Newbury Park, CA: Sage.

Naleppa, M. J. (1996). Families and the institutionalized elderly: A review. *Journal of Gerontological Social Work, 27,* 87–111.

National Association of Social Workers. (1995). *Encyclopedia of social work* (19th ed., pp. 95–106). Silver Spring, MD: NASW.

National Council on the Aging. (1981). *Aging in the eighties: America in transition.* Washington, DC: National Council on the Aging.

Neighbors, H. W., Jacobson, J., Bowman, P. J., & Gurin, G. (1983). Stress, coping and black mental health: Preliminary findings from a national study. *Prevention & Human Services, 2*(3), 5–29.

Neugarten, B. L. (1975). The future and the young-old. *The Gerontologist, 15*(1).

Neugarten, B. L. (1979). Time, age, and the life cycle. *American Journal of Psychiatry, 136*(7), 887–894.

Neugarten, B. L. & Neugarten, D. A. (1987). The changing meanings of age. *Psychology Today, 21*(5), 29–33.

Newman, B. M. & Newman, P. A. (1987). *Development through life: A psychosocial approach.* Chicago, IL: Dorsey Press.

O'Conner, B. P. & Vallerand, R. J. (1994). Motivation, self-determination and person-environment fit as predictors of psychological adjustment among nursing home residents. *Psychology and Aging, 9,* 189–94.

O'Rand, A. M., Henretta, J. C., & Krecker, M. L. (1992). Family pathways to retirement. In M. Szinovacz, D. J. Ekerdt, & B. H. Vinick (Eds.), *Families and retirement* (pp. 81–98). Newbury Park, CA: Sage.

Palmer, D. S. (1991). Co-leading a family council in a long-term care facility. *Journal of Gerontological Social Work, 16,* 121–134.

Palmore, E. (1981). Facts on aging quiz—Part 2. *The Gerontologist, 21,* 432–437.

Palmore, E., Fillenbaum, G. G., & George, L. K. (1984). Consequences of retirement. *Journal of Gerontology, 39*, 109–116.

Pillemer, K. & Finkelhor, D. (1988). The prevalence of elder abuse: A random sample survey. *The Gerontologist, 28*, 51–57.

Pillemer, K. & Finkelhor, D. (1989). Causes of elder abuse: Caregiver stress versus problem relations. *American Journal of Orthopsychology, 59*, 179–87.

Pillemer, K. & Moore, D. W. (1989). Abuse of patients in nursing homes: Findings from a survey of staff. *The Gerontologist, 29*, 314–320.

Poon, L. W. (1985). Differences in human memory with aging: Nature, causes, and clinical implications. In J. E. Birren & K. W. Schaie (Eds.), *Handbook of the psychology of aging* (2nd ed., pp. 427–462). New York: Van Nostrand Reinhold.

Pyka, G., Lindenberger, E., Charette, S., & Marcus, R. (1994). Muscle strength and fiber adaptations to a year-long resistance training program in elderly men and women. *Journal of gerontology: Medical Science, 49*, M22–M27.

Quinn, W. H. & Hughston, G. A. (1984). *Independent aging: Family and social systems perspectives*. Rockville, MD: Aspen.

Regier, D. A., Boyd, J. H., Burke, J. D., Rae, D. S., Myers, J. K., Kramer, M. Robins, L. N., George, L. K., Karno, M., & Locke, B. Z. (1988). One-month prevalence of mental disorders in the United States. *Archives of General Psychiatry, 45*, 977–986.

Riddick, C. C., Cohen-Mansfield, J., Fleshner, E., & Kraft, G. (1992). Caregiver adaptations to having a relative with dementia admitted to a nursing home. *Journal of Gerontological Social Work, 19*, 51–76.

Riley, M. W., Johnson, M., & Foner, A. (1972). *Aging in society: Vol. 3., A sociology of age stratification*. New York: Russell Sage Foundation.

Robbins, S. P., Chatterjee, P., & Canda, E. (1998). *Contemporary human behavior theory: A critical perspective for social work*. Boston: Allyn & Bacon.

Robertson, J. F. (1995). Grandparenting in an era of rapid change. In R. Bleiszner & V. H. Bedford (Eds.), *Handbook of aging and the family* (pp. 243–260). Westport, CT: Greenwood Press.

Rose, A. M. & Peterson, W. H. (1965). *Older people and their social world: the subculture of aging*. Philadelphia, PA: F. A. Davis.

Rowles, G. D. (1980). Growing old "inside:" Aging and attachment to place in an Appalachian community. In N. Datan & N. Lohmann (Eds.), *Transitions of aging* (pp. 153–170). New York: Academic Press.

Ryff, C. D. (1984). Personality development from the inside: The subjective experience of change in adulthood and aging. In P. B. Baltes & O. G. Brim, Jr. (Eds.), *Life-span development and behavior* (vol. 6, pp. 244–281). Orlando, FL: Academic Press.

Ryff, C. D. & Heincke, S. G. (1983). The subjective organization of personality in adulthood and aging. *Journal of Personality and Social Psychology, 44*, 807–816.

Safford, F. (1980). A program for families of the mentally impaired elderly. *The Gerontologist, 20*, 656–660.

Scheibel, F. (1992). Aging and the senses. In J. E. Birren, R. B. Sloane, & G. D. Cohen (Eds.), *Handbook of mental health and aging* (2nd ed., pp. 252–306). San Diego, CA: Academic Press.

Schiller, B. R. (1998). *The economics of poverty and discrimination* (7th ed.). Upper Saddle River, NJ: Prentice-Hall.

Schlossberg, N. K. (1981). A model for analyzing human adaptation to transition. *Counseling Psychologist, 9*(2), 2–17.

Schneewind, E. H. (1990). The reaction of the family to the institutionalization of an elderly member: Factors influencing adjustment and suggestions for easing the transition to a new life phase. *Journal of Gerontological Social Work, 15*, 121–136.

Shanas, E. (1979). The family as a social support system in old age. *The Gerontologist, 19*(2), 169–174.

Silverstone, B. & Hyman, H. K. (1982). *You and your aging parent; The modern family's guide to physical, emotional, and financial problems* (2nd ed.). New York: Pantheon Books.

Smeeding, T. M. (1990). Economic status of the elderly. In R. H. Binstock & L. K. George (Eds.), *Handbook of aging and the social sciences* (3rd ed., pp. 362–381). San Diego, CA: Academic Press.

Sussman, M. (1976). Family life of older people. In R. H. Binstock & E. Shanas (Eds.), *Handbook of aging and the social sciences.* New York: Van Nostrand Reinhold.

Sussman, M. (1985). The family life of old people. In R. H. Binstock & E. Shanas (Eds.), *Handbook of aging and the social sciences* (2nd ed.). New York: Van Nostrand Reinhold.

Szinovacz, M. (1986–87). Preferred retirement timing and retirement satisfaction in women. *International Journal of Aging and Human Development, 24*(4), 301–317.

Tatara, T. (1992). *Institutional elder abuse: A summary of data gathered from state units on aging, state APS agencies, and state long-term care ombudsman programs.* Washington, DC: National Aging Resource Center on Elder Abuse. In T. Tatara (1995). Elder abuse. In R. L. Edwards (Ed.) (1995), *Encyclopedia of social work* (19th ed., Vol. 1) (pp. 834–842). Washington, DC: National Association of Social Workers.

Tatara, T. (1993). *Summaries of the statistical data on elder abuse in domestic settings for FY90 and FY91.* Washington, DC: National Aging Resources Center on Elder Abuse. In T. Tatara (1995). Elder abuse. In R. L. Edwards (Ed.) (1995), *Encyclopedia of social work* (19th ed., Vol. 1) (pp. 834–842). Washington, DC: National Association of Social Workers.

Taylor, R. J. (1986). Religious participation among elderly blacks. *The Gerontologist, 26*(6), 630–636.

Tinsley, H. E., Teaff, J. D., Colbs, S. L., & Kaufman, N. (1985). System of classifying leisure activities in terms of the psychological benefits of participation reported by older persons. *Journal of Gerontology, 40,* 172–178.

Treas, J. (1977). Family support systems for their aged. *The Gerontologist, 17*(6), 486–491.

Uhlenberg, P., Cooney, T., & Boyd, R. (1990). Divorce for women after midlife. *Journal of Gerontology: Social Sciences 45,* S3–S11.

Uhlenberg, P., & Myers, M. A. P. (1981). Divorce and the elderly. *Gerontology, 21,* 276–282.

U.S. Bureau of the Census. (1983). *America in transition: An aging society.* Current population reports, Series P-23, No. 128. Washington, DC: U.S. Government Printing Office.

U.S. Bureau of the Census. (1990). *Statistical abstract of the United States, 1990* (110th ed.). Washington, DC: U.S. Government Printing Office.

U.S. Bureau of the Census. (1993). *Statistic abstract of the United States: 1993* (113th ed.). Washington DC: U.S. Government Printing Office.

U.S. Bureau of the Census. (1996). *65 + in the United States.* Current population reports, special studies, Series P-23, No. 190. Washington DC: U.S. Government Printing Office.

Vaillant, G. E. (1979). Natural history of male psychologic health: Effects of mental health on physical health. *New England Journal of Medicine, 301*(23), 1249–1254.

Veroff, J., Douvan, E., & Kulka, R. A. (1981). *The inner American. A self-portrait from 1957 to 1976.* New York: Basic Books.

West, R. L., & Crook, T. H. (1990). Age differences in every-day memory: Laboratory analogues of telephone number recall. *Psychology and Aging, 5,* 520–529.

Woodruff, D. S. (1985). Arousal, sleep, and aging. In J. E. Birren & K. W. Schaie (Eds.), *Handbook of the psychology of aging* (2nd ed., pp. 261–295). New York: Van Nostrand Reinhold.

Zarit, S. H., & Whitlock, C. J. (1992). Institutional placement: Phases of the transition. *The Gerontologist, 32,* 665–672.

3 Social Problems and Policies and the Elderly

■ ■ ■ ■ ■ ■ ■ ■ ■ ■ ■ ■ ■ ■

Anne J. Kisor, Edward A. McSweeney, and Deborah R. Jackson

A number of policies have been formulated that specifically allocate or regulate resources for the elderly. At the economic level, policies and practices such as company retirement practices, and stereotypes concerning the capabilities and competencies of the elderly, have a direct impact on the life conditions of older persons. At the biological level, age does eventually lead to changing capabilities and competencies that in turn require attention to health care and finances. In one sense, an anthology on the elderly as well as a discrete unit on social policy imply a certain kind of ageism that is not desirable. However, these political, economic, and biological facts call for a discussion of policy addressing the special needs of the elderly.

For purposes of clarity, social policy will be defined as: *the authoritative allocation or regulation of resources by elected or appointed public officials to be used by a specific group of people* (Beverly & McSweeney 1987). The group in this instance is the elderly population. Using this definition limits discussion to official decisions that determine the allocation and the regulation of resources. Resources include cash, in-kind programs, services, education, and health care. This chapter explores some of the major problems faced by older persons in the areas of finances, health care, and independent living, and it describes policies that address these areas. In addition, critical issues that may need to be confronted by future policy will be identified.

Demographics of the Elderly

Policy issues regarding the elderly have become increasingly complex with the changing demographics of society. Our population is living longer with the fastest growing age group being the oldest-old (eighty-five and older). Some statistics will help illustrate the degree of change in society. According to the American Association of Retired Persons (AARP) and the Administration on Aging (AoA) (1998), in 1997, the older population, defined as persons aged sixty-five or older, numbered 34.1 million, or 12.8 percent of the U.S. population. This number represents an increase of 9.1 percent since 1990, compared to a 7 percent increase for the under sixty-five population. Since 1900, the percentage of Americans aged sixty-five or older has tripled from 4.1 percent in 1900 to 12.8 percent in 1996. In addition, the older population itself is getting older. In 1996 the sixty-five to seventy-four age group was eight times larger than in 1900; the seventy-five to eighty-four age group was sixteen times larger, and the eighty-five plus group was thirty-one times larger. The older population is expected to continue to grow in the future and may represent 21.2 percent of the population by 2030.

These figures clearly demonstrate that the sixty-five and older age group has become and will continue to be a substantial part of our population. The policy questions that need to be explored relate to the quality of life available to this group. They deal with the financial well-being, health, and ability of the elderly to live independently. Before addressing the problems and policies related to these areas, this chapter seeks to develop an understanding of the political environment that has influenced the welfare of older Americans.

A New Political Environment

The Great Depression brought striking economic and political changes that forced Americans to modify attitudes toward their government. The attitude that "government is best that governs least" was converted into the attitude that the federal government should exercise its constitutional authority "to provide for the general welfare." The Social Security Act of 1935 was the first commitment by the federal government to provide welfare programs, and it remains the mainstay of public programs designed to assist older people (Dobelstein 1996). The White House Conferences on Aging and the Older Americans Act have had a profound influence on shaping the policies involving older people and determining the way in which services are offered to the aging.

The future of age-based policy is now in question. This is evident by the trend away from universal eligibility and entitlements along with "downsizing" and declining federal commitment to provision of social services. Older persons as a group escaped the 1980s federal retrenchment relatively unscathed. However, federal programs, such as Medicare, that traditionally support older persons were major targets in the 1995–1996 budget debate and continue to be the focus of bipartisan attention. Aimed at reducing the growth of federal commitment, this represents a shift in the philosophical framework of social welfare and social insurance.

The White House Conferences on Aging

The passage of the Social Security Act marked a growing political movement among older people. During the 1940s and 1950s, funds were appropriated to study the problems facing the elderly, a National Conference on the Aging was held, and a Federal Council on Aging was established. Voluntary associations of older people also developed.

In 1961, the first White House Conference on Aging was held in Washington to develop a blueprint for action on aging. The second and third conferences took place in 1971 and 1981. Before each conference, local and state meetings convened to discuss a wide variety of policies. These policy issues were summarized into major areas for deliberation by the conference delegates who then made recommendations to improve the lives of older people.

Because the participants of the White House Conferences on Aging have been the direct beneficiaries of the policy recommendations, the conferences constituted a new base of political organization for the elderly. In May 1995, the fourth White House Conference on Aging was convened to create a vision for national policy on aging for the twenty-first century. In all, fifty-one resolutions were adopted by the delegates. The top ten resolutions (those acquiring the most votes) were:

- Keeping Social Security sound, now and for the future.
- Reauthorizing and preserving the integrity of the Older Americans Act.
- Preserving the nature of Medicaid.

- Alzheimers research.
- Ensuring the future of the Medicare program.
- Ensuring the availability of a broad spectrum of services.
- Preserving advocacy functions under the Older Americans Act.
- Financing and providing long-term care services.
- Expanding and enhancing opportunities for older volunteers.
- Assuming personal responsibility for the state of one's health (DHHS 1996)

The 1995 White House Conference on Aging resolutions were characterized by the theme of aging as a lifelong process involving all generations (Greene 1997), a key factor in future policy making.

The Older Americans Act

The Older Americans Act was enacted into law in 1965. Title I enumerates the objectives of the act:

1. An adequate income in retirement in accordance with the American standard of living;
2. The best possible physical and mental health without regard to economic status;
3. Suitable housing available at costs older people can afford;
4. Fully restorative services for those who need institutional care;
5. Opportunity for employment with no discrimination because of age;
6. Retirement in health, honor, and dignity;
7. Pursuit of meaningful activity including cultural and recreational opportunities;
8. Efficient community services that provide social assistance in a coordinated manner;
9. Immediate benefit from proven research knowledge that can maintain and improve health and happiness;
10. Freedom, independence, and the free exercise of individual initiative in planning and managing their own lives.

Unlike other policies discussed in this chapter, the Older Americans Act was not designed to transfer resources or funds to the elderly. Instead, the act gave governmental authority to provide better coordinated and more effective public resources for older people, and provide a structure for government authority to coordinate resources (Dobelstein 1996). This structure has come to be known as "the aging network."

An important component of the aging network is the Administration on Aging (AoA), created under Title II of the act. AoA is a department of the federal government for developing new or improved programs and activities to help older people. It serves as a clearinghouse for information related to the problems of older people, administers the grants available under the act, and stimulates more effective use of existing resources and available services. The Older Americans Act also requires coordination and planning of aging services at the state and substate levels. Each state has designated a State Unit on Aging (SUA), which in turn, designated a single public or private, nonprofit agency as the Area Agency on Aging (AAA) for each planning area of the state.

The AAA is an important resource for gerontological social workers. AAAs provide social services to older people either directly or by contracting with other agencies and organizations. The AAA also serves as a clearinghouse of information on other resources available to older persons in the community.

Currently over seven hundred area agencies on aging operate at regional and local levels, with advisory boards that include older persons. In addition, there are direct service providers in local communities that offer a range of services such as information and referral, transportation, outreach, homemaker services, day care, nutrition education and congregate meals, legal services, respite care, and senior centers.

Although the Older Americans Act was designed to serve all persons over sixty years old, it has been criticized for serving primarily nonpoor or newly poor older persons rather than meeting the needs of the long-term poor older people (Minkler & Estes 1984). From initial passage, this principle of universalism has been the subject of debate in terms of legislative intent, and difficulties inherent in practical implementation such as the "scatter shot" approach to reaching a random proportion of those in need (Gelfand & Bechill 1991). For example, senior centers tend to serve the more affluent and healthier white population. The mission of the Older Americans Act must be fulfilled in the face of a rapidly growing consumer base of frail elderly—a virtual "service revolution" in transition from senior centers and congregate meal sites to in-home services (Hudson 1994). In addition, an argument is that too much money has been spent on planning and coordinating services and on jobs and research funds for professional gerontologists (Hudson 1994). Despite these criticisms, the Older Americans Act has had far reaching positive effects on the delivery of much needed services to the elderly.

Several years overdue, the current reauthorization process was stalled by partisan disagreement over distribution of Title V senior community service employment funding, targeting of low-income minorities, and funding formulas for senior centers, meal sites, and other programs. Congress is currently considering a bill introduced in 1999 by the minority party (Democrats). Key features of this bill include: restructuring of Title II (Area Agencies on Aging); major reductions in Title IV (Training and Research) and dismantlement of Title VII (Vulnerable Elder Rights Protection).

Financial Well-Being

The Problems

The overall financial picture for the elderly has improved dramatically over the past thirty years, yet there is great disparity between rich and poor. Poverty among the aged has decreased by 300 percent and real income has increased by 69 percent (Hudson 1997). The major sources of income for older persons in 1997 were Social Security (reported by 91 percent), income from property (63 percent), public and private pensions (41 percent), earnings (21 percent), and public assistance (6 percent). The median net worth (assets minus liabilities) of older households ($86,300), including those seventy-five years and older ($77,700), was well above the U.S. average ($37,600) in 1993 (AARP & AoA 1998). In addition, the poverty level for older persons is now lower than that of younger age cohorts. In 1997, about 3.4 million older persons, or 10.5 percent (down from 12.4 percent in 1986), were below the poverty level, which compares to 10.9 percent. Yet, in spite of improvement in economic well-being, almost one-fifth (17.0 percent) of the older population was poor or near-poor in 1997.

What accounts for these seemingly disparate set of statistics? According to Torres-Gil (1992), it is representative of the deepening chasm between vulnerable racial and gender subgroups and the more affluent elderly. Although the financial status of the elderly has been helped by political measures, not all elderly persons have benefitted equally. There are distinct differences by both race and gender obscured by reliance on aggregate figures. According to AARP and AoA (1998), the median income of older persons in 1996 was $17,768 for males and $10,062 for females. The median income for whites was $29,470, for African Americans, $21,328, and for Hispanics, $21,068. One of every eleven (9.0 percent) of elderly Whites was poor in 1997, compared to (26.0 percent) of elderly Blacks and (23.8 percent) of elderly Hispanics (AoA & AARP 1998). Forty percent of older black women who lived alone were poor in 1996 (AoA & AARP 1998). These statistics demonstrate that race and gender are important variables in financial well-being.

The Policies

SOCIAL SECURITY

In contrast to European countries with comparable levels of socioeconomic development, the United States has been slow to develop income policies affecting the elderly population. The Social Security Act of 1935 was the first major policy enacted to provide financial assistance to the elderly. Essentially, the act is based upon an implicit guarantee that the succeeding generations will provide for the elderly through their contributions to Social Security, and that individuals have earned the right to a retirement benefit through their work experience and their contributions to the system. Under the 1935 law, only 60 percent of the labor force was entitled to earn future retirement benefits. Since that time, coverage has been expanded so that 95 percent of the labor force contributes and is entitled to retirement benefits under the Social Security Law. Social Security has played a major role in decreasing the poverty rate among older Americans from over twice the national average to less than the national average (U.S. Bureau of the Census 1995).

Despite the public assumption, Social Security was not intended to be a full and adequate retirement income. The intent was to create a minimum base that would be supplemented by other retirement pensions and savings developed by the individual worker. However, Social Security constitutes the majority of income for most older persons (National Committee to Preserve Social Security and Medicare 1997), and reliance on Social Security rises dramatically with age (FamiliesUSA 1997). In 1972, in recognition of the significance of Social Security pensions to the financial well-being of the elderly, a system of indexing benefits to take account of inflation was established (Estes et al. 1983). This system is commonly called COLA (Cost of Living Adjustments).

When first established, the Social Security system was administered as an independent agency by three commissioners. Currently, the Social Security Administration (SSA) is part of the Department of Health and Human Services. Social Security is funded through separate trust funds from revenues raised equally by a separate tax on employer and employees. This management system has led to a number of issues and problems. The method of financing is dependent on the state of the economy at any given time period so that during a recession period, high unemployment and low productivity result in less revenues collected from employees and employers. In addition, the system is influenced by the demographic trends in the population. For example, the continued growth in the size of the elderly population and a proportionate decrease in the number of contributing workers have placed additional stress on the ability of the system to remain solvent and pay out promised benefits to retired workers. In fact, the ratio of contributing employees to recipient beneficiaries is projected to drop from 3.3 to 2.0 by 2030 (Quinn 1996).

Due to these economic and demographic problems, the solvency of the Social Security Fund became questionable in the early 1980s. The following changes in the Social Security Act are a result of this situation.

1. Cost of living adjustments are deferred for six months.
2. Increases in the normal retirement age from the present sixty-five will be made, beginning with those reaching the age of sixty-two in the year 2000. The new age will be sixty-six years in 2009–20, and rising to sixty-seven for those reaching that age in the year 2027 and beyond.
3. Beginning in 1990, the retirement earnings test for persons at the normal retirement age up to age seventy is liberalized by changing the "$1-for-$2" reduction in benefits for earnings above the annual exempt amount to a "$1-for-$3" basis.
4. Increases will be made in the credit for postponing claiming benefits beyond the normal retirement age from 3 percent per year for persons reaching age sixty-five in 1983–89, to 8 percent for persons reaching normal retirement age in 2009 and thereafter.
5. Several changes have been made to liberalize benefits which primarily affect women; for example, increasing the benefit rate for disabled widow(er)s aged fifty to fifty-nine from 50 to 71.5 percent depending upon age at disablement to a uniform 71.5 percent. These changes have had a major positive effect on the solvency of the Social Security Trust Fund.

The aging of the baby boom generation and resulting shift in age composition of the general population to those retired has tremendous implications for the future of Social Security. Although Social Security is now running sizable annual surpluses, by one estimate the trust fund is projected to be depleted (under current law) by 2029 (Quinn 1996). Three major policy proposals are offered to prevent insolvency: increase in payroll taxes; continued modifications of the retirement age; and pursual of either full or partial privatization (Quinn 1996). The most controversial proposal, privatization, now receives support, although opponents predict that women and low-wage workers would be negatively impacted through reduced returns on contributions (Williamson 1997).

SUPPLEMENTAL SECURITY INCOME
Supplemental Security Income (SSI) was enacted into law in 1972 to provide a national minimum income to the elderly living at or near poverty level. Historically, the elderly poor were provided financial assistance under the 1935 Social Security Act through the Old Age Assistance Program (OAA). This program, however, was available to each state on a matching basis so that the amount available in any given state was dependent on the amount appropriated by that state for the program. In addition, each state administered its

own OAA program. Consequently, there was substantial variation in the amount of individual benefits, and in the eyes of some, a good deal of inequity (Estes et al. 1983). The 1972 amendment establishing SSI was intended to eliminate the variability and the inequities.

The SSI program is financed fully by the federal government and administered by the Social Security Administration. States may supplement the amount of the federal grant at their discretion. In 1996, the average SSI grants were $484 per month per individual at age sixty-five and $726 per couple over that age (U.S. Department of Health and Human Services 1997). Both averages compute to below the official government poverty level for either a household of an older individual living alone or for an older couple. SSI administration also raises questions about equity for beneficiaries with low-income levels because of overlap with Social Security (Dobelstein 1996). Social Security benefits are considered income for determining SSI eligibility; receipt of SSI is offset by a decrease in Social Security payments (NCOA 1997). SSI does not adequately provide for those elderly living below the poverty level. A compounding fact is that at least 50 percent of low income elderly who could receive SSI benefits are not enrolled in the program because of the perceived stigma of the program as "welfare" (National Council on Aging 1997).

RETIREMENT PENSIONS AND LAWS

About 41 percent of the elderly receive some income from public or private pensions in addition to Social Security (AARP & AoA 1998). Employer-sponsored pension plans expanded rapidly after World War II, and by 1984 an estimated 795,000 private pension plans were in operation (Andrews 1987). In addition, state and local governments sponsor 2,600 pension plans and the federal government has 38 separate retirement plans.

Regulation of these plans falls under the 1974 Employee Retirement Income Security Act. This act established a ten-year vesting standard. Vested pension benefits are earned by the employee by satisfying specific service requirements (in this case, ten years of pension plan participation) and they cannot be revoked by the employer (Employee Benefit Research Institute 1985). By 1980, about 90 percent of employer plans had adopted the ten-year vesting plan. The Employee Retirement Income Security Act also regulated portability, a feature which enables employees to carry pension benefits from plan to plan.

The distinction between defined benefit plans and defined contribution plans is an important one. The former provides an employee a specific pension benefit at retirement, as for example, a certain percentage of salary per year of service under the plan. The latter, in contrast, does not guarantee a specific pension at retirement but ensures that plan contributions are made according to specific rules. Benefits may be provided as an annuity or through a lump sum distribution at retirement at the *discretion of the employer*. Under the Employee Retirement Income Security Act, lump sum distributions from defined contribution plans were permitted before retirement.

The Tax Reform Act of 1986 made two changes to ensure that a greater number of workers would receive pension benefits at retirement. The first change was to reduce the minimum vesting period from ten years to five years. The second change imposed penalty taxes on the consumption of distributions prior to retirement to ensure that vested benefits would be protected and not spent before retirement. A good deal of the interest in five-year vesting was in response to the increased labor force participation of women, whose average job tenure continues to be lower than that of men.

The pension systems outlined above tend to perpetuate systematic inequities by income, ethnic minority status, and sex, with lower income workers, and frequently women and minorities likely to be in jobs that exclude pension plans. In many ways, private and public pension plans tend to favor white males in technical, professional, or managerial positions (Crystal 1986). A study conducted by Woods (1996) provides new evidence about the unequal distribution of pension benefits among the aged, confirming that benefits are highly concentrated among higher income groups. Pension coverage reaches less than half of the labor force—those employed in full-time jobs—and only 40 percent of retirees receive pension benefits (FamiliesUSA 1997). In addition, there is concern over the stability and solvency of pension plans and retirement adequacy. In response, the National Council on Aging has recommended that the Pension Benefit Guarantee Corporation (PBGC) should ensure that private pension participants are informed about underfunded plans (NCOA 1997).

EMPLOYMENT

In 1997, about 12 percent of the older population were either working or actively seeking work (AARP & AoA 1997). Approximately half (54 percent) of the workers over sixty-five in 1995 were employed part-time—5 percent of men and 63 percent of women. Projected population figures showing a progressively aging society demonstrate a need for expanded federal response in the area of opportunities for future older workers (Miranda 1988a). Lammers (1983) suggests that these demographic conditions create an "economic imperative" for expanded employment among older persons (p. 126).

By the early 1980s, federal involvement with older workers was focused on three primary areas of interest: one of a legal nature, the other two concerning the employment of the elderly poor (Rich & Baum 1984). Legally, older workers were not protected from discrimination in employment in the Civil Rights Act of 1964. In 1967, Congress enacted the Age Discrimination in Employment Act, with the basic purpose of promoting employment based on ability rather than on age (Rich & Baum 1984). Employers of twenty persons or more came under the act, and in 1974, federal, state, and local government employees were included. The age limit for mandatory retirement was raised to seventy years in 1978, and in 1986, mandatory retirement was eliminated except for a few special circumstances (Eglit 1989). The passage in the early 1990s of the Older Workers Protection Act overturned a Supreme Court decision that older employees' benefits are not protected by the ADEA. In addition, the Americans with Disabilities Act provides civil rights protection for the disabled, important as the number of elderly with disabling conditions increases.

The most visible federally supported employment program for older persons, in this case, those who are fifty-five or older, is the Senior Community Service Employment Programs (SCSEP) (Miranda 1988b). This program is funded under Title V of the Older Americans Act, and emphasizes on-the-job training. The objective is to place trained workers in permanent, unsubsidized jobs (Lowy 1991). The program is restricted to low-income persons (125 percent of the poverty level or less) who also are unemployed (Dobelstein 1996). The SCSEP is the nation's largest older-worker program, with 65,000 low-income workers (National Council of Senior Citizens 1997).

Another area of interest in the employment of the elderly is part of the Job Training Partnership Act (JTPA) which focuses on older workers. A special provision of the act requires that a 3 percent "set-aside" of a state's allotment for training is targeted for older workers. This program also is limited to the economically disadvantaged, defined as those with an income below the poverty level. Title III of the Act, the dislocated workers program, was replaced by the Omnibus Trade Act (Miranda 1988b).

Health

The Problems

One policy issue is the amount of income received by the elderly. A second issue is expenditures by elderly people. Many older people have health care needs, including expensive evaluations, medications, and procedures. These expenditures can quickly erode personal resources of those people without adequate insurance. For example, in 1995, 28.3 percent of older persons assessed their health as fair or poor compared to 10 percent of persons under age sixty-five. One-third of all older persons reported that they were limited by chronic conditions, and had a severe disability (AoA & AARP 1998). Over 4.4 million (14 percent) had difficulty in carrying out activities of daily living (ADLs) and 6.5 million (21 percent) reported difficulties with instrumental activities of daily living (IADLs) (AoA & AARP 1998).

With more chronic conditions than younger age groups, the elderly use a disproportionate amount of health care resourses. Older persons averaged more visits to doctors in 1994 than did persons under sixty-five (eleven visits vs. five visits). The elderly accounted for 36 percent of total personal health care expenditures in 1997. Benefits from government programs, primarily Medicare and Medicaid, cover about two-thirds of the health care expenditures of older people (AARP & AoA 1997). Consequently, those government programs are of the utmost importance in providing health care for the elderly and are a major part of the federal budget.

The Policies

MEDICARE

In 1965, Congress added Title XVIII, or Medicare, to the Social Security Act. The purpose of Medicare is to provide older people protection against the heavy cost of hospital, nursing home, and physician care. The two basic components of Medicare are Hospital Insurance (Part A) and Supplemental Medical Insurance (Part B). Each of these components is directed toward acute care, as opposed to long-term care which is a growing need because of chronic illness.

The Hospital Insurance Component (Part A) is financed through the Social Security payroll tax and is available to all older persons who are eligible for Social Security benefits. This coverage pays for up to ninety days of hospital care, and for a restricted amount of skilled nursing home care and home health services. Recipients are responsible for the first day of hospital care and for co-payments for hospital stays that exceed sixty days. Supplemental Medical Insurance, or Part B, is financed through general tax revenues and by an additional monthly premium paid by participants. This coverage reimburses for physician services, hospital outpatient services, limited home health care, and diagnostic laboratory services. Because of the differences in health situations among the elderly, and especially with the growing number of elderly living beyond the age of seventy-five, the expenditures for Medicare in the older population vary widely.

Problems are inherent in the Medicare system. One problem is that Medicare pays less than actual health care costs. Medicare pays for 80 percent of allowable charges and not the actual amount charged by many health providers, although some providers, agree to accept "assignment," that is, what Medicare will pay. The elderly who are participating in both Part A and Part B of Medicare must pay the remaining 20 percent of expenses and an annual premium.

A second problem is the complexity of the system. Medicare has become so complicated that many older people do not understand how it works or what benefits it provides. There are several types of cost sharing and seemingly arbitrary distinctions between covered and noncovered services. A third problem is the limitation in what actually is covered. The major limitation of Medicare is its focus on acute care and the exclusion or limited coverage of prescription drugs, and the majority of nursing home and home care. Medicare has also been criticized on the grounds that it provides more benefits to upper- and middle-income people as compared to lower-income elderly who tend to have greater burdens of illness and disability. Not only can the more affluent elderly better afford supplemental private health insurance, but they also can better afford increasing Medicare co-payments and premiums than lower-income elderly. Some critics argue that a two-tier system of health care delivery is becoming the trend. One level is for those people with private health insurance and Medicare. The other level is for those who have no private insurance and rely on Medicaid and public charity or do without health care altogether (Torres-Gil 1992).

Medicare costs are of particular interest to policy makers. This system is frequently blamed for spiraling health care costs, in particular, hospital costs. Health care payment mechanisms provide little incentive for physicians or patients to reduce use of costly medical technology or out-patient care. Some critics maintain that Medicare benefits the providers of health care more than the older people with chronic health needs (Harvard Medicare Project 1986). While there is general agreement on the need to hold down Medicare costs, there are problems with the choices available for this process. One of the choices has been to increase substantially the amounts of co-payments paid by the elderly, which places a disproportionate burden on the less affluent.

Another choice has been a system of prospective payment, whereby payment is determined by the diagnostic category in which each patient is placed. This system was created in 1983 and is called Diagnostic Related Groupings (DRGs). Under the former actual cost based system, hospitals were paid more if they provided more services over a longer period of time, resulting in higher subsequent costs. Under the DRG system, a hospital loses financially if it keeps patients longer than necessary, or provides unnecessary tests or services.

Problems exist with this cost-saving system. One is the fact that this system applies to Medicare patients only and not to private pay patients. Hence hospitals may feel pressured to limit Medicare patients' access to services and to discharge them too quickly (Estes, Swan, & Associates 1992). A second problem is the DRG system does not take into account the severity of an individual's illness within a given diagnostic category. For example, if two older people are hospitalized for the same type of heart surgery, one may take longer than the other to recover for a variety of reasons.

The DRG system puts increased pressure on hospitals to discharge people earlier. In turn, this situation puts pressure on families, nursing homes, and home health care agencies to provide higher levels of care than in the past. Since many families and home health care agencies cannot provide the more complex service, premature discharge leads to the "revolving door" pattern of more patients repeating hospital stays (Estes, Swan, & Associates 1992).

A number of proposals for change in the Medicare program have been offered to address some of these problems. Proposals range from suggesting that health care be rationed, to those involving the changing of Medicare procedures and regulations. Procedure and regulatory changes include generating new sources of revenue, removing the prohibition against reimbursement for preventive care, and shifting from an age-based to a needs-based Medicare system (Hudson 1998). Proposals include far-reaching revisions, including a proposal that Medicare cover the cost of extended nursing home care and provide more generous coverage of long-term care in out-patient settings, such as home health care and mental health services. The most sweeping proposal is one that calls for a national health insurance system that would finance a comprehensive health care system regardless of age (Cockburn 1986). This principle was encompassed in the Health Security Act of 1993 that failed to be passed by Congress.

The debate over the cost of Medicare to consumers was temporarily settled in the late 1980s. Under pressure from elderly constituents to have adequate protection from escalating health care costs, Congress passed an amendment to Medicare, the Catastrophic Coverage Act, in June 1988. Many services, such as long-term care, were not covered under the legislation. Because the legislation did not address the health care needs of the under-sixty-five population, policymakers established the first seniors-only tax so that older persons would have to pay for *their* new coverage. The "seeds of discontent were sown" (Pollack 1990, 2) with that decision and the Catastrophic Coverage Act was ultimately repealed.

An important recent trend in Medicare is the growth of "managed care" provided through health maintenance organizations (HMOs), accelerated by the rising cost of supplemental insurance (FamiliesUSA 1996). Voluntary enrollment of Medicare recipients in managed care was projected to reach 7 million in 1999 and 15 million recipients by 2007 (Congressional Budget Office 1997). HMO health plans combine coverage of health care costs and delivery of health care for a prepaid premium. HMOs generally require patients to select a primary care physician (PCP) that serves as the point of coordination for care and referrals to specialists or the hospital.

Ideally, HMOs provide coordinated preventative care at a lower cost to both the patient and the federal government. From inception in the late 1980s, it was anticipated that Medicare HMOs would provide an organizational framework for care system coordination characterized by primary care, disease prevention, and health promotion—in essence, to improve the quality of care for elderly beneficiaries (Kirkiman-Liff 1999). However, current evidence of improved quality of care and outcomes is not dramatic (Wagner 1996). Further, the centerpiece of managed care, service coordination, can have the undesired effect of restricting flexibility for consumers. For example, patients are penalized with higher out-of-pocket costs for seeking care without a referral or outside the HMO network. The gate-keeper function of the PCP can erect an unnecessary barrier to social workers, counselors, and other providers of psychosocial services, as well as to specialist physicians seen on an on-going basis (Kirkiman-Liff 1999). In addition, there is a recognized geographic bias to the payment system. Medicare payments to managed care plans are based on what is spent per person on traditional Medicare health care in that area; payments to urban-area managed care plans are higher, enabling them to offer more services. In response to these criticisms, the Balanced Budget Act of 1997 included provisions to alter managed care by offering more choices for recipients and redistributing payments to rural areas. What is not clear for the future is how energetically managed care providers will compete for the business of growing subpopulations of elderly persons—more older, frail, and poor minorities.

Spiraling Medicare costs continue to plague legislators and policymakers alike. The financial health of the hospital trust fund (Part A), financed by payroll taxes, is questionable; by one estimate depletion is projected for the year 2002, long in advance of the major impact of demographic shifts (Quinn 1996). Unlike Social Security, there is the potential for immediate catastrophic consequences as Medicare problems are "on the doorstep" (Quinn 1996, 17). After much debate, Congress, in an effort to balance the budget by 2002, passed the Balanced Budget Act (BBA) of 1997 (Public Law 105-33), signed into law by President Clinton. This legislation, by garnering a savings of $115 billion, enacts the most significant changes to Medicare since its inception thirty years ago (GSA 1997). The Health Care Financing Administration (HCFA), the federal agency responsible for overseeing Medicare and Medicaid, reports that the legislation:

- extends the life of the Medicare trust fund and reduces federal spending;
- increases health care options, particularly with respect to HMOs, for older persons;
- improves benefits for staying healthy;
- fights Medicare fraud abuse;
- develops prospective payment systems for home health providers and skilled nursing facilities (HCFA 1997).

To complement changes to the law brought by the Balanced Budget Act, Congress appointed the Bipartisan Medicare Commission to make recommendations by 1999 on implementation of Medicare reform. The issues that the commission heard included: social missions of Medicare; revenues and payment reforms; the role of Medicare in long-term care; fee-for-service options; expansion of consumer flexibility; and public education (Older Americans Report 1997). The commission adjourned in 1999 without making a single recommendation to Congress.

Time will show whether the BBA is successful in trimming Medicare costs. The future solvency of Medicare rests on the interaction of a variety of factors: additional legislative changes, the continued existence of a budget surplus, the overall health of the economy, the viewpoint of Congressional leadership, and the political view of the sitting President.

MEDICAID

Medicaid also was enacted in 1965 as a federal and state program of medical assistance for the needy poor, regardless of age. It is the principal health insurance provided for the poor who meet the eligibility requirements. Overall, 72 percent of all Medicaid spending in 1995 was for the blind, disabled, and elderly; however, these groups represent only 27 percent of the program's beneficiaries (National Academy on Aging 1997). Intended for the poor, Medicaid has become the primary long-term care program for middle-class elderly by paying for a large portion of publicly funded nursing home care (Torres-Gil 1992, 45). Medicaid paid more than half (52 percent) of the total nursing home bill of $69.6 billion in 1994 (FamiliesUSA 1997).

Medicaid is different from Medicare since both federal and state funds are involved and administration is by local departments. This difference is important for two reasons. One is that Medicaid carries the stigma of being a welfare program. The second is that there is variability among states in terms of eligibility requirements and the array of health care services that are covered. In one sense, it is better to be poor and ill in some states than in others.

Federal regulations dictate that certain conditions must exist for state participation in the Medicaid program. Each state must provide for hospital inpatient care, physician services, skilled nursing care, laboratory and X-ray services, home health services, hospital outpatient care, family planning, and rural health clinics. In addition, many states provide up to thirty-two optional services. However, these services are subject to the economic cycles that each state experiences.

Although Medicaid usage by the elderly is only 6 percent of the total usage of the program, 12 percent of the total Medicaid costs are attributed to home care for the elderly (Winterbottom, Liska, & Obermaier 1995). The factors causing this disproportionate usage are the same as those for Medicare. In addition, Medicaid is the primary public source for funding nursing home care. Nursing home costs are increasing and are the fastest growing category of Medicaid expenses.

The Medicaid system has been criticized on several grounds. One of the criticisms is that Medicaid encourages over-utilization of nursing homes and benefits the major corporations that own an increasing percentage of nursing homes. Another criticism is that this system perpetuates economic injustice since a number of physicians refuse to accept Medicaid patients on the grounds that allowable fee reimbursement is below prevailing service costs. In addition, the number of Medicaid beds in nursing homes is limited so that Medicaid patients often have to wait in line behind more affluent patients.

The most frequently criticized and publicized regulation of the Medicaid program is the so-called spend-down qualification. This requirement forces patients to first exhaust their own resources, excluding house and car, on medical expenses until their remaining resources are below the income levels set for eligibility for the Medicaid program. This requirement works to impoverish even middle-class older patients and their spouses, especially wives. If the person in the nursing home is the husband who has been the primary income earner during their marriage, any pension income in his name must be used to pay Medicaid. This situation leaves his spouse with little or no income to support herself. Since annual nursing home costs average over $30,000, most patients quickly deplete their personal resources with the majority ending up on Medicaid within one to two years after admission. To protect the financial stability of the surviving spouse, a "spousal impoverishment" provision was added to Medicaid that increased the monthly income and overall assets the spouse in the community could retain (FamiliesUSA 1997).

Due to escalating costs, Medicaid also received dramatic spending cuts of $13 billion in the Balanced Budget Act of 1997 (Waxman & Alker 1997). A major change was the elimination of a standard federal reimbursement for nursing home care, leaving states free to set their own rates. This recommendation to "block grant" Medicaid provides a specific lump sum of money to each state with relatively few rules about how the money should be spent. In addition, states can now mandate that Medicaid beneficiaries enroll in a managed care program without a federal waiver (Waxman & Alker 1997). Additionally, the managed care revolution has had a greater impact on Medicaid than Medicare (FamiliesUSA 1997). States are rapidly transitioning out of fee-for-service programs into managed care as a cost savings device.

LONG-TERM CARE

Long-term care encompasses a range of services to meet the physical, social, and emotional needs of older people with chronic illnesses or disabilities that interfere with their independence and ability to perform activities of daily living. These services can be provided within an institutional setting such as a hospital or nursing home, community senior centers and adult day care, or the patient's own home by homemaker services or respite care. Long-term care is most frequently provided on an unpaid, informal basis by family and friends (National Academy on Aging 1997).

The Medicaid program in each state remains the largest third-party purchaser of nursing home care in the United States, and long-term care is 35 percent of the Medicaid budget (FamiliesUSA 1997). This structure puts a heavy burden on the individual states in financing Medicaid. In 2018, it is estimated that there will be 3.6 million elderly persons in need of a nursing home bed, up 2 million from the current figure (National Academy on Aging 1997). While nursing home use has grown steadily in the past thirty years, community-based services have increased dramatically in the last ten years; home health care and nonmedical home care are the fastest growing components of long-term care (National Academy on Aging 1997). There are two important pieces of policy introduced in 1987 that explain this expansion in community care: the prospective payment system reduced the length of hospital stays; and Medicare was revised to include expanded coverage of home care services. Yet current methods of financing health care for the elderly, namely Medicare and Medicaid, are not geared to provide community-based care. Less than 6 percent of Medicaid expenditures go to home health care services, and Medicare only covers skilled nursing for the acute care needs of the homebound elderly for a limited period of time. The public policy agenda of the National Council on Aging (NCOA) for the new millennium acknowledges the bias toward institutional care in its recommendations for changes in long-term care:

1. The federal government should provide incentives to states to:
   - reformulate long-term care programs away from the institutional bias in care;
   - provide consumers with a greater choice to enable them to remain at home as long as possible;
   - develop policies that recognize the central role of family in provision of services;
   - cover adult day care under Medicare;
   - oppose copayments on home health that would bar access for low-income beneficiaries;
   - improve quality standards for home and community-based care services;
   - rethink eligibility to include functional need as well as medical necessity.

2. States should establish and pay for care management systems consistent with national standards and federal guidelines.
3. Long-term care provisions should achieve a balance between flexibility for consumers and the security of guaranteed basic comprehensive benefits;
   - include health promotion and disease/disability prevention services in long-term care;
   - strengthen private long-term care insurance standards, extend coverage to include adult day care and home care, and make it more affordable and accessible to low-income older persons.

PRIVATE INSURANCE

In 1961, before the advent of Medicare, elderly persons paid 11 percent of their income on health care; by 1994, this had risen to 24 percent (FamiliesUSA 1996). Poor elderly persons spend, on average, one-third of their income (34 percent) on out-of-pocket health care costs (FamiliesUSA 1996). Beginning in 1996, Congress at least partially addressed the problem by protecting low-income elderly persons from out-of-pocket Medicare costs through the Qualified Medicare Beneficiary (QMB) program, where Medicaid picks up the cost for those recipients at or below 135 percent of the poverty line.

Because of the limited coverage of Medicare, many older persons who can afford it have purchased private medical insurance, sometimes referred to as Medigap policies. However, even these Medicare supplemental insurance policies do not cover long-term nursing home care, and Medicaid will pay for these services only after individuals have depleted their resources, fulfilling the spend-down qualification. According to the National Academy on Aging (1997), nursing home expenditures exceeded $36 billion in 1996, with the elderly and their families paying about half that amount. Private long-term care insurance is designed to finance these potentially catastrophic expenses. Older persons with means have sought protection from cost-sharing requirements through purchase of additional private insurance for deductibles, copayments, and noncovered benefits. However, in 1995, less than 6 percent of long-term care was paid for by supplemental insurance.

The Omnibus Budget Reconciliation Act of 1990 (OBRA 1990) required standardization of Medigap insurers to ten types of plans. The market for insurance policies is steadily growing along with the cost to the consumer. In 1995, for example, large numbers of elderly had 23 percent increases in Medigap policies, far in excess of cost-of-living increases (FamiliesUSA 1996).

Living Independently

The Problems

Although financial well-being and good health are important to one's ability to live independently, so are other factors, such as adequate housing, nutrition, and transportation.

Older people spend a higher percentage of their income on housing than younger people and their housing is generally older and less adequate (AARP & AoA 1997). Some of their housing problems include affordability; overcrowding; architectural barriers; minimum building standards; and access to shopping, transportation, and needed services (House Select Committee on Aging & Senate Special Committee on Aging 1987).

Many older Americans are at nutritional risk. Physical changes, such as decrease in metabolism or the senses of taste and smell, can prevent older people from receiving proper nutrition. Certain social factors, such as social isolation, loneliness, and depression, also can increase nutritional risk (Cicenas & Foltz 1988).

Meeting the transportation needs of the elderly is becoming a more serious issue. The number of older persons continues to increase, and the number of older persons living in the suburbs is beginning to outnumber those living in the central cities. In addition, the heavy dependence on travel by personal automobile becomes less feasible as the lifespan increases.

The Policies

HOUSING

Housing policy and programs for older people have tended to get less attention than income security and health care. There are a number of reasons to explain this phenomenon. From one perspective, an adequate income should make it possible for an individual to own or rent housing. From another perspective, the majority of older people live with relatives, so that housing is not an urgent need to be met. In addition, the cultural value placed on individual home ownership in the United States works against the interest in government owned or financed housing for the elderly. Some statistics will help illustrate these points.

In 1997 the majority (67 percent) of older noninstitutionalized persons lived in a family setting (81 percent of older men and 57 percent of older women). About 7 percent were not living with a spouse but were living with children, siblings or other relatives. About 32 percent of all noninstitutionalized older persons lived alone in 1995, but the percentage of women living alone was substantially higher than that of men—42 percent of women as compared to 17 percent of men.

The primary approach to providing housing for the elderly involves subsidizing builders where units sell or rent for less than the prevailing market price. Section 202 of the Housing Act of 1959 has provided housing for moderate income older persons. Under Section 202, low-interest loans are made to nonprofit corporations or to nonprofit consumer cooperatives. Half of the elderly poor spend 50 percent of their income on housing; 37 percent of federal subsidized housing units in 1996 (1.4 million units) were occupied by older persons (National Council of Senior Citizens 1997). Under Section 236 of the same act, builders are provided other means of supplying rental and cooperative housing to low and moderate income people. One approach allows the builders to lower their housing costs through interest reduction payments. In another approach, the federal government gives landlords the difference between the market rental cost of a housing unit and the 25 percent of a tenant's income assumed to be available for rent.

Older people also benefit from other policies such as property tax exemptions, energy assistance, and home equity conversions. In recent years, the focus in the area of housing has been on maintaining what already exists and to make better use of existing housing resources through home-sharing, accessory apartments, and home equity conversions. The trend is to meet older people's housing needs through adapting existing communities and neighborhoods rather than through expensive housing programs.

In recent years, the concept of "aging in place" in the Continuing Care Retirement (CCRC) setting, has influenced the retirement market as a bridge between housing and long-term care. (Kane & Wilson 1993). CCRCs are residential wings or detached housing affiliated with nursing homes, adult foster care homes or family care homes, congregate care, or even home-sharing arrangements. With lifetime care available, residents can move to a more intensive level of assistance and treatment as their needs warrant. However, CCRCs tend to be available to higher income elderly who can afford the costly entrance and monthly service fees (Kane & Wilson 1993).

NUTRITION

Since nutrition is such a fundamental need to support life, it is no wonder that the largest single program of the Administration on Aging is the nutrition program (Rich & Baum 1984). Nutrition services are provided under Title III of the Older Americans Act, and they include congregate meals and home-delivered meals.

The congregate meals program is designed to induce older people to get out of their homes and into social interaction with others. Meals are provided at a "nutrition site," such as senior center. Participants are also given information about nutrition and community resources available to them (Dobelstein 1996). For those who are unable to leave their homes, separate funding is provided for the home-delivered meals program. The programs are available to those sixty or older, and to their spouses, even if the spouses are not sixty years old (Dobelstein 1996).

Both of these programs are offered in-kind to the older person. The Older Americans Act prohibits charging for the meals, but older persons are encouraged to make a contribution. Cost sharing for meals has become an important policy issue in Older Americans Act reauthorization. During the 1980s the Administration on Aging encouraged providers to actively solicit meal contributions to compensate for a federal funding slowdown (Kassner 1992). During the 1991 reauthorization period, an amendment was presented that would have permitted providers of meal services to charge fees based on ability to pay for meal recipients above 200 percent of the poverty line (Older Americans Report 1991). The amendment was soundly rejected on the grounds that nutrition services were already well supported by voluntary contributions. The meal cost-sharing debate remains active in spite of the fact that $171 million was collected from voluntary contributions in FY 1995 (Benson 1997). Popularity of the program is based largely on the fact that it is not income based and encourages a sense of ownership by meal recipients and communities (Benson 1997).

TRANSPORTATION

Almost 10 percent of the funds from the Older Americans Act are used for transportation services, with additional help being provided through the Urban Mass Transit Act and the National Mass Transportation Act. In 1973, Title IV of the Older Americans Act was amended to include funds for a special study and demonstration projects to examine and devise new ways to help meet the transportation needs of older people. In 1975, priority services were mandated for the first time, and transportation services were targeted as a priority. In addition, the 1975 amendments authorized state and area agencies on aging under Title III to enter into cooperative agreements with other agencies providing programs such as Titles VI, XIX, and XX of the Social Security Act. This attempt to provide structured and efficient transportation for older people has never really been successful, and the issue of transportation as an unmet need for the elderly remains as a difficult policy problem.

Future Policy Issues

Although the elderly in general have fared relatively well from social policies in the United States, subpopulations of older persons continue to experience ill health, low income, and social isolation. Current public policies benefitting the aged do not account for the vast differences that exist in the older population, for example, functional ability by age group or economic differences between sexes and among minority groups.

DIVERSITY AND AGING

Non-white ethnic groups will comprise the fastest growing subgroups of elderly between 1990 and 2050. During this period, the proportion of elderly is expected to grow as follows: White, 80 percent; African-American, 199 percent, Asian and Pacific Islands, 885 percent, and Latinos, 921.5 percent (AoA & AARP 1998). Non-white groups also tend to disproportionately fall into the poor and near-poor categories, and depend upon Social Security as their sole source of income. What are the future policy implications of this demographic shift? First and foremost, there is likely to be a growing number of poor elderly or those who fall at the margins of sufficiency. This trend, coupled with continued questionable public support for income maintenance programs, may place increasing numbers of older persons in jeopardy.

Given the growing scarcity of economic resources and these income disparities, policymakers will be confronted with the issue of "age versus need." That is, should future public policies be universalistic in nature so that programs and services are offered to all on the basis of their "elderly" status? Or would particularistic policies, those that target benefits to the elderly in the greatest need, be a feasible policy alternative?

One potential danger of reforms based on need is that they may increase competition between groups who must vie for scarce resources. There will likely continue to be competition for a shrinking pot of dollars. A more advantageous strategy is for the elderly and their advocates to focus their energies upon policies that would benefit all Americans, such as on a cost-effective national health insurance program, rather than singling out the aged as a special, different, and dependent group (Torres-Gil 1992). Apart from the gaps in coverage for younger populations, those with histories of low wages, poor health, limited education, and marginal family and social supports will continue to arrive at old age with these problems (Hudson 1994).

Much of the policy debate involves the fiscal tension encompassing old-age programs. Rising costs, the increasing number of uninsured, and growing gaps in health care signal the need for ongoing health reform. Medicare and Medicaid problems are part of a larger policy dilemma—the provision of health care in America, a concern that has proven difficult to successfully address through social policy. The failure of the Medicare Catastrophic Coverage Act demonstrated the poor feasibility of a policy that requires the relatively "well-off" elderly to contribute funds to help their poorer counterparts.

Faced with rapidly increasing costs, legislators and policymakers turn to policy solutions that are rooted in the themes of fiscal austerity and declining federal responsibility. It will be important to observe the policy consequences, both intended and unintended, of the Balanced Budget Act and other legislative changes made to federal policy. This will be particularly important with respect to the impact on the poor and near-poor elderly that rely primarily on Medicaid for their health care needs. There is little current evidence to suggest that savings are possible in Medicaid without adversely affecting beneficiaries' eligibility, access to services, and quality of care received (Weiner 1996).

Health and Long-Term Care

Several issues of major national importance are relevant to the provision of long-term care in a rapidly aging society. The first issue involves the methods by which long-term care services are purchased, such as fee-for-service, prospective payment systems, and health maintenance organizations. A "case-mix" payment system which recognizes differences in the costs of caring for patients with different needs is offered as the best compromise to address appropriate resources for each patient's needs, administrative feasibility, and equitable reimbursement.

The second issue involves the place in which care should be provided to older persons and the functionally impaired. The number of older persons needing long-term care across the continuum is expected to increase dramatically in the next thirty years. Although nursing homes are likely to remain at the hub of the long-term care system, the spectrum and availability of alternatives for care need to be expanded. It will be important to continue to pursue policy options that provide access to affordable quality care for *all* elderly and to maintain a balance between institutional and community care alternatives. This will require the reexamination of financing methodologies that still tend to favor institutional over community care options. Options would include a fully developed array of both home health and community services. Concern also is expressed about the somewhat arbitrary criteria used to determine the appropriate level of care for patients. Case management activities will be important to address this problem, and new assessment instruments need to be developed to help in this new form of triage and advocacy. It will also be important to pursue policy options that support family caregivers such as tax credits and direct services. Services such as respite, home care services, and information and referral will help families sustain efforts to care for an older relative and prevent premature institutionalization.

The third area is the amount and cost of long-term care. Issues include the number of nursing home beds needed, governmental funding for home care, Certificate of Need restrictions on new nursing home beds, and the question of additional funds to nursing homes thereby improving quality of care. These topics address the trade-off between cost and quality in long-term care.

Employment, Retirement, and Income Security

The solvency of Social Security in the future remains a central concern, along with the threat of economic dependency. Wide income and poverty variations occur within elderly groups, and aggregate figures tend to hide large pockets of poor and near-poor. Retirement benefits, particularly government and private pensions, tend to go to those best equipped to command higher wages: educated, skilled, white males (Torres-Gil 1992, 101). In the area of employment and retirement, researchers for the Congressional forum discussed the problems associated with the combination of people "living longer and working shorter." They suggested that policy must change to encourage a view of aging that considers the potential of later life rather than focusing on older people as an economic and social burden. A recommendation is to scrutinize the provisions of pensions systems that can make them undesirable with regard to future policies for an aging society. If the trend toward early retirement continues, eventually the average worker will spend more time in retirement than in the labor force.

Another recommendation for aging policy has to do with the supervision and management of pension funds. Individuals have the right to protect their funds from intentional mismanagement or from ineptitude. Pension policy in which a tripartite control of interest between employees, the employers, and the public good is offered as a way of protecting pensions funds, and expanding the options for the older worker in deciding when to retire.

As older workers are gently pushed out of their jobs, it becomes more and more difficult for those who want to continue working to find new jobs. Displaced older workers have two major options: retirement or low-paying, dead-end jobs. Specialized employment agencies and clearinghouses for older workers need to be developed, as well as more flexible work scheduling and personnel practices. In order to confront the prejudices of employers and the fears of workers, more scientific evidence on the productivity of older workers needs to be produced.

Housing

Future housing policies should take into consideration the needs of the current generation of vulnerable old-old elderly and the emerging "new" aged. These policies also must attend to dwelling-specific problems, such as dwelling inadequacies, excessive expenditures, overcrowding, and dwelling-use problems, such as inadequacies of housing associated with limitations due to physical functioning. Assisted living, group residential homes that provide assistance with activities of daily living (ADLs), has emerged as a cost-effective alternative to expensive nursing home care. The present supply of elderly housing should be protected through state or federal government programs and funding support, and the existing stock of specialized housing for older persons needs to be enlarged and/or rehabilitated.

An Unfinished Agenda

As Estes et al. first noted in 1983, two forces continue to shape aging policy: fiscal austerity (the belief that scarcity of resources should govern public policy), and federalism (issues about the appropriate roles of federal, state, and local governments). Four major questions for the future of aging policy under these two forces are relevant. The first question involves the extent to which aging interest groups will ally with a broader base of action and become concerned with more generic issues that will inevitably affect older persons. Without addressing broader policy issues, the elderly may find their future shaped by the advocacy of others.

The second question addresses the extent to which elected officials at the state and local levels are likely to accept the growing shift of the federal government to place responsibilities on state and local governments. The social problems they must confront are becoming increasingly difficult. As the impact of federal and state cutbacks eventually are felt "at home," elected officials are increasingly put on the political "hot seat."

The third question relates to the "age vs. need" issue. Will the interests of the wealthy and the middle class continue to dominate public policy for the aging? Few national aging organizations have aligned themselves exclusively with the low-income, minority elderly or with older women. Aging advocacy has primarily been targeted toward improving benefits to a broad base of the elderly regardless of race, gender, or economic status. As financial and political pressures mount, class and age differences in public policy may become even more pronounced. Finally, what are the human consequences of fiscal austerity and aging? We need to obtain an accurate portrayal of how policies are felt and experienced by vulnerable subgroups of the elderly.

From another perspective, Hudson (1995) reflects on the resiliency of age as the "master policy variable" in defining the future of social policy for older persons. Indeed, in recent years aging policy has experienced a virtual "sea change" with reforms in Medicare and Medicaid and the focus on the solvency of Social Security. Alternatives to age as the primary eligibility criterion include means-testing (both economic and functional) and continued privatization of services that Hudson views as attempts to limit benefits and "re-residualize" the old (Hudson 1997).

How will social policies treat older persons in the new millennium? Will their "favored status" further erode? How will policy-makers address the needs of an increasingly diverse older population where "one size fits all" policy approaches no longer apply? These are but a few of the critical policy questions that gerontological social workers should have a role in addressing.

Discussion Questions

1. Social Security retirement income is financed through employer-employee taxes. Why should able-bodied hard-working adults pay for the retirement income of older people?
2. Some authors suggest that the Social Security retirement system should be abandoned in favor of private individual retirement savings plans. What are the advantages and disadvantages of this approach?
3. Medicare provides limited payment for health care to older people covered by Social Security. Medicaid provides limited payment for health care for people, including older people, who meet criteria of financial need. Discuss the reason(s) for having these two separate health care programs.
4. Why has long-term care traditionally been viewed as meaning institutional care in a nursing home? What other possibilities might best meet the needs of older people requiring long-term care?
5. Why is transportation becoming a significant and major problem for older people? Why does it seem so difficult to provide a satisfactory solution to this problem?
6. What policy challenges will the increasing diversity of older persons bring?
7. What have the effects of budget cutbacks and the shift of responsibility from the federal government to the states had on policy?

Experiential Learning

Activity: Perceptions of Older People

Our perceptions of certain groups of people influence governmental policies. This exercise helps students become aware of their own views of older people. It helps demonstrate how stereotypes about older people influence policies for the elderly.

Take a copy of the Aging Perceptions Scale (figure 3.1). Check the column that best describes your perception of older people. Mark items based upon your initial impression or feeling. After completing all the items, sum your scores. Each check receives the number of the column; for example, four checks in column three are scored 12. Sum the items and divide by 32 (the number of items). This mean score represents an overall impression of older people. The lower mean scores represent a more positive image of older people. Use your scores and answers as a basis for a discussion with other students of perceptions of older persons.

Case Studies

See Appendix B for guidelines in analyzing gerontological social work practice.

Case 1: Closures at Colfax State Mental Hospital

"They're cutting back nine hundred employees at Colfax State," Reginald Triddy exclaimed as he stared at the morning paper. "This article states that cuts will be made mainly in geriatric programs and adult psychiatric services resulting in the closure of the geriatric treatment center," he continued to his wife. "The situation will have a big impact on our programs."

Throughout that day, Reginald could not get the story out of his mind. As the Executive Director of Regional Area Agency on Aging (R-AAA) in Franklin, he knew that because Colfax was only twenty-five miles away, persons who were deinstitutionalized would certainly flee to the closest metropolitan area with its more available resources of services, shelter, and food. Later in the week, after receiving a telephone call from a board member about this news story and what it would mean to R-AAA, he decided that some of these issues must be addressed by his Board of Directors.

The R-AAA had been designated in 1974 by the State Department for the Aged with the approval and sanction of local governments to plan, coordinate, and administer services to the elderly under the Older Americans Act. Along with the other twenty-eight State Area Agencies on Aging, R-AAA was established as an advocate of elderly persons in developing appropriate responses to their needs. In its region, R-AAA assumed responsibilities for the city of Franklin (population: 140,000), located in a south central state, and the five surrounding counties (population: 300,000), which have varying suburban and rural characteristics. Each county has its own governmental board of elected supervisors.

Over the years, the R-AAA has supported many services to the elderly such as senior centers, homemaker services, information and referral, transportation, adult day care, legal assistance, home repairs and weatherization, a discount program, emergency services, crime prevention program, a newsletter to thirty thousand people, and outreach services. City and county government officials have come to depend on R-AAA for technical assistance and expertise regarding programs for elderly citizens. Recent favorable publicity given to the ombudsman of the agency for ferreting out two greedy nursing home operators has added region-wide luster to the agency's reputation. The closing of Colfax State means an influx of discharged patients could increase the number of older people beyond what the agency's services can adequately handle.

Instructions: Below are listed a series of polar adjectives accompanied by a scale. You are asked to place a check mark along the scale at a point which in your judgment best describes older people. Consider each item a separate and independent judgment. Do not worry or puzzle over individual items. Do not try to remember how you marked earlier items even though they may seem to have been similar. It is your first impression or immediate feeling about each item that should be recorded.

	1	2	3	4	5	
Progressive						Old-fashioned
Consistent						Inconsistent
Independent						Dependent
Rich						Poor
Generous						Selfish
Productive						Unproductive
Busy						Idle
Secure						Insecure
Strong						Weak
Healthy						Unhealthy
Active						Passive
Handsome						Ugly
Cooperative						Uncooperative
Optimistic						Pessimistic
Satisfied						Dissatisfied
Expectant						Resigned
Flexible						Inflexible
Hopeful						Dejected
Organized						Disorganized
Happy						Sad
Friendly						Unfriendly
Neat						Untidy
Trustful						Suspicious
Self-reliant						Dependent
Liberal						Conservative
Certain						Uncertain
Tolerant						Intolerant
Pleasant						Unpleasant
Beautiful						Grotesque
Aggressive						Defensive
Exciting						Dull
Decisive						Indecisive

Scoring:

Total number of checks in Column 1 _____ × 1 = _____
Total number of checks in Column 2 _____ × 2 = _____
Total number of checks in Column 3 _____ × 3 = _____
Total number of checks in Column 4 _____ × 4 = _____
Total number of checks in Column 5 _____ × 5 = _____

Total = _____ divided by 32 = _____
Mean Score

■ **Figure 3.1**   The Aging Perceptions Scale (Wilson et al. 1982)

Reginald decided that he needed support at the next board meeting. He called back Dr. Trebor, a retired university professor, and asked him if he would be willing to discuss the situation at the next meeting. Dr. Trebor readily agreed and at the meeting the following day, he eloquently addressed the issues and dangers as he saw them. Reginald thought, "I could not have said it better myself." But he became alarmed when the majority of the board members sat in a stony silence following Dr. Trebor's remarks. In fact, the chairman was ready to move on to another topic when Mrs. Roofer, the former Director of the CAP agency, quietly began a discourse on what happened to the city of Franklin fifteen years ago when the state cut funds for Southern Mental Hospital. She said that she was "appalled at the plight of people who were forced to flee to the city to get services and housing wherever they could. It was dreadful, and if we are not careful, we will see the creation of the next generation of street people and bag ladies in Franklin. Only this time, they're all going to be elderly. I, for one, want to see R-AAA do something!"

This powerful speech moved members of the board to begin searching for answers. The board finally recommended that Reginald come to the next board meeting with the following: an assessment of the impact that such a closure and reduction of services might have on Franklin and its service delivery system.

Reginald researched the situation thoroughly and presented this report to the next meeting. The Franklin area had 25 percent of the nursing home beds and 29 percent of the home for adult beds in the entire state. Previous studies had already shown high numbers of deinstitutionalized persons living in this area of the state. Approximately 285 older people would need care either in nursing homes or homes for adults following the closure of Colfax. Colfax State Mental Hospital was located in a neighboring region, where the Bullet Area Agency on Aging, in a small community of twenty-five thousand, had similar responsibilities as R-AAA. While it would have an economic and employment impact on this community, Reginald also believed it raised questions for the board of the Bullet AAA regarding the disposition and rights of elderly patients residing in their region.

Following a lively discussion with the board, Reginald suggested that R-AAA might wish to propose a joint task force with the Bullet AAA on deinstitutionalization of the elderly.

Source: Schneider, R. L., Decker, T., Freeman, J., & Syran, C., *The Integration of Gerontology into Social Work Educational Curricula* (Washington, DC: Council on Social Work Education, 1984).

Case 2: The Advent of a Nursing Home Advocacy Group

"I don't want anyone interfering with my nursing home. Someone from the ombudsman program came in several years ago—she acted like a military sergeant." That remark was typical of the sentiment in a small northern town about the possibility of forming a community nursing home advocacy group.

As a social work member of the County Commission on Aging, Fran Randolph suggested that the commission further operationalize its advocacy function by exploring ways of promoting the welfare of nursing home residents in the county. The ensuing discussion led to unanimous agreement that some kind of local initiative was needed to address the issues that had emerged. Several commissioners described incidents that they knew of firsthand, or had learned about from others, where the rights of residents had been abridged. Other concerns surfaced as well. For example, questions were raised about waiting lists for nursing home placement and whether or not nursing homes were discriminating against Medicaid patients in favor of private-pay patients with their admissions policies.

Obviously, the commission lacked a great deal of information. The commission director was instructed to invite representatives from the nursing homes in the county to attend the next commission meeting as a first step toward getting more information, from their perspectives, on the concerns that had emerged.

The Commission on Aging was created by the County Commission in 1974 to develop and coordinate programming in aging at the local level. The COA is responsible to the Area Agency on Aging that is located in an adjoining county in the northern part of an industrial midwestern state.

Fran is in her third three-year term on the COA. She has become increasingly troubled by what she perceives as an inadequate safeguard procedure for nursing home operations. She feels the need to increase advocacy efforts for nursing home residents. The Area Agency on Aging has traditionally viewed an advocacy program as a low priority program for funding purposes. In recent years, the welfare of nursing home residents in this region has been the sole responsibility of state inspectors operating out of the state capitol, which is several hundred miles away (during winter months, on-site inspections are even more irregularly scheduled due to frequent inclement weather).

With administrators from each of the nursing homes in the area in attendance at the next commission meeting, Fran raised the issue of the need for a local advocacy group. The administrators' response was less than enthusiastic. Confrontation was minimized by emphasizing the potential that a local group could have for helping to promote the welfare of residents. She also emphasized a collective concern about the recent rejection by state officials to expand the number of nursing home beds in the county. Agreement was reached on an important part of the process for resolving complaints, that is, any problems would be handled locally, if at all possible, with outside officials called in as a last resort.

The first organizational meeting for an advocacy group (which was widely publicized in the media and through direct contact with community agencies and groups) attracted representation from a broad spectrum of the community (nursing home staff, community-mental health, private home health care, public health, hospital, clergy, and two "consumers"—family members of residents in area nursing homes).

Meeting at least once a month since September 1995, the Community Nursing Home Committee has: secured standing committee status under the County Commission on Aging (a strategy designed to gain legal access to nursing homes); completed and disseminated a brochure type guide to nursing homes and alternatives in the county; recruited and trained two groups of candidates for volunteer companionship services to residents; gathered statistical data in preparation for political activism to demonstrate the inequity of the state formula used to allocate the number of nursing home beds in the state; and completed the planning for implementation of an Alzheimer's Support Group in cooperation with one of the senior centers.

In cooperation with the state ombudsman project staff, the committee is planning a training session in advocacy, problem solving, and complaint resolution. The Area Agency on Aging has agreed to defray some of the expenses to be incurred in bringing the ombudsman staff to the area to conduct the training. With the training, the on-site advocacy function should be fully operational by 1994.

With the completion of several projects, membership numbers have fluctuated from meeting to meeting recently. However, a core of nine or ten regulars are in attendance at each committee meeting, so the training program should generate new interest and greater participation in the committee's work.

Source: Nancy P. Kropf.

Case 3: The Relocation of Mr. Linwood

"My father thinks of Bonnie Manor as his home," Sue Massey said through tears. "I don't understand why he has to leave. He doesn't either and he is very depressed about leaving his friends." This conversation was the opening about Maxwell Linwood's discharge from the Bonnie Manor Nursing Home.

Marcie Coates, Boswell County Social Worker in charge of elderly relocation, knows this story too well. The state's nursing home screening had rated Max as too healthy for a nursing home and had given the social worker ten days to arrange alternate placement. The Massey's live in a small house; Sue Massey has severe arthritis, and her husband does not want Max to live with them. Marcie had located two board and care facilities which had a vacancy, but distance and financing were proving to be barriers. On top of everything else, the local county supervisors were making elderly placement a political issue. Marcie's new assignment as a placement specialist for elderly persons was challenging her social work training and experience.

Other older nursing home residents had found themselves in similar situations. This new screening system started when the state Medicaid program found itself with a $153 million deficit in its 1998–99 budget. A decision was reached to put into place a statewide pilot program that had been operating in Vantage City for two years. All applicants to nursing homes had been carefully screened by a team of nurses, social workers, and consulting physicians with a well-tested screening instrument, plus the advice of the professional team. An estimated $5 million of Medicaid money was saved in the first six months, so the experiment moved to screening persons already residing in nursing homes. If a patient's functional capacity and nursing needs were deemed inappropriate for nursing home services, the patient was discharged and the local social services social worker was given ten days to relocate the patient. This part of the Vantage City Medicaid project saved an additional $2 million. With the current deficit heading for even larger numbers, the state's Medicaid officials put the screening program into place statewide.

Boswell County prepared for the Medicaid screening team by assigning Marcie Coates as a Relocation Specialist. Her job description included working with the long-term care providers, coordinating public agency activity, and counseling the elderly patient and family to make the transition as smooth as possible. Boswell County is basically rural, with a large geographic territory and only two urbanized areas—Newton Falls (25,000) and Mariett (18,000). The county AAA had begun to develop some in-home services for the elderly, but in general, resources were scarce. There was one small bus company that ran through the area once a day and makes a daily trip from Newton Falls to Vantage City, the state capitol, eighty-five miles away. Bonnie Manor is the only nursing home in Boswell County, and it has a 125-bed capacity. It is privately owned by an old Boswell family and has the respect and support of local physicians. There are six small board and care type facilities in Boswell. Three of them have 8 or fewer beds; a fourth one has recently been cited by the regional licensing agency as not meeting fire safety regulations and was being required to install a sprinkler system if it was to stay open. A fifth 30-bed facility was in the county seat of Newton Falls and had a good reputation as being clean, fire safe, and developing an active mental health component. The son of a local county supervisor had bought the facility five years ago and planned to expand his operation. The sixth board and care facility was about thirty miles away from Newton Falls. It was owned by a retired minister and his wife and was noted for the vegetables they grew and allowed the residents to sell in town.

Marcie Coates recognized that Boswell County would need to encourage more long-term residential facilities. The population was growing older and more and more elderly would need shelter. The Mariett Baptist Church was considering converting the old elementary school into a home for the elderly and several private investors were doing market studies of Boswell County. Marcie was also working with the county AAA to expand in-home services. Newton Falls and Mariett have had noon meal home delivery programs for five years. The county in-home homemaker service was new this year. The five workers were kept busy covering the whole county. There was some public criticism of the program when two of the workers had constant car problems and missed many service days. But in general, there was support and they hoped to double the case capacity this year. The Methodist Church of Newton Falls has a senior citizens center. It has a very active quilting group, a bingo game two days a week, and a daily hour "hike" before lunch. The other major resource is the local women who earn their living by caring for elderly.

Source: Barbara B. Jameson and Nancy P. Kropf.

Annotated Bibliography

American Association of Retired Persons and Administration on Aging. (1997). *A profile of older Americans.* Pub. no. PF3049(1297)–D996.
  This fourteen-panel summary in brochure format provides an excellent summary of the demographics of the older population.
Andrews, E. S. (1987). Changing pension policy and the aging of America. *Contemporary Policy Issues, 5,* 84–97.
  Reviews the effects of the pension provisions of the 1986 Tax Reform Act. The author concludes that in the long term, the pension provisions will benefit older people.
Callahan, D. (1987). *Setting limits. Medical goals in an aging society.* New York: Simon & Schuster.
  The author attempts to spark debate and influence policy by examining the proper goals of medicine in our rapidly aging society. Callahan argues that we as a nation are crippling our financial stability by spending a disproportionate amount of resources extending the lives of the elderly without regard for quality of life.
Estes, C. L., Swan, J. H. & Associates. (1993). *The long term care crisis: Elders trapped in the no-care zone.* Newbury Park, CA: Sage.
  Looks at the effect of the Medicare prospective payment system (PPS) implemented in 1985. The authors compile research to demonstrate the profound effect this policy has on the delivery of long-term care services to the elderly, particularly the transition from hospital-based to community-based care.
Hudson, R. B. (Ed.). (1995). The future of age-based public policy. *Generations, 19* (3), 1–80.
  This special journal edition examines old age as a policy variable and whether old age remains a viable proxy for "negative events" associated with the need for benefits. Articles examine alternatives to age as a policy criterion as it applies to different populations of elderly,

population dynamics, policy arenas and the place of age, public and private prospects, and age and eligibility.

Hudson, R. B. (Ed.). (1997). *The future of age-based public policy.* Baltimore, MD: Johns Hopkins University Press.

Investigates the arguments and issues surrounding successful and popular age-based programs. The authors examine alternative ideological perspectives on age-related policy; differing levels of need within subpopulations of old persons and between old and young persons; and the characteristics of our major age-based and age-related programs, such as Social Security, Medicare, Medicaid, and the Older Americans Act.

Minkler, M. & Estes, C. L. (Eds.). (1991). *Critical perspectives on aging: The political and moral economy of growing old.* Amityville, NY: Baywood.

The authors apply a political economy of aging framework to the analysis of such diverse problems and issues as the politics of generational equity; the "biomedicalization" of old age; and how public policy is made.

Kane, R. A. & Wilson, K. B. (1993). *Assisted living in the United States: A new paradigm for residential care for frail older persons.* Washington, DC: American Association of Retired Persons Public Policy Institute.

The authors provide an overview of the growth of assisted living, generally associated with Continuing Care Retirement Communities, as a cost-effective alternative to institutional care that provides autonomous living for older persons. They describe how assisted living programs vary by resident characteristics and organizational sponsorship. The study also considers resident outcomes and how assisted living can meet the needs of low- and middle-income older people.

Pynoos, J. (1984). Setting the elderly housing agenda. *Policy Studies Journal, 13,* 173–184.

Explores how broader economic and political issues define the nature of the housing problem. Concludes that interest groups of older people will have to expand their advocacy efforts if housing as a problem is to become a priority need.

Ross, C. M., Danziger, S., & Smolensky, E. (1987). Interpreting changes in the economic status of the elderly, 1949–1979. *Contemporary Policy Issues 5,*(5), 98–112.

Analyzes changes in the economic well-being of the elderly using data from the Decennial Censuses of 1950 through 1980. The conclusion is that the economic well-being of elderly cohorts generally increases with age.

Saltz, C. C. (Ed.). (1997). *Social work response to the White House Conference on Aging.* New York: Haworth.

This book compiles the contributions of social work to the 1995 WHCoA, bringing together a policy agenda for gerontological social work for the next century. Topics include: productive aging, quality of life, mental health needs, changing families and family care, and gerontological social work education.

Social Security Bulletin. (1997). *Fast facts and figures about Social Security,* 50 (5).

Provides an excellent statistical survey on Social Security recipients and financial amounts. Figures are presented by population category, facilitating review of Social Security participation by older people and the amount of payments to them.

Torres-Gil, F. M. (1992). *The new aging: Politics and change in America.* Westport, CT: Auburn.

The author discusses the interface of three forces that define the "New Aging": claims upon government based on generation and mutual reciprocity; diversity (racial/ethnic, economic, geographic) within the aging population; and longevity and an increasing lifespan, and related ethical and philosophical concerns.

Wood, J. B., Hughes, R. G., & Estes, C. L. (1986). Community health centers and the elderly: A potential new alliance. *Journal of Community Health, 11,* 137–46.

Reviews the factors underlying Community Health Centers' strategic advantage in expanding services to the elderly, the evolution of federal policy, and the response to current policy that promotes autonomous existence for many agencies. The discussion is based on findings from studies conducted between 1982 and 1985.

General Bibliography

Binstock, R. H. (1983). The aged as scapegoat. *Gerontologist, 23,* 136–143.

Binstock. R. H. (1985). The oldest old: A fresh perspective on compassionate ageism revisited. *Millbank Memorial Fund Quarterly: Health and Society.*

Cook, F. L. & Kramek, L. (1986). Measuring economic hardship among older Americans. *The Gerontologist, 1* (26), 38–47.

Daniels, N. (1988). *Am I my parent's keeper? An essay on justice between the young and the old.* New York: Oxford University Press.

Haber, C. & Gratton, B. (1994). *Old age and the search for security.* Bloomington, IN: University of Indiana Press.

Jones, A. (1984). Prospective payment: Curbing Medicare costs at patient's expense? *Generations,* 9(1), 19–21.

Minkler, M. & Estes, C. (1991). *Critical perspectives on aging: The moral and political economy of growing old.* Amityville, NY: Baywood.

National Research Council. (1988). *The aging population in the twenty-first century: Statistics for health policy.* Washington, DC: National Academy Press.

Newcomer, R. J., Lawton, M. P., & Byerts, T. O. (1986). *Housing an aging society.* New York: Van Nostrand Reinhold.

Olson, L. K. (1984). Aging policy: Who benefits? *Generations,* 9(1), 10–14.

Scitovsky, A. (1985). Medical costs in the last year of life. *Generations* 9(4), 27–29.

Storey, J. R. (1983). *Older Americans in the Reagan era: Impacts of federal policy changes.* Washington, DC: Urban Institute Press.

Storey, J. R. (1986). Policy changes affecting older Americans during the first Reagan administration. *The Gerontologist,* 26(1), 27–31.

U.S. General Accounting Office. (1991). *Long term care: Projected needs of the baby boom generation.* Washington, DC: U.S. Government Printing Office.

Vladeck, B. (1980). *Unloving care: The nursing home tragedy.* New York: Basic Books.

References

American Association of Retired Persons & Administration on Aging. (1997). A profile of older Americans. Publication No. PF 3049 (1297). D996. Washington, DC: U.S. Government Printing Office.

Andrews, E. S. (1987). Changing pension policy and the aging of America. *Contemporary Policy Issues, 5,* 84–97.

Benson, W. F. (1997). *Testimony before the Subcommittee on Early Childhood, Youth and Families, Hearing on the reauthorization of the Older Americans Act.* U.S. House of Representatives Committee on Education and the Workforce. Washington, DC: U.S. Government Printing Office.

Beverly, D. P. & McSweeney, E. A. (1987). *Social welfare and social justice.* Englewood Cliffs, NJ: Prentice-Hall.

Buchanan, R. J. (1987). Medicaid reimbursement of long-term care: A survey of 1986 state policies. *The Journal of Long-Term Care Administration,* 15(4), 19–27.

Callahan, D. (1986). Health care in the aging society: A moral dilemma. In A. Pifer & L. Bronte (Eds.), *Our aging society: Paradox and promise* (pp. 319–339). New York: Norton.

Catastrophic-costs bill is sent to White House. (1988). *Congressional Quarterly Weekly Report,* 46(24), 1606–1611.

Cicenas, D. & Foltz, M. B. (1988). Specialized nutritional support for older Americans. *Aging Network News,* 5(4), 4, 6.

Cockburn, A. (1986). Health care: Sowing the seeds of revolution. *Gray Panther Network,* pp. 3–5.

Congressional Budget Office. (1997). *The economic and budget outlook, fiscal years 1998–2007.* January. www.cbo.gov

Crystal, S. (1986). Measuring income and inequality among the elderly. *Gerontologist, 26,* 56–59.

Davis, K. (1986). Paying the health-care bills of an aging population. In A. Pifer & L. Bronte (Eds.), *Our aging society: Paradox and promise* (pp. 299–318). New York: Norton.

Dobelstein, A. W. (1996). *Social welfare policy and analysis* (2nd ed.). Chicago: Nelson-Hall

Eglit, H. (1989). Ageism in the work place: An elusive quarry. *Generations, 13*(2), 31–35.

Employee Benefit Research Institute. (1985). *Fundamentals of employee benefit programs.* Washington, DC: EBRI.

Estes, C. J., Newcomer, R. J., Benjamin, A. E., Gerard, L., Harrington, C., Lee, P. R., Lindeman, D. A., Pardini, A., Swan, J. H., & Wood, J. B. (1983). *Fiscal austerity and aging: Shifting government responsibility for the elderly.* Beverly Hills, CA: Sage.

Estes, C. J., Swan, J. H., & Associates. (1993). *The long term care crisis: Elders trapped in the no-care zone.* Newbury Park, CA: Sage.

Gelfand, D. E. & Bechill, W. (1991). The evolution of the Older Americans Act: A 25 years review of the legislative changes. *Generations, 15*(3), 19–22.

Greene, R. R. (1997). Emerging issues for social workers in the field of aging: White House Conference Themes. In C. C. Saltz (Ed.), *Social work response to the White House Conference on Aging* (pp. 79–88). New York: Haworth.

Harvard Medicare Project. (1986). Special report. The future of Medicare. *New England Journal of Medicine.*

House Select Committee on Aging & Senate Special Committee on Aging. (1987). *Legislative agenda for an aging society: 1988 and beyond.* (HSC on Aging Pub. No. 100–664, SS Committee on Aging, Pub. No. 100-J). Washington, DC: U.S. Government Printing Office.

Hudson, R. B. (1994). The Older Americans Act and the defederalization of community-based care. In P. H. K. Kim (Ed.), *Services to the aging and aged* (pp. 45–75).

Hudson, R. B. (1995). The history and place of age-based public policy. *Generations, 19*(3), 5–10.

Hudson, R. B. (Ed.). (1997). *The future of age-based public policy.* Baltimore, MD: Johns Hopkins University Press.

Hudson, R. B. (1998). 1997 Kent Lecture: The reconstitution of aging policy. *Gerontology News.*

Justice, D. E. (1995). The aging network: A balancing act between universal coverage and defined eligibility. *Generations, 19*(3), 58–62.

Kane, R. A. & Wilson, K. B. (1993). *Assisted living in the United States: A new paradigm for residential care for frail older persons.* Washington, DC: American Association of Retired Persons Public Policy Institute.

Kassner, E. (1992). The Older Americans Act: Should participants share in the cost of services? *Journal of Aging and Social Policy, 4*(1/2), 51–71.

Kirkiman-Liff, B. (1999). Medicare managed care and primary care for frail elders. In F. Ellen Netting & F. G. Williams (Eds.), *Enhancing primary care of elderly persons.* New York: Garland.

Knight, B. & Walker, D. L. (1985). Toward a definition of alternatives to institutionalization for the frail and elderly. *The Gerontologist, 25,* 358–363.

Lammers, W. W. (1983). *Public policy and the aging.* Washington, DC: CQ Press.

Lane, L. F. (1985). Private long-term care insurance. *Long-Term Care Currents, 8*(3), 9–12.

Lombardi, T. (1985–87). Nursing home without walls. *Generations, 9,* 21–23.

Lowry, L. (1991). *Social policies and programs on aging.* (2nd ed.). Prospect Heights, IL: Waveland Press.

Marcus, L. J. (1989). Universal health insurance in Massachusetts: Negotiating policy compromise. *Journal of Aging & Social Policy, 1*(1/2), 33–59.

Minkler, M. & Estes, C. (1984). *Readings in the political economy of aging.* Farmingdale, NY: Baywood.

Miranda, M. R. (1988a). The older worker: Current and future prospects. *Aging Network News, 5*(6), 5.

Miranda, M. R. (1988b). The older worker. *Aging Network News, 5*(7), 5, 12.

National Academy on Aging. (1997). *Facts on long-term care.* Washington, DC.: Gerontological Society of America.

National Committee to Preserve Social Security and Medicare. (1997). *Facts at your fingertips*. Washington, DC: NCPSSM.

National Council on Aging. (1997). *Public policy agenda*. www.ncoa.org/

National Council of Senior Citizens. (1997). *Where we stand on the issues*. www.ncsc.org/

Newcomer, R. J., Lawton, M. P., & Byers, T. O. (1986). *Housing an aging society*. New York: Van Nostrand Reinhold.

Older Americans Report. (1991, May). Slants and trends. Silver Spring, MD: Business Publishers, Inc.

Older Americans Report. (1997, October). *Experts look at priorities for bipartisan Medicare Commission*. Silver Spring, MD: Business Publishers, Inc.

Pollack, R. F. (1990). Policy perspectives alter the catastrophic catastrophe. *Journal of Aging & Social Policy, 2*(3/4), 1–4.

Quinn, J. F. (1996). *Entitlements and the federal budget*. Washington, DC.: National Academy on Aging.

Rich, B. M. & Baum, M. (1984). *The aging: A guide to public policy*. Pittsburgh, PA: University of Pittsburgh.

Torres-Gil, F. M. (1992). *The new aging: Politics and change in America*. Westport, CT: Auburn.

U.S. Bureau of the Census. (1995). *Income, poverty and the valuation on noncash benefits: 1993*. Current Population Reports, Series P60–188. Washington, DC: U.S. Department of Commerce.

U.S. Department of Health and Human Services. (1997). Fast facts and figures about Social Security. Washington, DC: U.S. Government Printing Office.

U.S. Department of Health and Human Services, Health Care Financing Administration. (1997). *Balanced budget amendment*. www.hcfa.gov

U.S. Department of Health and Human Services, Social Security Administration. (1997). *SSI Income Program Recipients*. www.ssa.gov

U.S. General Accounting Office. (May). *Long-term care insurance: Coverage varies widely in a developing market*. (GAO/HRD-87-80). Washington, DC: GAO.

U.S. Senate Special Committee on Aging. (1986). *Aging America: Trends and projections*. Washington, DC: U.S. Department of Health and Human Services.

Wagner, E. H. (1996). The promise and performance of HMOs in improving outcomes in older adults. *Journal of the American Geriatric Society, 44*, 1251–1257.

Waxman, J. & Alker, J. (1997). *Balanced budget bill enacted*. Washington, DC: FamiliesUSA.

Weiner, J. M. (1996). Can Medicaid long-term care expenditures for the elderly be reduced: *Gerontologist, 36*(6), 800–811.

Williamson, J. B., Shindul, J. A., & Evans, L. (1985). *Aging and public policy: Social control or social justice?* Springfield, IL: Charles C. Thomas.

Williamson, J. B. (1997). A critique of the case for privatizing Social Security. *Gerontologist, 37*(5), 561–571.

Wilson, C. P., Hasan, S. Z., & Martin, L. L. *Mental health—rural aging: multidisciplinary curriculum*. Lexington: University of Kentucky College of Social Work, 1982.

Winterbottom, C., Liska, D., & Obermaier, K. (1995). *State-level Databook on health care access and financing*. Washington, DC: Urban Institute.

Woods, J. R. (1996). Pension benefits among the aged: Conflicting measures, unequal distributions. *Social Security Bulletin* (May).

4 The Research Process and the Elderly

■■■■■■■■■■■■■■■
Michael J. Sheridan and Anne J. Kisor

Increasing our understanding of aging and related issues is particularly critical at this point in our history. A dramatic shift in the profile of our citizens is taking place with the most significant demographic trend in this century being the extraordinary increase in the number of older adults. Since 1900, the percentage of Americans sixty-five and older has tripled (4.1 percent in 1900 to 12.8 percent in 1996), and overall number of elders has increased nine times (from 3.1 million to 29.2 million). This demographic shift is expected to continue into the next century with predictions that by the year 2030, 70 million of our citizens will be sixty-five or older, representing 20 percent of the population. If current fertility and immigration levels remain stable, the only age groups expected to experience significant growth in the next century will be those past age fifty-five (American Association of Retired Persons 1997).

Two major factors are related to this demographic shift, referred to as "the aging of America" (Torres-Gil 1992). One factor is the continued extension in the expected lifespan. For example, a child born in 1996 can be expected to live twenty-nine years longer than a child born in 1900. The second factor contributing to changing demographics is the aging of the large cohort born during the postwar baby boom. During the early 2000s, these baby boomers will reach their later years. An examination of demographic trends also reveals that the elderly population is disproportionately female and consists more and more of the very old, those persons who are eighty-five and above. Both of these developments have major social implications associated with the special needs of single older women, and health and quality of life issues in the very old.

Social workers will be called upon to meet a variety of challenges stemming from these demographic realities. A need exists for policy and program developments at both the micro and macro levels to deal constructively with the issues of growing older. Examples of issues important to social workers are health care and quality of life; housing, transportation and physical environments; attitudes toward aging and elder abuse; retirement and leisure time concerns; changing family structures, work patterns and caregiver arrangements; needs of special populations, such as the mentally or physically disabled, women, and minority groups; nutrition, exercise and stress management; mental health, substance abuse, and suicide; and long-term care options. Research will play a major role in building the general knowledge base on aging, as well as contributing to theory development and informing practice. Effective social work practitioners will need to participate in gerontological research and develop ways to integrate emerging knowledge into their professional practice.

Overview of the Research Process

The Nature of Social Research

Most writings on the nature of research proceed through a step-by-step overview of the research process, usually beginning with problem formulation and ending with data analysis and dissemination of the findings. This chapter on social research and aging will also follow this format as it is the clearest way to address a complex subject. However, just as problems for study do not exist simplistically in real life, neither does the actual practice of social research. When actually setting up and conducting a research study, decisions made at one point in the process have an effect on other phases of the project. For example, the choice to study guardianship for the elderly will influence decisions about sampling (whom should we target as subjects?), the timing of measurement (should we follow these subjects over months or years or get information one time?), how we collect the data (should we interview the elderly and their guardians or analyze court records?), and how we analyze the data and present the results (would a summary of statistical results be the most useful or should we provide case scenarios using a more narrative approach?). A study on guardianship in which elderly persons are interviewed at one point in time would be very different from a study analyzing court records over a year period. The decisions governing how a study will be conducted is a function of the questions or hypotheses which are formulated by the researchers.

Furthermore, research studies are not conducted in a vacuum. Two different contexts have an impact upon any research project. One context concerns the body of knowledge, or the "state of the art," of any particular topic. In gerontological research, this refers to both current theoretical perspectives and existing empirical knowledge about aging. Every research project should be rooted in what is known. Equally important, the study must contribute to the existing literature by identifying and researching gaps in the current understanding of the phenomenon. The second context consists of the variety of social forces, such as political, economic, and religious, that dictate what any society considers to be important or valued. The societal context affects the entire research process from the initial choice of the research topic to the dissemination and utilization of results. The fact that this text is being published is evidence that aging has been targeted as an important topic in our society.

Research is not a linear, step-by-step enterprise. The research endeavor involves multiple and overlapping decisions and choices. The whole process takes place in a complex atmosphere of knowledge and societal rules. Social research, including gerontological research, is part of a dynamic exchange involving what is currently known about an issue and the importance of that issue to society.

Basic versus Applied Research

Scientific investigations can generally be labeled as being either basic or applied research. Basic or "pure" research is categorized as a study whose purpose is primarily to advance knowledge or develop theoretical formulations. This type of research is conducted to add to the understanding of the topic and does not claim to have any immediate application to policy or practice. Applied research, on the other hand, is designed with some practical outcome in mind and carries an assumption that the results can be utilized to benefit some element of society. Quite often this distinction is not clear cut, as findings from basic research often provide useful information to policymakers and practitioners and results from applied research contribute to ongoing theory development. Within any research project, there is often an integration of these two general purposes.

Both types of research are appropriate gerontological studies. A need exists to both further our overall knowledge on aging and develop feasible and effective programs and services for the elderly. As understanding of the biological, psychological, social, and spiritual aspects of aging grows, the ability to address the problems, needs, and concerns of the elderly and their families will increase. Furthermore, researchers potentially utilize the same methods and procedures available through the scientific method in both basic and applied research projects. Social workers can employ knowledge from both types of research to increase their expertise and effectiveness with older clients.

Phases of the Research Process

Problem Formulation

The journey from an initial interest in a topic to formulation of a clearly stated, feasible problem is an important step in the research process. The problem statement serves as the foundation for the remainder of the research and guides the decisions the researcher needs to make along the way. For example, suppose you know you want to do a study on "the aspects of aging." Initially, this appears to be a reasonable choice of a research topic that targets an area you want to investigate. But then someone starts asking questions, such as: "Which aspects . . . physical or health issues, work or career changes, leisure time and retirement adjustments, changes in family responsibilities, living arrangements, psychosocial problems, or what exactly?" or "What do you mean by aging . . . people of a certain age or people who are experiencing certain changes?" or "Are you going to study the elderly themselves or social responses to aging or services provided for this group?" or "Who's interested in this topic and the results?" This journey of clearly formulating a research problem generally involves three steps: (1) selecting a research problem; (2) shaping and refining the problem; and (3) evaluating potential problems in conducting the project.

SELECTING A RESEARCH PROBLEM

There are a variety of factors that go into the initial selection of a research topic. Monette, Sullivan, and DeJong (1998) list several general sources of research problems that are applicable to research in gerontology. First of all, many topics are chosen because the researcher is particularly interested in some aspect of the subject. For example, a researcher may have his eighty-year-old mother living with him and decides to investigate three-generation living arrangements. Another researcher's father may have Alzheimer's disease and, thus, she is interested in research in this area. A particular problem may be selected because of a personal interest by the researcher.

Another stimulus for new research projects is prior research. All research projects have limitations and often produce additional questions to be answered. One project may report effective treatment interventions with the problem of elder abuse, but all the research participants were from white, middle-class families. Another researcher may decide to replicate these efforts with a different group of people to test whether this intervention is effective with Latino or low-income elderly. Another researcher may question the research findings of a study of companion care because there were methodological weaknesses, which leads him or her to study the same subject using a more rigorous design. These projects are a replication or modification of existing studies.

Some research projects are conducted to test existing theory. Although basic research is specifically designed to test theory and expand or revise theoretical formulations, issues related to theory can also serve as problems for applied research. Findings from two different programs for the elderly that appear to contradict accepted theory can lead to further investigation and modification of that theory. Newly introduced theory can lead to changes in policy which produce a need to do applied research at the program evaluation level. Theory from other areas, such as concepts on social support for the chronically mentally ill, may be tested in specific applications to an elderly population.

Another major source of research problems is in the area of program efforts and practice. Evaluation research focuses on the effectiveness or efficiency of some program, such as "Meals on Wheels" or an intergenerational day care program. Clinical research has the goal of studying the effects of different therapeutic interventions. For example, a study may be conducted on the use of different family therapy approaches with three generation households in order to inform practitioners about the most effective way to work with this family constellation. Practical questions of what works and how it works with which people are program and practice concerns that are appropriate for research efforts.

SHAPING AND REFINING THE PROBLEM

The next step in problem formulation is to transform a general area of interest into a working statement of the problem or a researchable problem. A problem statement should be conceptually clear, specific and precise, and appropriate for different audiences (Babbie 1998). These criteria are important as the problem statement serves to clarify the researcher's thinking, communicate the problem to others, and provide a guide for the rest of the research process (McCauley 1987). This process of focusing, narrowing, and refining is one that involves a number of activities over a period of time (Monette, Sullivan, & DeJong 1998). One of the key steps in this process is to identify and define the concepts targeted by the research topic. The specific tasks of this stage involve clearly defining the meaning of a concept and narrowing the focus of the concept so that it is something that can be obtained and measured in a single study. For example, the health status of the elderly is of interest to gerontologists. However, health status is a concept which is broad. Does the research intend to measure physical or mental health, for example? Will health status be measured as absence of a disease process or presence of health promotion activities? In choosing a clear and concise definition of the concept, researchers can make decisions about how health status will be measured.

When the concepts of the study are clear and measurable, previous literature that relates to the topic is reviewed. This step enables the researcher to become familiar with the current state of knowledge, identify existing gaps or problems in the literature, and target potentially useful procedures or measurement approaches for the study. Additionally, a review of previous work allows one to see how other researchers have stated their research problem. They can serve as models for formulating the current problem statement. For example, "What is the role of Medicaid in nursing home care?" suffers from lack of specificity and conceptual clarity (e.g., what is meant by role?). A better problem statement for this issue would be "What is the current role of Medicaid in nursing home care across the states in terms of characteristics of the population served in nursing homes, including patterns of length and stay; the characteristics of new admissions; and the variability of state expenditures, bed supply, and reimbursement?" (McCauley 1987, p. 54). This problem statement specifically defines how "role" is to be operationalized or measured, serves as a guide for the steps in the research process, and clearly communicates the focus of the study to others. Once the problem statement is formed into a clear working statement, possible problems in doing the research must be addressed before the project is begun.

EVALUATING POTENTIAL PROBLEMS

McCauley (1987) identifies four criteria in determining potential problems in carrying out the research project. First is the question of *feasibility*. Do the state of knowledge and research techniques available allow for a scientific investigation of this problem? Can the project be completed in the context that the researchers find themselves? Is there enough expertise, experience, authority, access to subjects or data, needed resources, etc.? What other issues must be addressed to assess if the problem is researchable? A research project that has inherent problems related to feasibility faces a high probability of being either poorly done or never completed at all.

Secondly, there is the issue of *costs*. Every research project requires financial resources. Variations in design, sample size, and methods greatly affect the overall financing required. Some budget areas to consider include staff time, supplies, computer usage, equipment, facilities, printing or duplication, travel, agency overhead, and payment to research participants. If outside funding is required for conducting the research, the project needs to be assessed for its potential to attract such funding. Resources must be available and agreements made about funding for every aspect of the research prior to the launching of the project.

Thirdly, the project should be assessed in terms of its *utility*. Utility is "the probability that the research will lead to the desired outcomes" (McCauley 1987, p. 48). Utility addresses both the ability of a research project to contribute to existing knowledge and the practicality of implications to be derived from the findings. Can changes realistically be expected to occur given the results? What needs to be done to increase the utility of the findings? Are there administrative, political, social, or fiscal realities which may affect the use of the results? Since applied research is conducted in order to provide benefit to some element of society, the research project needs to be evaluated for its potential to enable this goal.

And lastly, the project should be assessed for the overall *impact*. This criterion is defined as "the importance, degree, and scope of changes that can be expected from the study" (McCauley 1987, p. 48). Does the project address an important issue? How many people will it affect? How valuable are the changes that may occur as a result of the project? Will there be any negative consequences? Both the short-term and long-term effects of the project should be considered. Once the topic is selected, the problem statement clearly defined, and the project assessed for potential problems, the researcher is ready to determine the overall design to be used in conducting the study.

Research Design

The research design is the strategy or game plan concerning how proposed research questions will be answered or research hypotheses tested (Reid & Smith 1989). Although each

■ **Table 4.1**   Potential Threats to Research Validity

Extraneous Variable	Definition
INTERNAL VALIDITY	
History	Events occurring between the first and second measurement
Maturation	Processes occurring as a function of the passage of time per se
Testing	Effects of multiple measurement
Instrumentation	Changes in measuring instrument, observers, or scorers
Statistical Regression	Persons chosen because they are very high or very low on a variable will tend to score closer to the mean on the next measurement
Selection	Procedures used to choose participants can result in many extraneous differences among groups
Mortality or Experimental Attrition	Differential lose of participants from treatment and control groups
Placebo Effect	Effects due to unspecified aspects of the independent variable
EXTERNAL VALIDITY	
Persons	Findings observed with one group may not apply to others
Setting	Findings observed in one setting may not be found elsewhere
Treatment	Findings based on one set of treatment conditions may not hold true under other circumstances
Measures	Findings based on one instrument may not be found when using a different tool purportedly measuring the same construct
Historical Time	Findings observed at one time may not be found in other time periods

Sources: McCauley 1987; Monette, Sullivan, & DeJong 1998; Reid & Smith 1989.

research project is developed according to particular purposes, there are several issues that must be addressed in designing any study. Four dimensions important when designing a research project are: (1) threats to validity; (2) purpose of the proposed research; (3) timing of data collection; and (4) types of designs.

THREATS TO VALIDITY

The design of any study affects the validity of the findings. The overall validity of a study is increased by focusing on both internal and external validity. Internal validity refers to the degree to which the results can be explained by the variables studied versus effects of other factors. External validity refers to the extent to which generalizations from findings in the study sample can be made to some larger population (Monette, Sullivan, & DeJong 1998). Table 4.1 summarizes the various threats to internal and external validity.

With internal validity, the major goal is to reduce the possibility that the results were due to some factor not investigated by the study. For example, a nursing home has identified the need to increase social interaction among the residents and decides to start a recreation hour after dinner. This program involves a variety of activities, such as bingo, dancing, and singing sessions, which are designed to facilitate socialization among residents. Staff note that after a month of this program, less people are staying in their rooms in the evening and there seems to be more interaction taking place at other times of the day as well. The staff concludes that the program has met its goal. But are there other factors that may be responsible for the results? Is it really the recreation hour which has increased socialization? During the first week the recreation hour began, another event happened which may have had an effect upon the socialization patterns of the residents. The program was started during the spring right after the clocks were set for daylight savings time. Thus, there were more hours of daylight during the evening and warmer weather, which is conducive to being up and about—other possible reasons for increased socialization: The internal validity of the design of the study is threatened because there is no way to determine which factors played a significant role in the noted changes in resident behavior. The internal validity could have been increased by introducing the program to a randomly selected sample of the residents and comparing their behavior to other residents who were not involved in the program. This use of a control group would increase the likelihood that the observed changes were due to the recreational activities and not some other untested factor.

External validity concerns the ability to apply or generalize the results of the study to other people, situations, or conditions. In the nursing home example above, external validity would be enhanced by checking what effects the recreation program has on residents with varying medical conditions, in different types of nursing homes, or with different levels of outside social support. External validity cannot be established during a single study, but requires a series of studies that focus on the same variable—in this case, the recreation program. In consequent studies, key variables are purposefully altered to determine the effects. In any study, there is a trade-off between enhancing internal validity while increasing external validity. The researcher is challenged with balancing demands in both areas.

PURPOSE OF THE PROPOSED RESEARCH

There are generally three purposes, or functions, that are used to classify any applied research project (Monette, Sullivan, & DeJong 1998). Most studies generally combine one or more of these functions. The first is an *exploratory-formulative* function when research is used to gain a preliminary understanding of some phenomenon or to support the generation of concepts, hypotheses, and theories. This type of research is utilized when little is known about a topic, but exploration is needed to determine possible important variables or factors. For example, a local senior citizen center has noticed a sharp decline in the number of elderly who are participating in their program. The staff really does not have an understanding about why attendance is decreasing and decides to contact previous attendees to find out possible reasons for this decline. They discover that a variety of reasons are given, including changes in the bus line, ill health, and boredom with some of the activities at the center. The findings produced variables for forming hypotheses about the declining participation, as well as possible solutions for the problem. The key concept in exploratory-formulative designs is that the research yields ideas about what is *possible*, rather than probable.

A second purpose of research is that of *description*. Although all studies provide some descriptive information, some designs purposefully attempt to break down the whole into the various parts and study these relationships. For instance, in the above example, the staff decides to find out whether there is a definite relationship between changes in the bus line and the decline in attendance. By pinpointing the residences of the seniors who have stopped coming to the center, they discover that indeed most of the absent members do live in the neighborhood where the bus routes have been changed. Staff now have some specific information about the relationship between available transportation and use of needed services. These results lead them to consider implementing a plan to convince the city transportation services to reinstitute this bus line. However, at this point, their descriptive design has told them what is *probable*, but they do not know whether there is a cause-effect relationship between the change in bus lines and center attendance. In order to make this assessment, they must use a design that addresses the third function of research.

Explanatory research provides evidence that associations between different factors are causal. This design goes a step further than descriptive research, which demonstrates how different factors are related or occur together. In order to infer a *cause-effect* relationship, three criteria must be met. These are: (1) factor A is related to factor B (the change in bus routes and decline in participation occur together); (2) that factor A occurred prior to factor B (the change in the bus routes happened before the noted decline in attendance); and (3) there are no other factors that are associated with factor B (that there are no other reasons that the senior citizens stopped coming to the center). For this last criterion, the staff would have to use a research design that determines timing of events, and controls for or rules out other possible reasons for the decline in partic-ipation. For example, they could compare attendance before and after the change in the bus line and assess the level of participation of senior citizens from other neighborhoods where bus transportation is not a problem. Cause-effect relationships are never "proven" in an absolute way, but are deduced or inferred based on whether these three criteria have been met.

TIMING OF DATA COLLECTION

The timing of data collection refers to different kinds of scheduling decisions that must be made by the researcher. The first decision has to do with whether measurement occurs be-fore or after the presumed causative or independent variable. For example, nutrition classes or home companions may be predicted to increase the well-being of the elderly. If measure-ment is taken before the independent variable is introduced, the design is considered "prospective" or "projected." If measurement is only obtained after the occurrence of the in-dependent variable, it is a "retrospective" or "ex post facto" design. Since many studies do not have an explanatory purpose, but are exploratory or descriptive in nature, there is no distinction of independent versus dependent variable, and measurement is called "undiffer-entiated" (Reid & Smith 1989).

The timing of data collection also has to do with the number of times data are gathered. Some research questions can be answered with a single data collection strategy, known as cross-sectional studies, while others require multiple times of measurement, known as lon-gitudinal research. Research that primarily addresses differences between or among individ-uals, groups, programs, or conditions can utilize cross-sectional techniques. For example, service usage between older men and women would employ a design which measures the number of men and women using services at one point in time. Research projects that ex-amine stability or change over time require a longitudinal design. For example, different pat-terns of services between men and women over time is an example of a longitudinal design. Both cross-sectional and longitudinal approaches are needed to adequately study various aspects of aging and gerontological issues.

TYPES OF DESIGN

The general purpose of the research and the timing of data collection determine the specific type of research design that is appropriate for a study. Generally, designs can be placed on a continuum between nonexperimental and experimental categories. Additionally, studies used to plan and implement programs and policies are called macro research. The following summary briefly reviews the kinds of designs available for different research purposes (McCauley 1987; Monette, Sullivan, & DeJong 1998).

Nonexperimental Designs: These designs have the advantage of gathering information about the way things exist in the real world. Events are studied as they naturally occur. These designs usually gather data through either question-answer formats or through observation. The types of nonexperimental design are listed below:

Question/Answer
Survey: A one-time approach used to gather information on a variety of subjects. For example, do the elderly know which services exist within their communities?

Panel: A multiple measurement design which measures the same group of people at each measurement point. For example, asking the same group of people about available services every five years to assess their knowledge at different points in time.

Trend: Multiple measurements which use different cohorts of subjects. For example, measuring service knowledge among sixty year olds in 1985 and a group of sixty year olds in 1995.

Observation
Structured observation: A design where relationships or interactions are observed between different groups of people. For example, an observation of the type of communication which takes place between nursing home staff and residents.

Participant observation: A strategy in which the researcher actually experiences the subject of the study. For example, the situation of living in and becoming a resident of a senior citizen housing project.

Ethnographic Interview
An approach with the goal of understanding the subjective experience of some phenomenon. For example, interviews with residents about their experience in moving to and residing within a nursing home.

Experimental Designs: Unlike nonexperimental studies, experimental designs manipulate or contrive some type of situation. While experimental designs are more artificial, they are able to control for a large number of variables.

Between subjects: These studies make comparisons between different groups. Most commonly, one group will be exposed to some stimulus or situation and the other group will not. For example, eating habits between two groups of widows are compared, having one group which received a course on nutrition and one group which did not. The goal of the research is to see whether one group differs from the other.

Within subjects: These studies make comparisons of subjects before and after some event or stimulus. For example, the measurement of the number of calories consumed by a group of widows before and after attending a nutrition class. The goal in this research is to see whether changes have taken place within the participants.

Macro Designs: Research approaches which are used to plan, implement, and evaluate programs for the elderly are called macro research designs. These approaches can employ any of the various research designs to investigate needs, resources and services for elderly clients. Two of the most common approaches are summarized below:

Needs assessments: These studies attempt to gain information about the extent of some felt need, obtain an accurate picture of available resources and assess the fit between what is available and what is needed. For example, older people may be asked about their needs for transportation or housing services.

Program evaluations: These designs provide feedback about current program functioning and can be used to modify and improve program operations. Program evaluations also assess whether a particular program is effective in meeting established goals and objectives. For example, a congregate meal program can be evaluated to determine whether it is meeting the goal of providing lunches to low income elderly in the community.

A research project can be designed in many different ways. The type of design chosen is a function of the type of issues or questions of the study. Regardless of the type of design, whether nonexperimental, experimental, or macro research, decisions about who to include in the study must be made.

Sampling

Simply stated, sampling is the process of selecting the subjects or data sources for a study. Before enumerating the steps in the process, delineation between two concepts should be made: units of analysis and sources of data. *Units of analysis* are the "specific elements whose characteristics we wish to describe or explain and about which data will be collected" (Monette, Sullivan, & DeJong 1998, p. 78). In social research these elements are generally people or services and can be either individuals, families, groups, organizations, communities or programs. Another way of thinking of it is to ask the question, who or what are we gathering the data *about?*

Sources of data are the people or resources which will be used to get information about the targeted unit of analysis (Monette, Sullivan, & DeJong 1998). Sometimes the unit of analysis and the source of data are the same, such as when individuals are asked about some aspect of themselves. Often, however, the source of data is different from the unit of analysis. For example, individual members are often asked to assess their families or information is gathered about clients from existing records. The question for this step of the process is to ask, *from whom* or *from what* will the data be secured? If the source is a person, then he or she is called a subject or participant. When the source is something other than a person, it is generally referred to as a data resource, data base, or existing data. Sampling pertains to selecting sources of data, whether that source is a person or an inanimate object. The following discussion introduces the three general steps in the sampling process.

DEFINING THE POPULATION

The first step in sampling is to delineate all the possible cases within a population of the study in order to draw a sample from this larger aggregate. A common question asked about sampling is, if we can target all the possible cases, why not study the entire population? In some instances studying the whole population is appropriate and a sample is not needed. However, often a smaller subset of the total population is needed because of feasibility and accuracy. Gathering data from all members of a population may be impossible, for example, all people in the United States over age sixty-five. Secondly, samples can yield more accurate results than studies investigating the entire population (Babbie 1998). Sampling can increase the ability to gather more in-depth data, has less possibility of error, and involves a shorter data collection time period which enhances the relevancy and value of the findings (McCauley 1987).

When a population can be targeted, generally specified parameters and characteristics have been established. Examples of workable populations may include elderly residents residing in X senior citizen housing during a specified year, participants in a senior's recreation program during the past five years, or records of elderly clients receiving disability funds in a local social service agency during the past year. The population should be described with enough precision so that clarity exists about who or what is included and not included in the target population.

DEVELOPING A SAMPLING FRAME

Once the population has been clearly defined, the next step is to develop a sampling frame. A sampling frame is a list of all the elements, or units, in a population. Sometimes the list is already available, such as a roster of all the residents of a nursing home, while other times the list is created, such as the names of all students at a local university who are sixty-five or older. A sampling frame needs to meet these criteria: "(1) contains a unique identifier for each member of the population; (2) includes no duplications, and (3) has no nonpopulation members" (McCauley 1987, p. 126). These conditions are important because the sampling frame needs to accurately represent the targeted population from which the sample will be drawn. Findings which emerge from this sample can only be generalized back to the original population and not beyond the parameters established. For example, results drawn from a sample of residents at one nursing home can only be applied to that particular facility and not to residents from all nursing homes in the area.

Once the sampling frame has been developed, the researcher is ready to draw the sample, which is to select the desired subjects. Before this step is begun, two decisions must be made: (1) How large should the sample be? and (2) Which sampling technique should be used? Decisions about sampling size are based on a number of factors, such as the number of variables being investigated, the type of statistical analysis that will be used, the availability of participants, and the costs involved. While it is beyond the purpose of this chapter to discuss the multiplicity of factors involved in determining sampling size, there are several resources available that provide guidelines in this area (Bryman & Cramer 1990, Rosenthal & Rosnow 1991, Sudman 1976).

Choosing an Appropriate Sampling Technique

PROBABILITY SAMPLING

The third step, that of selecting a sampling technique, refers to choosing one of two general categories of samples: probability or nonprobability. *Random* or *probability* samples are those in which each member or element of the population has an equal and known chance of being selected. There are several types of random sampling procedures.

Four types of probability samples are summarized below. An example of each procedure is given to illustrate how that type of sampling would be performed for an evaluation of a Foster Grandparent Program in a certain county.

1. **Simple Random Sampling:** This type of sampling is the most basic probability sampling procedure. This method assigns a number to each member of the population and by some randomized procedure, draws the elements of the sample.

    Example: Assign a number to all Foster Grandparents in the county where the Foster Grandparent program is located. Use a random number table (which is available in standard research texts), or generate a list of random numbers using a computer program, to select fifty Grandparents for a program evaluation study.
2. **Stratified Random Sampling:** This sampling method is used when a certain characteristic is important for the study. The population is divided into groups by that characteristic and a simple random sample is drawn from all strata.

    Example: Stratify Foster Grandparents by gender. Assign numbers to all the men and all the women. Randomly select twenty-five Grandmothers and twenty-five Grandfathers for the study.
3. **Systematic Sampling:** This procedure is used when a sample is being pulled by hand, such as client files or case records. The starting place is selected randomly, then every Nth element is chosen (for example, every tenth case file). The interval between the different elements varies depending on the desired size of the sample. An important caution with using this procedure is to understand how the sampling frame is constructed. For example, if client records are ordered by a certain characteristic, such as severity of a physical condition in a hospital, the final sample may be skewed from over- or under-representation of that characteristic.

    Example: In the study of a Foster Grandparent program, centralized office files on all Grandparents in the county can be a sampling frame. Randomly choose the initial file, then pull every tenth file (if the total number of files is five hundred) until all fifty cases have been selected.
4. **Cluster Sampling:** This procedure is frequently used when a large geographical area will be sampled. This method is accomplished in two stages. First, certain "clusters" or areas are randomly selected. Second, the elements themselves are selected from the chosen clusters.

    Example: The evaluation of the Foster Grandparent program will take place within a statewide study. The desired sample size is two hundred grandparents. Randomly select ten counties in the state that have Foster Grandparent programs. Next, randomly select twenty grandparents in each of these counties for the total sample.

In all four random sampling approaches, the results from the sample can be inferred or generalized to the population from which it was drawn. In the examples of sampling within a county program, findings could be generalized only to grandparents within that county. Within the example using the statewide sampling method, results could be generalized to grandparents in that state.

NONPROBABILITY SAMPLING

In the second general sampling category, that of *nonrandom* or *nonprobability* samples, every element in a population does not have an equal and known chance of being selected. These approaches are used when there is no need to make inferences to a larger population or there is some difficulty in defining the targeted population and developing a sampling frame.

Four nonprobability sampling procedures are summarized below. An example is given of a study which would employ a nonprobability procedure to describe the social support systems of older gay men. No one sampling frame can be used to secure a sample from this population. An example of each procedure will be used to illustrate how the methods would secure a sample for this research project.

1. *Purposive Sampling:* This method involves selecting subjects based upon their known characteristics without any type of random selection procedure. However, the researcher may have to go through some type of agency or organization where known cases can be secured.

   Example: Contact a gay advocacy group in the community. Ask someone familiar with the group to identify thirty men in the community who are gay, over age fifty-five, and willing to participate in the study.
2. *Snowball Sampling:* This approach is used when it is difficult to target potential subjects but a few have been identified who meet certain criteria. The known subjects are asked to nominate others who would fit the sample characteristics.

   Example: Ten men have been identified through a gay advocacy group who meet the sample characteristics of having primarily male sexual partners and being over age fifty-five. These ten men are asked to identify additional men who have these same characteristics.
3. *Quota Sampling:* This procedure involves obtaining a certain number (quota) of subjects with specified characteristics. This technique is often used to target subjects in a particular geographical location or involved in a particular event.

   Example: Attend a national gay pride rally. Approach men who appear to be above a certain age. Ask the men their age, and if they are fifty-five or older, ask them to participate in the study. Continue this procedure until the desired number in the sample has been obtained.
4. *Availability Sampling:* The final and most frequent type of nonprobability sample is choosing subjects who are readily available to the researcher. This procedure is known as accidental, convenience, or availability sampling. Subjects are selected solely on the basis of being available. This factor may bias the sample in ways different from the other elements in the population. Differences between the sample group and the larger population need to be considered.

   Example: The researcher advertises the study through a local gay paper. Subjects who meet the criteria of being gay and over fifty-five are asked to contact the researcher.

In all four nonprobability sampling approaches, the results from the sample cannot be inferred or generalized to any larger population. Results can be interpreted only at the study sample level. For example, findings from the study that recruited older gay persons through a local gay newspaper can be applied only to the actual study participants themselves. To determine how much these findings hold true for other groups of gay older persons would require further research.

Measurement

Measurement is defined as "careful, deliberate observations of the real world for the purpose of describing objects and events in terms of the attributes composing a variable" (Rubin & Babbie 1997, p. 129). While sampling concerns selection of data sources, decisions related to measurement focus on selecting procedures for capturing what is being studied.

SELECTING VARIABLES

Measurement provides the bridge between the conceptual world and the real world and is a critical point in the research process. For example, if the concept of a study is response to loss in the lives of the elderly, decisions about measurement dictate how "response" (such as emotional, mental, or physical reactions) and "loss" (such as decline in physical, emotional, or mental functioning, death of loved ones, changes in lifestyle, or historical changes) are defined. Operationalization is the process of determining the exact measurement procedures of a concept and involves selecting particular indicators targeted for study. When operationalization has taken place, an abstract "concept" becomes a specified and measurable "variable."

The focus of any research project is to describe or explain variations in some targeted phenomenon. The term "variable" focuses on variation or differences. Therefore, a variable is "an operationally defined concept that can take on more than one value" (Monette, Sullivan, & DeJong 1998, p. 32). Examples of variables include age, religion, gender, attitudes about aging, marital status, level of mental functioning, degree of life satisfaction, number of social supports, number of social outlets, or quality of patient care.

SELECTING MEASURES

Once the variables have been targeted, the next step is to select or develop adequate measurements. Two issues should be addressed in this process. One concerns determining the level of measurement of the data produced by the measure. The second pertains to using various criteria in order to evaluate the adequacy and suitability of the measure.

1. The *level of measurement* refers to the kind of data that are produced by the measurement of any variable. Variables can be scaled in many different ways and, thus, yield different types of data. This point is important because the level of measurement determines the types of statistical analyses used and the conclusions that can be drawn from the data. There are four levels of measurement: nominal, ordinal, interval, and ratio. These four levels differ in the extent to which the attributes of the variable take on the properties of the real number system. At one end of the continuum, that of nominal measurement, the numbers that are assigned to responses or categories are completely arbitrary and do not correspond to any true number value. For example, a

question on marital status could have four possible responses (1 = married/domestic partner; 2 = single; 3 = divorced or separated; and 4 = widowed). These four categories could just as logically be numbered in the reverse order (1 = widowed; 2 = divorced or separated; 3 = single; and 4 = married/domestic partner). At the other end of the continuum, that of ratio measurement, the number assigned corresponds exactly to the mathematical meaning of that number in the real number system. An example of ratio data is the number of home visits in a month by a visiting nurse. In this case, an answer of 0 means no visits, an answer of 2 means two visits, an answer of 4 means four visits, and so on. Table 4.2 provides a summary of the levels of measurement, including their properties and gerontological examples.

2. The adequacy and suitability of a measure can be assessed from a variety of different vantage points. *Validity* refers to the extent to which a measurement tool captures what it was intended to measure. For example, in a study of social supports of the elderly the measurement tool must actually assess this variable and not some related variable, such as life satisfaction or well-being. There are three general types of validity (content, criterion, and construct validity), which yield different information concerning the adequacy of a measure in this area. *Reliability* refers to the precision and consistency of a measurement tool, or the extent to which a measure yields the same results over repeated applications. For example, in a study of decline in health status, the changes noted over time need to be attributed to true changes in health status and not inaccuracy of the measurement tool. There are generally three different approaches to estimating reliability which evaluate different aspects of this dimension (stability, equivalence, and homogeneity).

The researcher interested in aging should become knowledgeable of the numerous measures that have been specifically designed for use with older subjects. An excellent resource for such instruments is Kane and Kane's (1981) text on assessing the elderly. This volume includes measurements of: (1) physical functioning (e.g., Cornell Medical Index, Cumulative Illness Rating Scale, Index of Activities of Daily Living, Rosow Functional Health Scale); (2) mental functioning (e.g., VIRO Orientation Scale, Mental Status Questionnaire, Geriatric Interpersonal Evaluation Scale, Beck Depression Index, Nurses Observation for Inpatient Evaluation); (3) social functioning (e.g., Social Networks Assessment Questionnaire, Role Activity Scales, Bennett Social Isolation Scales, Exchanges of Support and Assistance Index, Family APGAR); and (4) multidimensional aspects of aging (e.g., Sickness Impact Profile; Older Americans Resources and Services [OARS]; Comprehensive Assessment and Referral Evaluation [CARE], Patient Appraisal and Care Evaluation [PACE]). Other important standardized measurement instruments used with older persons for both clinical and research purposes include: The Duke Health Profile (Parkerson, Broadhead, & Tse 1990); the Geriatric Depression Scale (Yesavage & Brink 1983); the Self-rating Depression Scale (Zung & Zung 1986); and the Life Satisfaction Index-Z (Neugarten, Havighurst & Tobin 1961).

The complex nature of multi-dimensional concepts used in gerontological research, such as quality of life or well-being, may often require the use of multiple instruments in order to operationalize different subdomains. Pinpointing an objective standard for these concepts has traditionally been a slippery slope for researchers. In their compilation of conceptual and empirical work on this topic, Birren, Lubben, Rowe, and Deutchman (1991) stress the utility of designing studies that use multiple measures to capture subtle dimensions

■ **Table 4.2**   Variables and Their Levels of Measurement

Level of Measurement	Properties	Examples in Gerontology
Nominal variable	A variable takes on different values, and the numbers which are assigned are arbitrary. Larger and smaller values do not imply more or less of the attribute. Different values represent distinct categories and are not on a continuum.	Category responses in which different categories are distinct. Sex: 1 = Male, 2 = Female, or 1 = Female, 2 = Male Institutional Care: 1 = Yes, 2 = No, or 1 = No, 2 = Yes Marital status: 1 = Single, 2 = Married/ domestic partner, 3 = Divorced, 4 = Widowed, 5 = Other
Ordinal variable	A variable takes on a range of values, and larger numbers indicate more of the attribute while smaller numbers indicate less of the attribute. Different values represent a rank ordering along a continuum.	Attitudes and opinions, many self-report measures and preferences. Religiosity: 0 = Not at all religious, 1 = Somewhat religious, 2 = Very Religious Ability to Dress Self: 1 = Must have caregiver dress, 2 = Can dress self with some help from caregiver, 3 = Can dress self with no help Perceived Need for Senior Citizens Center: 1 = Not needed at all, 2 = Little need, 3 = Neutral, 4 = Some need, 5 = Very much needed
Internal variable	A variable takes on a range of values, and numbers are assigned so that equal distances in amount reflect equal differences in numbers which are assigned. The numbers fall along a continuum and have an arbitrary zero point.	Intervals with arbitrary zero point. Body Temperature: 98, 99, 100. Calendar Time: days of the week, months of the year.
Ratio variables	A variable takes on different values along a continuum. Equal distances represent equal differences in the amount of the attribute. An absolute zero point is apparent.	Intervals which have absolute zero point. Number of children: 0, 1, 2, 3, etc. Number of elderly clients: 3, 10, 25, etc. Income per year (in dollars): $0–millions! Number of community resources for elderly: 2, 10, 15, etc.

Source: McCauley 1987 (modified).

of quality of life. However, in addition to examining what is known about the reliability and validity of the instrument prior to its use, it is also important to carefully select brief measures in order to avoid burdening older respondents (Steiner et al. 1996).

Sometimes the researcher is interested in some variable for which there are no previously developed measures. In these cases, a decision might be made to construct a measurement device. This process is complex and time consuming and requires attention to a variety of issues inherent to test construction. The researcher would be well advised to consult readings offered by a number of experts on the subject prior to taking on this task (Miller 1991; Mueller 1986; Oppenheim 1966; Stanley & Hopkins 1972). However, a few general guidelines to formulating questions or items will be offered here (Monette, Sullivan, & DeJong 1998). First, items or questions need to be clear, direct, and nonambiguous. Generally, the present tense should be used unless asking about the past or the future, in which case the directions should clearly state this perspective. Questions or items should not include more than one thought or idea. Reading level of the subjects should be underestimated rather than overestimated. Avoid using jargon or vague terms. Instead, attempts should be made to use language with which the elderly are familiar. Finally, any developed instrument should be pretested in order to identify and correct problems before using the measure in your study. In designing or selecting a measurement tool, the researcher needs to pay attention to the method of data collection proposed. The type of data collection which will be used will have an effect upon the type of measurement system used in the research. The following section discusses various options of data collection with a particular emphasis on issues related to gerontological research.

Data Collection

There are basically three ways that data or information can be collected: by (1) asking questions; (2) observing behavior, and (3) analyzing existing data. All three of these data collection approaches are appropriate for gerontological research. However, one method, or a combination of methods, usually emerges as the most appropriate for a particular study depending on the stated research problem, the targeted population, and the available resources.

ASKING QUESTIONS

Researchers ask questions of subjects either by administering a questionnaire or by conducting an interview. Use of a questionnaire requires that the subject respond directly to some written form of questions, while interviews involve having the interviewer ask the questions. In both approaches, items can be focused on thoughts, feelings, or behaviors either in the past, present, or future. The following provides an overview of both methods, including advantages and disadvantages of each.

1. The use of *questionnaires* is probably the most common method used by researchers. The standard approach is to compile a list of potential subjects, mail the questionnaire to these people, and request that they complete and mail the form back to the researcher. Other ways to distribute questionnaires include handing the forms out in person, placing the questionnaires in some appropriate location and designating a place to return them, or including them in product packaging. Sometimes these alternative methods increase the likelihood of a good response rate, which is the percentage of the total sample who return the questionnaire. Obtaining a good response rate is important in survey research to increase the likelihood that the results are representative and provide an accurate picture of the targeted sample.

With elderly respondents, three issues are especially important in gathering timely and accurate survey data. One is the validity of the instrument including size and density of print. Questionnaires for older respondents need to have larger print and denser print setting. A second issue is the length. The older respondent may take longer to complete a survey due to visual impairment, motor skill impairments, or general fatigue levels. Surveys which are fairly simple, with larger and darker print, will be easier for the older respondent to complete. A third issue is to include a cover letter which explains the purpose of the survey. Since the elderly frequently fear victimization, provide enough information to decrease this kind of worry. Information such as the researcher's credentials, the purpose or benefits derived from the study, and how the respondent's address was obtained are helpful and will increase response rate.

2. The second approach to asking questions is to conduct either *face-to-face* or *telephone interviews* with subjects. The central process in conducting either type of interview is interpersonal communication. Well-trained, experienced interviewers can be a key factor in obtaining quality information. As McCauley (1987) notes, good interviewers can encourage potential respondents to participate, assess and report back information about the interview context, respond to interviewee questions or concerns, identify and resolve problems, guide the interview process, and ensure that responses are in line with the researcher's intent. Many of the factors designed to increase a good response rate with questionnaires also apply to interviews, such as sharing with the interviewee information about the research, explaining why they were selected, and telling them how important their participation is to the project. In terms of ordering questions, however, there are definite differences between questionnaires and interviews. In interviewing, the interviewer should start with nonthreatening questions first, such as demographics, and save more difficult questions for later on in the process (Monette, Sullivan, & DeJong 1994).

There are advantages and disadvantages to all data collection approaches. Table 4.3 provides an overview of the advantages and disadvantages of questionnaires, face-to-face interviews, and telephone interviews. These elements apply to any research study, but there are additional factors that are especially important in surveying older respondents. Deficits in reading and writing ability, which create problems in completing questionnaires, are potentially evident in an elderly sample as older persons tend to have less education and poorer visual acuity than younger cohorts. Problems with completeness of responses may also be more prevalent with an older population. In a study by Leinbach (1982) which compared mail survey, face-to-face, and telephone interview results, the proportion of missing data for the mail surveys was more than four times greater than for the other techniques. Moreover, different data collection methods can also yield varying participation rates. In a recent survey of elderly participants, an initial response rate of 63 percent using mailed surveys increased to 93 percent when nonrespondents were contacted using face-to-face methods (Norton, Breitner, & Welsh 1994).

Interviewing older persons involves other important factors to consider. Face-to-face interviews that utilize a field approach, such as going door-to-door, may be negatively affected by fear which keeps older residents from participating in the interview or even answering the door. Face-to-face interviewers in other settings, such as nursing homes or day care centers, may experience difficulties in data collection due to problems with hearing,

■ **Table 4.3** Advantages and Disadvantages of Different Data Collection Approaches

Questionnaires

(+) Can tap large numbers of people	(−) Requires literacy and facility in English
(+) Can tap geographically diverse population	(−) Must be sufficiently simple to understand based on written instructions
(+) More inexpensive and quicker than interviews	(−) No chance to explain or probe further
(+) Can ask more personal questions because of privacy	(−) No assurance that targeted respondent was actually the one who completed survey
(+) Eliminates problem of interviewer bias	(−) Answers cannot be considered independent because respondent may have read ahead
	(−) Nonresponse bias; Those who responded may differ significantly from those who did not

Face-to-Face Interviews

(+) Can motivate respondents to give more accurate and complete info	(−) More expense, including training, travel, and equipment costs
(+) Can explain or probe further	(−) Takes longer to collect data on each respondent
(+) Does not require literacy and can use multilingual interviewer or interpreter for non-English-speaking respondents	(−) If data collection period takes an extended time may have intervening effect of external events
(+) Can control that targeted person respond in a certain order	(−) Possible interviewer bias, including misinterpretation or misrecording
(+) More flexible than questionnaires, can change style of interviewing based on needs of study	(−) Possible variation in instructions among interviewers
(+) Can collect observational data	(−) Respondents may reveal less due to lack of privacy

Telephone Interviews

(+) Travel time and costs eliminated	(−) Must be relatively short duration, about twenty minutes; some elderly even less
(+) Can tap more respondents than in face-to-face, but less than surveys	(−) Cannot take in observational data, only auditory
(+) Fewer interviewers needed, reduced supervision, training costs	(−) Cannot include subjects without a telephone which may include many elderly, especially lower income elderly
(+) Can still reach illiterate and non-English-speaking subjects	(−) May yield less personal information than questionnaire, but more than face-to-face
(+) Can still explain and probe	

Observational Techniques

(+) Can provide deeper, richer, or more comprehensive data	(−) Possible effect of observer bias
(+) Allows study of behavior that otherwise may be inaccessible	(−) Problem of observer's overidentifying with subjects
(+) Can collect data on both verbal and nonverbal behavior	(−) Lack of structure in unstructured field observation makes exact replication impossible
(+) Much observational research is longitudinal, can trace changes over time	(−) Sometimes difficult to quantify, e.g., field notes most often descriptive
	(−) Ethical issues re: consent and disclosure of purpose of research in some approaches
	(−) Little or no control over variables in setting
	(−) Because of physical and time limitations, most often done with small samples

■ **Table 4.3** *Cont'd.*

Analysis of Existing Data	
(+) Lower costs because data are already available	(−) Variable quality of data, can't control conditions of data collection
(+) Nonreactivity, no study effects on subjects	(−) Possible incompleteness of data, gaps in individual data or sets of data
(+) Can measure inaccessible subjects, e.g., deceased or institutionalized	
(+) Amendable to longitudinal studies	(−) Possible lack of comparability over time due to changes in way data defined or collected
(+) Access to large sample sizes, sometimes problem with too much data	(−) Have to accept how variable was operationalized, may not fit your definition
	(−) Possible systematic bias in what data was collected

Source: Monette, Sullivan, & DeJong 1998.

vision, speech, mobility, mental status, or some other functional or health deficit of the subjects (McCauley 1987). In some cases, the participants cannot be directly interviewed and an informant is needed to obtain the information. Some interview schedules are designed to include an initial assessment of whether the participant or an informant should be used (Center for the Study of Aging and Human Development 1978). An additional consideration in interviewing older persons is response bias, or the tendency for answers to questions to be influenced by things other than their true feelings, beliefs, and behaviors (Monette, Sullivan, & DeJong 1998, p. 161). This is particularly important when measuring the psychosocial well-being of older persons (Cappeliez 1989; Carstensen & Cone 1983).

Telephone interviews also run the risk of encountering difficulties related to health or functioning deficits, such as a hearing problem or an inability to talk at length on the phone (McCauley 1987). Kulka, Herzog, and Rodgers (1980) report that older persons are more affected than younger subjects by the length of telephone interviews. However, telephone data collection, using computer-assisted technology, has been used successfully with older participants. Dorfman, Lubben et al. (1995) conducted 45-minute long telephone interviews with older persons to screen for depression. The researchers noted, though, that participants had to be English speaking and have telephone service. These types of requirements for participation act to screen-out poorer ethnic subgroups of older persons from the sample. In a study of older Virginians, about 5 percent of persons sixty or older did not have phones. This rate doubled for older nonwhite Virginians with about 11 percent of the group having no telephone (McCauley, Arling, Nutty, & Bowling 1980). These specific age-related factors, along with other advantages and disadvantages of different approaches, should be carefully considered when selecting a particular data collection method.

OBSERVING BEHAVIOR
Sometimes observing events is the preferred method of data collection. This method can be used with both quantitative and qualitative research. In observational methods, the researcher actually sees or hears behavior as it happens. Observational methods can be a

flexible approach since various aspects of the process can be modified to fit the situation. One aspect concerns the degree of structure, which can range from little structure to the use of a highly structured observational coding schema or checklist. When the purpose of the study is to explore and generate ideas and concepts, an unstructured approach is best. When the research is addressing a specific question or attempting to test hypotheses, the structured format is most appropriate (Monette, Sullivan, & DeJong 1998).

Another aspect of observational research is the degree of participation of the observer. The observer can remain completely unobtrusive, as when he or she is hidden behind a two-way mirror, or be much more apparent, as when he or she participates in the activities being studied. When the researcher is playing the role of complete observer there is far less chance of influencing the subjects or interfering with the process, but data collection is limited to what can easily be observed and there is no chance to tease out the meaning of events. On the other end of the continuum, that of participant observer, there is the definite danger that the researcher will affect the environment, but there is the benefit of the researcher being able to obtain data about the subjective experience of subjects. Between these two extremes are approaches that involve varying degrees of participant observation (Monette, Sullivan, & DeJong 1998).

The third aspect of observational techniques is the amount of disclosure the researcher makes to the subjects concerning the true purpose of the research. In either the unobtrusive or participant observer role, the researcher can withhold information about the nature of the research and the fact that the subjects are being observed to informed consent in any study. Ways of dealing with this issue are to either inform the subjects about the purpose of the research at the beginning of the project or share this information with them at the end of the study. This latter approach is probably the most practical to use when there is a danger of biasing the results if subjects know they are being studied beforehand (Monette, Sullivan, & DeJong 1998).

As with questionnaires and interviews, observational techniques also have different advantages and disadvantages as data collection approaches (see table 4.3). Beyond these general characteristics, there are a few particular guidelines in using observational approaches with older persons. If the researcher plays the role of participant observer, he or she must first gain the trust of the subject and progress slowly in building relationships. This practice is particularly true in institutional settings where residents encounter a variety of people with whom they must interact. MacPherson (1988) discusses the implications of the role of participant-as-researcher in gerontological research, particularly when the researcher shares key characteristics of the group under study. Her study of a support group of menopausal women was both complicated and enhanced by the fact that she was a member. MacPherson brought experiential insight to her study, yet at the same time faced the dilemma of maintaining objectivity in representing her findings. An additional guideline is about the coding schema used with older subjects. In developing a coding schema or checklist of targeted behaviors, the researcher should be fully familiar with the sphere of possible behaviors most typical of an elderly population. If this step is not taken, the risk of including non-relevant behaviors and excluding appropriate behaviors of this age group increases.

ANALYZING EXISTING DATA

Sometimes information relevant to the proposed research question or hypothesis already exists and all that is required is to carefully organize or reanalyze these data. McCauley (1987) notes three ways that existing information can be utilized in a research project: (1) as a sole source of data, such as using census data to conduct a feasibility study of congregate housing for older persons; (2) as one component of the research, such as examining a hospital's record system for data on a patient's age, reason for admission, level of functioning, and length of stay, to add to interview data on patient satisfaction with services; and (3) as validation of data collected by other means, such as cross-checking census data to determine whether a sample of older persons reflects the characteristics of the larger elderly population from which it was drawn.

There are several sources of existing data that may be tapped in doing gerontological research (McCauley 1987). Most federal, state and local government agencies as well as private organizations collect data on an ongoing basis. Examples include vital registrant information, such as birth, death, marriage data; agency records, such as mental health client records, hospital discharge plans; and census data (see, for example, Neal, Carter, & Morgan 1996). Although data from existing records can be a fruitful source of information, the researcher should not assume that all such data are entirely accurate, complete, or consistent. This fact is especially true of agency records, as evidenced by a study of nursing home admission contracts that revealed inconsistencies between promises made by the facility in the contract and actual delivery of services to the resident (Kisor 1996). Agency policies, habits, time constraints, and other factors may lead to inaccuracies in such records (McCauley 1987).

Another major source of existing data is information from previous research, including studies conducted by others or by the researcher. One benefit of using such data bases is increased efficiency, as the data are often in a form that can be directly analyzed. The reanalysis of data collected for another research project is called secondary analysis. There is a wealth of available data for researchers to use to answer their own research questions. Universities, government agencies, and private organizations have national data archives on various topics of interest related to policy questions such as: health care, long-term care service patterns, and health care service utilization. Some of the more significant national data sets include: National Health and Nutrition Examination Survey (NHANES III); the National Health Interview Study (NHIS); the Longitudinal Study on Aging (LSOA); the National Nursing Home Survey (NNHS); the National Medical Care Utilization and Expenditure Survey (NMUES); and the Long Term Care Chanelling Demonstration (CHANELLING). In addition, the University of Michigan maintains the National Archives of Computerized Data on Aging (NACDA), a collection of the nation's largest library of computer readable data on aging.

Secondary analysis is a rapidly growing area in gerontological research due to the ease with which data can be obtained. Further, probability sampling methods are often used, enabling the researcher to generalize findings to larger populations of older persons. Some data sets are also longitudinal, meaning that the research question can be assessed by looking at changes over time. An example of gerontological research conducted using the technique of secondary analysis is a study conducted by Wolinsky, Johnson, & Stump (1995). The authors used data from the Longitudinal Study on Aging, released in 1993, to study health services utilization over time. This data set is based on interviews with 7,527 randomly sampled older adults and consists of key variables that either predispose or enable older persons to use health care services.

No data should be used without careful evaluation, as it is important to weigh any concerns of recency and credibility prior to beginning the study (Stewart & Kamins 1993). It is also critical to evaluate whether the sample size will allow for analysis according to respondent characteristics. For example, if the researcher wanted to compare health care utilization rates among different racial or ethnic groups, then the data set must first be assessed for sample adequacy. In his 1995 study, LaVeist reviewed forty-four national data sets and found the majority to be adequate for analysis involving African Americans, but not for Hispanics, Native Americans, or Asian Americans.

Reports disseminated through the mass media can also be used as a source of data for analysis. This data source includes magazine and newspaper articles, radio and television programs, or documentaries. These sources are especially good for tapping current thoughts or opinions related to aging. Two problems may exist when analyzing data from the mass media. One is the validity and reliability of such reports, as they can be considerably influenced by the opinions and views of the persons producing them. Also, the data from these sources are generally not in a form that is easily analyzed. The researcher usually has to transform these data into a usable form.

A final source of existing information is expressive materials, including novels, autobiographies, diaries, letters, paintings, plays, and films (McCauley 1987). These types of data allow the researcher to tap thoughts and feelings not generally available through other sources. As with media data, there are issues concerning reliability and validity, as well as generalizability due to the fact that the individuals who produce expressive materials may not be representative of the larger population. Although these problems exist with expressive materials, they offer unique information as demonstrated by a study by Demos and Jache (1981) in their analysis of age themes in humorous greeting cards and Berman's (1988) analysis of personal journals of older persons as they confront developmental issues of later life. In both studies, expressive material provided a perspective not usually captured by other methods.

Regardless of the source of data, there are certain advantages and disadvantages in using existing information (see table 4.3). In using this data collection method there are no additional factors that specifically pertain to doing gerontological research and researchers should consider this generally underutilized data source. Attention is now given to the final phase in the research process, which is analyzing the data and disseminating the results.

Data Analysis and Dissemination of Findings

SELECTING ANALYTICAL TECHNIQUES

After the data have been collected, the next step is to make sense of this information through the application of some analytical procedure. The goal in data analysis is to reduce, describe, and interpret information so that it can be communicated to and used by others. The general goal of data analysis, and the specific procedures utilized, are the same regardless of the age of the participants. There are no particular guidelines in analyzing data drawn from elderly respondents. Given the overall goal of data analysis, there are two general types of analysis: quantitative and qualitative.

For much applied research, the researcher will employ some type of quantitative or statistical analyses, which involves the use of descriptive and inferential statistics. In descriptive statistics, various characteristics of the study sample are described. Descriptive techniques can summarize individual variables, examine associations between variables, or explore differences in the same variable among different groups (Monette, Sullivan, & DeJong 1998). For example, descriptive statistics can provide information on the average age of residents at a nursing home, the range in income of the elderly in a given city, or the association between gender and feelings about having to hire a caregiver. Descriptive statistics can yield much information about the sample in the study but do not produce knowledge about the population from which that sample was drawn. In order to gain information about this larger context, inferential statistics are employed, which are designed to make and evaluate generalizations from the data about some targeted population. For example, researchers might want to know if there is a significant relationship in the larger population between race and particular health care problem, or whether there are significant differences between men and women regarding their participation in bereaved spouse support groups. In both cases, inferences are made from the investigated sample to a larger population of elderly based on inferential statistics. Of course, generalizations from findings to a larger population can only be done if probability sampling methods were utilized in the study design.

Quantitative statistical analysis often relies on the use of computer programs to compute the necessary statistics. However, some research projects can produce meaningful results without the use of sophisticated computer analyses. An example of this level of quantitative analysis is an undergraduate social work project conducted at Virginia Commonwealth University. A student completing her field placement at the Area Agency on Aging Meals on Wheels program wondered about the absence of client representation on the agency's board. When she asked staff about this concern, she was informed that there was little consumer interest in serving on the board. The student received permission to conduct a telephone survey of agency consumers to determine their level of interest and to identify possible barriers to involvement. The survey yielded simple descriptive data easily analyzed with the aid of a hand calculator. The student displayed her findings in visual form using bar graphs and pie charts, and presented her findings to the agency. Results showed that a number of consumers were interested in board service and would be able to participate if transportation were provided to meetings. Based on these findings, board membership was expanded to include agency clients. Using a simple approach to quantitative analyses, this modest applied research project led to important changes in agency policy and increased empowerment for agency consumers.

Qualitative analysis is another approach to studying a research problem and examining the resulting data. It involves data in the form of words, pictures, descriptions, or narratives (Monette, Sullivan, & DeJong 1998). Qualitative analysis is appropriate for data collection methods that yield data not easily codified into quantitative form (such as field notes or interview tapes). Qualitative analysis also provides rich information and subjective meaning not always accessible through quantitative methods. For example, a different perspective is gained on the process of aging from ten hours of in-depth interviewing of twenty older subjects than from completed questionnaires from five hundred subjects. Qualitative approaches are also useful in exploratory studies where there is little information on a topic.

In relation to research on aging, Reinharz and Rowles (1988) explain that:

> Qualitative gerontology is concerned with describing patterns of behavior and processes of interaction, as well as revealing the meanings, values, and intentionalities that pervade

elderly people's experience or the experience of others in relation to old age. In addition, qualitative gerontology seeks to identify patterns that underlie the life worlds of individuals, social groups, and larger systems as they relate to old age. (p. 6)

There are many different qualitative techniques available to the researcher, among them: case studies, in-depth interviewing, participant observation, ethnography, and content analysis. Choice of techniques depends on the nature of the research question and the aims of the researcher. As with quantitative research, there are particular guidelines to follow. Qualitative gerontological research requires that careful attention be paid to the data collection process to make sure the data supply a foundation for an analysis of meaning (Reinharz & Rowles 1988). The raw data have to be arranged into some organized form that can be interpreted and shared with others.

Content analysis is a useful qualitative technique because it offers a way to organize large amounts of written or spoken information. For example, Archer and MacLean (1993) used content analysis in conjunction with in-depth interviewing to examine perceptions of husbands and sons performing the caregiving role for older women. Content analysis involves a process where the researcher looks for typical or normal patterns and general themes in the data, as well as deviations or atypical cases (Babbie, 1998). This requires going back and forth between the data and preliminary findings until a final analysis or understanding emerges (Reinharz & Rowles 1988). Producing verbatim transcripts of narratives for analysis can be a very time-consuming process. Once the raw data are in a usable form, they must be unitized into words, themes, major characters, or sentences and paragraphs (Monette, Sullivan, & DeJong 1998).

Another qualitative method commonly used in gerontology is reminiscence, or review of life narratives. Used both as a clinical intervention to aid well-being (Luborsky 1993) and a research tool, reminiscence involves providing a forum for the older person to share personal meanings of life experiences. As a qualitative technique, it involves examining stories in the older person's language told in response to structured interview questions (Butler 1968). As Luborsky (1993) points out, it is important to consider that we view these life narratives in "fragments" selected by the researcher or author (p. 446). Methods for this type of research have become more rigorous (e.g., Haight & Webster 1995), and reminiscence offers a key way to study an older person's subjective views of the world. For example, Berghorn, Shafer, Holmes, and Quadagno (1986) used reminiscence to study nursing home residents perceptions of the ability to control aspects of their lives in an institutional setting.

In sum, there are a range of techniques available to conduct research and to increase our knowledge of aging. Selection of methods depends on many criteria including the research question, the state of the knowledge on the topic, and feasibility issues. It is important to emphasize that quantitative and qualitative methods are not incompatible. In fact, sometimes it is appropriate to use them in tandem, because diversity in methods yields a deeper understanding of the question under study. Moreover, combining methods has the effect of compensating for the shortcomings of each method (Reinharz & Rowles 1988). In his 1988 study, Pillemer used a combination of closed- and open-ended questions to capture the experience and meaning of physical maltreatment to actual victims of physical abuse. By combining methods, Pillemer was able to generalize his findings to a larger population of older persons and capture the richness of the personal meaning of elder abuse.

Reporting the Results

After analysis is complete, the final step is to share what has been learned with others interested in the topic, or to "translate dry findings into meaningful conclusions via effective communication" (McCauley 1987, p. 214). The research project is not completed until the findings have been disseminated to those groups who either want or need to know the study results. This final step is particularly crucial in applied research as the original intention is to create knowledge that has a practical purpose or use in the real world. McCauley (1987) suggests three general guidelines in reporting research findings:

1. *Focus on the Original Problem:* The research was conducted with a particular purpose in mind. Sometimes researchers lose sight of the original problem because of new interests in side issues that emerged during the process or as a reaction to the deluge of data. However, in reporting the findings, the focus should be on whether the goal of the research has been met and the targeted question answered. If the problem was important enough to be studied, the findings are important enough to be communicated.
2. *Focus on the Audience:* For any research project, a number of different people should have the research findings made available to them. There are several options for disseminating results such as professional journals or popular magazines, national conferences, through agency administrators and staff, local gatherings of concerned citizens or various media programs. In each case, the task of the researcher is to relate the findings in the most meaningful way to the particular audience who can use the information from the study.
3. *Communicate Effectively:* Communication of results may entail a lengthy written report or a thirty-second news blurb. Whether through a report or an oral presentation, a researcher should be able to summarize what was done and what is being recommended in one concise, synthesizing sentence. This preparation involves good planning and organization of materials and some time spent making decisions about writing or presentation style. Effective communication increases the likelihood that findings will be utilized.

At the point of the dissemination of findings, the research process has come full circle. Study results increase the understanding and knowledge about a topic and feed back into the cycle of theory, research, and practice. This ever-evolving process allows speculation about issues related to aging, investigation about specific concerns, and translation of knowledge into action. Although the scientific method is a major tool used in this process, the focus of gerontological research concerns human beings and human lives. For this reason, social work values play an important part in developing ethical guidelines for conducting research and targeting those issues of highest priority. The following section discusses special issues in research on aging.

Special Issues in Gerontological Research

Ethical Concerns

Research impacts people's lives in two different ways (Monette, Sullivan, & DeJong 1998). First, during the process of conducting research, people are asked to answer questions, to perform certain behaviors, or to be observed in different aspects of their lives.

Sometimes research can evoke strong emotions or reactions that may have negative consequences. Secondly, the findings and conclusions of research projects affect people's lives because the results are used in developing policy and programs in human services. Research influences what services are offered, how programs are structured, what techniques are used, and what people are helped. Due to the potential to greatly impact individuals, families and groups, the researcher has a clear responsibility to conduct a project with attention to ethical concerns. The topic of ethics covers many specific issues and situations which arise during the research process. Due to the diversity and complexity of research, there are no clear-cut rules for conducting research in an ethical way. However, Monette, Sullivan, and DeJong (1998) identify nine ethical issues to consider in planning and conducting human service research.

1. *Informed Consent.* This issue refers to telling potential research participants about all aspects of the research so that they can make an informed decision concerning their own participation. In gerontological research, potential participants may not be able to fully participate in this process due to disabilities or deficits in physical or mental functioning. In these cases, decisions need to be made concerning whether there is another person who can ethically give this consent and what the impact of this decision will be on the participant.
2. *Confidentiality.* Confidentiality pertains to assurances that specific individual responses will not be made available to public sources. This issue entails protecting the identity of participants or distorting information that could potentially identify the participant. Maintaining confidentiality requires that the researcher not allow access by others to information shared in confidence. In gerontological research, "others" may be the funding source for the study, the nursing home staff, or family members. Often numbers are assigned to data as they are collected and any connecting information to particular people is destroyed.
3. *Privacy.* This issue refers to the participant having control over when and under which condition the data will be collected. Although linked to confidentiality, privacy is specifically concerned about how the research is conducted. Intrusions into the lives of the elderly is a particularly sensitive issue, especially for those who reside in some type of institution. Researches should build in methods which protect privacy and allow the subject as much control as possible during his or her participation in the project.
4. *Physical or Mental Distress.* Researchers should avoid exposing participants to physical or mental distress or danger. If there is a potential for distress, this fact should be addressed while the researcher is obtaining informed consent. Social research rarely involves possible physical harm, although concern should be taken to ensure that elderly participants are not overtired or discomforted by the process. If there is a potential for mental or emotional distress, the researcher should assess the participant's state during a debriefing period. If distress is noted, it might be necessary to inform relevant persons, such as the participant's family, care provider, or other professionals.
5. *Issues Related to Sponsored Research.* Often research is sponsored and funded by a third party. An agreement must be drawn up between the sponsor and the researcher concerning the rights and obligations of the parties involved prior to the initiation of the project. Certain safeguards should be addressed at this point. One is that there will be no conditional publication of results, such as only publishing results if they turn out a

certain way. Secondly, although the researchers may use the data for other purposes beyond the sponsored research project, the focus of the study should not be altered so that it no longer meets the sponsor's needs. And thirdly, the sponsorship of the project should be a fact that can be shared with potential participants during the process of obtaining informed consent, as this may influence their decision to participate.

6. *Honest Disclosure of Results.* Dissemination of findings is part of the research process. The researcher is ethically bound not to disclose inaccurate, deceptive, or fraudulent research results. This obligation includes careless errors as well as purposeful deception. Results also need to be reported thoroughly, so that a comprehensive picture of the findings is available.

7. *Scientific Advocacy.* This refers to the degree to which the researcher advocates particular uses of the research data. This issue is controversial with many researchers holding the position that once that study has been published it is part of the public domain and there is no longer any control or responsibility for the researcher. Others argue that they have a duty to promote the constructive utilization of results. In any event, advocacy should be tempered with objectivity so that the pursuit of knowledge is not jeopardized.

8. *Protecting Vulnerable Clients.* Human service clients are often targeted as subjects for research and may find themselves vulnerable to pressures to participate, especially in projects conducted by the organization providing them with services. Elderly clients are one of the groups that may be targeted frequently as research participants. This issue involves voluntary and informed consent. Can these clients give consent freely or are there pressures to participate, such as promise of services? Sometimes researchers must decide to abandon a research project in the interests of ensuring truly voluntary informed consent.

9. *Withholding Treatment for Research Purposes.* Sometimes the need for a control group necessitates withholding treatment from one group of people in order to test the effectiveness of the treatment with another group. Some believe it is unethical to withhold services that may have some positive benefit. Another argument is that until the effectiveness of the treatment is investigated, it is unknown whether anything of value is being withheld. Alternatives exist to withholding treatment, such as using clients on a waiting list to serve as the control group or offering alternative services which are equally promising to the two groups and investigating the differences between the interventions. In any event, the researcher needs to weigh the potential risks and benefits in decisions relative to withholding treatment in a research project.

Diversity Issues

There is no one true or universal experience of aging. To attempt to characterize aging in broad categories or norms obscures the growing diversity of older Americans. For example, aggregate data on income can cloud differences between socio-economic groups such as poor and near-poor. Researchers must recognize that heterogeneity characterizes the aging process and that our definitions of aging are in a constant state of evolution.

The focus of research related to gerontological research should reflect the aging population itself. Currently, racial and ethnic subgroups comprise the fastest growing category of older Americans (AARP 1997). This growing population is becoming more divergent in characteristics and needs than ever before (Torres-Gil 1992). There is a well-established and growing body of literature on needs and use of services by racial and ethnic subgroups of older persons. This literature focuses largely on concerns such as the need for formal home and community long-term care, where ethnicity is an important predicting factor for service use (Hennessy & John 1996; Jackson & Mittelmark 1997; Mui & Burnette 1994). As demographic changes continue to shape the aging population, it remains essential to gather research data from a culturally relevant or "ethnogeriatric" perspective. Researchers must also be mindful of the need to examine smaller and more underrepresented groups of older persons, such as American Indians (Markides 1998), and expand beyond "stereotypical categories" such as race to probe the diversity of characteristics within racial groups (Gibson & Stoller 1998). It is also important to involve older persons in the research process itself in order to develop meaningful and culturally relevant services. Delgado (1996) designed his study of needs of Puerto Rican elderly by including an advisory committee of targeted beneficiaries and having them directly involved in all phases of the project.

Monette, Sullivan, and DeJong (1994) emphasize that there can be significant methodological considerations at all phases of the research process that impact diversity issues and research with older persons. In particular, it is critical in the problem formulation phase that the research question be conceptualized with culture and/or personal characteristics taken into account. For example, the concept of "caregiver stress" may take on very different meanings depending upon whether the older persons under study are white, African American, American Indian, or Southeast Asian. Or, the concept of "functional independence" may mean something completely different to an older person who experienced onset of a disabling condition at an early age with another who just recently had a stroke.

Another important methodological concern is sampling and "rare event status" where, due to residential segregation, racial minorities that live in largely white areas are relatively small in number. Small sample sizes make it difficult to assess differences of opinion and behavior, and thus it is easy to falsely conclude that the group is homogenous (Monette, Sullivan, & DeJong 1998). To avoid this pitfall, it may be necessary to take special consideration with sampling techniques. For example, Becerra and Zambrana (1985) suggest that snowball sampling may be an appropriate way to reach greater numbers of Latinos. This sampling technique may also be a way to locate samples of marginalized older persons such as the homeless.

Diversity and culturally relevant research extends to other characteristics such as sexual orientation, socio-economic status, disability status, and gender. Research on these topics is beneficial to both micro and macro social work practice with older persons. It helps to discount myths of aging and provides data related to the unique needs of older persons as individuals. For example, Dorfman and his associates (1995) surveyed a group of heterosexuals and a group of gay and lesbian older persons and found no difference in the level of social support but a profound variation in the source of support. Specifically, heterosexuals tend to rely on family members while gays and lesbians develop a friendship structure for support. Data from this type of research provides the information necessary to revise models of health and social service delivery and target needs more appropriately and efficiently (Mui & Burnette 1994, p. 190). Research that captures the diversity of aging also provides data to develop appropriate program alternatives and practice approaches.

Contemporary Issues

As stated previously, the proportion of the elderly in the United States has been growing considerably and is projected to increase into the next century. Other changes in our country interact with the "aging of America" to produce new issues and problems affecting everyone. Generally, these developments can be discussed as "micro" issues, which focus on the individual, the family and small groups, or "macro" issues, which concern the larger social, economic, and political context of people's lives. The following paragraphs review three examples of contemporary issues in gerontology, targeting one micro and macro issue for each topic. Examples of possible research questions for each area are offered.

CAREGIVING

An issue that has emerged as a critical concern is the whole arena of caregiving. As the proportion of older people increases and family patterns continue to change, who will care for our older citizens? From a micro perspective, one concern is the stress and strain that occurs within the family members of the elderly, especially the adult child of an aging parent. Often this person has parenting responsibilities for his or her own children while simultaneously being the primary caregiver for an elderly parent. This group has been labeled the "sandwich generation" to illustrate the pressure they feel from two generations of family members. A research project might assess the effectiveness of a self-help group designed to provide support and alleviate the physical and psychological consequences of stress experienced by adult-child caregivers.

A macro issue related to caregiving is existing policy and programs within the workplace. Although there has been some recognition of employees as caregivers of children, less attention has been paid to the reality that these same employees may also be caring for aging parents. Policies and programs that reflect an awareness of this reality include flexible work hours, sick leave options that allow for care of a sick family member including parents, and an on-site adult day care center. A research project in this arena would be a needs assessment conducted at the workplace to ascertain which policies and programs would be the most helpful to employees in their struggle to balance the demands of work and family.

RETIREMENT

A second contemporary issue is the complexity of changes and concerns related to retirement. In past generations, people were not expected to live long beyond their work years. Due to changes in our life expectancy, a person may face ten, twenty, even thirty years of remaining life past their involvement in work. A micro focus might target individual functioning in the retirement years, including physical, mental, and psychological aspects. A potential research question related to this issue might concern the factors associated with a productive and satisfying retirement? This research project might explore such areas as social support, use of leisure time, community involvement, and family contact.

From a macro perspective, a critical issue is the whole structure of fiscal support for retiring citizens. Given demographic shifts, an issue has emerged about the supply of younger workers to contribute adequately to retirement funds, such as Social Security or pension plans. There is a need to reexamine policies and programs related to retirement, such as considering raising the age of retirement to reflect changes in the life cycle. Research in the form of a policy analysis could explore the impact of proposed changes in policy and programs prior to implementation.

QUALITY OF LIFE

A third critical area is quality of life in the later years. This issue includes a whole set of concerns related to extension of the lifespan, including changes in the major causes of death. Previously, most people died from infectious, acute diseases of relatively short duration. Acute diseases, excluding violent deaths, have declined over the last eighty years of this century resulting in a shift to more chronic causes of death, such as diseases of the heart, circulation, and various forms of cancer. The consequence of this shift is that although people are living longer, a greater number are living their last years in less than optimal health. A micro concern is how individuals and families cope with debilitating, chronic health problems, and the demands produced by increased longevity of the mentally and physically disabled. A research project might examine the effects of long-term, chronic illness on the elderly and their significant others, including an investigation of typical coping mechanisms used to deal with this situation.

A macro focus related to quality of life is prevention and wellness promotion. If people are living longer, what resources are needed to increase the likelihood that these years will be quality ones? Greater attention to providing information and services to all age groups is needed to emphasize the promotion and maintenance of well-being, health, and self-care. A macro research project in this area might be a program evaluation of nutrition services aimed toward lower-income families, which provides information concerning healthy eating habits. Data from such an evaluation can be utilized to improve the existing program or implement similar programs with other groups.

In summary, this chapter has provided an overview of the research process, delineated the steps involved in conducting research, and discussed some of the existing issues in current gerontological research. The concerns related to aging are increasingly crucial in contemporary society, as dramatic shifts in the profile and patterns of our social fabric are occurring. Research can provide a foundation for both social work theory and practice, providing useful tools in meeting the challenges that lie ahead for persons of all ages.

Discussion Questions

1. What are the steps of the research process? For each step, what are the special concerns of gerontological research?
2. What are examples of nonexperimental, experimental, and macro research designs?
3. What are some of the potential problems in collecting data from an elderly sample? What are some possible strategies for dealing with these problems?
4. What are particular ethical concerns in conducting research with the elderly? What are some of the guidelines to ensure an ethical approach when conducting research with this population?
5. In addition to the examples provided, what contemporary issues are possible topics for research? For each issue, what is an example of a micro and a macro research project?
6. Why is it important to keep issues of diversity in mind in all stages of the research process?
7. What are some advantages of qualitative approaches in gerontological research?

Experiential Learning

Activity: How to Get the Information: Different Approaches to Data Collection

Nursing home care is expensive. Some residents pay for their own care. Such payment is called private pay. Most residents who have fewer economic resources have stays paid by Medicaid. When a nursing home provides care to both types of residents, differences in the quality of care may exist. A question for a research project could be: "Is there a difference in quality of care between private-pay and Medicaid patients in a selected nursing home?"

The class is divided into four groups; each group is assigned one of the following data collection approaches: (1) Questionnaire, (2) Interview, (3) Observational Technique, and (4) Analysis of Existing Data. Each group, given the assigned approach, is asked to make decisions concerning:

1. How "quality of care" would be operationalized.
2. What data sources would be utilized (perceptions of staff/residents, behavior of staff/residents, client folders, facility logs, etc.).
3. What specific data elements would be collected given the particular data collection approach.
4. What data collection resources would be needed to obtain the data.
5. What would be the advantages and disadvantages to this data collection method.

After the small group tasks are complete, the class as a whole is convened to discuss the group process and decisions. What was easy to decide? What was difficult? When did they need further information to make an informed decision? What was the process of decision-making like? How does the selected data collection approach affect the proposed study? What are the possibilities/problems of combining methods?

Case Studies

See Appendix B for guidelines in analyzing gerontological social work practice.

Case 1: Social Support and Nursing Home Adjustment: A Gender Issue?

The Shadylawn Nursing Home is a 120-bed facility located in a metropolitan area on the East Coast. The home has been in operation for almost ten years and provides convalescent and long-term care for the elderly. Two full-time social workers are on staff to provide psychosocial services to residents, including initial assessment and orientation, service planning and provision, and discharge planning. One of the major concerns for staff at the time of admission is enhancing the resident's adjustment to the facility. Some of the clients make the transition with relative ease, many experience at least some initial difficulties, and a sizable minority never seem to adjust to their new surroundings.

One of the social workers, Don Jackson, noted that the male residents appeared to have more adjustment difficulties than the female residents. He discussed this impression with his co-worker, Nancy Patterson, and the two decided to investigate the matter further. They first decided to find out whether Don's perceptions were indeed accurate and then try to pinpoint what factors seemed to make adjustments easier for both men and women.

After reading through other studies in the gerontological literature concerning nursing home adjustment, they located an interview schedule that explored various indicators of adjustment. This questionnaire included items about perceptions of quality of care, involvement in activities, satisfaction with the facility, and related factors such as degree of functioning, social supports, private-pay versus subsidized care, and prognosis for discharge. They contracted with a local professor at a School of Social Work to help them analyze the data and decided to conduct the interviews themselves.

Don and Nancy determined that 100 of the 120 nursing home residents would be able to respond to the interview questions. Each interview took about a half an hour to administer. The remaining twenty residents had physical conditions that made this process burdensome and were not included in the study. They also decided that they would equally divide the interviews between them, with each interviewing half the women (76) and half the men (34). Don and Nancy agreed that this practice would lessen the chance that the particular interviewer would affect the responses in a particular way. Over the next several months, they conducted the interviews resulting in data from about 95 residents. Three of the women and two of the men of the original sample had either been discharged or died.

When the results were analyzed, Don's original perception was supported. Women significantly reported better adjustment scores than men. These scores were measured by ratings of quality of care, reported satisfaction with the facility and services, and involvement in program activities. When variables potentially related to adjustment were analyzed, two factors emerged as significant: degree of outside social support (more social support, higher adjustment) and prognosis for discharge (higher likelihood of discharge, higher adjustment). Men and women did not differ significantly as to prognosis for discharge, but they did differ in terms of available social support, with women reporting much more contact with friends and family than did the male residents.

Don and Nancy began to plan strategies for increasing the social contact of male residents since greater degrees of contact with others helped in adjustment to the facility. One service that was developed was weekly visits by youngsters from a local day care center, which often resulted in the development of special "grandparent-grandchild" relationships. Don and Nancy observed positive changes in the attitudes and behaviors of the residents involved in these activities. Although it seemed that the program was a success, the two social workers decided to reinterview the male residents within a few months to see if their adjustment rating had been positively affected by this intervention.

Source: Michael J. Sheridan.

Case 2: Women's Support Services: Who Uses What?

"I've been noticing that we've provided more services to older women lately. I wonder if we should start a service specifically for older clients?" Sharon Mulligan, a social work intake specialist, asked this question at the staff meeting of a YWCA's Women Support Services meeting.

Eight years ago, the YWCA in a midsized midwestern city began a Women's Support Services program. This program has the mission of assisting women in the community who have experienced or are at risk of experiencing domestic violence, rape, or incest. The program offers counseling, a temporary shelter for women and their children, referrals to medical and legal services, support groups and preventative education to the public, and community professionals. Since the program started, the number of clients using services has increased by 120 percent.

Within the last year, Sharon Mulligan has noticed that more older women are being referred for services. Last year, seventeen women over age fifty-five used program services. While compiling the annual reports, Sharon discovered that thirty-eight women in the over fifty-five age group had used services this current year. Sharon had thought that she was performing more intakes on older women, but she had not imagined that the increase was so dramatic. She became very interested in the fact that a greater number of older women were using services.

At the staff meeting, other staff members also became interested in services to older women. Sharon had started to question whether the structure of current programs met the needs of the older women. Another staff person raised the question about which services these older women were using. For example, do older women use the same services as younger women, or do these women only use one or two certain services? This question sparked an additional question for Sharon. She began to wonder if these older women were as satisfied with the services provided by the Women's Support Services as their younger counterparts. Since all clients fill out an evaluation form on the services that they used, Sharon suggested that the staff should analyze the evaluation forms of older clients and younger clients and see if any differences could be determined.

Sharon volunteered to undertake this small research project. She began by asking these questions: Do older women use the same services as younger women? Are older clients as satisfied with the services provided by the Women's Support Services as are younger clients? Only clients which have used services within the last year were included in this study. Sharon chose to analyze the evaluation forms kept in the client's files. Her sampling frame was the intake list which included all clients who had used a service of the Women's Support Services in the past year. She stratified this list by age with older clients being women fifty-five and over and younger women being everyone fifty-four and younger. After choosing a total sample size of forty elements, she randomly chose twenty of the older group and twenty from the younger group and pulled the files for the forty women.

In the next step of this research project, Sharon read through the existing data on the evaluation forms. She discovered that fifteen of the older clients had requested prevention information about rape and crime against women. Only five of the older group had used services for those who had already experienced a violent crime. The number of older women who wanted information on prevention was much higher than the number of younger women. The younger group had more frequently requested services because of experiencing rape or abuse (eighteen out of twenty). Both groups of women were equally satisfied with the services they received; however, each group represented different types of service needs.

Sharon reported this information at the next staff meeting. She observed that the question about satisfaction with using services was less relevant than the fact that older women were using different services than were the younger women. While both younger and older women were satisfied with the services received, Sharon questioned whether education should be planned to include more information about older women and prevention. The staff was invested in redesigning the education curriculum and out-reach program to include a greater number of older women.

Source: Nancy P. Kropf.

Annotated Bibliography

Belsky, J. (1984). *The psychology of aging: Theory, research and practice*. Monterey, CA: Brooks/Cole.
> Designed to meet the needs of undergraduate students studying aging. Integrates research in discussions of theory and practice.

Birren, J. E., Lubben, J. E., Rose, J. C., & Deutchman, D. E. (Eds.). (1991). *The concept and measurement of quality of life in the frail elderly*. New York: Academic Press.
> A series of conceptual writings and research studies aimed at defining and measuring quality of life. It provides a body of knowledge that defines the concept of quality of life in later years, outlines issues of measurement, evaluates existing interventions, and suggests future research directions.

Bloom, M., Duchon, E., Frires, G., Hanson, H., Hurd, G., & South, V. (1971). Interviewing the ill aged. *The Gerontologist, 11*, 292–299.
> Presents practical advice for interviewing the ill elderly. Special interview strategies are provided which are designed to obtain successful interviews with subjects having limitations.

Gelfand, D. E. & Barresi, C. M. (Eds.). (1987). *Ethnic dimensions of aging*. New York: Springer.
> This book focuses on race and ethnicity as it pertains to the experience of older Americans. Part II (Research and Ethnic Dimensions of Aging) includes an interesting variety of research—the elderly Hmong in the United States; religious commitment in the American Jewish community; Amish families; Finnish sunbelt migrants; a comparison of social support among African American, Mexican, and Chinese elderly; and well-being of aged Japanese Canadians.

Gibson, R. C. & Herzog, A. R. (1984). Rare element telephone screening (RETS): A procedure for augmenting the number of black elderly in national samples. *The Gerontologist, 24*, 477–482.
> A description of an innovative sampling technique designed to increase access to elderly African American subjects through contact with younger respondents of a previous study. Method represents a practical, inexpensive way to obtain a nationwide sample of older African Americans.

Glanz, D. & Neikrug, S. (1997). Seniors as researchers in the study of aging: Learning and doing. *The Gerontologist, 37*(6), 823–827.
> The course, developed by Bar-Ilan University Brookdale Program in Applied Gerontology, described in this article teaches elders social gerontology by allowing them to conduct research as active participants in a process of their own design and to generate reports on social issues of importance to the elderly.

Haight, B. K. & Webster, J. D. (Eds). (1995). *The art and science of reminiscing: Theory, research, methods, and applications*. Washington, DC: Taylor and Francis.
> A comprehensive series of articles related to theory, recent research, and methodologies for examining older adults and reminiscence. The chapters on research provide information on methods for collecting and analyzing qualitative data on older persons' life stories.

Hawthorne, V. M. (1994). Aging, health, and health care—issues and data for secondary analysis: An interdisciplinary approach. *Gerontologist, 34*(4), 447–449.
> Identifies limitations of current research on aging and data for secondary analysis. Concerns about the quality of the data include the lack of longitudinal data.

Kane, R. A. & Kane, R. L. (1981). *Assessing the elderly: A practical guide to measurement*. Lexington, MA: Lexington Books.
> Focuses on conducting research in the area of long-term care. Measures of physical, mental, and social functioning, as well as multidimensional measures, are included.

LaVeist, T. A. (1995). Data sources for aging research on racial and ethnic groups. *Gerontologist, 35*(2), 150–161.
> The results of analysis of available data sources supported by federal agencies, specifically the adequacy of sample size for research on minority groups. The author found that the majority of the forty-four data sets reviewed are large enough to conduct research on African American elderly but not other groups such as Hispanics, Asian Americans, and Native Americans.

Lee, G. R. & Finney, J. M. (1977). Sampling in social gerontology: A method of locating specialized populations. *Journal of Gerontology, 32*, 689–693.

Presentation of research writing using a low-cost sampling and method designed to tap non-institutional elderly subjects. Includes detailed description of methods and results.

Luborsky, M. R. (1993). The romance with personal meaning in gerontology: Cultural aspects of life themes. *The Gerontologist, 33*(4), 445–452.

Discusses how to enhance the benefits of life narratives as a qualitative technique, but criticizes the idealization of stories and their benefits. The authors point out that settings and form can constrain their value as research data.

Mangen, D. J. & Peterson, W. A. (Eds.). (1982–1984). *Research instruments in social gerontology*, Vols. 1–3. Minneapolis: University of Minnesota Press.

Provides a comprehensive review of existing instruments in gerontology. Descriptive information, including data on reliability and validity, of the instruments is presented.

McCauley, W. J. (1987). *Applied research in gerontology*. New York: Van Nostrand Reinhold.

An excellent overview of the research process in conducting applied gerontological research. Covers issues, approaches, techniques, and resources particularly relevant to research on aging.

Ray, R. E. (1996). A postmodern perspective on feminist gerontology. *The Gerontologist, 36*(5), 674–680.

This article argues the need for research in feminist gerontology informed by postmodern and poststructuralist theories that challenge the assumption that reason can provide an objective, reliable, and universal foundation for knowledge. Postmodern questions for research include: defining "old woman"; how language constructs gender in gerontology; what metaphors or image of old women are perpetuated in gerontology; and what role do the elderly themselves play in research.

Reinharz, S. & Rowles, G. D. (1988). *Qualitative gerontology*. New York: Springer.

Provides a selection of qualitative methods (in-depth interviewing, field study, participant observation, and ethnography) and their application through exemplars of research. Both the process and substance of qualitative research are reviewed. The book also contains commentaries on qualitative techniques to generate debate.

Romeis J. C., Coe, R. M., & Morley, J. E. (Eds.). (1996). *Applying health services research to long term care*. New York: Springer.

Contains health services evaluations of basic issues in long-term care settings, studies about the effects of HMOs and managed care, and research on the effects of policy on outcomes in nursing homes. In addition, the final section of the book illustrates applications of health services research to the issue of integration of long-term care services.

Schaie, K. W., Campbell, R. T., Meredith, W., & Rawlings, S. C. (Eds.). (1988). *Methodological issues in aging research*. New York: Springer.

Presents selected papers from the National Institutes of Health 1984 Workshop on Methodological Issues in Aging Research. Identifies several methodological problems particular to aging research and discusses approaches to these problems in the area of sampling and generalizability, participant observation, measurement, and longitudinal research.

Special Issue: Qualitative methodology. *Research on Aging*, (1998) *17*(1), 3–116.

In this special journal edition, the authors report that qualitative studies are under represented in gerontology, while the methodology raises important questions about context, process, and cultural meaning. The articles cover a range of relevant topics such as: the way in which qualitative research is a true discipline; the technique of self-reflexivity and analysis of potential bias; principles for evaluating qualitative sampling; and the issue of objectivity in quantitative methods.

Strain, L. A. & Chappell, N. L. (1982). Problems and strategies: Ethical concerns in survey research with the elderly. *The Gerontologist, 22*, 526–531.

Good basic overview of major ethical issues in conducting research with older persons. Includes such topics as obtaining informed, voluntary consent, protecting privacy, avoiding harm, maintaining honesty and meeting the needs of participants.

Zsembik, B. A. (1994). Ethnic and sociodemographic correlates of the use of proxy respondents: The National Survey of Hispanic Elderly People, 1988. *Research on Aging, 16*(4), 401–415.

Considers the use of a spouse, child, or other adult as a proxy respondent for older Latinos. Implications are discussed, including the use of this technique to improve response rates.

General Bibliography

Anderson, M., Foreman, M. D., Theis, S. L., & Lelia B. (1997). Unanticipated results of continuity of care research with the elderly—part 1: Design issues. *Western Journal of Nursing Research, 19*(4), 406–413.

Anderson, M., Foreman, M. D., Theis, S. L., & Lelia, B. (1997). Unacticipated results of continuity of care research with the elderly—part 2: Health system issues. *Western Journal of Nursing Research, 19*(4), 531–535.

Binstock, R. H. & Shanas, E. (Eds.). (1985). *Handbook of aging and the social sciences.* New York: Van Nostrand Reinhold.

Binstock, R. H. & Spector, W. D. (1997). Five priority areas for research on long-term care. *Health Services Research, 32*(5), 715–730.

Birren, J. E. & Shaie, K. W. (1996). *Handbook of the psychology of aging* (4th ed.) New York: Van Nostrand Reinhold.

Borkan, G. A. & Norris, A. H. (1980). Assessment of biological age using a profile of physical parameters. *Journal of Gerontology, 35,* 177–184.

Butler, R. (1968). The life review: An interpretation of reminiscence in the aged. In B. Neugarten (Ed.), *Middle age and aging.* Chicago: University of Chicago.

Carp, F. M. & Carp, A. (1980). Person-environment congruence and sociability. *Research on Aging, 2,* 395–415.

Center for the Study of Aging and Human Development. (1978). *Multidimensional functional assessment: The OARS methodology* (2nd ed.). Durham, NC: CSAHD.

Chapleski, E. E., Lamphere, J. K., Kaczynski, R., Lichtenberg, P. A., & Dwyer, J. W. (1997). Structure of a depression measure among American Indian elders: Confirmatory factory analysis of the CES-D Scale. *Research on Aging, 19*(4), 462–485.

Demos, V. & Jache, A. (1981). When you care enough: An analysis of attitudes toward aging in humorous birthday cards. *The Gerontologist, 21,* 209–215.

Deniston, O. L. & Jette, A. (1980). A functional status assessment instrument: Validation in an elderly population. *Health Services Research, 15,* 21–34.

Ferraro, K. F. (1980). Self-ratings of health among the old and the old-old. *Journal of Health and Social Behavior, 21,* 377–383.

Fillenbaum, G. G. (1979). The longitudinal retirement history study: Methodological and substantive issues. *The Gerontologist, 19,* 203–209.

Fry, C. L. & Keith, J. (Eds.). (1980). *New methods for old age research: Anthropological alternatives.* Chicago: Loyola University of Chicago Center for Urban Policy.

George, L. K. (1979). The happiness syndrome: Methodological and substantive issues in the study of social psychological well-being in adulthood. *The Gerontologist, 19,* 210–216.

Gilford, D. M. (Ed.). (1988). *The aging population in the twenty-first century. Statistics for health policy.* Washington, DC: National Academy Press.

Grigsby, J. S. (1996). The meaning of heterogeneity: An introduction. *Gerontologist, 36*(2), 145–146.

Henretta, J. C. (1979). Using survey data in the study of social stratification in late life. *The Gerontologist, 19,* 197–202.

Kempen, G., Steverink, N., Ormel, J., & Deeg, D. (1996). The assessment of ADL among frail elderly in an interview survey: Self-report versus performance-based tests and determinants of discrepancies. *Journals of Gerontology—Series B: Psychological and Social Sciences, 51*(5), P254-260.

Krause, N. (1996). Welfare participation and self-esteem in later life. *The Gerontologist, 36*(5), 665–673.

Lawton, M. P. & Herzog, A. R. (1989). *Special research methods for gerontology.* Amityville, NY: Baywood.

Leinbach, R. M. (1982). Alternatives to the face-to-face interview for collecting gerontological needs assessment data. *The Gerontologist, 22,* 78–82.

Lemke, S. & Moos, R. (1980). Assessing the institutional policies of sheltered care settings. *Journal of Gerontology, 35,* 96–107.

Macey S. M. & Schneider, D.F. (1995). Frailty and mortality among the elderly. *Journal of Applied Gerontology, 14*(1), 22–33.

Marshall, V. W. (1995). The next half-century of aging research—And thoughts for the past. *Journals of Gerontology—Series B: Psychological and Social Sciences, 50*(3) S131–S133.

Nesselroade, J. R. & Ford, D. H. (1985). P-Technique comes of age: Multivariate, replicated, single-subject designs for research on older adults. *Research on Aging, 7,* 46–80.

North Carolina Rural Aging Program Staff. (1998). *Rural health and aging research: Theory, methods, and practical applications.* Amityville, NY: Baywood.

Pfeiffer, E. (1975). A short portable mental status questionnaire for the assessment of organic brain deficit in elderly patients. *Journal of the American Geriatric Society, 23*(10), 433–441.

Pietrukowicz, M. & Johnson, M. (1991). Using life histories to individualize nursing home staff attitudes towards residents. *The Gerontologist, 31,* 102–106.

Post, J. A. (1996). Internet resources on aging: Data sets and statistics. *The Gerontologist, 36*(4), 425–429.

Post, J. A. (1996). Internet resources on aging: Ten top web sites. *The Gerontologist, 36*(6), 728–733.

Prager, E. (1995). The older volunteer as a research colleague: Toward "generative participation" for older adults. *Educational Gerontology, 21,* 209–218.

Reinharz, S. & Rowles, G. (1988). *Qualitative gerontology.* New York: Springer.

Schaie, K. W. (1977). Quasi-experimental research designs in the psychology of aging. In J. E. Bitten & K. W. Schaie (Eds.), *Handbook of the psychology of aging* New York: Van Nostrand Reinhold.

Schelle, J. F., Uman, G. C., Kulvicki, A. D., Lee, K. O. H., & Ouslander, J. (1997). Selecting nursing home residents for satisfaction surveys. *The Gerontologist, 37*(4), 543–550.

Seltzer, M. M. (1985). Research in social aspects of aging and developmental disabilities. In M. P. Janicki & H. M. Wisniewski (Eds.), *Aging and developmental disabilities: Issues and approaches.* Baltimore, MD: Paul H. Brooks.

Smit, J., Deeg, D. II., & Schmand, B. A. (1997). Asking the age question in elderly populations: A reverse record check study. *Journals of Gerontology—Series B: psychological and Social Sciences, 52*(4), P175–177.

Streib, G.F. (1983). The frail elderly: Research dilemmas and research opportunities. *The Gerontologist, 23,* 40–44.

Tanjasiri, S. P., Wallace, S. P., & Shibata, K. (1995). Picture imperfect: Hidden problems among Asian Pacific Islander elderly. *The Gerontologist, 35*(6), 753–761.

Villeponteaux, L. & DeCoux, V. (1998). Self-report of functional abilities in older adults with mental retardation: ADLs and IADLs. *Journal of Applied Gerontology, 17*(1), 53-66.

Wallace, S. P., Levy-Storms, L., Kingston, R. S., & Andersen, R. M. (1998). The persistence of race and ethnicity in the use of long term care. *Journal of Gerontology, 53B*(2), S104–112.

Wolinsky, F. D., Johnson, R. L., & Stump, T. E. (1995). The risk of mortality among older adults over an eight-year period. *The Gerontologist, 35*(3), 328–339.

Zarit, S. H. (1980). *Aging and mental disorders: psychological approaches to assessment and treatment.* New York: Free Press.

References

Archer, C. K. & MacLean, M. J. (1993). Husbands and sons as caregivers of chronically ill elderly women. *Journal of Gerontological Social Work, 21*(1/2), 5–23.

American Association of Retired Persons. (1997). *A profile of older Americans.* Washington, DC: AARP.

Babbie, E. R. (1998). *The practice of social research* (7th ed.). Belmont, CA: Wadsworth.

Becerra, R. M. & Zambrana, R. E. (1985). Methodological approaches to research on Hispanics. *Social Work Research and Abstracts, 21,* 42–49.

Berman, H. J. (1988). Geropsychology and the personal journal. In Reinharz, S. & Rowles, G. D. (Eds.), *Qualitative gerontology* (pp. 47–63). New York: Springer.

Berghorn, D., Shafer, F., Holmes, D., & Quadagno. J. (1986). The effect of reminiscing on the perceived control and social relations of institutionalized elderly. *Activities, Adaptation, and Aging, 8*, 95–110.

Birren, J. E., Lubben, J. E., Rowe, J. C., & Deutchman, D. E. (Eds.). (1991). *The concept and measurement of quality of life in the frail elderly.* New York: Academic Press.

Bryman, B. & Cramer, D. (1990). *Quantitative data analysis for social scientists.* London: Routledge.

Butler, R. (1968). The life review: An interpretation of reminiscence in the aged. In B. Neugarten, (Ed.), *Middle age and aging.* Chicago: University of Chicago Press.

Cappeliez, P. (1989). Social desirability response set and self-report depression inventories in the elderly. *Clinical Gerontologist, 9*(2), 45–52.

Carstensen, L. L. & Cone, J. D. (1983). Social desirability and the measurement of psychological well-being in elderly persons. *Journal of Gerontology, 38*(6), 713–715.

Center for the Study of Aging and Human Development. (1978). *Multidimensional functional assessment: The OARS methodology* (2nd ed.). Durham, NC: CSAHD.

Demos, V. & Jache, A. (1981). When you care enough: An analysis of attitudes toward aging in humorous birthday cards. *The Gerontologist, 21*, 209–215.

Delgado, M. (1996). Aging research and the Puerto Rican community: The use of an Elder Advisory Committee of intended respondents. *The Gerontologist, 36*(3), 406–408.

Dorfman, R. A., Lubben, J. A., Mayer-Oakes, A., Atchison, K., Schweitzer, S. O., DeJong, F. J., & Matthias, R. E. (1995). Screening for depression among a well-elderly population. *Social Work, 40*(3), 295–305.

Dorfman, R., Walters, K., Burke D., Hardin, L., Karanik, T., Raphael, J., & Silverstein, E. (1995). Old, sad and alone: The myth of the aging homosexual. *Journal of Gerontological Social Work, 24*(1–2), 29–45.

Fries, J. F. & Crapo, L. M. (1981). *Vitality and aging: Implications of the rectangular curve* (pp. 59–67). San Francisco: Freeman.

Gaitz, C. M. & Scott, J. (1975). Analysis of letters to "Dear Abby" concerning old age. *The Gerontologist, 15*, 47–50.

Gibson, R. C. & Stoller, E.P. (1998). Applied gerontology and minority aging: A millenial goal. *Journal of Applied Gerontology, 17*(2), 124–129.

Haight, B. K. & Webster, J. D. (Eds). (1995). *The art and science of reminiscing: Theory, research, methods, and applications.* Washington, DC: Taylor and Francis.

Hennessy, C. H. & John, R. (1996). American Indian family caregivers perceptions of burden and needed support services. *Journal of Applied Gerontology, 15*(3), 275–293.

Jackson, S. A. & Mittelmark, M. B. (1997). Unmet needs for formal home and community services among African American and white older adults: The Forsyth County aging study. *Journal of Applied Gerontology, 16*(3), 298–316.

Kane, R. A. & Kane, R. L. (1981). *Assessing the elderly: A practical guide to measurement.* Lexington, MA: Lexington Books.

Kish, L. (1965). *Survey sampling.* New York: Wiley.

Kisor, A. J. (1996). Nursing facility agreements: An analysis of selected content. *Journal of Applied Gerontology, 15*(3), 294–313.

Kulka, R. A., Herzog, A. R., & Rodgers, W. L. (1980). *Age differences in the effect of telephone and personal interviewing made on the survey interview process.* Paper presented at the 33rd meeting of the Gerontological Society of America, San Diego, California.

LaVeist, T. A. (1995). Data sources for aging research on racial and ethnic groups. *The Gerontologist, 35*(2), 150–161.

Leinbach, R. M. (1982). Alternatives to the face-to-face interview for collecting gerontological needs assessment data. *The Gerontologist, 22*, 78–82.

Luborsky, M. R. (1993). The romance with personal meaning in gerontology: Cultural aspects of life themes. *The Gerontologist, 33*(4), 445–452.

MacPherson, K. I. (1988). Dilemmas of participant-observation in a menopause collective. In Reinharz, S. & Rowles, G. D. (Eds.), *Qualitative gerontology* (pp. 184–196). New York: Springer.

McCauley, W. J. (1987). *Applied research in gerontology*. New York: Van Nostrand Reinhold.

McCauley, W. J., Arling, G., Nutty, C., & Bowling, C. (1994). *Final report of the statewide survey of older Virginians* (Research Series No. 3). Richmond: Virginia Commonwealth University, Virginia Center on Aging.

Markides, K. S. (1998). Challenges to minority aging research in the next century (editorial). *Journal of Applied Gerontology, 17*(2), 129–133.

Miller, D. C. (1991). *Handbook of research design and measurement* (5th ed.). New York: McKay.

Monette, D. R., Sullivan, T. J., & DeJong, C. R. (1998). *Applied social research: Tool for the human services*. (4th ed.). New York: Holt, Rinehart & Winston.

Mueller, D. (1986). *Measuring social attitudes*. New York: Columbia.

Mui, A. C. & Burnette, D. (1994). Long-term care service use by frail elders: Is ethnicity a factor? *The Gerontologist, 34*(2) 190–198.

Neal, M. B., Carder, P. C., & Morgan, D. L. (1996). Use of public records to compare respondents and nonrespondents in a study of recent widows. *Research on Aging, 18*(2), 219–242.

Neugarten, B. L., Havighurst, R. J., & Tobin, S.S. (1961). The measure of life satisfaction. *Journal of Gerontology, 16*, 134–143.

Norton, M. C., Breitner, J. C. S., & Welsh, K. A. (1994). Characteristics of nonresponders in a community survey of elderly. *Journal of the American Geriatrics Society, 42*, 1252–1256.

Oppenheim, A. N. (1989). *Questionnaire design and attitude measurement*. New York: Basic Books.

Parkerson, G. R., Broadhead, W. E., & Tse, C. J. (1990). The Duke Health Profile: A 17-item measure of health and dysfunction. *Medical Care, 28*, 1056–1072.

Pillemer, K. (1988). Combining qualitative and quantitative data in the study of elder abuse. In Reinharz, S. & Rowles, G. D. (Eds.), *Qualitative gerontology* (pp. 256–273). New York: Springer.

Reid, W. J. & Smith, A. D. (1989). *Research in social work*. New York: Columbia University Press.

Reinharz, S. & Rowles, G. (1988). Qualitative gerontology: Themes and challenges. In Reinharz, S. & Rowles, G. D. (Eds.), *Qualitative gerontology* (pp. 3–33). New York: Springer.

Rosenthal, R. & Rosnow, R. L. (1991). *Essentials of behavioral research: Methods and data analysis* (2nd ed.). New York: McGraw-Hill.

Rubin, A. & Babbie, E. (1997). *Research methods for social work* (3rd ed.). Pacific Grove, CA: Brooks/Cole.

Schaie, K. W., Campbell, R. T., Meredith, W., & Rawlings, S. C. (Eds.). (1988). *Methodological issues in aging research*. New York: Springer.

Stanley, J. C. & Hopkins, K. D. (1972). *Educational and psychological measurement and evaluation*. Englewood Cliffs, NJ: Prentice-Hall.

Steiner, A., Rabue, K., Stuck, A. E., Aronow, H. U., Draper, D., Rubenstein, L. Z., & Beck, J. C. (1995). Measuring psychosocial aspects of well-being in older community residents: performance of four short scales. *The Gerontologist, 36*(1), 54–62.

Stewart, D. W. & Kamins, M. A. (1993). *Applied social research methods series, Volume 4. Secondary research: Information sources and methods* (2nd ed.). Newbury Park, CA: Sage.

Sudman, S. (1976). *Applied sampling*. New York: Academic Press.

Torres-Gil, F. (1992). *The new aging: Politics and change in America*. Westport, CT: Auburn House.

Wolinsky, F. D., Johnson, R. L., & Stump, T. E. (1995). The risk of mortality among older adults over an eight-year period. *The Gerontologist, 35*(3), 328–339.

Yesavage, J. A. & Brink, T. L. (1983). Development and validation of a geriatric depression screening scale: A preliminary report. *Journal of Psychiatric Research, 17*, 37–49.

Zung, W. W. & Zung, E. M. (1986). Use of the Zung Self-Rating Depression Scale in the elderly. *Clinical Gerontologist, 5*(1–2), 137–148.

■ ■ ■ ■ ■ ■ ■ ■ ■ ■ ■ ■ ■ ■ ■

Margaret M. Robinson

Case management is a practice model used for many years in the helping professions, especially social work. The professional roots of case management were heavily influenced by social and economic changes in this country. As our lives became more complex, the interaction of need and service became more complicated. The current era of privatization of social programs and "downsizing" of mandated services has increased the need for case managers. Today, few agencies are equipped to handle all of the needs of their clients. Case management services are needed to address the complexity of need and service provision.

As defined by the National Association of Social Workers (NASW 1992), social work case management "is a method of providing services whereby a professional social worker assesses the needs of the client and client's family, and, when appropriate, arranges, coordinates, monitors, evaluates, and advocates for a package of multiple services to meet the specific client's complex needs" (p. 7). The case management model of service is applicable to many types of clients including long-term mentally ill, children, families, elderly, and institutionalized individuals. While case managers are used in many settings, they are especially important in the field of gerontology. Given the possibility of complex medical, social, economic, and legal issues inherent in the aging process, case management practice provides a model that identifies issues, assesses needs, provides links with services, and follows-up on progress so that the best possible services are offered to the elderly individual.

This chapter provides an overview of case management and addresses how this practice model is used in specific gerontological settings. Although several models exist, this chapter employs Rothman's (1994) comprehensive model of general case management. Various tasks and roles of the case manager are described from the beginning phase of identifying a client to evaluation of the service plan.

Case Management Practice

Historical Perspective

The development of case management parallels the evolution of the practice of social work. Case management practice in human services began as early as 1863 with the need to coordinate services for children and the development of the first Board of Charities (Weil & Karls 1985). The plight of poor and orphaned children and widowed adults in the late 1800s in the United States is well-documented (Trattner 1989). As society began to respond to poverty, disease, and abuse, agencies developed to address these difficulties.

By the beginning of the twentieth century, social problems largely became a responsibility of churches that ministered to the poor, but need quickly outstripped available resources. In 1901, Mary Richmond developed a clinical model that marked the beginning of professional case management. Additionally, the model initiated by Jane Addams at Hull House utilized case management techniques to keep track of the poor with a goal to connect the needy with available services in the community (Weil & Karls 1985).

During the 1920s, the Community Chest Movement necessitated further coordination of services. Means-tested eligibility played an important part in Community Chest services. Knowledge of eligibility requirements was essential for care coordination. The child guidance movement also emphasized a care coordination approach that was very similar to case management. Individual and community hardships that arose as a result of the Great Depression and World War I and II contributed to demand for case management services. Coordination of scarce resources became a critical issue. Massive unemployment during the Great Depression, particularly among African American and blue-collar workers, left many families without food, clothing, medical care, heating, and shelter (Day 1988). Returning World War II soldiers had employment, medical, and psychological needs. Both an assessment of the soldiers' needs and eligibility for services were necessary. Case management services were developed to handle the diverse and complex problems of veterans (Weil & Karls 1985). Professionals began to appreciate the relationship between case management, or care coordination services, and assessing and addressing needs in an increasingly complex service environment.

As a result of social, medical, and demographic changes, an emergence of different case management models developed in the 1970s. The term "case management" began to appear in the literature during the early part of the decade and was used in professional language in 1974 (Weil & Karls 1985). An increase in homelessness, deinstitutionalization, poverty, Vietnam veterans, and individuals with HIV/AIDS contributed to the further rise in the need for case management services (Rose & Moore 1995). Additionally, the aging of the population and the growing numbers of individuals with chronic disease contributed to a need for a system that could both coordinate and share needs (Anker-Unnever, & Netting 1995). Recently, the shift to managed care in health services has also highlighted the need for case managers in medical settings. In a managed care service context, the case manager may have the role of coordinating services, as well as containing health care costs.

Traditionally, the focus of social work assessment and service is on the person-in-environment (PIE) configuration (Germain 1991). In this model, the social work case manager assesses health and functioning needs of an older client, and also addresses psychosocial functioning and sources of formal and informal support. While it is one of the oldest models of social work practice, case management continues to be an important professional role in the current service delivery system.

Case Management in Gerontology

Case management is an important practice model with older adults. As individuals age, they begin to require services from various service delivery systems. For example, an older woman who has health problems such as high blood pressure and diabetes may need to be under the care of multiple health provides (e.g., physician, nurse, nutritionist). She may also need to access public welfare in order to receive Medicaid or be involved in community services by participating in a congregate meal program and a senior volunteer program. In all, this older woman may see as many as six service providers in three different service delivery networks.

As one might imagine, this arrangement can be confusing and can create bureaucratic or access barriers for older adults.

Case managers work with older clients in a variety of settings. Many programs within the aging service network include a case management component. Specific types of settings that employ gerontological case managers are senior centers, home health care, and nursing home Medicaid-waiver programs. However, case managers in age-integrated settings may also work with older clients. For example, case managers in developmental disabilities or mental health settings may be working with more older adults, as clients experience increased life spans. Therefore, social work case managers in numerous service settings will find that older adults are part of the caseload.

Case managers link clients to services and advocate on the client's behalf when barriers to access are experienced. Emlet (1996) provides the example of older adults with AIDS, who number over one-half million in the United States. Linking the older HIV client to an appropriate service may be difficult since many HIV programs are designed for younger cohorts. Grandparents who are raising their grandchildren are another group that often has difficulty accessing services (Burton 1992; Minkler et al. 1993). Although 1.5 million children live in primary care of their grandparent (AARP 1995), many of these caregivers do not have legal custody and are not able to access services for the children.

Case management with older adults may also introduce some complex, ethical issues. One dilemma occurs when the case manager must judge whether an older adult is competent to make independent decisions, for example, continuing to live in the community with limited resources, being noncompliant with medical treatment, or staying in an unhealthy or unsafe situation. Another dilemma is balancing responsibility between the agency and the client. This type of conflict arises in such situations as, for example, when an agency tries to reduce costs and a client needs to receive services past the designated time limit. With managed care, case managers increasingly have to make decisions about service that balance the needs of the client and the budgetary and time constraints that are imposed on programs that serve older adults.

Core Case Management Function Applied to Gerontological Social Work

Although many models of care management services exist, there are common core functions that are found throughout the models as described by White (1986).

- *Case Finding*—determining eligibility for services.
- *Assessment*—determining the needs and resources of clients.
- *Service Planning*—constructing service goals to meet the needs of clients.
- *Coordination*—constructing a plan that links various formal resources and informal supports.
- *Follow-up*—monitoring to ensure that services in the service plan are being provided.
- *Reassessment*—reevaluating whether the plan is sufficient, or whether changes in the client's condition or services/support are still available.

The following case example illustrates some of these core functions of case management. Mrs. Jones, an eighty-four-year-old widow, was able to live alone and care for herself until she fell in her home, breaking her leg. The hospital discharge planner contacted the local area

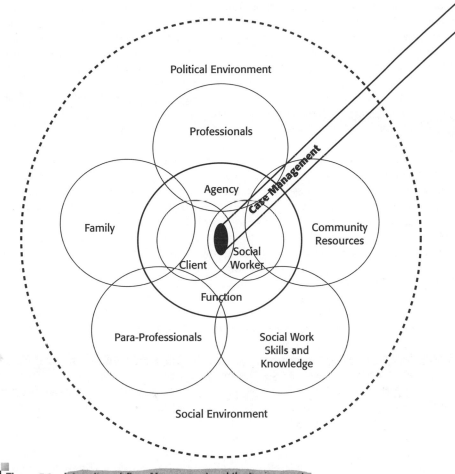

■ **Figure 5.1** Interaction of Case Management and the Environment

agency on aging (AAA), a network of services that includes a case management program. The case manager visited Mrs. Jones at the hospital to determine her postdischarge needs. These will include several forms of support such as: a nurse aide, a volunteer to do her shopping, and a home aide to help her clean and cook. The case manager also assesses informal services available to the client. Importantly, Mrs. Jones has a neighbor who can provide informal support by bringing in the mail and doing some errands. The case manager's role is to set up the formal services and monitor effectiveness. The case manager will also reevaluate Mrs. Jones's recuperation progress to determine when services can be terminated.

Case management occurs within the interaction of various components including social work knowledge, agency function, community resources, professional and paraprofessional support, and family. In figure 5.1, the case management process is depicted as taking place within a particular political environment (what types of case management programs will be funded, for example), and social environment (for example, service provision model chosen by agency). The supposition is that the core functions of case management act as an "anchor" for the intersection of political environment, social environment, community resources, social work skills and knowledge, family, professional and paraprofessional workers, agency function, client, social worker, and service delivery.

Although general case management shares certain core functions, there are some important differences among case management models. Case management is also referred to as care management, managed care, care coordination, continuing care coordination, continuity coordination, service integration, and service coordination (Secord 1987). It is also important to realize that case managers may come from disciplines other than social work. While case management is one of the primary domains of social work, nurses also claim the term "case management." However, nurse case managers frequently do not offer the same services as social work case managers. Nurses are involved in coordinating patient care between several different kinds of medical needs, including both inpatient and outpatient services. However, social or environmental needs may not be addressed (Cronin & Maklebust 1989). For example, once a patient is out of the hospital, nursing case management ceases. Adjustment back to a new home or to a nursing home environment may not be included in the nursing case management plan. While some of the roles of nursing case managers and social work case managers may overlap, social work's focus is more a biopsychosocial model. For example, the social work case manager will assess a client's adaptation to a new health status or role, the impact on family caregivers, and the financial needs that a health problem may cause. If any of these or related issues develop, the case manager will identify resources such as a caregiver support group.

One way of classifying case management models is by the focus of service that is provided by the case manager (Goodman 1987). Rose and Moore (1995) delineate case management models as "client driven" versus "provider driven." In a client-driven model, the clients are actively involved in constructing the service plan. Strengths are identified and developed and used to guide the development of the case plan (Sullivan & Fisher 1994; Whitley, White, Kelley, & Yorke 1999). Goals are derived directly from the client's needs and wishes, and both informal and formal supports are utilized. Evaluation is then determined by the amount of autonomy, self-confidence, and use of informal networks that the client develops. This model is common in providing services to clients with developmental disabilities. As parents age, they may become less able to manage the tasks of caring for a son or daughter with a disability. In a client-centered planning process, the case manager often invites the family and other sources of support (e.g., close friends, minister/rabbi) to a series of meetings to determine future care plans. This process includes discussions about possible options, such as having the person with a disability move into a supervised living situation, or bringing assistance into the home, such as respite care. In all phases of case management, the wishes, desires, and goals of the family are critical components in constructing a service plan.

A similar model of case management, one that also focuses on the client, is the consumer-driven model. Riley, Fortinskey, and Cogburn (1992) developed a consumer-centered, negotiated case management model for home care quality assurance. In this case management model, the emphasis is on the outcome of the entire plan of care, not just on the effectiveness of discrete services. This model involves a fundamental change in the way that case managers think about clients, who are conceptualized as the consumer of services.

This model includes four main components: consumer assessment, care planning, monitoring, and assessment of services. Within each of these areas, the consumer is expected to exercise choice, be provided access to a broad range of services within his or her community, be physically safe and free from exploitation, and maintain opportunities to relationships and community participation.

Case manager characteristics are important in this model. Nufer, Rosenberg, & Smith (1998) found that elderly clients responded best to case management services when treated with respect and dignity. Further, elderly clients expected services that were timely, adequate, delivered with enthusiasm, and sensitive to consumer needs. In contrast, clients are "acted upon" in the provider-driven model. The case manager's goal is to identify problems and manage them. Case managers may act as "eligibility case managers" or "gatekeepers" to determine whether a client can access agency resources. The client is then expected to comply with the service plan developed by the case manager. An example is a substance abuse treatment program where a case manager determines eligibility for an inpatient program. Based upon the information about the client's health, level of addiction, and type of insurance that he or she carries, the individual will be admitted to the program for a certain length of time. Primarily, the evaluation is determined not by how well the client attains his or her goals (e.g., detoxification) but instead on units of services and cost containment. Until recently, there was largely anecdotal information on the effectiveness of case management. However, it has been found that case managers are able to help reduce hospitalizations for the elderly and to enhance their feelings of safety and comfort at home (Bernabei, Landi, Gambassi, Sgadari, et al. 1998). Netting and Williams (1999) sought to integrate case managers with physicians. Case managers were viewed by the physicians as an advocate for clients and a resource allocation mechanism to contain the cost of care as well as an enhancement of primary care for the elderly. The case manager's ability to understand family dynamics and to serve as the "eyes and ears" of the physician was very important to the physicians who came to appreciate and utilize case managers. Vanchieri (1998) also reported increased patient satisfaction when case managers became an ancillary to the physician.

A "task-centered" case management model specifically for older adults has been developed by two social workers (Naleppa & Reid 1998). The focus of task-centered case management is on specific tasks that can be taken to ameliorate the problems that a client is experiencing. To the greatest extent possible, the case manager gives the client (or clients' family) responsibility for following through on tasks prior to the next session. For example, a family may be having difficulty trying to decide whether an older family member should move into a nursing home. One task may be to have the family visit three nursing homes within a two week period. For each facility, the family prepares a list of advantages and disadvantages. During the next session, the case manager reviews this information with the family and establishes the next task, which could be setting up a follow-up visit with the most acceptable facility or selecting three additional facilities if none were satisfactory. This model emphasizes the self-determination of the client and clearly establishes roles and goals.

As described here, case management involves the interrelationship of all components of a client's life. Since most aging services include a variety of providers, the case manager must involve and interact with a variety of other professionals and paraprofessionals. Importantly, the service plan will combine formal and informal resources to address the needs of the older client.

Case Management Tasks and Roles

The range of tasks that a case manager may perform is directly related to the agency function and client need. Each task may include several different roles. The case manager may be required to provide counseling, linking of services, coordination of resources, and advocacy for the same client.

Rothman (1994) developed a comprehensive model of client-driven case management. While applicable in any case management setting, the breadth and flexibility of this model is particularly useful in aging services. The needs of older adults, as well as adults with disabilities, are complex. Rothman's model includes the interaction of skills, knowledge, and resources that provide comprehensive case management addressing the complex needs of elderly clients. Gerontological case managers can "plug" their client into any part of the model and understand the roles, tasks, and possible services needed. This model is shown in figure 5.2.

Rothman's model begins with either outreach or referral to an agency. In concert with the client-driven framework, the client is directly involved in the process. In addition to determining eligibility for services, intake includes a psychological, medical, and social assessment of the client. After goal setting, service planning, resource identification, and indexing co-exist to provide the best services for the client. Service coordination, or linking an individual to needed services provided by other agencies or by informal support services, completes the identification and planning phase of the model. Final core functions include monitoring for service effectiveness and reassessment when appropriate. Outcome evaluations allow both the worker and the client to understand the accomplishments.

Rothman (1992) delineated several important complementary tasks to accompany case management core functions outlined in the model.

Case finding

- Client identification and outreach—bringing clients into the case management program. The tasks include both intake and referral as clients come to the agency from a wide variety of sources. At the point of intake or referral, assessment of eligibility begins.
- Intake—gathering information about the client, including current functioning and psychosocial history. Intake may also include a decision about what additional information on the client is needed.

Assessment

- Individual assessment or diagnosis—determining needs and resources of client. This assessment may include psychological, physical, and mental capabilities. Assessment tasks also include gathering information from a variety of sources, including the client, family, and other professionals involved with the client.

Service planning

- Goal setting—constructing goals and objectives that will address the needs of the client. This task involves understanding and synthesizing information gained in the assessment phase, reviewing the information in conjunction with client input. Obtainable, objective goals are needed for future monitoring and evaluation.

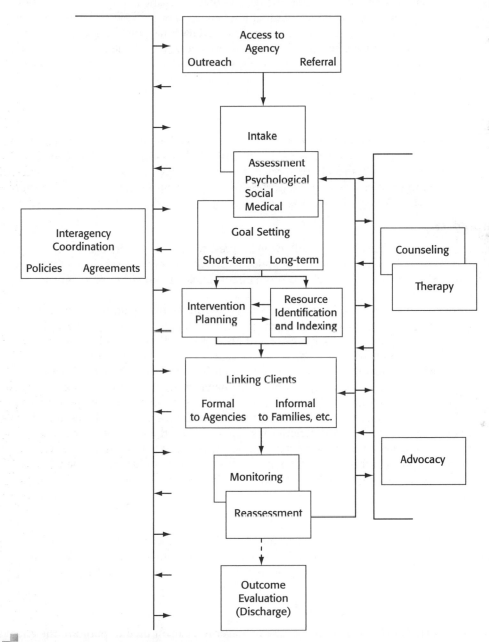

Figure 5.2 Rothman Case Management Model

■ Resource identification—determining formal and informal resources that are available in the environment. At this point, the task involves assessing resources discovered in the initial assessment function. Coordination between new and old resources is essential.
■ Service planning—constructing a plan that identifies how various resources can achieve goals that have been established by case manager and client. The case management must interweave resources, needs, wishes, and assessment to form a viable service plan. If any one element of the process is neglected, the resulting service plan has less chance of being successful.

Coordination

■ Linking clients to needed services and supports—assisting client to become involved with various services, including making referrals, helping client complete eligibility process, and so on. If tasks in the previous functions have been successfully completed, coordination will be a facilitation process. When previous tasks were not successfully completed, coordination may involve returning to an earlier function.

Follow-up

■ Monitoring service delivery—following progress toward service goals to determine that the client is receiving services. The tasks involved in monitoring service delivery include assessing both the service and the client. Difficulty on either part can lead to holes in the service plan.
■ Reassessment—reevaluating service goals to determine if the plan needs to be modified due to a change in a client's situation or problems with service provision. Reassessment is an ongoing process. Reassessment ensures that the service plan continues to meet the needs of the client.
■ Advocacy—acting on behalf of a client to eradicate any barriers to services that may exist. This task is also an ongoing one. Case managers should address gaps in service delivery and use their knowledge and expertise to advocate for new or different services.
■ Evaluation (individual level)—determining a client's progress toward established goals. For example, has the client's functioning improved? At the point of evaluation, the task may include termination or redesigning the service plan to ensure a better or more appropriate service plan. Changes both in services offered and in the needs of the client contribute to the importance of the task of evaluation.

The tasks delineated by Rothman provide the basic framework for the generalist case management model. Specific operationalization of core functions and tasks necessary to successfully complete each function in Rothman's case management model is different for older adults. The following section applies these tasks to gerontological social work. Additional frameworks are also introduced to supplement Rothman's generalist model.

Referral, Intake, and Assessment

Norris and Hill (1991) state that the case manager role is best used to optimize the client's and the family's abilities to meet their needs. The goal is to increase or maintain the client's quality of life. The two initial steps in this process are: (1) connecting with the older adult and (2) gathering preliminary information through the assessment process.

■ **Table 5.1**   Knowledge Needed for Quality Case Management

Knowledge of	Area
Physical/Health Issues	Physical/biological changes in aging
	Symptoms and implication of illnesses and diseases common among older people
	Common medications used by elders, their effects, side-effects, signs of misuse/abuse
	Health promotion and disease prevention issues for older people
	Nutrition issues and the impact of nutrition problems on elders
Psychological/Mental Health	Psychological processes related to aging
	Issues related to death, dying, bereavement, and how to work with these issues
	The cognitive processes related to aging
	Cognitive disorders
	Normal developmental issues over the life span
	Family dynamics and understanding family relationships
	Elder abuse issues
	Issues related to working with younger, disabled populations
Social Issues/Resources	Social issues related to aging
	Legal issues
	Understanding policies that influence the lives of elders
	Resources available in the community to assist with needs of elders
	Resources available in the community to assist with the needs of younger, disabled people

Source: Diwan, Berger & Ivy 1996.

One of the first roles of the case manager is that of outreach worker. Outreach can take many forms and is determined by the mission of the agency (Diwan, Berger, & Ivy 1996). If the gerontological social worker is employed in an agency that brokers services (e.g., refers clients outside of the agency), the role of outreach will be to assess the client and find needed services. If the outreach worker is employed by a facility that provides direct service to the elderly, the role will be that of screening the client to ascertain eligibility (Goodman 1987).

After the older client is connected to the agency, the intake process begins. Diwan, Berger, and Ivy (1996) offer several broad categories of knowledge that are needed to complete the intake process. These categories include: physical/health issues, psychological/mental health, and social issues/resources. Older clients, especially the frail elderly, may have many health and functional issues. These health problems and/or medication interactions can cause or contribute to psychological problems (e.g., disorientation, agitation, depression). During an intake, the case manager needs to use good practice skills, such as engaging the client, clarifying the situation, responding to the client as a unique individual, and exploring negative as well as positive aspects of the client's situation (Rothman 1994). Therefore, gerontological case managers need to have good practice skills as well as a solid foundation in social work values. Table 5.1 outlines the specific areas that Diwan, Berger, and Ivy (1996) propose that the gerontological social worker needs to know to provide quality service.

During an assessment, the case manager may use assessment instruments to aid in the determination of several areas of functioning and need. Mosley and DeWeaver (1998) critiqued client scales that are appropriate for case management with the elderly. These include the Symptom Checklist {SCL-90-R} (Deragotis, Lipman, & Covi 1973), which measures a variety of difficulties include depression and anxiety; the Life Satisfaction Index-Z (Neugarten, Havighurst, & Tobin 1961), which assesses life satisfaction in older adults; the Rosenberg Self-Esteem Index (Rosenberg 1979), which measures self-esteem; and the Symptom Questionnaire (SQ) (Kellner 1987), which measures psychopathology and well-being. In addition, Mosely and DeWeaver (1998) suggest that case managers also perform a qualitative evaluation of their clients. A structured or semistructured interview to assess both instrumental and emotional/cognitive needs will enlarge and enrich the understanding of strengths and needs of an older client.

Therapeutic skills may also be necessary in case management with elderly individuals and their families (Johnson & Rubin 1983; Lamb 1980). Psychosocial issues can present barriers to using services and need to be addressed by the case manager. Examples of clinical aspects of case management with frail elders include dealing with issues of loneliness, losses, coming to grips with their aging process, and managing their own sense of independence (Soares & Rose 1994).

Here is an example of case management with an older client where the worker uses clinical skills, and collects information about the client and available resources: Mr. Payne is a seventy-six-year-old American Indian who has lived alone for many years and does not want people to bother him. He has started losing his eyesight, and his relatives fear for his safety. At the time that the case manager met Mr. Payne, he was adamant that he did not want to move. Although he was initially resistant to help from any services, the case manager developed a positive relationship by learning about his reason for remaining independent as possible. The worker came to understand that Mr. Payne's resistance to using services is related to his sense of what an older man, specifically an older American Indian man, should be able to accomplish. In addition, the case manager began to construct an impression about the type of assistance that might be acceptable to Mr. Payne, such as cooking and cleaning. Those areas were both problems due to declining sight.

After determining the need for service, the case manager worked to connect Mr. Payne to homemaking resources, which he eagerly anticipated. Unfortunately, his Social Security was insufficient to cover these costs, and he did not qualify for any other funds. In collecting information about the client, however, the case manager discovered that he owns land on the Cherokee Indian Reservation. Even though he does not live there, he may be entitled to a distribution of tribal funds.

At this point in service provision, the role of the case manager is to help Mr. Payne discover if he is eligible for these funds. If he is eligible, the next role is to link Mr. Payne with the agencies that distribute the monies. When funds have been secured, the case manager would return to a linking role in helping Mr. Payne to find the appropriate home care worker. Finally, the case manager would continue to monitor and evaluate the success of the arrangement and the quality of Mr. Payne's health.

As this example illustrates, several areas are important to case management with Mr. Payne. The first is knowledge of resources currently used, such as appointments with physicians, recent visits to emergency rooms, and participation in senior service programs. Second, some dimensions of psychological functioning may also be critical, such as sleep

■ **Table 5.2**   Case Management Dimensions and Levels

Dimensions	Levels
Living arrangement	alone, with spouse, with family
Residence	hotel, apartment, family's home
Interaction with informal supports	good relationship, strained relationship
Level of informal ADL support	minimal, moderate, or extensive
Arthritis	slow, moderate, high severity
Stroke	residuals low, moderate, high severity
Diabetes	low, moderate, high severity
Pulmonary disease	low, moderate, high severity
Heart disease	low, moderate, high severity
Dementia	low, moderate, high severity
Medical stability	stable, moderately stable, unstable
Functional status	minimum, moderate, major impairment, total impairment except eating, total impairment
Client preference	has no preference, has a preference
Behavior	no problem, managed with some effort, noncompliant with treatment, noncompliant and yells, totally noncompliant and hits
Continence	no problem, minor, moderate incontinence, total incontinence
Day health care attendance	attends 2, 3, 4, 5, 6, 7 days a week
In-home supportive care	receives no in-home care, receives in-home supervision, receives AM/PM care 7 days a week
Day health center demand	attendance below, at, or over capacity
Communal living facilities	placements below, at, or over capacity
Home care department	few overnights cases, moderate number of overnight cases, many overnight cases
Staff burden level	few "heavy care" cases, moderate number of "heavy care" cases, many "heavy care" cases

Source: Hennessy 1993, p. 335.

disorders, disorientation, or memory loss. These symptoms may indicate a need for a more thorough assessment for depression, dementia, or other condition. Third, social knowledge should also be included, such as an understanding of the completion of advance directives and frequency of contact with family members and other sources of support. Together, these provide a person-in-environment (PIE) assessment of the client (Anker-Unnever & Netting 1995).

Service Planning: Developing a Strategy for Action

As the case manager gathers information about current needs and resources, this information is constructed into a case plan that identifies service goals. However, it is important to be aware that the process of assessment is ongoing, culminating in a reassessment after completion of the case plan. Hennessy (1993) provides a framework for an ongoing assessment process useful for work with older adults. The dimensions of the assessment include information from all members of the case management team—social workers, nurses, home health care providers, and doctors.

Hennesey (1993) provides an example of a case plan using the ongoing assessment process.

The client is an eighty-five-year-old Chinese female, Mrs. Hu, who lives alone in a single-room occupancy (SRO) hotel. She has received a moderate amount of assistance with Activities of Daily Living (ADLs) from her informal supports with whom she has a strained relationship. Her medical problems include congestive heart disease, requiring medication for chronic peripheral edema and lung congestion, and minimal residual effects from a stroke suffered a year ago. The client has been hospitalized more than a week within the past month for exacerbation of chronic disease, and she occasionally experiences urinary incontinence during the day. She needs help with some Instrumental Activities of Daily Living (IADLs), especially cooking, cleaning, and shopping, and needs supervision for bathing. Mrs. Hu frequently yells at staff and other clients and is noncompliant with her care plan (refuses to take medications).

She attends the day health center five days a week and receives A.M. or P.M. care only to supervise medications or assist with meal preparation. The client does not have a strong preference about remaining in her current living situation or in maintaining the current service plan. In analyzing resources that are available, the case manager gathered information about current services. Attendance at the day health center is at capacity but Communal Living has several available beds. The Home Care department currently has a moderate number of cases requiring overnight stays. The day health center currently has many "heavy care" cases with numerous crises during the past three months. (p. 336)

The case plan for this client should incorporate the desires and resources of this client into an organized plan of action that targets appropriate services that will address her complex needs. In reviewing the assessment of Mrs. Hu, the case manager develops an overall picture of Mrs. Hu as a woman who is difficult, yet lonely. She has some moderate impairment but appears to easily alienate her helpers. Based on Mrs. Hu's decision to stay in her home, the case manager develops a case plan with Mrs. Hu that includes both increasing formal and informal supports and commitment from Mrs. Hu to be more cooperative.

This example, and that of Mr. Payne, highlights both relationship and multicultural issues in case management. Perceptions of the need for services can be related to both worker and client identity and cultural background. While Mr. Payne was able to accept assistance with housekeeping and cooking, an older woman might have more difficulty with these two areas, since these are traditionally female tasks. Case managers should assess how things such as ethnicity, gender role expectations, and functional and cognitive limitations impact service preference and utilization. For example, a hearing impaired elderly client may be frustrated and refuse to return to a senior center with large crowds. The noise of a crowd may make using his hearing aid impossible. Having a male attendant may be very difficult for an elderly Asian woman. A male attendant may violate culture norms around the relationships between men and women. An elderly African-American man may be uncomfortable with both Caucasian male or female attendants. Cultural issues are relevant to work with clients of all ages.

Intervention planning involves using the assessment to develop a case plan that is comprehensive and doable. In the process of developing the case plan, the case manager should begin to determine appropriate techniques for accomplishing the goals. The client should be involved in the case planning as much as possible. Case plans developed with, rather than for, a client are far more likely to succeed. Older adults need and respond well to an opportunity to have input into their care and control over their lives.

Age: 85 years
Ethnicity: Chinese
Living Arrangement: Lives alone
Interaction with Informal Supports: Has a strained relationship
Level of Informal IADL Support: Moderate impairment—Needs moderate help from informal
   helpers for cooking, cleaning, and shopping
Stroke Residuals: Low severity from a stroke suffered one year ago
Heart Disease: Has congestive heart disease, resulting from edema and lung congestion
Behavioral Manageability: Noncompliant and yells
Day Health Care Attendance: Attends five days per week
In-home Supportive Care: Receives no in-home supportive care
Day Health Care Demand: Attendance is at capacity
Community Living Facilities Demand: Placement is below capacity
Staff Burden Level: Many "heavy care" cases

■ **Figure 5.3**   Dimensions of Case Assessment with an Eighty-Five-Year-Old Woman (Hennessy 1993)

Service Coordination: Defining and Linking

After an assessment is performed and a case plan is developed, the next step in case management is to identify resources for the client. The linking phase of case management is not simply a referral function. Linking clients to agencies includes assertive implementation, such as providing transportation, accompanying the client to the agency, and possibly assisting with intake in another agency (Rothman 1992). Case managers should develop resources on a ongoing basis. In his subsequent book on case management, Rothman (1994) identifies the maintaining of information about resources, as well as keeping current on their available services and participation guidelines, as an essential part of case management. Service coordination depends upon the ability of the case manager to be familiar with the rapidly changing array of services and providers.

In the beginning of the provision of services, case managers need to understand client barriers to services. Applebaum and Christianson (1988) described several common service delivery problems that case managers and their clients faced. These problems included poor quality of service, incomplete service delivery, exploitation of clients, and high turnover among homemaker/personal care workers. The trend is to rely on case managers to monitor and evaluate services. Consequently, an additional task/role is monitoring providers and exposing serious deficiencies in service delivery.

An essential part of defining and linking services is understanding the function of the agency. This information should include access and eligibility for services, as well as knowledge of fee structure. In the process of gathering this information, the case manager should assess quality of the service provided, climate and accommodations of the agency, and key people in the system (Rothman 1994). The case manager should provide personal support for the client as they are linking to the various services. This action is especially important for older adults. Navigating the maze of providers and services is not always easy for the case manager. As the following example illustrates, it can also be overwhelming for the older adult.

Mr. Quincy has several medical problems and has been referred to several specialists. He also attends a Senior Center and receives Social Security and home health services. His case manager did a good job of linking him to the various services but did not follow up with him about the services. Mr. Quincy has to navigate all of the providers himself. Consequently, he frequently shows up for an appointment on the wrong day or goes to the Senior Center on the days he is to be home for home health services. As this example illustrates, linking services includes not only identifying sources but helping the client navigate, negotiate, and structure them.

Informal links are often as important as formal connections, and case managers should explore possible options with the older client. In addition to linking with community resources, other possible resources include consulting with families and other caregivers, and monitoring and expanding social networks of the client, such as extended family, the church, friends, and neighbors (Kantor 1989). Family caregiving beliefs as well as individual relationships between family members (such as a strained relationship between two older siblings) may preclude the helping process and require further assessment.

Ethnic differences in family styles may further define the roles that family members will play in case management with old adults. Kropf, Nackerud, and Gorokhovsky (in press) discuss how cultural issues factor into case management with older adults from former Soviet Union (FSU) countries. After the collapse of the Soviet Union, many families from the FSU emigrated to the United States. Often, a condition to leave their homeland included a mandate to take older family members to the United States so these older adults would not be dependent on government aid. Case managers in this country find that adult children are less likely to make caregiving decisions about their older Soviet parents, since parental relationships are seen as primary across the life span. Even in adulthood, sons and daughters are reluctant to take action that is against the wishes of an older parent.

Making Optimal Use of Informal Resources in Case Management

Friends and neighbors can be excellent natural helpers as they are often in proximity to the older adult. However, the client may not want friends and neighbors to know of his or her circumstances. The client is generally the best person to help the case manager identify appropriate friends and family, allowing the client to retain some control over personal information. Rothman (1994) lists several dimensions useful for assessing informal helping networks:

Size: How many people comprise the informal network of an older client?

Helpfulness: What type of assistance can the members provide an older client? Do the members have the resources and capability to provide the type of assistance that is required by an older client?

Durability: How strong are the ties between the older client and the members of the network? Are these lasting or transient relationships?

Accessibility and Proximity: Are the members available to the older client when he or she needs their help? Do they live in the same community, for example?

Reciprocity: Do the members receive something from the older client (e.g., support, love, assistance) in return?

The case manager needs to define all possible networks and assess their helpfulness in light of the client's goals and needs. These informal networks can be extremely helpful in working with older adults. Neighbors can provide informal services, such as grocery shopping, transportation, home maintenance, or health monitoring. These services are often critical in allowing the older adult to continue to live at home.

Linking older adults frequently includes connections between both formal and informal systems. The following case situation of Mrs. Peters provides an example of how these two distinct systems blend together with the coordination of the case manager.

Mrs. Peters is a seventy-six-year-old, blind, and diabetic African-American woman. Her daughters live two blocks away from her and checked on her daily. She has been blind for twenty years as a result of complications of her diabetes. She had been an active member of her church and had received many informal support services from the members, including fellowship, running errands, and some minor home repairs. With these sources of assistance, Mrs. Peters was able to function well in her own home until recently. About two months ago, however, her health steadily declined as a result of a fall within her home. She was hospitalized, and it was recommended that she be discharged to a nursing home. Mrs. Peters did not want to go. She feared losing her independence and her kinship and church network.

The tasks for the case manager then became working with Mrs. Peters to accept the need for the placement and linking her with her support services so that the relationships could continue even after the move from her home. Although Mrs. Peters did move to a nursing home, the case manager coordinated with her family and church friends to maintain the positive relationships. Friends from church spend time at the nursing home, and her family members take turns having Mrs. Peters for short visits. In this way, Mrs. Peters receives the health care she needs while retaining a vital connection to the community.

Service Monitoring: Reassessment and Outcome Evaluation

Informal and formal linkages that the case manager develops relate directly to the quality of the service that the client receives. After the linkages are developed and the care plan is in place, the role of the case manager is one of monitoring and reassessment. Netting (1992) states that unless quality monitoring, adequate reassessment, and evolving case planning occur, the client may develop "false hope" (p. 163). Promised services may not materialize; subsequently, case plans may fail.. Case managers see the whole picture of both informal and formal linkages and services and therefore are in the best role to provide oversight for the case plan.

The primary tasks included in the case monitoring phase are systematic contact with the agency service providers and with informal supports (Rothman 1994). The case manager appraises the situation to determine if the case plan is being followed or if a change in the service plan is needed. The change in the case plan may be prompted by several reasons, such as a change in the client's physical status (e.g., sustained an accident or fall), mental status (e.g., progression of Alzheimer's disease), social relationships (e.g., illness or death of primary care provider), or financial status (e.g., capitation of service eligibility). When these types of changes occur, the case manager needs to reassess the service plan to include new components that address the evolving issue. Kerr and Birk (1988) propose that the monitoring function may also include cost analysis. Part of the monitoring process is determining if other, specifically less expensive, services are available for the client.

Client Contact Card

Name	Date
Type of Contact	
Contact Support	
Goal of Contact	
Monitoring Tasks	
Results	
Follow-up	

■ **Figure 5.4** Client Contact Card (Rothman 1994, p. 186)

Ongoing monitoring by the case manager is also useful in identifying specific service areas that are difficult for the client to negotiate and assess (Nishimoto, Weil, & Theil 1991). Case management services include phone contacts to facilitate and follow-up with referrals, case conferences with other agency staff, accompanying clients to various service agencies, and providing support and encouragement to the client to follow through on a referral or an ongoing service plan. When problems are noted across clients of different agencies or with different situations, there may be a strong incentive for some additional action to make these services more accessible or comprehensive. Advocacy becomes an important part of the linking and case plan functions of case management. Rothman (1994) describes advocacy as an assertive approach to assisting a client. The case manager may function as an ad-

Home Visits to Clients	Office Visits by Client	Telephone Calls to Client	Collateral Contacts

■ **Figure 5.5**   Visiting Record (Indicate Dates) (Rothman 1994, p. 186)

vocate when an older client is being denied services, such as an older women with mental retardation who is deemed ineligible to attend a senior center. However, the case manager may also be an advocate to promote more comprehensive services where gaps exist. In many rural areas, for example, there is a lack of services for elderly adults. The role of the case manager becomes one of advocating for the development of these services, such as respite care, transportation, or recreational options (Ginther et al. 1993).

Kemper (1990) suggests that case management agencies are in a good position to monitor services. Case managers routinely have contact with both the clients and the service providers; therefore, they know what services are being given and the quality of these services. Because of multiple client involvement, they can assess the consistency of quality of services. Rothman (1994) provides some examples of monitoring forms that help the case manager.

Figure 5.4 is an example of a Client Contact Card that provides a summary of what takes place during each contact with a client and progress toward goals. It allows the case manager to record the chronological progress of monitoring efforts. Figure 5.5 provides a form that can provide a cumulative record of what the case manager has done and serves as a gauge of the amount and intensity of contact with clients. This process may lead to the development of a different case plan as this example indicates. Mr. Mullen is an elderly gentleman who is confused and often not oriented to time or place. Ms. Mitchell, the case manager, has been working with him for several months. In reviewing her visiting record, the case manager realizes that Mr. Mullen has become increasingly confused and contacts have become almost daily. She is beginning to question the safety of leaving Mr. Mullen alone. However, there have been no collateral contacts except with Mr. Mullen's daughter, Bonnie, who lives three hundred miles away. Ms. Mitchell realizes that the next step in the case management process may be to find, assess, and implement informal services for Mr. Mullen.

Home Visits to Clients	Office Visits by Client	Telephone Calls to Client	Collateral Contacts
3/12/98		March 5, 18, 30, 1998	Bonnie Wood, 4/1/1998
4/13/98		April 6, 15, 22, 29, 1998	
5/20/1998		May 1, 5, 8, 10, 13, 15, 19, 22, 25, 28, 31, 1998	
6/15/1998		June 2, 5, 6, 8, 10, 13, 14, 1998	

■ **Figure 5.6** Completed Client Visiting Record (Rothman 1994, p. 186)

Another evaluation tool for case managers and clients is Goal Attainment Scaling (GAS) (Grinnell 1997), which is widely used to monitor case progress. As figure 5.7 indicates, areas of change are delineated and a series of accompanying goals are developed. The expectation of goal attainment is also recorded to assess the subjective aspect of case progress. Figure 5.8 provides an example of the implementation of the GAS. Monitoring and reassessment is not always an easy task. Lack of client motivation, loosely formulated goals, and client resistance often can compromise an effective monitoring and reassessment strategy.

The consistent process of monitoring and reassessment allows the case manager to know when and if termination of services is appropriate. For some frail elderly, case management services will continue until death. However, many elderly need case management services as a result of an unexpected medical condition, such as a broken leg, or an unplanned life event, such as a death of a spouse. These services may be short term, and termination of service is appropriate. At this time, an overall evaluation of case management services is needed. Although evaluation is listed as a final task, in reality, the best time to start an evaluation is at the beginning of the case management process (Issel 1995). If the evaluation commences at the beginning of the process, not only will the evaluation be more focused and congruent, but the evaluation will be tied to the established service goals.

Ethical Considerations in Case Management

Ethical issues can arise from the tension between agency function and client self-determination. This division raises the question about whether the client or the agency is the primary focus of service delivery. Managed care has helped to create an environment where cost, not client, is paramount. In managed care settings, the case manager functions

Client's name: _____

Date of goal negotiation with client: _____

Check (✓) goal levels for above date.

Follow-up dates: _____

GOALS

ATTAINMENT LEVEL	1	2	3
Much less than expected (−2)	_____	_____	_____
Less than expected (−1)	_____	_____	_____
Expected level of goal attainment (0)	_____	_____	_____
Better than expected (+1)	_____	_____	_____
Much better than expected (+2)	_____	_____	_____

■ **Figure 5.7**   Goal Attainment Scale (GAS) Form (Grinnell 1997, p. 197)

as the service gatekeeper to decrease provider risk and keep costs below established payment levels (Austin 1993; Grusky et al. 1997). Consequently, case managers may have become the gatekeepers for service provision (Bull & Kane 1996). This gatekeeper function includes the question of who gets and who does not get services. The primary issue, for the case manager, becomes whether services are designed to facilitate client access to services (person-driven model) or to contain costs (provider-driven model). These difficult choices are a reality of managed care environments.

Client self-determination is an important ethical issue for case managers working with elderly adults. Often, as in the case of Mrs. Peters, elderly adults may not want what they perceive as interference in their lives. They view case management services with suspicion, assuming that the goal is to "put them in a home." How then does a case manager decide to

Client's name: <u>John Doe</u>

Date of goal negotiation with client: <u>January 12, 1999</u>

Check (✓) goal levels for above date.

Follow-up dates: <u>February 22, 1999, March 29, 1999, April 29, 1999</u>

GOALS

ATTAINMENT LEVEL	1 HOUSING	2 SELF-CONTROL	3 APPOINTMENTS
Much less than expected (−2)	Client is homeless	✓ Daily temper tantrums	Fails to keep all appointments
Less than expected (−1)	✓ Has to share room and cannot afford his own room	Temper tantrums twice a week	Is late for all appointments but keeps half of them
Expected level of goal attainment (0)	Has own room, within means	Can control tantrums, only one per month	✓ Can keep four out of five appointments on time
Better than expected (+1)	Own housekeeping apartment within means	Only one, brief outburst of temper, once every month	Can keep eight out of nine appointments
Much better than expected (+2)	One-bedroom apartment, within means, in nice part of town	No more uncontrolled, unexpected, and unjustified outbursts of temper	Can keep all appointments on time

■ **Figure 5.8** An Example of a Goal Attainment Scale Used in an Outpatient Department of a Community Mental Center (Grinnell 1997, p. 197)

go against the wishes of the client? If the client is in danger, the decision may be simple. But what if there is no immediate danger? What if the client is coherent, disabled, barely able to take care of him- or herself, but adamant that he or she does not want to move? Or what if a family's preference is different from the preference of the client?

To follow an earlier case example, what if the family of Mr. Payne was advocating for relocation to a nursing home? Although he was losing some of his functional ability because of problems with his eyesight, he was not in imminent danger. The case manager may frequently have to make a decision that is ethically difficult by weighing the pros and cons of client self-determination versus quality of life and safety issues. Established social work ethical standards provide an important guideline, yet the case manager may sometimes find him- or herself in a "gray area."

Family and friends can also present ethical concerns for the case manager. Often, family and/or friends think that they know best for the elderly client. Case managers must ask themselves who is the primary client and what are their responsibilities to others involved with an elderly adult. Ethical decisions are not always easy to make. Case managers who work with the elderly need to be aware of the ethical dilemmas they may face. Making ethical decisions requires a combination of social work values, intervention knowledge, and a commitment to client self-determination.

Conclusion

Case management is a function at the very heart of social work practice. As a method, it is a widely used, effective, and comprehensive model of service provision. As defined by Rothman, case management provides a framework for linking services, negotiating service providers, assessing client needs, monitoring the provision of services, assessing progress, and evaluating outcomes. It is most effective when the process is completed from beginning to end; that is, from outreach and referral to outcome evaluation. Further, case management provides a conduit for blending formal and informal services to bolster client strengths.

Case management is an important tool for gerontological social work. It is a model that is especially effective and appropriate for older clients as the range of needed services can be substantial. This model epitomizes the "person-in-environment" focus of social work and allows the social worker to explore and implement a wide range of services.

Discussion Questions

1. What are the major tasks and roles involved in case management? How do these tasks interrelate? How are these tasks and roles critical to gerontological case management?
2. Ethical considerations are important in case management. What are some of the ethical considerations? How might ethics and agency goals compete?
3. Goals are intimately related to outcomes. Discuss the importance of goal development in case management. What psychosocial factors are important for the case manager to remember in the process of goal development and assessment?
4. What role does the initial assessment play in the development of goals? In outcome evaluation?
5. What case management skills are necessary for linking and referral? Why?
6. One ethical issue in case management is cost containment and service provision. How does the case manager make the decision to offer a service to one client but not to another? How can the case manager ethically deny service to anyone based on cost?

Experiential Learning

Activity: Goal Attainment Scaling with Mr. Samms

Read the brief description of Mr. Samms, review the section on Goal Attainment Scaling, and develop a plan for him.

Mr. Samms is a sixty-eight-year-old alcoholic who lives by himself in public housing. His income is a combination of Social Security retirement, work retirement, and a small disability pension from the plant where he worked for twenty years. About eight months ago, Mr. Samms fell on the job and permanently injured his leg. Although he always drank heavily, his drinking has increased since the loss of his job. On a usual day, he drinks a quart of alcohol and spends much of his time and money at the local bar. While he was working, he managed on his own for many years. The leg injury coupled with liver problems, skin cancer, and failing eyesight have contributed to his being unable to live alone without help. He could cook for himself, but rarely does. His weight has dropped twenty-five pounds in the past six months.

Due to his health problems, Mr. Samms's physician referred him for home health services. After several visits to his home, the home health case manager noted the need for several different services. Mr. Samms agreed to home health services, regular doctor's visits, and attending Alcoholics Anonymous. However, after a month of intervention, none of the goals had been met. Mr. Samms agreed to the services, but did not follow through with visits to the doctor or attend AA meetings. Further, the home health aid has never been able to catch Mr. Samms at home. Appointments were made but never kept.

QUESTIONS FOR DISCUSSION OR ANALYSIS

1. Reformulate the goals of Mr. Samms to include his unwillingness to keep his doctor's appointments and attend AA meetings. What are the new service goals for Mr. Samms?
2. Part of case management is determining what barriers prevent the client from attaining his or her goals. What might be some of the difficulties with the goals that the case manager and Mr. Samms agreed on?
3. What additional services might benefit Mr. Samms? Are these services readily available? Write one or two goal statements about how these services would be helpful.
4. Older alcoholics like Mr. Samms might be reluctant to attend AA because there are no meetings specifically for older adults. As the case manager, how would you advocate for this resource in your community?

Experiential Learning

Activity: Case Management Model of Intervention

Use figure 5.2, Rothman Case Management Model, for this activity. Listed below are four situations of older adults that could be part of a case manager's client load. Review figure 5.2 and answer the set of questions at the end of the activity for each client.

JERRY

Jerry is a sixty-two-year-old man who has mental retardation. He has attended the same day activity program for thirty years and enjoys his work very much. About six weeks ago, he fell and suffered a broken arm. Although he has recovered, the activity center is terminating him, citing possible risks such as additional falls. He lives in a group home, and the administrator states that there is not staff coverage for him to stay home during the day. Jerry has no family as his parents are dead, and there is no contact with his one brother. The vocational counselor at the day program contacted you, a case manager in developmental disabilities.

ANNA

Anna is an eighty-three-year-old woman who lives alone in a medium sized southern city. Anna recently had a car accident when she was driving home from church. This is the second accident she has had in six months. Although no one was injured, her daughter is very concerned about her mother's safety. Anna refuses to give up driving, stating that she will have no way to get around to the stores, her church, and her volunteer work at the local hospital. Her daughter contacted you at the local council on aging to see if there is anything that can be done.

OLIVIA

Olivia is a sixty-eight-year-old woman who lives in a two bedroom apartment in a public housing complex. About one month ago, her daughter was incarcerated on drug, prostitution, and robbery charges, and she will be in prison for several years. Olivia's three grandchildren, ages twelve, seven, and four have moved into the apartment with her. Olivia has a limited income, surviving on Social Security. She also has some health problems, including high blood pressure and an enlarged heart. These conditions forced her to retire last year from her job on the housekeeping staff at a hotel. You are the case manager for the housing authority and are concerned about Olivia's ability to care for her three grandchildren.

ROBERTO

Roberto is a seventy-one-year-old immigrant from Mexico who moved to the United States with his son's family about seven years ago. The family consists of his son and daughter-in-law, five grandchildren, and one great grandchild. Roberto has no written or spoken English skills. Within the last month, Roberto has been experiencing some health problems and has stopped attending Mass, which was one of his few social outlets. His priest contacted you, a case manager at Catholic Social Services about Roberto. His priest also informed you that Roberto is a very stubborn man, and practices faith healing and refuses to see a doctor. However, his condition is worsening, and the priest is very concerned.

QUESTIONS

Review figure 5.2, and answer the following questions for each case:

1. How did the client get connected to you as the case manager? Are there any potential problems in having the older adult case management services?
2. What types of information are important to gather about this client during intake? What are the sources you can use to gather this information, besides from the client him- or herself?
3. How would you summarize the problem(s) that the client is experiencing? Identify two or three goals that you would work on with this client.
4. What formal and informal resources are available for this client? How would these accomplish the goals that you have constructed?
5. To what services would you link this client? Can you foresee possible barriers? If so, how could you act as an advocate on this client's behalf?
6. At the reassessment, what might be some possible changes that would need to be considered for this client in the service plan?
7. How would you measure success with this client?

Case Studies

See Appendix B for guidelines in analyzing gerontological social work practice.

Case 1: Losing Your Home

Mrs. Edwards is a seventy-six-year-old widow. She lives alone in a run-down, two room house. It has been her home for over fifty years. The house has been condemned by the city, and Mrs. Edwards is being forced to move. Social Services sent a social worker to investigate the problems with a goal of getting Mrs. Edwards to move to an apartment in the city housing authority complex.

The social worker noted that Mrs. Edwards is a lively, aware, engaging woman. Mrs. Edwards is determined not to move and feels that the city has no right to make her leave her home. She feels that she is safe, has her friends nearby, and that she should decide where she wants to live her final years. The social worker tried to explain why the city condemned the house. The foundation is crumbling, there are unpatchable holes in the roof, the floor boards are rotten, and the pipes leading to the sewer are leaking. The house is about fifty-three years old, but it was not built well initially and is not salvageable.

Upon further discussion, the social worker found out that Mrs. Edwards promised her husband that she would always live in this house. She feels that she "owes it to her late husband" to honor his wishes. Her two children, while wanting to see her safe, also feel that her moving would betray their father.

Case 2: The Grief Process

Mr. James, a sixty-five-year-old African American man, is dying of skin cancer. The cancer is concentrated in the face and neck area of his body. He has lost his left ear, half of his face, and his nose. He keeps a handkerchief over the left side of his face so visitors will not have to look at the devastation.

Mrs. James has kept her husband at home and has nursed him for many years. However, in the past two months, the cancer has spread more rapidly. Mr. James needs increasingly stronger doses of pain medication. The James's have two children, one son and one daughter. They are both successful small-business owners in California and live several hundred miles away from their parents. The family, including Mr. James, realize that he is dying. The children have visited, with their families, in the last two months and said their good-byes.

The couple have spent all of their savings on treatments for Mr. James. He has undergone both chemotherapy and radiation, but neither has been successful. The time has arrived to have Mr. James enter a hospice program. However, the closest facility is a private one, and the James's cannot afford it. A state-run hospice is about two hours away from their home. Mrs. James cannot drive that distance by herself, and transportation would become a major problem.

If Mr. James goes into the hospice, it is likely that he will not see his wife again. They both know that he will never come home again. They have called you at the local council on aging, as you had worked with this couple when they attended activities at the senior center. They do not know what to do and have asked that you help them make a decision.

Case 3: Is Moving Home an Option?

Mrs. Diaz had been in a nursing/rehabilitation home for six weeks. She developed multiple sclerosis when she was twenty-two years old. The condition got progressively worse, and at the age of sixty, she entered a nursing/rehabilitation home.

When the social worker first met Mrs. Diaz, she was angry and hostile. She did not want to be there and was furious with her family for "placing her in an INSTITUTION!" Mrs. Diaz had requested a meeting with the social worker to help her get home. Upon reading the case file, the social worker discovered that Mrs. Diaz was wheelchair bound, could not bathe herself, could not cook for herself, and could not take care of any personal needs. The family had hired a half-time helper for her, but were no longer able to afford the help.

Mrs. Diaz is convinced that the family was plotting against her, that she still had lots of money, and her family just wanted to protect their inheritance. She tries to convince you that she has plenty of neighbors and true friends who would gladly help her.

On your first visit to her son, the only child, you discover that he has been shouldering the burden of his mother's care almost exclusively by himself. Her godchild, who also stands to inherit from her, helps as much as possible. But she has problems with her own mother and cannot help consistently. Mr. Diaz, the son, loves his mother very much, but is afraid that if she comes to live with him and his family, it will break the family apart. When Mrs. Diaz was in her apartment alone, she called her son night and day to help her. He virtually begs you to help keep his mother in the home.

Annotated Bibliography

Anker-Unnever, L. & Netting, F. E. (1995). Coordinated care partnership: Case management with physician practices. *Journal of Case Management, 4*(1), 3–8.

    The authors propose that case managers become an extension of the physician when dealing with the elderly adult with chronic conditions. They present a screening instrument that can be used on the telephone to begin an initial assessment, with in-depth information gathered by the MSW or RN case managers. Coordination with a physician allows the health care plan to become part of the client's overall case plan.

Diwan, S., Berger, C., & Ivy, C. (1996). Supervision and quality assurance in long-term care case management. *Journal of Case Management, 5*(2), 65–71.

    Supervision of services is linked with quality of the services offered in a case management environment. They propose indicators of quality of case management. Additionally, the authors discuss variation in the delivery of services as a result of many factors.

Hennessy, C. H. (1993). Modeling case management decision-making in a consolidated long-term care program. *The Gerontologist, 33*(3), 333–341.

    This article provides a multidimensional model of assessment in case management. The assessment model is comprehensive and related to the risk of institutionalization and selection of a care plan. The model is currently being used in long-term geriatric care as a cost-saving and quality-promoting mechanism for delivery of service.

Issel, L. M. (1995). Evaluating case management programs. MCN: *Journal of Maternal/Child Nursing, 20*(March/April), 67–74.

    Issel provides guidelines for the evaluation of case management programs. She proposes that evolution start in the beginning of the program. In outlining nine key questions, she provides the reader with an excellent starting point for both an evaluation and a case plan. Finally, Issel suggests that outcome indicators be set in the beginning of the evaluation plan.

Moore, S. T. (1990). A social work practice model of case management: The case management grid. *Social Work, 35*, 385–480.

Moore proposes that when service integration is high and resources are low case managers become the mechanism for rationing services. When both service integration and resources are high, case management has a marketing function. If resources are high and integration is low, a brokering model of case management is important. Case management takes on a developmental role when both service integration and resources are low.

Naleppa, M. J. & Reid, W. J. (1998). Task-centered case management for the elderly: Developing a practice model. *Research on Social Work Practice, 8*(1), 63–85.

Naleppa and Reid developed and field tested a task-centered model of case management. The authors integrated a specific intervention protocol with established case management core functions. They further propose that their model addresses the lack of clearly defined practice guidelines for case management with elderly clients.

Netting, F. E. (1992). Case management: Service or symptom? *Social Work, 37*(2), 160–164.

Netting provides a brief overview of case management, its history, and contemporary models. The article also examines macrochallenges for social work case management. She questions whether case management is being used to cover up the problems of the health care system. Maintaining a client-centered approach in an era of a cost-obsessed environment is a challenge for social workers.

Riley, P. A., Fortinskey, R. H., & Cogburn, A. F. (1992). Developing consumer-centered quality assurance strategies for home care: A case management approach. *Journal of Case Management, 1*(2), 39–48.

Quality assurance models for case management are scarce. The authors propose a model for consumer-centered quality assurance. Interviews were conducted with business leaders and with home care consumers and their families. Focus groups were held with consumers, case managers, and home health nurses. Quality assurance is a regular, integrated part of case management.

Rothman, J. (1992). *Guidelines for case management: Putting research to professional use.* Itasca, IL: Peacock.

This book is Rothman's first about case management. He goes into great detail about case management, practice roles, and linking to both formal and informal agencies. Rothman also discusses staff and training issues. He proposes a model of case management evaluation and a methodology for the inquiry. Finally, Rothman presents us with practice guidelines that are extremely useful in learning case management.

Rothman, J. (1994). *Practice with highly vulnerable clients: Case management and community based practice.* Englewood Cliffs, NJ: Prentice-Hall.

This second book of Rothman's takes the model developed in his first book, enlarges it, and applies it to a particularly vulnerable clientele. He uses a psychosocial, ecological approach to case management that works well with both individuals and groups. The book is well written and very useful in teaching or learning case management practice.

General Bibliography

AARP (1995). Grandparents raising their grandchildren. *Perspectives in Health Promotion and Aging, 10,* 6–7.

Applebaum, R. & Christianson, J. (1988). Using case management to monitor community-based long term care. *Quality Review Bulletin, 14*(7), 227–231.

Anker-Unnever, L. & Netting, F. E. (1995). Coordinated care partnership: Case management with physician practices. *Journal of Case Management, 4*(1), 3–8.

Austin, C. B. (1992, February). When the whole is more than the sum of the parts: Case management issues from a systems perspective. Paper presented at the First International Long-term Care Case Management Conference, Seattle, WA.

Austin, C. D. (1993). Case management: A systems perspective. *Families in Society: The Journal of Contemporary Human Services, 74,* 451–459.

Bull, M. J. & Kane, R. L. (1996). Gaps in discharge planning. *The Journal of Applied Gerontology, 15*(4), 486–500.

Burton, L. M. (1992). Black grandparents rearing children of drug-addicted parents: Stressors, outcomes, and social service needs. *The Gerontologist, 32*, 744–751.

Cronin, C. J. & Maklebust, J. (1989). Case-managed care: Capitalizing on the CNS. *Nursing Management, 20*(3), 38–47.

Day, P. J. (1988). *A New History of Social Welfare*. Englewood Cliffs, NJ: Prentice-Hall.

Degenholtz, H. B., Kane, R. A., Kane, R. L., & Finch, M. (1999). Long-term care case managers' out-of-home placement decisions: An application of hierarchical logistic regression. *Research on Aging, 21*(2), 240–274.

Derogotis, L., Lipman, R., & Covi, L. (1973). The SCL-90: An outpatient psychiatric rating scale. *Psychopharmacology, 1*, 13–38.

Diwan, S., Berger, C., & Ivey, C. (1996). Supervision and quality assurance in long-term care case management. *Journal of Case Management, 5*(2), 64–71.

Emlet, C. A. (1996). Case managing older people with AIDS: Bridging systems-recognizing diversity. *Journal of Gerontological Social Work, 27*(¹/₂), 55–71.

Galambos, C. M. (1997). Resolving ethical conflicts in providing case management services to the elderly. *Journal of Gerontological Social Work, 24*(4), 57–67.

Germain, C. (1994). Using an ecological perspective. In J. Rothman, *Practice with Highly Vulnerable Clients: Case Management and Community Based Practice* (pp. 39–56). Englewood Cliff, NJ: Prentice-Hall.

Ginther, S. D., Webber, P., Fox, P. J., & Miller, L. (1993). Predictors of case management for persons with Alzheimer's disease. *The Journal of Applied Gerontology, 12*(2), 139–154.

Goodman, C. C. (1987). The elderly frail: Who should get case management? *Journal of Gerontological Social Work, 11*(3/4), 99–113.

Grinnell, R. M. (1997). *Social Work Research and Evaluation: Quantitative and Qualitative Approaches*. Itasca, IL: Peacock Publisher, Inc.

Grusky, O., Podus, D., Webster, C., & Young, A. S. (1997). Measuring the cost and outcome effects of case management teams. *Research in the Sociology of Health Care, 14*, 305–325.

Hennessy, C. H. (1993). Modeling case management decision-making in a consolidated long-term care program. *The Gerontologist, 33*93) 333–341.

Issel, L. M. (1995). Evaluating case management programs. *MCN, 20*(2), 67–74.

Johnson, P. J. & Rubin, A. (1983). Case management in mental health: A social work domain? *Social Work, (January/February)*, 49–55.

Kantor, J. (1989). Clinical case management: Definition, principles, components. *Hospital and Community Psychiatry, 40*(4), 361–368.

Kellner, R. (1987). A symptom questionnaire. *The Journal of Clinical Psychiatry, 48*, 268–274.

Kemper, P. (1990). Case management agency systems of administering long-term care: Evidence from the Channeling Demonstration. *The Gerontologist, 30*(6), 817–824.

Kerr, M. H. & Birk, J. M. (1988). A client-centered case management model. *Quality Review Bulletin, 14*(9), 279–283.

Kropf, N. P., Nackerud, L., & Gorokhovsky, I. (In press). Social work practice with older Soviet clients. *Journal of Multicultural Social Work*.

Lamb, H. (1980). Therapist-case managers: More the brokers of services. *Hospital and Community Psychiatry, 31*(11), 762–764.

Minkler, M., Driver, D., Roe, K. M., & Bedian, K. (1993). Community interventions to support grandparent caregivers. *The Gerontologist, 33*, 807–811.

Moore, S. T. (1990). A social work practice model of case management: The case management grid. *Social Work, 35*, 385–480.

Moroney, R. M., Dokecki, P. R., Gates, J. J., Haynes, K. N., Newbrough, J. R., & Nottingham, J. A. (1998). *Caring and Competent Caregivers*. Athens: University of Georgia Press.

Mosley, P. G. & DeWeaver, K. L. (1998). Empirical approaches to case management: In J. S. Wodarski & B. A. Thyer (Eds.), *Handbook of Empirical Social Work Practice, Vol. 2* (pp. 393–412). New York: John Wiley & Sons.

Naleppa, M. J. & Reid, W. J. (1998). Task-centered case management for the elderly: Developing a practice model. *Research on Social Work Practice, 8*(1), 63–85.

NASW (1992). *NASW Standards for Social Work Case Management.* Washington, DC: NASW.

Netting, F. E. (1992). Case management: Service or symptom? *Social Work, 37*(2), 160–164.

Netting, F. E., Warrick, L. H., Christianson, J. B., & Williams, F. G. (1994). Determinants of client termination in hospital-based case management programs. *Journal of Case Management 3*(2), 74–80.

Netting, F. E. & Williams, F. G. (1999). Implementing a case management program designed to enhance primary care physician practice with older persons. *Journal of Applied Gerontology, 18*(1), 25–45.

Neugarten, B. L., Havighurst, R. J., & Tobin, S. S. (1961). The measurement of life satisfaction. *Journal of Gerontology, 16,* 134–141.

Nishimoto, R., Weil, M., & Theil, K. (1991). A service tracking and referral form to monitor the receipt of services in a case management program. *Administration in Social Work, 15*(3), 33–47.

Norris, M. K. & Hill, C. (1991). The clinical nurse specialist: Developing the case manager role. *Dimensions of Critical Care Nursing, 10*(6), 346–353.

Nufer, Y., Rosenberg, H., & Smith, D. H. (1998). Consumer and case manager perceptions of important case manager characteristics. *Journal of Rehabilitation, 64*(4), 40–46.

Parker, G. (1992). *With This Body: Caring and Disability in Marriage.* Buckingham, England: Open University Press.

Rapp, C. A. & Chamberlain, R. (1985). Case management services for the chronically mentally ill. *Social Work, 30,* 414–412.

Riley, P. A., Fortinskey, R. H., & Cogburn, A. F. (1992). Developing consumer-centered quality assurance strategies for home care: A case management approach. *Journal of Case Management, 1*(2), 39–48.

Rose, S. M. & Moore, V. L. (1995). Case management. In R. L. Edwards & J. G. Hopps (eds.), *Encyclopedia of Social Work,* (19th Ed.), 335–340. Washington, DC: NASW Press.

Rosenberg, C. (1995). Controversies in case management. *Journal of Long Term Home Health Care, 14*(3), 37–42.

Rosenberg, M. (1979). *Conceiving the Self.* New York: Basic Books.

Rothman, J. (1992). Guidelines for case management: putting research to professional use. Itasca, IL: F. E. Peacock Publishers, Inc.

Rothman, J. (1994). *Practice with Highly Vulnerable Clients: Case Management and Community Based Practice.* Englewood Cliffs: Prentice-Hall.

Secord, L. J. (1987). *Private case management for older persons and their families: Practice, policy, potential.* Excelsior, MN: InterStudy.

Soares, H. H. & Rose, M. K. (1994). Clinical aspects of case management with the elderly. *Journal of Gerontological Social Work, 22*(3/4), 143–156.

Stephens, M. A. (1993). Understanding the barriers to caregiver's use of formal services: The caregiver's perspective. In S. H. Zarit, L. I. Pearlin, & K. W. Shaie (Eds.), *Caregiving systems: Formal and informal helpers.* Hillsdale, N.J.: Lawrence Erlbaum.

Sullivan, W. P. & Fisher, B. J. (1994). Intervening for success: Strengths-based case management and successful aging. *Journal of Gerontological Social Work, 22*(1/2), 61–74.

Trattner, W. I. (1989). *From poor law to welfare state: A history of social welfare in America.* (4th Ed.). New York: The Free Press.

Vanchieri, C. (1998). Eye on the elderly. *Hospitals and Health Networks, 72*(12), 54.

Weil, M. & Karls, J. M. & Associates. (1985). *Case management in human service practice.* San Francisco: Jossey-Bass.

White, M. (1986). Case management. In G. L. Maddox (Ed.), *The Encyclopedia of Aging* (92–96). New York: Springer.

Whitley, D. M., White, K. R., Kelley, S. B., & Yorke, B. (1999). Strengths-based case management: The application to grandparents raising grandchildren. *Families in Society: The Journal of Contemporary Human Services, (March/April),* 110–119.

II   Service Settings

6   Home Health and Community Services

Nancy P. Kropf

Home health and community care services are important components of a comprehensive long-term care system. These services support many older people who find themselves with limited resources and health concerns. For example, a sixty-five-year-old widow who breaks her hip may no longer to able to manage her household alone. A seventy-five-year-old man who has his driver's license revoked may be unable to shop for groceries or medications. Unfortunately, a common consequence for an older person needing assistance is placement into a nursing home. Community or home care is advocated as an alternative to nursing home placement, with about 20 percent of all placements in nursing homes judged to be inappropriate or preventable (AARP 1997; Kane & Kane 1994). Many older people who receive some type of support are able to remain in their own homes and communities. Support can come from a variety of sources—from those in a person's informal network, such as family, friends, and neighbors, or from a formal network, such as home health programs and community care services.

Social workers provide important services in home and community care systems. They are instrumental in assessing needs and linking a person with appropriate support systems. For example, the sixty-five-year-old woman may be eligible for a visiting homemaker and a health aide to assist with household and medical tasks. The seventy-five-year-old man may have neighbors who agree to take him on their weekly shopping trip. He also could be transported to a meal site for a daily lunch program. Combining support from family, friends, and formal programs can delay or prevent nursing home placement. Effective social workers utilize the informal and formal support networks to help many older people remain in their own homes and communities. Social workers contribute to one of the most important goals in long-term care, which is maintaining the independence of the older person.

Home Health and Community Care Services in Long-Term Care

Definition of Long-Term Care

Long-term care is often misconstrued to mean nursing home care. Nursing homes are an important part of long-term care, but the total system is not limited to institutional services. The following is offered as a more generic definition of long-term care.

> Long-term care can be defined as those services designed to provide diagnostic, preventative, therapeutic, rehabilitative, supportive and maintenance services on a recurring or continuous basis for individuals of all age groups. These services are provided in a variety of institutionalized and noninstitutionalized care settings, including the home, with the goal of promoting the optimal level of physical, social and psychological functioning. Individuals in need of long-term care services are defined as persons who have chronic physical and/or mental impairments. (Virginia Long-Term Care Council 1985, p. 2).

Individuals with some limitations in functioning may also benefit from long-term care services. This definition includes much broader services than those provided within a nursing home.

Continuum of Long-Term Care Services

A comprehensive long-term care system usually includes diverse and flexible services which are provided along a continuum of care. Figure 6.1 is a schematic representation of an array of services recommended for a comprehensive long-term care system (Brody & Masciocchi 1980). As depicted, the continuum can be broken into three services settings. One type, institutional settings, provides a twenty-four-hour residential service. These places are most appropriate for individuals who need continuous, intermittent or acute treatment. The second type, community care programs, provides services (including health, nutritional, legal or social assistance) to older people at various sites around the community. The third type is home health services. These services are provided within someone's home by an agency representative or social worker. The continuum of care represents services to individuals with multiple or severe impairments, to people who require nursing home care, and to the elderly who have minimal needs, such as a place to socialize with others.

Social workers in the long-term care system are employed in a variety of settings, such as hospitals, nursing homes, governmental agencies, or home health care agencies. They are responsible for performing many different functions, depending upon the goals of their agencies and the needs of their clients. In determining a long-term care service plan for an older client, the social worker must assess how the client's unique needs can be met while preserving the greatest autonomy for the person. A major role of all social workers in this system is continued assessment of the changing needs of their clients and linkage to the resources which best address those needs.

Reasons for Home Health and Community Care Services

DEMOGRAPHICS

The number of older people has been growing dramatically. Current predictions indicate that this growth will continue into the next century. One reason for the increased interest in long-term health care is the increasing number of older people in society. Between 1900 and 1996, the over sixty-five age group has increased (from 3 million to 3.9 million people). Future projections indicate that the over sixty-five population will continue to increase. By 2030, there will be about 70 million persons, more than double the number in 1996. In the year 2000, people over 65 years represent 13% of the population. By 2030, this estimate rises to 20%. (Administration on Aging 1997a). These figures forecast a society with a larger ratio of older people, especially those who are the "oldest-old." Not only can our society expect to have more older members, but our oldest members will be represented in even greater numbers than previously.

Advancing age by itself does not necessarily mean there will be a greater need for long-term care services. However, certain health conditions are more prevalent in the older population. As people age, the number of chronic conditions such as arthritis, cardiac problems, or dementia also increases. In 1992, more than half (53%) of the over 65 population reported at least one disability that impaired the ability to carry out Activities of Daily Living

Array of Services		Setting
Most restrictive State mental hospital Acute care, general hospital Chronic care hospital Rehabilitation hospital Skilled nursing facility Intermediate care facility Housing — Group home Personal care home Foster home Domiciliary care home Boarding home Congregate care home • with meals • with social services • with medical service • with housekeeping Retirement villages • with life care • with services		Institutional
Hospice Respite care Geriatric day rehabilitation hospital Day care Sheltered workshop Congregate meals Community mental health Senior citizen center Geriatric medical services • dental service • podiatry service Legal services Protective services		Community
Visiting nurse Homemaker Home health aide Chore services **Least restrictive** Meals delivered		In home

 Figure 6.1   Long-Term Support System

(ADLs) or Instrumental Activities of Daily Living (IADLs) (Administration on Aging 1997a). When these limitations occur, assistance from family, friends, or service programs can help prevent or delay placement into a nursing home for the older person.

Psychosocial Issues

The increase in impairments of older people affects more than just biological or physical functions. Social workers with elderly clients need to assess the psychosocial implications of their clients' limitations. For example, the seventy-five-year-old man who loses his driver's license also loses a sense of independence. Social workers help older clients receive services which best address their physical and psychosocial needs. This seventy-five-year-old man may be referred to a social worker for a meal program since he can no longer get to a grocery store. However, effective social work practice with this man will address not only his need for meals but also his need for independence.

An important part of psychosocial adjustment to receiving services is the value that older people attach to their home environment. Most older people desire to remain in their own homes and communities—places which have real and symbolic value. While many older people begin to experience limitations in functioning, many others resist leaving their own homes and communities. The desire to feel connected to others is a part of human nature, regardless of a person's age. With support from an older person's family, friends, neighbors, and established services, even frail people are able to remain at home. Psychosocial issues of aging are as important as physical issues when service needs are assessed.

Family caregivers of older people need to be considered in the evaluation of the psychosocial issues of aging. Most older people who need assistance in daily living receive support from family members. Family caregiving is estimated to compromise 80 percent of total care of the elderly (Home Care Facts 1997). Older people are not "dumped" into nursing homes because their families do not want to help in care. Families continue to provide care to older members, many of whom are frail. The importance of family caregiving cannot be underestimated since this support may be the reason that many impaired older people stay out of residential institutions. A study by Silverstone and Burack-Weiss (1982) found that nursing home residents had substantially less family support than did the community dwelling elderly. The severity of health conditions varied less dramatically between the two groups. Psychosocial issues of long-term care support include family issues since this support frequently prevents or delays nursing placement for an older person.

Health Care Costs

Health care costs for the aging population are major long-term care issues. Much of this change has to do with the changing structure of health care services. Before the creation of Medicare and Medicaid in 1965, home care consisted of a few hospital geriatric programs and charitable visiting nurse associations. Insurance coverage was rare or limited. Significant expansion happened in 1980 when Congress erased Medicare limits on the number of home visits, eliminated the requirement for prior hospital stays, and opened the door to for-profit providers (Meyers 1997b). In addition, patients are being discharged more quickly from hospital settings, and high-tech care has been introduced to home health.

Concomitantly, Medicare home health usage and costs have risen sharply. Home health care service agencies increased from 5,700 in 1990 to 9,800 in 1996. During this same time frame, the percentage of Medicare beneficiaries jumped from 5.6 to 10.1 percent, and spending zoomed from $3 billion to $16 billion per year (Meyers 1997a). With the increased number of older adults, these trends are expected to increase into the next century.

Managed care is a factor in the changing structure of health care services. Due to increased rates of spending, cost containment has become a prominent goal in service delivery. Managed care companies have become key providers in health care services, which impacts older adults who are involved in home and community programs. Cost containment, or service capitation, can potentially place older adults in disadvantaged positions since many require multiple and ongoing health care services. In addition, the "bottom line" for managed care companies is cost effectiveness based upon outcome-based performances (Leavenworth 1995). As O'Brien and Flannery (1997) state, "Disadvantages [of managed health care] include the fact that the patient is seldom the center of attention. This is reflected in the need to reduce cost by keeping the doctor at the gate to restrict patient access to specialty services. This often places the patient in a conflict with the physician's need to make a living" (pp. 14–15). In addition, cost limits would also disproportionately affect those older adults who are in the highest risk groups for nursing home admission such as the oldest-old, not married, or women from minority groups (Freedman 1999).

Informal Support Networks

Most support of an older person is supplied by the family. The family unit is just one of the components of an informal support network. A definition of an informal network is a series of linkages along which information, emotional reassurances, and services flow to and from a person and his or her exchange relationships. These services may be economic, social, or emotional (Hooyman 1983). The members of an informal network usually have emotional ties to an older person. A paid housekeeper, for example, maintains a different relationship with an older person than does a daughter or neighbor who assists with cleaning. Members of informal networks provide important services to elderly people and their contribution needs to be acknowledged and supported. Highlighting important issues for social workers, the following section will review some of the systems included in an informal support network.

Family Caregiving

The family is the primary and preferred source of support for older people in the United States. Cantor (1985) describes the structure of support operating in our society as "hierarchal-compensatory," with family as the most preferred source of assistance, followed by friends, and lastly governmental or formal agencies. Within this structure, an older person would probably receive the majority of support from family, with friends compensating for functions not performed by family. Any remaining gaps would be filled by formal agencies, such as health care or meal services. Within the family structure, various members provide different functions and support for an older member (Wenger 1984). The majority is provided by either a spouse or an adult child. Additionally, most family caregivers are women (Day 1985). This role has been termed "the unexpected career" since the lives of caregivers can be altered dramatically by the responsibilities and impact of care provision (Aneshensel, Pearlin, Mullan, Zarit, & Whitlatch 1995).

Most families will undertake major sacrifices to provide care for an older member. Even when the person is impaired, families make great attempts to continue to provide care (Cantor 1985; Shanas 1979). Caregiving has many rewards but also includes demands. Social workers and other professionals need to be extremely sensitive to the stresses and strains of caregiving. Identifying the demanding aspects of caregiving is an initial step in social work interventions planned to buffer or relieve stress. Caregiving strain can be categorized into these types: financial, physical, or emotional (Zimemr & Mellor 1982). Financial strain emerges from the actual expense of caregiving, for medications, or gas to take the older person shopping. Financial strain also occurs from the "opportunity cost" of care—the things which someone gives up to assume a caregiving role. For example, a daughter who quits a job to care for her mother gives up the money from employment. In this example, the daughter is relinquishing her "opportunity" to receive a salary. This type of stress is particularly difficult for women, who often face difficult decisions about their employment. Compared to men, female care providers are more likely to quit their jobs, cut back on work hours, or decline job promotion or advancement opportunities (Anastas, Gibeau, & Larson 1990; Scharlach, Lowe, & Schneider 1991). This situation can cause problems for women in late life, as this pattern reduces their ability to save for their own old-age benefits (Kingston & O'Grady-LeShane 1993). Hopefully, this trend may be changing as greater numbers of adults are involved in eldercare roles. In a small study of employed caregivers, Lechner and Gupta (1996) reported that between 1988–1992, greater numbers of adults expected that their workplace would provide them with assistance with their caregiving demands. This type of support may allow care providers to remain in the workforce and decrease economic stress of eldercare.

Physical exertion is another type of strain in caregiving. Physical demands of caregiving can be great. Someone who requires assistance in toileting or bathing needs to be lifted, moved, and positioned. Continued assistance can result in injuries for the caregiver. Since the majority of family caregivers are spouses or adult children, they may be experiencing some physical limitations themselves (Day 1985). A situation of a sixty-five-year-old providing care to an eighty-eight-year-old parent is one of the "younger-old" person caring for the "older-old." The multiple demands on a caregiver's time contributes to physical strain. The stress of trying to juggle responsibilities becomes exhausting and physically draining. Many caregivers work full time jobs, have children, and assist an older parent. Little time is left for these people, often called the "sandwich" generation, to attend to their own health needs, such as exercising and eating balanced meals.

A third type of strain experienced by family caregivers is emotional. Having a personal relationship makes the experience of caregiving emotionally charged. Since some people are quite frail, fears of hurting the older person are common. Decision-making becomes a source of strain when the responsibility of health or residential decisions are assumed by the caregiver. What happens, for example, when a son thinks his mother should not continue to live alone, but his mother refuses to move? These decisions become even more complicated when other family members choose sides and may split families into factions. Guilt and conflict can ensue for a family. The constant progression of certain ailments is highly emotional for a family. For example, a grandparent with Alzheimer's disease may not be able to remember the names of the grandchildren or even recognize their faces. The potent relationship between family caregivers and an older member increases the emotional components of care.

Social workers helping older clients and their families need to be sensitive to the strains of caregiving. In some types of illness, such as dementia, caregiver stress may be especially acute across all aspects of care (Ory, Hoffman, Yee, Tennshedt, & Schulz, 1999). Understanding family issues is an important part of social work practice with the aging population. Certain programs and services can "help the helpers" provide support. Providing caregivers with information about caring for an older person is educational. Information on the normal aging process, medical conditions, possible community resources, and interaction with professional and medical staff have been found to be useful. A second program deals with emotional aspects of care. Support groups give caregivers a place to socialize with others, vent feelings, and get away from providing care for a few hours.

While these interventions are beneficial for families, financial strain may continue to be a problem since public policy in America does little to assist caregiving families. Social workers and other professionals should advocate for policy to provide some kind of financial support. Specific proposals include subsidies to families who provide care, increased coverage of home health services by Medicare, Medicaid, and private insurance, and more flexibility in employment schedules of caregivers.

Friends and Neighbors

Friends and neighbors are other resources within an older person's informal support network. Even when older people have interactions with adult children, nearby friends and neighbors may be better suited to perform certain tasks (Cantor 1979). Frequently friends live closer to an older person than do family members and are able to respond quickly in cases of emergency. When a family lives a long distance away, they rely on information from neighbors about their relative's functioning. A neighbor who notices that newspapers are piling up on a porch or a friend who notices that cigarette butts are being extinguished on living room chairs can provide information about the individual's functioning. Friends and neighbors are main sources of support for older people with no family (Cantor 1979). For example, a couple may ask the widow who lives next door to holiday dinners. Friends from church may assist the woman by transporting her to services. Even when family members are involved, friendships allow people to have different types of relationships. Friends provide a sense of intimacy, especially important when an older person loses a significant other, such as a spouse (Hooyman 1987).

Since friends and neighbors are important resources in an older person's network, they should not be overlooked in social work practices with older people. These people are familiar faces for an older person and provide a connection to the larger society. Just looking out a window and knowing the names of people passing on the street can be a source of security, assistance, and comfort for an older person. Social workers can foster supportive relationships between an older person and neighbors. Social workers must also be sensitive to an older person's desire to remain connected to friends and communities.

Religious Affiliations

In addition to family, friends, and neighbors, older people belong to various voluntary groups. Religious affiliations with churches and synagogues are the most common type of voluntary organization for older people (Huttman 1985). Religious ties continue to be important sources of support for older people, especially for the current cohort who were raised during a religious era. Besides providing spiritual and fellowship benefits, many churches and synagogues have special programs for older members. These programs include outreach ministries to homebound or hospitalized members, special transportation to worship services, special services for the hearing or visually impaired, and meals or grocery supply programs.

The church may be an important, and overlooked, source of support for certain segments of the older population. For African American elders, the church can collaborate with formalized service to provide more comprehensive and accessible services (Morrison 1991). For older people in rural areas where there are few agency support programs, churches are major resources in providing community elderly with services (Hancock 1987). A program by Catholic Social Services in New Mexico, for example, organized an Outreach Program for community elderly. This program is run through various churches but is linked to a community agency that provides training and consultation to volunteer service providers (Anker & Trumbower 1985). Volunteers are also used as referral sources for the elderly who need additional services, such as therapy or financial assistance. These churches provide a vital outreach service to link community elderly with needed programs and services.

Self-Care Groups and Mutual Help Systems

Self-care and mutual help groups, while not limited to the elderly, may have special relevance for this age group. "Self-care refers to actions that individuals take to promote their own well-being or that of their families and friends. Mutual help groups are comprised of individuals who share a common condition and meet to give each other support" (Bernadette, Wright, Minkler, & Fullarton 1981, p. 50). A major advantage of both groups is the emphasis on self-determination of the members, who actively participate and structure the group experiences. Some gerontologists stress the need for more of these kind of groups, since too frequently projects are started and maintained by professionals, not older members (Haber 1983). An example of a mutual help system is a monitoring group for recently diagnosed diabetics who help each other stay on diets and take medications. Another example is the STAES program in St. Louis. This program trains elderly volunteers to provide services such as telephone reassurance, socializing, and shopping assistance to other elderly community members. Additionally, these volunteers maintain regular contact with assigned neighbors and are sources for referrals if other needs arise (Morrow-Howell & Ozawa 1987). Self-care and mutual help systems allow elderly participants to be both recipients and providers of service to others.

Although self-care and mutual help groups have the goal of members helping one another, social workers are important components of a successful system. Social workers are instrumental in identifying a need for a group and assisting members with the group's organization. Social workers are trained in group process and supervising volunteers. Skills in these areas are assets in starting and maintaining self-care and mutual help systems. Social workers also are sources of referral for potential members. Being active in groups benefit elderly clients by promoting their own problem solving and health promotion process.

Summary

An informal network includes family, friends, neighbors, and members of voluntary groups. Each of these are actual or potential resources for an older person. Social workers can be involved with all these informal groups. Because social workers are trained in understanding family dynamics, group processes, community organization, and volunteer management, they possess knowledge and skills to intervene in a variety of ways within an informal network. For example, family caregivers can be linked to respite services that buffer the strains of caregiving. Friends and neighbors can be used as information sources about an older person's functioning. Churches and synagogues can be organized to provide a telephone reassurance program. Since the majority of care for an older person is provided by informal systems, effective social work practice includes support to members of this network.

Formal Support Networks

Formal support networks are those services and agencies which are established to meet the needs of older people. Agencies in the formal service network include governmental agencies, state agencies, or public systems. Formal network services also include private non-profit agencies, such as Catholic or Jewish Social Services, and proprietary agencies such as private clinics or private in-home nursing services. The formal service network may provide services such as nursing care, social work or housekeeping. This relationship between a formal service provider and an older person is different from that of members of the informal network who maintain a more personal bond. Social workers are employed in most formal agencies. Because the formal service network is large, complex, and confusing, social workers in community agencies must be familiar with the different agencies available to the older client, the services they provide, and any eligibility requirements to use the services.

An important issue is how this formal network interfaces with an established informal support network of the clients. In addition, greater information about patterns of utilization of in-house and out of house services is also needed as different client factors are associated with various types of formal services (e.g., Ozawa & Teng 1999). Formal services do offer numerous benefits to clients, such as being staffed by trained professionals, having special equipment, and receiving money from the government. The current philosophy of service delivery is to have agencies and professionals bolster existing support mechanisms, such as families and friends, and fill in the service gaps or service need. For example, a daughter believed that her aging mother should be called daily. However, restrictions at the daughter's job prevented her from placing calls. The daughter contacted an agency to discuss this problem. The agency social worker linked the daughter to a telephone reassurance program sponsored through a local church. Now the phone program contacts the mother on weekdays and the daughter continues to make weekend calls. This type of collaboration by information and formal supports meets the needs of the aging person and assists the caregivers. Due to the burgeoning number of older adults who require some degree of support, the issues about costs, quality of care, and interface of formal and informal support systems continues to be paramount (Montgomery 1999).

Home-Based Services

Home health care services are those which are provided to people within their own home. These services are needed because of a functional limitation which prevents the older person from leaving home. For example, a person who is bedridden cannot get out to receive services in the community. Even though a person is quite frail, home-based service may provide more appropriate assistance than hospitals or nursing homes. Here is a brief summary about current home care services (Home care facts 1997):

■ An estimated 7 million Americans receive home care services. A disproportionate share are women who are older than seventy-five years of age. In 1994, 43 percent of Medicare home users had annual incomes under $10,000

■ Medicare is the biggest single payer of home care services, accounting for 38 percent of in-home programs in 1992.

■ In-home services vary by region of the country. In 1993, home health care agencies in nineteen states averaged 97.2 Medicare visits per patients, while agencies in other states averaged 36. The southeastern region had the most visits, with agencies in Tennessee, Alabama, Mississippi, and Georgia averaging 93 visits.

■ Fraud does exist in home health care billing procedures. Federal investigators believe that 10 percent of all home care bills submitted to Medicare and Medicaid are fraudulent, which translates into about $2.2 billion annually.

■ Although home care has the goal of cutting institutional costs, there have actually been about 15 percent increases in costs. However, carefully targeted home and community-based care recently has reduced nursing home use and lowered costs by a range of 9 to 23 percent in three states.

The goal of home-based services is to decrease, delay, or prevent nursing home or hospital admission. Services provided within the home assist an elderly person in a variety of ways. Homebound people typically require multiple services provided by a number of health care providers. For example, nurses and physical therapists assist with medication and muscle rehabilitation. Home health aides assist with less complicated medical procedures, such as changing bandages, positioning or transferring. Homemakers attend to personal care areas, such as meal preparation, dressing and housekeeping. Home-based people may require any or all of these services, depending on their abilities and supports.

In 1994, about 8 percent of Medicare beneficiaries used home health care services. The average number of visits per year was sixty-five, which is an increase from fifty-two visits in 1994. The usage rates (upper 10 percent received more than two hundred visits during the calendar year and received assistance with 2.4 out of 5 activities of daily living [eating, bathing, toileting, transferring, and dressing] and 3.5 out of 6 instrumental activities of daily living [shopping, managing money, using the phone, light housework, heavy housework, meal preparation]. Over the period 1995–2000, the average number of home health visits per user is expected to increase to eighty-two. The total Medicare payments for home health care will reach close to $27 billion (Mauser 1997).

When older people cannot leave their homes, they are not able to get groceries or prepare meals, and they may not even feel like eating properly. Meals on Wheels is a meal delivery program to home-bound individuals. This program serves one or two meals per day to people unable to get around in the community. The primary function is to prepare and deliver meals, but it has the added function of providing home-bound elderly with a few minutes of social visiting. The Administration on Aging (1997b) reports that during fiscal year 1994, 113 million home-delivered meals were provided to 877,000 homebound elderly people. Most of the meals are delivered by volunteers who deliver to the same individuals daily. An established route has the added advantage of allowing the volunteers to monitor the homebound person. Many of these volunteers are themselves older people. Older volunteers for this program become the service providers to other older people in a self-help arrangement benefiting both the volunteer and the homebound elderly.

Social workers in home health care are often responsible for coordinating the various professionals and organizations involved in caring for a home-bound client. Often social workers act as liaisons for clients with health care agencies and insurance providers, including Medicaid and Medicare. Social workers help the family and client adjust to service providers entering the home and providing care. Reassessment of clients' needs are an on-going part of social work in home-based care. Clients who are improving may need some services reduced while other clients may need additional services over time. An effective service plan needs to adapt to the changing needs of the clients and their informal supports.

Social workers in home health care also need to be aware of potential limitations of these services. Many private insurance companies do not provide coverage for services within a client's home. Medicare and Medicaid funds also have restrictions on what type of home service can be reimbursed. Medicare policies do not consider social work as a primary service. Social work services are covered only if they are ordered by a physician. As already discussed, this area of health services has changed dramatically in recent years. Continued changes in coverage are expected (Meyer 1997a). Another problem is the unavailability of health care services. Rural areas or poorer communities may not have the necessary resources to provide a well-integrated home health care service.

Community Services

Unlike home health services, community programs provide services to many older people simultaneously. This system has two major benefits: it is able to provide services to a large number of people and it gives older people an opportunity to socialize with peers. Two types of community services will be discussed. One type is the care services offering temporary supervision or assistance for an older person and temporary relief for the caregivers. Care programs serve those elderly with mental or physical impairments which prevent them from staying alone. The second type of community service is congregate programs which mainly attract the older person with preserved functional and mental abilities. These programs are provided at various community sites where older individuals gather together to receive a service, such as a meal. Unlike home-based services, community programs are designed for the elderly who are ambulatory or mobile.

CARE SERVICES

Community care sites provide temporary care for the elderly person allowing their caregivers to attend to other tasks, such as working, shopping, socializing, or relaxing. These services have an added advantage over home care services because the people have an opportunity to socialize with others. The following paragraphs review the different types of community programs available for the elderly and their caregivers.

For caregivers of an impaired person, leaving the home for any reason may mean finding and paying someone else to provide temporary care to an impaired family member. Even small trips to the grocery store can become complicated, involved, and costly. Respite care services provide relief for caregivers enabling them to use time for something other than caregiving. A definition of respite care is "short-term temporary care for disabled or chronically ill people living at home" (Joyce, Singer, & Isralowitz 1983, p. 153). There are many models of respite services, some provided within a person's home and others at some community site. Community respite care can be in adult foster care or nursing homes. For example, a family going on vacation can arrange for an elderly parent to stay in respite while they are away. In-home respite is usually for a short time, perhaps a few hours so a couple can have a night out together. Used on a regular basis, respite services can help prevent or decrease the feeling of entrapment by caregivers. Having periodic breaks from the responsibility of providing care, family members can attend to tasks, to personal matters, or simply have a needed break.

Adult day care centers provide a supervised environment for the elderly who are unable to remain alone. Although similar to respite care, day care centers require regular attendance while respite services are scheduled around certain times or events. Many caregivers use adult day care because they are working and must be out of the home. Most day care centers are small, averaging fifteen to twenty clients with a staff ratio of 1:5 or 1:7. Maintaining this size and ratio prevents the development of an institutional atmosphere (Gelfand 1984). Day care centers typically provide some type of programming for their participants, such as crafts or other individual or group projects. Individual plans are drawn up for participants of the centers based upon medical, social, and functional assessments. Staff is available to assist day care participants with special needs, such as ambulation, taking medications, or toileting.

A newer model of day care is the intergenerational center. In this setting, older adults and children are brought together in the same program. The goal of this model is to provide an opportunity for increased interactions between the generations. The benefit for older adults is to fill meaningful roles with younger generations. Over the past decade, there has been tremendous growth in this service model (Ames & Youatt 1994). Unfortunately, there has been more attention paid to the children who participate in this type of program than to the older adults. Dellman-Jenkins (1997) outlines a model program that is designed to enhance the older adults' participation in this type of setting. Specific dimensions of a quality intergenerational model include: orientation for both children and older adult participants, older adults making decisions about how they can relate to the children, adequate training for staff, and adequate evaluation of shared activities between participants of both ages to determine which ones are successful.

Hospices provide services to the terminally ill. While not specifically designed for older people, this population is frequently diagnosed with conditions appropriate for hospice care. Since these programs deal with the terminally ill, or those for whom there are no cures, the focus of care is providing comfort measures for the patient and the family. Issues of bereavement and grief are discussed openly with patients and families, and the hospice team assists in making appropriate plans. Hospice teams use an interdisciplinary approach, providing physical, social, emotional, and spiritual care. Teams usually include a physician, nurse, social worker, clergy member, and volunteers (Williams & Anderson 1986). As with respite services, care can be provided within the person's home or within various community structures such as a hospital or community health agency. Since 1989, Medicare hospice benefits have been available to terminally ill nursing home residents. Over the past decade, hospice has become more commonly available to these older adults as well (Petryek & Mor 1999). Regardless of the setting, hospice care promotes the quality of life for patient and family, not just the extension of life.

CONGREGATE PROGRAMS

Congregate programs provide services to the elderly and opportunities for socializing at various community sites. Two types of congregate programs will be discussed: the Congregate Meal Program and the Multi Purpose Senior Center.

The Congregate Meal Program is a federal program authorized in 1973 by the Older American Act. This program provides a hot meal for the elderly at various places within the community. Typical meal sites include churches, school cafeterias, or senior centers. This program provides for the nutritional needs of older persons who may be at high risk for malnutrition. Barriers to proper nutritional eating include inadequate finances to purchase food, inability to prepare or purchase groceries, or the lack of desire to eat. Eating involves psychosocial factors; people who are depressed or lonely may have less desire to eat. Congregate meal sites address both the nutritional and social aspects of eating. While all people over sixty years of age are entitled to this program, sites are planned with special attention to low-income older people. Many people take advantage of the congregate meal program. In 1994, 127 million meals were served to 2.3 million older adults nationally (Administration on Aging 1997b). Frequently, meal sites provide some programming on issues or activities of interest to the elderly. Examples of typical offerings are a lecture by a dietitian on low-cost meal preparation, organized card games or health promotion exercises.

The Multi Purpose Senior Center is another type of congregate program. These centers were established by the Older American Act and began receiving federal funding in the mid 1970s. Senior centers follow a holistic approach to the health of older people, offering an array of services within a centralized location (Gelfand & Gelfand 1982). Senior centers are found within local communities across the nation. They provide older community members a place to gather, socialize and receive services and information. While different locations stress different programs based upon community needs and desires, program offerings fall into two major categories (Gelfand 1984). One type is recreation/education programs. Seniors can choose from activities, such as drama, lectures, arts and crafts, physical fitness, and many others. The second type of program focuses on services delivered through the center. Representatives from community agencies such as Social Security, legal centers, or housing authorities often have hours within senior centers. Community services such as meal programs, health screenings, or day care, can be delivered within the center. Multi Purpose Senior Centers provide opportunities for community seniors to become involved with others and receive needed services at accessible locations.

Many of the community programs outlined above have social workers on staff. Depending upon program goals, the social workers may become involved in a variety of services. For most community programs, a major issue is transportation to and from the community site. Social workers may be involved in coordinating transportation for clients or linking with other community agencies for shared services. Community advocacy and organization tasks are other ways social workers coordinate transportation. For clients who use public transportation possible froms of assistance include a reduced rate for people over sixty years, arranged stops close to community programs, and accessible transportation vehicles for people with physical limitations. Transportation coordination between families, such as Share-a-Ride program, is an additional idea for social work intervention.

Besides transportation coordination, social workers in community services play a major role in coordinating services for program clients and families. For example, a single daughter who lives with her eighty-five-year-old father relies on day care services while she works. Her work schedule varies and she frequently works in the evenings or on weekends when the day care center is closed. Social workers knowledgeable about other forms of respite care in the community can assist the daughter in structuring a plan so her father is cared for while she works these shifts. Figure 6.2 is a problem/solution inventory which can be used as a checklist by social workers and families (Hooyman 1983). Possible problems of the elderly person are identified along with ways of solving the problems. Families should be encouraged to use these resources to prevent strain and stresses of caregiving.

Summary

Social workers in community systems are frequently involved with families or caregivers of the older clients, as well as with the clients themselves. Sometimes work with the families involves discussions and assurances about the quality of services provided. With respite care, for example, the social worker may have to plan the transition of a family into a service (Ellis 1986). Families planning on using a respite placement for any length of time may have reservations or guilt about going away and leaving a parent in a nursing home. Introducing the family to the system gradually by discussing the specific respite program, visiting the respite location and perhaps arranging a trial stay allows both family and older member to become familiar with the surroundings before a longer respite time is planned.

Home-based and community services are cost effective and humane methods of serving the health, social, and emotional needs of the elderly. While community programs serve people who have some mobility, even frail people are assisted by home-based services. Social workers have important functions in coordinating and delivering these services.

Model Programs

Over the past several years, various types of home and community services have been initiated to help prevent institutionalization of older adults. The following section provides examples of various services that have been successful in achieving this goal. Many employ social workers in service delivery, and others should be part of social workers' referral networks if available in their community.

Options for Elders

As a result of the Medicaid waiver project, the expansion of state home care programs, and the growth in Medicare, the number and type of home care services have expanded. However, these programs may not be organized in a manner that is rational and accessible to older adults who need them. During 1989–1991, Ohio initiated the Options for Elders

Problem	Possible community resources
Difficulty arranging transportation to employment, volunteer site, senior center, medical appointment, etc.	Carpools with neighbors, families of other older people, fellow volunteers or workers. City provisions for older people: reduced bus fares, taxi cab scrip, "Trans-Aide." Volunteer services: Red Cross, Salvation Army, church organizations for emergency or occasional transportation.
Living alone and fearing accidental injury or illness without access to assistance.	Telephone check-up services through local hospitals, or friends, neighbors, or relatives. Postal alert: register with local senior center; sticker on mail box alerts letter carrier to check for accumulation of mail. Newspaper delivery: parents of the delivery boy or girl can be given an emergency phone number if newspapers accumulate. Neighbors: can check pattern of lights on/off.
Needs assistance with personal care such as bathing and dressing.	Private pay for hourly services: home aides from private agencies listed in phone book. Visiting Nurse Association: services will include aide services when nurses are utilized. Medicaid/Medicare: provisions for home aides are limited to strict eligibility requirements, but such care is provided in certain situations. Student help: posting notices on bulletin boards at nursing schools can yield an inexpensive helper. Home sharing: sharing the home with another person who is willing to provide this kind of assistance in exchange for room and board.
Needs occasional nursing care and/or physical therapy.	Visiting nurse: services provided through Medicare or Medicaid or sliding scale fees; must be ordered by a physician. Home health services: private providers; Medicare and Medicaid reimbursement for authorized services. Veterans Administration Hospital Home Care: for veterans over sixty years old for specific situations.
Difficulty cooking meals, shopping for food, and arranging nutritious diet.	Home-delivered meals: "Meals on Wheels" delivers frozen meals once a week, sliding fees. Nutrition sites: meals served at senior centers, churches, schools, and other sites. Cooperatives: arrangements with neighbors to exchange a service for meals, food shopping, etc.
Not enough contact with other people; insufficient activity or stimulation; loneliness and boredom.	Senior centers: provide social opportunities, classes, volunteer opportunities, outings. Church-sponsored clubs: social activities, volunteer opportunities, outings. Support groups: for widows, stroke victims, and general support. Adult day care: provides social interaction, classes, discussion groups, outings, exercise.
Difficulty doing housework.	Homemaker services: for those meeting income eligibility criteria. Service exchanges: with neighbors and friends, e.g., babysitting exchanged or housework help. Home helpers: hired through agencies or through employment listings at senior centers, schools, etc. Home sharing: renting out a room or portion of the home, reduced rent for help with housework.
Forgetful about financial affairs; eyesight too poor for balancing checkbook and reading necessary information.	Power of attorney: given to friend or relative for handling financial matters. Joint checking account: with friend or relative for ease in paying bills. Volunteer assistance: available from the Red Cross, Salvation Army, church groups, senior centers, and other organizations.
Needs assistance with will, landlord-tenant concerns, property tax exemptions, guardianship, etc.	Senior citizens' legal services. Lawyer referral service: offered by the county bar association. City/county aging programs: hotlines for information and assistance in phone book.

Figure 6.2 Problems/Solution Inventory *Source:* Hooyman 1983.

Demonstration Project described by Applebaum and Mayberry (1996). The goal was to develop a coordinated service system for individuals who required in-home care. This type of service, called channeling models of care, has been established to reduce nursing home placements and contain costs of home care (Kemper 1990).

The program uses a single entry point model for anyone who requires long-term care assistance. Service requests range from information only to provision of services. Based on the initial service request, callers are assigned to a Basic, Ongoing, or Case Management level of care. Basic assistance is defined as short-term needs (less than eight weeks), Ongoing level is for those who require services for a longer period of time but need low levels of case management. The Case Management level assists individuals with more extensive service needs or care management. The combined costs for monthly service and case management was about $258 for Basic assistance, $236 for Ongoing, and $574 for Case Managed clients (Applebaum & Mayberry 1996; Applebaum, Ciferri, Riley, & Molfenter 1991). These data suggest that this case management program can provide clients with the level of service that is needed within a reasonable cost structure.

On Lok Senior Health Services

On Lok is located in San Francisco with particular focus on comprehensive and culturally sensitive health care needs of Asian American adults. Often, the individuals who use this service are immigrants who speak no or limited English and have health care beliefs that are not valued in the American health model. On Lok provides an array of service from meals to acute hospitalizations based upon the needs of the individual participant. Evaluations of cost and quality suggest that this model has been successful in reducing the need for institutionalization and providing quality services (Van Steenberg, Ansak, & Chin-Hansen 1993). On Lok encourages participants to make autonomous health care decisions, and most continue in the program until their death (Der-McLeod & Hensen 1992).

Senior Home Repair and Maintenance Programs

As older adults experience health declines, many are unable to maintain upkeep of their homes. Unfortunately, this can create safety problems and can lead to home accidents or unsafe environments. In research on home modifications, Tideiksaar (1990) reported that these changes accounted for a 72 percent decrease in falls in the elderly. In a national exploratory survey of programs, Osterkamp and Chapin (1995) identify three types of home repair and service models that are available for older adults. These are:

- On-going handyman service. Usually sponsored by a community aging agency or church related group. Volunteers (often retired men) provide a range of repairs from unclogging drains to repairing roof leaks. Example of this type of program: "Mr. Fixit," sponsored by the Senior Multi-Purpose Center in Flemington, New Jersey.
- Seasonal home maintenance. Usually community efforts sponsored by a volunteer center service group, with donations from area business or organizations. Group members may rake leaves, trim shrubs, or cut lawns of older adults. Example of this type of program: "Paint the Town," in Boise, Idaho, where one day each year, community volunteers paint older or disabled adults' homes.

- Intergenerational programs. Typically involve students from schools or youth groups who receive service or academic credits for projects. Student volunteers assume a variety of tasks with adults or peers that benefit older adults. Example of this type of program: "Serve Our Seniors," in Arlington Heights, Illinois, collaborative project of the school district and community agencies, partially funded by the Charles Stewart Mott Foundation. These students do tasks such as installing smoke detectors, cleaning gutters, or exterior painting for older adults in their community.

Gatekeeper Programs

Every day, older adults may come into contact with natural supports in the community who can function as a source of information and referral. These natural "gatekeeper programs" have been established in several communities nationwide. Examples of natural gatekeepers are newspaper carriers, meter-readers, postal carriers, or bank tellers. These are individuals who can provide information about changes in an older person's level of functioning or identify potential problems such as piled newspapers, broken windows in the home, or un-retrieved mail. In both Seattle and Virginia, companies (banks, power companies) partner with aging services to train natural gatekeepers to signs of concern with older adults. These employees learn potential problem signs and make referrals to appropriate sources for further investigation. These types of programs can provide a point of contact for at-risk older adults, especially those individuals who are isolated. One evaluation of this type of program determined that 40 percent of a geriatric case psychiatric program were isolated older adults who were chronically mentally ill (Raschko 1991).

Telemedicine

Technological advances have changed many aspects of society, including the provision of in-home services. Telemedicine, which includes various components such as telephone, radio communications, and interactive video, has increased rapidly over the last few years and has the potential to cut costs and increase the efficiency of in-home health care workers. For example, a network links patients to nurses in four sites in Hays, Atwood, and Lawrence, Kansas, and Kansas City, Missouri. Cost reductions have decreased patients' visits to their physicians by substituting telemedical evaluations in the home for on-site ones (Jones 1996). Although the evaluation data are just preliminary at this time, Medicaid pays $35 for an initial consult and $9 for additional ones. Traditional on-site Medicaid consults are $62. In Kaye's (1997) estimate of potential cost savings, reductions may be achieved in the areas of fewer emergency room visits, physician office visits, or in-home consults. Telemedicine is not confined to only health-related evaluations, however. An examination of a psychometric evaluation for mental status (using the Mini-Mental Status Examination) can be conducted via telemedicine (Montani et al. 1996). Due to the potential to increase access for quality care, and simultaneously control costs, telemedicine appears to have important benefits for older adults' health care (Kropf & Grigsby 1999).

These models are a sample of the programs around the country providing community based long-term care. They reflect the effort of professionals responding to the need for consolidated and comprehensive services. Hopefully, additional models and demonstration projects will influence policymakers and service providers to consider community and home-based services as viable, cost-effective, and humane methods of caring for our elderly population.

Discussion Questions

1. What is a definition of long-term care? Why are home health and community care programs important components of a long-term care system?
2. What are three areas of stress and strain for family caregivers? How can social workers intervene to minimize or buffer the stress of caregiving?
3. How is a formal support network different from an informal network?
4. How do home health and community care services differ? What are typical social work functions in both kinds of services?

Experiential Learning

Activity: Where Has My Time Gone?

In the following exercise, you will become sensitized to the amount of time caregivers of the elderly spend performing that role. First, outline a typical week. Then, adjust this schedule to provide caregiving tasks for an elderly relative. Choose a typical week in your life, and fill in the worksheet (figure 6.3) with activities performed within the time slots for each day of the week. For example, classes could be filled in for Monday/Wednesday/Friday, 9 AM–Noon.

Now, read the following story:

You are the only relative who lives in the same town as your Aunt Emily. She is seventy-four years old and widowed. She is in the hospital with a broken hip which occurred when she slipped on ice outside her apartment. She is about to be discharged and cannot live by herself for at least three months. Since no other relatives are available to help, she is coming to live with you while she convalesces. She currently gets around with a walker but requires help in the following areas:

- Preparing meals
- Dressing and undressing
- Bathing
- Toileting
- Dispensing medication, which needs to be refrigerated. She takes her medication orally at breakfast, lunch, and dinner.
- Laundering clothes

On a second copy of the Activity Worksheet, plan what your week would look like if you had to fit these caregiving responsibilities into your regular week's activities. Fill out the second sheet by altering your schedule to assist Aunt Emily.

After you have competed the worksheets, assess how your life would change if you became a caregiver of an older person. What activities were cut out to make room for caregiving tasks? How much personal time is left? How would you feel if you had to assume the caregiving schedule?

Time	Sunday	Monday	Tuesday	Wednesday	Thursday	Friday	Saturday
Midnight–6 A.M.							
6 A.M.–9 A.M.							
9 A.M.–Noon							
Noon–3 P.M.							
3 P.M.–6 P.M.							
6 P.M.–9 P.M.							
9 P.M.–Midnight							

■ **Figure 6.3**   Where Has My Time Gone? Activity Worksheet

Case Studies

See Appendix B for guidelines in analyzing gerontological social work practice.

Case 1: A Healthy Mrs. Heath

"I'm tired of being in this hospital and want to go home." These are the first words Mrs. Heath tells Ann Blake, the hospital social worker.

Mrs. Heath is a sixty-three-year-old widow who lives alone in an apartment. She is currently hospitalized for a fractured leg. She was admitted two days ago after falling in her church parking lot. Her private insurance policy fully covers any medical problems and is expected to heal successfully. Her discharge date is scheduled in one week. However, Mrs. Heath will need assistance after her discharge. Ann Blake, the hospital social worker, has been contacted to assist in discharge planning for this patient.

Mrs. Heath is expected to have her leg in a cast for a month after her release from the hospital. Her physician predicts that she will be able to walk with a walker soon after her return home. Due to her lack of strength and the size of her cast, he thinks her mobility will be limited while she uses her walker. She needs to return to the hospital biweekly to monitor the healing process and to have the cast setting checked.

Mrs. Heath tells the social worker that she gets along well with others in her apartment complex where most of the residents are retired and widowed. After the death of her husband four years ago, she moved into this complex so she wouldn't be so lonely. She and her husband were "always on the go" and she felt lost right after his death. She and the other widows in the apartment complex socialize frequently. They go shopping together, eat out, and see movies. Her room is already beginning to fill with cards and plants from her friends. She is anxious to return to her apartment and resume her life activities. Although she has two adult children, both are married, work, and have families. Her son lives in another state, and her daughter is several miles away. Although Mrs. Heath has a good relationship with both children, she does not want to convalesce in their homes. She stated that she would "go crazy living there. I'm used to my own place now, you know. Right after Arnie, my husband, died, I stayed with my daughter for a month. What a mess! I love my grandkids and my poor granddaughter had to move out of her room so I could have a place to stay. A twelve-year-old girl needs her own room. I was out of place. No, I won't go back there to stay. I'm used to my apartment with my friends and my beautiful kitty, Sugar."

Mrs. Heath has expressed much frustration with this accident. She is particularly worried that she may not be able to prepare meals, attend to personal hygiene, and drive her car. Mrs. Heath is active in a number of groups, including her church, a senior citizens club, and her group of women friends. She receives a good pension from her husband's employment and is financially secure. As the hospital social worker, Ann Blake is responsible to make sure that Mrs. Heath has the assistance she needs after her return home.

Source: Nancy P. Kropf.

Case 2: The Pressing Needs of Mrs. Preston

"My mother has been acting different lately. Her behavior really has me concerned." Alice Marshall begins to describe the unusual way her mother has been acting.

Mrs. Preston, Alice's mother, is a seventy-eight-year-old widow. She has lived alone since her husband's death twenty years ago. She is in good health, except for high blood pressure which is controlled by diet and medication. She gets along well with her neighbors, all of whom she knows by name. Her favorite activities are baking, watching TV, and going for walks. Until recently, she has been managing her household well.

Two months ago, neighbors contacted Alice with concerns about Mrs. Preston. On three or four occasions, neighbors observed her walking through the neighborhood in her pajamas and slippers. She has also accused the newspaper and postal carriers of trying to break into her house, although she has known these people for years.

Alice describes changes within her mother's normal housekeeping routine. Her mother was an immaculate housekeeper. Recently things have been out of order. Dirty clothes are piled in corners of the room. Dishes caked with food are stacked on living room furniture. Numerous hazards were discovered in the kitchen, such as newspaper placed on top of the burners. All the pots were badly burned, and black ants were crawling over the counter and dirty dishes. "But the hardest part," Alice stated, "is her denial. She insists that the pans have been scorched for years. I know that's not true. One Saturday I spent the entire day cleaning her house. I washed the dishes, laundered her clothes, sprayed the ants. One week later, the place was a mess again."

Alice contacted her brother who lives in town. For two weeks they have been taking turns going to see their mother daily. Since both have jobs and families, these trips are demanding of their time. Alice has also started to prepare meals for her mother as she suspects that her mother is not eating properly. Alice is worried that her mother needs more assistance than she and her brother can provide. She concludes with the statement, "Even though she doesn't want to, Mother may have to move to a nursing home."

Source: Nancy P. Kropf.

Annotated Bibliography

Aneshensel C. S., Pearlin, L. I., Mullan, J. T., Zarit, S. H., & Whitlatch, C. J. (1995). *Profiles in caregiving: The unexpected career.* San Diego, CA: Academic Press.

    Reports on a study of caregivers of older adults with dementia. Included are topics on experience with stress, impact on interpersonal relationships and roles of the care provider, transition to institutional care, and dealing with death of the family member. Also included are interventions that can benefit care providers and implications for public policy.

Barton, L. J. (1997). Comparing the options. *American Demographics, 19,* 48–49.

    Compares various housing and service options for older adults. The author compares advantages and disadvantages of each, and gives an estimate of cost. The major categories that are covered are: independent living, independent assisted living, home health care, continuing care retirement communities, assisted living, and board-and-care homes.

Cox, E. O. & Dooley, A. C. (1996). Care receivers' perception of their role in the care process. *Journal of Gerontological Social Work, 26*(1/2), 133–152.

    This article takes a unique perspective in exploring the role of the care recipient. The study examined a sample of black, white, and Hispanic care recipients about their experience in care provision. Several areas were important for the sample including the relationship that they shared with the caregiver and the ability to accept their limitations and disabilities. Surprisingly, no one in the sample had discussed issues of their role in the caregiving process with a social worker.

Feldman, P. H. (Ed) (1999). *Journal of Aging and Health, 11*(3).

    The entire issue of this journal relates to goals and effectiveness of home-based services. Articles deal with family issues, efficacy of services, and resource allocation.

Henry, M. E. & Capitman, J. A. (1995). Finding satisfaction in adult day care: Analysis of a national demonstration of dementia care and respite services. *Journal of Applied Gerontology, 14,* 302–320.

    This study was designed to determine levels of satisfaction of informal caregivers who had relatives participate in ten dementia specific day care sites. The researchers determined that satisfaction with services is complex and involves the level of functioning of the older adult and aspects of the site such as cost and programming.

Hughes, B. (1995). *Older people and community care: Critical theory and practice.* Philadelphia, PA: Open University Press.

    Two agenda items converge as the theme for this book and tackle both practice and policy issues. One is the context of community care to provide older people with both social and health care services. The author also discusses ageism and the impact of this form of oppression on community care resources and programs.

Jette, A. M., Smith, K. W., & McDermott, S. (1996). Quality of Medicare-reimbursed home health care. *The Gerontologist, 36,* 492–501.

    With the increase in home health providers, this research reviewed case records to determine adequacy of care for clients. Serious quality deficiencies were note in about 15 percent of the home health care episodes, which could have potentially problematic outcomes for the older adult. The most common problem that was reported was difficulty in delivering prescribed nursing or therapy services.

O'Brien, R. C. & Flannery, M. T. (1997). *Long-term care: Federal, state, and private options for the future.* New York: Haworth Press.

    Policy issues that impact long-term care are covered at both national and state levels. In a section on alternative programs, state-by-state coverage of long-term care initiatives is summarized.

General Bibliograpy

Anastas, J., Gibeau J., & Larson, P. (1990). Working families and elder care: A national perspective in an aging America. *Social Work*, *35*, 405–411.

Davit, J. K. & Kaye, L. W. (1996). Supporting patient autonomy: Decision making in home health care. *Social Work*, *41*, 41–50.

Donovan, R., Kurzman, P. A., & Rotman, C. (1993). Improving the lives of home care workers: A partnership of social work and labor. *Social Work*, *38*, 579–585.

Freedman, M. (1994). Helping home bound elderly clients understand and use advance directives. *Social Work in Health Care*, *20*, 61–73.

Gilson, S. F. & Casebolt, G. J. (1997). Personal assistance services and case management. *Journal of Case Management*, *6*, 13–17.

Greene, R. R. & Knee, R. I. (1996). Shaping the policy practice agenda of social work in the field of aging. *Social Work*, *41*, 533–560.

Haddad, A. M. (1994). Reaching a right and good decision: Ethical decision-making and the front-line worker. *Generations*, *18*, 75–77.

Kaye, L. W. (1997). Telemedicine: Extension to home care? *Telemedicine Journal*, *3*, 243–246.

Kingston, E. & O'Grady-LeShane, R. (1993). The effects of caregiving on women's Social Security benefits. *The Gerontologist*, *33*, 230–239.

Osterkamp, L. B. & Chapin, R. K. (1995). Community-based volunteer home-repair and home-maintenance programs for elders: An effective service paradigm? *Journal of Gerontological Social Work*, *24*(1/2), 55–75.

Penning, M. J. (1995). Cognitive impairment, caregiver burden, and the utilization of home health services. *Journal of Aging and Health*, *7*, 233–253.

Stull, D. E., Cosbey, J., Bowman, K., & McNutt, W. (1997). Institutionalization: A continuation of family care. *Journal of Applied Gerontology*, *16*, 379–402.

Tully, C. T. & Sehm, S. D. (1994). Eldercare: The social service system's missing link? *Journal of Gerontological Social Work*, *21* (3/4), 117–132.

Van Steenberg, C., Ansak, M., & Chin-Hansen, J. (1993). On Lok's model: Managed long-term care. In C. Barresi and D. Stull (Eds.), *Ethnic elderly and long-term care* (pp. 178–190). Springer.

Verhey, M. P. (1996). Quality management in home care: Models for today's practice. *Home Care Provider*, *1*, 180–185.

Wallace, S. P., Campbell, K., & Lew-Ting, C. (1994). Structured barriers for the use of formal in-home services by elderly Latinos. *Journals of Gerontology*, *49*, S253–S263.

References

Administration on Aging. (1997a). *Facts on aging*. Washington, DC: A. A.

Administration on Aging (1997b). *Fact Sheet: Elderly nutrition program evaluation 1993–1995*. Washington, DC: A. A.

American Association of Retired Persons. (1997). Ensuring a responsive long-term care system: New challenge for a new century. *Perspectives in Health and Aging*, *12*(1), 1–6.

Ames, B. & Youatt, J. (1994). Intergenerational education and service programming. *Educaitonal Gerontology*, *20*, 755–764.

Anastas, J., Gibeau, J., & Larson, P. (1990). Working families and elder care: A national perspective in an aging America. *Social Work*, *35*, 405–411.

Aneshensel, C. S., Pearlin, L. I., Mullan, J. T., Zarit, S. H., & Whitlatch, C. J. (1995). *Profiles in caregiving: The unexpected career*. San Diego, CA: Academic Press.

Anker, L. & Trumbower, J. A. (1985). Congregations reach out to the homebound. *Aging*, no. 351.

Applebaum, R., Ciferri, W., Riley, T,. & Molfenter, C. (1991). Evaluation of the implementation of Ohio's options for elders demonstration. Oxford, OH: Miami University, Scripps Gerontology Center.

Applebaum, R. & Mayberry, P. (1996). Long-term care case management: A look at alternative models. *The Gerontologist, 35,* 701–705.

Bernadette, M., Wright, L. D., Minkler, M., & Fullarton, J. (1981). Self-care and mutual help. *Report of the technical committee on health maintenance and health promotion.* White House Conference on Aging. Washington, DC: U.S. Government Printing Office.

Brody, S. J. & Masciocchi, B. A. (1980). Data for long-term care planning by health systems agencies. *American Journal of Public Health, 70*(11).

Cantor, M. H. (1979). Neighbors and friends: A overlooked resource in the informal support system. *Research on Aging, 1*(4).

Cantor, M. H. (1985). Families: A basic source of long-term for the elderly. *Aging,* no. 349.

Day, A. T. (1985). Who cares? Demographic trends challenge family care for the elderly. *Population Trends and Public Policy.* Washington, DC: Population Reference Bureau, Inc.

Der-McLeod, D. & Hensen, J. C. (1992). On Lok: The family continuum. *Generations, 16*(3), 71–72.

Dellman-Jenkins, M. (1997). A senior-model of international programming with young children. *Journal of Applied Gerontology, 16*(4), 495–506.

Freedman, V. A. (1999). Long term admissions to home health agencies: A life table analysis. *The Gerontologist, 39,* 16–24.

Gelfand, D. E. (1984). *The aging network* (2nd ed.). New York: Springer.

Gelfand, D. E. & Gelfand, J. R. (1982). Senior centers and social support networks. In P. Biegel & A. Naparstek (Eds.), *Community support systems and mental health.* New York: Springer.

Haber, D. (1983). Promoting mutual help groups among older persons. *The Gerontologist, 23*(3).

Hancock, B. L. (1987). *Social work with older people.* Englewood Cliffs, NJ: Prentice-Hall.

Home care facts. (1997). *Hospital & Health Networks, 71*(9), 24.

Hooyman, N. (1983). Social Support networks in services to the elderly. In J. K. Whittaker & J. Garbarino (Eds.), *Social support networks: Informal helping in the human services.* Chicago, IL: Aldine.

Hooyman, N. (1987). *The importance of social supports: Family, friends, and neighbors.* Unpublished document.

Huttman, E. D. (1985). *Social services for the elderly.* New York: Free Press.

Irwin, T. (1982). Home health care: When a patient leaves the hospital. *Public Affairs Pamphlet,* no. 560.

Jones, E. (1996). New horizons beckon to home health industry. *Telemedicine and Telehealth Networks, 2,* 18–24.

Joyce, K., Singer, M., & Isralowitz, R. (1983). Impact of respite care on parents' perceptions of quality of life. *Mental Retardation, 21*(4).

Kane, R. C. & Kane, R. A. (1994). Effects of the Clinton health reform on older persons and their families: A health care systems perspective. *The Gerontologist, 34*(5), 598–605.

Kaye, L. W. (1997). Telemedicine: Extension to home care? *Telemedicine Journal, 3,* 243–246.

Kemper, P. (1990). Case management agency systems of administering long-term care: Evidence from the Channeling Demonstration. *The Gerontologist, 6,* 817–824.

Kingston, E. & O'Grady-LeShane, R. (1993). The effects of caregiving on women's Social Security benefits. *The Gerontologist, 33,* 230–239.

Kropf, N. P. & Grigsby, R. K. (1999). Telemedicine for older adults. *Home Health Care Services Quarterly, 17,* (4), 1–11.

Leavenworth, G. (1995). Trends in home health care. *Business & Health, 13*(3), 155–156.

Lechner, V. M. & Gupta, C. (1996). Employed caregivers: A four-year follow-up. *Journal of Applied Gerontology, 15*(1), 102–115.

Mauser, E. (1997). Medicare home health initiative: Current activities and future direction. *Healthcare Financing Review, 18,* 275–291.

Meyer, H. (1997a). Home (care) improvement. *Hospitals & Health Networks, 71*(8), 40–42.

Meyer, H. (1997b). Home health on the high wire. *Hospitals & Health Networks, 71*(14), 26–29.

Montani, C., Billaud, N., Couturier, P., Fluchaire, I., Lemaire, R., Malteere, C., Lauvernay, N., Piquard, J. F., Frossard, M., & Franco, A. (1996). "Telepsychometry": A remote psychometry consultation in clinical gerontology: Preliminary study. *Telemedicine Journal, 2,* 145–150.

Montgomery, R. J. V. (1999). The family role in the context of long term care. *Journal of Aging and Health, 11*, 383–416.

Morrison, J. D. (1991). The black church as a support system for black elderly. *Journal of Gerontological Social Work, 17*(1/2), 105–120.

Morrow, Howell, N. & Ozawa, M. N. (1987). Helping network: Seniors to seniors. *The Gerontologist, 27*(1).

O'Brien, R. C. & Flannery, M. T. (1997). *Long-term care: Federal, state, and private options for the future.* New York: Haworth.

Ory, M. G., Hoffman, R. R., Yee, J. L, Tennstedt, S., & Schulz, R. (1999). Prevalence and impact of caregiving: A detailed comparison between dementia and non-dementia caregivers. *The Gerontologist, 39*, 177–185.

Osterkamp, L. B. & Chapin, R. K. (1995). Community-based volunteer home-repair and home-maintenance programs for elders: An effective service paradigm? *Journal of Gerontological Social Work, 24*(1/2, 55–75.

Ozawa, M. N. & Tseng, H. Y. (1999). Utilization of formal services during the ten years after retirement. *Journal of Gerontological Social Work, 31*(1/2), 3–20.

Petrisek, A. C. & Mor, V. (1999). Hospice in nursing homes: A facility-level analysis of the distribution of hospice beneficiaries. *The Gerontologist, 39*, 279–290.

Raschko, R. (1991). Spokane community mental health center elderly services. In E. Light and B. D. Lebowitz (Eds.), *The elderly with chronic mental illness.* New York: Springer.

Scharlach, A., Lowe, B., & Schneider, E. C. (1991). *Elder care and the work force.* Lexington, MA: D.C. Heath.

Shanas, E. (1979). The family as a social support system in old age. *The Gerontologist, 19*(2).

Silverstone, B. & Burack-Weiss, A. (1982). The social work function in nursing homes and home care. *Journal of Gerontological Social Work, 5*(1/2).

Tideiksaar, R. (1990). Environmental adaptions to preserve balance and prevent falls. *Topics in Geriatric Rehabilitation, 5*, 28–32.

Van Steenberg, C., Ansak, M. N., & Chin-Hansen, J. (1993). On Lok's model: Managed long-term care. In C. Barresi and D. Stull (Eds.), *Ethnic elderly and long-term care* (pp. 178–190). New York: Springer.

Virginia Long-Term Care Council. (1985). *Study of the public and private cost of institutional and community based long-term care.* Richmond, VA: VLTCC.

Wenger, G. C. (1984). *The supportive network: Coping with old age.* London: George Allen and Irwin.

Williams, J. & Anderson, H. (1986). Hospice. *Caring, 5.*

Zimmer, A. H. & Mellor, M. J. (1982). The role of the family in long-term home health care. *Pride Institute Journal of Long-Term Home Health Care, 1*(2).

7 Hospital Discharge Planning

■ ■ ■ ■ ■ ■ ■ ■ ■ ■ ■ ■ ■ ■

Sherry M. Cummings, with Deborah R. Jackson

Hospitals provide much of the acute health care of the elderly, and over a third of all nursing home admissions originate from hospitals. Unfortunately, it has been estimated that more than 20 percent of nursing home placements are inappropriate (Hooyman & Kiyak 1996). Given this fact, it can be seen that decisions made in hospitals about elderly persons' discharge plans can have significant implications. Older persons enter the hospital more often and stay longer than those under age sixty-five. Although the elderly make up 12.5 percent of the U.S. Population, they account for 42 percent of hospital stays (U.S. Senate, Special Committee on Aging 1991). While the average length of stay for patients aged sixteen to forty-four years is 4.6 days, persons sixty-five years and over average 8.7 days for each hospital stay (U.S. Department of health and Human Services 1992). For this reason the hospital social worker inevitably becomes involved in discharge planning for elderly patients. Their sheer numbers, complexity of their problems, and their vulnerability make older persons highly visible in the hospital setting. With the current emphasis toward community rather than institutional care, effective discharge processes are becoming increasingly more important in providing a high quality level of care (Waters 1987).

Social workers have played a pivotal role in health care ever since hospital social work was first introduced at Massachusetts General Hospital in 1905 (Abramson 1981). The discharge planning role however was once viewed as a nonprofessional task and considered a "stepchild" function of the hospital social worker (Davidson 1987). Recently, concerns about cost containment in health care have brought about a rediscovery of discharge planning "as a truly professional role that demands the highest abilities of assessment and intervention" (Blumenfield 1986, p. 52). Discharge planning requires basic social work knowledge of crisis intervention, interviewing, community resources, advocacy, family system functioning, geriatrics, death and dying, and systems theory (Bender 1987; Blumenfield & Rosenberg 1988).

Care provided by health care professionals is usually oriented toward the individual patient. Social workers, however, must be prepared to assist individual patients and their families within institutions, communities, and among many different professionals. Social workers provide leadership in interdisciplinary collaboration and the coordination of services and linkages for the patient to services both within and outside of the hospital setting (Saltz & Schaeffer 1996). The hospital is often a point of access to other services and serves as a vital component of the long-term health care of the elderly and as a primary setting for social work practice with older persons (Blumenfield 1982).

Overview of Discharge Planning

Definition

There are many possible answers to the question, "What is discharge planning?" A hospital administrator may say that discharge planning is a service that helps protect the organization's solvency (Davidson 1978). Hospital accrediting organizations and governmental agencies emphasize discharge planning as a mechanism for containing costs and assuring quality (Jessee & Doyle 1984). Patients and families may view discharge as a right (DeRienzo 1985), or as an unnecessary intrusion (Crittenden 1983).

Discharge planning can be defined as a "complex professional task that involves determining patient needs and wishes, assessing family resources and preferences, facilitating communication among relevant parties, and working with community agencies" (Proctor & Morrow-Howell 1990, p. 45). From a broad perspective, discharge planning may be defined as "a multidisciplinary approach to providing coordinated services to patients and their families in order to ensure continuity of care for the patient from hospital to home, from hospital to another facility, or from service to service within the hospital" (Shields 1987, pp. 1–2). The Joint Commission on the Accreditation of Health Care Organizations (1996) notes that discharge planning is an interdisciplinary effort aimed at identifying patients' continuing physical, emotional, social, and environmental needs and is responsible for arranging services to meet these needs.

An "adequate" plan for continuity of care after discharge should address both the medical and psychosocial needs of the patient and should maximize the patient's independent functioning and potential for wellness (Buckwalter 1985; Muenchow & Carlton 1985). Colerick and George (1986) add another dimension, which is especially important when dealing with elderly patients, and argue that an adequate after-care plan not only maximizes patient functioning and well-being, but does so "without jeopardizing quality of life for the caregiver" (p. 493). Drawing upon these concepts, an adequate discharge plan may be understood as one that counteracts the disabling effects, whether medical, functional, or emotional, of an illness or disability without jeopardizing caregiver well-being.

The Impact of DRG's and Managed Care

In 1983 the existing retrospective cost-of-service reimbursement model for Medicare was replaced with reimbursement based upon diagnostically related groups (DRGs). Rather then reimbursing hospitals for the costs incurred during a patient's stay, Medicare now reimburses hospitals a fixed amount based upon the patient's diagnosis. Hospitals that keep patients longer than the number of days established by the DRGs incur a financial loss. On the other hand, hospitals that are able to promptly discharge patients and, thereby, provide care at a cost below the established DRG, gain financially (Berkman 1988). Because of this reality, the introduction of DRGs resulted in a heightened emphasis on the importance of discharge planning as a means of efficiently moving patients out of the acute care setting and into the community for recuperation. The introduction of DRGs did result in decreased length of patient stays. Studies show that, while the average length of stay (LOS) was 9.6 days in 1983, by 1990 it had decreased to 6.4 days (U.S. Department of Health and Human Services 1992). There is concern, however, that as a result patients are being released from the hospital in a less stable condition and with greater after-care needs (Hooyman & Kiyak 1996; Kosecoff et al 1990).

The trend toward reduced LOS and the provision of needed continuing care in the community after discharge have further increased with the growth of managed care. Currently, almost 60 percent of the U.S. Population is covered by some type of managed care system. The number of elderly enrolled in Medicare HMOs has also begun to rise. Congressional projections suggest that within the next few years, 40 percent of the elderly will opt for managed care (Angus et al. 1996). Because inpatient's days represent one of the most expensive aspects of health care provision, managed care organizations have striven to further reduce patients' LOS. One study found that managed care organizations resulted in the reduction of patient LOS by 17 percent (Robinson 1996). Some argue that the continued decrease in length of hospital stays results in insufficient lead time to plan for discharge and negatively affects continuing patient care. In one study of hospital health care workers, 27 percent of the physicians and 13 percent of the social workers felt that patients were being discharged prematurely (Bull & Kane 1996). A recent national survey found that over 80% of caregivers encountered problems during the discharge planning process (vom Eigen, Walker, Edgman-Levitan, Cleary & Delbanco 1999). Patients, family members, and discharge planners are all under mounting pressure to swiftly develop effective after-care plans for persons with increasingly complex needs.

Four Recurring Themes

Definitions of discharge planning are abundant, and within these definitions are four recurring themes: discharge planning as a process, as a multidisciplinary activity, as a mechanism for ensuring continuity of care, and as a means of cost containment.

PROCESS

Discharge planning, as a special form of social casework, is a systematic, problem-solving process. The tasks involved in this process are (Blumenfield 1986):

- identifying people who need discharge planning;
- assessing their needs;
- identifying resources available to meet those needs;
- collaborating with the patient, family, and health care team, and
- developing and implementing a plan of action.

The discharge planning process should begin early, ideally, upon the patient's admission to the hospital. Timely discharge planning helps to alert hospital staff to the patient's after-care needs and gives the patient and family time to accept the fact that posthospital care will be required. It also gives the discharge planner time to explore resources and arrange for needed care (Haddock 1991). The process does not end with the patient's discharge from the hospital. Follow-up is important to ensure that the discharge plan is effectively meeting the patient's and family's needs (Berkman, Walker, Bonander & Homes 1992; Naylor et al 1999).

To illustrate this problem-solving process, consider the case of Mr. Sykes, an eighty-three-year old widower who enters the hospital with a severe respiratory infection. Due to his age and the fact that Mr. Sykes live alone, the social worker considers him at high risk. An assessment soon after Mr. Sykes' admission reveals that he has two sons and a daughter who have been "seeing about" their father. Mr. Sykes wants to go home when he is well enough, and his children are willing to care for him in his home. For Mr. Sykes, his "problem" is his illness and hospitalization. His financial situation, living environment, and social support system do not need social work intervention. For the social worker, Mr. Sykes' case is a relatively uncomplicated one. He was screened as a high-risk, but assessed as having resources available to meet his needs. He, his family, and his health care team agree that he should return home after discharge. After his discharge, the social worker will follow up on Mr. Sykes' medical condition and on the extent to which his adult children are able to continue their care as he needs them.

MULTIDISCIPLINARY COLLABORATION

Historically, discharge planning has been a role for hospital social workers. Entry of nurses into the role is a relatively new phenomenon. According to the guidelines of the Joint Commission of Accreditation of Health Care Organizations (JCAHCO) (1996), both nursing and social services may be involved in the process. It is no wonder that "turf" has become an issue in the field of discharge planning.

Social workers involved in discharge planning are members of a health care team. The team may be composed of all or some of the following: primary physician, nurse, utilization review coordinator, patient educator, dietitian, pharmacist, and physical, occupational, respiratory, and speech therapists. The social worker is responsible for coordinating the contributions of the team (Society for Hospital Social Work Directors of the American Hospital Association 1986) so that patients and their families will receive coordinated services (Shields 1987).

No one can be schooled in every area pertinent to a patient's situation. If discharge planning is to have a holistic approach, collaboration with health care professionals from a variety of disciplines is essential. Discharge planning is also to include the patient and the patient's family. It is the role of social workers and other health care professionals to help the patient and family develop and adapt to the plan of care (Joint Commission of Accreditation of Heath Care Organizations 1996; Saltz & Schaeffer 1996). Discharge planning is not something done to or for a patient but a collaboration of professionals and informal supports.

CONTINUITY OF CARE

Few patients are discharged from the hospital without needing some continuation of treatment. They may require as little as a special diet and rest. But for many older patients who often have several chronic health problems, continuity of care after hospitalization may mean the difference between returning to their level of functioning prior to illness, or returning to the hospital.

As illustrated in Fig. 7.1, everyone who enters an acute care setting is discharged in one of four ways: returning home without supports, returning home with assistance from the family or community services, going to an alternative care facility, or through death (Zarle 1987). If the patient recovers, the discharge planner uses his or her expertise to help structure a plan to meet the needs of the patient after leaving the hospital.

Patient-centered discharge planning must involve both patient and family in decision making to incorporate their needs and expectations. This type of collaborative decision making is important. The discharge plan is designed to ensure the patient's safety, well-

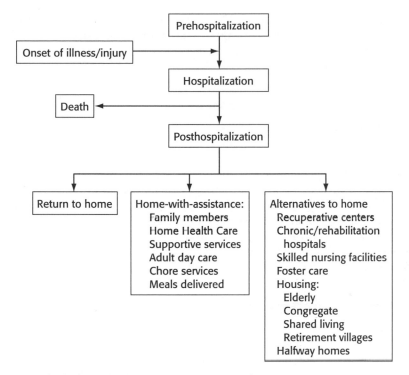

■ **Figure 7.1**   Continuing Care Planning Continuum   *Source:* Zarle 1987, p. 3.

being, and is an essential component of the continuing care process (Bull & Kane 1996; Chakrabarty, Beallor & Pelle 1988). The expectation of reasonable continuity of care is so important to the discharge planning process that it is included in the standards issued by JCAHCO (1996).

COST CONTAINMENT

Discharge planning is a pivotal component of hospitals' efforts to increase efficiency and cost effectiveness. Social workers have joined other researchers in exploring the discharge planning processes and the impact on hospital resource utilization. Studies show that prompt and comprehensive discharge planning are associated with shorter hospital stays. In fact, these studies report that efficient and thorough discharge planning can reduce patients' LOS by two to five days (Evans, Hendricks, Lawrence-Umlauf & Bishop 1989; Liebergall 1999). When patients are discharged from the acute-care setting and are able to receive continuing care in a less medically intense environment, health care dollars are conserved. It is important, however, that discharge planning results not only in shorter hospitals stays but also in effective after-care that meets patients' medical and psychosocial needs. Inadequate after-care plans may result in a deterioration in the patient's condition and costly readmissions to the hospital (Berkman & Abrams 1986). Studies have found that prompt and comprehensive discharge planning is related to an increase in patients' health status

(Haddock 1991; Soskolne & Auslander 1993), higher levels of patient satisfaction (Haddock 1991) and decreased readmissions (Naylor et al 1999). Therefore, efficient and effective discharge planning can help contain costs by reducing patient LOS and by preventing avoidable readmissions.

Aims and Objectives of Discharge Planning

Despite differences among hospitals in staffing, policies, and procedures of discharge planning, several objectives are common to all. Commonly described goals include: (1) delivery and coordination of needed services in the after-care environment; (2) reinforcement of patient gains made in the acute-care setting; (3) enhancement of the patient's ability to deal with limitations as a result of his or her illness; (4) maintenance of the patient in the post-discharge environment at the highest level of health and social functioning possible; (5) prevention and alleviation of unnecessary stress on the patient and family; (6) reduction of financial burden on patients, families, the hospital, and third party payers; and (7) promotion of efficient use of the continuum of care (Dash, Zarle, O'Donnell & Vince-Whitman 1996; Morrow-Howell, Proctor & Mui 1991; Volland 1988; Zarle 1987).

Basic Principles of Discharge Planning

All discharge planning efforts should be guided by four general principles: (1) use of a patient- and problem-centered approach; (2) coordination of professionals; (3) linking community resources to the patient; and (4) advocacy for the patient.

Patient and Problem-Centered Approach

What may be practical for one person or family may be counterproductive or useless for another. Developing a discharge plan that the patient is able and willing to implement requires patient and family input. Research findings indicate that lack of patient and family involvement in discharge planning may result in the patient's needs not being adequately met in the postdischarge environment (Morrow-Howell, Proctor & Mui 1991). In addition, patient and family members' satisfaction with discharge plans have been linked to the level of their involvement in the development of those plans (Cox 1996; Proctor, Morrow-Howell, Albaz & Weir 1992).

Using this patient-centered approach, the social worker also needs to focus on the anticipated consequences of the medical problems. For example, will the patient be able to resume normal activities? If not, how will the patient and family be affected mentally, physically, and socially? By anticipating these effects, the social worker can help the patient learn to cope effectively with the inherent problems of his or her situation.

Coordination and Linkage

Social workers have an important role in coordinating different professionals within a hospital and linking community resources to a patient. Discharge planning involves input from a variety of sources, such as patients, families, and professionals. Often, the social worker is the only professional talking with all of these sources, and so is in a perfect position to assume the role as "director" or coordinator of their input. The goal of the social worker is then to "channel the information into a workable discharge plan" (Crittenden 1983, p. 10).

Unlike many other health care professionals whose work is done primarily within the hospital setting, the social worker also must function within the community as it relates to the patient. He or she serves as a bridge between the hospital and the community. One tool that is helpful to physicians, patients, families, and staff in planning for continuing care after hospitalization, is a list of community resources. Social workers provide a vital link for the patient between hospital and community through appropriate referral and use of these community resources (Lawrence 1988).

Advocacy

Advocacy is fundamental to the social work role in discharge planning. First and foremost, the social worker is an advocate of the patient. Patients and family members need to understand and cooperate with the medical care system to receive the full benefit of hospitalization, and to be informed of their rights. The social worker also serves to communicate the patient's expectations and needs to the health care professionals involved. Effective communication with patients, families, hospital staff, and resource providers has been identified as a key component of successful discharge planning (Bull 1994).

Case advocacy goes beyond the hospital. Discharged patients may have difficulty obtaining the governmental or community programs they need. Through personal contacts and linkages, the social worker can help patients and their families to gain access to services (Lurie 1982).

Social workers must be knowledgeable about community resources to develop effective discharge plans. As they work with patients and their families, they may discover gaps in those resources such as transportation or nutritional services. Social workers are responsible for monitoring discharge plan outcomes and participating in the development of programs designed to fill current resource gaps in the after-care environment (Blumenfield & Rosenberg 1988).

Components of Discharge Planning

Working with Staff

Discharge planners need to know which patients should receive discharge planning, and which staff members are to be involved in the process. They need access to patients and to other staff members.

Access to Patients

Traditionally, discharge planners have had access to patients by a referral from a physician who requests discharge planning intervention. Currently, an automatic access system or case-finding technique is often incorporated into discharge planning policies. This newer system directs staff energies towards patients who require earlier intervention and intensive attention from discharge planners (Volland 1988). Using this case-finding technique, the social worker often sees the patient before a diagnosis has been reached. High-risk patients are identified early in their hospital stay through established high-risk screening criteria. Some factors that place patients at high risk include (Fitzig 1988; McNulty 1988):

- multiple medical diagnoses
- seventy years of age or over and living alone
- previously or newly diagnosed as disabled
- history of repeated admissions
- admitted from a skilled nursing facility or an intermediate care facility
- dependent in activities of daily living
- disoriented, confused, forgetful
- requires wound care
- complex medication schedule
- speech, occupational, physical, or respiratory therapy
- no apparent family involvement or problems with social situation
- comatose
- victim of a severe accident

Generally, any combination of two or more of these factors justifies an early assessment of the patient's situation.

Timeliness is essential to meet the demands for better utilization of the medical system. Discharge planning should begin on the day of admission to a hospital. In addition, the discharge planner must have a consistent and reliable system for finding patients so that all patients who meet established discharge planning criteria have access to the same services and benefits (Crittenden 1983).

Finally, a system of access to patients should include the premise that biological and psychosocial needs are interrelated. Resources and limitations in both of these areas should be assessed and addressed together. The discharge planner needs to understand the interrelationship of the medical problem and the patient's and family's psychological relationships and social situation (JCAHCO 1996).

ACCESS TO MEDICAL STAFF

Initial responsibility for a discharge plan rests with the patient's primary physician (Rehr 1986). As noted earlier, hospital staff representing many different disciplines may be involved in the development of a discharge plan. Given the large variety of persons involved in the discharge planning process, it is not surprising that disagreements may arise. Research suggests that disagreements are present in at least one-third of the cases, and that the majority of these cases involve conflict between family members and staff (Abramson, Donnelly, King & Mailick 1993). In order to reach a resolution, the social worker must maintain good relationships and open communication with the medical staff. The social worker can help interpret and explain divergent views and assist the involved parties in reaching a consensus.

The discharge planner also needs to work closely with the physician as part of an interprofessional collaborative team. Older people frequently have multiple and complex social and psychological needs. The team approach has been shown to be an effective discharge service delivery model for serving this patient population (Berkman, Campion, Swagerty & Goldman 1983).

Each profession represented in the collaborative team has different responsibilities to fulfill and priorities to meet in serving hospital patients. The discharge planner needs to facilitate the collaboration of the team by minimizing problems of territoriality. After all, the professions share a common goal: excellent patient care and the patient's return to optimum health (Saltz 1992).

Working with the Patient and Family

The heart of discharge planning is working with the patient and family to identify discharge problems, and then to formulate and implement a discharge plan. "Family" may be those who have no blood ties with the patient but who provide support and are trusted by the patient. The family relationship is so important to the discharge planning process because it influences the extent of the role that staff need to play during hospitalization and discharge process (Bennett & Beckerman 1986).

Goals

The discharge planning process is designed to meet the many needs of the patient and family. It consists of seven primary goals (Crittenden 1983; Zarle 1987):

Goal 1: Educating the patient and family about the functions of discharge planning.

Many patients and families are unfamiliar with the concept of discharge planning. During the first visit, the discharge planner needs to explain the process, and emphasize the patient's and family's importance as members of a problem identification and problem solving team. The helping relationship is reinforced by assuring the patient and family that a discharge plan will not be done to or for them but with them.

The patient and family need to understand that discharge planning means thinking about leaving the hospital and convalescing as the physician orders. They need to be informed that physicians, not discharge planners, decide when patients leave the hospital. They also should be oriented to the idea that discharge planners work as a part of a team that includes the physician, other hospital staff, and the patient and family.

Goal 2: Helping patients and families to emotionally adjust to the patient's diagnosis and prognosis.

Before practical matters can be effectively discussed, the patient and family members must accept the patient's diagnosis and the long-term implications of this diagnosis. The ability to evaluate options and decide on a course of action may be compromised if the patient or family has not fully acknowledged the nature and consequence of the disease. Denial of the diagnosis and related prognosis can make assessment, decision making, and treatment planning impossible (Teusink & Mahler 1984). Some family members may not be willing or ready to accept the diagnosis given by the doctor and may accuse health professions of exaggerating the patient's symptoms (Dippel 1991). Given this fact, discharge planners must assess the patient's and family's ability to emotionally accept the reality of the illness before engaging them in the actual planning process. Fear, lack of information, grief, turmoil over the loss of significant roles, or anxiety about the assumption of caregiving activities may present barriers to patients and family members. Additionally, previous conflict between the patient and caregiver or among family members may resurface during hospitalization and impede the discharge planning process (Cauffield, Moye & Travis 1999). The social worker may need to engage in brief counseling around these issues. Referrals to the hospital chaplain and to community-based support groups may also prove useful.

Goal 3: Assisting the patient and family to identify practical and psychosocial problems for discharge.

After understanding the function of discharge planning, the patient and family need to focus on the practical problems created by illness. What needs must be met after the patient leaves the hospital in order to continue prescribed medical care in an appropriate setting? The medical diagnosis and prognosis create a framework for establishing needs. Through a process called partialization, that is, focusing on particular problems in a time-limited situation, the discharge planner discusses with the patient and family their practical needs related to the medical problem.

The discharge planner must sort out what the patient and family need and want, and what the physician and medical staff consider necessary. Practical problems of how, where, and by whom a patient's needs will be met can then be addressed. One of the most difficult tasks of this stage of discharge planning is to hear the "possible" from patients and staff, and to weight that against the "probable" based on available resources.

Once practical problems such as patient education, equipment, and home or institutional planning have been addressed, the discharge planner needs to move into psychosocial issues. Sudden or chronic illness alters the perception of the patient and family and influences their thoughts, feelings, and behaviors. If psychosocial issues are not addressed, patient and family may feel overwhelmed by the experience of illness, hospitalization, and readjustment.

Goal 4: Assisting the patient and family to meet practical and psychosocial problems for discharge.

Once the patient and family and the discharge planner have identified the practical problems which must be faced, alternative resources need to be presented. Ideally, the patient and family contact resources and make arrangements as much as possible, and the discharge planner provides direction and support about where to call or go, whom to see, and what to request.

Often patients and families are so caught up in illness that they do not realize that their feelings of anger, fear, or anxiety are normal. The discharge planner can provide psychosocial support by (Crittenden 1983):

■ listening;
■ encouraging verbalization;
■ reassuring the patient and family of those behaviors that are normal and helpful;
■ educating the patient and family about the facts of their situation and helping them understand how to work on it;
■ observing actions, reactions of patient and family as they work on the problems; and
■ identifying ego strengths and coping mechanisms and reinforcing them.

Goal 5: Formulating the discharge plan.

The next step of discharge planning is to formulate the actual discharge plan (see figure 7.2). This step involves the coordinated effort of the medical staff and patient and

Patient's Name:_____

History #:_____

Discharge Date:_____ Floor:_____

Closed Case: Yes ( )   No ( )

I. Patient Information Prior to Admission

Address:_____

_____

Responsible Relative:_____

Telephone: _____

II. Patient was discharged to:

Home	*Institution*
( ) Own	( ) Acute Hospital
( ) Relative	( ) Chronic Hospital
( ) Foster Care	( ) Rehab. Hospital
( ) Boarding Home	( ) Residential Treatment
( ) Group Home	( ) Nursing Home
( ) Other	( ) 1/2 way, 1/4 way
	( ) State Mental Hospital
	( ) Other

Name:_____

Address:_____

_____ Telephone:_____

III. Referrals to Community Resources completed:

1. ( ) Home Health
2. ( ) Financial/Environmental Support
3. ( ) Counseling Agencies
4. ( ) Training/Rehab. Agencies
5. ( ) Residential/Day Care
6. ( ) Equipment
7. ( ) Other

Agency information

Name:_____

Address: _____

_____

Service Requested:_____

_____

Name:_____

Address: _____

_____

Service Requested:_____

_____

Social Worker:_____

History #:_____

IV. Pending Placement: Yes ( )   No ( )

If there is a temporary arrangement state final plan including approximate date of placement:_____

_____

V. Factors Complicating Discharge Planning: (Explain)

1. ( ) Patient Condition:_____

_____

_____

2. ( ) Community Resources:_____

_____

3. ( ) Patient/Family:_____

_____

4. ( ) Hospital:_____

_____

_____

5. ( ) Other:_____

_____

_____

VI. Anticipated Problems with this Case Postdischarge: Yes ( )   No ( )
If yes, explain:

_____

_____

_____

_____

_____

Plan to Address Potential Problem:

_____

_____

_____

_____

_____

VII. Other Interventions Planned:

_____

_____

_____

_____

_____

_____

■ **Figure 7.2**   Sample Discharge Plan   *Source:* Lawrence 1988, p. 148.

family. Formulation of the plan moves from consideration of problems and potential solutions to specifying where, when, and what is going to happen upon discharge. The discharge planner assumes the role of coordinator of the plan and documents the complete plan on the patient's record.

Goal 6: Implementing the discharge plan.

Implementing the discharge plan requires flexibility on the part of the discharge planner and the patient and family. Problems often arise during actual implementation of the plan that require creative problem solving and changes or substitutions. Discharge planners must expect problems during implementation. A familiarity with community resources is a valuable tool for rescuing a discharge plan that goes awry. If substituting resources is not possible, the patient and family, discharge planner, and physician must consider the consequences to the patient of postponing some details of the discharge plan.

Goal 7: Monitoring the discharge plan through follow-up.

Some hospitals do not believe they have the time or resources to devote to follow-up activities (Berkman, Walker, Bonander & Holmes 1992). Many discharge planners do not receive any feedback about the effectiveness of the discharge plan unless the patient or caregiver call back to complain or the patient is rehospitalized (Bull & Kane 1996). But follow-up, whether by telephone, by questionnaire, or in person, is essential for the continuation of high-quality care. Follow-up helps to reinforce continuity of care and assures the patient and family that problems that arise after discharge will be addressed. This process may also help ease the fear and anger experienced by patients and family members due to the suddenness of a discharge following a shortened hospital stay (Haddock 1991; Naylor et al 1999). In fact, social work departments are required to have a system for monitoring and evaluating the quality and appropriateness of patient care (Coulton 1986). A method to monitor the effectiveness of discharge planning needs to include internal program evaluation and effectiveness at the community level, and the patient's and family's perception of the usefulness of the discharge planning process (Kaye & Leadley 1985). As the current economic climate in health care has resulted in shorter lengths of stay, patients and families are apt to feel new stresses, frightened, angry, abandoned, or unprepared for self-care. Follow-up can ease these feelings and provide much-needed support (Rossen 1984).

The Discharge Planning Interview

An essential tool for working with the patient and family is the discharge planning interview. Discharge planners should have a course in basic interviewing skills as part of their professional preparation. The discharge planner acts as a facilitator in the interview, moving the conversation while extracting and channeling information.

CHARACTERISTICS OF THE INTERVIEW

There are time limits, often time pressure, on discharge planning. Much needs to be accomplished in a short time. In an emergency, discharge planning may need to take place within an hour, and often, must be accomplished within two or three days. The interview must be structured to get the necessary information and give adequate assistance within the available time.

Interviews can take place in various locations and have a variety of forms. Interviews are often held at bedside, sometimes with minimal privacy. The discharge planner must be able to interview under distracting conditions and focus attention on the patient and family. Much interviewing, particularly with families, occurs over the telephone. The discharge planner needs to exercise courtesy while obtaining information and giving assistance and support. The discharge planner needs to have courtesy, persistence, and patience when having to interview when not invited or wanted. If the patient and family are resistant, the physician may help to stress the importance for planning to leave the hospital.

Consistent with the seven goals for working with the patient and family, the interview needs to be both problem oriented and person oriented. The discharge planner must listen for concerns of the persons with the needs, as well as identify those needs and problems. An active and accurate listening process within a problem-solving orientation is a critical method in obtaining information from an interview.

FRAMEWORK OF THE INTERVIEW

Interviewing is both a method and a process. The method is the framework or steps you follow in obtaining information you need. The process is the dynamics: what happens between people and between you and those people during the interview? How do the facts emerge? How do things develop? How do they "feel?" In an interview, the discharge planner is a facilitator moving the conversation and extracting and channeling information.

The discharge planner's interviewing method should include the following (Crittenden 1983):

- **Opening:** Introduce yourself and your function. Indicate to patient and family awareness of their problem and desire to help the patient not only leave the hospital but also do well at home and return to some normalcy in daily living. State needs commensurate with this goal as seen by staff, physician, and yourself.
- **Development:** Ask for patient and family input and reaction. Restate their perceptions in concrete terms in a mutually agreeable way.
- **Assessment:** Notice patient and family dynamics and interaction with you and one another. What feelings or reactions are expressed overtly or covertly? Where do conflicts occur in perception, opinion, or communication? What issues are avoided or downplayed or overstated? Where is there uncertainty, anxiety, or insecurity? Where is there lack of knowledge or understanding?
- **Reaction:** Channel conversation, advise or structure, guide with facts and relevant information. Encourage support and communication between patient, family, and the hospital. Suggest and reinforce ways of dealing with practical problems.
- **Construction:** Lead the patient and family into stating a plan for discharge needs and ongoing care. Introduce them to wellness as a goal for their living.
- **Close:** Summarize, agree on the next meeting or telephone call, and the details that will be finalized or ready by then.

Working with Facts (Assessment)

Discharge planning is an excellent example of social work's distinctive focus on the person in transaction with the environment (Rauch & Schreiber 1985). The assessment factors that need to be considered before a discharge plan can be formulated (figure 7.3) include characteristics and abilities of the patient as well as characteristics and resources of the environment to which the patient will return.

Figure 7.3 Assessment Factors to Be Considered before Discharge Planning *Source:* Jupp & Sims 1986.

ABOUT THE PATIENT

Good discharge planning needs to be both patient- and problem-centered, so information must be gathered *from* the patient as well as *about* the patient. The initial interview with the patient and family can be more sensitive and productive if the discharge planner is already acquainted with the patient's medical problems and treatment plan.

Information to Obtain from the Hospital Chart. As summarized in table 7.1, the hospital chart can provide valuable information about the patient's medical history, current problems, treatment, and progress.

MEDICAL TEAM MEMBERS TO CONSULT

An important function of discharge planners is to coordinate the contributions to the discharge planning process by the members of the multidisciplinary team. Table 7.2 summarizes the kind of information that each team member can provide about the patient.

■ **Table 7.1** Information to Obtain From Hospital Chart

History and physical	A resumé of patient's medical history and current medical problem with anticipated goals to be accomplished by hospitalization.
Physician's orders	Treatment and activity ordered for the patient, usually on daily basis; includes orders for diet, medication.
Physician's progress notes	Daily notation of medical progress of patient with note of special problems; anticipated discharge may be noted.
Nursing notes	A record of daily care of patient with any significant problems or reactions indicated.
Vital signs sheet	Usually included near nursing notes; indicates progress of patient's temperature and blood pressure; deviations from average, such as a drop in blood pressure or a rise in temperature, usually indicate complications.
Pharmacy sheet	Included in many hospital charts; lists patient's medications along with frequency and dosage; a good indicator of what patient will need at home.
Consultation sheets	Communication from one physician to another indicating problems and a diagnosis and prognosis, and usually recommendations for treatment.
Paramedical progress	One or several sheets from services and therapists, such as social services; physical, speech, or occupational therapy citing patient's treatment and progress.
Face sheet	Includes admitting data and specific information about the patient: age, sex, marital status, address; employer or job; source of insurance; primary attending physician; room assignment, and diagnosis. Other information may be included also.
Other information	Included at the end of many hospital charts. Gives information sent from another hospital or emergency room, a nursing home, a home care program. Any of this may have valuable information for the discharge planner; for example, a patient returning to a nursing home will probably return to the same one. Name, address, and phone number are available if there are transfer records.

Source: Crittenden 1983.

ENVIRONMENTAL AND COMMUNITY RESOURCES

In addition to knowing the patient, the discharge planner needs to know the environment to which the patient will be returning and the resources that are available in the community. An essential tool for the discharge planner is a list of the community resources. Table 7.3 summarizes potential patient needs upon discharge and the types of agencies and organizations that may be available to fulfill those needs.

Because agencies, personnel, and guidelines change periodically, an important task for the discharge planner is to update available resources every few months. In addition to referring a patient to resources appropriate for the patient's age, financial and medical condition, and specific need, the discharge planner needs to assure that the existence and guidelines of an agency are current.

There is certain information that patients and families need for each referral in order to get the kind of help they need (Crittenden 1983):

a. the proper name of the resource or agency;
b. a correct phone number;
c. the times when the resource may be called or visited;
d. the name of a contact person;

■ **Table 7.2** Medical Team Members to Consult for Information about the Patient

Team Member	Information
Primary physician	Synopsis of the case and patient's history; present diagnosis and anticipated treatment; probable discharge date; discharge order and follow-up care (including medications, activity limits, self-care, and return visits or out-patient referrals or therapy); social information relevant to case.
Nurse	In-hospital progress and treatment; patient functional ability; attitudes, emotions, and adjustment of patient and family; family support and notable problems; anticipated medical problems on discharge; education needed by or given to the patient for continuing care and treatment.
Utilization review coordinator	For Medicare/Medicaid patients, adequacy of documentation of patient's progress and appropriateness of stay; anticipated barriers to discharge; and termination of federally or state-funded benefits; expected letters of denial; avenues of appeal of denial and procedures for same.
Physical therapist	Physical limitations; anticipated rehabilitation potential; progress in therapy; anticipated length of therapy and outpatient needs; medical equipment needed for outpatient use, including specifications for same; education or training needed by family; home care therapy visits, if needed and how often.
Occupational therapist	Progress in activities of daily living (ADL) training and special assistive devices needed; rehabilitation potential; need for outpatient care or home care services; family training needs.
Respiratory therapist	Anticipated breathing difficulties and degree ADL is affected; training and education needed by patients or family; equipment needed for outpatient use; rehabilitation potential and outpatient or home care follow-up.
Speech therapist	Rehabilitation potential and prognosis for adequate communication with others; special devices or equipment needed; family training needs; outpatient or home care follow-up.
Social services	Emotional, intellectual assessment; counseling needs of patient and family; family and patient problems such as socialization, emotional support, community resources.
Patient educator	Status of patient's ability to perform self-care and treatment; understanding of medical situation and convalescent needs (diet, activity level, medication and medication use, self-understanding about depression, stress, and role of emotions in illness).
Dietitian	Plan for patient's diet; special restrictions for salt, calories, or other factors; instruction given, materials given.
Pharmacist	Information on medications; reactions to medications.

Source: Crittenden 1983.

e. the type of information that the agency will need;
f. the limits of services the agency or resource can provide; and
g. cost of service.

As a consequence of updating the resource list and working with patients and families to fill their needs, the discharge planner is likely to discover gaps in services in the community. Unfortunately, the patient and family may ascribe the limitation of resources to the social worker (Bennett 1984). The discharge planner needs to be involved in documenting and working to eliminate real service gaps (Blumenfield 1986).

■ **Table 7.3**   Environment and Community Resources

Need	Agencies and Organizations
Physician services	Local medical society.
Nursing services	Home health agencies; professional registries for in-home care; nursing homes; psychiatric care centers.
Rehabilitation services	Organizations and societies by specific diagnosis (American Cancer Society, for example); county and state medical and paramedical societies; state vocational rehabilitation department.
Clinical laboratory and radiology services	County and state medical or paramedical societies.
Nutrition	Meals on Wheels or Meals to Homebound programs; senior citizen centers.
Social services	County Department of Public Social Services.
Education	Organizations and societies by specific illnesses (American Heart Association, Arthritis Foundation); public library; federal Department of Health, Education and Welfare; local colleges, universities; local hospitals or clinics for educational programs or groups.
Transportation	Local transit programs, taxis; local organizations that provide service to the handicapped; senior centers; programs such as Dial-A-Ride, Medi-ride; local ambulance companies.
Financial assistance	State and federal benefits programs (Medicare, Medicaid, Social Security); local unemployment and welfare offices for general relief; specific societies such as American Cancer or Easter Seals that may make short loans or grants.
Pharmaceutical services	Local pharmaceutical society; special senior programs at chain pharmacies such as Rexall; American Assn. of Retired Persons (AARP).
Equipment or prosthetic needs	Local businesses in hospital equipment, oxygen service, prosthetics; local medical society, specific organizations such as Arthritis Foundation, American Cancer Society, or Easter Seals; equipment provided by Medicare and Medicaid.
Domestic assistance	Local employment agencies; home health agencies; the Homemaker Chore Program or similar Medicaid programs; societies for specific diseases that may help train, locate, or finance help, such as ALS (amyotrophic lateral sclerosis) Society, American Cancer Society; day-care centers or programs at country or state level or sponsored by community organizations.
Housing	Local or county organizations that list housing resources such as senior helplines or hotlines, renters' association, aid to handicapped agencies or Easter Seals, HUD local office, and real estate organizations; state licensing agencies for list of licensed retirement hotels and board/care facilities; local churches may have church housing; the American Red Cross and Salvation Army sometimes aid with emergency housing.
Legal services	Local or county bar association.
Employment	Employment agencies; human resources development (unemployment) offices; state or federal programs for retraining; vocational rehabilitation office of state; local senior programs that may have employment possibility listings.

Source: Crittenden 1983.

A major area of work with older patients is helping them to obtain financial assistance. The discharge planner must be familiar with entitlement programs for older people and spend a large amount of time giving entitlement information (Blumenfeld 1982). Providing written information to the patient and family can be helpful in reducing the repetition of information. The information must be kept current, however, and the discharge planner must have a sound grasp of current entitlement information (Bennett 1984).

Considerations for Effective Discharge Planning

Barriers to Timely Discharge

New pressures for cost containment provide hospitals with incentives to shorten patients' lengths of stay. One cost-containment measure which has affected discharge planning is Medicare's prospective system under which hospital rates are predetermined by the patient's diagnostic category (diagnosis-related groups or DRGs). This system permits less time to work with patients in the hospital, and underscores timely discharge as an important task for social workers.

As stated previously, the growth of managed care has led to further reductions in patients' LOS and a heightened interest in the discharge planning process. In addition to reduced length of time in which to work with patients and families, there are several kinds of barriers that may prevent timely discharge (Abramson, Donnelly, King & Mailick 1993; Blazyk & Canavan 1985; Bull & Kane 1996; Proctor & Morrow-Howell 1990).

Patient Problems
- patient unable to manage own affairs
- patient confusion
- difficulty in working with the patient
- change in patient's medical condition
- patient or family refuses to leave the hospital

Family Related Problems
- lack of family availability
- difficulty in working with the family
- family's denial of the patient's condition and/or prognosis
- disagreement among family members

Communication Problems
- communication breakdown between staff and patient
- lack of communication among team members
- communication gaps between patient and/or family and hospital staff
- communication gaps between hospital staff and staff of referral agencies

Internal Hospital Problems
- treatment not completed due to personnel or equipment failure
- inadequate or confusing documentation
- inaccessibility of personnel (i.e., physician unavailable)
- poor preparation or coordination of details by discharge planner
- ageism among hospital health care professionals

Community Resource Problems
- lack of financial resources by patient and family
- lack of coverage by Medicare/Medicaid for needed services/resources
- lack of family or support group to care for patient
- unavailable beds in intermediate care or skilled nursing facilities

- needed resources not available in patient's community
- lack of transportation

Freak-of-Nature Problems
- natural phenomena (i.e., blizzards, fires, flood, etc.) that make implementing discharge plans impossible

In some cases, such as with freak-of-nature problems, there is little the discharge planner can do to predict or prevent delay in discharge. But other obstacles can be targets for intervention. Educating staff on the importance of necessary paperwork, the proper completion of forms, and on the limitations of community resources can minimize certain factors that delay patients' discharge most often (Schrager, Halman, Myers, Nichols & Rosenblum 1978).

Ethical Issues

Due to the continuing decrease in patients' LOS, patients are being discharged with higher levels of dependency and a greater need for skilled care. In this environment, social workers are expected to work more rapidly than in previous eras to develop plans for patients who are increasingly frail (Cummings & Cockerham, 1997); Kosecoff et al. 1990). Ethical dilemmas arise as discharge planners work to address the needs of the patient while also attending to the competing demands of the hospital, the medical staff, and the patient's family.

Ethical dilemmas result when the worker experiences a "pull of divergent loyalties, interests and desires between individuals and groups," and when "acting on one moral conviction means behaving contrary to another or when adhering to one value means abandoning another" (Blumenfield & Lowe 1987, p. 48). In discharge planning ethical dilemmas may arise when there is a conflict between ethical principles; competition among role obligations to the patient, family, staff members, or the hospital; the need to choose between unsatisfactory options; and difficulty in determining the risks and benefits of a particular action (Abramson 1988; Aroskar 1980; Mizrahi & Abramson 1985; Proctor, Morrow-Howell & Lott 1993).

A conflict may arise when the patient and family's wishes for discharge clash with what the social worker and hospital staff believe is best for the patient. The patient and family, for example, may strongly state their desire for the patient to return home without supervision, while the social worker doubts the patient's ability to safely live alone. In such a case, the social worker may become caught between the desire to promote patient *autonomy* (a fundamental value described in the *NASW Code of Ethics*, 1993) and the *desire to protect* the patient from harm. In such a case, the social worker must weigh the benefits and risks present in each of these divergent plans. The social worker must also consider that a plan that protects a patient from harm may also be one that causes significant emotional anguish if it involves changes to which the patient is firmly opposed. One choice may result in physical harm, while the other may produce emotional pain. The social worker, therefore, may be faced with two equally unsatisfactory options.

Patients and family members often need education and support in order to emotionally accept the patient's diagnosis. Sufficient time to search for needed resources is also critical. Because of the hospital's financial need to quickly discharge the patient, however, the social worker may become trapped between the desire to provide the patient/family with the needed assistance and the economic pressure to promptly expedite a discharge plan. This type of struggle represents a fundamental conflict between loyalty to the patient or family and loyalty to the hospital.

A conflict in loyalty may also arise when the patient and family do not agree on the discharge plan. The *NASW Code of Ethics* directs social workers to consider first their responsibility to their client. However, when an elderly patient is functionally dependent or cognitively impaired, the family must assist with the decision making and also with the provision of after-care. In this situation, who should be considered the client? Is the client the elderly patient, the family providing care, or both the patient and family who may be equally effected by the discharge plans? No clear-cut answer exists to this problem or the many other dilemmas faced by discharge planners.

The ambiguity that lies at the heart of many ethical dilemmas defies quick or easy answers. In order to work through these conflicts, social workers should take the time to carefully analyze the problem and work toward an acceptable solution. Social workers who choose to skirt over these difficult issues may experience burn-out and feelings of guilt.

When analyzing ethical dilemmas it is helpful for social workers to follow a five-step model (Abramson 1983; Aroskar 1980; Cummings & Cockerham 1997). The first step is to identify the background facts surrounding the dilemma, such as the patient's medical, functional, and financial status and the caregiver's physical, emotional, and financial resources. Secondly, the social worker should consider the central decision-making elements. Who is involved in the decision making and what are the abilities and roles of each party? How much time is available in which to make the decision? Third, examine alternate courses of action. The benefits and risks of each option must be weighed. Fourth, consider the value system of the involved parties. What values do you, the patient, the family, and involved medical staff believe to be the most important? These values may not be the same. It is important not to assume that the values you see as having the greatest priority are also the ones held most dearly by others. Clarification of the values of the parties involved helps to avoid painful miscommunications and misunderstandings. The fifth and last step involves deciding upon a course of action and monitoring the consequences. The social worker must make a decision based upon the knowledge and insight gained from the steps noted while recognizing that no perfect solution may exist. However, taking the time to carefully work through the dilemma may enhance social workers' confidence that they did all that was possible and that they made the best possible decision given the situation.

Legal Issues

In addition to ethical issues, hospital social workers are also involved in matters of a legal nature such as release of information, informed consent, determination of competency, and the execution of advanced directives. Regarding release of information, concerns may impact social workers differently than they do other hospital professionals. Within the hospital, charts are strictly confidential and available to the medical team providing the patient's care. But social workers participating in the discharge planning process are often involved in transferring patients to agencies or facilities in the community. Generally, the hospital will have a policy requiring the patient to sign a Release of Medical Information form so that social workers can supply medical and psychosocial information to professionals outside of the hospital.

Sharing information with the spouse or next-of-kin usually is not a problem but permission should be gained from the patient. Medical records are liable to subpoenaed if the patient initiates a lawsuit against the hospital or any members of the medical team (Crittenden 1983).

Health care workers also have a legal and ethical obligation to provide patients with the information that is necessary for them to make an informed decision about their health care. Such standards should also apply to discharge planning decisions. Social workers should provide patients and family members with complete information about after-care options so that patients/families clearly understand the alternatives available to them. Informed consent entails more than obtaining a signature on a medical form or providing a patient with brochures about available resources. It involves a process of communication in which health care workers translate information into terms that patients can understand (Zukerman 1988). Armed with such information patients can then make decisions that they believe are in their own best interests and that conform to their own desires.

Since early in this century our legal system has asserted that every adult who is of sound mind has a right to determine what will happen to his or her own body. Individuals who have reached the age of majority (usually eighteen years) are legally presumed to be competent and have the right to make their own decisions and act on their own behalf (Zukerman 1988). Legally, adults are empowered to make their own choices regardless of the wisdom of theses choices. However, in a hospital setting the legal presumptions of competency and autonomy are often overlooked when the patient is elderly.

Unfortunately, there are no clear legal standards for making decisions regarding an individual's competency (Smith 1996). However, family members may petition the court for guardianship of the patient's finances and/or person if they fear that the patient is truly no longer competent to make his or her own decisions. When no family members are present, the hospital social worker may also petition the court to appoint a guardian for a patient. A guardianship involves a legal determination by the court that an individual is not competent. When a guardian is appointed, the individual is stripped of legal rights as an adult. Guardianships may be helpful when a patient is incompetent and is making decisions which may be harmful to self or others. A legal guardian is empowered to work with the discharge planner and interdisciplinary team to make decisions about after-care on the patient's behalf. However, since a guardianship does eliminate an individual's legal rights as an adult, this process should not be entered into without careful consideration and thorough exploration of all other alternatives.

Advanced directives are legal documents that enable individuals to state in advance what medical treatments they would or would not want applied should they be unable to communicate their desires to a health care team. The presence of advanced directives may eliminate the need for the pursuance of a guardianship. However, only about 9 percent of Americans have executed advanced directives (Smith 1996). Hospital social workers are often the persons responsible for educating patients and relatives about these choices. A "living will" is a document that enables individuals to indicate in advance whether they do or do not wish to be started on or maintained on "extraordinary measures" in the event of a terminal illness or a coma with no hope of recovery. A person may indicate, for example, that he or she would not want artificial nutrition or hydration to be applied. Discharge planners should be aware of the contents of advanced directives and ensure that the discharge plan will not negate the desires indicated in these documents. A person whose living will indicates that she or he does not want artificial nutrition should not be sent to a nursing home that has a policy of extending patients' lives as long as medically possible. A "durable power of attorney of health care" allows individuals to name someone as their appointed decision-maker in health related matters should they be unable to perform this function themselves. In situations in which a patient is not competent, the person named as the decision maker does have the legal ability to make decisions on the patient's behalf.

The many legal issues faced during the discharge planning process create a need for social workers to utilize the hospital attorney as a resource for the discharge planning team (Mullaney & Andrews 1983). The hospital attorney may prove useful in several situations:

■ clarifying the legal principles involved in aspects of patient care that require a determination of the patient's right to choose a less than optimal discharge plan, family responsibility, transfer to a nursing home, and financial assets to pay for care;
■ clarifying the responsibilities of the social worker to the patient and to the hospital regarding these patient care situations;
■ developing a good quality discharge plan for patients with whom it is nearly impossible to plan because of their mental, physical, or social deficits; and
■ advocating for the discharge planner and the hospital in cases in which a patient is competent but uncooperative, by enforcing the need for decision making; and advocating for patients by insuring appropriate representation and protection of their individual rights.

Discharge planning provides social workers with a challenging opportunity to integrate their knowledge and skills. Social work education is ideal preparation for the discharge planning process. In order to be effective discharge planners, social workers must be skilled in assessment, interviewing, collaboration, and advocacy. A thorough knowledge of community resources as well as a good working relationship with these resources is also essential. These skills are an integral part of social work education. In order to be effective discharge planners with older patients, in addition to the skills acquired in an undergraduate social work program, social workers need to become knowledgeable about the field of gerontology. What are the realities of aging? What are the special needs of older patients? What special considerations for effective discharge planning are posed by older patients? What are the legal and ethical issues involved in working with older patients?

As the population continues to age, gerontological education will become an increasingly important partner to social work education. Hospital social workers will be faced with more and more older persons who need discharge planning and other social work services. Social workers who are well grounded in aging will be vital to the delivery of high quality care of older persons.

Discussion Questions

1. The guidelines of the Joint Commission of Accreditation of Hospitals (JCAH) state that both nursing and social work are to be involved in the discharge planning process. Why should both professions have responsibility for the discharge plan? What problems does joint responsibility pose?

2. The American Hospital Association includes "continuity of care" in its patients' Bill of Rights. Why is continuity of care so important to the patient? To the hospital?
3. What should the social worker do if the patient, the patient's family, and the primary physician all disagree about the plan for patient care after discharge from the hospital?
4. What type of information is needed about each community resource in order for the social worker to provide an accurate and appropriate referral?
5. How is the discharge planning interview the same or different from other interviews conducted by social workers?

Experiential Learning

Activity: Identifying Medical and Psychosocial Problems

Study the following list of patients:

A. A thirteen-year-old girl with a broken leg in a waist-to-ankle body cast.
B. A thirty-five-year-old postman, father of four, who has a severe gastric ulcer, probably related to nervous stress.
C. A fifty-seven-year-old female school teacher, living alone, with chest pains diagnosed as angina (coronary artery disease).
D. A ninety-two-year-old man with fever, dehydration, and malnutrition, who lives in an apartment on skid row.
E. A twenty-three-year-old welfare mother with seven children, one a newborn.
F. A sixty-seven-year-old man, a retired banker, with a slight stroke that left a residual slight weakness in the left arm and leg.
G. A forty-seven-year-old single parent with a recent diagnosis of acute leukemia.
H. A seventy-two-year-old woman, married, with two broken toes.

1. Construct a table using the following headings: Patient, medical problem, medical needs, social needs, psychological needs. Then fill in the table for each patient. (One has been done for you.) Please be creative and draw from your own experiences and common sense to infer possible medical, psychological, and social needs. You may find it helpful to consult a medical dictionary, such as *Taber's Medical Cyclopedia*.

Patient	Medical Problem	Medical Needs	Social Needs	Psychological Needs
A	broken leg with waist-to-ankle cast	cast care, X-rays, cast changes, visits to physician for followup, wheelchair, bed reset, pain relief	all daily needs: food, bath, toilet, dressing, companionship, and recreation	help with anxiety, anger, and depression relating to illness, especially isolation from friends and school

Source: Crittenden 1983, pp. 47–49.
Note: The object of this exercise is not to make you a medical diagnostician. It is to help you think about needs other than the medical problem—needs arising from the medical problem that may affect discharge planning.

2. Assume you were the hospital social worker involved in making discharge plans for each patient in the table. You would need to "prioritize" your work. In other words, you would have to decide which cases needed the most immediate attention and organize your work accordingly. You would need to consider questions such as these (please answer):

a. Which case would be most likely to need a lot of medical care once the patient left the hospital?
b. Which case would be of most concern to utilization review?
c. Which case(s) might need a visiting nurse?
d. Which cases might need nursing home care?
e. Which cases have the greatest social need for a support group or help from community agencies?
f. Which case would be most likely to need a lot of patient education to deal with illness?
g. Which case would be most likely to need ongoing counseling help to deal with illness?
h. Which cases do you think would be likely to be discharged from the hospital after a short stay?
i. Having answered the above questions, which case would you, as a discharge planner, work on first?

Suggested Answers to Activities
1.

Patient	Medical Problem	Medical Needs	Social Needs	Psychological Needs
B	severe gastric ulcer	Treatment and observation for ulcer, good diet; stress reduction and pain control, appropriate medication; rest	disability insurance as other income help for family during illness	help with tension, fear, or depression; reassurance
C	angina, mild	medicines for cardiac problems; special diet; rest; education about illness and how to manage it	a less demanding work-load	help with fear of heart attacks; stress-reduction techniques
D	fever, dehydration, and malnutrition	diagnosis of cause of fever; fluids and food to restore body to optimum health	adequate shelter and personal care; a support group; financial aid, possible facility placement	assessment of mental status; emotional support to discontinue drinking; help with possible depression
E	childbirth	postpartum care for baby and mother; medical supervision, diet, rest for both; education in birth control	assessment of personal living situation and family history, including financial, housing, diet and nutrition, education, health, work situation; support groups in community and family	emotional support; assessment of basic behavior, mother-child relationships, adult social relationships

Patient	Medical Problem	Medical Needs	Social Needs	Psychological Needs
F	stroke	physical therapy; medication for circulatory system; education about illness, diet; cane or walker	support group or family help in recovery	help with fear or concern of body failure or image change; anger or depression over illness and loss
G	acute leukemia	chemotherapy, diet, rest and long-term doctor supervision and possibly hospitalization for symptoms of disease including fever, weakness; education about illness for self as well as family	good support group; help with children; adult to care for domestic details; financial assistance	help to cope with life-threatening disease and prolonged hospitalization and illness; probably fear, anger, depression, stress; lot of reassurance and emotional support

Source: Crittenden 1983, pp. 47–49.

Note: The object of this exercise is not to make you a medical diagnostician. It is to help you think about needs other than the medical problem—needs arising from the medical problem that may affect discharge planning.

2. a. G, A, D
   b. D
   c. A, D, G, F
   d. D, G
   e. D, G, C
   f. G, F
   g. G, F
   h. H. E
   i. D (due to Medicare/utilization pressures and probable short-term acute treatment needs)

Case Studies

See Appendix B for guidelines in analyzing gerontological social work practice.

Case 1: Balancing Patient's Rights and Needs with Family Responsibility and Limitations

The hospital admission of Mr. D., seventy, was precipitated by a fire in the patient's bedroom; smoke inhalation exacerbated his condition of chronic obstructive pulmonary disease. At the time of admission, Mr. D. was ambulatory with the aid of a cane, and required some assistance with activities of daily living. Social work intervention was initiated within two days of admission. The referral source was a community health agency whose staff had some knowledge of the patient and questioned the safety of the home environment.

The hospital social worker assessed Mr. D. as oriented but mildly confused. Mr. D. provided conflicting information at times, and became argumentative and hostile with little provocation. Mr. D. refused to follow directions, presenting management problems for nursing and physician staff. Efforts by the social worker to plan for his discharge and continuing care were met with indifference by Mr. D. He did not acknowledge any need for care after discharge, and seemed not to understand his medical condition. Mr. D. maintained that he would return to his daughter's home, with his daughter assuming the role of primary caretaker.

Miss D., the daughter, did not visit or call during the first two weeks of the patient's hospitalization. The social worker secured Mr. D.'s permission to contact his daughter. Although when contacted she agreed to a meeting and discussion of discharge plans for Mr. D., she failed to keep this scheduled appointment, as well as four subsequent ones. In her telephone talks with Miss D., the social worker observed signs of alcohol abuse. Miss D. was unaware of time and dates, speech was slurred at times, nonsensical. Miss D. did not visit her father, and she blamed this on transportation difficulties.

Mr. D.'s medical and mental status improved; discharge would be possible in the near future. With her permission, a home visit was made to Miss D. The home was in disarray; Miss D. was noticeably intoxicated; empty liquor bottles were evident. Miss D. maintained that she was able to care for her father, but would honor his decision if he chose not to return to her home. She refused an offer of intervention for her alcohol problem.

The social worker assessed the home situation as unsafe for Mr. D. Although greatly improved, Mr. D. still required assistance with activities of daily living. Alternatives for discharge were presented to the patient; he was insistent on discharge to the home of his daughter.

The social worker questioned his ability to make decisions. Mr. D. had demonstrated impaired reasoning and judgment throughout the hospital stay. He continued to disregard medical information and instruction without exhibiting comprehension of the information.

The question of Mr. D.'s ability to represent himself became the deciding factor in planning. The psychiatric consultation requested by the social worker dictated acceptance of Mr. D.'s decision for discharge albeit to a situation which seemed unsafe. Discharge alternatives were again presented by the social worker and refused by Mr. D. He was discharged to his daughter's home with a referral for visiting nurse services.

As Mr. D. was found able to represent himself, his decision had to be honored. Consultation with the hospital attorney confirmed this. The attorney stressed the importance of documenting efforts to offer Mr. D. other alternatives. However, as he was a competent adult, his choice could not be challenged.

Following discharge, Mr. D. was home with his daughter for four months. The patient's physical condition and the home situation deteriorated. Mr. D. was readmitted with a diagnosis of chronic pulmonary insufficiency. His mental status was impaired. During the third week of hospitalization, Mr. D. was declared incompetent following the procedures described earlier. Mr. D.'s grandson was appointed guardian. Mr. D. was discharged to his home.

Source: Mullaney & Andrews 1983, pp. 57–59.

Case 2: Working with Families

Mrs. M. is an eighty-seven-year-old, Orthodox Jewish widow admitted to the hospital for internal bleeding and anemia. Mrs. M. had been living at home while she suffered from a variety of chronic conditions. She had been cared for by an eight-hour/day home attendant. Overseeing her care was her fifty-seven-year-old, married son, who lived nearby.

During the patient's hospitalization, her son stayed at the hospital all day, everyday. Mrs. M. suffered one medical crisis after another with the physician needing to do a variety of procedures and nursing staff being particularly attentive. The patient was quite ill and inaccessible to interview. Mr. M. spent most of the time reading religious books, but he would jump up to meet a physician or nurse entering his mother's room to ask questions, suggest changes in procedures, or discuss the merits of particular foods for his mother. Staff began to avoid entering Mrs. M.'s room unless absolutely necessary. They also had problems restraining Mr. M. from feeding his mother. Staff had warned Mr. M. of risks in trying to give his mother food since she was restricted to a special diet. However, he persisted in trying to urge her to eat ice cream or soup brought from outside. Staff became frustrated and angry in trying to deal with the son both because of his behavior in the hospital and their belief that he was acting out of guilt for having let his mother become so ill before being brought to the hospital.

The unit social worker was asked to see Mr. M. to help staff deal with the problems. Mr. M. was difficult to get to know. His orthodoxy contributed to the discomfort he had speaking with women and the social worker needed to respect such feelings. He was eventually able to respond to discussion about his concerns and needs and explained how fearful he was of the discomfort his mother was having, and his anger that the doctors couldn't seem to do more for her. He felt that no one was talking to him and that he was helpless in the situation, for he never knew when the physician would be around or when something new would happen. Mr. M. was almost frantic in his need to do something. Praying in the hall outside his mother's room was one thing he felt he could do, and trying to force her to eat in order to regain strength was another.

The social worker met with staff and was able to reframe Mr. M.'s behavior to the staff, from that of inscrutable, angry, and ungrateful, to frightened, overwhelmed, and lacking direction. House staff and nurses were engaged in considering ways to help Mr. M. with his problems while attempting to do the most they could for the patient. It was agreed that the intern in charge of Mrs. M.'s care would schedule a specific time each day to meet Mr. M. Setting limits on Mr. M.'s demands, yet attempting to give him information and support appropriately was suggested by the social worker as a way of providing structure that would help the patient's son.

The social worker also suggested that the team attempt to find some roles for Mr. M. to fill his need to do something. It was suggested that Mr. M. read to his mother and help feed her the specific diet provided by the hospital.

By providing more understanding of the patient's son and indicating that his needs could help in caring for the patient, the social worker was able to engage the staff in thinking creatively together. Providing structure in which to work with this family member and some role for him to play helped him to cope with the hospitalization of his mother and become ready to actively help in planning for his mother's eventual discharge.

Source: Blumenfield 1982, pp. 47–48.

Case 3: Balancing Conflicting Demands and Pressures

Mr. G. came to the hospital quite confused, weak, and unable to walk. He was a seventy-two-year-old, Hispanic man whose wife had died eight years before and who had been living since that time with one of his married daughters. Upon Mr. G.'s admission to the hospital, the daughter spoke to the social worker and discussed her feelings of being overwhelmed with his care and her inability to go on providing care. Her own children, aged four, eight, and ten, needed her attention, the space in her apartment was cramped, and tensions had increased between her and her husband.

Throughout Mr. G.'s hospitalization, his daughter's plaintive cry ran in counterpoint to his continuing improvement. Mr. G. proved a rewarding patient for staff. With medication changes and improvement in the heart problems, Mr. G.'s mental status improved. He remained with moderate disorientation and confusion, but he was able to respond appropriately in general and evidenced an engaging personality. He was cheerful, optimistic, and amusing. With a great deal of nursing input, Mr. G. started to walk and provide his self-care with minimal assistance.

With the dramatic improvement, everyone was hopeful that Mr. G. could return to live with his daughter. All staff, including the unit social worker, began to press for such a discharge plan. However, the daughter, while guilty and most unhappy, remained adamant that Mr. G could not continue to live in her apartment. The social worker began to receive calls from another daughter and son of the patient and was able to arrange a meeting with all the patient's children who were clearly at odds around the planning.

Mr. G. expected to return to his daughter's although he acknowledged that his grandchildren were sometimes loud and bothersome. He also thrived on the attention given him by staff and responded to the interchange with the other patients in his room.

The social worker needed to help the family sort out their conflicting needs in regard to the patient. All three adult children were unhappy about sending their father to a nursing home, yet the brother and single sister could not agree to provide either a home or more aid for their father. The daughter who had been caring for him was still viewed as the logical person to continue such care, but her plight became clearer as the social worker met with her. Finding Mr. G. an apartment of his own and providing help there was ruled out as not only something difficult to do but something he had been unable to adjust to even years earlier. The fact that now Mr. G. needed direction, assistance, and help in orientation twenty-four hours a day made such a plan quite unrealistic.

The family agreed to apply for his admission to a nursing facility near them so they could visit frequently. They found it difficult to discuss these plans with Mr. G. and needed help in including him in the planning.

The social worker was pressured by the family to "go ahead and make the arrangements." She was also pressured by the staff who were invested in this patient and who felt nursing home placement was inappropriate. The patient, while speaking of returning to his daughter's, was also somewhat aware of his comfort in the hospital. The social worker was not without bias and wanted this patient, who had improved so much, to return to the community.

Source: Beaver and Miller 1985.

However, the role of the social worker in planning discharge is to help to effect what is possible once the needs of the patient and resources at his disposal are known. The social worker had to work with the family to help them come to a plan of action. At the same time she helped them discuss this plan directly with the patient. Mr. G. was initially unhappy with the thought of not returning to his daughter's home. Because of the chance she had had to work through some of her ambivalent feelings with the social worker, the daughter was able to cope with Mr. G.'s disappointment and to help him see some positives in the proposal. The possibility of this being a temporary plan was discussed.

The social worker also had to work with staff who were angry at this plan and therefore at her for "allowing" it. The fact that families cannot be "told" what to do, as well as the ramifications of this particular family's interactions, were shared with staff. The feelings of investment in this patient and the fears that his improvement was "wasted" had to be acknowledged and dealt with. The hospital experiences that had been so positive for Mr. G. were features that would continue in a long-term institution.

Annotated Bibliography

Berkman, B., Millar, S., Holmes, W. & Bonander, E. (1991). Predicting elderly cardiac patients at risk for readmission. *Social Work in Health Care, 16,* 21–38.

    Older patients with cardiac disease are at high risk for physical deterioration after discharge and suffer frequent readmission. This study identified three variables that predicted readmission within three months: marital status, coping abilities, and patient age. Using these three factors, the accuracy for predicting readmission was 61 percent.

Clemens, E. L. (1995). Multiple perceptions of discharge planning in one urban hospital. *Health & Social Work, 20,* 254–261.

    Explores how the discharge planning process was perceived by both discharge planners and family care providers. Planners overrated several factors related to the caregiving process and discharge plans. In addition, excessive concerns by hospital staff about patient safety after discharge may override patients' right to autonomy and choice.

Cooper, L. (1991). Adult discharge planning and nursing home placement: A study of risk factors for quality assurance. *Australian Clinical Review, 11,* 95–102.

    Two groups of patients were included in a study of outcomes of the discharge planning process to compare characteristics of patients who were admitted to nursing homes and those who returned to the community. One important finding was that patients who were discharged to nursing homes had delayed referrals to the social workers, which prolonged and complicated the discharge planning process.

Cummings, S. M. & Cockerham, C. (1997). Ethical dilemmas in discharge planning for patients with Alzheimer's disease. *Health & Social Work, 22,* 101–108.

    As social workers are faced with the complex tasks of discharge plans for patients with Alzheimer's disease, there is the potential for complications in the discharge planning process. This article presents a clinical model to help social workers identify, organize, and evaluate information relevant to discharge planning and determine an appropriate course of action.

Dobrof, R. (1991). DRGs and the social worker's role in discharge planning. *Social Work in Health, 16,* 37–54.

    Cost-containment measures have mixed consequences for the hospitalized patient and health care worker. This article examines the impact of DRGs on the work environment and practice of hospital social workers. In addition, strategies are proposed to enhance the social worker's ability to provide comprehensive, coordinated services within the context of cost-containment strategies.

Haddock, K. S. (1994). Collaborative discharge planning: Nursing and social services. *Clinical Nurse Specialist, 8,* 248–252, 288.

Sixty-four patients participated in a study to determine the effects of a structured discharge planning process using a collaborative design between nurse and social workers. After discharge, patients were telephoned to determine their satisfaction and services received. Patients involved in the collaborative program were more satisfied, had shorter lengths of stay and fewer readmissions, and received more services.

Kadushin, G. (1996). Elderly hospitalized patients' perceptions of the interaction with the social worker during discharge planning. *Social Work in Health Care, 23,* 1–21.

This article reports on a study of older patients' perceptions of the discharge planning process. Results indicate that many patients were confused about the role of the social worker, and that environmental problems exist in the discharge planning process. Recommendations are offered for practice and additional research.

Oktay, J. S., Stinwachs, D. M., Mamon, J., Bone, L. R. & Fahey, M. (1992). Evaluating social work discharge planning services for elderly people: Access, complexity, and outcome. *Health & Social Work, 17,* 290–298.

This study analyzed the extent to which older patients most in need of posthospitalization receive services and the effectiveness of the discharge plan. Results suggest that only a minority of patients who return to the community use social work services while hospitalized, but those who do have posthospitalization service needs. In addition, social work services were effective in reducing the level of unmet needs in nursing, medication, and physical therapy.

Proctor, E. K., Morrow-Howell, N., Albaz, R. & Weir, C. (1992). Patient and family satisfaction with discharge plans. *Medical Care, 30,* 262–275.

This study explored factors that impact patient and family satisfaction with discharge plans. Patient rating of discharge plans were related to their degree of involvement in decision making, their social supports, and their physical condition. Family ratings were somewhat different and related to the planning process, discharge destination, and length of hospitalization.

General Bibliography

Abramson, J. S. (1990). Enhancing patient participation: Clinical strategies in the discharge planning process. *Social Work in Health Care, 14,* 53–71.

Abramson, J. S., Donnelly, J., King, M.A. & Mailick, M.D. (1993). Disagreements in discharge planning: A normative phenomenon. *Health & Social Work, 18,* 57–64.

Bull, M. J. (1994). Patients' and professionals' perceptions of quality in discharge planning. *Journal of Nursing Quality Care, 8,* 47–57.

Bull, M. J. & Kane, R. L. (1996). Gaps in discharge planning. *Journal of Applied Gerontology, 15,* 486–500.

Cox, C. B. (1996). Discharge planning for dementia patients. *Health & Social Work, 21,* 97–104.

Cummings, S., Kelly, T .B., Holland, T., & Peterson-Hazen, S. (1998). Development of a brief needs inventory for caregivers of hospitalized elderly (NICHE). *Research on Social Work Practice, 8(1),* 3–10.

Feigin, R., Cohen, I. & Gilad, M. (1998). The use of single-group sessions in discharge planning. *Social Work in Health Care, 26,* 19–38.

Iglehart, A.P. (1990). Discharge planning: Professional perspectives versus organizational effects. *Health & Social Work, 15,* 301–309.

Kadushin, G. & Kulys, R. (1993). Discharge planning revised: What do social workers actually do in discharge planning? *Social Work, 38,* 713–726.

Lockery, S. A., Dunkle, R. E., Kart, C. S. & Coulton, C. J. (1994). Factors contributing to the early rehospitalization of elderly people. *Health in Social Work, 19,* 182–191.

Morrow-Howell, N., Proctor, E. K. & Mui, A. C. (1991). Adequacy of discharge plans for elderly patients. *Social Work Research & Abstracts, 27,* 6–13.

Proctor, E. K. & Morrow-Howell, N. (1990). Complications in discharge planning with Medicare patients. *Health & Social Work, 15,* 45–54.

Saltz, C. C. & Schaeffer, T. (1996). Interdisciplinary teams in health care: Integration of family care-givers. *Social Work in Health Care, 22*, 59–70.

Soskolne, V. & Auslander, G. K. (1993). Follow-up evaluation of discharge planning by social work-ers in an acute-care medical center in Israel. *Social Work in Health Care, 18*, 23–49.

Tennier, L. D. (1997). Discharge planning: An examination of the perceptions and recommendations for improved discharge at the Montreal General Hospital. *Social Work in Health Care, 26*, 41–60.

Volland, P .J. (1988). (Ed.). *Discharge planning: An interdisciplinary approach to continuity of care.* Ow-ings Mill, MD: National Health Publishing.

References

Abramson, J. S. (1988). Participation of elderly patients in discharge planning: Is self-determination a reality? *Social Work, 33*, 443–448.

Abramson, J. S., Donnelly, J., King, M. A. & Mailick, M. D. (1993). Disagreements in discharge plan-ning: A normative phenomenon. *Health & Social Work, 18*, 57–64.

Abramson, M. (1981). Ethical dilemmas for social workers in discharge planning. *Social Work in Health Care, 6*, 33–42.

Abramson, M. (1983). A model for organizing an ethical analysis of the discharge planning process of the chronically impaired older person from an acute care hospital to the community or an institu-tion. *Social Work in Health Care, 9*(1), 45–52.

Angus, D. C., Linde-Zwirble, W. T., Sirio, C. A., Rotondi, A. J., Chelluri, L., Newbold, R. C., Lave, J.R. & Pinsky, M.R. (1996). The effect of managed care on ICU length of stay. *JAMA, 276*, 1075–1082.

Aroskar, M. A. (1980). Anatomy of an ethical dilemma: The theory. *American Journal of Nursing, 80*, 658–663.

Bender, S. J. (1987). The clinical challenge of hospital-based social work practice. *Social Work in Health Care, 13*, 25–34.

Bennett, C. (1984). Testing the value of written information for patients and families in discharge planning. *Social Work in Health Care, 9*(3)

Bennett, C., & Beckerman, N. (1986). The drama of discharge: Worker/supervisor perspectives. *Social Work in Health Care, 11*(3), 1–12.

Berkman, B. (1988). Quality assurance, utilization review, and discharge planning. In P.J. Volland (Ed.), *Discharge planning: An interdisciplinary approach to continuity of care* (pp. 255–277). Owings Mill, MD: National Health Publishing.

Berkman, B. & Abrams, R. D. (1986). Factors related to hospital readmission of elderly cardiac pa-tients. *Social Work, 99–103.

Berkman, B., Campion, G. W., Swagerty, E. & Goldman, M. (1983). Geriatric consultation team: Al-ternate approach to social work discharge planning. *Journal of Gerontological Social Work, 5*(3), 77–88.

Berkman, B., Walker, S., Bonander, E., & Holmes, W. (1992). Early unplanned readmissions to social work of elderly patients: Factors predicting who needs follow-up services. *Social Work in Health Care, 17*, 103–119.

Blazyk, S., & Canavan, M. M. (1985). Therapeutic aspects of discharge planning. *Social Work, 489–496.

Blumenfield, S. (1982). The hospital center and aging: A challenge for the social worker. *Journal of Gerontological Social Work, 5*, 1–2, 35–60.

Blumenfield, S. (1986). Discharge planning: Changes for hospital social work in a new health care cli-mate. *Quality Review Bulletin, 12*(2), 51–54.

Blumenfield, S. & Lowell, J. (1987). A template for analyzing ethical dilemmas in discharge planning. *Health and Social Work, 12*, 47–56.

Blumenfield, S. & Rosenberg, G. (1988). Towards a network of social health services: Redefining dis-charge planning and expanding the social work domain. *Social Work in Health Care, 13*, 31–39.

Buckwalter, K.C. (1985). Exploring the process of discharge planning: Application to the construct of health. In E. McClelland, K. Kelly & K. C. Buckwalter (Eds.), *Continuity of care: Advancing the concept of discharge planning* (pp. 5–10). Orlando, FL: Grune and Stratton.

Bull, M.J. (1994). Patients' and professionals' perceptions of quality in discharge planning. *Journal of Nursing Quality Care, 8,* 47–57.

Bull, M.J. & Kane, R. L. (1996). Gaps in discharge planning. *Journal of Applied Gerontology, 15,* 486–500.

Cauffield, C. A., Moye, J. & Travis, L. (1999). Long term marital conflict: Antecedents to and consequences for discharge planning. *clinical Gerontologist, 20,* 82-86.

Chakrabarty, C., Beallor, G. N., & Pelle, D. (1988). A multidisciplinary approach to continuity care planning. In P.J. Volland (Ed.), *Discharge planning: An interdisciplinary approach to continuity of care* (pp. 153–170). Owings Mill, MD: National Health Publishing.

Code of Ethics of the National Association of Social Workers. (1993). Washington, DC: National Association of Social Workers.

Colerick, E. J. & George, L. K. (1986). Predictors of institutionalization among caregivers of patients with Alzheimer's disease. *Journal of the American Geriatrics Society, 34,* 493–498.

Coulton, C. J. (1986). Implementing monitoring and evaluation systems in social work. *Quality Review Bulletin, 12*(2), 72–75.

Coulton, C. J. (1988). Prospective payment requires increased attention to quality of post hospital care. *Social Work in Health Care, 13,* 19–30.

Cox, C.B. (1996). Discharge planning for dementia patients. *Health and Social Work, 21,* 97–104.

Cummings, S. M. & Cockerham, C. (1997). Ethical dilemmas in discharge planning for patients with Alzheimer's disease. *Health and Social Work, 22,* 101–108.

Crittenden, F. J. (1983). *Discharge planning for health care facilities.* Bowie, MD: Robert J. Brady.

Dash, K., Zarle, N. C., O'Donnell, L. & Vince-Whitman, C. (1996). *Discharge planning for the elderly: A guide for nurses.* New York: Springer.

Davidson, K. W. (1978). Evolving social work roles in health care: The case of discharge planning. *Social Work in Health Care, 4*(1), 43–54.

DeRienzo, B. (1985). Discharge planning. *Rehabilitation Nursing, 10*(4), 34–36.

Dippel, R. L. (1991). The caregivers. In R. L. Dippel & J. T. Hutton (Eds.), *Caring for the Alzheimer's Patient.* Golden Age Books.

Evans, R. L., Hendricks, R. D., Lawrence-Umlauf, K. V. & Bishop, D. S. (1989). Interventions and Medicaid patients' length of hospital stay. *Health and Social Work, 14,* 227–282.

Fitzig, C. (1988) Discharge planning: Nursing focus. In P. J. Volland (Ed.), *Discharge Planning: An interdisciplinary approach to continuity of care* (pp. 93–118). Owings Mill, MD: National Health Publishing.

Haddock, S.K. (1991). Characteristics of effective discharge planning programs for frail elderly. *Journal of Gerontological Nursing, 17,* 10–13.

Hooyman, N. & Kiyak, H. A. (Eds.). (1996). *Social gerontology: A multidisciplinary perspective.* Boston: Allyn and Bacon.

Jessee, W .F. & Doyle, B. J. (1984). Discharge planning: Using audit to identify areas that need improvement. *Quarterly Review Bulletin, 10*(12), 552–555.

Joint Commission on Accreditation of Health Care Organizations. (1996). *Hospital Accreditation Standards.* Oakbrook Terrace, IL: JCAHCO.

Kaye, C. & Leadley, V. (1985). QA and discharge planning: Ongoing process at Niagra General. *Dimensional Health Services, 62*(6), 35–36.

Kennedy, L., Neidlinger, S. & Scroggins, K. (1987). Effective comprehensive discharge planning for hospitalized elderly. *The Gerontologist, 27,* 577–580.

Kosecoff, J., Kahn, K. I., Rogers, W.H., Reinisch, E. J., Sherwood, M. J., Rubenstein, L. V., Draper, D., Roth, C. P., Chew, C. & Brook, R. H. (1990). Prospective payment system and impairment at discharge: The "quicker and sicker" story revisited. *JAMA,* 1980–1983.

Lawrence, F. P. (1988). Discharge planning: Social work focus. In P.J. Volland (Ed.), *Discharge planning: An interdisciplinary approach to continuity of care* (pp. 119–152). Owings Mills, MD: National Health Publishing.

Liebergall, M., Soskolne, V., Mattan, Y., Feder, N., Segal, D., Spira, S., Schneidman, G., Stern, Z., & Israeli, A. (1999). Preadmission screening of patients scheduled for hip and knee replacement: impact on length of stay. *Clinical Performance and Quality Health Care, 7,* 17–22.

Lurie, A. (1982). The social work advocacy role in discharge planning. *Social Work in Health Care, 8*(2), 75-85.

McNulty, E. G. (1988). Discharge planning models. In P. J. Vollard (Ed.), *Discharge Planning: An interdisciplinary approach to continuity of care* (pp. 21–50). Owings Mill, MD: National Health Publishing.

Mizrahi, T. & Abramson, J. (1985). Sources of strain between physicians and social workers: Implications for social workers in health care settings. *Social Work in Health Care, 10,* 33–51.

Morrow-Howell, N., Proctor, E. K., & Mui, A. C. (1991). Adequacy of discharge plans for elderly patients. *Social Work Research & Abstracts, 27,* 6–13.

Muenchow, J. D. & Carlton, B. B. (1985). Evaluating programs of discharge planning. In E. McClelland, K. Kelly & K. C. Buckwalter (Eds.), *Continuity of care: Advancing the concept of discharge planning* (pp. 149-159). Orlando, FL: Grune and Stratton.

Mullaney, J. W., & Andrews, B. F. (1983). Legal problems and principles in discharge planning: Implications for social work. *Social Work in Health Care, 9*(1), 53-62.

Naylor, M. D., Brooten, D., Campbell, R., Jacobsen, B. S., Mezey, M. D., Pauly, M. V. & Schwartz, J. S. (1999). Comprehensive discharge planning and home follow-up of hospitalized elders: A randomized clinical trial. *JAMA, 281,* 613–20.

Proctor, E. K. & Morrow-Howell, N. (1990). Complications in discharge planning with Medicare patients. *Health and Social Work, 15,* 45–54.

Proctor, E. K., Morrow-Howell, N., Albaz, R. & Weir, C. (1992). Patient and family satisfaction with discharge plans. *Medical Care, 30,* 262–275.

Proctor, E. K., Morrow-Howell, N. & Lott, C. L. (1993). Classifications and correlates of ethical dilemmas in hospital social work. *Social Work, 38,* 166–177.

Rauch, J. B., & Schreiber, H. (1985). Discharge planning as a teaching mechanism. *Health and Social Work, 10*(3), 208–216.

Rehr, H. (1986). Discharge planning: An ongoing function of quality care. *Quality Review Bulletin, 12*(2), 47–50.

Robinson, J. C. (1996). Decline in hospital utilization and cost inflation under managed care in California. *JAMA, 276,* 1060–1064.

Rossen, S. (1984). Adapting discharge planning to prospective pricing. *Hospitals, 58*(5), 71, 75, 79.

Saltz, C. C. (1992). The interdisciplinary team in geriatric rehabilitation. Implications for training. *Journal of Social Work Education, 18,* 135–144.

Saltz, C. C. & Schaeffer, T. (1996). Interdisciplinary teams in health care: Integration of family caregivers. *Social Work in Health, 22,* 59–70.

Schrager, J., Halman, M., Myers, D., Nichols, R. & Rosenblum, L. (1978). Impediments to the course and effectiveness of discharge planning. *Social Work in Health Care,* 491), 65–79.

Shields, L. (1987). *A training and resource handbook for hospital discharge planners.* Richmond, Virginia: Department for the Aging.

Society for Hospital Social Work Directors of the American Hospital Association. (1986). The role of the social worker in discharge planning. *Quality Review Bulletin, 12*(2), 76.

Soskolne, V. & Auslander, G. K. (1993). Follow-up evaluation of discharge planning by social workers in an acute-care medical center in Israel. *Social Work in Health Care, 18,* 23–49.

Smith, G. P. (1996). *Legal and health care ethics for the elderly.* Washington, DC: Taylor and Francis.

Teusink, J. P. & Mahler, S. (1984). Helping families cope with Alzheimer's disease. *Hospital and Community Psychiatry, 35,* 152–156.

U.S. Department of Health and Human Services. (1992). 1990 summary: National hospital discharge survey. *Vital and Health Statistics of the National Center of Health Statistics, 210,* 1–6.

U.S. Senate, Special Committee on Aging. (1991). Report. Washington, DC: U.S. Government Printing Office.

Volland, P. J. (1988). Model for decision making in the discharge planning process. In P. J. Volland (Ed.), *Discharge Planning: An interdisciplinary approach to continuity of care* (pp. 279–302). Owings Mill, MD: National Health Publishing.

vom Eigen, K. A., Walker, J. D., Edgman-Levitan, S., Cleary, P.D. & Delbaco, T. L. (1999). Carepartner experiences with hospital care. *Medical Care, 37,* 33–38.

Waters, K. (1987). Discharge planning: An exploratory study of the process of discharge planning on geriatric wards. *Journal of Advanced Nursing, 12,* 71–83.

Zarle, X. (1987). *Continuing care: The process and practice of discharge planning.* Rockville, MD: Aspen Publications.

Zukerman, C. (1988). Ethical and legal issues. In P.J. Volland (Ed.), *Discharge Planning: An interdisciplinary approach to continuity of care* (pp. 317–336). Owings Mill, MD: National Health Publishing.

8 Nursing Homes

Stephen D. Stahlman with Anne J. Kisor

While social workers have been employed in health care settings since 1905, their involvement in nursing home facilities is a recent phenomenon dating to the 1960s. Nursing homes are one of many facilities which provide long-term care to elderly individuals. Long-term care refers to health, personal care, and social services delivered over a sustained period of time to persons who have lost or never achieved some capacity for self care (Kane & Kane 1987). Long-term care, whether continuous or intermittent, strives to provide care for the elderly in an environment which supports a high degree of autonomy for the older person.

While other age groups are recipients of long-term care services, the elderly constitute the largest consumers of long-term care, primarily through nursing home placement (American Association of Retired Persons 1998). In the past, long-term care referred specifically to institutional placement. Today the term implies a continuum of services such as home health care, respite care, hospice care, and other services that are provided to meet the needs of the elderly.

Over the past twenty years, there has been an increase in the number of persons over 65 as well as an increase in the number of nursing homes. These increases have provided new opportunities for social workers in health care. They have also raised questions concerning the quality and cost of health care, the role of the social worker in nursing home facilities, and the bioethical dilemmas that have been created by advances in medical technology.

This chapter provides a description of nursing homes that includes characteristics of residents, levels of care, and staffing patterns. Three models of social work practice in working with the elderly are presented. Issues that relate to health policy and professional practice are also discussed. Lastly, future issues that affect the quality, cost, and access of care are considered.

Nursing Home Demographics

Development of Nursing Homes in Health Care

While the growth of the modern day nursing home is a post-1930s phenomenon, the practice of providing care to elderly in private homes dates back to the early 1900s. Pegal (1981) indicates that at the beginning of the 1900s, as many as one thousand such homes existed. Most of these homes were owned and operated by philanthropic, charitable organizations and churches. Many of the homes for the elderly at the turn of the century were a result of various immigrant self-help groups who wished to provide for their own. These homes were primarily custodial in nature and most often referred to as convalescent or rest homes. Most were small and the administration consisted of family operations. Nearly half the homes had

Grateful acknowledgement is given to Kathie Manning, Secretary of the Department of Social Work, Indiana Wesleyan University, for her invaluable assistance with this chapter.

no financial requirements for payment. In some homes, residents who were able bodied were expected to contribute their share of work around the facility (Pegal 1981).

Few changes occurred in long-term institutional care for the elderly from the early 1900s to the 1930s. The Social Security Act of 1935 was instrumental in the creation and development of the modern day nursing home. Title I of the Social Security Act established grants-in-aid to states, and Old Age Assistance (OAA) established federal responsibility for the care of the helpless by providing financial assistance (Vladeck 1980). Even though cash assistance was given to the elderly, the provisions made clear that benefits would not be provided to individuals who were residing in any public institution, such as a poor farm or almshouse. This act signaled the end of the poor farms and almshouses and marked the beginning of older living alternatives for the elderly. Beginning to emerge were proprietary homes which provided services to the elderly, who now had resources to pay for such services.

Since the 1930s, the nursing home industry has experienced phenomenal growth due to the increase of health care needs of the elderly population. The reasons for this growth are varied and complex. Over the past fifty years, the advances in medical technology have increased longevity. Since more people are living longer, there has been an increase in the number of chronic conditions that are present among the elderly. In addition, a growing number of families have two wage earners outside the home, reducing the possibility for providing home care for aging parents. As society continues to become increasingly mobile, children may be unable to provide care for an aging parent.

Federal grants and loans were also made available, events which encouraged nursing home growth. The Hill-Burton Act of 1946 is an example of one such program. This government-sponsored program initially provided direct grants for the construction of 350,000 beds in over six thousand health care facilities. In 1954, giving further incentives for growth, the Hill-Burton Act was amended to provide grants for the construction of nonprofit nursing homes.

The amendments of the Social Security Act in 1965, commonly known as Medicare and Medicaid, significantly changed the way in which health care for the elderly would be paid. The purpose of the Medicare program was to provide a health insurance plan for those over the age of sixty-five. The Medicare program is federally funded while Medicaid, on the other hand, is a federal/state partnership program designed to provide health care to certain disadvantaged and low income groups. A large percentage of Medicaid funding is spent on nursing home care. In 1995, 63 percent of nursing home residents relied on Medicaid (38 percent) and Medicare (25 percent) as their primary source of payment (Dey 1995).

In response to concern over poor conditions, and modeled after the ground-breaking Institute of Medicine report (1986), the Nursing Home Reform Law of the Omnibus Budget Reconciliation Act (PL 100-203) was passed in 1987. Arguably the legislation with the most significant regulatory impact on the nursing home industry since the Hill-Burton Act, this law changed virtually all significant federal requirements for Medicare and Medicaid certification. The foundation of OBRA 87 is improved quality of care and quality of life for older persons in institutional settings. Important provisions include: expanding residents' rights; improving resident assessment and care planning; reducing the use of chemical and physical restraints; and upgrading training and licensing requirements of personnel.

The term "nursing home" typically refers to residential facilities in which at least 50 percent of the residents receive nursing services (Beaver & Miller 1985). Homes that receive reimbursement from Medicare or Medicaid must be certified by the federal government. The data from the 1995 National Nursing Home Survey reveal that 69.7 percent were

Table 8.1   Selected Nursing Home Characteristics, 1995

Nursing Homes	Beds		Current Residents			
Facility characteristic	Number	Percent Distribution	Number	Beds per Nursing Home	Occupancy Number	Rate
All facilities	16,700	100.0	1,770,900	106.0	1,548,600	87.4
Ownership						
Proprietary	11,000	66.1	1,151,700	104.7	989,700	85.9
Voluntary nonprofit	4,300	26.7	468,100	108.9	420,800	89.9
Government and other	1,400	8.2	151,000	107.9	138,100	91.5
Certification						
Certified by Medicare and Medicaid	11,600	69.7	1,378,400	118.08	1,213,700	88.0
Certified by Medicare only	1,000	6.1	59,600	59.6	50,000	83.9
Certified by Medicaid only	3,400	20.1	280,300	82.4	240,600	85.8
Not certified	700	4.2	52,600	75.1	44,300	84.2
Bed Size						
Less than 50 beds	2,800	16.8	87,300	31.2	71,100	81.4
50–99 beds	5,900	35.6	430,400	72.9	373,300	87.9
100–199 beds	6,700	40.1	902,500	134.7	794,200	88.0
200 beds or more	1,300	7.5	350,800	269.8	305,000	86.9
Census Region						
Northeast	2,900	17.1	378,800	130.6	346,700	91.5
Midwest	5,600	33.1	564,400	100.8	494,900	87.7
South	5,500	32.8	572,700	104.1	495,000	86.4
West	2,800	16.6	254,900	91.0	212,000	83.2
Affiliation						
Chain	9,100	54.3	978,000	107.5	857,300	87.7
Independent	7,600	45.5	788,200	90.7	689,100	87.4

Source: Adapted from National Center for Health Statistics data (Strahan 1997).

both Medicare and Medicaid certified. Further analysis indicates that 6.1 percent were certified only by Medicare, while 20.1 percent were certified only by Medicaid. A very small percent (4.2) had no certification at all (Strahan 1997).

Nursing home sponsorship falls into three categories. The most frequent type of sponsorship is proprietary ownership, designed specifically for profit. Other nursing home facilities may be identified as voluntary nonprofit, which generally are sponsored by nonprofit religious institutions. The third type of sponsorship is by the government. These facilities are run by state and local municipalities. Nursing homes within a Veterans Administration Hospital would be an example of this kind of facility.

A recent trend over the past ten years indicates a 12.6 percent decrease in the number of nursing homes but a 9 percent increase in the number of available beds. In other words, there are fewer nursing homes but the average number of beds per home has increased since the 1985 survey was conducted. See table 8.1 for a summary of selected characteristics of nursing home facilities.

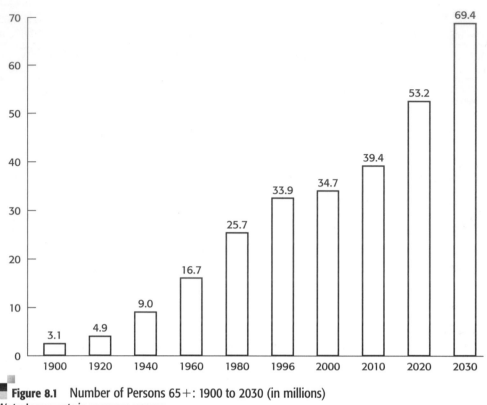

Figure 8.1   Number of Persons 65+: 1900 to 2030 (in millions)
Note: Increments in years are uneven.
Source: Based on data from the U.S. Bureau of the Census.

Resident Profile

In 1997 the number of persons over the age of sixty-five numbered 34.1 million, representing 12.7 percent of the United States population (AARP 1998). Of this number, there were 21.0 million elderly women and 14.0 million elderly men, or a sex ratio of 143 women to every 100 men. This number represents an increase of 9.1 percent since 1990. During this same time period, the under sixty-five population increased 7 percent. The elderly population itself is becoming an older population, with the fastest growing cohort being those individuals over eighty-five years of age. It is anticipated that the number of elderly will continue to grow, with the most rapid increase expected to be between the years 2010 and 2030, when the "baby boom" generation joins the ranks of the elderly (AARP 1998). Figure 8.1 illustrates the projected growth of the elderly population.

While it is important to understand the current projected growth of the elderly population, it is equally important to note that only a small percentage of this population is living in institutionalized care at any given point in time. Currently, only about 4 percent of the population (1.4 million) over the age of sixty-five live in institutional care settings, most of which are nursing care facilities. However, the percentage of elderly that live in nursing care facilities dramatically increases with age. For example, only 1 percent of those between the ages of sixty-five and seventy-four live in such a facility, while 15 percent of those over the age of eighty-five live in a nursing care facility (AARP 1997). The life-time risk of entering a nursing home for the average American is substantial. For persons who turned sixty-five in 1990, it is projected that 43 percent will enter a nursing home at some point (Kemper & Murtaugh 1991).

What are the characteristics of a "typical" resident in nursing home care? Nearly 90 percent of all nursing care patients are over the age of sixty-five; over 35 percent are eighty years or older. In 1995, residents were predominantly white and female (Strahan 1997). The number of residents per population sixty-five years of age or older has declined over the last several years. The small increase in the number of nursing home residents compared to previous years is a result of the tremendous growth in the number of home health care agencies. The number of home health care agencies in 1994 numbered eleven thousand (Strahan 1997).

From this description, the "typical" resident in a nursing home can be described as a poor, white elderly female, suffering from chronic conditions, who dies in the institution. Additional facts about the nursing home population include (Dey 1997):

- They are generally very old. Eighty-two percent are seventy-five years or older.
- They are generally female. Seventy-five percent of nursing home residents are women.
- Most are widowed. Sixty-six percent of nursing home residents (37.3 percent of males and 75.5 of females) have experienced the death of their spouse.
- Most are white. Eighty-nine percent of nursing home residents are white, 8 percent are African American, 2 percent are Latino and the remainder are Asian American and Native American.
- Most have chronic or crippling disabilities that require assistance with activities of daily living (ADL).

Today the resident population of nursing homes shows some changing characteristics, a situation based in part on the implementation of the policy of Diagnostic-Related Groups (DRGs). The DRG system reimburses the hospital a flat fee based exclusively on the diagnostic category assigned to the patient. Hospitals are paid a predetermined price, based on the average cost of treating a patient with a particular diagnosis. The number of days of coverage and the rate of payment will differ for a patient with cardiac problems from someone with kidney failure.

Since the inauguration of the DRGs in 1984, the average length of stay in hospitals has decreased (AARP 1998). The concern of whether hospital patients are being released prematurely has implications for the nursing home population. If patients still need acute medical services, the nursing home becomes a possible alternative. In fact, nursing home populations are becoming more acutely ill and debilitated. This population will require greater specialization and more intensive care from nursing home staff.

Staffing Patterns

The personnel employed by a nursing home work in various departments and contribute to the overall goals and needs of the resident population. The size and number of personnel vary considerably depending on the level of care and size of the total institution.

The following is an overview of the various departments and responsibilities that are found in most nursing home facilities and required by OBRA (1987).

DIETARY DEPARTMENT

The dietary program is responsible for planning and preparing the food served in a nursing home in accordance with state licensure regulations (and federal certification requirements if it is a certified facility). Special diets must be ordered by a physician.

- **Dietitian**—expert in planning menus, diets and dietary procedures. The dietitian is responsible for setting up special diets, as well as maintaining proper nutritional levels for residents.
- **Food services supervisor**—responsible for the daily preparation of foods, special diets, etc. He or she uses the menus developed by the dietitian.

ACTIVITIES DEPARTMENT

Most nursing homes have an activities program. An activities program is a requirement for certification of ICFs and SNFs. Activities should be planned to be appropriate to the needs and interests of the residents and to enhance the quality of life.

- **Recreational therapist** (also called Activities Coordinator or Activities Director)— responsible for developing, scheduling and conducting programs to meet the social and diversional needs of residents such as outside speakers, music, games, outings, parties, etc. Must be licensed or registered (OBRA 1987).

NURSING SERVICES

Nursing Services generally include RNs, LPNs, and nursing assistants/orderlies. These are the people who provide direct care to the residents.

- **Director of nursing (DON)**— a registered nurse (RN) who oversees the entire nursing staff, including nursing supervisors, licensed practical nurses, nurses aides and orderlies. The DON is responsible for quality and safety in patient care.
- **Nursing supervisor** (also called charge nurses)—responsible for nursing care to residents on a floor, or in an area or section, or the nursing home during a particular shift. May be an RN or LPN.
- **Registered nurse (RN)**—a nurse with a minimum of two years of nursing school training and licensure.
- **Licensed practical nurse (LPN)**—a person who has completed one year vocational training in nursing. May be in charge of nursing in the absence of an RN. LPNs often administer medications and perform treatments.
- **Certified nurse aide**—the staff member that provides most of the hands-on care given to residents of nursing homes. Must have completed a mandatory training and certification process.

ADMINISTRATION

The administration unit of a home may include the nursing home administrator, secretarial staff, accounting, and admissions. The nursing home administrator is usually required by state law to be in the home a certain number of hours per week.

- **Nursing home administrator**—is responsible for overall (fiscal, legal, medical and social) management and operation of the facility. Must be licensed by the Board of Nursing Home Administration to operate a nursing home. This individual is ultimately responsible for all nursing home activities.
- **Medical director**—is the physician who formulates and directs overall policy for medical care in the nursing home. Usually only part-time (in the facility for 3-5 hours/month).

SOCIAL SERVICES

Social Services departments are responsible for identifying the emotional, social, and medically related needs of the patient. An assessment of each resident's needs should be found in his or her record, and needed services should be incorporated into the care plan. If the services are not provided by the home, there are usually policies and procedures for referral.

- **Social worker**—a licensed professional trained to identify and respond to medically related and emotional needs of residents. Smaller facilities (less than 120 beds) generally have a part-time social worker and an outside consultant.

HOUSEKEEPING AND LAUNDRY

Members of the housekeeping staff are usually responsible for basic housekeeping chores such as vacuuming floors, dusting, emptying waste cans, and cleaning furnishings. Most nursing homes have laundry facilities and provide clean bed linens and towels. The homes are also equipped to launder residents' clothing.

OTHER MEDICAL STAFF

- **Medical director**—responsible for implementation of all resident care policies, resident accidents and incidents, ancillary services (e.g., radiology), use and release of clinical information from resident charts, and overall quality of care.
- **Attending physicians**—directly responsible for the care of residents. Residents must either choose their own physician or have one assigned by the nursing home to supervise their care.
- **Podiatrist**—specializes in the diagnosis and treatment of diseases, defects and injuries of the foot.
- **Dermatologist**—specializes in the diagnosis and treatment of diseases, defects and injuries of the skin.
- **Ophthalmologist**—specializes in the diagnosis and treatment of diseases, defects and injuries of the eye.
- **Physical therapist (PT)**—trained in restoring the function of muscles in arms, legs, backs, hands, and feet through movement, exercises or treatment. Usually a consultant to the facility. Sometimes physical therapy assistants carry out the plans of the therapists.
- **Occupational therapist**—trained to conduct therapy to restore the fine muscles of the hands and arms.
- **Consultant pharmacist**—required, in a consultant capacity, to conduct an annual review for all residents using psychotropic drugs (e.g., antidepressants or anti-anxiety drugs).
- **Psychologist**—specializes in diagnosis and treatment of mental health disorders and mental illness.

■ **Dentist**—responsible as a consultant for routine dental care and, in some cases, emergency care.

Models of Social Work Practice

In response to the demand for social services for residents in nursing homes, several social work practice models have been developed that provide frameworks for assessment and intervention with the elderly population in nursing home care. A description and discussion is provided below of three specific models: auxiliary function model, advocacy model, and intergenerational family model.

Auxiliary Function Model

Silverstone and Burack-Weiss (1983) have developed a model specifically for working with the frail elderly. The frail elderly are identified as "the old old (over seventy-five) and other persons over sixty who suffer from impairments or enervating conditions that can temporarily or permanently interfere with autonomous functioning" (p. 5). The auxiliary function model is based on a systemic view of human behavior. Problems and solutions associated with aging are viewed as multi-dimensional rather than linear cause and effect. In addition, this model employs a problem-solving framework to gather appropriate information and formulate a plan of action based on the data gathered.

With the frail elderly population, loss and depletion is a major theme. Silverstone and Burack-Weiss (1983) identify the various losses as primary and secondary losses. Primary depletion refers to those losses which are biological in nature. These losses may be external or internal. Examples of primary depletions include the sensory changes such as diminished eyesight, hearing or speech, and mental impairments.

Secondary depletions refer to those losses that are experienced by the elderly that accompany biological aging or are imposed by the age structure of our social system and other environmental deficits. For example as people age, the likelihood of the death of a spouse is increased. While secondary depletions are not confined to the frail elderly, they are experienced in greater frequency with this group. Additional examples of secondary depletions include changes in work status through retirement, loss of significant others, and financial changes.

Since the number of losses or depletions may be extensive, the desired goal of the auxiliary function model is to maximize the frail elderly person's adaptation through support. A supportive environment includes the use of significant others such as family, neighbors and friends. Within the context of this model, every effort is made to restore what is lost and conserve strengths and assets available to the frail elderly. Special attention is given to the adaptive response of the frail elderly. The responses to the primary and secondary depletions determine in part the level and type of intervention that is needed. Three specific responses to adaptation have been identified by Silverstone and Burack-Weiss (1983):

■ The first adaptive response to depletion is that of *restitution*. "Restitution is the process of recovering a function that has been lost even if at a slightly diminished level" (p. 18). Restitution can occur through healing, spontaneous remission, or external intervention.

- The second adaptive response to loss is that of *compensation*. Compensation involves substituting for a lost object or increasing the function of an unimpaired part of the organism. For example, by using crutches, a person who has a leg amputated would increase the usage of his or her hands. For depletions that occur at the secondary level, the compensation may include the development of new friendships to compensate for the death of significant others.
- The third adaptive response to primary and secondary depletion is *accomodation*. Accommodation should only be considered when restitution and compensation are not possible for the frail elderly. For example, when mental and physical disabilities have become chronic and the level of functioning has diminished significantly, restitution or compensation may be impossible. Accommodation may increase dependence, but services and support should be introduced to sustain the elderly person's functioning as much as possible.

Since the auxiliary function model focuses on the replacement of depletion, the degree to which restitution and compensation is possible is significantly influenced by the amount of resources that are available to provide support.

The function of the social workers in the auxiliary function model is to individualize the particular needs of each client. These tasks can be accomplished by preparation of a written statement identified as the study, assessment, and plan (figure 8.2). The study, assessment, and plan serve as an organizing tool, a method of accountability, and a vehicle of interpersonal communication. The written statement identifies the various depletion of losses, the way the client has responded to such losses, and the development of short and long range objectives and corresponding tasks.

After the study, assessment, and plan have been completed, the role of the social worker is to identify those support systems which will be used to carry out the auxiliary role. In many situations, this role will be performed by the family.

Advocacy Model

Many opportunities are provided in the nursing home setting for social workers to be advocates for the elderly resident. An advocate is a person who acts on behalf of another person when someone is not able to act on his or her own behalf. Hancock (1990) indicates that the social worker may carry out the role of patient advocate and "identify rules, regulations, practices and policies that are inconsistent with the rights of nursing home residents, or with the provision of care for the residents and to work toward their change" (p. 179).

Many nursing home practices affect patient care. These include hiring practices which allow the employment of unqualified personnel, inadequate staffing, and any policy which would violate legal rights of residents. The social workers must work cooperatively with the nursing home administrator. However, in the role of resident advocate, the social worker must bring to the attention of the administrator those policies and conditions that impinge and violate the rights of residents. (See figure 8.3 for Residents Rights in Nursing Homes.)

Besides the nursing home, the advocacy role extends to the community. The linkage between the nursing home facility and the community is a most important one. Hamilton et al. (1998) describe a useful intergeneration program for involving the community. Communities can provide assistance and input through advisory boards. The community may be

1. Study
   A. Overview
      (1) Presenting problem and precipitating event
      (2) Referral source
      (3) Client profile (fact sheet)
         (a) Age, sex, marital status, race, religion
         (b) Family constellation
         (c) Socioeconomic and cultural influences
         (d) Environmental influences
      (4) Client and family behavior in interview situation
      (5) Professional contacts and consultation arranged
   B. Depletion and Losses
      (1) Individual functioning
         (a) Activities of daily living
         (b) Problem-solving capacities
         (c) Affective and interpersonal behaviors
      (2) Environmental functioning
         (a) Physical surroundings
         (b) Family: resources and problem-solving capacity
         (c) Service organizations
         (d) Other informal resources
   C. Previous Adaptation
      (1) Developmental and situational crises
      (2) Life-style
      (3) Family exchange patterns
2. Assessment
   A. Summary of study
   B. Interpretation: Reformulation of problem
3. Plan
   A. Long range objectives
   B. Short range goals
   C. Social work tasks

■ **Figure 8.2** Outline of Study, Assessment, and Plan

an important source of needed volunteers that help to link the facility with the surrounding area. In addition, educational programs can serve as an excellent marketing tool to provide information about programs and services that are available to the elderly in the community. One area often overlooked is the contributions the elderly can make to the community through such programs as Adopt A Grandparent.

Hancock (1990) identifies the Ombudsman program, National Citizens' Coalition for Nursing Home Reform, residents' councils, and legal rights of nursing home residents, as specific programs that promote advocacy for nursing home residents. The National Citizens' Coalition for Nursing Home Reform is a national organization formed in 1975 that seeks to improve long-term care systems and quality of life for residents. The Ombudsman program is federally mandated under the Older Americans Act. The nursing home ombudsman is an advocate for residents who have concerns about nursing home policy and operation. The scope of the ombudsman's advocacy efforts was broadened by OBRA 87 that provided for increased access to records and the daily operations of the facility. For example, the facility must allow the ombudsman (with permission of the resident or resident's legal representative) access to the residents clinical records. The nursing home residents' council is another federally mandated program. This council is a forum for the expression of resident concerns or input into policymaking in the facility.

Intergenerational Family Model

The model of intergenerational family treatment is an approach that can be used whenever an older adult is part of the family constellation (Greene 1986). The model focuses on treating the older adult within the context of the family unit. One basic element in this model is the functional age of the older client. Functional age refers to the adaptational capacity in the biological, psychological, and sociocultural areas (Greene 1986). "An assessment of the individual from this perspective allows the caseworker and family alike to understand the structure of life and daily living habits of the older adult" (p. 19).

When biopsychosocial changes occur in the older adult, changes also take place with other family members. Without realizing how the issues affect the entire family system, social workers cannot adequately address the older person's problems. Interventions are designed to assist family members in their adaptation to functional age changes of an older family member. Family participation in treatment is encouraged. Social workers who employ the functional age model organize and interpret client information to arrive at a family-focused biopsychosocial assessment. The assessment includes how the changes in functioning of the older adult have altered the balance within the family system. Interventions are introduced that help restore individual and family functioning.

Issues for Social Work

Social workers in nursing home care are faced with many practice and policy concerns that have a direct effect on the clients they serve. They have an obligation to clients to be informed about practice and policy issues that affect programs and services. Policy issues such as Medicare and Medicaid costs, standards for nursing home care, and impact of diagnostic related groups (DRGs) are discussed below. Practice issues that have been identified for discussion include interventions with families, ethical decision making, and an interdisciplinary approach of working with the elderly.

Policy Issues

MEDICARE AND MEDICAID COSTS

The Amendments to the Social Security Act of 1965 (Title XVIII and XIX), commonly known as Medicare and Medicaid, significantly changed the way in which health care of the elderly would be paid. The Medicare program provides a health insurance plan for those over age sixty-five. Medicaid provides medical assistance for low income persons who are aged, blind, disabled or members of families with dependent children.

Only a very small percentage (8.1 percent) of the Medicare dollar is spent on skilled nursing home care (Health Care Financing Administration 1996). Medicare does not

Some people think that nursing home residents surrender the right to make medical decisions, manage funds, and control their activities when they enter a nursing home. This is not true. As a nursing home resident, you have the same rights as anyone else and certain special protections under the law. The nursing home must post and provide new residents with a statement that details each resident's rights. New residents also have these specific rights.

Respect: You have the right to be treated with dignity and respect. You have the right to make your own schedule and bedtime, and to select the activities you would like to attend (as long as it fits your plan of care). A nursing home is prohibited from using physical and chemical restraints except when necessary to treat medical symptoms.

Services and Fees: The nursing home must inform you, in writing, about its services and fees before you enter the home. Most facilities charge a basic rate that covers room, meals, housekeeping, linen, general nursing care, recreation, and some personal care services. There may be extra charges for personal services, such as haircuts, flowers, and telephone.

Managing Money: You have the right to manage your own money or to designate someone you trust to do so. If you allow the nursing home to manage your personal funds, you must sign a written statement that authorizes the nursing home to manage your finances, and the nursing home must allow you access to your funds. Federal law requires that the home protect your funds from any loss by having a bond or similar arrangement.

Privacy, Property, and Living Arrangements: You have the right to privacy. In addition, you have the right to keep and use your personal property, as long as it does not interfere with the rights, health, or safety of others. Your mail can never be opened by the home unless you allow it. The nursing home must have a system in place to keep you safe from neglect and abuse, and to protect your property from theft. If you and your spouse live in the same home, you are entitled to share a room (if you both agree to do so).

Guardianship and Advanced Directives: As a nursing home resident, you are responsible for making your own decisions (unless you are mentally unable). If you wish, you may designate someone else to make health care decisions for you. You may also draw up advance directives. A Durable Power of Attorney will designate your legal guardian if you ever become incapable of making your own decisions. You may also make your end of life wishes known in a living will.

Visitors: You have the right to spend private time with the visitors of your choice at any reasonable hour. You have the right to make and receive telephone calls in privacy. The nursing home must permit your family to visit you at any time. Any person who provides you with health or legal services may see you at any reasonable times. Of course, you do not have to see anyone you do not wish to see.

Medical Care: You have the right to be informed about your medical condition and medications, and to participate in your plan of care. You have the right to refuse medications or treatments, and to see your own doctor.

Social Services: The nursing home must provide each resident with social services, including counseling, mediation of disputes with other residents, assistance in contacting legal and financial professionals, and discharge planning.

Moving Out: Living in a nursing home is voluntary. You are free to move to another place. However, nursing home admission policies usually require that you give proper notice that you are leaving. If you do not give proper notice, you may owe the nursing home money based on the home's proper notice rules. Residents whose nursing home services are covered by Medicare and Medicaid do not have to give the nursing home proper notice before moving out.

■ **Figure 8.3** Resident Rights in a Nursing Home

Discharge: The nursing home may not discharge or transfer you unless:

- it is necessary for the welfare, health, or safety of others,
- your health has declined to the point that the nursing home cannot meet your care needs,
- your health has improved to the extent that nursing home care is no longer necessary,
- the nursing home has not received payment for services delivered, or
- the nursing home ceases operation.

If you have any concerns about the nursing home in which you live, call your local long-term care ombudsman or your State's survey agency.
Source: Health Care Financing Administration (1996).

■ **Figure 8.3–Cont'd.** Resident Rights in a Nursing Home

provide for the type of custodial care typically provided in nursing homes. By contrast, a much higher percentage of the Medicaid dollar is spent on nursing home care. Combined, Medicare and Medicaid financed $3.58 billion, or a little more than a third, of all health care expenditures for 1996 (Health Care Financing Administration 1997). Federal and state spending by the Medicaid program funded 35.8 percent for hospital care and 25.4 percent for nursing home care.

National health care expenditures have risen dramatically in recent years. The obvious question is how are rising health care costs going to be paid for? Several efforts have been initiated to control the spiraling costs of health care: freezing physician's fees, prospective payments like DRGs, mandatory establishment of rate setting commissions, and prior authorization of non emergency care for Medicaid patients. Other programs include the establishment of Health Maintenance Organizations (HMOs) and Preferred Provider Organizations (PPOs). The reasons for the dramatic increase in the health care expenditures are complex and varied. Rising demands and costs for health care have been created by the Medicare and Medicaid programs of the 1960s. The increase in the number of elderly which require an increasingly larger percent of the health care dollar, and the level of medical technology which has created additional diagnostic tests and procedures all fuel the fires of increased costs.

EFFECTS OF DRGs

One particular plan aimed at cost containment directly affecting the elderly is the Diagnostic Related Group System (DRGs). Enacted in 1983 by Congress, the DRGs is a government program designed to provide incentives for cost containment of Medicare expenditures. Hospitals are paid a predetermined price for their services, a price based on the average cost of treating a patient with a particular diagnosis. Since hospitals are reimbursed a flat rate, efforts must be made to make sure real costs do not exceed the amount that is reimbursable.

One particular concern of health care professionals is the effect the DRGs will have on the quality of patient care. Since the implementation of the DRGs, the nationwide length of stay in hospitals has decreased. In 1990 the average length of stay was 9.0 days compared to 7.1 days in 1995 (Health Care Financing Administration 1996). While this decrease in the average length of stay may signify greater efficiency of hospital use, many health care professionals fear that patients are being discharged "sicker and quicker."

Antiher concern is that hospitals discourage admissions of seriously ill patients who require a longer length of stay than allowed under the DRG system. Such patients have been identified as "outliers" because they fall outside the range of reimbursement allowed by the DRG system. Hospitals may avoid seriously ill patients who will likely require a longer length of stay and will therefore most likely cost more than prospective payments allow. This trend has serious negative implications for the elderly since the severity of illness and number of chronic conditions both increase with age. While the intended effects of DRGs are to contain the spiraling cost of health care, patients who are discharged prematurely will create additional caregiving burdens on nursing homes, families, and community resources. Essentially, the onus of care has shifted from acute care settings to community-based home health care. Demand for such services may put some older persons in jeopardy of falling into a "no-care zone" (Estes, Swan, & Associates 1993).

CERTIFICATION REQUIREMENTS

Facilities that receive Medicaid or Medicare reimbursement must be certified. The certification requires compliance with minimal standards for care as set forth by the federal government. To be eligible for reimbursement under the Medicaid and Medicare programs, facilities must meet Requirements for Participation set by federal regulations (Edelman 1993). These include:

1. **Compliance with federal, state, and local laws.** It involves checking all licenses and registrations of facility staff (e.g., administrator, dieticians, etc.) and compliance with life safety rules and regulations.
2. **Governing body and management.** A facility must have a written policy for resident care that covers every aspect of medical and psychological treatment. This policy must be reviewed annually. There are also standards that pertain to disclosure of ownership, staffing patterns, and staff development.
3. **Medical direction.** A facility must have a Medical Director who is responsible for implementing a resident care policy. The director ensures that medical care is in compliance with federal and state regulations and meets the residents' needs.
4. **Physician services.** A resident may be admitted to a facility only through recommendation of a physician and must remain under the care of a physician throughout the resident's stay. The resident must be thoroughly examined within forty-eight hours after admission. The examining physician must prescribe a plan for medical and personal care and review that plan periodically. This plan is subject to peer review and should be adjusted as the resident's condition changes.
5. **Resident assessment.** Uniform assessment using the Minimum Data Set (MDS) and Resident Assessment Protocols (RAPs) is required. These instruments have a strengths-based, as opposed to a deficit-based, focus. Thorough assessment provides the means for individualized and comprehensive care planning.
6. **Nursing services.** Skilled Nursing Facilities must have a Director of Nursing; a registered nurse on day duty, seven days a week; a charge nurse on each shift to supervise nursing activities; and a licensed practical nurse on duty twenty-four hours a day. Each resident should have a written plan of care. The director of nursing and

the medical director review and revise the plan and make sure it is carried out. This plan of care includes a resident's diet, medication, physical therapy, physical limitations, and psychosocial needs. Only an RN, LPN, a doctor, or a staff member with appropriate training can administer drugs. The drugs must be kept in a safe place, labeled, and dispensed according to a doctor's order. A complete record of each dosage and its effects must be kept. The physician who prescribes medication must do so in writing and review the orders frequently. Medication cannot be used as a convenience for staff members. Residents may use their own drugs with the approval of a physician.

7. **Dietetic services.** The facility must also have a dietitian or a staff member responsible for nutrition who consults a dietitian regularly. The dietitian should consult with residents' physicians in determining any special needs. Restrictions should be noted in writing in the medical record. Those residents who need help eating must receive it. Residents also have a right to make suggestions about their diets and the dietitian must take into account each resident's "food preferences and eating habits." Any change in a resident's eating habits should be noted for the physician.

8. **Special rehabilitative services.** Residents must be able to receive necessary rehabilitative treatment. If the facility cannot provide this service, it must enable the resident to get the service, or specify that it does not offer rehabilitation. The facility is responsible for helping residents to achieve the widest range of motion possible and, at the same time, adjust to their physical limitations.

9. **Pharmaceutical services.** The facility should have someone who is responsible for the distribution of drugs. If this person is not a pharmacist, the facility must periodically consult with a pharmacist. There should be a periodic review of all drugs prescribed to a resident to ensure the drugs are working properly, without undesirable side effects.

10. **Laboratory and radiological services.** Facilities should either provide or arrange for the provision of X-rays, blood tests, and emergency treatment. Doctor's orders are needed for these services. Orders should be documented in the resident's care chart with a dated doctor's signature.

11. **Dental services.** Facilities should refer residents to dentists. They should help residents get to and from such services and keep the results of all tests as part of the resident's medical record. Facilities are responsible for daily oral hygiene and the maintenance of dentures.

12. **Social services.** Facilities must have a qualified social service worker on hand or must have someone who acts as a liaison with a social service agency in the community. This person helps develop resident care plans and attends to residents' psychosocial and emotional needs. The worker maintains contact with each resident's family and informs them of the resident's rights.

13. **Resident activities.** The regulations are not specific with regard to residents' activities. The purpose of an activities program is to create an environment that is as near to normal as possible, thereby encouraging persons in a facility to exercise their abilities. An activities program should provide physical, intellectual, social, spiritual, and emotional challenges much in the same way that everyday life in the community provides challenges. All that the standards require is that the facility provide

adequate space, facilities, and an activities director. Residents may refuse to participate if they wish. Physicians must approve an activity plan and can limit residents' activities if they consider it medically necessary.

14. **Medical records.** The Medical Director and the Director of Nursing must maintain medical records for each resident. These are confidential and must contain notes on every aspect of the resident's medical condition and treatment. They must be up-to-date and signed. Only a doctor may make medical judgments. After each visit, the attending physician should note the resident's condition and review the plan of treatment, in writing, in the resident's medical record.

15. **Transfer agreement.** Nursing homes must have transfer agreements with a hospital so that when their residents require more skilled care, the homes can assist residents in receiving such care.

16. **Physical environment.** The physical environment of the facility must meet the standards of the Fire Code and the Life Safety Code.

17. **Infection control.** Each facility must have an infection control plan that is practiced regularly. Staff members should receive infection control preparedness training.

18. **Utilization review.** Facilities are required to have utilization review committees to ensure that quality care is provided efficiently, appropriately, and cost effectively. They focus primarily on expenditures and review residents' records and conditions to make sure that the facilities provide the appropriate level of care. They monitor treatment and residents' care plans. Members of the committee come from the staff of the facility and from the local community. They are physicians and health professionals, and they offer an evaluation of the medical needs of the resident. The utilization review committee should work closely with the administrative staff on the home to facilitate necessary changes in resident care. The facility must have an operational discharge planning program that adheres to requirements for reasonable grounds for discharge under regulations, and the resident's right to notice of discharge and his/her right to appeal.

19. **Preadmission screening and annual resident review (PASARR).** Facilities must screen all residents prior to admission, and then on an annual basis, to prevent inappropriate placement for older persons with mental illness or mental retardation. Mental health services for appropriately placed residents are mandatory.

20. **Nurse aide training.** A key feature of the reform law's mandate to improve quality of care was to ensure proper training and certification of nurse aides. Aides employed by a facility for more than four months must be trained and competent.

21. **Charges to resident funds.** Facilities are required to disclose to residents what charges are not included in the daily rate. Facilities may not charge for any services mandated by the reform law. In addition, facilities may not impose a charge for routine personal hygiene items or laundry services.

In addition, each state requires SNF and ICF facilities to be licensed. The state regulations vary from state to state, but must conform to the Federal regulations for certification.

The purpose of state and federal regulations is to ensure that the facility has the *capacity* to provide adequate care. The regulations require that the building itself meets safety requirements, that procedures be established for infection control, that facilities employ staff or consultants with certain formal credentials, and that medical records meet certain requirements (Kane & Kane 1987). The regulations provide only minimal expectations for staffing and operation. OBRA 87 also provided for improvements in survey, certification, and enforcement procedures for federal and state surveyors.

Social workers should be familiar with the federal requirements for social services in nursing homes. Nursing homes are required to provide medically related social services to attain or maintain the highest practicable physical, mental, and psychosocial well-being of the resident (OBRA 1987). Facilities with an excess of 120 beds must maintain a full-time "qualified" social worker. The reform law indicates that a qualified social worker must have either a BSW or a bachelor's degree in a human services field, including, but not limited to, sociology, special education, rehabilitation counseling, and psychology. Estimates of residents with mental health problems range from 50 percent to 80 percent, leaving questions as to whether the minimum requirements for a qualified social worker actually provide for the skills necessary to meet this need (Tirrito 1996). In her 1996 study, Tirrito found that nursing home social workers do not have adequate knowledge about managing behavioral symptoms or identifying mental health problems and are therefore not meeting the needs of some residents.

Practice Issues

STANDARDS FOR SOCIAL WORK PRACTICE

The National Association of Social Workers (NASW) developed standards of social work practice in long-term care facilities in 1981. According to these standards, social work objectives for long-term care include the following (NASW 1981):

1. Provide direct social services to residents, their families, and significant others.
2. Assist residents, families, and significant others to utilize appropriately and receive maximum benefit from the facility and the community-based social and health resources on a continuum throughout the stay of each individual from preadmission to discharge or death.
3. Strengthening communications between residents, their families, and significant others, and the program or facility staff.
4. Assisting the facility to achieve and maintain a therapeutic environment essential to the optimal quality of life and independent functioning of each resident and to provide for maximum participation of residents in planning activities and policies.
5. Promoting facility-community interaction through encouraging community involvement in the facility and resident and staff involvement in the community, developing linkages with a wide range of community resources, and participating in the assessment of the need for and planning for other long-term and health care resources.

These basic standards were improved upon by the passage of the reform law in 1987 that expanded the role of social workers in nursing homes. Social workers perform an array of functions in assisting residents to maintain or improve their ability to manage their needs.

INTERVENTION WITH FAMILIES

Contrary to the myth that older people are isolated and alienated, the family is the primary source of social support for older people. The immediate family tends to be the major source of help during illness and the extended family ties the elderly to the community (Dobrof 1989). The availability of family is often a major determinant of whether an older person lives in a nursing home or in the community. For every older person living in a nursing home, two or more equally impaired elderly live with and are cared for by family (Hooyman & Kiyak 1996).

The decision to move a loved one into a nursing home facility is not easy. The social worker often works with the family members to assist in the transition. Mixed feelings of relief, guilt, anger, and loss are common. The social worker must be prepared to deal with the family's response to nursing home placement. The family can also be a tremendous source of information during the admission stage. The following questions can give the social worker insight concerning future interventions and also provide an opportunity for family members to discuss the crisis of institutionalization. These include: What were the major disabilities? What kind of assistance in daily living did the new resident require prior to admission? What were some of the problems and stresses each family member faced and how did they try to cope with them?

Once the placement has been made, the social worker can be instrumental in providing families with instruction about the nursing home, establishing a mutual support group with other family members, and providing information on the particular disease or condition of the family member. The social worker should ensure that the family members are active participants in the care planning process. The need for the family to keep in regular contact with the resident should be also emphasized. Lustbader and Hooyman (1994) indicate that nursing home residents who have regular visitors receive better care than those who are not frequently visited by friends or family members. When staff are aware that family members will follow up on a resident's request, they are likely to fulfill it more quickly than they would in the absence of this expectation. The importance of the social worker working with family members from the preadmission screening through discharge cannot be overemphasized. The family's involvement in the life of their loved one ideally continues after the placement has been made.

ETHICAL DECISION MAKING

While social workers perform various roles in the nursing home, all will be confronted with situations and circumstances requiring decision-making skills in bioethics. Broadly defined, bioethics refers to the ethical decisions that are made in health care. Blumenfeld and Lowe (1987) indicate that an ethical dilemma can occur when there is a pull of divergent loyalties and interests. An ethical dilemma exists when acting on one moral conviction means behaving contrary to another one or when adhering to one value means abandoning another.

The expanding technologies of the medical field have increased the complexity of ethical decision making. The introduction of new technologies, such as organ transplants, in vitro fertilization, genetic screening, and life-sustaining support systems have led to increased complexities that could not have been possible even twenty-five years ago. These technological changes have made possible the ability to maintain life almost indefinitely through artificial life support systems. Once the cessation of a heart beat determined death, but now, as a result of the advances in medical technology, the criteria for determining when death occurs have been the subject of much debate. As the level of medical technology advances, so does the level of complexity involving ethical decision making. The social worker who is employed in a nursing home must come to grips with such questions as: What action should be taken in life and death situations? Who should make such decisions and under what circumstances? What criteria should be used to arrive at a chosen course of action? How much and when should information be shared with residents with terminal conditions? Who should make decisions when the resident is unable to decide for him or herself? These are only a few of the many ethical questions that social workers confront in nursing homes facilities. Recent legislation has helped provide guidance in addressing these ethical dilemmas. The Patient Self-Determination Act (PSDA), passed by Congress in 1990, requires all facilities receiving Medicare or Medicaid to provide residents with written information at admission about advance directives and the right to refuse treatment (Zwahr et al. 1997). Advance directives include living wills and legally binding surrogate decision-making powers such as a durable power of attorney. Many nursing home residents now have advanced directives that document their preferences for care in future situations where they may be unable to voice their needs. Social workers are generally actively involved in the admission process and may take a leading role in exploring whether the resident has an advanced directive, and in explaining rights under the PSDA.

Guidelines can be offered to assist the social workers with such difficult decisions. While not providing specific responses to specific issues, the National Association of Social Workers (NASW) Code of Ethics provides useful guidelines relevant to the worker's obligations to client, staff, and the profession. The common theme that is present within social work and health care is the underlying concern about right and wrong with respect to the duties and obligations of the social worker.

Social workers who work in nursing homes deal with difficult ethical issues in practice, especially in the area of admissions. In a survey of 348 American Homes for the Aging, 82 percent reported that they were confronted with ethical issues in the admission process (Lewis 1990). Schneider and Kropf (1996) have constructed a model to help social workers sort through the various aspects of ethical problems in long term care. This model is based upon following the principles of: *autonomy* of the older adult, *beneficience* for the health and well-being of the person, and *justice* as related to the impact upon others in the nursing home. While ethical decisions have no clear answers, examining these three factors can help provide a framework for critical thinking and reflection upon the admission process.

Complex ethical decisions may be compounded when the social worker in nursing homes feels inadequate as a result of not being prepared to make such decisions. As opportunities continue to grow for social workers in nursing home facilities, service providers must be knowledgeable and appropriately trained in employing ethical decision-making skills.

SUPPORTING RESIDENT RIGHTS

An important focus of the reform law is the increased emphasis on resident rights and resident involvement in his or her plan of care. The right to quality care and quality of life is codified in federal law. Further, residents are to be actively protected from abuse and neglect and from the unnecessary use of chemical and/or physical restraints.

The social worker is the primary conduit for delivery of medically related social services. These services can include, for example (DHHS 1995):

- making arrangements for obtaining needed adaptive equipment, clothing, and personal items
- maintaining contact with the family (with resident permission) to report on changes in health, current goals, discharge planning, and encouragement to participate in care planning
- assisting staff to inform residents and those they designate about the resident's health status and health care choices and their ramifications
- making referrals and obtaining services from outside entities (e.g., talking books, absentee ballots, community wheelchair transportation)
- assisting residents with financial and legal matters (e.g., applying for pensions, referrals to lawyers, referrals to funeral home for preplanning arrangements)
- providing or arranging provision of needed counseling services
- through the assessment and care planning process, identifying and seeking ways to support residents' individual needs and preferences, customary routines, concerns, and choices
- building relationships between residents and staff, and teaching staff how to understand and support residents' individual needs
- promoting actions by staff that maintain or enhance each resident's dignity in full recognition of each resident's individuality
- assisting residents to determine how they would like to make decisions about their health care and whether or not they would like anyone else to be involved in those decisions

A central practice goal for social workers in the nursing home setting is to provide services that support resident autonomy and self-determination. The National Association of Social Workers (1993) has identified clinical indicators to monitor the quality of resident care that can assist the social worker in supporting residents rights.

INTERDISCIPLINARY APPROACH

While the role of a social worker may vary from facility to facility, one commonality is membership on a health care team. A nursing home social worker is a member of a team that provides a "therapeutic community" to meet the needs of the residents. The team consists of nursing staff, rehabilitation therapists, and social workers. Collaboratively, the team identifies short- and long-term goals, meets on a regular basis to assess progress, and reevaluates or formulates new goals appropriate to client care. One particular contribution that the social worker makes to the team is providing a social history of residents. The social history includes background information about family, medical information, and other information relevant in meeting the psychosocial needs of the resident. After the social history is completed, a care plan is developed, and short- and long-term care goals are established. Care plans are periodically reviewed and updated by team members to ensure that the psychosocial needs are being met.

Future Trends

As social workers in nursing home care look to the future, what changes can be anticipated? As previously indicated, the elderly population, particularly those over age seventy-five, will continue to grow, a fact making it likely for continued growth in nursing home care, particularly in skilled nursing facilities. Although the need for nursing home care will continue to expand, several changes arise concerning issues of quality, access, and costs of providing care for the elderly.

QUALITY OF CARE

Quality of care has traditionally been difficult to define. Government approaches to upholding quality include licensing, certification, inspection of care, the Ombudsman program, and training and certification of personnel. The reform law of 1987 is an attempt to take a comprehensive and holistic view of quality care where medical, psychological, and social needs are intertwined. This legislation delineates specific criteria that act as proxy indicators by which quality of care can be measured. These indicators reflect all aspects of the resident's daily life in the facility. In this way, federal standards ensure that the nursing home provides quality care.

Future tasks in maintaining quality of care in nursing homes include monitoring both the positive and negative outcomes of the reform law. Consumer advocacy groups such as the National Citizens' Coalition for Nursing Home Reform and professional organizations like the National Association of Social Workers continue to be in the forefront of these efforts.

ACCESS TO CARE

The combination of the rapidly growing number of older persons and high nursing home occupancy rates almost guarantees that access to care will continue to be an issue for the future. There is concern that access to nursing home care may prove more difficult for some older persons than others. For example, in the past, facilities have often avoided residents needing heavy care, or exhibiting a behavior problem, or financed by Medicare (Kane & Kane 1987). In addition, some argue that African Americans and other minorities are discriminated against in the admission process (see, for example, New York State Advisory Committee to the U.S. Commission on Civil Rights 1992).

One specific strategy to improve access to care along medically related grounds is preadmission screening. Under the reform law, the purpose of screening is to prevent inappropriate placement and to protect consumers from being denied admission on unwarranted grounds. For example, an older person with dementia cannot be refused admission to a nursing home due to behavioral difficulties. Dementia, while a crippling disease that markedly impairs the cognitive processes, is not classified as mental illness and cannot therefore be cited as a reason to refuse admission to an otherwise eligible older person.

Long-term care is viewed as fragmented, uncoordinated, and challenging for the older person to negotiate alone. Consumers have difficulty gathering information about existing programs and services. Case management consists of a "package" of services to meet an individual's need in allocating resources across a community or catchment area. Case management can be offered by many organizations such as hospitals, Area Agencies on Aging, family service agencies, or private case manager agencies. This can result in considerable confusion that exists within the case management system. Issues that remain important to consider include:

- Is case management useful without additional services or without additional money to pay for services? The answer to this question depends on whether the major problems of long-term care are getting information about services in the community, or paying for them.
- Can case management appropriately be done by organizations that also provide service?
- Does this introduce a conflict of interest?
- To what extent should case mangers build expectations of family care into a plan?
- To what extent should case managers use the client's preferences as the basis for a plan?

Attention to these specific issues will enhance case management as a service method for older clients.

COST OF CARE

Another issue that will affect nursing home care in the future is the cost and payment of care. Current tax revenues are not expected to meet increased expenditures. Changes will need to be made in the way health care is financed. Since nursing homes consume a major portion of the health care dollar, policies must be developed to ensure that adequate financing is available for meeting the needs of the residents. Future efforts to limit the nursing home sector will include limiting the supply of nursing home beds, changing the way nursing homes are paid, and substituting less expensive community care for more expensive care in facilities.

As costs continue to grow, there is a danger that adequate health care services will not be available. Society may experience an unwillingness to pay for care since a large portion of health care costs are financed by state and federal governments. Federal expenditures for health care for the elderly have skyrocketed in the last decade, requiring that policymakers address alternative models for providing care. In an effort to control government costs, new sources of revenue must be generated. Long term care insurance is now widely available to the consumer but risk to companies remains substantial until more actuarial data are available.

Conclusion

The elderly are the fastest growing age group in our society and will continue to show steady growth into the twenty-first century. The increase in this population group will necessitate the expansion and creation of programs to meet the biopsychosocial needs of the elderly. As the number of those over the age of seventy-five increases, so will the demand for nursing home care. The changing demographics will provide many challenges for the social work profession. Social workers in nursing homes must be appropriately trained to meet the psychosocial needs of the elderly. This training must include knowledge of social work practice with the elderly, skills for ethical decision making, and the ability to advocate for and on behalf of clients. Social workers must also accept the challenge of developing policies that are in the best interests of the elderly.

While no one can predict the future, the outlook for social workers in nursing home care can be viewed with cautious optimism. As the profession of social work continues to increase the knowledge base for practice with elderly in nursing home care, it is expected that additional knowledge, technologies, and instruments will be developed that more effectively meet the psychosocial needs of nursing home residents. Social workers will be called upon to meet these challenges on behalf of the elderly population.

Discussion Questions

1. How do social workers incorporate their values and skills into a nursing home setting?
2. Over seventy percent of nursing homes are owned by profit-making enterprises. In what ways might this affect the quality of care?
3. What are DRGs and how might they affect the care of the elderly in nursing homes?
4. What are some of the important changes created by the nursing home reform law (OBRA 87)?
5. What are some ethical issues social workers encounter in nursing homes?
6. Can the public perception of a nursing home ever be changed? How?
7. Mrs. J., a seventy-eight-year-old resident of a nursing facility, has recently had a feeding tube inserted. She has been in a coma for two weeks. Mrs. J.'s daughter wants the tube removed, but the physician refuses. What ethical issues are present in this scenario?
8. What is case management?

Experiential Learning

Activity: Fantasy Exercise

Imagine that you are an eighty-year-old person, and you have come to live in a nursing home. It was difficult for you to leave your home, but you and your doctor, your family, and your friends have come to believe that you really need the help that you can get from a skilled nursing facility. Your safety, social, nutritional, and housekeeping needs are being taken care of in the nursing home.

For the purpose of this exercise, you can only keep seven of the privileges listed below. Place an (X) in front of the seven which are *most important to you*. If the most important things to your happiness are *not* listed, you may add two choices by writing them in the space marked "Other." These will be included in your final list of seven. You will have ten minutes to complete this part of the activity. A discussion will follow.

_____ The privilege of taking frequent trips and visiting with family and/or friends outside the nursing home.

_____ The privilege of engaging in some gainful activity every day, similar to what you did in your home or apartment.

_____ The privilege of keeping pictures of your family and small, treasured mementos close to you.

_____ The privilege of defining your own schedule, i.e., making noise, staying up late, not getting dressed in the morning, etc.

_____ The privilege of being considered a sexual being and of being able to entertain friends in sufficient space and with privacy.

_____ The privilege of keeping and preparing food any way you please.

_____ The privilege of bringing favorite pieces of furniture from your home or apartment and of having your living space be a reflection of your personality (including not being particularly neat).

_____ The privilege of having a pet.

_____ The privilege of living in a heterogeneous community where you regularly come into contact with people of different ages and races, including children.

_____ The privilege of monitoring your own health; to keep, take, or refuse to take medications.

_____ The privilege of making totally independent decisions, with yourself and your close family and friends as the only people's opinions to consider.

_____ The privilege of choosing how you will spend your time.

_____ The privilege of having space and supplies to work on your hobby.

_____ The privilege of being alone and having absolute peace and quiet.

_____ The privilege of grieving for loss of home and independent living status.

_____ The privilege of receiving considerate, respectful care, with your privacy and need for independence inviolate.

_____ The privilege of living in an environment where it is okay to talk about and discuss your fears and feelings about aging, life, and death.

Other: _____

_____

_____

After a ten-minute period, share with classmates your choices and the reasons why those items were so important. During the session, it should be pointed out that placement in a nursing home can often be a major assault on a person's autonomy.

Case Studies

See Appendix B for guidelines in analyzing gerontological social work practice.

Case 1: The New Admission

Fred Marks is an eighty-five-year-old widower who has lived alone in a small rented house since his wife's death fifteen years earlier. He is admitted to the nursing home following hospitalization from a fall resulting in a fractured hip. It is unlikely that he will be able to return home, as he has no living relatives and the community has a weak support system. Mr. Marks is bewildered by the sheer number of people he encountered the morning of his admission. The administrator welcomes him absentmindedly and quickly reads a booklet aloud to him, entitled *The Legal Rights of Nursing Home Residents*. He is then wheeled to his bedroom where he is distressed to find a roommate who is disoriented and confused, and who bursts unaccountably into laughter or profanity at intervals.

An aide then escorts Mr. Marks in his wheelchair to an "activity room," which seems a mile from his room. The aide disappears and a kind-appearing woman tries to engage him in working a puzzle. He does not express his feeling of being insulted, but as soon as her back is turned, he wheels himself into the corridor. He has no idea which way to go until an aide passes and gives directions so loudly that he is embarrassed, for his hearing is unimpaired.

_____

Source: Hancock 1987

The new resident toys with the food on his plate at lunch. He is accustomed to having lunch, usually a peanut butter sandwich and milk, in front of the television while he looks at the noon news show. Sitting at a table with six other people is a new and unenjoyable experience. Even if he felt like eating, the clamor of trays is giving him a headache. The lady across from him is having trouble chewing. Seeing the food dribble over her chin makes Mr. Marks feel a little queasy. He looks at his watch and sighs, for he is going to miss nearly all of the noon news.

The afternoon is slow. Even the veterans' hospital had more interesting afternoons. He had enjoyed swapping stories with the other veterans. When he was at home, he took a walk every afternoon, rain or shine. In nice weather he walked to a park about two miles away. Sometimes he sat on a bench with a couple of old cronies, if they were well enough to be outside. Other times he watched the children. He often took bread to toss to the birds. That seems a long time ago.

A nurse taps his shoulder and announces that it is time for the evening meal. He realizes he had dropped off to sleep, sitting in his chair. He looks closely at the nurse; he has not seen her before, which means the second shift has arrived. He looks at his watch. Dinner at five o'clock. He has been eating his evening meal at seven o'clock ever since he can remember. He isn't hungry, but there is really nothing else to do. Clattering dishes, so many voices, somebody's angry voice. The food looks all right but it tastes so different he can hardly swallow it. He takes a few bites, then quits. He keeps getting lost when he tries to find his way back to his room.

It's now 5:30. Mr. Marks wonders what he will do until 11:00, his usual bedtime. When he is at home and it's summertime, he weeds the garden in the cool evening air. He smiles, thinking about his neighbor's cat, a feisty gray tom that was forever prowling in his garden, but never did any harm.

The evening seems interminable. He doesn't want to go to the activity room, but the aide insists, saying the "able-bodied" are "supposed" to be in the activity room. He wonders why he is considered able bodied, until he recalls the rooms he has passed and the inert bodies lying in bed. He is introduced to a large number of people who seem to take little interest in him, with the exception of one woman. She believes she lived next door to him in Louisville. Even though he explains he has never even visited that city, she is not convinced and keeps asking him whether he remembers the corner grocer, the neighborhood soda shop, and so on.

He lies awake that first night for what seems like hours. His roommate wakes up, goes to the bathroom, and then tries to crawl in Mr. Mark's bed. Even though this does not happen again, Mr. Marks finds himself waiting, each time there is a noise on the other side of the room, for the stranger to return. Other noises are also disturbing: rubber soles padding against the floor, doors slamming, a sudden scream, a wail of abandonment. He finally drifts into an uneasy sleep.

Case 2: Socialization for Mrs. Sanders

The Sanders family, two sons and their wives, was upset that their mother, age eighty-five, was becoming increasingly disorganized and confused when they visited her in the nursing home. They were particularly upset because the home wished to move her to a floor where

Source: Adapted from Silverstone & Burack-Weiss 1983.

she could receive more protection due to a decrease in her ability to ambulate. The family felt that this segregation would only worsen her condition, and she would be depressed by living with "the sick people." The social worker met with the four family members and gave each of them time to vent and state their opinion; the social worker pointed out the limitations of the institution in caring for this kind of resident. She noted the fact that the elder Mrs. Sanders would become increasingly isolated on her present floor since she was being rejected by residents and would have more activities and companionship on the new floor.

With the problem outlined, both sons agreed to fill the social gap by visiting more regularly to aid in the care of their mother. They made a commitment to take her to their homes as frequently as possible for visits, take her out on other visits from the home, including other residents when possible, and be helpful to staff in her direct care when they were there. The wives supported their husbands in this commitment. Mrs. Sanders was particularly pleased.

With these commitments, the problem was redefined and the social workers, after talking with staff, agreed to make a tentative commitment to keeping Mrs. Sanders where she was for the time being. The new plan worked well for nine months, at which time the sons felt that their commitment was too much for them since Mrs. Sanders was growing worse, and she was moved to another floor. However, the extension of this time for socialization was a meaningful one for all involved, including the sons and Mrs. Sanders.

Case 3: A Move for Mrs. Marshall?

Mr. Marshall is a self-referral to the senior center. Mr. Marshall is eighty-three and is seeking nursing home placement for his seventy-nine-year-old wife, due to the fact that she was becoming increasingly difficult to care for. He learned of the social worker's services through a center newsletter. Clearly in conflict about the move, he had spent a sleepless night following an angry scene with his wife, who was reportedly both confused and incontinent.

Mr. and Mrs. Marshall are an African-American couple, originally from Alabama, and married for sixty years. The husband is a former postal employee, now retired for eighteen years. His wife is a former part-time sales clerk who retired with her husband. They are supported adequately by a government pension and Social Security. For the past three years, the couple have lived in a public housing project for seniors after the neighborhood they had resided in all their married years had been razed. Devout Baptists, the Marshalls have not attended church since moving to their new home and have no contact with their neighbors.

The couple have two middle-aged married sons, a lawyer living in Atlanta and a businessman living in Chicago. They visit their parents a few times a year and talk with them weekly on the phone. There are six grandchildren, but no other close family members. Mrs. Marshall's sister, who lived nearby, died one year ago.

One office visit with Mr. Marshall, two home visits with the couple, and one telephone call to each son (with the Marshall's permission) were conducted for the purpose for assessment and planning. A medical examination was obtained for both Mr. and Mrs. Marshall,

Source: Adapted from Silverstone & Burack-Weiss 1983.

who had not seen a physician in many years. A psychiatric examination and nursing con-sultation were also arranged for Mrs. Marshall.

Mr. Marshall appeared quite frail in the interviews. Although he seemed alert and so-cially appropriate, he was openly distraught that he could no longer manage on his own. In interviews, Mr. Marshall appeared at times angry and at times quite tender toward his wife, who appeared physically well cared for, confused, ingratiating, and inappropriately cheerful and unconcerned about their circumstances.

Annotated Bibliography

Brody, E. (1977). *Long term care of older people: A practical guide*. New York: Human Sciences Press.
    Represents one of the first attempts to provide guidelines for the provision of long-term care for the elderly.
Coile, R. C. (1993). Future trends, health care reform and the outlook for long term care. *Journal of Long Term Care Administration*, 6–10.
    An excellent discussion of health care reform and long-term care. Predictions are made con-cerning the future of funding long-term care.
Dolenc, D. & Dougherty, C. (1985). DRGs: The counterrevolution of financing health care. *Hastings Center Report*, 15, 19–20.
    An excellent overview and discussion of the implementation of the DRGs. The authors pro-vide a discussion of the long-term effects of DRGs.
Green, R. (1982). Families and the nursing home social worker. *Social Work in Health Care*, 7, 57–67.
    Provides an excellent discussion about the importance of working with the family in nursing home placement.
Kane, R. A. & Kane, R. L. (1987). *Long term care: principles, programs, and policies*. New York: Springer.
    Excellent review and summary of research in long-term care. Good overview of policies and programs and how they affect the elderly.
Kodner, D. L. (1993, Winter). Long term care 2010: Speculations and implications. *The Journal of Long Term Care Administration*, 82–86.
    Good review of the long-term care of the future. Specific attention is given to the discussion of a shift to home care and community based services.
Koff, T. H. & Bursac, K. (1995). *Long term care: An annotated bibliography*. Westport: CT: Greenwood Press.
    Excellent bibliography that provides a variety of articles on long-term care, including institu-tional and community based care. Administrative issues of nursing home care are also included.
Kruzich, J. M. & Powell, W. E. (1995). Decision-making influence: An empirical study of social work-ers in nursing homes. *Health and Social Work*, 20(3), 215–223.
    The authors present findings of a survey of ninety social workers employed in nursing homes re-garding their perceived influence in organizational decision making.
Leutz, W. N., et al. (1991). Adding long term care to medicare: The social HMO experience. *Journal of Aging and Social Policy*, 3(4), 69–87.
    Provides a review of model projects that utilize community long-term care. Also presents an overview of Social Health Maintenance Organizations.
Liu, K., Doty, P., & Manton, K. (1990). Medicaid spend down in nursing homes. *The Gerontologist*, 30, 7–15.
    Good discussion of the process of "spend down" to access public assistance. Data is used from the National Long Term Care Surveys.
Parham, I. (Ed.). (1993). *Gerontological social work: An annotated bibliography*. Westport, CT: Green-wood Press.
    An excellent bibliography that covers a variety of topics on working with the elderly. The se-lected topics include clinical issues, educational issues, and medical issues.

Peterson, K. J. (1987). Changing needs of patients and families in long-term care facilities: Implications for social work practice. *Social Work in Health Care, 12,* 37–49.

    With an increase in chronic conditions among the elderly and the creation of DRGs, this article examines how the needs of the elderly have changed in the nursing home setting.

Quadagno, J., Mayer, M. H., and Turner, J.B. (1991). Falling into the Medicaid gap: The hidden long term care dilemma. *The Gerontologist, 31,* 521–526.

    Good discussion of those individuals that are just above the Medicaid cutoff but have insufficient resources for needed services. Possible solutions are proposed.

Schneider, E. L., & Guranlnik, J. M. (1990). The aging of America: Impact on health care costs. *Journal of the American Medical Association, 263*(17), 2325–2340.

    Provides an excellent discussion of the specific health care needs of the "oldest" old. Possible solutions are examined to meet the specific needs of the fastest growing group of elderly.

U.S. General Accounting Office. (1991). *Long term care: Projected needs of the aging baby boom generation.* Report to the special needs committee on aging, U.S. Senate. Washington, DC: U.S. Government Printing Office.

    This report projects long-term care needs of the "baby boomer" generation that will join the ranks of the elderly between 2018 and 2060.

General Bibliography

Applebaum, R., & Austin, C. (1990). *Long-term care case management: Design and evaluation.* New York: Springer.

Blieszner, R., & Bedford, V. H. (Eds.) (1995). *Handbook of Aging and the Family.* Westport, CT: Greenwood Press.

Brannon, D. (1992). Toward second-generation nursing home research. *Gerontologist, 32,* 293–294.

Brody, E. (1985). *Mental and physical health practices of older people.* New York: Springer.

Burack-Weiss, A., & Brennam, F. C. (1991). *Gerontological social work supervision.* New York: Haworth Press.

Coe, M., Wilkenson, A., & Patterson, P. (1986). *Preliminanry evidence on the impact of DRGs dependency at discharge study.* Portland, OR: Northwest Oregon Health Systems.

Coons, D., Mace, N., & Whyte, T. (1996). *Quality of life in long-term care.* New York: Haworth Press.

Dey, A. N. (1997). *Characteristics of elderly nursing home residents: Data from the 1995 National Nursing Home Survey. Advance data from vital and health statistics; no. 289.* Hyattsville, MD: National Center for Health Statistics.

Davis, M. A. (1991). *On nursing home quality: A review and analysis.* Medical Care Review, 48, 129–166.

Dreher, B. (1987). *Communication skills for working with elders.* New York: Springer.

Erwin, K. (1996). *Group tech for aging adults: Putting geriatric skills enhancement into practice.* Washington, DC: Taylor & Francis.

Foner, N. (1994). *The Caregiving Dilemma: Work in an American Nursing Home.* Berkeley: University of California Press.

Funk, S. G., Torquist, E. M., Champagne, M. T., & Wiese, R. A. (Eds.) (1993). *Key Aspects of Caring for the Chronically Ill.* New York: Springer.

Germaine, C. (1984). *Social work practice in health care: An ecological perspective.* New York: Free Press.

Gutheil, I. (Ed.) (1994). *Work with older people: Challenges and opportunities.* New York: Fordham University Press.

Hendricks, J. (Ed.) (1995). *The Meaning of Reminiscence and Life Review.* Amityville, NY: Baywood.

Kane, R. A. (1993). *Assisted living in the U.S.: A new paradigm for residential care for frail older persons.* Washington, DC: American Association of Retired Persons.

Kane, R. A., & Caplan, A. L. (Eds.) (1990). *Everyday ethics: Resolving dilemmas in nursing home life.* Springer: New York.

Kane, R. A., & Caplan, A. (Eds.) (1993). *Ethical conflicts in the management of home care: The case managers dilemma.* New York: Springer.

Katz, P. R., & Calkins, E. (Eds.) (1989). *Principles and practice of nursing home care.* New York: Springer.

Katz, P. R., Kane, R. L, & Mezey, M.D. (Eds.) (1993). *Advances in long-term care,* vol. 1, 2. New York: Springer.

Katz, P., Kane, R. A., & Mezey, M. (Eds.) (1995). *Quality care in geriatric settings.* New York: Springer.

Kodner, D. L., (1993). Long term care 2010: Speculations and Implications. *The Journal of Long Term Care Administration,* 82–86.

Koff, T. H., & Bursac, K. M. (1995). *Long term care: An annotated bibliography.* Westport, CT: Greenwood Press.

Kruzich, J. M. (1986). The chronically mentally ill in nursing homes: Policy and practice issues. *Health and Social Work, 11,* 5–14.

Madeleine, G. (1991). *Social work and social work services as defined in Medicare law and regulations, citations analysis and summary.* Washington, DC: National Association of Social Workers.

March, C. S. (1997) *The complete care plan manual for long-term care.* (Revised Ed.). Chicago: American Hospital Publishing.

Monk, A. (Ed.) (1990). *Handbook of gerontological services.* New York: Columbia University Press.

Mitty, E. L. (1992). *Quality imperatives in long term care: The elusive agenda.* New York: National League for Nursing Home Press.

National Association of Social Workers. (1993). *NASW clinical indicators for social work and psychological services in nursing homes.* Washington, DC: NASW.

Rehr, H. (1985). Medical care organization and the social service connection. *Health and Social Work, 10,* 145–257.

Roberts, C. (1989). Conflicting professional values in social work and medicine. *Health and Social Work, 14,* 211–218.

Schneider, R. L., & Kropf, N. P. (1996). The admission process in nursing homes: A clinical model for ethical decision-making. *The Journal of Long Term Home Health Care, 15*(3), 39–46.

Suzman, R. M., Willis, D.P., & Manton, K. G. (Eds.) (1992). *The Oldest Old.* New York: Oxford University Press.

Strahan, G. W. (1997). *An overview of nursing homes and their current residents: Data from the 1995 National Nursing Home Survey. Advance data from vital and health statistics;* no 280. Hyattsville, MD: National Center for Health Statistics.

Thomas, W. H. (1996). *Life worth living.* Action, MA: VanderWyk & Burnhan.

Vourlekis, B., Gelfand, D., & Greene, R. (1992). Psychosocial needs and care in nursing homes: Comparison of views of social workers and home administrators. *Gerontologist, 32,* 113–119.

Wunderlich, G. S., Sloan, F. A., & Davis, C. K. (Eds.) (1996). *Nursing Staff in Hospital and Nursing Homes: Is It Adequate?* Washington, DC: National Academy Press.

References

American Association of Retired persons. (1998). *A profile of older Americans: 1997.* Washington, DC: Program Resources Department, U.S. Department of Health and Human Services.

Ball, R. (1985). Medicare: A strategy for protecting and improving it. *Generations, 14,* 9–12.

Blumenfield, S., & Lowe, J. (1987). A template for analyzing ethical dilemmas in discharge planning. *Health and Social Work, 12,* 47–56.

Department of Health and Human Services, Health Care Financing Administration. (1995, June). *State operations manual.* Washington, DC: Author.

Dey, A. N. (1997). *Characteristics of elderly nursing home residents: Data from the 1995 National Nursing Home Survey. Advance data from vital and health statistics;* no. 289. Hyattsville, MD: National Center for Health Statistics.

Dobrof, R. (1989). Staff and families: Partners in caring for the institutionalized aged. In P. Katz & E. Calkins (Eds.), *Principles of nursing home care.* New York: Springer.

Dolenc, D., & Dougherty, C. (1985). DRGs: The counter-revolution in financing health care. *Hastings Center Report, 15,* 19–29.

Edelman, T. S. (1993). The nursing home reform law: The federal response. *Clearinghouse Review* (Aug.–Sept.), 454–458.

Estes, C. L., Swan, & Associates, (1993). *The long term care crisis: Elders trapped in the no-care zone.* Newbury Park, CA: Sage.

Gehrke, J., & Wattenberg, S. (1981). Assessing social services in nursing homes. *Health and Social Work, 6,* 12–25.

Greene, R. (1982). Families and the nursing home social worker. *Social Work in Health Care, 7,* 57–67.

Greene, R. (1986). *Social work with the aged and their families.* Hawthorne, NY: Aldine de Gruyter.

Hamilton, G., Brown, S., Alonzo, T., Glover, M., Mensereau, Y., and Wilson, D. (1998). Building community for the long term: An intergenerational commitment. *The Gerontologist, 39,* 235–238.

Health Care Financing Administration. (1996a). *Guide to choosing a nursing home.* Publication No. HCFA 02195. Washington, DC: HCFA.

Health Care Financing Administration. (1996b). *HCFA statistics: Highlights.* Washington, DC: HCFA.

Health Care Financing Administration. (1997). *Health care expenditures.* Washington, DC: National Health Statistics Group.

Hooyman, N. & Kiyak, H. (1996). *Social gerontology: A multi-disciplinary perspective.* (4th ed.). Boston: Allyn & Bacon.

Institute of Medicine. (1986). *Improving the quality of care in nursing homes.* Washington, DC: Academy Press.

Iverson, L. (1986). *A description and analysis of state preadmission programs.* Minneapolis: MN: Interstudy, Center for Aging and Long-term Care.

Kane, R. A., & Kane, R. L. (1987). *Long-term care: principles, programs, and policies.* New York: Springer.

Kemper, P., & Murtaugh, C.M. (1991). Life time use of nursing home care. *New England Journal of Medicine, 324*(9), 595–600.

Lewis, M. (1990). *Results of the AAHA membership survey on ethics.* New York: Fordham University Third Age Center.

Lustbader, W., & Hooyman, N. (1994). *Taking care of aging family members.* (2nd Ed.) New York: Free Press.

Meadors, A., & Wilson, N. (1985). Prospective payment system for hospital reimbursement. *Hospital Administration Currents, 29,* 3.

Meyer, C. H. (Ed.). (1986). *Social work with the aging.* Silver Spring, MD: NASW.

Morreim, H. (1985). The MD and the DRG. *Hastings Center Report, 15,* 30–39.

National Association of Social Workers. (1981). *Standards for social work services in long-term care facilities.* Silver Spring, MD: NASW.

New York State Advisory Committee to the U.S. Commission on Civil Rights. (1992, November). *Minority elderly access to health care and nursing homes.* Albany, NY: Author.

Omnibus Budget Reconciliation Act of 1987 (OBRA 87), Pub. L. No. 100–203, 101 Stat. 1330 (1987), amending 42 U.S.C. §§ 1995 I - 3(a) - (h) Medicare and 1396r(a) - (h) Medicaid.

Pegal, C. (1981). *Health care and the elderly.* Rockville, MD: Aspen Publications.

Reamer, F. (1985). The emergence of bioethics in social work. *Health and Social Work, 10,* 271–281.

Schneider, R. L., & Kropf, N. P. (1996). The admission process in nursing homes: A clinical model for ethical decision-making. *The Journal of Long Term Home Health Care, 15*(3), 39–46.

Schneider, R., & Kropf, N. (1987). *Virginia Ombudsman program: Professional certification curriculum.* Richmond, VA: Virginia Department for the Aging.

Silverstone, B., & Burack-Weiss, A. (1983). *Social work practice with the frail elderly and their families: The auxiliary function model.* Springfield, IL: Charles C. Thomas.

Smyer, M. (1980). The differential usage of services by impaired elderly. *Journal of Gerontology, 35,* 249–255.

Strahan, G. W. (1997) An overview of nursing homes and their current residents: Data from the 1995 National Nursing Home Survey. *Advance data from vital and health statistics;* no 280. Hyattsville, MD: National Center for Health Statistics.

Tirrito, T. (1996). Mental health problems and behavioral disruptions in nursing homes: Are social workers prepared to provide needed services? *Journal of Gerontological Social Work, 27*(1-2), 73–87.

Vladeck, B. (1980). *Unloving care.* New York: Basic Books.

Zwahr, M. D., Park, D. C., Eaton, T. A., & Larson, E. J. 91997). Implementation of the Patient Self-Determination Act: A comparison of nursing homes to hospitals. *Journal of Applied Gerontology, 16*(2), 190–207.

III Special Populations

9 Older Persons of Color:
Asian/Pacific Islander Americans, African Americans, Hispanic Americans, and American Indians

■ ■ ■ ■ ■ ■ ■ ■ ■ ■ ■ ■ ■ ■ ■
Joyce O. Beckett and Delores Dungee-Anderson

The term "old people" is used categorically to describe individuals at a certain age or beyond. Typically implied is that all persons who meet this criterion are alike. In reality, however, the elderly are a highly diverse population group among whom heterogeneity cannot be overemphasized. When the combination of ethnicity and minority status is added, being elderly is, at best, a unique life-stage experience and often results in oppression. This chapter will examine the dual membership status of individuals who are both elderly and belong to minority groups in the United States.

There are many oppressed groups which comprise the elderly population; however, discussion in this chapter is limited to (1) Asian/Pacific Islander Americans, (2) African Americans, (3) Hispanic Americans, and (4) American Indians. These groups comprised 13 percent of the elderly in 1990 and are expected to be 25 percent of the elderly by 2025 (AARP 1996).

Though each of these groups has a distinct history, they all share the common experience of oppression in the United States. They have customs, values, traditions, and sometimes, languages that differ from dominant society and from each other. They have identifiable physical characteristics which make them easy targets for discrimination and exclusion from mainstream America.

The Aging Process

Senescence, or aging, is a cultural, behavioral, psychological, chronological, social, and biological process. No matter what definition is used, the aging process is highly individual. Definitions of aging shape the perceptions, preferences, beliefs, and behavior of all persons and, frequently, the treatment of older persons. In America, being "old" is associated with certain culturally unpleasant occurrences such as physical decline and death, and as a result, interactions with elderly persons may be uncomfortable, and/or individual elderly may be treated with less than respect. Caucasian elderly men, for example, may experience discrimination for the first time in their lives simply because they have become "old." For persons of color, the negative conditions and reactions associated with aging may be the last stage in a life history of oppression, powerlessness, and low status. Elderly persons of color tend to lead more difficult lives as aging may compound or intensify discriminatory treatment. In addition, the stresses associated with being a minority group member can accelerate the aging process so that minorities may be faced with aging concerns at a much earlier point in life than majority persons.

Individual characteristics and the nature of the aging process itself make it difficult to define or measure when a person is considered "old" or "elderly." For example, when chronic ailments and disabilities are considered, many American Indians are old at age forty-five. Because definitions and measures vary with circumstances, this chapter relies on the data sources definition of "aged" which ranges from forty-five to sixty-five years.

Overview of Elderly Persons of Color

Ethnic diversity is increasing within the elderly population. The 1990 census counted 31.1 million elderly aged sixty-five or older, reflecting a 22 percent increase between 1980 and 1990 (U.S. Bureau of Census 1992b). In 1990, one in ten elderly persons were persons of color. Of the total elderly population in 1990, about 28 million were Caucasian, 2.5 million African American, 1.1 million Hispanic, 450,000 Asian/Pacific Islander, and 116,000 American Indian/Eskimo/Aleut. To understand how elderly persons of color are likely to experience life in the United States, it is important to appreciate the context in which these individuals matured. Those who are sixty-two or older in 1998 were born in 1936 or earlier, about at least thirty years before the Civil Rights era of the sixties. They are removed by at least one generation or more from immigration, slavery, conquest, and/or forced labor. Each group has a history of hostile induction into American society with experiences often limited to the ghetto, barrios, reservations, and/or enclaves.

The majority of these elderly persons of color are all too familiar with oppression in most aspects of their lives. They grew up in an historical era when resources, roles, and status were determined almost exclusively by race and ethnicity and when both legal and de facto discrimination and segregation were the rule rather than the exception. These experiences have directly influenced their orientation to life and perception of the world. It is well known that some direct consequences of oppression, such as poverty or low income levels, are predictors of other problematic psychosocial factors such as poor nutrition, poor housing, increased stress, and decreased access to health care and other social services (Kerner, Dusenbury, & Mandelblatt 1993). These and other repercussions of systematic and pervasive oppression have influenced and continue to influence the relationships elderly persons of color have with one another and the Anglo majority.

That elderly persons of color have coped and survived despite the overwhelming barriers is a testament to their strengths. They have learned to live with and overcome adversity and scarcity. They have developed coping strategies, such as reliance on the extended family and the development of community networks, that have buffered them from the harsh Anglo world.

Demographic and socioeconomic characteristics provide a snapshot of the current experiences of elderly persons of color and are compared and contrasted in this section.

Asian/Pacific Islander Americans

Asian/Pacific Islander American (APIA) elderly have received little attention in social work literature and as consumers of social services. Several factors help to explain this occurrence. First, the designation APIAs includes several culturally distinct and diverse groups. There is little agreement, even among governmental institutions, about which groups to designate as APIA. The discussion in this section will rely primarily on the definition of the U.S. Census Bureau which is congruent with that of the Council on Social

Work Education and National Association of Social Workers. However, the general litera-ture often does not specify which groups are defined as APIAs.

A second reason is that, unlike the other population groups of color, APIAs are not a protected group under the definition of "socially and economically disadvantaged" persons. Public Law 95–507 specifically excludes APIAs from this category (U.S. Commission on Civil Rights 1979). This results in the exclusion of APIAs from programs that are specifi-cally targeted toward the poor elderly persons of color.

A related third factor is the prevalent reference to APIAs as the "model minority" and "super minority" ("America's Super Minority" 1986). They also have been compared with and pitted against other ethnic groups in the United States. The successes of APIAs were greatly exaggerated in the mass media during the 1980s. For, example, as Ross-Sherrif (1992) reports, two popular television news programs aired special segments on the success of APIAs in 1986. In 1987, a television magazine-format program presented a glowing re-port of the academic achievements of this group in America. This designation suggests APIAs have been able to overcome prejudice and oppression, the proof being that as a group their socioeconomic characteristics are similar to or exceed those of caucasian Amer-icans. This stereotype has become the basis for several unfounded assumptions, including that APIAs do not have problems, are able to care for their own, and do not need or desire social services. The socioeconomic situation and the history of elderly APIAs in this coun-try do not support this myth. Like other persons of color, they have been and continue to be victims of discrimination and oppression. Although the myth of the "model minority" has opened windows of opportunity for Asians who are considered intelligent and hard working, it has also resulted in efforts to close doors by attempting to set quotas on the num-bers of APIAs entering institutions of higher learning. Despite the support of family, friends, co-nationals, and ethnic community organizations, some APIAs experience stress and psychosocial consequences at the group, family, and individual levels (Ross-Sheriff 1992). Berry (1988) also has described the acculturative stress and related mental health problems of Southeast Asian refugees. Similarly, unlike European immigrants, APIAs faced quotas which for decades (1882 to 1965) limited their entry into the United States. A ma-jority of APIA elderly were impacted in a variety of ways by the U.S. policy. Many were forced to leave family members behind or make difficult choices related to their decisions to emigrate to America. Furthermore, once they were in America, prejudice and racism not only continued but escalated for some groups of APIAs. Among elderly Japanese Ameri-cans, for example, the climax of this discrimination was their internment from 1941 to 1946. During those years, all persons with as little as one-eighth Japanese blood, whether American citizens or not, were evacuated from their homes and herded into "relocation camps" or concentration camps. They lost millions in property and income (Lum 1984, 1986; Weeks 1984).

Fourth, the perceived positive situation of APIAs rests to some extent on the erro-neous use of data for all APIAs. When APIAs are treated as a homogeneous group, impor-tant differences are masked, such as bimodal distributions on most social characteristic indicators. For example, when one looks at occupation or income, APIAs concentrate at the top and the bottom levels. An arithmetic average camouflages these extreme scores and perpetrates the myth of "average" or "above average" achievement on social indicators. Once the data are disaggregated, the elderly are one group that emerges as having some special concerns.

A fifth factor is the scarcity of historical and contemporary national data. Statistics from the Census, for instance, do not report on APIAs as a separate group until 1980 (Kim 1983). Even in 1998, there was no consistent effort to include APIAs as a separate group when national or local data are considered. Therefore, it is difficult to find statistical information on elderly APIAs.

African Americans

African Americans have received relatively little attention in the gerontological literature, despite the fact that they constitute America's largest and most underprivileged persons of color group. Knowledge of the history of their immigration to this country is necessary for understanding their place in contemporary American society. African Americans began coming to the United States in the early 1600s along with the first white settlers. While many were free or indentured servants similar to a number of Caucasians, a large majority came involuntarily as slaves. As the need for labor increased, especially in agriculture, fewer African Americans were free, and laws were enacted to support the institution of slavery (Watson 1983).

There are at least two immigration patterns for African Americans. One is that they came directly to the United States from Africa. The other is that they moved from an African country to another country—frequently the Caribbean Islands or South America—and later migrated or were brought to the United States.

All African Americans can trace their roots to Africa. They represent a number of African countries which have had and continue to have distinct cultures and languages. Even in the same country, Africans lived in tribes with different dialects. Currently, African countries reflect their own indigenous historical culture and the culture of the European countries which colonialized them. Thus, variant customs and dialectical vestiges remain today among African American population subgroups that have been relatively isolated from the majority population.

In the United States, many of the current elderly African Americans grew up in the rural, agricultural South where they had few rights and privileges. Laws as well as customs prevented them from actively participating in and receiving rewards from the larger society. In many cases, their children have moved to larger cities and to the North and Midwest seeking better opportunities, which has ended a major source of social support for the elderly in these regions. Another group of African American elderly comprises those born in the West Indies. There is little, if any, empirical data that have compared conditions between U.S. mainland-born and West Indies–born African-American elderly in this country. Only recently, Lyons (1997) offered a comparison between the social support systems of both groups. She did not find data to dispute the position that although major societal changes and positive gains have occurred during the lifetimes of U.S. mainland and West Indies born African American elderly, both continue to be disadvantaged groups that do not share equally in any facet of American society.

Hispanic Americans

Historically, Hispanic groups have been "ignored or considered as insignificant by social scientists and policymakers" (Maldonado 1979, p. 176). The Census Bureau projects a 600 percent growth rate among elderly Hispanics in less than fifty years (Miranda 1988). The needs of this population are increasingly important to recognize and address.

More than one out of twenty Americans are of Spanish origin. They share the common group label of "Hispanic" or "Latino." Americans of Central or South American, Mexican, Puerto Rican, Cuban, and European descent (Spain) share the Hispanic designation.

Mexican Americans, widely referred to as Chicanos, Latin Americans, and/or Spanish Americans, are the largest Hispanic American subgroup. They have a long history in the United States beginning in the early days of European exploration before the nation was formed. Historical accounts document the founding of Sante Fe, New Mexico, more than a decade before the Pilgrims landed at Plymouth (Shaffer 1984). Their ancestry can be traced back to the Spanish conquest of the indigenous populations of Central America and the merging of these Spanish conquerors with those populations to form the Mexican people.

Puerto Ricans are the second largest Hispanic subgroup and originate from the island of Puerto Rico, located about a thousand miles from Miami. The original inhabitants of the island became extinct while the Spanish settlers, who imported African slaves, merged with the slaves to form the group currently called Puerto Ricans (Shaffer 1984).

Cubans came to the United States in large numbers in four major waves of immigration. The most recognized wave was the Cuban Refugee Program which was in operation from 1965 to 1973 (Cuban Refugee Program 1974). During this period the United States and Cuba cooperated to run daily shuttle flights to the States to reunite families separated during earlier open immigration periods. Approximately 300,000 Cubans settled in the United States during this wave. Considering the diverse origins of the three largest subgroups of Hispanic Americans, it is obvious that, when combined with the smaller subgroups of Spanish origin, the total Hispanic-American population is widely divergent.

The majority of Hispanic elderly have settled in four states. Those from Mexico and Central America are found predominantly in California and Texas. Florida has a large Cuban population, and New York has attracted many immigrants from Puerto Rico and the Caribbean Islands (American Association of Retired Persons 1987).

American Indians

American Indians are recognized as the first inhabitants of North America and the first ethnic group to be subordinated to the Europeans. The American Indian population includes Indians, Eskimos, and Aleuts (AARP 1995). The majority of American Indians who survived contact with Europeans were removed from their ancestral homes and resettled on reservations restricted to certain areas in the country.

At that time and currently, American Indians have a diversity of life-styles, languages, religions, kinship systems, and political organizations. For example, as Shaffer (1984) notes, at the time of the first European contact in North America, American Indian inhabitants spoke at least three hundred tribal languages. Approximately half are still used in the United States.

Clusters of American Indian population groups which include the elderly are located in large urban centers such as Pittsburgh, Minneapolis, Tulsa, Denver, Oakland, and Tacoma. Other large population concentrations are located in Alaskan villages, in rural and semirural areas, and on reservations in southern and southeastern areas of the United States. There is a total of twenty-five states in which there are large concentrations of American

Indian elderly sixty-five years of age and older. Included among these states are California, Oregon, Texas, North Carolina, and Florida (AARP 1995).

In comparison with other racial and ethnic minorities in the United States, an understanding of the uniqueness of the American Indian population becomes crucial. American Indians retain both a legal and constitutional status that differs from other persons of color. This difference impacts the provision of services to American Indian elderly (National Indian Council on Aging 1981b).

The Constitution, a number of court decisions, and federal laws together award important powers of self-government to federally recognized tribes of American Indians. Tribes living within the boundaries of federally recognized reservations possess many of the features of sovereignty that characterize American state and local governments. Tribes retain the right to adopt a form of government of their own choosing, to define tribal membership, regulate domestic relations of members, and to tax and control the conduct of tribal members on reservations. The National Indian Council on Aging (NICOA) (1981b) also suggests that the notion of self-determination is inherent in the possession of these powers. As distinct legal and cultural units, American Indian tribes are legally sanctioned to determine their own futures within the parameters of the United States law.

The elderly who live on reservations or in Alaskan native villages are governed by tribal policies and may experience differences in the quality of life compared to the single American Indian elder who lives in and is governed by the laws of individual states. As political jurisdictions, states have powers of taxation and are consequently able to legislate and support local programs for their elderly. Tribes do not have the resources to operate in this fashion. Congress and the Bureau of Indian Affairs make the final policy and financial decisions on questions of need for older American Indians. As a result, they have less access to government assistance than "other persons of color," which increases their risks of substandard housing, poverty, malnutrition and poor health (AARP 1995).

Demographics

Size and Growth

The proportion of the population that is elderly varies considerably by race and ethnic origin. As shown in table 9.1, there is a smaller proportion of older African Americans (8 percent) than whites (14 percent). This difference is a result of African Americans having a higher fertility rate and a higher mortality rate than Caucasians. Among African Americans, more children are born and fewer persons live to reach sixty-five (AARP 1995; U.S. Senate, Special Committee on Aging 1986). At about age seventy, an interesting phenomenon occurs. African Americans who survive to this age have a life expectancy almost identical to Caucasians. At more advanced ages, African Americans actually have a greater life expectancy, so that the life expectancy for African American men and women at age eighty-five exceeds that for Caucasian men and women. No simple explanation has been given for this "age cross over" (U.S. Bureau of the Census 1987; AARP 1995; Hooyman & Kiyak 1993; U.S. Senate et al. 1991).

During the 1700s and 1800s, slavery was a major force that changed the size of the African American population. In the first census of 1790, about 757,000 people were reported as African American. In 1860, just before the Emancipation Proclamation, the census counted almost 4.4 million African Americans, a six fold increase. This phenomenal

Table 9.1   Socio-Demographic Characteristics of the Elderly (65+ years) of Color

Race	Sex	Sex Ratio	1991 Life Expectancy in years[†]	1992 Median Income[‡]	Percentage Below Poverty Line[*,‡]	1990 Age 65+ years[*,§]	1990 Education[*] No Formal	High School
Caucasian:	Male	67	72.9	$18,980	9%	14%	1%	56%
	Female	100	79.6	$10,904				
Asian/Pacific Islander American:	Male	82	No Data	N/A	12%	6%	10%	47%
	Female	100						
African American:	Male	63	64.6	$11,331	26%	8%	4%	27%
	Female	100	73.8	$7,798				
Hispanic American:	Male	71	No Data	$11,509	21%	5%	10%	27%
	Female	100		$6,877				
American Indian:	Male	73	67*	N/A	N/A	5%	10%	34%
	Female	100						

*Data for males and females
[†]U.S. Bureau of the Census 1996
[‡]U.S. Bureau of the Census 1999
[§]American Association of Retired Persons 1996

increase was due directly to importation and the encouraged high fertility rates (Watson 1983).

The increase in the African American population has continued although at a slower rate than during slavery. In 1990 there were 25 million African Americans. The rate of growth among the African American elderly surpasses both that of the total African American population and of younger African Americans. African Americans have a higher proportion of elderly than any other group of color. In 1990, 8 percent of African Americans, 6 percent of Asians, 6 percent American Indians, and 5 percent of Hispanic Americans were sixty-five years old and over (AARP 1995).

Many of today's elderly African Americans grew up in the rural, agricultural South where they had few rights and privileges. Laws as well as customs prevented them from actively participating and receiving rewards from the larger society. In many cases, their children moved to larger cities and to the North and Midwest seeking better opportunities. Although African American elderly have lived through major societal changes and positive gains, they continue to be a disadvantaged group that does not share equally in any facet of American society.

With the exception of native Hawaiians, all other APIA groups immigrated to the United States and experienced both oppression and racism. Native Hawaiians also experienced oppression and racism but were colonized in their own homeland. As Mokuau (1991) notes, the severity of the historical oppression of these groups is reflected in such events as the internment of Japanese Americans during World War II, exclusion acts preventing Chinese from becoming citizens in the early 1900s, and the abrogation of native Hawaiian government and religion since the arrival of Westerners in 1778. Refugee populations in the 1970s and 1980s, such as the Vietnamese, Laotian, and Hmong, displaced from their own countries because of war, also suffered poverty and maladjustment in the United States (Mokuau 1991). APIAs are a relatively small group and are not dispersed throughout the United States. This group has accounted for less than 2 percent of the American population and has constituted 5 percent of American persons of color. The large concentration (93 percent) of Asian Americans in the metropolitan areas of a few states supports the stereotype of an "invisible minority." The majority of APIAs reside in five states: California, New York, Texas, Hawaii, and Illinois. Implications for these states with high-density APIA population groups include the existence of ethnic enclaves as well as the demonstration of high levels of racism because of the increased visibility of persons of color (Beaver 1983; Mokuau 1991; AARP 1995). In 1990, approximately 6 percent of the APIA population in America was sixty-five or older.

The actual breakdown of APIA elderly residence is 60 percent living in the two western states of California and Hawaii (AARP 1995; Kim 1983; Yu 1980). In Virginia and Louisiana, APIAs constitute the smallest proportion of minority elderly since only 3.1 percent and 3.7 percent, respectively, were sixty-five and over in 1980 (AARP 1987). Overall, Japanese constitute the largest portion, one-third, of elderly APIAs.

Hispanics are the fastest growing minority population group in the United States. They are largely concentrated in urban areas (Becerra & Shaw, 1984; U.S. Bureau of the Census 1987). In March 1987, there were 18.8 million Hispanics in the United States who were noninstitutional civilians. This is an increase of approximately 700,000 in only one year.

Approximately 5 percent or about 1.2 million of the Hispanic elderly are sixty-five years of age or over. Of this number, approximately 94,000 are eighty-five and older (AARP

1995). Consequently, as a group, Hispanic Americans are a relatively young population. (See table 9.1.)

The proportion of elderly among the American Indian population has grown faster than in other groups of color. Between 1980 and 1990, the number of elderly increased by 52 percent. This figure is more than twice the increase for African American or Caucasian elderly. (U.S. Bureau of the Census 1993).

American Indian elderly comprise about 5 percent of the American Indian population in the United States. Approximately 114,000 American Indians are over the age of sixty-five. Of these, about 42,000 are eighty-five years and over. Beginning at age forty-five, they suffer a higher incidence of chronic health problems and functional impairments than the general elderly population in the United States. Those individuals who are forty-five and over show startling similarities across several dimensions, to the non-American Indian population over age sixty-five (NICOA 1981a). (See table 9.1.)

Education

In our society in general, level and type of education are indicators used to help measure socioeconomic status. Lower educational achievement is a factor that has influenced the socioeconomic status of many elderly persons of color. For the large percentage of those who have left the work force for retirement and/or other age-related reasons, education has assumed added relevance to the extent that it tends to represent a benchmark of the ability to function within complicated societal social service and other care systems for the elderly (White 1997).

A higher proportion of older persons with color have no formal education. Asian Americans, Hispanic Americans, and American Indians all have an illiteracy rate of 10 percent, ten times the rate of Caucasians (1 percent). In 1990, only 27 percent of Hispanic elderly had completed high school (AARP 1995) (See table 9.1.)

Among the Hispanic subgroups, older Cubans were found to have a higher level of education than older Puerto Ricans or Hispanics of Mexican descent (Becerra & Shaw 1984). This finding is explained by the large number of Cubans of higher socioeconomic status who fled Cuba for this country during the unrest of the 1960s. Puerto Rican immigrants were found to have less formal education than any racial or ethnic group studied while Hispanics of Mexican origin living in the Southwest have the highest illiteracy rate in the nation for elderly individuals (Leonard 1967).

Approximately 34 percent of American Indians are high school graduates and about 10 percent have no formal education at all (AARP 1995). Only 4 percent of African American elderly have had no formal education despite the severe limitations to educational resources they experienced in U.S. school systems. Only 27 percent of African Americans have completed high school compared with 56 percent of Caucasian elderly (AARP 1995).

Of all minority elderly, APIAs have the greatest percentage of high school graduates (47 percent). Yet, this figure is still significantly lower than the proportion of Caucasian elderly graduates (56 percent). Even though recent Asian/Pacific Islander immigrants include a significant proportion of well-educated professionals, the percentage of those lacking formal education (10 percent) is still substantially greater than for Caucasian elderly (1 percent).

Heterogeneity

Of the four elderly groups discussed in this chapter, African Americans are the only ones who are not defined or described in any of the literature or government documents. The literature assumes that everyone knows who African Americans are. This situation reflects the myth that African Americans are a homogeneous population. In reality, African Americans vary on many dimensions including the amount of time they have lived in the United States, their country of origin, and their immigration patterns. For example, some elderly African Americans have lived in the United States all their lives and may be eighth or ninth generation Americans. Others have recently immigrated to the United States from non-African countries like Haiti or from African countries such as Ghana or Nigeria. They may not speak English. There is little or no appreciation of the rich cultural differences among the various ethnic groups within the literature. It is important for understanding and intervention to consider these differences. For example, an older African American who has recently moved to the United States from Haiti and speaks no English would likely have different concerns than an elderly African American who has lived in this country all his or her life.

APIAs are a diverse group. According to the Asian American Health Forum, Inc. (1990), Asian Americans have geographical origins in over twenty countries. They represent more than sixty different ethnicities and a multitude of languages and dialects. The heterogeneous nature of Pacific Islander groups is easily reflected in the distinctive languages, traditions, and values of the Polynesian, Micronesian, and Melanesian island cultures found throughout the 64 million square miles of the Pacific Ocean (Mokuau 1991). Similarly, APIA elderly are also diverse and can be divided into at least five groups (Lum 1996).

1. retired single males, mainly Chinese and Filipino, who were denied marriage because of immigration restrictions;
2. elderly females, mainly Japanese who entered the country as picture brides;
3. immigrants or Americans born during the early 1900s;
4. parents who accompanied their children to America from China, Taiwan, Korea, and the Philippines during the last two decades; and
5. persons who came to America in recent years with their families as a result of the Vietnamese and Cambodian wars.

There are unique historical and contemporary influences on each of these five groups as well as on each ethnic group among the Asian Americans.

The Hispanic population in this country is racially heterogeneous and is comprised of several population subgroups of Spanish origin. Each subgroup is identified by place-of-origin but may include Caucasians, persons of African descent, American Indians, Asians, and Pacific Islanders of Spanish ancestry. Although demographic data on the subgroups are independently estimated, all subgroups are also statistically combined to comprise the larger group of Hispanic Americans. Included in the Spanish surname group are individuals of Mexican, Puerto Rican, Cuban, Central American, South American, and Spanish origin (Torres-Gil & Negm 1980; U.S. Bureau of the Census 1996).

Discussion of American Indian elderly as a group is difficult because "Indian groups are extremely diverse, with important tribal differences" (Gelfand 1982, p. 29). Although most

American Indian elders identify first on the basis of tribe, many of those who live on reservations further identify themselves with a particular band within their tribe (Dukepoo 1980; Treas 1995). For example, an elder may be a member of the Cahuilla band of the Mission tribe. American Indian elderly also differ in their "degree Indian." The concept of blood quantum or "degree of Indian blood" is a "means of establishing ties with the Indian community." However, this situation poses a unique and specific problem for American Indians by inserting "legalisms into ethnic identification" which impact on one's eligibility for services (Dukepoo 1980, p. 28).

Most research on American Indian elderly has been conducted on samples from reservations even though less than one-fourth of this group live on reservations (Stuart & Rathbone-McCuan 1988). An important exception is a 1981 study conducted by the National Indian Council on aging. Among its national representative sample of American Indians, several lived in urban centers and a large concentration were also located in small, rural villages. The large number of tribes represented and the varied geographical residences underscore that American Indian elderly are as heterogeneous as their ethnic group counterparts (NICOA 1981a). Efforts to estimate the characteristics and needs of American Indian elderly "are complicated by population dispersion and varying definitions of who is an Indian" (Stuart & Rathbone-McCuan 1988, p. 240).

Economics

Income and Poverty

Inadequate income is the most prevalent concern for elderly persons of color. According to some, the lack of adequate economic resources is a primary cause of every other problem elderly face (Burt, 1993; Cuban American Council, 1996; U.S. Bureau of the Census, 1993). For example, Stanford and Du Bois (1992) state that low income results in poor health, poor nutrition, more stress and fewer coping resources. While poverty tends to be a transitory state for many younger Americans, it becomes a continuing fact of life for many elderly persons of color. Employment and marriage, two strategies that move many beyond the poverty level, are less available to older persons and especially to persons of color. Discrimination because of age, gender, and race restricts employment opportunities, and the shortage of potential spouses limits marriage as an avenue to economic improvement.

Ethnic elderly persons have substantially lower earned incomes than their Caucasian counterparts. In 1998 (see Table 9.1) median income for African American elderly males was 60 percent of that of Caucasian males. Median income of Hispanic elderly males was about the same as that of African American elderly males. African American elderly females had a median income somewhat above that of Hispanic elderly females. Women in all groups had substantially lower incomes than comparable men, and women of color made less than Caucasian women. Incomes of African American women totaled 41 percent of those of Caucasian males, and the income of Hispanic females was 36 percent of that of Caucasian males. In the general population, however, compared to other groups of color, the income of APIAs is nearest that of Caucasians. In 1998, median incomes of APIA males were 95 percent of those of Caucasian males, and APIA females' income was 75 percent of that of Caucasian males; the comparable statistic for African American males was 74 percent and for African American females was 64 percent. Elderly persons of color also have a higher proportion in poverty than do Caucasians. (Figures from U.S. Census Bureau, 1999).

African Americans are the poorest of the poor regardless of the indicator used. They have a higher poverty rate and a lower income than Caucasians (AARP 1995). For example, in 1990 the poverty rate among African American elderly (34 percent) was more than triple the rate of Caucasian elderly (10 percent). Hispanic elderly had double the poverty rate (22.5 percent) of Caucasian counterparts (Administration on Aging 1996). (See table 9.1.)

The harshness of the situation becomes more apparent when one considers the "economically vulnerable," those individuals with income between the poverty level and twice the poverty line. Evidence is clear that poor people do not live as long as the nonpoor and that they suffer disproportionately from complications also affected by other variables such as gender and race. The oldest are the poorest, and the youngest old are the most economically secure (White 1997). Elderly women have a higher poverty rate than men. About one-third (33 percent) of elderly African-American women are poor, a percentage three times that of elderly Caucasian women (11 percent) (Ball & Whittington 1995). Marital status is also strongly associated with poverty. Older women tend to outlive men and, therefore, are more likely than men to be unmarried. Data suggest that older Caucasian men fare better financially than older Caucasian women, older Caucasian women are better off than older African-American men, and older African-American women living alone constitute the poorest group among the elderly (White 1997).

As with most elderly persons of color in the United States, overall, a greater percentage of APIA elders have incomes below the poverty level than do Caucasian elders (AARP 1995). However, APIA within-group income level variations are also noted in overall income. For example, elderly Asian Indians (17.4 percent) and Chinese (15.9 percent) are those who most often fall below the poverty level (Liu & Yu 1985). Lower percentages (9.3 and 9.5, respectively) are noted for the elderly Japanese and Filipinos who are the poorest members of their own ethnocultural groups (Liu & Yu 1985; Makuau, 1991). However, across all ethnocultural groups, APIA elders residing in rural areas have poverty rates as high as 40 percent in comparison with other groups of elderly persons of color (Makuau 1991; AARP 1995). (See table 9.1.)

As Aleman (1997) reports from findings of Trevino, Moyer, Valdez, & Stroup-Benham (1991) the Hispanic population as a whole is disproportionately represented in the lower economic strata and Hispanic elders follow this pattern. Elders are in the lower socioeconomic level because they have spent their lives in low-paying and seasonal employment. As a result, they are without medical insurance, and less likely to have financial resources from investments, accumulated savings, and other assets.

Elderly Hispanic women are less likely to have worked outside the home. Among those who did work for pay, two-thirds worked at unskilled, service-sector, or farm-sector jobs. Such an employment history supports the notion of "multiple jeopardy" that has also been associated with African American societal conditions. Aleman (1997) further concludes from the arguments of Gelfand (1982) and Jackson (1970) that like other ethnic elders, Hispanic elderly have also experienced triple areas of biopsychosocial jeopardy—"being old, belonging to a persons-of-color group, and being poor." Additionally, Hispanic elderly are also noted for their psychosocial experience as victims of sexism, a fourth area of "jeopardy" for this population group.

Hispanic elderly are particularly vulnerable to loss of employment income. They often do not collect income maintenance supplements. Language barriers, pride, lack of information about the bureaucratic process and about available services, and distrust of the federal government, because of past discrimination, all add to their reluctance to seek assistance. Fear of problems related to citizenship status is another major issue (Torres-Gil & Negm 1980; Torres-Gil 1992). For the elderly Hispanic illegal aliens who have worked in the United States, the fear of discovery prohibits their exploration of governmental income maintenance supplements. Twenty-three percent of Hispanics were below the poverty level in 1990 (AARP 1995).

Twenty percent of American Indian elderly sixty-five years old or over live below the official poverty line compared to 10 percent of Caucasians in this same age group (see table 9.1). In urban areas, 14 percent of American Indian elderly were in poverty. In nonmetropolitan areas, the proportion is even higher, 24 percent in 1990 (AARP 1995). Because the American Indian is "old" at age forty-five, the chronic ailments and disabilities suffered result in loss of economic earning power and a decrease in an already poor quality of life. The extended family is affected along with the individual (NICOA 1981a; U.S. Bureau of the Census 1993). Interesting is that since the 1970 census a 10 percent increase of American Indian elderly have fallen below the national poverty level. Despite the fact that in the years 1970–1980 when American Indian elders were designated "a target population" to receive entitlement program services, more than ten-thousand joined the ranks of the impoverished (NICOA 1986).

Sources of Income

Employment

In general, as persons reach their late fifties, participation in the labor force falls and those who remain employed usually have higher unemployment rate and reduced occupational mobility. These trends are intensified for the elderly persons of color, especially African Americans. The extent of labor force participation for African American men over age sixty-five was identical to the rate for older Caucasian (12 percent) men (AARP 1995). This rate has fallen more rapidly than for Caucasians in recent years. Historically, participation of African American women in the labor force has been considerably higher than for Caucasian women. Over the last thirty years, however, the rates have converged. (AARP 1990; AARP 1995; U.S. Department of Labor, 1988).

The historically high unemployment rates for younger African American men help to explain the fact that older African American men have lower levels of lifetime labor force participation. Long periods of unemployment due to discrimination and other reasons cause many African American workers to leave the labor force altogether and stop looking for work. These persons are classified as discouraged workers and are not counted among the unemployed. Not only do African American men have less lifetime work experience, they are also more likely to leave the workforce earlier than Caucasians (AARP 1995).

For older (fifty-five years plus) workers who did not work at all during the previous year, African American men are a little more likely than Caucasian to fall into this category. The differences among women are negligible. One distinct racial difference, however, is that African Americans are far more likely than Caucasian counterparts to cite illness or disabilities as their reason for not working. These physical ailments are often related to the heavy physical types of work African Americans have engaged in during their work lives (AARP 1995; Social Security Administration 1996).

These findings and other research indicate that African Americans are more likely than Caucasians to retire involuntarily. Poor health and less demand for African American workers, as shown in the unemployment rates, force many African Americans to retire early. Because of inadequate retirement income, poor health status, and other factors, African Americans are consistently more dissatisfied with retirement than Caucasians (AARP 1995) and often return to work after retirement.

Despite their age, many older persons attempt to augment their incomes by working. Again, persons of color fare worse than whites. African American elderly workers, for example, are more likely than their Caucasian counterparts to be unemployed, underemployed, or working in lower paying positions. For instance, in 1992 African Americans age fifty-five to sixty-four were at least twice as likely as Caucasians to be unemployed or earning as little as 56 percent of the wages paid to Caucasians (AARP 1995).

About 16 percent of the APIA elderly over age sixty-five participated in the labor force in 1990 (AARP 1995). These people who were working or actively looking for work compares to 12 percent of Caucasian older workers (AARP 1997). Even at seventy-five years of age and older, approximately 16 percent of APIAs work (Kim 1983; Bureau of the Census 1993). These persons are primarily self employed and working in service areas and farming.

The percentage of Hispanic elderly who are in the labor force is about the same, (12 percent versus 13 percent), as for the white population. However, elderly Hispanics suffer from greater unemployment (9 percent) than whites (5 percent) (AARP 1995).

Approximately 12 percent of American Indians continue working after age sixty-five (AARP 1995). A national profile shows that of those American Indian elderly who were employed, 65 percent were semi-skilled, unskilled, or farm workers (NICOA 1981b). The unemployment rate among reservation elders tends to be higher than for those living in urban area (Dukepoo 1980).

Social Security and Pensions

Social Security benefits are a key source of income for most elderly (93 percent). Elderly of color are, however, less likely to receive Social Security benefits than Caucasians. For example, 93 percent of Caucasians compared to 86 percent of African Americans and 84 percent of Hispanics received benefits in 1995 (AARP 1998). In addition, the amount of benefits for elderly of color is smaller. This disparity is primarily explained by the type of employment ethnic elderly held. They worked in minimum or low-wage occupations that were either not covered or only partially covered by Social Security or other pension program benefits (Social Security Administration 1995).

The importance of the Social Security income for elderly persons of color is more grave when one considers that it is often the only income these elderly receive, while many Caucasians have other sources of income such as assets, earnings, private pensions, and interest. In 1995, for example, one-third of Caucasians received pensions compared to one-fourth of African Americans and one-fifth of Hispanics. The differences were even greater for interest income; 70 percent of Caucasians had interest income compared to 33 percent of African Americans and 32 percent of Hispanics. Elderly persons of color are more likely than Caucasians to receive Supplemental Security Income; 3 percent of Caucasians, 14 percent of African Americans, and 18 percent of Hispanics received SSI in 1995 (AARP

1998). The availability of SSI is beneficial but limited. Many elderly recipients of SSI remain well below the poverty level (OWL 1998). Yet, SSI prevented some elderly from falling beneath the poverty level; three to eight times more African Americans and Hispanics would have moved into poverty without income from SSI (Namkee 1997). Many elderly of color who are eligible for SSI, however, do not apply for it. Their reasons vary including not wanting to do all the paperwork to not wanting to be on public welfare. During their entire work lives, APIAs are more likely to be self-employed. When this group does retire, they are usually ineligible for Social Security and private pension benefits.

Overall, elderly Hispanics are less likely to receive retirement income from private pensions and private savings than are Caucasian elderly. Although their most common source of post-retirement income is Social Security, still only 84 percent of Hispanic elderly receive Social Security compared to 93 percent of all elderly in 1995 (AARP 1998). Aleman (1997) cites Chase's (1990) findings that 66 percent of Hispanic elderly received Social Security and 4 percent received Supplemental Security Income in 1990. Given that Hispanic elderly are disproportionately represented among groups in poverty, their underutilization of income maintenance programs is noteworthy. Uneven work histories, low employment in manufacturing, professional, or blue collar work associated with few pension plans and the inability to have accumulated savings are realities that preclude income from these sources (Becerra & Shaw 1984). Older Hispanics who retire due to a disability face another economic barrier. The strict definitions of disability often preclude them from eligibility for SSI benefits.

Another factor which reduces the level of benefits is the method by which Social Security is calculated. The amount payable is determined by adding incomeless years into an average yearly income. Consequently, elderly Hispanics like African Americans, who may not have held regular employment or who were unemployed during the normally high earning period of late middle age are severely penalized (Becerra & Shaw 1984).

Income for American Indian elderly largely comes from Social Security or Supplemental Security Income benefits. However, in keeping with the complex status of American Indians in this country, several factors complicate or prevent these income supports under existing federal programs. With little formal education, many American Indian elderly fail to complete the application process or, because of the complexity of rules and regulations, they do not apply for entitlements under Social Security or Veterans Administration programs. Further, some of the regulations create special hardships. For example, tribal dividends governed by treaty regulations must be counted as income when SSI eligibility is determined. In addition, the Social Security program requires documentation of quarters worked, of marriage, and of age (NICOA 1981b). Needless to say, "story telling" and verbal renditions of births, deaths, and marriages do not substitute for official written documentation and thereby abort the application process.

Living Arrangements and Social Support

Housing

Housing is the most expensive budgetary item for the elderly. Yet, there is a lack of attention to housing for the elderly (Gilderblom & Mullins 1995). Almost half of the elderly spend at least 45 percent of their income for shelter. The availability of suitable, affordable housing for elderly of color is rare. Long waiting lists exist, especially in urban areas where many elderly of color live. Waiting time of 3 to 5 years is not unusual (Pynoos et al. 1995). This time frame discourages elders of color from applying.

Federal cutbacks and prohibitive rents further reduce the availability of suitable housing. The reduction in funding for housing has resulted in a substantial decline in the erection of federally assisted and other public housing for the elderly. For instance, there have been substantial reductions in availability of federally subsidized housing at the same time that rental rates have increased (Pynoos et al. 1995).

Whether owners or renters, African American elderly have major housing problems. Even during the recent economic expansion, the rate of home ownership among African Americans has declined (Gaberlavage & Citro 1997). Those fortunate enough to own homes (63 percent of African Americans compared to 78 percent of Caucasians) may face unaffordable and escalating property taxes and maintenance costs (Hooyman & Kiyak 1996). Among both homeowners and renters, African Americans are considerably more likely to have substandard and unsuitable housing (one-third of elderly African American compared to one-eighth of older Caucasians). These housing units may lack plumbing, central heat, air conditioning, and kitchen facilities (AARP 1995).

African American elderly are more likely than Caucasian to be widowed, divorced and separated. Thus, they are less likely than other ethnic groups and Caucasians to live without a spouse (Himes 1992; Himes et al. 1996). In 1990, 23 percent of African American males and 37 percent of African American females lived alone (U.S. Bureau of the Census 1996). They, however, usually reside in a household with family or with unrelated persons rather than live alone. It is not unusual to find children and younger persons residing in African American families headed by an elderly individual or couple. An African American elderly person living with a grown child, usually a daughter, is also a rather common occurrence (AARP 1997; Himes 1992; Carstenson 1993). The nurturing role, particularly among older African American women, seems to be a dominant one.

Although most APIAs prefer to live with family, many elderly live alone. As a group, fewer aged APIAs (19 percent) than Caucasians (30 percent) live alone. When one looks at subgroups, however, another picture emerges. Some APIAs are more likely than Caucasians to live alone. Over one fourth (26 percent) of Chinese American elderly men and greater than two-thirds (67 percent) of the women, live alone. Half of all Japanese households outside of the West have only one person and (70 percent) of these are women living alone. Almost one-third of the Filipino elderly live alone (Kim 1983). Many of these people would like to share homes and help each other; however, specific social policies prevent such mutual interdependence. For instance, Supplemental Security Income is reduced if persons live with others whether they are ethnic friends or kin (Lacayo 1991). In 1990, 8 percent of APIA men and 16 percent of APIA women lived alone (U.S. Bureau of the Census 1996).

The actual physical living arrangements of Hispanic elderly, such as sharing residences with kin either as primary household heads or as dependents, represent an important family characteristic. However, mutual aid and informal support within the extended network system are also significant for this cultural group. Hispanic Americans have a highly integrated kin network and tend to live in close proximity to their kin. Most Hispanic elderly, however, do not live in extended families (Torrez 1996).

Seventy-two percent of Hispanic elderly were found to live with at least one family member. This figure is slightly higher than the 69 percent of comparable Caucasians who live with family (AARP 1987). However, among the old-old, eighty plus, differences among the groups in living with a spouse disappeared (Lubben & Becerra 1987). This finding is likely explained by the large number of widows among all ethnic groups in this older age category. In 1980, over 80 percent of Hispanic elderly lived in metropolitan areas located mainly in four states, each with different concentrations of Hispanic elderly groups. While the majority of Hispanic elderly in California and Texas are from Mexico and Central America, Florida attracts the Cuban population, and New York receives a large number of immigrants from Puerto Rico and the Caribbean Islands. Other states such as Colorado, Arizona, and New Mexico also have fairly large populations of Hispanic elders. Earlier research indicates that the Hispanic elderly tend to be a relatively stable residential population (Sotomayer 1975; Torres-Gil et al. 1977; Valle & Mendoza 1978; Sotomayer 1997; AARP 1995).

Compared with older Caucasian, elderly Hispanics live in poorer quality housing. Regional differences also have been observed. An early study cited housing as "best in the West and worst in the South" (Bell, Kaschau, & Zellman 1976). Elderly Hispanics of Mexican descent living in the central United States were three times more likely to live in poorer quality housing than those Hispanics in California and Arizona. Elderly Hispanics from Southern states were about five times more likely to live in substandard housing when compared with elderly Hispanics in western states.

Becerra and Shaw (1984) point out that because low-income elderly Hispanics tend to live with kin more often than other elderly groups of color and Caucasians, the lack of housing units large enough to accommodate extended family living arrangements poses additional housing problems for several of the subgroups. For example, elderly Hispanics of Cuban descent have long lived in overcrowded conditions because of the extended family tradition and small housing size typically in low-income urban centers. Puerto Rican elderly also must move and find their own housing units because of limited space in crowded housing units in the inner cities of the northeast (Becerra & Shaw 1984). Large numbers of these subgroups in inner city areas are seriously affected by the many economic and environmental problems that tend to characterize nonaffluent urban areas. When compared to Caucasian elderly, they usually are among the first groups affected by inflation resulting in forced relocations. Depending upon general demographic population shifts, elderly Hispanics may be among the first to be dispossessed and relocated (Torres-Gil & Negm 1980).

Based on either a preference to live in close proximity to other Hispanics or the need to find low-income housing, many rural elderly Hispanics have moved to areas of high Hispanic concentrations. These ethnic enclaves or barrios embody characteristics of both rural and modern urban lifestyles. This type of community setting may soften the blow of culture discontinuities resulting from acculturation, urbanization, and the move away from traditional neighborhood social interactions (Becerra & Shaw 1984).

Approximately half or more of American Indian elderly live in the states of Oklahoma, California, Arizona, New Mexico, and Texas. An additional one-quarter or more live on reservations and in Alaskan Native villages. The remaining elderly, somewhat less than one-quarter percent, live in states along the Canada border (AARP 1995).

Most American Indians do not live on reservations. About 96 percent of American Indian elderly live in households in their communities. Multigenerational households are very common (U.S. Bureau of the Census 1993). Housing stock is generally old and dilapidated, and approximately 26 percent occupied by the elderly was built prior to 1939. The National

Indian Council on Aging (1986) found that one-quarter of their sample of 712 elderly American Indians slept in bedrooms occupied by three or more persons. Few of these homes had heat (20 percent), water (24 percent) or indoor toilets (15 percent).

The proportion of American Indian elderly in nursing homes is low and decreases as age increases. This trend is most noticeable among those eighty-five years and over (oldest-old) where 13 percent live in nursing homes compared to 23 percent of white elderly (AARP 1987). Shorter life expectancies contribute to this phenomenon.

Marital Status

The majority of elderly men of color are married while the majority of women are widowed. Overall, elderly of color are less likely than Caucasians to be married and more likely to be widowed and divorced (AARP 1995).

The marital status of elderly persons of color is related to life expectancy. No matter what ethnicity or race, women outlive men. The life expectancy for minorities is usually less than for Caucasians. For example in 1991 the life expectancy at birth for Caucasian men was 72.9 years; Caucasian women, 79.6 years; African American men 64.6 years; and African American women 73.8 years. Since women outlive men, they are more likely to become widowed (U.S. Bureau of the Census 1996).

As among Caucasians and other non-APIA persons of color, the majority of elderly APIA men are married and the majority of women are widowed. APIAs, however, have a larger proportion (7.5 percent) of never married men than Caucasians or any other group of persons of color. This situation is a consequence of immigration laws that prohibited Chinese women and children from accompanying men to the United States (AARP 1995).

Among older males, African Americans are more than twice as likely as Caucasians to be divorced or separated and a smaller percent live with their wives (AARP 1995).

Family Life

Familial support and expectations (Kobata, Lockery, & Moriwaki 1980) vary within each ethnic group, social class, and subculture. For many ethnic communities, however, the role of family in all its forms is still a viable and significant support system (Alvarez & Bean 1976; Price 1976; Solomon 1976).

In many African American families, the younger generation respects and reveres the older persons. These favorable attitudes help account for the fact that fewer African American elderly (3 percent) than Caucasians (5 percent) are institutionalized (AARP 1995). The racial difference increases with age. For persons 85 and over, who are more likely to be widowed and in need of long-term physical and medical assistance, 12 percent of African Americans as compared to 26 percent of Caucasians are institutionalized (AARP 1987; National Caucus and Center on Black Aged 1987). Other factors relating to black underutilization of nursing homes and other long-term facilities are (National Caucus and Center on Black Aged 1987; Morrison 1995):

■ prohibitive high costs
■ racial discrimination

■ reluctance of African Americans to seek institutional care because of the media accounts of the poor conditions in the facilities

■ the African American extended family provides a number of persons to share in the responsibility of caring for the ill elderly.

Family life among elderly APIAs can differ in many ways. Characteristics such as the length of stay in America, country of origin, socio-economic status, geographical region, marital status, fluency in English, and history of conflict with the majority in America must be considered.

The current solo living situation of some APIA elderly is quite different from their historical family pattern. Traditionally, the APIA family has been a close social unit which provided support, security, and a sense of meaning for its members. Roles were strictly and formally assigned. Elderly family members were respected and cared for in multigeneration households. The roles of the elderly included aiding their children and grandchildren in achieving positions of wealth and status. The elderly willingly sacrificed themselves to care for their descendants and to teach the younger generation. In return, the elderly were respected and consulted about all major family decisions. China, for example, has been described as a gerontocracy because of the revered position of the elderly in the family (Lum 2000).

In addition to the family, the clan developed historically in the United States as an informal source of support for APIAs. The associations representing various provinces of the old country or based on last names, developed in urban America. These organizations symbolized the power of a strong extended family. In some instances they served as social service agencies by providing food, shelter, employment, and protection to new immigrants along with an opportunity for socialization (Lum 2000). For various reasons, the clan has become less important and less able to cope with current social problems of the inner city, such as over-population due to immigration, inadequate housing, unemployment, crime, and increasing health problems (Lum 2000). The demise of clan associations and the increased mobility of second and third generation immigrants and American-born persons of Asian of Pacific Island decent have left many older APIAs without their traditional social supports. Many also have lost their important family role of guide and consultant for the younger generations. Some elderly have responded by using the familiar strategies of relying on other APIAs, and, in this case, on other elderly APIAs who remain nearby in the urban areas.

Various research has yielded contradictory results about the role of the elderly in the Hispanic family (Becerra & Shaw 1984). The Mexican-American Hispanic subgroup is by far the largest, and as a result, the focus in the literature has mostly been on the Mexican-American elderly residing in the Southwest. Therefore, existing data of elderly Hispanics can only suggest general patterns of family life because the lifestyles of the subgroups are different. However, a significant ethnic value is the idealized role given to the extended family members by relatives, with the godparent playing an especially important family role (Becerra & Shaw 1984; Lubben & Becerra 1987).

Evidence suggests that Hispanic elderly in this country believe in the extended family orientation more than other minority elderly groups. This way of life is used as a determinant of family ties, frequency of contact, and degree of closeness of family ties (Bengston & Burton 1980). The ethnic value of family orientation for Hispanic elderly in both the country of origin and in the United States grew out of socioeconomic needs. "Family" meant an extended, multigenerational group of persons with specific social roles ascribed to members of each group to help meet the requirements of survival for the entire family group. Thus, the extended family network has included grandparents, aunts, uncles, cousins, lifelong family friends, and godparents.

An important characteristic of the traditional Hispanic-American family of Mexican descent is the subordination of the younger to the older. It is argued that older people receive more respect from youth and children than is characteristic in Anglo homes. Such respect is noted in the behaviors, manners and patterns of speech of younger to older Hispanics. This pattern is noted even among children whose older siblings have higher authority and greater power in the family than do younger ones (Mindel and Habenstein 1981).

Recent data, however, have pointed to the erosion of intergenerational and lateral interdependence or "familism" in the Hispanic family network (Mindel 1981; Torrez 1996). In areas where neighborhood friends and churches provide some support services, the function of the family in providing for socioeconomic needs is shifting as other institutions increasingly assume such functions (Becerra & Shaw 1984; Torres-Gil 1976). The plight of younger Hispanics looking for better employment opportunities contributes to family erosion. Seeking better employment may force them to leave their elders behind. For example, in rural areas, a large percentage of elderly remain members of extended family units at a significantly higher rate than do their Caucasian counterparts. The socioeconomic barriers that their younger family members experience may actually increase their dependency on natural support networks. Finally, the acculturation of the younger generation in a society which places a high premium on youth and on liberal mores may offset the once-valued roles of older Hispanics and devalue lateral interdependence.

Family life among American Indian family networks also assumes a structure which is radically different from other extended family units in Western society. For example, the accepted structural boundary of the European model of family life is the household. An extended family is defined as three generations within a single household. In contrast, American Indian family networks are structurally open and assume a village type characteristic. Family extensions include several households representing significant relatives in vertical and horizontal kinships. A large network may easily encompass two hundred persons and span three generations. Such networks are characteristically divided in units with each unit having at least one responsible and obligated adult available as family head (Red Horse, Lewis, Feit, & Decker 1978).

The extended family often serves as a major instrument of accountability. Standards and expectations which maintain group solidarity through enforcement of values are established. This structure contributes to a conservative cultural pattern as the vehicle of transmission of cultural attributes prevents "contamination" from the wider society.

The elderly, or the grandparents, retain official and symbolic leadership in family communities. Each of these active processes is sanctioned by children and their parents. As Red Horse et al. (1978) suggest, official leadership is characterized by a close proximity of grandparents to family. Such leadership may be observed in the behavior of children who seek daily contact with grandparents and by grandparents who monitor parental behavior. Based on this structure, American Indian elders have an official voice in child-rearing methods. Parents rarely overrule corrective measures from their own parents.

Symbolic leadership, reflecting immense respect for the elderly, is seen in the incorporation of unrelated elderly into the family. This practice more frequently occurs during the absence of a natural grandparent, but it is not necessarily limited to or dependent on this absence. Symbolic leadership may be observed in the behavior of children and parents who select and virtually adopt elders as grandparents. Symbolic grandparents do not invoke strong child-rearing sanctions. Because their acceptance is sought, their norm-setting standards are seldom ignored (Red Horse et al. 1978).

Regardless of the geographic movements of tribes and intertribal marriages occurring over time, American Indian family network dynamics have remained intact. The extended family network remains constant despite family lifestyle patterns which indicate the emergence of a distinct American Indian community that does not easily admit outsiders. Thus the maintenance of cultural characteristics and values tends to be transmitted with relative ease.

The world of American Indian elderly to a large extent has been limited to reservations. This situation has been especially true for American Indians in the rural areas of the South and Southwest. Reverence and attachment to the land as well as treaties with the U.S. government which have provided designated areas of land have contributed to the value of the extended open family structure (Birren & Sloane 1980). Family ties have been strong and far reaching, contributing to decreased socializing outside the family. Despite close family ties, there appears to be less trust and more unhappiness about family relationships among American Indian elderly than among Caucasian elderly, as American Indians are challenged to allocate deficient resources among their large numbers (NICOA 1981a).

Health

Physical and Mental Well-Being

In general, elderly persons are more likely than younger persons to have physical and mental health problems and to need health services. This is especially so when race and ethnicity are considered. The elderly, however, underutilize mental health services and instead turn to family, friends, and medical providers (Proctor et al. 1996).

Regardless of the criteria used, older African Americans have poorer health than elderly Caucasians. Overall, African Americans have more illnesses and are more debilitated by an illness (Escarce & Puffer 1997). For example, African Americans are more likely to develop high blood pressure, to have more kidney failure, and to die by stroke as a consequence of the hypertension (AARP 1995). African Americans seek medical care less frequently, receive less preventative care and rely more on self diagnosis and treatment. When they do obtain medical help, African Americans are more likely than Caucasians to rate their health as "poor" or "fair" (Kington & Smith 1997).

Inadequate income is a pivotal factor in the poor health status of African Americans. Actually African Americans begin and end life in a poorer health state than Caucasians. This fact is supported by the differential life expectancy and death rates. The economic deprivation throughout African Americans' lives has a cumulative influence that peaks with old age. With less income, African Americans have poorer nutrition and few opportunities for preventive health measures. They tend to have worked in low status jobs which provide inadequate health insurance benefits. In addition, among those with limited resources and competing needs, health care is postponed until an illness reaches crisis proportion (Woodruff 1995).

After reviewing decades of literature on how African Americans utilize mental health facilities, Davis (1998) found the following trends:

■ African American populations with major mental illness drop out of services at a significantly higher rate than do Caucasians.
■ African American populations use fewer treatment sessions for their mental health problems than do Caucasians.
■ African American populations enter mental health treatment services at a later stage in the course of their illness than do Caucasians.
■ African American populations underconsume community mental health services of all kinds.
■ African American populations overconsume inpatient psychiatric care in state hospitals, using it at twice the rate of corresponding Caucasian groups.
■ African American populations are more often misdiagnosed by mental health practitioners than are Caucasians.
■ African American people are more often diagnosed as having a severe mental illness than are Caucasians. (p. 56)

Literature suggests there are several reasons for African Americans being diagnosed with more severe mental health problems. Flaskerud and Hu (1992), Lawson et al. (1994) and Garrison (1993) suggest that diagnostic errors, cultural differences in language and training orientation of clinicians are the culprit. The tendency of African Americans to delay treatment is another possibility. In addition to other factors, the delay of treatment may be related to lack of transportation. It is interesting that the treatment of African Americans also differs from that of Caucasians. African Americans are more likely to be hospitalized while Caucasians with the same symptoms are seen in outpatient facilities, and African Americans are more likely to get medication while Caucasians are more likely to participate in "talk" therapy (Markides & Mindel 1987; Snowden and Cheung 1990; Snowden and Holschuh 1992). Discrimination is also a reason to consider for the differential diagnosis and treatment of African Americans. This perspective posits that older African Americans are actively steered to public mental health facilities and away from private psychiatric hospitals and nursing homes used by many Caucasians. Some researchers suggest that state mental hospitals function as nursing homes for African Americans since these facilities are the only ones routinely available (Barresi and Stull 1993). Instead of turning to mental health professionals, African Americans diagnosed with mental disorders are more likely to turn to their clergy (Brown et al. 1995).

Relatively little national data are available about the health and mental health status of APIA elderly and few research studies address these issues (Sotomayor 1997; Uba 1994; Yamashiro & Matsuoka 1997). An even smaller amount of literature focuses on the diverse subgroups of the APIA elderly (Miah and Kahler 1997; Sotomayor 1997). The literature that exists shows that the picture of the health status of APIA elderly is complex. As a group, elderly APIAs have higher rates of some diseases such as tuberculosis, hepatitis, anemia, and hypertension than Caucasians (AARP 1996; Browne & Broderick 1996). They, however, report fewer activity limitations and better general health status than Caucasians (Sotomayor 1997). Certain groups of elderly APIAs have the best health in the country. For example, Chinese and Japanese Americans have longer life expectancies than Caucasians

(Browne & Broderick 1996). Although APIAs have physical health problems, they are reluctant to use medical services and often delay seeking these services until they are acutely ill (Browne & Broderick 1996).

Literature suggests that elderly APIAs as a group, like other elderly of color, are more likely than Caucasians to have mental health concerns, less likely to use mental health services and terminate earlier if they utilize the services (Kang & Kang 1995; Browne & Broderick 1996; Koa & Lam 1997). Elderly Chinese American women have a suicide rate 10 times that of Caucasian women. The rate for elderly Chinese, Japanese, and Filipino men is higher than for Caucasian men (Browne & Broderick 1996). The differences in these rates may reflect cultural differences. Among several elderly APIA groups, suicide is seen as an act of honor. APIAs are more likely than Caucasians to be diagnosed with severe mental disorders such as psychosis (Browne & Broderick 1996; Yamashiro & Matsuoka 1997). They are less likely, however, to be admitted to private psychiatric hospitals and general hospitals with psychiatric units (Davis 1998). Elderly APIAs are also more likely than Caucasians to be misdiagnosed. The Western cultural values of personal autonomy and independence often become a part of the definition of *normal*. When persons such as elderly APIAs who value interdependence and obedience are evaluated, they are often diagnosed as "dependent personalities" or "passive aggressive" (Wodarski 1992). These diagnoses can reflect cultural differences rather than abnormal behaviors.

Mental health symptoms differ among elderly APIA groups. For example, elderly Korean immigrants have the highest incidence of depression compared to other elderly APIAs (Kim & Kim 1992). As expected, the life experiences of specific elderly APIA groups are related to their particular mental health symptoms. Recent immigrants have higher rates of depression than other APIA groups. Southeastern Asian refugees, such as the Cambodians, experience the trauma of evacuation, immigration and resettlement; many experience multiple losses. Their reactions include depression and post-traumatic stress disorders (Murase 1995).

Discrimination, immigration, acculturation, exclusion, and racism are some factors that can influence the physical and mental well-being of APIA elderly and their help-seeking behavior. They may also account for differences among APIA groups and between APIAs and Caucasians. There are many reasons APIA elderly underutilize physical and mental health care services. These include language barriers and its related isolation, reliance on the extended family, limited resources, transportation barriers, cultural differences from Western service providers in viewing problems and expectations for intervention. Japanese Americans, for example, have a different style of communication than that expected by a Western service provider. Japanese Americans value implicit, nonverbal, intuitive communication over the expected explicit, verbal, and logical communication (Wodarski 1992). Financial resources are also an important concern. Kim and Kim (1992) reported that almost half of the elderly Koreans did not have any health insurance, not even Medicaid and Medicare.

Many Hispanics do not perceive mental health services as a solution to emotional or family difficulties they may experience. The reasons for the underutilization of services are numerous. Language barriers, cultural and social class differences between therapist and clients, an insufficient number of mental health facilities, overuse or misuse of physicians for psychological problems, reluctance to recognize the urgent need for help, and a lack of awareness of the existence of mental health services and their purpose are reasons cited in the literature to explain Hispanics' underutilization of both health and mental health services (Ho 1987).

It has been noted that Hispanic Americans rely strongly on family and consider family members as primary sources of support. Accordingly, traditional family roles are important, and responsibility is taken seriously. This belief creates some difficulty for the male head of household to admit that he is experiencing problems in efforts to provide for the family. Before the seeking of outside help is considered, godparents or compadres usually are consulted. Seemingly, different problem areas direct the seeking of certain types of help. For example, if the family problem is marital, the compadre of marriages may be sought for mediation (Ho 1987). In the Hispanic family of Puerto Rican origin, the padrino is used as a mediator. A padrino is an "individual in a higher position within the family structure and who has a personal relationship with the family for whom he provides material needs and emotional guidance" (Ho 1987, p. 127).

Additionally, Catholicism plays a vital role in the lives of Hispanic Americans, and priests, folk healers, and religious leaders are often strong resources for families in times of difficulty and stress. The Hispanic-American family may distortedly view the mental health therapist as omnipotent because of a perceived association of roles between a healer, the priest, and the therapist. A reliance on these sources of help and a less than clear understanding of the nature and type of mental health services offered by localities may contribute to a significant underutilization of mental health services.

On the other hand, the physical and mental health care services available to Hispanic elderly are inferior both in quality and quantity. Some observers have suggested that physicians are often perceived by some Hispanic elderly of Mexican descent as a cure all or as a centralized health resource for all illnesses not treatable in the home. When asked reasons for consulting a physician during the preceding year, men sixty and older cited diabetes, gastrointestinal diseases, musculo-skeletal arthritis, and hypertension as reasons to consult a physician. Women over sixty cited hypertension, diabetes, flu, and colds. Approximately 50 percent of the respondents said they received home health care provided by a relative or friend. The relatively high use of this resource may be attributed to the cost of other care, alienation from or lack of access to various forms of institutional care, the positive support of family and friends, and the reliance on folk medicine or faith healers (Torres-Gil & Negm 1980).

American Indian elderly have significant physical and mental health problems and, as has been noted, become functionally "old" before the general elderly population (NICOA 1981a). Data from the Indian Health Service show that the average life expectancy for American Indians is only sixty-five years, eight years less than that for Caucasians (AARP 1987). Several factors may account for this difference. The majority of American Indian elderly seldom see a physician, and when they do, they tend to be more ill than Caucasian elderly who seek medical care. A large number of those needing medical services often live in rural isolated areas and do not have access to transportation. For some elderly, where services are accessible, a different cultural understanding of disease processes and a tradition of ritual for healing often prevent efforts to seek help from physicians.

The major health problems experienced by American Indian elderly are tuberculosis, diabetes, liver and kidney disease, high blood pressure, pneumonia, malnutrition, and sight impairment (AARP 1987; NICOA 1986). In other conditions of health impairment, American Indian elderly are at least as impaired as a representative sample of comparable Caucasian elderly taken from Cleveland (NICOA 1981a). Elderly American Indians also perceive their physical health as poorer than do their Caucasian counterparts.

Utilization of Services

Because of their stressful life experiences, African Americans are expected to have a greater need for mental health services than Caucasians but they actually underutilize mental health programs (Edinberg 1985; Sue 1981). In addition, a majority of those who seek services terminate prematurely and feel they are neither helped nor understood (Sue 1981).

There are at least three interactive factors that largely determine the rate and the way in which African American elderly utilize mental health services: characteristics of elderly African Americans; characteristics of mental health programs; and characteristics of mental health professionals. The issues related to each factor follow.

Elderly African Americans:

■ mistrust mainstream institutions.
■ rely heavily upon extended family ties, church organizations, and other informal mutual aid.
■ view therapy as "strange" and think it is a service for "crazy" people.
■ turn to formal services after all other sources of help have been exhausted, which is usually a time of crisis.
■ distrust therapists, especially Caucasian therapists.
■ prefer African American therapists, who are often not on staff, over Caucasian therapists.
■ feel therapists are not responsive to their needs and priorities.
■ often have multiple concrete problems, such as housing, low income, that influence their psychological functioning but are not addressed in some intervention plans.
■ may not have transportation to get to agencies.
■ accept their problems as an inevitable part of old age. (Beaver 1983; Edinberg 1985; National Caucus and Center on Black Aged 1987).

Mental health programs:

■ are located in inconvenient and inaccessible areas outside the central cities where most African American elderly reside.
■ do little or no outreach, education, or publicity to the African American community.
■ do not have elderly African Americans on advisory councils or in other roles where they could have input about service development and evaluation.
■ have few or no African Americans on staff.
■ do not train staff to work effectively with the African American elderly.
■ have poor coordination of services with other programs and services that the African American elderly use or need.
■ overlook concrete problems (housing, income, physical health) which influence the psychological functioning of the African American elderly.

- have physical settings which do not help African American feel welcome; for example, the lack of African American magazines in the waiting room.
- do not make home visits (Beaver 1983; Edinberg 1985; National Caucus and Center on Black Aged 1987).

Mental health professionals:

- have negative attitudes about serving African American elderly, which interfere with service delivery.
- are pessimistic about outcomes and communicate, often nonverbally, these feelings to the client.
- are ill at ease with elderly African Americans because they have had little previous contact with them and little training about effective intervention with African Americans.
- interact with and diagnose African American elderly often on the basis of negative stereotypes (Flaskerud & Hu 1992) resulting in misdiagnosis (Garretson 1993).
- often communicate with jargon that the African American elderly do not understand; they are too proud to ask for further clarification.
- view client problems as inevitable and a normal part of the aging process.
- have values and ways of interacting that are not congruent with the expectation of clients. For example, Caucasian professionals often call clients by their first name to show concern or closeness. Older African Americans especially, prefer the use of titles and the last names (for example, Mrs. Jones instead of Susie, Mr. Moore instead of Joe). (Beaver & Miller 1985; Brody 1985; Edinberg 1985).

This list is not exhaustive, but it does demonstrate that there are several contributors to low mental health utilization rates and premature service termination of elderly African Americans. This pattern of underutilization of services is not solely a mental health problem. While home health care, homemaker service, transportation, outreach, information and referral, congregate meals, and home delivered meals are specifically for the elderly, they attract few African American elderly. This situation occurs despite the fact that older persons of color have needs that are typically 2 to 3.5 times as great as Caucasian elderly (Davis 1998).

One notable precipitant of termination of services APIAs is differences in Western and American cultural values in help-seeking and help-giving processes. It has been noted that APIA clients often do not share certain values that implicitly undergird social work helping processes in America (Sue 1981). Valuing independence and self-determination over interdependence and family wishes or emotional expressiveness over inhibition is often conflictual for APIA clients. Further, many APIAs believe that having psychological problems is shameful and disgraceful and that the ability to control the expression of personal problems is a sign of maturity. Others believe that it is more socially acceptable to have a physical problem than a psychological problem. Aleman (1997) cites Wong's (1982) findings that APIAs are also more likely to use services when bilingual, bicultural personnel are employed in the service setting. Thus, barriers to access and continued utilization of social welfare, health, and mental health programs by APIA elderly appear to cluster in four categories, which also reflect the wider APIA population:

(1) lack of awareness of such programs, (2) distrust of the social service systems based on a variety of factors, (3) uncertainty how to navigate within the system(s), and (4) a preference for assistance from family or familiar others (Mokuau 1991). Further, availability of preferred alternatives is also important. In larger cities of the United States where Asian Americans are concentrated, folk medicines are often available. Also, many Asian elderly still order folk medications from their old countries and keep them for emergencies (Kim 1983).

The provision of services to the Hispanic elderly is often complicated by several variables. First, as has been pointed out, the Hispanic elderly are heterogeneous. The several subgroups have discrete nationalities with different dialects, cultures, and needs. Responses to services that are offered tend to cluster in different geographic locations; however, the reluctance of service organizations to develop appropriate interventions that are sensitive to the Hispanic culture act as barriers to services. Secondly, the needs of the subgroups usually remain unmet because there is a lack of trained bilingual, bicultural professionals to act as advocates in policy formulation and implementation. Consequently, the policies that are enacted and services that flow from them do not address group specific cultural factors.

A comprehensive network of services exists for the general population of American Indians in self-governed communities. The unique relationship tribes have with the federal government commands an array of resources from the Bureau of Indian Affairs, Indian Health Service, and the Department of Housing and Urban Development. Therefore, American Indian elderly are more likely to say that they live in subsidized housing and receive health and nutrition services more than a comparable group of their Caucasian counterparts (NICOA 1981a). They tend to use public services to a greater extent than Caucasians largely because there are no other alternatives to care. However, in comparison to the representative sample of Cleveland white elderly, American Indian elderly actually utilized the service system less (NICOA 1981a).

One significant explanation is that when extended family members have resources, American Indian elderly seek their help first. Mainstream heath care system is used only after the resources of the family network are exhausted (Red Horse et al. 1978; Red Horse 1991). Despite the comprehensive array of services offered and the preference for indigenous services, a majority of American Indian elderly will say that more services are needed than are provided. It is thus possible to conclude that the extent to which actual needs are met is inadequate. Services such as transportation, coordination, education, and employment were perceived as underprovided while others such as meal preparation, legal protection, personal care, and checking were either not wanted or felt to be not needed even when they were provided (NICOA 1981a). This leads one to question whether services to American Indian elderly are being provided under the assumption that their needs are the same as the dominant society and that cultural barriers do not affect the utilization of these sometimes indiscriminately offered services (NICOA 1981a).

Participation in Medicaid and Medicare Programs

The fact that poverty status is still linked to poor health among the elderly is surprising since the Medicare and Medicaid Programs provide health services to this group. These programs are insufficient to combat accelerating health care costs of elderly persons of color and are frequent recipients of budgetary cuts. In 1984, for example, the elderly were spending the same proportion (15 percent) of their income on health care as they did before these programs were established in 1965. Furthermore, the amount of benefits Medicaid and Medicare offer is constantly eroding. For example, the Medicare inpatient hospital deductible charge escalated from $204 in 1981 to $520 in 1987 (National Caucus and Center on Black Aged 1987).

Surprisingly, the majority of poor elders are not covered by these programs. In 1984, only one-third (36 percent) of the noninstitutionalized elderly poor had Medicaid protection. The amount of paper work and information, the complicated procedures, the desire to be self-sufficient, as well as suspiciousness of bureaucracy probably result in many eligible elderly not applying for these programs. Another element in the health problems of minority elderly is the gaps in the Medicare and Medicaid Programs. Services of particular importance for the elderly are not covered in many states. These include prescription drugs, physicals, eye glasses, hearing aids, dentures, custodial nursing home care, and homemaker services (National Caucus and Center on Black Aged 1987).

Even when Medicare services are available, there are differential patterns in their use according to race. There are many disparities between Caucasian elders and elders of color. For example, elderly of color have fewer mammograms and immunizations but are hospitalized more often and have higher mortality rates than Caucasians. This suggests that elderly of color may receive less primary and preventive care than whites (Gornick et al. 1996). Navarro's (1990) analysis of the first twenty years of the Medicare program indicated that racial disparities were disappearing in terms of visits to physicians and hospital discharges. More recent study, however, shows wide racial differences in the use of many medical and surgical services (Gornick et al. 1996). Some expect these disparities to increase with the managed care system (Davis 1998; Hernandez 1996; Ginzberg & Ostow, M. 1997; Morgan et al. 1997).

Working with Elderly Persons of Color

In general, the social worker must recognize and accept that many older ethnic clients concerned about survival issues seek intervention only as a last resort and with limited understanding of the traditional helping process. The worker must use the strengths and aspects of the culture to help the elderly minority client understand that the helping process is a mutual endeavor between two involved participants. Enhancing and maintaining health and preventing further disability in the elderly of color are the primary aims of social work intervention.

Assessment

In assessing the physical mental health status of elderly persons of color in general, social work practitioners must examine the total person and the physician and social environment. Not only the current presenting problem but the life situation, social and personal world, and values and life history of the client must be explored (Beckett & Coley 1987; Lum 2000). In consideration of and respect for cultural values and traditions, this task may be far easier said than done. Specifically, for example, APIA culture dictates that inner negative thoughts, feelings, and personal problems not be expressed (Tseng & Char 1974; Paniagua 1994; Lum 2000).

Since the success of our traditional treatment modalities depends heavily on eliciting such information, work with APIA minority elderly using traditional models could be severely hindered. Further, even though unacceptable thoughts and feelings are suppressed, physical illness is acceptable, and APIA who exhibit physical illness are given positive attention and concern. In addition, traditional Chinese medication links emotion to specific vicera, such as the heart to happiness and the liver to anger and nervousness (Kobata, Lockery & Moriwaki 1980; Butler et al. 1991). Such specific beliefs help to clarify and underscore the importance of close examination of the type of somatic complaints APIA elderly may present. The problem may be anxiety but expressed as discomfort in the lower back area, denoting possible problems with the liver. Such knowledge of APIA beliefs and customs are significant if intervention with the elderly of APIA descent is to be responsive and helpful.

Evidence suggests that some Hispanic elderly believe old age comes early because they associate it with the end of the work role. Since they have usually been employed in physically demanding jobs, they frequently must leave the work force relatively early. These cir-cumstances contribute to pessimism about the quality of life and often cause high levels of depression among the elderly. Also language barriers and poverty add to depression and must be considered both in assessment and in the planning stages of intervention with this group.

Assessment of American Indian elderly must consider that an individual American Indian's mental health is linked to a sense of selfhood which is accomplished by adherence to historical culture and transmitted primarily through family socialization (Levine 1976; Red Horse 1990; Harper & Lantz 1996). As American Indians leave the reservation to seek gainful employment, acculturation increases. Thus, the adoption of Anglo culture value, orientation, and behavioral norms has an impact on the psychological conflict in values and behaviors, and the individual's classification of the difficulty must be weighed carefully as intervention strategies are planned.

In summary, accurate assessment of the minority of color client or client system involves the client's classification of the problem as either an illness, a physical disorder, and/or lack of skill or resources. Because the culture of the client influences perceptions and labeling of problems as well as shapes expectations for intervention, discrepancies between these expectations and the worker's culturally determined expectations may lead to the client's early termination of services. The worker's basic task is to elicit the client's explanatory model, to fully understand the client's beliefs about the issues at hand, the personal and social meaning attached to them, and the expectations about what the client will do and what the worker will do. Worker and client can then jointly determine the therapeutic goals (Brown & Gil 1985; Butler et al. 1991; Harper & Lantz 1996).

Intervention

Social work intervention, in general, can be categorized into three types of preventive strategies: primary, secondary, and tertiary (Beaver & Miller 1985).

- **Primary prevention** is intervention in which the focus is the averting of problems before they occur. Primary prevention activities are those that promote well-being. Examples are good nutrition, stress management, and education.
- **Secondary prevention** is intervention given at the earliest sign of a problem. The aim is to avoid further deterioration as well as to assist people in developing

coping mechanisms that will help prevent new occurrences of similar dysfunctions in the future. Examples of secondary prevention are problem solving and teaching new strategies and new behaviors.

■ **Tertiary prevention** is intervention that includes intensive actions to limit further disability and to rehabilitate. An example of this type of intervention is finding a safe living situation for the elderly who can no longer live at home.

While these three types of intervention indeed contribute to the effectiveness of the helping process, intervention with the older ethnic client carries additional considerations that cannot be ignored if the clients' needs are to be met in a responsible and responsive manner.

It is important that those working with elderly persons of color be informed of the cultural milieu from which the client comes and to have some understanding of the relationship of this context to the majority culture (Wellons 1996). Social work practitioners should assume very little and test clinical judgments by requesting information and perspectives from the client. It is also important to realize that one cannot be an expert on all cultures. The most appropriate and ethically sound practice often requires consultation, and in some cases when confronted with an unfamiliar situation or culture and expediency of service is required, referral to someone more experienced with a particular group may be necessary. General considerations in working with the elderly client, as noted by Beaver (1983), include recognition and understanding of (1) the likelihood of any physical changes due to impairment, (2) interrelated economic, social, and personal concerns, (3) the issues of multiple losses and coping with and accepting such losses, (4) the likelihood of negative self-stereotype related to age, and (5) generational values about help-seeking and help-accepting behaviors (Mindel & Habenstein 1981; Butler et al. 1991).

Racial and/or ethnic factors or attitudes may influence the helping process with elderly persons of color. When or if such issues are observed or experienced, the practitioner should bring them out in the open to be explored with the client. Doing so may be uncomfortable for both the social worker and the client, but to ignore them would be disastrous and as unprofessional as refusing to recognize or deal with any other barriers that may impede effective helping processes.

The following is a set of specific recommendations offered by Grant (1995) for intervention with elderly persons of color. Each strategy appears clearly applicable across primary, secondary, and tertiary levels of social work intervention.

1. *Ensure that the client understands the helping process.* Elderly persons of color often have negative and unrealistic views regarding the content and processes of help. Practitioners should not assume that the client has knowledge of the helping processes or of the role of the practitioner and client. It is important to explore expectations and educate the client about the process before beginning. Professional jargon should be kept to a minimum.

2. *Be more active in the helping process.* Elderly persons of color demand a more active stance and may view a more passive stance as reflecting a lack of interest in their problems. Elderly clients with depressive disorders will not be able to bring much energy to the helping process, especially in the beginning stage, and will require more energy from the practitioner.

3. *Employ all available resources in the intervention process.* The biopsychosocial theoretical model implies that intervention is directed toward a number of areas. Consequently, referral to sources that furnish biological and social interventions in addition to psychological interventions are often made. Examples include medical intervention, physical therapy, help in the home, and the use of natural support systems in the community. Often elderly persons of color will require assistance and advice in accessing the many social institutions and public agencies they must utilize.
4. *Involve the family and other social supports in the helping process.* The term *family* is to be interpreted loosely and inclusively to include multiple generations, extended family, informal social networks of friends, and supportive institutions. Many of these care givers will also require some education about the practitioner's social work helping process with the elderly client (Grant 1995).

Further special considerations in working with the older ethnic client include sensitivity and understanding of racial cultural differences. For example, the social worker who works with the elderly black client, who has in all probability experienced overt and sanctioned discrimination, should give formal respect to that client. The use of titles and last names and the communication of appreciation of the *value* of self-sufficiency by the presentation of the services in question as a right and not a need serve to convey respect for the client and his or her dignity.

Accordingly, work with the elderly Hispanic client would initially focus on concerns about politeness in language. The worker would use formal forms of "you" and consult with the client as to how to refer to his or her ethnic group since there are several Spanish-origin groups. Also important in work with the elderly Hispanic client is permitting a *social relationship* to develop as a prerequisite to further work with the client. Mindel and Habenstein (1981) suggest that the client be permitted to set the pace with the initial focus largely on service requested and not the underlying problem.

Because Hispanic sex roles tend to be sharply delineated, with male dominant behaviors, elderly Hispanic clients may experience difficulty in sharing with a worker of the opposite sex. Thus, the arranging of same-sex practitioners to work with the elderly client exhibits sensitivity and understanding to discrete ethnic/cultural values and practices in cases in which the elderly client has not adopted Anglo-value orientations and behavioral norms. The worker's utilization of the aspects and strengths of the culture (roles and values) as part of the interventive strategy then becomes a specialized approach with attention to the client's own level of comfort.

In interventions with elderly APIA clients, it is also important for same sex workers to be assigned and for the workers to slow the pace of the helping process. It will take time for the elderly APIA client to develop a relationship with the worker and for formal services to be accepted or developed. The worker must pay attention to the cultural differences that signal respect. For example, the use of titles and the careful attention to issues of politeness as opposed to confrontation are likely to convey to the client he or she is respected. Older APIA clients tend to be very concerned with "saving face"; the worker must be careful to limit or avoid eye contact—a sign of respect in sensitive issues. Also, work with the elderly APIA client, in many situations, calls for the avoidance of touch as well as the understanding that a polite nod does not mean agreement.

Intervention with the elderly American Indian must take into account various tribal differences. Each will vary in terms of the significance of touch and eye contact. Across the tribes, however, it is important to establish relationships with both formal and informal community leaders, to be honest, and to avoid aggressive behavior and excessive talking. American Indian elderly value listening and revere age. When the worker is invited into the home of the elder American Indian, he or she must convey respect by listening well, by accepting refreshments, and by not looking around the home, which is a sign of disrespect (Mindel and Habenstein 1981).

The consideration of family network structure in working with the American Indian elderly client is a major component in understanding the client. Without such understanding, normal ethnic behaviors within the network relational field may appear questionable and bizarre to an outsider. Such behaviors may lead workers to raise questions of competency and responsibility about familiar behaviors within the network structure and lead to negative labeling of the family and its behavior (Red Horse et al. 1978). For example, permitting a young adolescent girl to visit and sleep unsupervised in the homes of a succession of adolescent males may be labeled neglect in another culture. The elders who permit it may be questioned. However, the American Indian family relational field can be extensive. Such males offer protection and preservation of honor to the adolescent girl as her most loyal brothers. The absence of understanding in a situation of this type can lead to serious gaffes by the social worker and create alienation in the helping attempt that may never be renegotiated.

Finally, because of discrimination, economic concerns, health issues and losses, and other issues, most elderly of color often have multiple concerns that need to be addressed. Working with older persons on these concerns, unfortunately, has tended not to be associated with creative methods or imaginative approaches in practice. One reason for the overall lack of creativity in working with the elderly is in part related to the influence of "ageism" (Thompson 1995). For example, the assumed primary role in working with the elderly is to promote "care." Therefore, if the focus is on "looking after" the elderly, a creative approach to the helping process is often seen to have little value or applicability.

However, in 1985, Beaver and Miller observed that many "creative and productive preventive helping efforts" (p. 226) had been developed by practitioners working directly with or on behalf of the elderly. They noted that these were necessary strategies that assisted in providing a comprehensive helping process. These efforts require an active level of involvement by the social worker and communicate to the elderly an interest in them and their concerns. Included in these efforts are:

■ Developing knowledge of cultural resources and teaching the elderly how to establish linkages with culturally sensitive agencies and organizations
■ Using group approaches with family members who are experiencing problems caring for older relatives by providing them with information about adult development, the aging process, and related culturally sensitive community resources
■ Providing information on safety to avoid victimization of elderly persons of color
■ Developing and implementing specific culturally based outreach programs for elderly groups of color.

These and other such "creative" strategies suggest that the social worker must use a wide lens for viewing and intervening with the elderly persons of color.

Direct service or clinical practice is not always sufficient; indirect service or social action and political strategies are also necessary. For elderly of color who have experienced various degrees of powerlessness, it is helpful to engage them in activities to help change their own and the larger environment (Butler 1997; Binstock 1999). Social workers can help these elders use their strengths and abilities to problem-solve and to influence events and institutions that affect their lives, such as Medicare policies. Clients might be encouraged, for example, to join local chapters of the American Association of Retired Persons or the Area Agency on Aging. The social worker must also make certain that the environment of the organization in which he or she works is sensitive and welcoming to the elderly person of color. Networks of practitioners must also advocate for political changes for the elderly of color (Green & Knee 1996).

Discussion Questions

1. Why are ethnicity and race important variables in understanding and intervening with the elderly?
2. Compare the socio-economic characteristics of the four ethnic groups of color (Asian/Pacific Islander Americans, African Americans, Hispanic Americans, and American Indians).
3. Design a social service program to serve one ethnic group of color. What need does each component of the program address? How does your program differ from a program already existing in your community?
4. Discuss five ways the aging experience for persons of color differs from that of Caucasians.
5. To what extent to you think the situation of elderly persons of color is a consequence of: (a) individual factors; or (b) structural factors? Why?
6. Does the key to improving the conditions of elderly persons of color lie in: (a) integration into the mainstream of American society; (b) in strengthening the sense of cultural identity among groups of elderly persons of color; or (c) in a combination of both a and b? Why?
7. For what reasons do you think elderly persons of color are discriminated against and/or oppressed in American society?
8. How would you redesign the Social Security benefits so they would be more equitable for elderly of color who have a significantly shorter life expectancy than the Caucasian majority?

Experiential Learning
Activity: Lifeline Exercise

SAMPLE LIFELINE

birth date	sister born	began school	graduate high school	today's date	college graduation	marriage	first child	retire date	death
10/5/80	6/20/82	9/2/84	6/3/98	1/15/00	6/3/02	6/03	2006	2040	12/31/2070

INSTRUCTIONS

This exercise puts your lifespan into clear perspective and focus. On an 8^1/$_2$ by 11 inch sheet, draw a horizontal line lengthwise in the middle of the paper. At the left end, put a slash and your birthdate. At the right end, put a slash and guess your deathdate. Between these two slashes, put a slash indicating today's date. Choose significant events and date them. (Students usually choose as the significant dates between birth and today's date such events as their graduation from high school, birth of a sibling or relocations. Other choices include significant deaths, beginning college, serious illness and other family changes such as divorce.) Then, between today's date and your deathdate, place slashes and dates, indicating significant events that you want to happen between now and the time you die.

After you complete your lifeline, initiate a discussion with other students who have also completed lifelines. Students have no difficulty with their birthdates but are resistant and frightened about selecting a deathdate. This is a good time to talk about death and fears of dying, relating it to how much more older persons must think about dying. We need to begin to accept death as a fact, and talking about death is helpful. It can be cathartic to talk for a few minutes about the fears and fantasies of what happens at death. Many students will acknowledge that they have never allowed themselves to think of their own deaths and doing so is like opening a door which they have always kept closed. As the discussion continues, you may hear responses such as, "I've never thought I'd die until recently." "I had a hard time accepting death until my father developed cancer. Seeing him suffer has made me begin to think about dying, his death and mine," or "it's not easy to talk about death over lunch, or at the dinner table."

Responses between today's date and the death date may include marriage, becoming a parent, losing weight, taking a world cruise, going back to school, moving into a home, retiring, beginning a career, caring for older parents, and so on. This prediction helps mobilize students to consider options and choices which they have and points up how much control they have in exercising those options.

ADDITIONAL ACTIVITY

Students should complete another lifeline. Each student should now assume that he or she is a person of color (APIA, African American, Hispanic, or American Indian). Discuss the problems students may have in completing this lifeline, for example, assigning a deathdate, determining the education level and identifying significant life events. Students should compare and contrast the lifelines of the four minority groups with their own lifelines. Include consideration of economic, social, and political differences.

Case Studies

See Appendix B for guidelines in analyzing gerontological social work practice.

Case 1: Mrs. Chan

Mrs. Chan, a sixty-five-year-old Chinese widow from Hong Kong, was referred to a community mental health center by a family physician, who had been unable to correct Mrs.

Source: Ho 1987.

Chan's insomnia and weight loss through medication. In addition to her physical problems, Mrs. Chan's symptoms included depression and lack of appetite and energy. She spent most of her time gazing motionlessly out the front window of her apartment.

The intake social worker described Mrs. Chan's reaction to her as mixed with shame and hopefulness. She remarked that Mrs. Chan feared "losing face" because of her situation and regretted greatly that she has been a "burden" to the social worker. Mrs. Chan spoke little English and displayed limited cooperation, according to the social worker.

Eight months ago, Mrs. Chan's husband died in Hong Kong. Five months ago her only son invited her to live with him and his family in the United States. Mrs. Chan initially was apprehensive about leaving her home, close friends, and relatives in Hong Kong, but due to Chinese social pressure and customs, she yielded to the idea of living with her son. She had not wanted her relatives and friends to suspect that her son did not want to take care of her.

Living with her son and family did not work well for her. Mrs. Chan and her daughter-in-law, an American-born Chinese, never seemed to get along with each other. They had open conflict about the role of a wife and the proper manner in which children should be disciplined.

Mrs. Chan's son, caught in the middle, developed a severe case of sleep disturbance. To protect her son's health, Mrs. Chan agreed to live in an apartment by herself. Mrs. Chan explained that the idea of living apart from her son was difficult for her. She would never have conceded to his idea of her living alone if she still lived in Hong Kong.

Case 2: Mr. Williams

Mr. Williams is a fifty-eight-year-old African American man who was referred to a family service agency by his minister. Mr. Williams, a retired military man, works irregularly as a construction worker. When not working, he has a tendency to drink heavily. When he drinks he often stays away from home for a couple of days. During the past two weeks, Mr. Williams had two serious car accidents, and he was found asleep in the car on a cold night. The minister felt Mr. Williams might be suicidal and in need of therapy. Mr. Williams refused to go to the local clinic, but the minister was able to persuade him to go to a family service agency.

Mr. Williams is married and has four children. Mrs. Williams, age fifty-six, is a Licensed Practical Nurse. The two older children, a son, age thirty-six, and a daughter, age thirty-three, are married and live out of state. The two younger children, a daughter, age twenty, and a son, age seventeen, are still at home. The daughter is a sophomore at a local college, and the son attends high school and is an excellent athlete. Both are excellent students.

Mr. Williams disclosed that his family had adequate income—wife's employment, his retirement benefits, and his irregular construction work. He, however, felt "out of place" in his own home. He thought his wife was an excellent mother and a busybody working all the time and attending church activities several times a week.

He went on to say that no one at home seems to notice him except when he was not there for a couple of days. This he said has been the situation ever since he retired from the service four years ago. Mr. Williams has reacted by initiating "fairly close" relationships with females whom he calls his "drinking buddies."

Source: Ho 1987.

Case 3: Mrs. Alvarez

Mrs. Alvarez, a sixty-nine-year-old motel housekeeper, has experienced a number of significant losses over the past six years. Six years ago, her husband of thirty-nine years died of a heart attack. The death was sudden and occurred shortly after Mrs. Alvarez returned home from work. Mr. Alvarez had been a laborer and had spent his last three years sporadically unemployed and unable to contribute to the family income. He routinely looked for work but was generally passed over for younger men in his neighborhood who seemed strong and in good health.

Mrs. Alvarez took her husband's death quite hard but managed to adjust to the loss with the help of her five grown daughters and a few close friends and relatives. She remained employed and found going to work kept her mind off her loneliness and the emptiness she experienced without Mr. Alvarez.

Approximately a year after Mr. Alvarez's death, Mrs. Alvarez's purse was snatched one evening as she walked to the bus stop from the motel on her way home. Although Mrs. Alvarez was not physically injured, she was emotionally traumatized. Her weekly pay of $117 had been taken along with her house keys and other important insurance papers she always carried in her purse. She had no money for food and was terrified to return to work. She became nervous and jumpy and was unable to sleep at night even though her oldest daughter had come over to the apartment and had seen to it that management had changed the locks and had issued Mrs. Alvarez a new set of keys.

Six months after the attack, Mrs. Alvarez gave up her apartment and moved in with her middle daughter. It was difficult for Mrs. Alvarez to give up her home in which she and Mr. Alvarez had raised their children. She had come to know the people and the neighborhood quite well, but she knew her fears were threatening her physical and mental health.

Mrs. Alvarez secured part-time work at a motel in the neighborhood in which her daughter lived. However, her continued flashbacks of the prior attack and the vision problems she was experiencing made holding the job too difficult for her. After giving up her job, Mrs. Alvarez spent much of her time in the house. Even so, she managed to maintain regular phone contact with two of Mr. Alvarez's sisters from the old neighborhood and with friends who also visited her occasionally at her daughter's home. Mrs. Alvarez seemed to be adjusting relatively well to these major social stresses. Her appetite was good, she maintained contact with her family and friends, and she found time to take short trips with her daughter.

Then, six months later, Mrs. Alvarez's daughter, her favorite and only unmarried child, died unexpectedly of a heart attack. Mrs. Alvarez was devastated but, with the help of her other children, managed to make arrangements for the funeral and attend to all of the legal documents. Mrs. Alvarez then moved in with her oldest after some conflict among her children about who had the room to "take in" Mrs. Alvarez.

Mrs. Alvarez has lost quite a bit of weight since her daughter's death. She sits around the house all day, does not answer the phone, takes no interest in her personal appearance, and is totally withdrawn. She rarely, if ever, smiles.

Source: Adapted from Beaver & Miller 1985.

Case 4: Anita Thundercloud

Anita was the elder within the family. She was a direct descendent of the most renowned chief of her band and enjoyed high status. She lived alone in a trailer. Shortly after her seventieth birthday, she became ill and unable to care either for herself or to perform routine household chores. A social worker arranged for Anita's admission to a rest home.

The family accepted this interventive plan without comment. Subsequently, however, this situation changed. Anita received regular visits at the rest home but these did not satisfy family needs. Anita became lonely for home, and the family became lonely for her. A ritual feast was held which Anita attended. Family concerns regarding her absence were expressed and a decision was made that she should remain at home.

The family developed its own helping plan. Each member was given a scheduled time period to provide homemaker services for Anita. Through this shift system, the family network assumed service responsibility. In this case, the family in the immediate vicinity consisted of ten households. Service providers ranged from thirteen-year-old grandchildren to fifty-eight-year-old children.

Source: Red Horse et al. 1978.

Annotated Bibliography

Angel, R. J. & Angel, J. (1997). *Aging and long term care in multicultural America*. New York: New York University Press.

This book explores the possibility for long-term U.S. care policies for racially and culturally diverse elderly which the authors suggest will help optimize choices in living arrangements and make the best use of community support systems for elderly persons sixty-five years and over.

Aponte, J., Rivers, R. V., & Wohl, J. (1995). *Psychological interventions and cultural diversity*. Boston: Allyn and Bacon.

This book provides a comprehensive overview of multicultural mental health intervention processes with elderly persons of color. It provides a detailed exploration of clinical expressions of problems-in-living across and within ethnic groups.

Ball, M. M. & Whittington, F. J. (1995). *Surviving dependence: Voices of African American elders*. Amityville, NY: Baywood.

A chronicle comprised of the stories of "being old, black, poor, and no longer able to manage alone." Highlights the complex relationships between poverty, race, health, gender, age, marital status, and the informal and formal care experience.

Barresi, C. M. & Stull, D. E. (Eds.). (1993). *Ethnic elderly and long-term care*. New York: Springer.

A survey of health issues in very diverse types of ethnic communities. Presents effective models for ethnic-sensitive care giving and offers multidisciplinary practice and policy recommendations for care.

Becerra, R. M. & Shaw, D. (1984). *The Hispanic elderly: A research reference guide*. Lanham, MD: University Press of America.

Details a list of Spanish language research instruments which have been used to assess the Hispanic elderly. Also discusses the knowledge gained from research among the elderly Hispanics and from Hispanics in general. There is an excellent overview of barriers that must be overcome when one is doing research with Hispanic elders. Helps to bridge the gap between the Hispanic elders' needs and the provision of culturally sensitive human services.

Beckett, J. O. & Coley, S. M. (1987). Ecological intervention with the elderly: A case example. *Journal of Gerontological Social Work, 11*, 137–157.

Discusses an intervention model, the ecological system's perspective, and a related tool, the eco map, all of which are particularly relevant for service delivery to the elderly, especially the African American elderly. The model is applied to a case of a black family.

Carillo, C. (9182). Changing norms of Hispanic families: Implications for treatment. In E. E. Jones & S. J. Korchin (Eds.), *Minority mental health*. New York: Praeger.

Examines the affective and cognitive process and rationales involved in Hispanic interactions. Widely held prejudicial views and their effect on the Hispanic community are explored.

Dressel, P. L. (1989). Gender, race, and class: Beyond the feminization of poverty in later life. *The Gerontologist, 28*(2), 177–180.

The feminization of poverty has the potential for both limiting and distorting the issue of old age poverty. Diversity contained within age, race, and gender groups must be acknowledged in order to facilitate a more complete understanding of poverty among the elderly and its policy implications.

Edinberg, M. (1985). *Mental health practice with the elderly*. Englewood Cliffs, NJ: Prentice Hall.

The book is divided into four sections: Processes of Aging (four chapters); Psychopathology and Assessment (three chapters); Interventions with the Aged (seven chapters), and Delivery of Mental Health Services (one chapter). Each section has material relevant to elderly groups of color. For example, one chapter in the first section has a discussion of characteristics and stereotypes of minorities of color and ways to overcome barriers to their receiving mental health services. A chapter in the third section has a useful paradigm for comparing and evaluating intervention with all elderly groups.

Furuto, S. M., Biswas, R., Chung D. K., Murase, K., & Ross-Sheriff, F. (Eds.). (1992). *Social work practice with Asian Americans*. Newbury Park, CA: Sage.

The authors use a variety of formats including synthesizing essays, reports of exploratory and ethnographic studies, case vignettes, census data analyses, and descriptive interpretive data about APIAs to support developing a network of culturally sensitive and competent social services. Attention is also pointedly drawn to conditions of APIA elderly and their need for social services.

Gelfand, D. E. & Barresi, C. M. (Eds.). (1987). *Ethnic dimensions of aging*. New York: Springer.

This book is divided into three sections: theory, research and practice, and policy. It includes chapters on each minority of color and other ethnic groups such as Amish, Greeks, and Jews. The book has a good discussion of the intersection of ethnicity and age and has a thirty page reference section.

Green, J. W. (1982). *Cultural awareness in the human services*. Englewood Cliffs, NJ: Prentice-Hall.

Offers significant concepts regarding APIA, African American, Hispanic and Native Americans and the provisions of social service. Types of help-seeking behaviors found among these groups and ethnic-sensitive social work practices are delineated.

Guttman, D. (1987). Ethnicity in aging: perspective on the needs of ethnic aged. *Social Thought, 13*(1), 42–51.

Discusses the needs of older ethnic Americans, with references to the existing literature on the subject. On the national level, concrete needs and their alleviation must be addressed through the building of coalitions and partnerships between often competing representatives of groups of color. On the local level, the leaders for the ethnic community must become aware of the real daily needs of the elderly and search for ways in which these needs can be met.

Ho, M. K. (1987). *Family therapy with ethnic minorities*. Newbury Park, CA: Sage.

Although this book focuses on family therapy with ethnic persons of color, it is also a repository of important information about these groups. For example, it addresses the following for each of the four groups of persons of color: values, sociocultural and demographic descriptions, family interaction, and help-seeking patterns. In addition, it compares and contrasts the four groups on these measures. It presents cases and discusses intervention with each group.

Jackson, J. S., Newton, P., Ostfield, A., Savage, D., & Schneider, E. (Eds). (1988). *The Black-American elderly: Research on physical and psychosocial health*. New York: Springer.

This state-of-the-art volume gathers, for the first time, what is currently known about aging African American populations in the United States. Topics range from epidemiology and demography to cultural, behavioral, economic, social, and biomedical aspects of aging. The authors compare African American elderly to the elderly of other racial and ethnic groups as well as discuss research.

Lee, J. K. (1986). Asian-American elderly: A neglected minority group. *Journal of Gerontological Social Work*, 9, 103–116.

Discusses the historical experiences, structural difficulties, and cultural barriers that prevent the APIA elderly from obtaining needed social services. It describes eight pieces of federal and state discriminating legislation from 1853 to 1942 which has negatively impacted the political, social, and economic status of APIA elderly. It also explains this group's under-utilization of social services.

Lyons, B. (1997). *Sociocultural differences between American born and West Indianborn elderly blacks: A comparative study of health and social service use*. New York: Garland.

A study which explores similarities and differences between native-born and Caribbean immigrant blacks in the use of community services and the nature of their respective needs from the formal service community. Areas explored in detail are church and religion, family structures, and experiences with and preferences for informal and formal supports.

Markides, K. S. & Mindel, C. H. (1987). *Aging and ethnicity*. Newbury Park, CA: Sage.

Organized into ten chapters, this book explores elderly Americans who are neither white nor middle class. The purpose is to synthesize ethnic research in social gerontology. Also includes an extensive reference section and an author's index. It is a valuable overview of the issues of today's ethnic elderly of color.

National Indian Council on Aging. (1981). *American Indian elderly: A national profile*. Albuquerque, NM. Administration on Aging, Office of Human Development Services, Washington, DC.

A comprehensive research effort that examines in detail and documents the conditions of life of Native-American people in the United States, including Alaska.

U.S. Commission on Civil Rights. (1987). *Asian-American discrimination issues, population and employment characteristics, and Indochina refugees by detailed origin. 1970s-85*. Washington, DC: U.S. Government Printing Office.

Examines APIA population characteristics and factors contributing to anti-APIA activity in the United States and presents demographic and socioeconomic data.

Yu, E. S. (1986). Health of the Chinese elderly in America. *Research on Aging*, 8, 84–109.

Reports and compares death rates, causes of death, and socioeconomic characteristics of Chinese Americans and Caucasians. While the Chinese had a lower death rate than Caucasians, place of birth had a greater effect than gender on the Chinese Americans. Suicide rates were higher for older Chinese-American women than for whites but there was no difference for men.

General Bibliography

Alvarez, D. & Bean, F. D. (1976). The Mexican-American family. In C. H. Mindel & R. W. Habenstein (Eds.). *Ethnic families in America: Pattern and variations*. New York: Elseveer Scientific Pub. Co.

Beaver, M. & Miller, D. (1985). *Clinical social work practice with the elderly*. Homewood, IL: Dorsey

Bell, J. L. (1991). *Chronic physical illness and depression among ethnic minority elderly*. New York: Garland.

Bernard, S. L. (1997). *Racial differences in perceptions of access to health care among the elderly*. New York: Garland.

Brown, L. B. & Gil, R. M. (1985). Social work practice with Hispanic groups. In L. Brown, J. Oliver & J. Alva (Eds.), *Sociocultural and service issues in working with Hispanic-American clients*. State University of New York at Albany: School of Social Welfare.

Brown, V. S. (1997). *The elderly in poor urban neighborhoods*. New York: Garland.

Coke, N. M. (1991). *Correlates of life satisfaction among the African American elderly*. New York: Garland.

Crain, M. (1997). *Medical decision-making among Chinese born and EuroAmerican elderly: A comparative study of values*. New York: Garland.

Devore, W. & Schlesinger, E. (1981). *Ethnic-sensitive social work practice*. St. Louis, MO: Mosby.

Dukepoo, F. C. (1980). *The elder American Indian: A cross cultural study of minority elders in San Diego*. San Diego State University: University Center on Aging.

Ho, M. H. (1987). *Family therapy with ethnic minorities*. Newbury Park, CA: Sage.

John, R. A. (1995). *Social integration of an elderly Native American population*. New York: Garland.

Kim, P. (1983). Demography of the Asian-Pacific elderly: Selected problems and implications. In R. L. McNeely & J. Cohen (Eds.), *Aging in minority groups*. Beverly Hills, CA: Sage.

Kobato, F. S., Lockery, S. A., & Moriwaki, S. Y. (1980). Minority issues in mental health and aging. In J. E. Birren & R. B. Sloane (Eds.). *Handbook of mental health and aging*. Englewood Cliffs, NJ: Prentice-Hall.

Lipshy, B. L. (1990). *Ethnic minority elderly and public policy bibliography*. San Diego, CA: National Resource Center on Minority Aging Populations.

Lubben, J. E. & Becerra, R. M. (1987). Social networks. In D. E. Gelfand & C. M. Barresi (Eds.), *Ethnic dimensions of aging*. New York: Springer.

Markides, K. & Mindel, C. (1987). *Aging and ethnicity*. Beverly Hills, CA: Sage.

Narduzzi, J. L. (1994). *Mental health among elderly Native Americans*. New York: Garland.

National Caucus and Center on Black Aged. (1987). *The status of the Black elderly in the United States*. Washington, DC: U.S. Government Printing Office.

National Indian Council on Aging. (1981). *American-Indian elderly: A national profile*. Albuquerque, NM. Administration on Aging, Office of Human Development Services, Washington, DC.

Shrestha, L. B. (1997). *Racial differences in life expectancy among elderly African Americans and whites: The surprising truth about comparisons*. New York: Garland.

Solomon, B. B. (1983). Social work with Afro-Americans. In A. Morales & B. W. Sheafor (Eds.), *Social work: A profession of many faces*. Boston: Allyn & Bacon.

Sue, D. W. (1981). *Counseling the culturally different: Theory and practice*. New York: Wiley.

Van Zandt, P. L. (1991). *The invisible woman: Women over age 85 in today's society*. New York: Garland.

Wright, B. (1994). *Self-help among the elderly: Formal and informal support systems*. New York: Garland.

References

AARP. See American Association of Retired Persons.

Adebimpe, V. (1981). Overview: White men and psychiatric diagnosis of black patients. *American Journal of Psychiatry, 138*, 279–285.

Administration on Aging. (1996). *AOA Update, 1*(5).

Aleman, S. (1997). *Hispanic elders and human services*. New York: Garland.

Alvarez, D. & Bean, F. D. (1976). The Mexican American family. In C. H. Mindel & R. W. Habenstein (Eds.), *Ethnic families in America: Patterns and variations*. New York: Elsevier Scientific Pub. Co.

American Association of Retired Persons. (1987). *A portrait of older minorities*. Washington, DC: AARP.

American Association of Retired Persons (AARP). (1995). *A portrait of older minorities*. Washington, DC: AARP.

American Association of Retired Persons (AARP). (1996). *A demographic profile of older minorities*. Washington, DC: AARP.

American Association of Retired persons (AARP). (1997). *A profile of older Americans*. Washington, DC: AARP.

American Association of Retired Persons (AARP). (1998). *Source of Income for Older Persons in 1995*. [online], Available: http: //research.aarp.org/econ/95income2.html.

America's super minority. (1986, November 26). *Fortune*, pp. 148–165.

Angel, R. J. & Angel, J. L. (1997). *Who will care for us? Aging and Long-term care in multicultural America*. New York: New York University Press.

Aponte, J., Rivers, R. V., & Wohl, J. (1995). *Psychological interventions and cultural diversity.* Boston: Allyn and Bacon.

Asian American Health Forum, Inc. (1990). Asian Pacific Islander Americans population statistics. San Francisco, CA.

Barresi, C. & Stull, D. (1993). Ethnicity and long-term care: An overview. In C. Barresi and D. Stull (Eds.), *Ethnic elderly and long term care.* New York: Springer.

Ball, M. M. & Whittington, F. J. (1995). *Surviving dependence: Voices of African American elders.* Amityville, NY: Baywood.

Beaver, M. L. (1983). *Human service practice with the elderly.* Englewood Cliffs, NJ: Prentice-Hall.

Beaver, M. & Miller, D. (1985). *Clinical social work practice with the elderly.* Homewood, IL: Dorsey.

Becerra, R. M. & Shaw, D. (1984). *The Hispanic elderly: A research reference guide.* Lanham, MD: University Press of America.

Beckett, J. O. & Coley, S. M. (1987). Ecological intervention with the elderly: A case example. *Journal of Gerontological Social Work, 11,* 137–157.

Bell, D., Kaschau, P., & Zellman, G. (1976). *Delivering services to elderly members of minority groups: A critical review of the literature.* Santa Monica, CA: Rand Corp.

Bengston, V. L. & Burton. (1980). *Familism, ethnicity and supports systems: Patterns of contrast and congruence.* A paper presented at the Western Gerontological Association, San Diego, CA.

Binstock, R. (1999). Challenges to United States policies on aging in the new millennium. *Hallyn International Journal of Aging, 1*(1), 3–13.

Birren, J. E. & Sloane, R. B. (Eds.). (1980). *Handbook of mental health and aging.* Englewood Cliffs, NJ: Prentice-Hall.

Brody, E. (1985). *Mental and physical health practices of older people.* New York: Springer.

Brown, D., Ahmed, F., Gray, L., & Milburn, N. (1995). Major depression in a community sample of African Americans. *American Journal of Psychiatry, 17,* 144–50.

Brown, L. B. & Gil, R. M. (1985). Social work practice with Hispanic groups. In L. Brown, J. Oliver, & J. Alva (Eds.), *Sociocultural and service issues in working with Hispanic-American clients.* Albany: State University of New York, School of Social Welfare.

Brown, T. R. (1973). Mental illness and the role of mental health facilities in Chinatown. In S. Sue & N. Wagner (Eds.), *Asian Americans: Psychological perspectives.* Palo Alto, CA: Science and Behavior Books.

Burt, R. M. (1993). *Hunger among the elderly: Local and national comparisons.* Washington, DC: The Urban Institute.

Butler, R. (1997). Living longer, contributing longer. *Journal of American Medical Association, 278,* 1372–1373.

Butler, R. M. & Sunderland, T. (1991). *Aging and mental health* (4th ed.). New York: Macmillan.

Butler, R. N. & Lewis, M. I. (1977). *Aging and mental health: Positive psychological approaches* (2nd ed.). St. Louis, MO: Mosby.

Carp, F. M. & Kataoka, E. (1976). Health care problems of the elderly of San Francisco's Chinatown. *The Gerontologist, 16,* 30–38.

Cartenson, L. (1993). Perspective on research with older families: Contributions of older adults to families and to family theory. In P. Cowan, D. Field, D. Hansen, A. Skolnick, & G. Swanson (Eds.), *Family self and society: Toward a new agenda for family research* (pp. 353–360). Hillsdale, NJ: Erlbaum.

Crandall, R. C. (1980). *Gerontology—A behavioral science approach.* Reading, MA: Addison-Wesley.

Cuban Refugee Program. (1974). *FACT sheet.* Washington, DC: U.S. Government Printing Office.

Davis, K. (1998). Managed care, mental illness, and African Americans. In G. Schamess & A. Lightburn (Eds.), *Humane Managed Care?* (pp. 51–64). Washington, DC: National Association of Social Workers.

Cuellar, J. (1990). *Aging and health: Hispanic American elders.* Stanford, CA: Stanford Geriatric Center's GEC Working Paper Series, Number 5.

Dohrenwend, B. P. & Dohrenwend, B. S. (1969). *Social status and psychological disorder: A casual inquiry.* New York: Wiley-Interscience.

Dohrenwend, B. S. (1970). Social class and stressful events. In E. H. Hare & J. K. Wings (Eds.), *Psychiatry epidemiology* (pp. 313–319). New York: Oxford University Press.

Dohrenwend, B. S. (1973). Social status and stressful life events. *Journal of Personality and Social Psychology, 9,* 203–214.

Dukepoo, F. C. (1980). *The elder American Indian: A cross cultural study of minority elders in San Diego.* San Diego, CA: San Diego State University, University Center on Aging.

Edinberg, M. A. (1985). *Mental health practice with the elderly.* Englewood Cliffs, NJ: Prentice-Hall.

Edwards, A. (1982). The consequences of error in selecting treatment for blacks. *Social Casework: The Journal of Contemporary Social Work, 63,* 429–433.

Escarce, J. & Puffer, F. (1997). Black-white differences in the use of medical care by the elderly: A contemporary analysis. In L. Martina and B. Soldo (Eds.), *Radical and ethnic differences in the health of older Americans* (pp. 180–212). New York: National Academy Press.

Fellin, P. & Powell, T. (1988). Mental health services and older adult minorities: An assessment. *The Gerontologist, 18,* 442–447.

Flaskerud, J. & Hu, L. (1992). Relationship of ethnicity to psychiatric diagnosis. *Journal of Nervous and Mental Disorders, 180,* 296–303.

Fried, M. (1975). Social differences in mental health. In J. Rosa & I. Zola (Eds.), *Poverty and health* (2nd ed.). Cambridge, MA: Harvard University Press.

Gaberlavage, G. & Citro, J. (197). *Progress in housing of older persons.* Washington DC: American Association of Retired Persons.

Garretson, D. (1993). Psychological misdiagnosis of African Americans. *Journal of Multicultural Counseling and Developments, 21,* 119–126.

Gelfand, D. (1982). *Aging: The ethnic factor.* Boston, MA: Little Brown.

Gilderbloom, J. & Mullins, R. (1995). Elderly housing needs: An examination of the American Housing Survey. *International Journal of Aging and Human Development, 40,* 52–72.

Ginzberg, E. & Ostow, M. (1997). Managed care: A look back and a look ahead. *New England Journal of Medicine, 336,* 1017–1020.

Gornick, M. E., Eggers, P. W., Reilly, T. W., Mentnech, R. M., Fitterman, L. K., Kuchen, L. E., & Vladeck, B. C. (1996). Effects of race and income on mortality and use of services among Medicare beneficiaries. *New England Journal of Medicine, 335,* 791–816.

Green, J. (1995). *Cultural awareness in the human services: A multi-ethnic approach* (2nd ed). Boston: Allyn and Bacon.

Green, R. & Knee, R. (1996). Shaping the policy practice agenda of social work in the field of aging. *Social Work, 41,* 553–560.

Harper, K. & Lantz, J. (1996). *Cross-cultural practice: Social work with diverse populations.* Chicago: Lyceum.

Hernandez, G. G. (1996). Managed care: A cultural perspective. *Minority Faces, 2*(1).

Himes, C. L. (1992). Future caregivers: Projected family structures of older people. *Journal of Gerontology, 47*(1), S23.

Himes, C., Hogan, D., & Eggebeen, D. (1996). *Journal of Gerontology, 51,* S42–S48.

Ho, M. H. (1987). Family therapy with ethnic minorities. Newbury Park: Sage.

Hollingshead, A. & Redlich, F. (1958). *Social class and mental illness: A community study.* New York: Wiley.

Jackson, J. (1970). Aged Negroes: Their cultural departures from statistical stereotypes and rural-urban differences. *Gerontologist, 10,* pp. 140–145.

Johnson, E. S. & Williamson, J. B. (1987). Retirement in the United States. In K. S. Markides & C. L. Cooper (Eds.), *Retirement in industrialized societies.* New York: Wiley.

Kart, C. S. (1981). *The realities of aging.* Boston, MA: Allyn & Bacon.

Kenner, J. F., Dusenbury, L., & Mandelblatt, J. S. (1993). Poverty and cultural diversity: Challenges for health promotion among medically underserved. *Annual Review of Public Health, 14,* 355–377.

Kessler, R. C. (1979). Stress, social status and psychological distress. *Journal of Health and Social Behavior, 20,* 100–108.

Kessler, R. C. & Cleary, P. D. (1980). Social class and psychological stress. *American Sociological Review, 45,* 463–478.

Kim, P. (1983). Demography of the Asian-Pacific elderly: Selected problems and implications. In R. L. McNeely & J. Cohen (Eds.), *Aging in minority groups.* Beverly Hills, CA: Sage.

Kingston, R. & Smith, J. (1917). Socioeconomic status and racial and ethnic differences in functional status associated with chronic diseases. *American Journal of Public Health, 87,* 805–810.

Kitano, H. (1969). Japanese-American mental illness. In S. Plog & R. Edgerton (Eds.), *Changing perspectives in mental illness.* New York: Holt, Rinehart & Winston.

Kobato, F. S., Lockery, S. A., & Moriwaki, S. Y. (1980). Minority issues in mental health and aging. In J. E. Birren & R. B. Sloane (Eds.), *Handbook of mental health and aging.* Englewood Cliffs, NJ: Prentice-Hall.

Lacay, C. (1991). Current trends in living arrangements and social environment among ethnic minority elderly. *Generations, 15,* 43–46.

Leonard, O. E. 91967). The older rural Spanish people of the Southwest. In E. G. Youmans (Ed.), *Older rural Americans* (pp. 239–261). Lexington: University of Kentucky Press.

Levine, I. M. (1976). *Ethnicity and mental health: A social conservation approach.* Washington, DC: White House Conference on Ethnicity and Mental Health.

Liu, N. T. & Yu, E. (1985). Asian Pacific Island American elderly: Mortality differentials, health status, and use of health services. *Journal of Applied Gerontology* 4(1), 35–64.

Loring, M. & Powell, B. (1988). Gender, race and DSM-III: A study of the objectivity of psychiatric diagnostic behavior. *JOurnal of Health and Social Behavior, 29,* 1–22.

Lubben, J. E. & Becerra, R.M. (1987). Social networks. In D. E. Gelfand & C. M. Barresi (Eds.), *Ethnic dimensions of aging.* New York: Springer.

Lum, D. (1983). Asian-Americans and their aged. In R. L. McNeely & J. L. Cohen (Eds.), *Aging in minority groups* (pp. 85–94). Beverly Hills, CA: Sage.

Lum, D. (1984). Toward a framework for social work practice with minorities. *Social Work, 27,* 244–249.

Lum, D. (1986). *Social work practice and people of color.* Monterey, CA: Brooks/Cole.

Lum, D. (1996). *Social work practice and people of color: A process approach* (3rd ed.). Pacific Grove, CA: Brooks/Cole.

Lum, D. (2000). *Social work practice and people of color* (4th ed) Belmont, CA: Brooks/Cole.

Lyman, S. (1974). *Chinese Americans.* New York: Random House.

Lyons, B. (1997). *Sociocultural differences between American-born and West Indian born elderly blacks: A comparative study of health and social service use.* New York: Garland.

Maldonado, D., Jr. (1979). Aging in the Chicano context. In D. E. Gelfand & A. J. Kutzik (Eds.), *Ethnicity and aging: Theory, research, and policy* (pp. 175–183). New York: Springer.

Markides, K. S. (1985). Minority aging. In B. B. Hess & E. W. Markson (Eds.), *Growing old in America* (3rd ed.). New Brunswick, NJ: Transaction.

Markides, K. & Mindel, C. (1987). *Aging and ethnicity.* Beverly Hills, CA: Sage.

Mindel, C. H. & Habenstein, R. W. (Eds.). (1981). *Ethnic families in America: Patterns and variations* (2nd ed.). New York: Elsevier Scientific Pub. Co.

Miranda, M. R. (1988). Hispanic aging: Issues for policy development. *Aging Network News, 5*(8), 5–6.

Mokuau, N. (Ed.). (1991). *Handbook of Social Services for Asian Pacific Islanders.* New York: Greenwood Press.

Morgan, R., Virgnig, B., DeVito, C., & Persily, N. (1997). The Medicare-HMO revolving door: The healthy go in and the sick go out. *New England Journal of Medicine, 337,* 169–175.

Morrison, B. (1995). A research and policy agenda on predictions of institutional placement among minority elderly. *Journal of Gerontological Social Work, 24,* 17–28.

Namkee, Choi. (1997). Racial differences in retirement income: The roles of public and private income sources. *Journal of Aging and Social Policy, 9,* 21–42.

National Caucus and Center on Black Aged. (1987). *The status of the Black elderly in the United States.* Washington, DC: U.S. Government Printing Office.

National Indian Council on Aging. (1981a). *American Indian elderly—A national profile.* Albuquerque, NM. Administration on Aging, Office of Human Development Services, Washington, DC.

National Indian Council on Aging. (1981b). *Indian elderly and entitlement programs: An accessing demonstration project.* Albuquerque, NM. Administration on Aging. Office of Human Development Services, Washington, DC.

National Indian Council on Aging. (1986). *Research project to derive and disseminate information on the health, housing and safety status of Indian elders*. Albuquerque, NM. Administration on Aging, Office of Human Development Services, Washington, DC.

Navarro, V. (1990). Race or class versus race and class: Mortality differentials in the United States. *Lancet, 336*, 1238–1240.

Neighbors, H. W. (1984). The distribution of psychiatric morbidity in Black Americans: A review and suggestions for research. *Community Mental Health Journal, 20*, 169–181.

Older Women's League. (1998). Path to poverty: an analysis of women's retirement income. In Carroll Estes and Meredith Minkler (Eds.). *Critical gerontology: Perspectives from political and moral economy* (pp. 299–313). Bayward Pub: Amityville.

Owens, C. E. (1980). *Mental health and Black offenders*. Boston, MA: Heath.

Paniagua, F. (1994). *Assessing and treating culturally diverse clients*. Thousand Oaks, CA: Sage.

Pope, H. G. & Lipinski, J. F. (1978). Diagnosis in schizophrenia and manic depressive illness. *Archives of General Psychiatry, 35*, 811–828.

Price, J. A. (1976). North American Indian families. In C. H. Mindel & R. W. Haberstein (Eds.), *Ethnic families in America: Patterns and variations*. New York: Elsevier Scientific Pub., Co.

Proctor, E., Morrell-Howell, N., & Dore, P. (1996). Functional dependency among elderly geropsychiatric patients discharged home after acute care. Paper presented at the 10th NIMH International Conference on Mental Health Programs in the General Health Care Sector, Bethesda, MD.

Pynoos, J., Reynolds, S., Salend, E., Rachman, A., & Jenkins, R. (1995). *Waiting for federally assisted housing: A study of the needs and experience of older applicants*. Washington, DC: American Association of Retired Persons.

Red Horse, J. G., Lewis R., Feit, M., & Decker, J. (1978). Family behavior of urban American Indians. *Social Casework, 59*, 67–72.

Red Horse, J. (1991). American Indian aging: Issues in income, housing and transportation. In *Aging and old age in diverse populations* (pp. 1–16). Washington, DC: American Association of Retired Persons.

Ross-Sheriff, F. (1992). Adaptation and integration into American society: Major issues affecting Asian Americans. In S. M. Furuto, R. Biswas, D. K. Chung, K. Murae, & F. Ross-Sheriff (Eds.), *Social Work Practice with Asian Americans*. Newbury park, CA: Sage.

Shaffer, R. T. (1984). *Racial and ethnic groups* (2nd ed.): Boston: Little, Brown.

Social Security Administration. (1998). *Income of Population 55 or older, 1966*. Washington, DC: Author.

Social Security Administration. (1995). Office of Research and Statistics, *Fast facts and figures about Social Security 1995*. Washington, DC: U.S. Government Printing Office.

Solomon, B. B. (1976). *Black empowerment social work in oppressed communities*. New York: Columbia University.

Sotomayor, M. (1975). Social change and the Spanish speaking elderly. In A. Hernandez & J. Mendoza (Eds.), *The national conference on the Spanish-speaking elderly*. Kansas City: National Chicano Social Planning Council.

Sotomayer, M. (1997). Aging: Racial and ethnic groups. In R. Edwards (Ed.), *Encyclopedia of Social Work*, 19th edition, 1977 Supplement, pp. 26–35. Washington DC: National Association of Social Workers.

Stanford, E. P. & DuBois, B. C. (1992). Gender and ethnicity patterns. In J. E. Birren, R. B. Sloane, & G. D. Cohen (Eds.), *Handbook of mental health and aging* (pp. 1–26). San Diego: Academic Press.

Stuart, P., Rathbone-McCuan, & B. Havens (Eds.), *North American elders: Untied States and Canadian perspective* (pp. 235-254). New York: Greenwood Press.

Sue, D. W. (1981). *Counseling the culturally different: Theory and practice*. New York: Wiley.

Sue, S. & McKinney, H. (1975). Asian-Americans in the community mental health care system. *American Journal of Orthopsychiatry, 45*, 111–118.

Sue, S. & Morishima, J. (1982). The mental health of Asian Americans. Special Committee on Aging. U.S. Senate. *Development in Aging*, Vol 3. San Francisco, CA: Jossey-Bass.

Sue, S. & Sue, D. W. (1974). MMPI comparisons between Asian-American and non-Asian students utilizing a student health psychiatric clinic. *Journal of Counseling Psychology, 21,* 423–427.

Torres-Gil, F. (1992). *The new aging: Politics and change in America.* Westport, CT: Auburn House.

Torres-Gil, F. & Negm, M. (1980). Policy issues concerning the Hispanic elderly. *Aging, 305/306,* 2–5.

Torres-Gil, F. M., Newquist, D., & Simonia, M. (1977). *Housing: The diverse aged.* Los Angeles: Andrus Gerontology Center, University of Southern California.

Trevino, F., Moyer, M. E., Valdez, B., & Stroup-Benham, C. (1991). *Health insurance coverage and utilization of health services by Mexican Americans, Mainland Puerto Ricans and Cuban Americans.* JAMA, 265(2), pp. 233–327.

Torrez, D. (1996). Independent living among Mexican American elderly: The need for social services support. In R. DeAnda (Ed.), *Chicanas and Chicanos in contemporary society* (pp. 87–95). Boston: Allyn & Bacon.

Treas, J. (1995). Older Americans in the 1990s and beyond. *Population Bulletin, 50*(2).

Tseng, W. & Char, W. (1974). The Chinese of Hawaii. In W. S. Tseng, J. F. McDeamott, & T. W. Maretzki (Eds.), *People and cultures in Hawaii.* Honolulu: University Press of Hawaii.

Uba, L. (1994). *Asian Americans: Personality patterns, identity and mental health.* New York: Guildford Press.

U.S. Bureau of the Census (1983). *America in transition: An aging society.* Washington, DC: U.S. Government Printing Office.

U.S. Bureau of the Census. (1985). *Current population reports.* Washington, DC: U.S. Government Printing Office.

U.S. Bureau of the Census. (1987). *Statistical abstract of the United States* (107th Edition). Washington, DC: U.S. Government Printing Office.

U.S. Bureau of Census. (1992a). *Current population reports, P 25-1092: Population projections of the United States by age, sex, race, and Hispanic origin: 1922–2050.* Washington DC: U.S. Government Printing Office.

U.S. Bureau of Census. (1992b). *Current population reports, P 23-178: Sixty-five plus in America.* Washington DC: U.S. Government Printing Office.

U.S. Bureau of Census. (1996). *Current population reports, Special Studies, P23-190, Sixty-five plus in the United States.* Washington DC: U.S. Government Printing Office.

U.S. Commission on Civil Rights. (1979). *Civil rights of Asian and Pacific Americans: Myths and realities.* Washington, DC: U.S. Government Printing Office.

U.S. Congress House Select Committee on Aging. (1987). *The plight of the Black elderly: A major crisis in America.* Hearing before the Select committee on Aging, House of Representatives, 99th Congress, Second Session. Washington, DC: U.S. Government Printing Office.

U.S. Department of Labor (1988). *Employment in perspective: Women in the labor force* (Report 756). Washington, DC: U.S. Government Printing Office.

U.S. Senate Special Committee on Aging in Conjunction with the American Association of Retired Persons, the Federal Council on the Aging and Administration on Aging. (1986). *Aging America: Trends and projections* (1985-86 ed.). Washington, DC.

U.S. Senate Special Committee on Aging, the American Association of Retired Persons, the Federal Council on Aging and the U.S. Administration on Aging (1991). *Aging America: Trends and projections* (rev. Ed.). Washington, DC: U.S. Department of Health and Human Services.

Valle, R. & Mendoza, L. (1978) *The elder Latino.* San Diego, CA: Campanile Press.

Watson, W. (1983). Selected demographic and social aspects of older Blacks: An analysis with policy implications. In R. McNeely & J. Cohen (Eds.), *Aging in minority groups* (pp. 42–49). Beverly Hills, CA: Sage.

Weeks, J. (1984). *Aging concepts and social issues.* Belmont, CA: Wadsworth.

Wellons, K. (1996). Aspects of aging in the twenty-first century. In P. Raffoul & C. McNeece (Eds.), *Future issues for social work practice* (pp. 117–124).

White, S. E. (1997). *The elderly living alone in America: A portrait.* New York: Garland.

Woodruff, L. (1995). Growing diversity in the aging population. *Caring, 14,* 4–9.

Yu, E. S. H. (1980). Philippino migration and community organization in the United States. *California Sociologist, 3,* 76–102.

10 Aging Women

■ ■ ■ ■ ■ ■ ■ ■ ■ ■ ■ ■ ■ ■ ■

Joyce O. Beckett and Robert L. Schneider,
with Etty Vandsburger and Ellen Stevens

Although legislation has been enacted to foster equal treatment of women in all areas of society, the need for attention to women's issues continues. Even though women in general, and aging women in particular, comprise a numerical majority in America, they are oppressed. Women are discriminated against in many areas, including the economic, education, health, mental health, and criminal justice systems.

Possibly the single most significant fact about aging is that the population of aging persons is overwhelmingly female; 60 percent of those sixty-five years of age and over are women. These women are the fastest growing segment of the population in the United States (AARP 1998). One of every six aging women is a person of color (AOA 1998). Among persons seventy-five and older, women comprise two-thirds of the population (Hess 1990). The ratio of women to men increases over the lifespan. Large numbers of women outlive their husbands, often by as much as two decades; and a significant number outlive their eldest son. The problems associated with aging, such as greater risk of chronic illness, reduced economic resources, increased poverty, increased caregiving and care needing, surviving one's relatives and closest friends, and increased risk of death and institutionalization are predominantly the problems of women (Administration on Aging 1998; U.S. Senate, Special Committee on Aging 1992).

Despite the rapidly rising number of aging women, research and social policy usually overlook this important group of the elderly. Attention to women and the elderly has usually failed to take the particular needs of aging women into account. For example, *The Encyclopedia of Social Work* (Edward 1995) does not include an entry for "older women" or "aging women" in the index. Thus, the reader is not directed to the few places in the book where these issues are discussed.

Definition of "Aging Women"

Who constitutes "aging women?" This is a difficult question to answer. Traditionally, age sixty-five has been the benchmark for delineating the elderly; it was used because it is the age at which most men retire from the labor force and the age when full Social Security benefits begin. The lives of many of the current cohort of aging women follow a pattern unlike that of men. These women may have worked before marriage and before the birth of the first child, but many withdrew from the labor force and returned home to care for their children. As the children matured and left home, and perhaps the husband died or divorce occurred, women often returned to work outside the home.

There are exceptions to this intermittent pattern of work. Many African American women and never-married women have a lifelong pattern of work similar to men, and some upper-class white women have never been employed outside the home. Nevertheless, the employment pattern for most aging women differs from the traditional male norm. The result is that retirement is not a good benchmark for the age at which women move into the status of the elderly.

In addition, age is more than a chronological occurrence. It has cultural, social, as well as biological components. In general, there seems to be a double standard about age which considers women old at an earlier age than men (Sontag 1972). Furthermore, women in the poorest stratum may be physically old by their thirties due to successive pregnancies, inadequate nutrition, and overwork (Crooks 1986). This chapter will use the age of the sources and literature discussed, which is usually sixty-two or sixty-five.

Midlife, the years between ages forty-five and sixty-five, is an important life stage for women and should also be the target for research and study. Midlife women face significant alterations in all areas of their lives—family, occupation, social, education, health, and finance. While it is a time for expansion and growth, it is also a period of role change as children usually grow up and leave home and parents and parents-in-law begin to have medical complications associated with the aging process. During this life stage, an appropriate foundation for personal and economic security must be built or expanded in order to prevent economic dependency and poverty in the subsequent life stage.

Discrimination and Bias

Most aging women are confronted with the double jeopardy of discrimination because of age and gender. Unlike Caucasian men, who may be initially subjected to prejudice because of age only in later life, Caucasian women cope with gender discrimination throughout their lives. Age compounds their oppression. Aging women face additional oppression because of characteristics such as race, class, and residence. An aging, lower class, African American woman who lives in the central city is likely to face multiple jeopardies.

In addition to discrimination, there is also age-sex bias. Three types of such bias have been noted (U.S. House of Representatives 1979):

1. *Expectation and distortion*—belief that certain behaviors fit certain ages according to sex. As a result, people tend to make their perceptions congruent with their expectations. For example, if one expects women to be ill during menopause, one sees them that way even through this view may be inaccurate.
2. *Restrictiveness*—people's behaviors are limited by what is perceived to be appropriate actions for their age and sex. For instance, a sixty-year-old woman beginning to work on a graduate degree or a fifty-year-old woman having her first child would likely be considered a "deviant."
3. *Negative attitudes*—people classified as old, no matter what age standard is used, may be seen as intellectually inferior, narrowminded, ineffective, and/or infirm.

Demographic Profile of Aging Women

The cohort of aging women in America has been largely invisible and the realities of their lives obscured by myths and neglect. Their life experiences are different from those of men. Even the Women's Movement did not define aging as a feminist issue until the late 1970s

(Hooyman 1986a). Nevertheless, aging women are the fastest growing segment of the American population. As Peter Morrison, a Rand Corporation demographer puts it, "Aging is disproportionately a woman's problem in our society" (Otten 1984, p. 1).

The following profile provides a description of the status, the conditions, and the actual circumstances of many aging women. These facts produce an overview of the reality confronted by aging women in American society.

- Aging women outnumber aging men three to two. In 1997, the sex ratio for aging persons was 143 women for every 100 men—20 million aging women versus aging men. This disparity increases with age; for age eighty-five and older, there were 248 women for every 100 men. Women also live longer than men. At age sixty-five, women have an average of nineteen years of life remaining, while men can expect to live another sixteen years (AARP 1998).
- In 1997, aging men were almost twice as likely (74 percent) to be married as aging women (42 percent) (AARP 1998). Aging men are several times more likely to remarry than women. The higher remarriage rate of widowers is the result of social norms supporting men's marriage to younger women and discouraging the opposite for women, and the surplus of women in the marriage market.
- Widowhood is the marital status of almost half (46 percent) of aging women and is also long lasting (AARP 1998). The average widow who does not remarry and dies a natural death will spend 18.5 years in this last portion of life. This period, as a woman alone following marriage, is longer than the period from entrance into first grade until marriage.
- Almost half (46 percent) of all aging women in 1998 were widowed compared to less than one-fifth (16 percent) of the men. There were over four times as many widows (8.5 million) as widowers (2.1 million) (AARP 1998).
- While most women over seventy-five are widowed, most men over seventy-five are married. The divorce rate for men over sixty-five is more than double the rate for women of the same age group. For men, that means a surfeit of women available for dating or marriage, but also, because there are few other unattached men around, there can also be stretches of intense loneliness. For aging women, the situation is just the opposite. They often find a supportive community of other aging women in similar situations, but they are less likely to find a spouse (AARP 1998).
- In 1997, the majority (66 percent) of older noninstitutionalized persons lived in a family setting. Approximately 10.7 million (81 percent) of aging men and 10.5 million (57 percent) of aging women lived in families. The proportion living in a family setting decreases with age. Of those eighty-five years and older, about thirteen percent (8 percent of men and 17 percent of women) were not living with a spouse, but living with children, siblings, or other relatives (AARP 1998).
- Aging persons living alone increased in number by 7 percent between 1990 and 1995 (AARP 1995). By 1997, 41 percent of aging women and 17 percent of aging men lived alone (AARP 1998).
- About 3.9 million aging workers were in the labor force in 1997, including 2.3 million men (17 percent) and 1.6 million women (8 percent). They constituted 2.9 percent of the labor force (AARP 1998).
- Approximately half (53 percent) of workers over sixty-five in 1997 were employed part-time; 46 percent of men and 63 percent of women were employed part-time (AARP 1998).

- The education level of aging persons continues to increase. The number who completed high school rose from 28 to 66 percent between 1970 and 1997. In 1997, about 13 percent of aging persons had four or more years of college (AARP 1998).
- Aging women are more likely than aging men to develop chronic diseases and to become disabled and frail (Administration on Aging 1998).
- Of the 20.8 million households headed by aging persons in 1995, 78 percent were owners and 22 percent were renters. Older male householders were more likely to be owners than were females (AARP 1998).
- Almost three-quarters of all aging persons below the poverty level were women. More than half of these women were not poor before the death of their husbands (Administration on Aging 1998). Among elderly widows, poverty rates are as high as 40 percent; the prospects for older African American single women are particularly bleak—seven in every ten of them live below the poverty line (Smith 1997).

This demographic profile of aging America illustrates many of the particular problems and circumstances facing aging women. It is evident that aging women are primarily the ones who experience loneliness, isolation, widowhood, part-time employment, few opportunities to remarry, and life in long-term care institutions. Service providers such as social workers must be aware of these data and intervene in ways that take into account the needs of this increasingly large group of aging individuals.

Family

There have been many changes during the twentieth century which influence the family life of aging women. These include an increase in life expectancy; the tendency until the 1960s toward earlier marriage; couples having fewer children; an increase in the education level, especially for women; increase in the number of women who work outside the home; increase in the divorce rate; and the removal of a mandatory retirement age (Hendricks & Hendricks 1986; Rix 1987). These events interact in complex ways to affect family life. For example, the increase in life expectancy has augmented the amount of time a couple is alone after the last child leaves home. It is also related to a greater likelihood of middle-age and aging women caring for their and/or their spouses' parents, often at a time when these caregivers have returned to the labor force.

Living Arrangements

The overwhelming majority (96 percent) of aging persons live in the community, mostly with family members. Below are some facts about the living arrangements in 1995 (AARP 1998).

- Aging men are much more likely than women to live in a family setting, 81 percent of men and 57 percent of women.
- Aging men are more likely to live with a spouse than older women, 77 percent of men and 48 percent of women.
- More aging women than men live with other family members—children, siblings and other relatives (8 percent of women and 4 percent of men).
- A small proportion of men (2 percent) and women (2 percent) live with nonrelatives.

- Aging women (42 percent) are almost three times as likely as aging men (17 percent) to live alone.
- Although a small percentage (4 percent) of aging persons lived in nursing homes in 1995, the percentage increases drastically with age, ranging from 1 percent for persons sixty-five to seventy-four, 5 percent for persons seventy-five to eighty-four and 15 percent for persons eighty-five and older. The vast majority (67 percent) of nursing home residents are aging women, reflecting their tendency to live longer and have more chronic illnesses than men.

Marital Status

Both age and gender are important determinants of marital status. Aging persons are less likely than younger to have never married and older women are less likely than men to be currently married (Hendricks & Hendricks 1986). Below are some facts concerning the marital status of aging persons with an emphasis on gender differences (AARP 1998).

- In 1997, aging women were less likely than aging men to be married, 42 percent of women and 74 percent of men.
- Aging women were almost four times as likely as aging men to be widowed, 46 percent of women and 16 percent of men.
- In absolute numbers, there were five times as many widows (8.5 million) as widowers (2.1 million) in 1997.
- The same *proportion* of aging women as aging men were never married (4 percent) and divorced (6 percent). The *number* of women who were widowed or divorced was substantially larger than the number of men, however.
- The number (2.2 million) of divorced aging persons is increasing dramatically; it soared nearly three times as fast as the aging population as a whole during the period of 1990 to 1997, 2.8 times for men, 7.4 for women.

DIVORCE AND WIDOWHOOD

Aging women are increasingly living without a spouse. Because of divorce and widowhood, more than 40 percent of the current generation of aging women live alone for nearly one-third of their adult lives. Women's average age of widowhood is fifty-six years and at age sixty-five, females have an average life expectancy of nineteen years (AARP 1998; Hooyman 1986a).

The primary negative consequence of widowhood and divorce is poverty, which is experienced by one-fifth of aging women living alone (AARP 1998). Aging divorced women usually do not share their ex-husband's pension or social security benefits. In addition, few of these women receive any property settlement. Moreover, divorced aging women have poorer health, higher mortality rates, and lower levels of life satisfaction than divorced men or married and widowed women (Hess & Waring 1983).

REMARRIAGE

Once widowed or divorced, aging women are much less likely than men to remarry. The possibility for remarriage dramatically decreases as women age. Barriers to aging women's remarriage include the substantial deficit of aging men because of their lower life expectancy, a small proportion of unmarried aging men, the cultural norm against women marrying younger men, and the societal expectation that men will marry younger women. The sex ratio dramatically underscores the scarcity of aging men. It increases with age and ranges from 121 women to every 100 men for the sixty-five to sixty-nine group to a high of 257 women per 100 men for persons eighty-five and older (AARP 1998).

Family Relations

The gender differences in marital status influence family relations among the aging. Because of the prevalence of widowhood, divorce, and rare instances of remarriage, aging women's family interactions revolve around vertical kinship ties to children, grandchildren, and the aging woman's parents. In contrast, aging men more often have strong horizontal ties to their current spouse. Aging women are not usually active in the day-to-day decisions of their children and grandchildren. But in times of crisis such as a child's divorce, aging women often provide important assistance. Since mothers are more likely to retain custody of children following divorce, maternal grandparents become more involved with their daughters and grandchildren.

A relatively large portion of aging women have no children; 25 percent of the women in their seventies have no surviving children. In addition to relationships with their surviving parents, interaction with female peers and friends have added importance for these women (AARP 1998). Childless widows, however, are often more lonely and dissatisfied than widows with grown children. The absence of children and spouse also increases their probability of institutionalization.

Whether married or not, aging women who have children have frequent contact with them. Sixty-two percent of these women have at least weekly visits and 76 percent talk on the phone at least weekly with their children. Moreover, 66 percent live within thirty minutes of a child (AARP 1997). Whether spouse, parents, or children, family members are an important dimension in the lives of aging women.

Caregiving

The family ties of women are possibly stronger than those of aging men. Women are socialized to adopt a nurturing role in which they provide support to their families throughout their lives. The caring roles of women in their later years usually include spouse, mother, grandmother, and caregiver to aging parents and parents-in-law and increasingly to their dependent children (Jennings 1987; Williams 1995). Due to the rising life expectancies, more aging women than in prior generations become great grandmothers or even members of five-generation families (AARP 1997; Kiyak & Hooyman 1999) The average age of informal caregivers is fifty-seven years. Three-quarters of caregivers share households with the care recipient (whose average age is seventy-eight years), while providing assistance for several years, usually seven days a week (Williams 1995, p. 102).

Women, some of whom may be sixty or seventy years of age, constitute almost 80 percent of the caregivers of disabled elderly relatives. These women usually are daughters, wives, and other relatives. Some of these caregivers provide services to persons who reside in their household while others care for relatives who live elsewhere. These women are the invisible laborers without whom neither the health system nor the patient could survive. The number of aging women who are the primary caregivers of grandchildren is growing. They are the caregivers for a majority of these 1.3 million children (Administration on Aging 1998).

Women's caregiving activities in the family are in addition to their own life stage tasks. Aging women's multiple roles and multigeneration caregiving responsibilities place them at risk of depression, exhaustion, financial difficulties, and physical and mental illness. They are sometimes referred to as the "hidden patient" (Fengler & Goodrich 1979, p. 11). Their own illness or death tends to result in institutionalization of the person(s) for whom they cared (Teresi, Toner, Bennett, & Wilson 1980; Hooyman & Kiyak 1996).

Just as the informal caregivers are predominantly women, so are formal caregivers of services to the elderly. Staffs of social service agencies, nursing homes, hospitals, and other institutions that serve the elderly are primarily female. Throughout the life cycle, women are dependent on other women whether these are unpaid caregivers, underpaid employees in social agencies, or recipients of the services. The result is that the conditions of aging persons, who are primarily women, must be central to the consciousness of all.

Sexual Orientation

Although there has been an exponential increase in research and literature on sexuality and sexual orientation, studies of aging gay men and lesbians are rare. This is so despite the fact that in 1982 it was estimated that there were about 3.5 million homosexual men and women over 60 (Rogers 1993). Most of the available research is primarily descriptive, examines myths and stereotypes, and concentrates on gay men rather than on lesbians (Berger 1982; Friend 1987). However, some literature is emerging that describes the lesbian experience more in-depth (e.g., Slater 1995).

The neglect of women is particularly problematic since some literature suggests the experiences of aging lesbians is quite different from that of aging gays. For example, lesbians tend to socialize in private circles and avoid public institutions of the gay community (Berger 1982). As lesbians age, it is reported, they are less concerned than gay men about a youthful appearance and sexual activity (Minnigerode & Adelman 1976; Slater 1995).

Some refer to aging lesbians as an invisible minority group (Almvig 1982; Kimmel 1978). Most aging lesbians spent the majority of their lives in a time where they were forced to conceal their sexual orientation (Shenk & Fullmer 1996). A result in old age is that these lesbians may be more isolated than gays from their age peers and younger homosexuals. Like other oppressed elderly, lesbians often face multiple jeopardies and discrimination due to age, gender, and an unpopular sexual orientation. The oppression is compounded even further for lesbians who are ethnic minorities of color. For example, the African American community is much less accepting of homosexuality than the Caucasian community (Dawson 1982; Friend 1984; Kimmel 1978; Tully 1995).

The ageism, heterosexism, genderism, and racism that lesbians face create unique conflicts and problems as well as successful coping mechanisms (Friend 1987; Tully 1995; Woodman 1995). Lesbians who live together, for example, have to contend with the economic pressure of having combined incomes and/or pensions which are usually less than the amount for male couples or heterosexual couples. Apart from tangible economic challenges, aging lesbians also face the internal conflict between personal and public definitions of lifestyle (Shenk & Fullmer 1996).

Aging lesbians face the compounded consequences of expectable age-related issues. For instance, a lesbian may find it difficult to manage a terminal or chronic illness when many health facilities exclude all except blood relatives. Fear of institutionalization may be intensified for at least two reasons. First, lesbians are less likely to assume their families will provide for them in old age (Dawson 1982). Thus, they anticipate the greater likelihood of institutionalization. Secondly, nursing homes and rehabilitation centers are often perceived to be unsupportive and hostile toward a homosexual lifestyle (Friend 1987). Another problem is the loss of a lover or partner. Families of a deceased lesbian may actively exclude the lover and homosexual friends of the deceased from funeral plans and participation in the services. This isolation frequently intensifies the grief process and increases the anger.

As they are among other oppressed, the problems and conflicts faced by lesbians may result in effective coping mechanisms which can facilitate successful aging. Homosexuality is reported to be functional in adjusting to old age in several ways. First, the successful handling and resolution of the sexual orientation and identity struggle that usually occurs in adolescence may provide a sense of "crisis competence" (Kimmel 1978). That is, the "coming out process" provides the individual with coping mechanisms which can be used in other crises in later life.

The consequences of the "coming out" may include family disruption, intense feelings, and sometimes alienation from family. Lesbians may subsequently rely less on nuclear family members and more on accepting extended family, friends, and other lesbians. These resources tend to serve as a "surrogate family" (Bell & Weinberg 1978).

Another consequence of a lesbian lifestyle that may be helpful in the aging process is role flexibility. It is reported that homosexuals are more likely than heterosexuals to achieve the potential for greater freedom to learn skills associated with society's stereotypical views of males and females. Greater flexibility in gender roles among lesbians suggests they are more likely to weather the life stage crisis and to have skills to manage loss and independent living (Dawson 1982; Friend 1987).

Crisis competence, gender role flexibility, and a broad family and community network can be helpful to aging lesbians. The literature that discusses these supports seems to assume that the women had a homosexual lifestyle at least since adolescence. It does not address the women who initially participate in homosexual relationships in their later years. These women often have been married and have grown children. They may turn to other women for emotional and sexual gratification after the death of their spouse, partly because of the lack of men. These homosexual experiences may cause ambivalence, depression, uncertainty, and shame. These consequences often exacerbate the normal crisis and tasks of the later life stages.

Economics and Aging Women

Socialization

The lifelong socialization encouraged by church, state, school, and family for passive, dependent female roles in marriage make women particularly vulnerable in old age when they may be alone. Traditionally, their role in marriage has been characterized by economic, social, and psychological dependency. Many accepted the societal norm of women as caretakers—wives, mothers, accountants, homemakers, unpaid family physicians, and assistants—who did not enter the world of work outside the home. Most women and men do not anticipate that women may spend years alone as widows or that women may have to function independently. The years they may have devoted to being wives, mothers, homemakers and the skills they have developed have been given low economic value in American society. Even among the never married and long-term divorced women, society reinforces a dependent role (Hooyman & Kiyak 1996; *Older Women* 1981).

Economic Dependency

Significant differences between aging women and aging men indicate a need for special attention to the particular situations in which so many aging women live. Women tend to be poorer and have fewer financial resources with which to support themselves in their later years. The low incomes of aging women are largely associated with a pattern of life-long economic dependence on men and with status changes that occur with old age (AARP 1988). The median income of aging persons in 1997 was $17,768 for males and $10,062 for females. Aging women in every age group were substantially more likely to be poor than men at the same age. Overall, only about 7 percent of the men sixty-five and older were poor compared to 13 percent of the women in 1997 (AARP 1998). The oldest women were the poorest. While women accounted for more than half (58.4 percent) of the elderly population in 1997, they accounted for nearly three-quarters of the elderly poor (AARP 1998).

The phrase "feminization of poverty" is also associated with aging women. Consider the following facts (AARP 1998; Administration on Aging 1998):

■ aging women have a higher poverty rate than aging men (13 percent vs 7 percent);
■ nearly three-fourths of the elderly poor are women;
■ women (22 percent) are half as likely as men (49 percent) to receive a pension and those who do receive a pension get half as much as men;
■ aging women living alone are at the greatest risk of poverty;
■ most women living alone have Social Security as their sole source of income;
■ women are the vast majority (74 percent) of aging recipients of Supplemental Security Income (SSI);
■ for elderly women, avoiding poverty is primarily associated with living in a married-couple household;
■ the situation for aging women of color is more bleak. Among aging women living alone, three-fifths of African Americans and two-fifths of Latinos live in poverty;
■ the sharp contrast between race and sex groups can be seen most easily when all aging Caucasian men are compared with all aging African American women; 39 percent of African American women lived in poverty while only 9 percent of Caucasian men of this age group were poor in 1989 (U.S. Bureau of the Census 1996).

Economic Insecurity

Economic security is essential for the well-being of every aging person. It is important to understand the causes of economic deprivation experienced by so many aging women. Discussed in the following section are factors that have determined the economic status of many aging women in America.

LIMITED EMPLOYMENT OPPORTUNITIES

Although mature women, aged forty-five to sixty-four, are participating more substantially in the work force, their occupational distribution is one of over-representation among part-time workers and concentration in low paying occupations and lower status jobs. Women over the age of fifty-four are disproportionately employed part-time or seeking part-time work. This is attributed to their inability to secure full-time work rather than a preference for part-time employment.

PAY INEQUITY

Historically and currently, in America, as in other countries, women's wages are less than men's despite the Equal Pay Act of 1963 and the Civil Rights Act of 1964. The focus of this legislation was ending the discrimination in employment based on sex, race, and national origin. Most women work out of economic necessity, yet Caucasian women earn about seventy cents for every dollar earned by Caucasian men. Minority women fare the worst. The wage disparity increases with age and education level. While Caucasian men's earning potential increases with age, women's earning potential stagnates and even declines in later years. Since women live longer than men and often have longer work careers, the wage discrimination is a crucial issue for aging women (AARP 1993; *Elimination of Sex and Race-Based Wage Discrimination* 1987; Kiyak & Hooyman, 1999).

Aging women are often victims of a particular synthesis of sexist, racist, and ageist prejudice in the labor market. They find employers unwilling to credit previous work experience and activities while out of the work force. Unwarranted assumptions of reduced trainability and productivity are often used to exclude the aging woman from jobs.

The economic status of aging women is a problem for which there are few easy answers. Policy makers in the public and private sectors are continuing to review alternative plans to reduce the economic deprivation experienced by so many aging women. Social workers will continue to face obstacles in assisting aging female clients to achieve economic security. Advocacy on their behalf should clearly be a priority in all forums of decision making, such as legislature and advocacy groups.

MARITAL DISSOLUTION

The problems of income maintenance among survivors of deceased workers or among divorced spouses affect primarily women since they tend to live longer, do not remarry as frequently, and have traditionally been in roles of economic dependency. For *widows*, the economic consequences may be as follows:

- Income from the husband's employment upon which the wife may be dependent is lost.
- The financial resources of the couple may have been greatly diminished or totally exhausted by the high costs of the husband's final illness and death. The total average death benefit left by husbands to widows is only $12,000, which includes all income from life insurance and Social Security and perhaps veteran's pensions. Fifty-two percent of all widows will have used up all available insurance benefits within eighteen months, and 25 percent have exhausted this resource within two months. Twenty-five percent of widows never receive all of their husband's benefits usually because they lack information to get access of these benefits. Social Security and benefit pensions may be inadequate or unavailable (Bound, Duncan, Laren, & Oleinick 1991; *Older Women* 1981; Tracy & Ozawa 1995).

For women who are *divorced* at mid-life or later, there are also economic consequences which may determine the quality of their remaining years:

■ Usually the husband has the highest and often the only income. When divorce occurs, that income is removed and child care and alimony payments are usually only a small part of the husband's income. Divorce and loss of the husband's income is a major cause of the movement of wives and children from middle class or lower class into poverty (Administration on Aging 1998).

■ Contrary to popular mythology, there are only a few wealthy divorcees. Most divorced women are thrown upon their own resources not only to support themselves but their children. Thus, they may be handicapped by limited employment opportunities, low wages, and the high costs of child-rearing in meeting current expenses and in building up economic security for their later years.

■ Provisions for payment of Social Security and pension benefits to divorced wives are limited.

■ Other benefits such as health insurance may be lost upon the termination of a marriage. Aging divorced women may have difficulty in securing alternative health coverage before they are eligible for Medicare at age sixty-five. In no-fault divorce cases, the assumption is that the woman can find employment and support herself, but the older a woman is and the longer she has remained out of the paid labor force, the more difficult is her search to find satisfactory employment (*Older Women* 1981).

PROBLEMS WITH SOCIAL SECURITY

The Social Security system does not cover everyone in the system equally. Someone who has been solely a homemaker or both an unpaid homemaker and a paid worker does not receive as good coverage as a person who has had a long-term and consistent employment pattern. Retirement benefits are based on average earnings over a lifetime. At the current time, benefits are averaged over a thirty-five-year period. This long averaging period results in lower average earnings for women compared to men because married women typically spend time out of the work force in homemaking and child care activities (Hardy & Hardy 1991).

A widow's benefits from Social Security is related to the standard of living that existed at the time of her husband's death rather than the standard of living at the time she went on the benefit rolls. Her benefits are based on his earnings index up to the year of his death. These benefits may be worth substantially less by the time the widow is eligible to receive them at age sixty-two.

A divorced woman's benefits under Social Security are usually 50 percent of the former husband's benefit. This amount may be inadequate for a person living alone since the spouse's benefit was intended as a supplement for a married couple. A divorced homemaker cannot receive a divorced spouse's benefit until the divorced husband reaches age sixty-two and retires. If he elects to continue working, she is ineligible for benefits until he retires. If she was married for less than ten years, she has no entitlement to her ex-spouse's benefits.

A major equity issue is the relative worth of Social Security benefits given to a dependent spouse who receives benefits through her husband's employment, and the benefits awarded to spouses who have themselves earned benefits, as a paid employee. The system clearly favors women who have remained at home and couples who have earned an income from the husband's work alone rather than when both spouses worked. The protection that an aging woman receives based on the years she was a paid worker cannot be added to the protection based on the years she was an unpaid homemaker. As a result, a previously employed woman may get no or only slightly higher benefits than she would have received as a dependent who had never worked. The money she personally pays into the system as a result of her own employment is not returned to her in benefits (Tracy & Ozawa, 1995; OWL 1999).

LIMITED ACCESS TO PENSIONS

In terms of pensions, less than half of the private sector is presently covered by an employee-sponsored pension plan; however, women are affected disproportionately. Aging women are only about half as likely as aging men to be covered by a pension plan, and those covered receive smaller benefits than aging men (Administration on Aging 1998). The different working patterns of men and women are reflected in the pension system because a large number of women work in retail or service industries which typically provide low pension coverage. Moreover, women often interrupt their careers for family obligations, and they are usually paid less than men, a situation which affects their pension checks.

Many women depend on their husband's pension to help see them through retirement. But what happens to the pension if the husband dies first? In many cases, the surviving spouse will receive no benefits even if her husband worked twenty or thirty years for the same company. For example, in a single life annuity arrangement that many companies use as a pension, payments will cease when the husband dies. If the husband has chosen a joint and survivor annuity, the monthly payment generally will be reduced, but the company will continue to pay after the death of either husband or wife. Many women whose husbands retired before the 1984 Retirement Equity Act did not learn until after the funeral that their husbands gambled on a higher benefit single life option, leaving their widows with no benefits at all (*Richmond Times-Dispatch*, May 13, 1984; Schwenk 1992).

Housing

Home ownership is one of the American dreams. While it can be an asset for some, it becomes a serious liability for some elderly persons, especially women living alone. Some facts about housing for the elderly are listed below with gender differences highlighted whenever possible.

- A majority of elderly men and women who were heads of households in 1995 owned their homes (78 percent owners, 22 percent renters) (AARP 1998).
- About 80 percent of aging homeowners in 1995 owned their homes free and clear (AARP 1997).
- Homes of elderly women living alone tend to be older and of lower market value than of elderly men or elderly couples (AARP 1998).
- Housing costs of older women living alone are a greater portion of their resources than for aging men or married couples (AARP 1998).

With fixed or diminishing incomes and the steadily rising costs of owning and renting, many aging persons, especially women, face "shelter poverty." "Shelter poverty" occurs when the costs of housing and fuel result in insufficient funds for other basic needs such as food and clothing. In almost 2 million households, total shelter costs comprise 85 percent of the total budget. Shelter poverty is even more likely among African American and Hispanic women, who are almost twice as likely to rent as are all other elderly (AARP 1998).

The housing situation combined with other factors can result in other problems for aging women. As mentioned earlier, aging women are more likely to live alone and have more chronic ailments than aging men. These women are often fearful of crime and react by restricting their activities so that they do not venture out to get needed medical and social services. In addition, a shortage of home- and community-based services to assist aging persons to live independently aggravates the problems these women face and can result in the need for institutionalization and long-term care.

Labor Force Participation

Possibly the greatest social change of the twentieth century has been the influx of women into the work force. The movement of women out of the home was a progressive rather than a sudden change and reflected differential patterns by age. It began about the turn of the century but has increased at a faster pace since World War II (Beckett 1982; Evans 1987). Aging women spearheaded the addition of the work role outside of the home. Their primacy reflects public attitudes about the activity of women as much as anything else. Attitudes about women working shifted first for aging women because they generally did not have young children; thus it was thought their home responsibilities would not be too adversely affected. In 1913, only 10 percent of all forty-year-old women worked compared to approximately 50 percent in 1987 (Licht 1988). During the postwar period the labor force rate of women fifty to fifty-four escalated from about 30 percent in 1950 to 50 percent in 1960 to almost 70 percent in 1990 (Gottlieb 1995; U.S. Bureau of the Census 1996).

Some aging women have worked for pay throughout their lives. Women with this employment pattern are more likely to be single, African American, and/or from working-class families. Urban African American women are the only group of married women who often have a high lifetime work rate. These women were excused from the prevalent attitude that a wife's place was in the home. African American women responded by eagerly taking the opportunity to work, usually in low paid service jobs, to help their family survive economically and to provide for their children's education (Beckett 1982; Evans 1987).

Aging women who wish to enter or reenter the work force meet formidable barriers. New and continuing family responsibilities, lack of documented employment experience, and disrupted work histories prevent many, especially the recently separated, divorced, and widowed, from securing employment outside the home (Benokraitis 1987; OWL 1998).

The movement of women into the work force is remarkable when one considers the discrimination they have had and continue to face. In addition to sex discrimination in employment, many women also face discrimination due to race, class, sexual orientation, or disability. When they reach middle age, the discrimination women face throughout their lives is compounded by age discrimination. Despite the fact that aging women are reliable workers with low turnover and low absentee rates, and laws that prohibit age and gender discrimination, differential treatment persists for aging women (Hatch 1990; OWL 1998).

Employment

- Middle-aged women (fifty-five to sixty-four) are entering the world of work in record numbers (OWL 1998).
- Middle-aged women (fifty-five to sixty-four) show a stronger preference than men to continue working even if they can afford to retire. In addition, many women in this age group who are not in paid employment regret their situation.
- About 4 million aging Americans (sixty-five and over) were in the labor force in 1997; they comprised 3 percent of the labor force. Forty percent were women (AARP 1998).
- Labor force participation of aging men decreased steadily until 1985 and stabilized—66 percent in 1900, compared with 16 percent since 1985. The rate for aging women has fluctuated (from approximately 8 percent in 1900 to 10 percent in the 1950s to 8 percent since 1988 (AARP 1997).
- Women accounted for 40 percent of the older (sixty-five plus) workers in 1993 (U.S. Bureau of the Census 1996).

Part-Time Employment

- Aging men and women are more likely than younger persons to work part-time. Yet, regardless of age, women are more likely to work part-time than men. In 1995, 51 percent of men and 63 percent of women worked part-time (AARP 1998).
- Among women, unemployment is higher for African Americans and Hispanics than among Caucasians; it is also higher for persons with less education (U.S. Bureau of the Census, 1996).
- Compared to younger people, aging male and female workers stay unemployed longer periods, are more likely not to find reemployment, and earn less in subsequent jobs (Beckett 1988; Stein, Doress, & Fillmore, 1987; U.S. Bureau of Census 1996).

Out of the Labor Force

- "Displaced homemakers" are a growing concern among aging women. This label describes women in their middle and older years who must support themselves for the first time because of separation, divorce, or widowhood. They often have no skills (Benokraitis 1987; Stein et al. 1987; Hooyman & Kiyak 1996).
- Almost one-third of aging women leave the labor force entirely by taking early retirement, despite the permanent reduction in Social Security benefits that results from retirement prior to age sixty-five (Tracy & Ozawa 1995).
- Family responsibilities are the primary reason women give who remain outside the paid work force or who prematurely leave their jobs. Aging workers, especially women, are concentrated in declining industries, such as manufacturing and textiles, which puts them at higher risk for job displacement (AARP 1998). In contrast, the nonworking men indicated ill health, retirement or no desire to work as their primary reasons (Gardner 1995; Shank 1988).

Health

Physical Health

The majority of aging women live active, healthy lives. Despite the gender differences in mortality rates, women die from the same primary causes as men: heart attacks, cancers, strokes, and respiratory disorders (AARP 1998). There are, however, gender differences in the incidence and severity of illness. Aging women experience higher rates of potentially disabling illness, such as arthritis, osteoporosis, hypertension, and diabetes. Women are more likely than men to have mobility problems, to be disabled, to be bedfast, and to be unable to perform essential self-care tasks. Because of the longer life expectancy, women often have to cope longer with chronic illness than do men (Guralnik et al. 1997; Hooyman & Kiyak 1996; Jan & Stoddard 1999).

These situations suggest that women's longevity brings risk of serious impairments in functioning and ability to perform the tasks of daily life. It is important to note that elderly women who face severe health problems are usually much older than elderly men. Men have health problems at an earlier age than women and are unlikely to reach the advanced age at which many women begin to have serious health problems. In addition, women are more likely than men to receive and comply with outpatient medical care when ill; for example, hypertensive women were twice as likely as men to be on medication (Jan & Stoddard 1998).

Income is an important determinant of a woman's health status as well as the quality of the health care she receives. Coverage by Medicare is no guarantee that aging women will receive quality health care. Their lower incomes mean they spend more of their disposable incomes than men on out-of-pocket expenses. Health care costs often push them into poverty. This is particularly severe since women have a higher risk of chronic diseases and disabling conditions than men, which ultimately may require long-term care, an expensive medical service. Thus women may not have the financial means for good health care. Not only does women's health care status differ from men's, their medical treatment for the same medical problems also differs. The Older Women's League (1999) reports a study that looked at a range of medical problems treated in acute care hospitals and found that women are less likely than men to receive a major diagnostic procedure. Women were also less likely to get major therapeutic procedures for thirty-two of sixty-two conditions. This shows that even though aging men and women have Medicare, physicians prescribe more diagnostic and therapeutic care for men in hospitals. This may be partly because men are more likely than aging women to have supplemented health insurance. Other findings indicate the explanation is more complex. For example, women are treated less aggressively than men after a heart attack; women are less likely than men to receive life-saving drugs for heart attacks; women are less likely than men to be included in clinical trials of heart attack treatment; and women are more likely than men to die in the hospital following a heart attack (AHCPR 1998).

Because of their incidence of chronic and disabling conditions, behavioral changes such as exercise programs, the use of assistive technology and prevention, screening and early testing are critical to aging women's health. For example 75 percent of those with breast cancer are fifty or over (Women and Aging Letter 1997). Yet two-thirds do not take advantage of mammograms and other preventive services for reasons such as cost, fear, belief that such services are not essential, or lack of referral by their physician (AOA, *Older Women* 1998). The type of physician turns out to be a critical factor in referrals. Aging women who have internists instead of obstetricians/gynecologists or family physicians receive more referrals to specialists and ancillary services, and spend substantially more on outpatient care (OWL 1999).

Insufficient income has several additional effects:

- Daily stress level is increased as one attempts to get basic needs met.
- The likelihood of sufficient exercise is reduced. Exercise can decrease stress levels and prevent physical and mental health problems. Many live in neighborhoods where they do not feel safe on the streets and have no access to indoor exercise facilities. Exercise also improves cardiovascular fitness and assists in monitoring weight, lowering the risk for disability (Taunton et al. 1996; Tully & Snowdon 1995).
- Many middle age women have no health insurance benefits.
- For postmenopausal women, the health benefits of estrogen replacement therapy (ERT) can be enormous. ERT contributes to preventing osteoporotic fractures, reduces heart disease, decreases mortality, and may reduce the risk of Alzheimer's disease. These health benefits outweigh the risk of endometrial and breast cancers (Paganini-Hill 1995; Schiefeling 1996) for those aging women that have access to medical care.

The health status of aging women also differs by race. African American aging women have more health problems and poorer general health than Caucasian women (AARP 1998). Physicians prescribe fewer medical diagnostic and intervention procedures for African American aging women than for Caucasians (OWL 1999). The incidence and severity of health problems also varies by race. More Caucasian women than African American aging women have beast cancer, but African American women are more likely to die from the disease. The reasons for this difference may include diagnosis at a more advanced stage of the disease, lack of access to state-of-the-art intervention, or possibly a biological predisposition to more aggressive tumors (AHCPR 1988). The incidence of another disease, osteoporosis, increases dramatically with age but varies by race and ethnicity. Asian American and Caucasian women have similar prevalence rates, while African American women have a substantially lower incidence (Jans & Stoddard 1999).

Even though current and immediate-future cohorts of aging women may continue to have poorer health and encounter more barriers to quality health care than men, these disparities should decrease in the more distant future. As women pursue lifelong careers and have higher levels of education age, they will have greater access to their own insurance and retirement income. These women are more likely to carry their regular exercise programs into their aging years. Physical exercise, for example, may result in less disability from diseases such as depression, heart attacks, osteoporosis, and arthritis and enhance their strength and mobility. Physical activity, increased positive self-images, and greater economic and social independence may enable aging women to become more active in their health care and have additional years of healthful independence. Unfortunately, for poorer women and persons of color, many barriers to better health may remain without new social policies and advocacy.

Mental Health

Research demonstrates the existence of a strong association between increase in age and first hospital admission rates for the elderly, and suggests an increase of the incidence of psychosis with age, with the rates being higher for aging women (Van Os, Howard, Takei, & Murray 1995). Especially among the aging, there is a close relationship between mental health problems and physical health status. Psychological symptoms may be a result of a physical illness and/or side effects from over the counter or prescribed medications as well as environmental changes and losses. Aging persons are more likely than younger to receive psychoactive drugs for their psychological symptoms. These drugs are the most commonly used treatment for psychiatric problems. Prescribing psychoactive medication for the elderly can be problematic for several reasons (Kaplan & Sadock 1998):

- Many disorders of aging persons vary from their clinical manifestations, causes, and physiology in younger persons
- Many disorders of the aging do not match the categories in DSM-IV.
- Psychoactive drugs have adverse behavioral and cognitive effects.
- There is no standard dosage for aging people; each dose must be determined individually; prescribing drugs for the elderly is an art not a science.
- Medications used to treat physical problems such as heart and pulmonary disorders cause psychiatric side effects.
- Complicated dosage regimens exist for multiple symptoms and illnesses.
- The elderly often use multiple medications (polypharmacy).
- The dosage may need to be changed as the person ages.
- Psychoactive drugs may have a high addiction potential.
- Insufficient pharmacological knowledge exists among primary care physicians, since there is little or no formal training in this area and in the use of psychotrophics for the elderly.
- Physicians often do not explain side effects of drugs to patients; when side effects do occur, patients make their own decision about medication or see another physician who is not told about the previous medication.
- Lack of communication and coordination exists between mental health and medical personnel.

There are several gender differences among the elderly with mental health problems. Gender variations appear in diagnosis, treatment, prescribing psychotherapeutic drugs, and reaction to stress. The biases of the medical and mental health professions are often more of a factor in these distinctions than are the actual conditions of elderly men and women (Butler, Lewis, & Sunderland 1991). Some of the variations by gender are noted below:

- After age sixty-five, women have a lower risk than men for mental health problems.
- Woman are more likely than men to receive mental health services.
- Women receive mental health services for a longer period of time than men.
- Men are at least three times as likely to attempt and to succeed in suicide.
- Women are more likely than men to be given psychoactive drugs.

■ Females have a lower hospitalization rate in *county* and *state* mental health facilities than men; but when private facilities are also considered, women comprise the majority of all hospitalized mental health patients.

■ A majority of those undergoing electroshock therapy are women.

■ Aging women are more likely than men to lose their spouses and are better able than men to successfully work through the normal grief and depression.

The most common mental disorders of the aging are depressive disorders, cognitive disorders, phobias, and alcohol use disorders. Aging persons also have a high probability of suicide and drug-induced psychiatric symptoms (Kaplan & Sadock 1998). Women have a higher prevalence of depression and anxiety disorders and men have a higher rate of substance abuse and antisocial problems (Proctor and Stiffman 1998). Depression is a commonly observed disorder. Depression decreases with age in both men and women, so aging persons are less likely to have depression than younger persons. Nevertheless, some experience an episode of depression for the first time in later life. Aging persons with depression are more likely than younger persons to report memory problems and physical complaints rather than emotional symptoms such as sadness. Women are nearly twice as likely as men to develop depression, and they are more likely to seek help and develop better coping mechanisms (National Policy and Resource Center on Women and Aging 1998).

Psychosocial predictors of depression in aging women include sense of mastery, level of social support, and the level of religious commitment (Bienefeld 1997). Studies indicate that, in women, a relatively strong internal locus of control is predictive of depression, especially when accompanied by impairment in general cognitive functioning (Van den Henvel, Smits, Deeg, & Beekman 1996). The second predictor of depression, social support, indicates that loneliness has a major negative effect on both moral and overall well-being (Deimling & Harel 1984; Lee & Ishi-Kuntz 1988). With the statistical probability of women outliving their husbands, the possibility of loneliness and depression are serious realities facing aging women. Religiosity, the third predictor of depression, is important in that it provides sustaining spiritual support. It also involves the benefit of social support available through association with a religious establishment (Johnson & Mullins 1989). It is important to note that most women with depression receive inappropriate care or no care at all (AHCPR 1998). With the increasing growth of gerontology, gerontological social work, and geriatric psychiatry, more aging women should have appropriate treatment available. Aging persons are less likely than younger persons to use mental health services. Even among persons who use these services, aging individuals use them at a substantially lower rate. Burns & Taube (1990) report that about one-third of aging persons receive services from mental health professionals. Mental health service utilization also varies with gender and race. Women are more likely to see mental health professionals than men. African Americans diagnosed with mental health problems more frequently turn to their clergy, friends, and relatives for help. Even after discharge from a hospital for a psychiatric disorder, the aging turn to family, friends, and medical providers rather than mental health professionals (Proctor & Stiffman 1998).

Long-term Care

Women are more likely than men to use long-term care services and to use them for a longer period of time (AHCPR 1998). This is partly because women have more chronic and severe medical problems than men. The lack of family can be a prime factor as well. Almost all of the aging women in nursing homes, for example, have no spouse and nearly half have no close relatives (Hooyman 1986a, 1986b). This suggests that women are likely to use long-term care services for both social and medical reasons.

Although aging persons have more chronic illnesses than young people, most with long-term care needs live in the community. Families provide the care to an overwhelming majority (84 percent of men and 79 percent of the women) of the disabled elderly who reside in the community. Only 5 percent (about 1.4 million) of all elderly reside in institutions. The proportion in institutions increases with age; for example, 2 percent of those sixty-five to seventy-four, but 9 percent of those seventy-five and older are in institutions (AARP 1997). These institutions vary from homes for the elderly, which provide custodial care and general supervision, to skilled nursing facilities.

Most (70 percent) of the disabled institutionalized elderly are women; for those eighty-five-years-old and above, 80 percent are women (Hendricks & Hendricks 1986; Hooyman 1986a, 1986b, 1986c; *Older Women—The Economics of Aging* 1981). The lack of family can be a prime factor of institutionalization. Almost all (90 percent) elderly women in nursing homes have no spouse and almost half have no close relatives (Hooyman 1986a, 1986b; *Women and Aging Around the World* 1985). These characteristics suggest that women are more likely to be institutionalized for social and medical reasons.

Despite the fact that the majority of institutional care residents are women, little has been written in America about the qualitative differences in men's and women's experiences in these institutions. Some literature shows that women are given more types of medication than men but that male residents are more likely than female to be given drugs as "chemical restraints" or "chemical straightjackets" (Brink 1979; Glantz et al. 1983; Milliren 1977). Research in Great Britain indicates men and women in long-term facilities have a different profile: men enter at an earlier age, are in better health, and are more mobile; women are less satisfied with residential life and feel more lonely and less useful. Women in institutions have lost a role that most men do not have—the domestic, housekeeper, or caretaker role.

For both men and women, misuse of drugs in long-term care facilities is problematic. They are among the highest users of medication and are also the greatest victims of drug misuse. The average nursing home resident receives five to twelve different drugs per day. Doses are missed, multiple doses given, and drug interactions are all too often. Drugs are given to counteract the side effects of other medications. A resident may receive a medical order for two drugs, one that treats diarrhea and the other for constipation; or one that is a diuretic and another for incontinence. These problems are related to thirty thousand long-term care resident deaths a year (Brink 1979).

Another problem is that long-term care is expensive. In 1990 long-term care costs averaged $25,000, making it the fourth largest health care expenditure category (AHCPR 1998). Many (80 percent) elderly and their families mistakenly think Medicare and/or private supplements cover the cost. Less than 2 percent of the costs are paid by these benefits (*A Profile of Older Americans* 1998). To receive Medicaid, a benefit that does pay for some long-term care in institutions, a person must either be poor or reduced to poverty in the process of trying to pay for care.

The long-term care of the elderly in institutions is increasingly a women's industry but administered by males. Low income women are both residents and low wage caretakers-persons without much power. The management and administration, positions that command higher salaries, are usually done by younger men, however (Boston Women's Health Book Collective 1984; Hooyman 1986b; *Women and Aging Around the World* 1985).

Obstacles to Good Health Care

As aging women turn to the health care system, they face some special obstacles to good care.

INADEQUATE RESEARCH

Until recently, medical research paid little attention to the health concerns of older women. Aging women were excluded from most research until the 1970s. For example, women were not added to the well-known Baltimore longitudinal study until 1978.

An increase in health research on women occurred during the 1990s. Examples of the increased interest in women include research programs and dissemination of information concerning women's health issues. The Agency for Health Care Policy and Research (AHCPR) funds and reports on health conditions especially important to women and the quality of care they receive (1998). Jans and Stoddard (1999) have compiled health data on women from a number of sources and include a substantial amount concerning aging women. The Administration on Aging created a Web site in 1999 devoted to aging women. These and other recent works also show an appreciation for the diversity among aging women by looking at the affects of such things as income, race, ethnicity, and residence.

Medical research still pays little attention to other issues such as occupational health concerns. Since medical research has not consistently addressed many important health concerns of aging women, health care practitioners have inadequate information about diseases facing aging women and about the treatment and prevention of these medical and psychiatric problems.

PRACTITIONER ATTITUDES

Physicians and other health care staff share our culture's negative attitudes, myths, and stereotypes toward aging persons. Medical personnel, like the general public, are personally ambivalent and frightened by aging and death. This ageism is complicated by sexism. Medical staff more frequently dismiss aging women's complaints and problems as neurotic and/or imaginary than those made by men. As one nurse put it: when a man complains of dizziness, he gets a workup; an aging woman gets Valium (Boston Women's Health Book Collective 1984). Classism and racism are other factors. Poor and minority women are more likely to be subjected to the negative attitudes and behaviors. These practices are less blatant with women who have ample financial resources and who have private physicians.

LIMITS OF MEDICAL MODEL TO CHRONIC ILLNESS

Diseases of the elderly are more often chronic than acute; they develop slowly, without a marked crisis point, linger for extended periods, often involve a number of body functions, have no single cause, and no cure. These illnesses do not respond to the daring surgery or high technological interventions that medical staff are trained to prefer. Some treatment is boring and ordinary—diet, braces, physical therapy, aspirin, environmental changes—and often time consuming and expensive. These treatments seldom spark the interest of health care providers and often the elderly are not seen as worth the time, energy, and cost.

If practitioners begin to see and acknowledge the limitations of the medical model, other and better solutions may be found for women's health concerns. For example, as long as menopause is seen as a deficiency disease or an endocrinological disorder, surgery (hysterectomies) or drugs (estrogen or tranquilizers) seem like reasonable remedies. If, however, menopause is seen as a transition or a turning point on the way to a new life stage, other remedies—exercise, diet, or stress reduction—may be more appropriate. In addition, Medicare, Medicaid, and private insurances do not adequately cover chronic conditions unless they require institutionalization.

INAPPROPRIATE SOURCES OF CARE

Presently no single medical specialty specifically addresses the health problems of aging persons or aging women. Although there is growing interest in the area of geriatrics, there is also a debate as to whether geriatrics should be a medical specialty or integrated with other medical specialties. Internists, family practitioners, and primary care physicians who may be skilled in the medical problems of aging women and who have a positive attitude are the most appropriate physicians for aging women. There is a shortage of physicians, however, for these specialty areas as well as for psychiatry.

There is also an insufficient number of geriatric centers and clinics. Those that do exist are usually located in large urban medical centers and thus not available to many elderly who live in the inner city or remote rural areas. They may have limited hours; for example, the recently developed clinic at Medical College of Virginia in Richmond is available only one afternoon a week.

MISDIAGNOSIS

Health care persons tend to assign the physical and emotional problems of the elderly to either aging or senility. Treatable causes such as poor nutrition, physical malfunctions, grief, or side effects of medication are rarely considered. These practices result in failure to treat reversible conditions or inappropriate treatment, such as tranquilizers, sedatives, antidepressants and hormones.

OVERPRESCRIPTION OF DRUGS

Many aging persons take several medications daily for multiple chronic conditions, often prescribed by different physicians. While the dosage may be technically correct, it may be inappropriate for several reasons. First, persons over sixty and women are more sensitive to many drugs and should take lower doses than younger persons and males. Second, the drug may have side effects such as depression and confusion. Third, drugs may interact with each other and cause additional health problems. Some medications are especially problematic for aging persons: reserpine, methyldopa, digitalis, procainamide, beta-blocking agents, all barbiturates, alcohol, and tranquilizers. Sharing a list of all medications with all physicians and coordination of health care can help alleviate these problems.

INSUFFICIENT ATTENTION TO PREVENTION

Treatment rather than prevention is usually the focus of health care. Thus, illnesses such as osteoporosis that are prevalent among women get little attention despite the fact that they are in great part preventable. For example, the following help to prevent osteoporosis: increased calcium intake, vitamin C and D supplements, increased exercise, not smoking, reducing the intake of alcohol, and refraining from the long-term use of steroid medications, such as corti-sone prescribed for diseases such as arthritis (AARP 1998). Attention to prevention should also focus on encouraging aging women to stay physically active and emotionally and cogni-tively involved in their surroundings, and to make independent decisions regarding their lives. Aging women should also be encouraged to maintain a support system of friends, become knowledgeable regarding finances, and seek professional help for physical and psychological problems (Jacobs 1994).

Transitions in Women's Lives: The Biopsychosocial Changes and Their Accumulative Effects

Aging is an inevitable part of the life cycle in which biological and physiological changes occur. The advance of age affects the brain and the nervous system, the immune system, the cardiovascular and respiratory systems, the senses, the reproductive system, changes in body composition, appearance, movement, and sleep patterns (Cavanaugh 1993; Fries 1989; Williams 1995). These changes have, in turn, a major effect on the psychological state of being. Social, environmental, and familial changes comprise another set of influential fac-tors to be considered.

For women, these physiological transitions are more dramatic. Many changes in the re-productive system that become manifest in advanced age actually start in middle age. The menopause and the loss of the ability to bear children are significant periods in women's lives. For women, the menopause is a symbol of the multiple mid-life issues they are facing (Jones 1994; Sheehy 1993), including the variety of physiological and psychological symp-toms due to decreases in hormonal levels. Common symptoms include hot flashes, chills, headaches, depression, dizziness, nervousness, and various aches and pains. Physical trans-formation as a result of aging has an especially hard impact on women because it is so visi-ble. For example, with advanced age, the body's basal metabolic rate slows down and is accompanied by a decrease in lean body tissue and an increase in fat. Wrinkles appear on the face and "aging spots" on the hands. Hair becomes thinner and grayer. Other changes may require the use of devices such as hearing aids, eyeglasses, pacemakers, canes, or walk-ers. These changes affect both appearance and body experience, perhaps resulting in lower self-esteem and a restriction of social interaction.

Although women experience such drastic physiological changes, it is important to note that there is no change in their desire to have sex (Strean 1993). While women with an av-erage age of 68.8 years revealed that the frequency of their sexual activity declined, their overall satisfaction with sex stays the same or increases with age (Cross & Drake 1993).

The Social, Environmental, and Familial Transitions in Women's Lives

The adult woman, along with her family, confronts major adaptational challenges in her life as she ages. Children leaving home, stress of her or husband's retirement, widowhood, grandparenthood, illness and dependency of an aging spouse or parent, adjustment to loss, and reorganization, are just some of the challenges.

Walsh (1980) identifies five major later life transitions and tasks that the aging woman faces. The first task involves "launching"; for families with children, this stage in the family life cycle starts when the last child leaves home. This transition is also termed the "empty nest" transition. The loss of the maternal role makes this passage especially crucial for women who identify their primary role as mothers. This stage presents the parents with the tasks of separating from their children and focusing on their marriage. This may affect the relationship between the couple and is especially stressful when an unsatisfying marriage exists.

The next task, retirement, is a major event in a woman's life, whether it is her own disengagement from the work world or that of her spouse. Retirement inevitably causes a reduction in income. Retirement may bring a loss of one's social network. In addition, long-established patterns of family interaction require adjustment. Daily routines require organization to reflect the increased time a retiree will spend at home and the qualitative and quantitative changes of marital interactions.

Another critical transition of aging is widowhood—losing a spouse is a common occurrence for older people. Women are four times as likely as men to become widows at an early age with many years of life yet ahead (Walsh 1980). For women who devoted their lives to caring for their children and husbands, accepting widowhood forces them to reevaluate themselves as individuals rather than a member of a couple. Means of deciding on financial matters are also altered as a result of entering widowhood. "Cycle into poverty" (Lewis 1997) is a risk middle-class women can face as widows, especially if their husbands suffered long, costly illnesses before their death.

A generally more rewarding life task is grandparenthood. For aging adults who have grandchildren, the experience of becoming a grandparent can be of great significance. It offers a variety of role possibilities and opportunities for meaningful interaction. Grandparents and grandchildren may enjoy a special bond that is not complicated by the responsibilities and conflicts inherent in the parent-child relationship (Walsh 1980). For women this period may be especially important, as it stimulates the reliving of earlier child-rearing experiences. However, in recent years, a growing number of grandparents have been forced to become the main caregivers for their grandchildren. The reasons for this lie in overwhelming problems that face the parents, such as succumbing to a prolonged illness like AIDS, drug addiction, divorce, and the financial constraints that accompany increased medical care.

The fifth later life transition is illness and dependency. Aging is accompanied by an increased incidence of disease and often by multiple age-related illnesses. Not surprisingly, illness is a prominent concern for most aging adults, especially for aging women who tend to live longer. Fear of losing physical and mental functioning, for contracting a chronic and painful ailment, and of slowly degenerating are common preoccupations, despite the fact that most elderly maintain good health care. Physical and mental deterioration may be exacerbated by depression and fears of loss of control (Walsh 1980), and as Rakowski, Fleishman, & Bryant (1993) demonstrate in their study, a high correlation exists between assessment of health and mortality among aging people. At this phase of life the risk of a spouse or a parent encountering health problems and subsequent dependency are high. This can have a serious effect on the aging woman, since the task of taking care of an ill spouse or parent is physically and emotionally draining.

There are also important modifying factors that affect physiological/biological and psychosocial well-being. Fries (1989) describes three basic aging principles that encourage applying the efforts of mind and body in aging. The first principle is maintaining independence. Independence and confidence are the foundation of preserving vitality. It is important for an adult to be able to make choices, avoid helplessness, make plans, and look

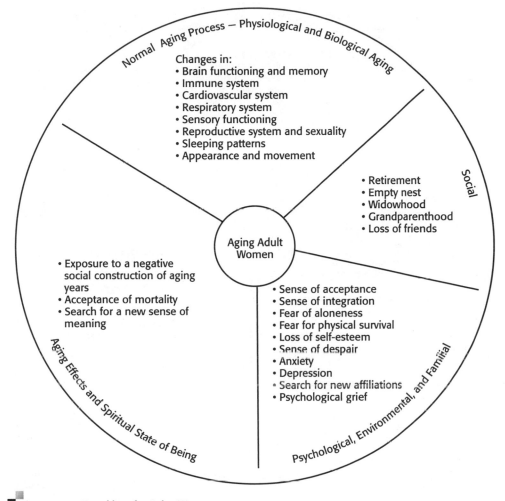

Normal Aging Process — Physiological and Biological Aging

Changes in:
• Brain functioning and memory
• Immune system
• Cardiovascular system
• Respiratory system
• Sensory functioning
• Reproductive system and sexuality
• Sleeping patterns
• Appearance and movement

Social

• Retirement
• Empty nest
• Widowhood
• Grandparenthood
• Loss of friends

Aging Adult Women

• Exposure to a negative
social construction of aging
years
• Acceptance of mortality
• Search for a new sense of
meaning

• Sense of acceptance
• Sense of integration
• Fear of aloneness
• Fear for physical survival
• Loss of self-esteem
• Sense of despair
• Anxiety
• Depression
• Search for new affiliations
• Psychological grief

Aging Effects and Spiritual State of Being

Psychological, Environmental, and Familial

■ **Figure 10.1**   Transitions for Aging Women

forward to the future. Johnson and Barer (1993) demonstrated that people age eighty-five or over were able to sustain a sense of well-being and maintain a sense of control despite physical and social losses.

"Moderate habits," the second principle, holds that healthy lifestyles are critical to maintaining good health. It is important to stop smoking, reduce alcohol consumption, and maintain adequate body weight. Data support the notion that a healthy diet prevents or delays the effects of aging and the onset of age-related diseases (Masor 1993; Undie & Friedman 1993; Williams 1995).

The third of Fries's principles involves the importance of keeping active. Exercise is central for good health. It tones the muscles, strengthens the bones, makes the heart and lungs work more efficiently, and helps increase vitality. Exercise eases depression and aids in maintaining good sleep patterns (Fries 1989; Williams 1995).

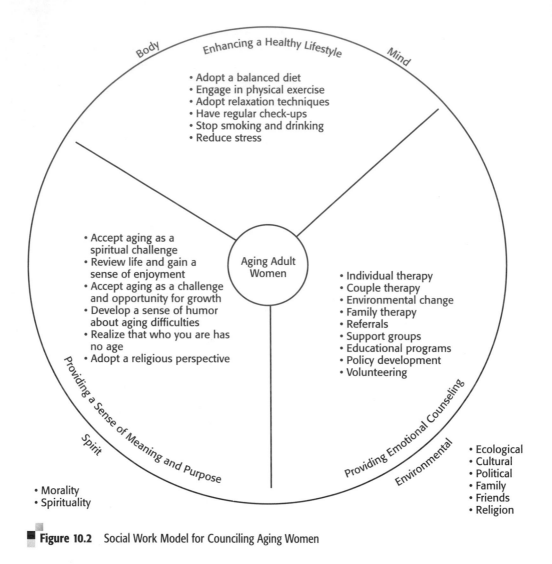

Figure 10.2 Social Work Model for Counciling Aging Women

Aging Women and the Social Worker's Role

Physical, social, and environmental changes all occur during the same period in an adult's life. As a result of their cumulative effects, many aging persons may feel overwhelmed by concerns with health, adaptation to physical deterioration, financial strains, changes in family situation, or the loss of a loved person and close friends. Social work intervention is oriented toward aiding the aging woman cope with or avoid emotional stress, become fulfilled, and gain a sense of empowerment. Mid-life and menopause can be a time of searching, transformation, and working on developmental tasks (McQuaide 1996). At this time of transitions and search for new meanings, social workers can be instrumental by providing guidance and facilitating the construction of a positive self-image (McQuaide 1996). Social workers can provide individual counseling and family therapy services, facilitate support groups, improve access to health care, initiate community services geared toward the unique needs of aging women, and provide referral services. An integrative model of intervention can modify the manner in which the aging person thinks, feels, and behaves. It is accomplished by providing emotional support, teaching coping skills, encouraging an internal sense of control, enhancing the capacity for problem solving, encouraging the right to make independent choices, and advocating a healthy lifestyle (Fries 1989; Pulliam, Plowfield, & Fuess 1996; Sherman 1981; Speroff 1996). The use of an integrative treatment model with the aging woman may result in improved morale and life satisfaction.

In addition to working with aging women on their psychosocial concerns, social workers can also act as advocates on behalf of their clients. Taking into account the financial risks that women are facing as they age and the possibility of inadequate health insurance, it is important for social workers to be actively involved in promoting policies that insure the well-being of aging women in this vulnerable stage of their lives.

The passage into older adulthood is a dynamic process that can be viewed as a period of change and growth, rather than the waning years of life. The social worker can advise the aging woman within the context of her genetic, biological, physiological, familial, sociocultural, and psychological uniqueness and recognize the active interrelationship and interconnectedness between the mind and the body.

Discussion Questions

1. Imagine you are in charge of the U.S. Department of Health and Human Services. How could information on gender differences in the elderly be useful to you? Describe one way you would use this information for policy development.
2. Discuss three demographic differences between aging men and women. How might each difference influence service delivery to aging persons?
3. Discuss two problems aging women face in securing physical and mental health services. What steps can be taken to overcome the problems?
4. Imagine you are the administrator of a multi-service agency. Plan a program that would be helpful to minority elderly women. What concerns would the program address? Why?
5. Do you think Social Security and other governmental benefits should be determined differently for women than men? Why?
6. Discuss two differences in the experiences in the aging lesbians and aging gays compared to heterosexuals of the same age cohorts. What significance do these differences have for the development of services targeted for homosexuals?
7. Divorce often has severe economic consequences for aging women. Explain how this social event is related to the economic status of aging women.

Experiential Learning

Activity: Clarifying Values—Old Versus Young

Values are very important factors in determining how each of us responds to other persons and situations. Self-awareness is a fundamental requirement for social work practice, particularly in regard to values. How would you respond to the specific situations listed below? What *criteria* do you use in responding to the circumstances? Are you *consistent* in your reasoning and logic? Are you more or less *comfortable* in the different situations? What values are present in each instance? Do you have one set of values for women and another for men? For young and for old?

How would you respond if:

1. _____ came to you and said she was contemplating marriage?
   a. Your twenty-one-year-old niece _____
   b. Your seventy-one-year-old grandmother _____
2. _____ told you he wanted to become a nurse?
   a. Your twenty-one-year-old nephew _____
   b. Your sixty-year-old uncle _____
3. _____ said she wanted to learn how to bowl?
   a. Your eighteen-year-old cousin _____
   b. Your eighty-year-old mother _____
4. _____ said she was joining an art class?
   a. Your sixteen-year-old sister _____
   b. Your seventy-three-year-old mother _____
5. _____ was planning to campaign actively for a presidential candidate?
   a. Your twenty-two-year-old niece _____
   b. Your seventy-five-year-old patient _____
6. _____ was going to start college after being out of school for years?
   a. Your thirty-year-old aunt _____
   b. Your sixty-year-old aunt _____
7. _____ wanted to set up a business?
   a. Your twenty-year-old client _____
   b. Your sixty-five-year-old client _____
8. _____ started coming home at two and three in the morning?
   a. Your twenty-one-year-old sister _____
   b. Your seventy-year-old grandmother _____
9. _____ wanted to buy an expensive computer?
   a. Your sixteen-year-old brother _____
   b. Your seventy-five-year-old grandmother
10. All _____ ever did for recreation was play cards?
    a. Your twenty-five-year-old cousin _____
    b. Your seventy-year-old aunt _____

Case Studies

See Appendix B for guidelines in analyzing gerontological social work practice.

Case 1: Mrs. Tish and Past Memories

It took us quite a while after Mrs. Tish's admission to understand that when she sat by the elevators, although blind, there was something in this situation that stimulated in her a desire to travel. It is not the usual kind of feeling that occurs in one of the residents when they become confused and dependent and want to accompany a departing volunteer or visitor. In these cases, the social worker can help by meeting the resident's need to be with somebody. After the visitor has departed, the social worker will tell the resident where she lives, what meal is next, and resettle her without any real difficulty.

However, Mrs. Tish's reaction was of panic and deep agitation. Although blind, Mrs. Tish hears well. She heard the elevator doors open and close and people coming and going. I was trying to picture what was making her so upset when she heard the sounds. When she said she wanted to get on "the train" and mentioned the name of a little town in Russia, I knew she had transported herself back in time to when she was a young girl sitting in a railroad station, waiting for a train. She seemed to be reliving the anxiety of having to get aboard despite all obstacles. We were not able to calm her by offering her reality information at that moment. We walked with her a long time until her agitation seemed to wear off and she was tired and ready to nap. I made sure when she awoke that she was told where she was and how long she had lived here. She would say, "Yes, I am an old woman now, and I do need help to put on my shoes." She would be back with us again.

We realized Mrs. Tish is a person who can slip easily into her past when the present is too confusing. When she is able to understand what is going on, she is clear about where she is and her present capabilities.

Now we do not take her to the elevators to sit and be with many other people to experience all the traffic and commotion, which triggers associations with which she cannot cope. We were wrong in thinking that everyone who is blind needed so much social stimulation. It might be right for some nonsighted people, but it was not right for Mrs. Tish. Now we seat her outside her room on the bench nearby, where the surroundings are simple for her to comprehend. She knows her bed, her table, and her clothing are nearby, and she is next door to Mrs. David. She recognizes the voices of the nurses who come by, and she talks with them while they are working.

Source: Adapted from Edelson, J. S. & Lyons, W. (1985). *Institutional care for the mentally impaired elderly.* New York: Van Nostrand.

Case 2: Confusion and Care

"Miss, Miss!" she beckoned to me. "Tell me, please, where am I?"

"Mrs. London," I said, "you are sitting outside your room, third floor of the Stuart Home for the Aged."

"What am I doing here?"

"You live here now, Mrs. London."

"I just woke up," she said "I don't know anything anymore. How long have I been here?"

"I think you and I have been here about the same length of time," I replied.

"How long is that?" she interrupted, looking at me more closely.

"About three and a half years."

"Do my children know that I am here?"

"Yes, your sons, Arthur and Joseph, come to visit you here, usually in the evening or on weekends."

"I think I am going crazy," she said with a heavy voice. "I can't remember anything."

"Mrs. London," I said, "there is nothing the matter with your ability to think very clearly." She seemed to be reflecting on what I had said.

"So," she replied, "I live here . . . So, what do you do here?"

"I work here. I work with the volunteers and the residents on the third floor."

"Do the nurses know me?"

"Yes, Mrs. London, they do know you, and they are here to help you. When you forget, they will help you."

"Do my children know I am here?" she asked again.

"They know," I said again, "and they visit you. Your sons who live in Beal City come to visit as often as they can. Your daughter Sarah lives out of town and she cannot come to Beal City very often."

"Are you sure?"

"Yes," I said. "Remember you used to live with Sarah and then you needed to have medical care and nurses to help you follow the doctor's instructions. The children and you decided that this was the best place to have people to look after you, and you came to live here at the Stuart Home for the Aged." She nodded.

I continued, "I can't remember the name of the university where Sarah's husband teaches, where you used to live. It is in the Midwest."

"Yes," she said, "I know where you mean, but my mind is like a cat; I can't remember the name either."

"That is why the nurses are here, Mrs. London, to help you remember other things you need to know and to help you do things you need to do."

"Thank you," she said. She pointed to a door. "That is my room?" I nodded. "Tell me," she asked, "what time is it?"

"It is 3:15 P.M. At 4:00 P.M., it will be time for supper and the nurse will come and invite you to eat."

"Well, I guess I could wait," she said, trying to make a joke. "I wouldn't starve. Thank you."

As I left her, I heard her calling to a nursing aide in the corridor in a characteristic fashion with which the staff is most familiar. "Nurse, nurse! When do they feed you here? I am hungry!"

Source: Adapted from Edelson & Lyons 1985.

Case 3: Decision Making and Long-term Care for Miss Perkins

Miss Perkins was a small, seemingly fragile woman who dressed in a stylish but dated fashion. She had been living in the same house for more than forty years. After the deaths of her two older, unmarried sisters who had shared the home with her, she continued to live alone. In spite of her many eccentricities, Miss Perkins was likable and personable. A well-to-do, socially prominent first cousin helped her financially, but took no sustained personal interest in Miss Perkins.

Spry and active all her life, Miss Perkins became increasingly anxious as she felt herself growing older and less steady on her feet. At the age of seventy-five, she reached out for help by applying for admission to a nearby nursing home. The idea of planning for the move was distasteful to her. The prospect of dismantling her beloved home, with its accumulated and cherished possessions of over half a century, was overwhelming and threatening to her.

Miss Perkins was quite lonely, had little money, and was undergoing tests for bleeding from the bowel. When the tests proved negative she decided not to enter the nursing home. Nevertheless, she was afraid to withdraw her application for fear she might need to be admitted at some future time. The social worker at the nursing home offered her deferred status. This meant that the nursing home encouraged her to remain in the community for as long as possible, that the social worker would be available to her when needed, and that she could be admitted if and when her circumstances required.

At intervals during the next few years, Miss Perkins' bowel problem would flare up; a flurry of phone calls and home visits would ensue and help to alleviate it. With each such incident Miss Perkins went through the process of conflict, doubt, hesitation, and indecision. She would review a number of alternatives and express her fears about group living— especially with people she didn't know. Repeatedly, the situation was resolved in favor of Miss Perkins staying in her own home a little longer. During this period the nursing home provided Miss Perkins with a variety of supportive services including telephone reassurance, friendly visiting, a hot lunch program, and transportation services whenever she needed to go to the doctor.

Miss Perkins was sustained by the knowledge that she could enter the nursing home if and when it became necessary. With the help of supportive services she remained in her own home for the next nine years, at which time she suffered a massive stroke and was immediately hospitalized. She died in the hospital less than three weeks later.

Source: Adapted from Beaver & Miller 1985.

Annotated Bibliography

Allen, J. & Pifer, A. (Eds.). (1993). *Women on the front lines: Meeting a challenge of an aging America.* Washington, DC: Urban Institute Press.

 A diverse series of essays and writings related to the experience of older women, organized through the Project on Women and Population Aging. Topics include the important social changes that accompany the growing number of aging women; the importance of addressing both pension and Social Security reform; and women as the connecting link across the generations.

Arber, S. & Ginn, J. (1995). *Connecting gender and ageing: A sociological approach.* Philadelphia, PA: Open University Press.

 This collection of theoretical and research articles examines social aspects of aging from a feminist perspective by focusing on the British and Canadian experience. In linking gender and aging, contributors base their ideas on the premise that gender roles are not static. They discuss this premise by examining the various experiences of men and women in both the public and private domains. The authors demonstrate the key point that aging women may develop a more "authentic" and fluid identity when no longer constrained by the generated role obligations within family and marriage.

Barusch, A. S. (1994). *Older women in poverty.* New York: Springer.

 This book is useful for the reader seeking knowledge of public policies' effects on the day-to-day lives of poor aging women. Barusch presents her findings from a nationwide study, and highlights the qualitative in-depth stories of seven diverse women. She discusses the relationship between poverty and self-concept, marriage, and caregiving. The author also reviews the major federal initiatives targeted to alleviate poverty and their relationship to the current status of aging women.

Burkhauser, R. V., Duncan, G. J., & Hauser, R. (1994). Sharing prosperity across age distribution: A comparison of the United States and Germany in the 1980s. *Gerontologist, 3*(2), 150–160.

Important articles in the Social Security debate, the authors' cross-national panel data shows that the economic growth of the 1980s was disproportionately allocated by age and gender. In both Germany and the United States, aging women remain the most vulnerable in society and in a much worse situation relative to older men.

Burkhauser, R. V. & Smeeding, T. M. (1994). *Policy brief No. 2. Social Security reform: A budget neutral approach to reducing older women's disproportionate risk of poverty*. Syracuse, NY: Syracuse University, Maxwell School Center for Policy Research.

This policy brief provides a readable summary of how aging women are vulnerable to poverty in spite of the successes of the Social Security system as a whole. The authors discuss important factors including the increased life expectancy of women and the decreased retirement age of men. They also offer policy solutions to this problem that do not involve large budgetary outlays.

Burton, L. M. (1996). Age norms, the timing of family role transitions, and intergenerational caregiving among African American women. *Gerontologist, 36*(2), 199–208.

Burton's article reports findings from two exploratory qualitative studies of the relationship between age norms, family role transitions, and the caregiving responsibilities of African American women. She found equitable distribution of caregiving responsibilities across the generations and discusses the implications for practice. This article is useful for building a knowledge base in women's issues related to ethnogeriatric practice.

Canetto, S. S., Kaminski, P. L., & Felicio, D. M. (1995). Typical and optimal aging in women and men: Is there a double standard? *International Journal of Aging and Human Development, 40*(3), 187–207.

The authors compared perceptions of aging among 232 young adults and 233 of their older relatives. They used nine assessment instruments to look at perceptions of typical aging and found that gender stereotypes were more important than aging stereotypes. For example, aging women were rated higher on the aspect of nurturance, while aging men rated higher on intellectual competence and independence. The authors attribute their findings to a double standard of aging.

Doress, P. & Siegel, D. (1987). *Ourselves growing older: Women aging with knowledge and power*. New York: Simon and Schuster.

Written by the authors of the popular book, *Our bodies: Ourselves*. Using a feminist perspective, it examines the neglected health and well-being concerns of middle-aged and aging women. One of the most in-depth and easy-to-read books on the topic. Divided into three sections: aging well; living with ourselves and others; and medical problems. While discussion of minorities of color are included, it would be easier for the reader if this material had been put together in one chapter. Nevertheless, this should be a required reading for all social workers. Written by and for women.

Dressel, P. L. (1988). Gender, race, and class: Beyond the feminization of poverty in later life. *The Gerontologist, 28*(2), 177–180.

The feminization of poverty has the potential for both limiting and distorting the issue of old-age poverty. Diversity contained within age groups and within gender groups must be acknowledged in order to facilitate a more complete understanding of poverty among the elderly and its policy implications.

Garner, J. D. & Mercer, S. O. (Eds.). (1989). *Women as they age: Challenge, opportunity, and triumph*. New York: Haworth Press.

Although published nearly a decade ago, this edited volume provides a solid framework of knowledge for the study of women and aging. It contains chapters on an international overview of aging women; multidisciplinary perspectives; special issues; and programs, policies and resources. The book is written by women, many of them social workers and feminists, in a style accessible to students, practitioners, administrators, and academics.

Gibson, D. (1996). Broken down by age and gender: "The problem of old women" redefined. *Gender and Society, 10*, 433–488.

In this theoretical article, the author reviews fundamental weaknesses in comparing the experience of aging women to that of men. According to Gibson, the use of a phallocentric approach undermines some of the positive aspects of women's process of aging. Gibson also outlines some of the uncharted areas of investigation of positive aspects of women and aging.

Goldburg, G. S., Kantrow, R., Kremen, E., & Lauter, L. (1986). Spouseless, childless elderly women and their social support. *Social Work, 31*(2), 104–112.

   A study of fifty-two spouseless, childless, elderly females living in a metropolitan area. The women included are never married, widowed, divorced, and separated individuals. Most of the women had developed substitute supports for the close kin they lacked. Implications for women who become less healthy are discussed along with the need to develop support from the younger generation.

Golub, S. & Freedman, R. J. (Eds.). (1985, Summer/Fall). Health needs of women as they age: Women and health. *Journal of Women's Health Care* (entire issue), 10 (2/3).

   The health needs of women as they age is the theme of this special double issue. Together, the ten articles provide an informative and thorough overview of the major problems that confront women beyond middle age, of how these health needs are being met, and of the problems that are not being adequately addressed by the medical care system. Problems such as osteoporosis, reproductive cancer, societal myths, negative stereotypes, psychological concerns of aging women, and issues relating to social policy are discussed. Together, the articles in this special issue emphasize the need for the health care delivery system to be prepared to meet the special health care needs of the aging woman.

Hess, B. (1985). Aging policies and old women: The hidden agenda. In A. S. Rossi (Ed.), *Gender and the life course* (pp. 319–331). New York: Aldine.

   Discusses the impact of social policies on aged women and effectively argues that public policy regarding the aged discriminates against women. Also discusses the gender differential impact of past and present policy in such areas as income maintenance, health care, and housing.

Jennings, J. (1987). Elderly parents as caregivers for adult dependent children. *Social Work, 32*(5), 430–433.

   Discusses some of the issues of a neglected group of caregivers (usually women) in our society—the elderly who are providing care rather than receiving it. Elderly caregiver parents of adult disabled children have similar concerns, when compared to other caregivers, including social isolation, lack of respite care, financial/economic needs, inadequate counseling and planning for the future of their dependents (adult disabled child). Research and practice implications are discussed.

Kahne, H. (1985–86). Not yet equal: Employment experience of older women and older men. *International Journal of Aging and Human Development, 22*(1), 1–13.

   Women aged forty-five and older make up almost 30 percent of the female civilian labor force and 40 percent of the labor force consisting of older, civilian workers.

MacDonald, B. & Rich, C. (1983). *Look me in the eye: Old women, aging, and ageism*. San Francisco, CA: Spinsters, Inc.

   This book contains a series of essays framed by the authors' experiences as older lesbian women. They write about topics important to them, including the stigma of old age, feminism and ageism, and women's issues from an international perspective.

Nolan, J. (1986). Developmental concerns and the health of midlife women. *Nursing Clinics of North America, 21*, 151–159.

   Reviews the literature of factors affecting the psychological health of middle-aged women. Topics considered include the impact of menopause, the empty nest syndrome, and the influence of work on mid-life women.

Porcino, J. (1983). *Growing older, getting better: A handbook for women in the second half of life*. Reading, MA: Addison-Wesley.

   Includes a discussion of many possible transitions for women forty years of age and older: grandparenthood, separation, divorce, widowhood, coping with aging parents, and securing employment. The second half ("Our changing bodies") discusses both normal developments, such as menopause, and common diseases (e.g., hypertension and various cancers). Well-researched and well-written, Porcino's work could be a text for a practicum on predictable transitions of aging, and also excellent bibliotherapy.

Sarton, M. (1973). *As we are now*. New York: Norton.

   In this novel, Sarton tells the moving story of Caro, a seventy-six-year-old retired school teacher who is placed in a nursing home by her brother. Caro enters a world of loneliness and despair, of brutality and humility, that she refers to as a "jail" and a "concentration camp for the old." Independent and intelligent, Caro is forced to confront what it is like to be stripped of her individuality. In the end, she takes control and rescues her dignity in the only way she sees possible.

Sheehy, G. (1991). *The silent passage*. New York: Simon and Schuster.

Sheehy shattered longstanding societal myths by presenting menopause as a beginning rather than as the end of womanhood. She equates the passage through menopause with a "second adulthood." Sheehy casts aside the stigma of menopause by viewing it as a normal passage, and by providing women with straightforward and reliable information. She also presents important information on hormone replacement therapy (HRT), hysterectomy, early menopause, African American women's experiences, and male menopause.

Sherman, S. R., Ward, R. A., & LaGory, M. (1988). Women as caregivers of the elderly: Instrumental and expressive support. *Social Work, 33*(2), 164–167.

Focused on two types of support provided by caregivers of the elderly: (1) instrumental, defined as tangible aid and service referral; and (2) expressive, defined as role models and confidants who provide a form of sharing. Interviews were conducted with a probability sample of 1,185 persons sixty years of age and older to determine the availability and gender of their caregivers. A majority reported having both instrumental and expressive support. Men were more likely than women to name their spouses as an instrumental helper; and the majority of caregivers and confidants named by the subjects were women. Implications for social workers of the predominance of women in support networks are outlined.

Shulman, S. C. (1985). Psychodynamic group therapy with older women. *Social Casework: The Journal of Contemporary Social Work, 66,*(10), 579–586.

Psycodynamically oriented groups can be a effective catalyst of growth for older patients. The discussion describes the first six years of an ongoing group for women, aged fifty-five to seventy, who were outpatients of a community mental health center. The formation of the group, the selection and orientation of its members, and the process that evolved are examined. Object relations theory is used to organize observations about the development of the group. Countertransference issues are discussed.

Siegenthaler, J. K. (1996). Poverty among single elderly women under different systems of old-age security: A comparative review. *Social Security Bulletin, 59*(3), 31–44.

Poverty among aging women who receive Social Security is an important issue, and this study assesses the pool of available comparative research on the topic from France, Germany, the Netherlands, Sweden, Switzerland, and the United States. In his assessment of the retirement benefit structures of these six Western industrialized countries, Siegenthaler critiques their effectiveness in preventing poverty.

Smith, J. P. (1997). *Policy brief No. 8. The changing economic circumstances of the elderly: Income, wealth and Social Security*. Syracuse, NY: Syracuse University Maxwell School Center for Policy Research.

This policy brief provides an excellent summary of current issues related to personal wealth of aging persons and Social Security reform. The author sheds light on the question of why the typical aging household has so little wealth and who are the "winners and losers" in the Social Security equation.

Turner, B. F. & Troll, L. E. (Eds.). (1994). *Women growing older: Psychological perspectives*. Thousand Oaks, CA: Sage.

This volume provides exemplars of current research as it pertains to the psychology of adult development and aging from the perspective of gender differences. The authors examine conceptual and theoretical developments germane to gerontological social work by focusing on social cognition, psychodynamic, and life span perspectives of women and aging.

United Nations. (1995). *Bulletin on Aging* (Nos. 2 & 3). New York: United Nations Secretariat.

A useful resource for those interested in women and aging from an international perspective, this special double issue of the *Bulletin on Aging,* published by the UN Programme on Ageing, is a follow-up to the 1995 Fourth World Conference on Women. The overview looks at global concerns such as widowhood, income security in old age, caregiving, and employment and women's contribution to the world economy. The bulletin also includes an article on the status of women in Asia and the Caribbean.

General Bibliography

Ahern, K. D. (1996). *The older woman: The able self.* New York: Garland.

Allen, K. R. & Chin-Sang, V. (1990). A lifetime of work: The context and meanings of leisure for aging Black women. *Gerontologist, 30,* 734–740.

Almvig, C. (1982). *The invisible minority: Aging and lesbianism.* New York: Utica College of Syracuse University Press.

Barker, J. C., Morrow, J., & Mitteness, L. S. (1998). Gender, informal social support networks, and elderly urban African Americans. *Journal of Aging Studies, 12,* 199–222.

Belgrave, L. L. (1989). Understanding women's retirement. *Generations, 13*(2) 49–52.

Butler, R. N., Lewis, M. L., & Sunderland, T. (1998). *Aging and mental health: Positive psychosocial and biomedical approaches* (5th ed.). Boston: Allyn and Bacon.

Calasanti, T. M. (1992). Theorizing about gender and aging: Beginning with the voices of women. *Gerontologist, 32,* 280–282.

Choi, N. G. (1996a). Older persons who move: Reasons and health consequences. *Journal of Applied Gerontology, 15*(3), 325–344.

Choi, N. G. (1996b). The never-married and divorced elderly: Comparison of economic and health status, social support, and living arrangement. *Journal of Gerontological Social Work, 26*(1–2), 3–25.

Coyle, J. M. (1997). *Handbook on women and aging.* Westport, CT: Greenwood Press.

Davis, N. D. (Ed.). (1993). *Faces of women and aging.* New York: Haworth Press.

Dressel, P., Minkler, M., & Yen, I. (1997). Gender, race, class and aging: Advances and opportunities. *International Journal of Health Services, 27,* 579–600.

Eckert, J. W. & Shulman, S. C. (1996). Daughters caring for their aging mothers: A midlife developmental process. *Journal of Gerontological Social Work, 25*(3/4), 17–32.

Essex, M. J. & Nam, S. (1987). Marital status and loneliness among older women: The differential importance of close family and friends. *Journal of Marriage and the Family, 49,* 93–106.

Faulkner, A. O. & Micchelli, M. (1988). The aging, the aged, and the very old: Women the policymakers forgot. *Women and Health, 14*(3/4), 5–19.

Fingerman, K. L. (1995). Aging mothers and their adult daughters' perspectives on conflict behaviors. *Psychology of Aging, 10,* 639–649.

Fulani, L. (Ed.). (1988). *The politics of race and gender in therapy.* New York: Haworth Press.

Furman, F. K. (1997). *Facing the mirror: Older women and beauty shop culture.* New York: Rutledge.

Garner, D. & Mercer, S. (Eds.). (1989). *Women as they age.* New York: Haworth Press.

Gass, K. (1987). Health of conjugally bereaved older widows: The role of appraisal, coping and resources. *Research in Nursing and Health. 10,* 39–47.

Gibson, M. J. (Ed.). (1987). *Income security and long term care for women in midlife and beyond.* Washington, DC: American Association of Retired Persons.

Ginn, J. (1998). Older women in Europe: East follows west in the feminization of poverty. *Ageing International, 24,* 121–122.

Gist, Y. J. & Velkoff, V. A. (1997). Gender and aging: Demographic dimesions. U.S. Bureau of the Census, International Programs Center, International Brief, IB/97/3.[on-line] att http://www.cencusgov/ipc/prod/ib-9703.pdf/

Goldberg, G., Kantrow, R., & Kremen, E. (1986). Elderly women and their social supports. *Social Work, 31,* 104–112.

Golub, S. & Freedman, R. (Eds.). (1985). *Health needs of women as they age.* New York: Haworth Press.

Gonyea, J. G. (1994). The paradox of the advantaged elder and the feminization of poverty. *Social Work, 39*(1), 35–41.

Grau, L. (Ed.). (1989). *Women in the later years.* New York: Haworth Press.

Hardy, M. A. (1993). The gender of poverty in an aging population. *Research on Aging, 15,* 243–278.

Harris, M. B. (1994). Growing old gracefully: Age concealment and gender. *Journals of Gerontology, 49,* 149–158.

Hartman, A. (1990). Aging as a feminist issue. *Social Work, 35,* 387–388.

Haug, M., Ford, A., & Sheafor, M. (1985). *Physical and mental health of aged women.* New York: Springer.

Hoeffer, B. (1987). Predictors of life outlook of older single women. *Research in Nursing and Health, 10,* 111–117.

Hooyman, N. R. (1999). Research on older women: Where is feminism? *The Gerontologist, 39,* 115–118.

Hong, J. & Seltzer, M. M. (1995). The psychological consequences of multiple roles: The non-formative case. *Journal of Health and Social Behavior, 36*(4), 386–398.

Hopper, S. V. (1993). The influence of ethnicity on the health of older women. *Clinics in Geriatric Medicine, 9*(1), 231–259.

International Social Security Association. (1998). The social security protection of older women: The hidden issue of the end of the century. *Ageing International, 24,* 49–61.

Lesnoff-Caravaglia, G. (Ed.). (1984). *The world of the older woman.* New York: Human Sciences Press.

Magaziner, J., Cadigan, D., Hebel, R., & Parry, R. (1988). Health and living arrangements among older women: Does living alone increase the risk of illness? *Journal of Gerontology, 43,* 127–133.

Mantecon, V. H. (1993). Where are the archetypes? Searching for symbols of women's midlife passage. Special Issue: Faces of women and aging. *Women and Therapy, 14*(1-2), 77–88.

Markson, E. W. (1995). Issues affecting older women. In L. A. Bond, S. J. Cutler, & A. Grams (Eds.), *Promoting successful and productive aging* (pp. 161–278). Thousand Oaks, CA: Sage.

McDougall, G. J. (1993). Therapeutic issues with gay and lesbian elders. Special Issue. The forgotten aged: Ethnic, psychiatric and societal minorities. *Clinical Gerontologist, 14*(1), 45–57.

Miller, J. (1986). *Toward a new psychology of women* (rev. ed.). New York: Harper Row.

Minkler, M. & Stone, R. (1985). The feminization of poverty and older women. *The Gerontologist, 25,* 351–357.

Mutchler, J. E. (1990). Household composition among the nonmarried elderly: A comparison of black and white women. *Research on Aging, 12,* 487–506.

Perkins, K. (1992). Psychosocial implications of women and retirement. *Social Work, 37*(6), 526–532.

Ramsey, J. L. & Blieszner, R. (1999). *Spiritual resiliency in older women.* Thousand Oaks, CA: Sage Publications.

Seymour, J. & Wattis, J. P. (1992). Alcohol abuse in the elderly. *Reviews in Clinical Gerontology, 2*(2), 141–150.

Sharpe, P. A. (1995). Older women and health services: Moving from ageism to empowerment. *Women and Health, 22*(3), 9–23.

Slevin, K. F. & Wingrove, C. R. (1998). *From stumbling blocks to stepping stones: The life experiences of fifty professional African-American women.* New York: New York University Press.

Social Security Administration. Office of Policy. (1998). Women and retirement security. [on-line] at http://www.ssa.gov/statistics/incpop55toc.html/

Souder, E. (1993). Alzheimer's disease and older women. *Journal of Women and Aging, 5*(3/4), 139–154.

Stevens, N. (1995). Gender and adaptation to widowhood in later life. *Ageing and Society, 15*(1), 37–58.

Verbrugge, L. & Madans, J. (1985). Social roles and health trends in American women. *Milbank Memorial Fund Quarterly: Health and Society, 63,* 691–735.

Warlick, J. (1985). Why is poverty after 65 a woman's problem? *Journal of Gerontology, 40,* 751–757.

Wolf, D. A. (1990). Household patterns of older women: Some international comparisons. *Research on Aging, 12,* 463–486.

Wu, Z. & Pollard, M. S. (1998). Social support among unmarried childless elderly persons. *Journal of Gerontology: Social Sciences, 55B,* S324–S335.

Yee, D. L. & Capitman, J. A. (1996). Health care access, health promotion, and older women of color. *Journal of Health Care for the Poor and Underserved, 7*(3), 252–272.

Feature-Length Films about Aging Women (Available on Video)

Antonia's Line (1996). After the end of World War II, a middle-aged woman returns to her home in Holland after being away for twenty years. She soon begins to restore "community" to the morally bankrupt village and its embedded patriarchy. She becomes the matriarch, resolving crises, rooting out evil, and drawing people to her through dinners served at her long family table.

Central Station (1998). A retired schoolteacher writes letters for the illiterate at the central rail station in Rio de Janeiro, Brazil. She befriends an orphaned boy and they go searching for his father in the interior of the country. Their journey becomes an emotional pilgrimage and the intergenerational relationship between them is compelling.

Driving Miss Daisy (1989). A wealthy widow is compelled to hire a chauffeur when her son realizes that she should not drive a car anymore. After initial hostility toward the African American chauffeur, she warms to his presence and he becomes an integral part of her life. After twenty-five years, she declares him to be her best friend.

Fried Green Tomatoes (1992). An aging woman resident of a nursing home is befriended by a middle-aged woman who returns to visit her after the old woman tells stories of her life in a small town in Georgia. The story focuses on love and friendship.

Strangers in Good Company (1993). Eight women are stranded in the Canadian wilderness when their bus breaks down. All of the women grow closer to each other and are able to expand their understanding of how to face the trials of old age.

Tea with Mussolini (1999). A group of older English women living in Italy when World War II breaks out are confronted with many decisions about what to do when they are evicted from their living quarters because they are considered dangerous aliens. The spirit and daring of the group is admirable and demonstrates a woman's role in times of danger and uncertainty.

The Trip to Bountiful (1985). An aging widow dreams of returning to her home in a small town in Texas. Her return triggers a significant life review.

The Winter Guest (1997). An aging Scottish woman's anxieties are exposed in a complex intergenerational relationship with her middle-aged daughter who is grieving her husband's death. At first, they are adversarial on every topic, but eventually, they begin to acknowledge each other's needs.

The Dance is an educational video about the life of an aging woman who is victimized by domestic violence. Available from Area Agency on Aging, Region One, 1366 East Thomas Road, Suite 108, Phoenix, AZ 85014. (602) 264-2255.

References

Administration of Aging. (1999). *Older women: A diverse and growing population*. Fact Sheet. [on-line]. Available: http://www.aoa.gov/factsheets/ow.html.

Administration on Aging. (1999). *Grandparents as caregivers*. [on-line]. Available: http://www.aoa.dhhs.gov/may97/grandparents.html/

AHCPR. *Women's health highlight*. (1999). Fact Sheet. AHCPR Pub. No 98-P004, May 1998. Agency for Health Care Policy Research, Rockville, MD. [on-line]. Available: http://www.ahcpr.gov/research/womenh1.htm.

Almvig, C. (1982). *The invisible minority: Aging and lesbianism*. Utica, NY: Syracuse University.

American Association of Retired Persons. (1993). *Facts about older women*: Income and poverty. Washington, DC: AARP.

American Association of Retired Persons. (1995). *A profile of older Americans*. Washington, DC: AARP.

American Association of Retired Persons. (1997). *A profile of older Americans*. Washington, DC: AARP.

American Association of Retired Persons. (1998). *A profile of older Americans*. Washington, DC: AARP.

Beaver, M. (1983). *Human service practice with the elderly*. Englewood Cliffs, NJ: Prentice-Hall.

Beaver, M. & Miller, D. (1985). *Clinical social work practice with the elderly*. Homewood, IL: Dorsey.

Beckett, J. O. (1982). Working women: A historical review of racial difference. *The Black Sociologist*, 9, 5–27.

Beckett, J. O. (1988). Plant closings: How older workers are affected. *Social Work*, 33,(1), 29–33.

Before you buy: A guide to long-term care insurance. (1997) Washington, DC: American Association of Retired Persons.

Bell, A. & Weinberg, M. (1978). *Homosexualities*. New York: Simon and Schuster.

Benokraitis, N. (1987). Older women and reentry problems: The case of displaced homemakers. *Journal of Gerontological Social Work, 10,* 75–92.

Berger, R. (1982). The unseen minority: Older gays and lesbians. *Social Work, 27,* 236–241.

Bienefeld, D., Koenig, H. G., Larson, D. B. & Sherrill, K. A. (1997). Psychosocial predictors of mental health in a population of elderly women: Test of an explanatory model. *American Journal of Geriatric Psychiatry, 5*(1), 43–53.

Boston Women's Health Book Collective. (1984). *The new our bodies, ourselves*. New York: Simon and Schuster.

Bound, J., Duncan, G., Laren, D., & Oleinick, L. (1991). Poverty dynamics in widowhood. *Journals of Gerontology, 46,* S115–S124.

Brink, T. L. (1979). *Geriatric psychotherapy*. New York: Human Sciences Press.

Brody, E. (1985). Women in the middle and family help to older people. *The Gerontologist, 25,* 19–30.

Bureau of the Census. (1980). *A statistical portrait of women in the United States: 1978*. Washington, DC: U.S. Government Printing Office.

Burkhauser, R. V., Holden, K. C., & Feaster, D. (1988). Incidence, timing, and events associated with poverty: A dynamic view of poverty in retirement. *Journal of Gerontology: Social Sciences, 43*(2).

Burns, B. & Taube, C. (1990). Mental health services in general medical care and in nursing homes. In B. Fogel, A Furing, & G. Gottlieb. (Eds.). *Mental health policy for older Americans: Protecting minds at risk*. Washington, DC: American Psychiatric Press.

Butler, R. (1975). *Why survive: Being old in America*. New York: Harper-Colophon.

Butler, R. & Lewis, M. (1976). *Sex after sixty*. North Miami, FL: Merit Publications.

Butler, R., Lewis, M., & Sunderland, T. (1991). *Aging and mental health* (4th ed.). New York: Macmillan.

Cavanaugh, J. C. (1993). *Adult development and aging*. Pacific Grove, CA: Brooks/Cole.

Chauncey, C. (1987). Shelter poverty and displacement. In P. Doress & D. Siegel (Eds.), *Ourselves growing older* (pp. 146–147). New York: Simon and Schuster.

Cherlin, A. (1987). Women and the family. In S. Rix (Ed.), *The American Woman 1987–88* (pp. 67–103). New York: Norton.

Comfort, A. (1976). *A good age*. New York: Crown.

Crooks, L. D. (1986). *The situation of older women around the world: An emerging issue*. Paper presented at International Conference on Social Welfare, Tokyo.

Cross, R. & Drake, L. (1993). Older women's sexuality. *Clinical Gerontologist, 12*(4), 51–56.

Dawson, K. (1982). Serving the older community. *SIECUS report* (pp. 4–6). New York: Sex Education and Information Council of the United States.

Deimling, G. T. & Harel, Z. (1984). Social integration and mental health of the aged. *Research on Aging, 6*(4), 515–527.

dePatie, C. (1980). Social security and the older woman. In V. C. Little (Ed.), *Women, work and age: Policy challenges*. Ann Arbor, MI: Institute of Gerontology.

Doress, P., Swenson, N., Cohen, R., Freidman, M., Harvis, L., & MacPherson, K. (1984). Women growing older. In The Boston Women's Health Book Collective, *The new our bodies, ourselves* (pp. 435–472). New York: Simon and Schuster.

du Rivage, V. (1984). Increasing poverty through federal policy change. In E. Snyder (Ed.), *Women, work and age: Policy challeges*. Ann Arbor, MI: Institute of Gerontology.

Edwards, R. (Ed.). (1995). *Encyclopedia of social work*. (19th edition). Washington, DC: National Association of Social Workers.

Elimination of sex and race wage discrimination: Policy statement. (1987). Silver Spring, MD: National Association of Social Workers.

Evans, S. (1987). Women in twentieth century America: An overview. In S. Rix (Ed.), *The American woman 1987-88* (pp. 33–66). New York: Norton.

Fengler, A. & Goodrich, N. (1979). Wives of elderly disabled men: The hidden patients. *The Gerontologist, 19,* 175–183.

Friend, R. A. (1984, June). *A theory of accelerated aging among lesbians and gay men*. Paper presented to the combined annual meeting of American Association of Sex Educators, Counselors and Therapists, and the Society for Scientific Study of Sex, Boston, MA.

Friend, R. A. (1987). The individual and social psychology of aging: Clinical implications for lesbians and gay men. *Journal of Homosexuality, 14*, 305–331.

Fries, J. (1989). *Aging well: A guide for successful seniors*. Reading, MA: Addison-Wesley.

Gardner, J. (1995). Worker displacement: A decade of change. *Monthly Labor Review*, 45–57.

Gelfand, D. & Barresi, C. M. (1987). *Ethnic dimensions of aging*. New York: Springer.

Glantz, M. D., Peterson, D., & Whittington, F. J. (Eds.). (1983). *Drugs and the elderly adults: Research issues*. Washington, DC: U.S. Department of Health and Human Services.

Gottlieg, N. (1995). Women overview. In R. Edwards. (Ed.). *Encyclopedia of social work* (19th edition). 2518–2528. Washington, DC: National Association of Social Workers.

Growing numbers, growing force: A report from the White House mini-conference on older women. (1980). Oakland, CA: Older Women's League.

Guralnik, J. & Fried, L. (1997). Disability in older adults: Evidence regarding significance, etiology, and risk. *Journal of the American Geriatrics Society, 45*, 92–100.

Guralnik, J. M., Leveille, S. G., Hirsh, R., Ferrucci, L., & Fried, L. P. (1997). The impact of disability in older women. *Journal of the American Medical Women's Association, 52*(3), 113–120.

Hagestad, G. (1986). The aging society as a context for family life. *Daedalus, 115*, 119–139.

Hardy, D. & Hardy, C. (1991). *Social insecurity*. New York: Villard Books.

Hatch, L. (1990). Gender at work at midlife and beyond. *Generations, 14*(3), 48–52.

Hendricks, J. & Hendricks, C. D. (1986). *Aging in mass society*. Boston: Little, Brown.

Hess, B. & Waring, J. (1983). Family relationships of older women: A women's issue. In E. Markson, *Older women*. Lexington, MA: Lexington Books.

Hess, B. (1990). Gender and aging: The demographic parameters. *Generations, 14*(3), 125.

Holden, K. C. (1988). Poverty, and living arrangements among older women: Are changes in economic well being under estimated? *Journal of Gerontology: Social Sciences, 43*(1).

Hooyman, N. (1986a). *Family caregiving of the elderly: A fact sheet*. Unpublished paper. Seattle: University of Washington, School of Social Work.

Hooyman, N. (1986b). *The older woman in America*. Paper presented at International Conference on Social Welfare, Tokyo.

Hooyman, N. (1986c). *Taking care: Supporting older people and their families*. New York: Free Press.

Hooyman, N. & Kiyak, H. (1996). *Social gerontology*. Boston: Allyn and Bacon.

Jacobs, R. H. (1994). His and her aging: Differences, difficulties, dilemmas, delights. *Journal of Geriatric Psychiatry, 27*(1), 113–128.

Jans, L. & Stoddard, S. (1999). *Chartbook on women and disability in the United States*. An Info Report. Washington, DC: U.S. National Institute on Disability and Rehabilitation Research. [on-line]. Available:http:www.infouse.com/disabiltiydata/.

Jennings, J. (1987). Elderly parents as caregivers for adult dependent children. *Social Work, 32*(5), 430–433.

Johnson, C. & Barer, B. (1993). Coping and a sense of control among the oldest old: An exploratory analysis. *Journal of Aging Studies, 7*(1), 67–80.

Jones, J. (1994). Embodied meaning: Menopause and the change of life. Special Issue. Women's health and social work: Feminist perspectives. *Social Work in Health Care, 19*(3/4), 43–65.

Jones-Witters, P. & Witters, W. (1983). *Drugs and society: A biological perspective*. Monterey, CA: Wadsworth.

Kaplan, H. & Sadock, B. (1998). *Synopsis of psychiatry* (8th Edition). Baltimore: Williams & Wilkins.

Kermis, M. (1986). *Mental health in late life*. Boston/Monterey: Jones and Barrett.

Kimmel, D. (1978). Adult development and aging: A gay perspective. *Journal of Social Issues, 34*, 113–130.

Kiyak, H. & Hooyman, N. (1999). Aging in the twenty-first century. *Hallym International Journal of Aging, 1*, 56–66.

Klemesrud, J. (1982, November 22). Older women: Their league gains strength. *New York Times*, B-12.

Lamy, P. (1978). Therapeutics and the elderly. *Addictive Disease: An International Journal, 3*, 311–335.

Lamy, P. (1983). Pharmacology and therapeutics. In M. D. Glantz et al., *Drugs and the elderly adult* (pp. 121–129). Washington, DC: U.S. Department of Health and Human Services.

Lee, G. R. & Ish-Kuntz, M. (1988). Social interaction, loneliness, and emotional well-being among the elderly. *Research on Aging, 9*(4), 459–482.

Lewis, M. I. (1997). An economic profile of American elder women. *Journal of American Medical Women's Association, 52*(3), 107–112.

Licht, W. (1988, February). How the work place has changed in 75 years. *Monthly Labor Review,* 19–25.

Marshall. (1980). *Last chapters: A sociology of aging and dying.* Monterey, CA: Brooks/Cole

Masor, E. (1993). Dietary restrictions and aging. *Journal of the American Geriatrics Society, 41*(9), 994–999.

McQuaide, S. (1996). Keeping the wise blood: The construction of images in a mid-life women's group. *Social Work with Groups, 19*(3/4), 131–144.

Milliren, J. W. (1977). Some contingencies affecting the utilization of tranquilizers in long-term care of the elderly. *Journal of Health and Social Behavior, 18*, 206–211.

Minnigerode, F. & Adelman, M. (1976, October). *Adaptions of aging homosexual men and women.* Paper presented at the Annual Meeting of the Gerontological Society of America. New York, NY.

National Center for Health Statistics. (1985). Annual summary of births, marriages, divorces and deaths, United States, 1984. *Monthly Vital Statistics Report, 33,* Department of Health and Human Services, Publication No. (PHS)85–1120, Hyattsville, MD: U.S. Public Health Service.

National Center for Health Statistics. (1985). *Monthly Vital Statistics Report, 34.* Hyattsville, MD: U.S. Public Health Service.

National Policy and Resource Center on Women and Aging. (1999). Half of America's women are not getting the mammograms they should. *Women and aging letter, 2* (May 1997). [on-line]. Available:http:www.aoa.dhhs.gov/elderpage/walmamogr/html.

National Policy and Resource Center on Women and Aging. (1999). Identifying and coping with depression. *Women and aging letter, 2* (January 1998). [one-line]. Available:http://www.aoa.gov/elderpage/waldepression.html.

Number of U.S. elderly growing rapidly. (1984). *Boston Globe,* May 31.

Older women and the labor force. (1984, June 6). Testimony of the Older Women's League (OWL) before the Joint Economic Committee.

Older women—The economics of aging. (1981). Washington, DC: George Washington University, Women Studies Program and Policy Center.

Older Women's League. (1999). *Gender and the social security system.* [on-line]. Available:htp///www.owl-national.org/Gender.html.

Older Women's League. (1999). *Women and medicare.* [on-line]. Available:http://www.ow.-national.org/MEDICARE.html

Otten, A. L. (1984). The oldest old: Ever more Americans live into 80s and 90s, causing big problems. *Wall Street Journal,* July 30.

Otten, A. L. (1985). Women continue to outlive men, but the female edge is narrowing. *Wall Street Journal,* June 5.

Paganini-Hill, A. (1995). The risks and benefits of estrogen replacement therapy: Leisure world. *International Journal of Fertility and Menopausal Studies,* 40(Suppl. 1), 54–62.

Pincus, J., Swenson, N., & Poor, B. (1984). Pregnancy. In The Boston Women's Health Book Collective, *The new our bodies, ourselves* (pp. 329–360). New York: Simon and Schuster.

President's Commission on Mental Health. (1978). *Final reports: Vol. 2. Task panel reports.* Washington, DC: U.S. Government Printing Office.

Pulliam, L. W., Plowfield, L. A., & Fuess, S. (1996). Developmental care: The key to the emergence of the older woman. *Journal of Obstetrics and Gynecology of Neonatal Nursing, 25*(7), 623–628.

Raymond, J. C. (1982). Medicine as patriarchal religion. *Journal of Medicine and Philosophy, 7,* 197–216.

Report of the mini-conference on older women. (1981). Prepared for the 1981 White House Conference on Aging, Washington, DC, MCR-18.

Report on the status of midlife and older women in America. (1986). Washington, DC: Older Women's League.

Richmond Times Dispatch. (1984). Women still have a tough time qualifying for pension plans. May 13.

Ricks, T. E. (1986). Men who live to a ripe old age find unexpected bonus: Lot of single women. *Wall Street Journal*, April 22.

Rix, S. (Ed.). (1987). *The American woman, 1987–88*. New York: Norton.

Rakowski, W., Fleishman, J. & Bryant, S. (1993). Self-assessment of health and mortality among older persons. *Research on Aging, 15*(1), 91–116.

Rogers, P. (1993, February). How many gays are there? *Newsweek*, p. 46.

Schiefeling, M. (1996). Menopause and postmenopause. Prognostic criteria in insurance medicine. *Verischerungsmedizin, 48*(4), 116–125.

Schwenk, F. (1992). Income and expenditures of older widowed, divorced, and never-married women who live alone. *Family Economics Review, 5*, 2–8.

Sex differences and aging. (1981). Washington, DC: National Institute on Aging.

Shank, S. (1988). Women's link to labor market grows stronger. *Monthly Labor Review* (March), 3–8.

Sheehy, G. (1993). *Menopause: The silent passage*. New York: Simon and Schuster.

Shenk, D. & Fullmer, D. (1996). Significant relationships among older women: Cultural and personal constructions of lesbianism. *Journal of Women and Aging, 8*(3/4), 75–90.

Sherman, E. (1981). *Counseling the aging: An integrative approach*. New York: Free Press.

Slater, S. (1995). *The lesbian family life cycle*. New York: Free Press.

Smith, J. P. (1997). *The changing economic circumstances of the elderly: Income, wealth, and Social Security*. Policy Brief #8. Syracuse, NY: Syracuse University Maxwell School of Citizenship and Public Affairs, Center for Policy Research.

Sontag, S. (1972). The double standard of aging. *Saturday Review of the Society, 95*, 29–38.

Speroff, L. (1996). Preventive health care for older women. *International Journal of Fertility and Menopausal Studies, 41*(2), 64–68.

Strean, H. (1993). *The sexual dimension: A guide for the helping professional*. New York: Free Press.

Stein, E., Doress, P., & Fillmore, M. (1987). Work and retirement. In P. Doress & D. Siegel (Eds.), *Ourselves growing older* (pp. 163–180). New York: Simon and Schuster.

Taunton, J. E., Rhodes, E. C., Wolski, L. A., Donelly, M., Warren, J., Elliot, J., McFarlane, L., Leslie, J., Mitchell, J., & Lauridsen, B. (1996). Effect of land-based and water-based fitness programs on the cardiovascular fitness, strength and flexibility of women aged 65-75 years. *Journals of Gerontology, 42*(4), 204–210.

Teresi, J. A., Toner, J., Bennett, R., & Wilson, D. (1980). *Factors related to family attitudes toward institutionalizing older relatives*. Paper presented at the 33rd Annual Scientific Meeting of the Gerontological Society of America, San Diego, CA, November.

Tracy, M. & Ozawa, M. (1995). Social security. In R. Edwards. (Ed.). *Encyclopedia of social work* (19th Edition). 2186–2195. Washington, DC: National Association of Social Workers.

Treas, J. (1977). Family support systems for the aged: Some social and demographic considerations. *The Gerontologist, 17*, 486–491.

Tully, C. (1995). Lesbians' overview. In R. Edwards. (Ed.). *Encyclopedia of Social Work* (19th Edition). 1591–1596. Washington, DC: National Association of Social Workers.

Tully, C. L. & Snowdon, D. A. (1995). Weight change and physical function in older women: Findings from the nun study. *Journal of the American Geriatrics Society, 43*(12), 1394–1397.

Undie, A. & Friedman, E. (1993). Diet restriction prevents aging-induced deficits in brain phosphoinositide metabolism. *Journals of Gerontology, 48*(2), B62–B67.

United Nations Development Program. (1979). *Women and the international economic order, Development issue paper for the 1980's*, No. 12. New York: UNDP, Division of Information.

U.S. Bureau of the Census. (1983): *America in transition: An aging society*. Current Population Reports, series P-23, No. 128. Washington, DC: U.S. Government Printing Office.

U.S. Bureau of the Census. (1996). Current population reports, special studies. *65 + in the United States*. Washington, DC: U.S. Government Printing Office.

U.S. House of Representatives Select Committee on Aging. (1979). *Midlife women: Policy proposals on their problems*. Washington, DC: U.S. Government Printing Office.

U.S. Senate, Special Committee on Aging. (1985). *Developments in aging: 1984*. Vol. 1. Washington, DC: U.S. Government Printing Office.

U.S. Senate, Special Committee on Aging. (1987). *Development in aging: 1986*. Vol. 1. Washington, DC: U.S. Government Printing Office.

U.S. Senate, Special Committee on Aging. (1982). *Aging America: Trends and projections*. Washington, DC: U.S. Department of Health and Human Services.

Van den Heuvel, N., Smits, C., Deeg, D., & Beekman, A. (1996). Personality: A moderator of the relation between cognitive functioning and depression in adults aged 55-85? *Journal of Affective Disorders, 41*(3), 229–240.

Van Os, J., Howard, R., Takei, N., & Murray, R. (1995). Increasing age is risk factor for psychosis in the elderly. *Social Psychiatry and Psychiatric Epidemiology, 30*(4), 161–164.

Walsh, F. (1980). The family in later life. In E. Carter & M. McGoldrick (Eds.), *The family life cycle: A framework for family therapy*. New York: Gardner.

Ward-Griffin, C. & Ploeg, J. (1997). A feminist approach to health promotion for older women. *Canadian Journal on Aging, 16*(2), 279–296.

Williams, M. E. (1995). *The American Geriatrics Society's complete guide to aging and health*. New York: Harmony.

Women and aging around the world. (1985). Washington, DC: American Association of Retired Persons and International Federation on Aging.

Woody, B. (1983). *Uncertainty and risk of low income black working women: Project summary*. Wellesley, MA: Wellesley College, Center for Research on Women.

Lesbian and Gay Elders: An Invisible Minority

■ ■ ■ ■ ■ ■ ■ ■ ■ ■ ■ ■ ■ ■ ■

Chrystal C. Ramirez Barranti and Harriet L. Cohen

Louise is gone. It's been four months now, and Margaret has been living with her brother Michael and his wife. She feels more depressed than ever. Michael doesn't realize what Louise was to her, and he can't understand the depth of her grief. She cries alone at night and struggles to hide her tears during the day.

Joe has one year until retirement. He had always thought it would be a joyful year in preparation for the many trips he and Paul planned. Paul started showing signs of forgetfulness a few years ago shortly after his own retirement. Now he needs almost constant supervision, and Paul wants to be with him. How can he explain this at his job? The Family Medical Leave Act doesn't apply to gay families, and he certainly hasn't been "out" at work.

Introduction

It is no longer news that the population of the United States is growing older. While this reality has become a focus of social work study and practice, there is probably no other "category" of individuals that is as subject to the bias of heterogeneity as the elderly. Limited attention has been given to understanding diversity in general among the aging population, and there has been even less attention given to identifying and understanding the needs of the growing population of lesbian and gay elders (Butler & Hope 1999; Rosenfeld 1999). Recognition and understanding of needs and issues that are unique to lesbian and gay elders is critical to improving the quality of care and quality of life for adults in late life.

The purpose of this chapter is to assist in filling this current void in the gerontological literature through a highlighted discussion of older gay men, who Berger (1996) calls "gay and gray," and lesbians, who Kehoe (1986a) refers to as the "triple invisible minority." The myths and stereotypes about older gay men and lesbians are addressed, and social work interventions to enhance and strengthen the quality of life for this population are presented. This chapter also describes social and health issues affecting gay and lesbian elders living in the United States. Finally, areas for future research and improved service delivery are presented.

Gay and Lesbian Elders—Who Are They?

Katherine reached over and tenderly moved the hair that had fallen across Gerty's forehead. It had been two weeks now since the massive stroke. Katherine, sixty-eight years old, was in good health. The jogger, hiker, and gardener of the two, she was always after Gerty to get more exercise. Gerty was the older of the two at age seventy-three, and they had lived together now for forty-two years. Sorrow fell over Katherine as she thought of the fear, sometimes shame, and almost always secrecy that shrouded their dedicated and fulfilling life together. Gerty was her life, her joy, and her reason for living. There was no word for it. "Roommate" was so vacant and "lesbian" was too terrifying. She knew only that she had to find a way to let the doctors and nurses know that they belonged together without jeopardizing Gerty's care and their safety. Katherine felt terribly alone and frightened.

Invisibility of the Population

During the lifetime of the current cohort of older gays and lesbians, it was unsafe for them to identify as gay, lesbian, and/or homosexual, and many never did. This generation of gay men and lesbians, who came out before the Stonewall riots in 1969 and before the 1973 American Psychiatric Association decision to remove homosexuality as a disease, were "labeled sick by doctors, immoral by clergy, unfit by the military, and a menace by the police" (Kochman 1997, p. 2). Often, they feared losing their jobs, homes, families, and friends. As a consequence, two women who shared housing were frequently perceived as "just friends" or as "spinsters." Gay men were more likely to hide their homosexuality by heterosexual marriages, yet continue to maintain sexual relationships with men. Quam (1993) states, "The heavy moral, social and legal injunctions against homosexuality have weighed heavily on this population of gay men and lesbians" (p. 10).

The issue of invisibility in the older population is evident in several ways. In a book of statistics on the gay/lesbian population, no reference is made to older gay men and lesbians (Singer & Deschamps 1994). Interesting statistics such as estimates of numbers of children with gay or lesbian parents are included; however, the reader is given the impression that gay men and lesbians disappear after the age of forty! Invisibility of subpopulations of this older group is even more pronounced. In *Social Services for Senior Gay Men and Lesbians* (Quam 1997b), the two chapters dealing with research and treatment are focused on older white gay men who enjoy good physical health and financial security. No reference is made to research about older lesbian women or ethnic or cultural minorities.

Unfortunately, the profession of social work has neglected the lives of older gay men and lesbian women in practice and research areas. Several factors can account for this omission. First, the gay culture may be seen as a youth-oriented one. While some social workers may be sensitive to issues of younger lesbians and gays, such as "coming-out" disclosure of sexual orientation to family and friends, and job discrimination, these issues are less likely to be realized with lesbian and gay elders. Another issue has to do with Americans' discomfort in discussing sex in general and specifically in recognizing the needs of older persons as sexual human beings. Even with social workers, ageism and homophobia can impair practitioners' assessment of issues related to sexuality and intimate relationships of older adults. When older lesbians and gays enter a nursing home, for example, they may be separated from their loving companions and partners because the facility does not recognize relationships between same-sex couples. In instances where the relationship is recognized, homosexual couples are denied rights extended to heterosexual married partners.

Due to ageism, older gay men and lesbian women may find themselves invisible to younger gay men and lesbians and to professionals such as social workers and gerontologists (Zack 1999). One of the most poignant myths that has been sustained by ageism is that older adults are asexual and perhaps even genderless. Gerontologists are just beginning to "acknowledge that older adults are sexual beings, and the prevailing assumption is that sexual means heterosexual" (Quam 1993, p. 10). The lack of recognition of the significance of sexuality to one's identity continues until death, has substantially limited gerontologists' view of older adults in general, and has resulted in the exclusion of gay and lesbian elders in research and practice.

Estimates of the Population

For several reasons, there is difficulty in calculating the actual number of older gay men and lesbian women. First, there are no reliable figures about the total number of gays and lesbians, young and old. In part, this is due to the bias in research instruments, which have no categories for lesbian and gay elders to indicate their identity, and also to the fear that these elders have about being visible as gay or lesbian in a homophobic and non–gay/lesbian affirming society (Kochman 1997). Those who have participated in research projects either belonged to lesbian and gay organizations or were willing to self-identify.

As a consequence of the invisibility of the population, research with gay men and lesbians has predominantly focused on samples of young and middle-aged people. In fact, research that has explored aging issues among gays and lesbians has often included individuals in their forties as participants (Quam & Whitford 1992). The current estimates of the older gay and lesbian population living in the United States range from a low of 1.75 million gays over the age of sixty-five years (Berger 1982) to a high of 3.5 million lesbian and gay people over the age of sixty (Dawson 1982). Jacobson and Grossman (in press) estimate that there are currently a minimum of 1,100,880 older lesbians living in the United States; however, many of these women have never identified themselves as "lesbians." According to one study, a respondent who was asked the question, "What word do you prefer to use to describe your emotional and/or sexual preference?" answered, "anything but lesbian" (Kehoe 1988, p. 46).

An additional challenge in defining this population in all of its true diversity is that research has been based on older gay men and lesbians who have been willing to self-identify or who participate in gay or lesbian organizations (Berger 1984; Cruikshank 1991; Galassi 1991; Jacobson 1995; Kehoe 1986b; Quam 1993). These individuals have been mostly white and middle class. Older gay men and lesbians from working-class and/or nonwhite backgrounds have been underrepresented in the statistics.

Historical Overview

> I was 22 when I joined the scene in the mid-40s after World War II. It was the beatnik era. You had musicians, artists, gay people and communists hanging out together. It was a raunchy scene and the bar where I hung out, the Black Cat, was a symbol of it. It was a dangerous place. There was the danger of being caught in a raid and publicly shamed. There was the physical danger from roving bands of soldiers and rowdies. . . . It seems hard to believe now, but really—what choice did I have? (Adelman 1986, pp. 12–13).

Understanding the social context experienced by the current cohort of lesbian and gay elders is crucial to understanding some of their unique needs and issues. These men and women spent a great deal of emotional and psychological energy on managing heterosexism and homophobia in a nonaffirming social environment (Rosenfeld 1999). Key historical events that have impacted the current cohort of lesbian and gay elders include the Great

Depression, World War II, the McCarthy Era, and the Stonewall Rebellion (Herdt & Beeler 1998; Mallon 1998; Rosenfeld 1999; Slater 1995). In addition, this group of men and women have lived through eras where homosexuality was pathologized, then de-pathologized as a psychiatric diagnosis.

In general, the historical social behavior toward gay men and lesbian women was unaccepting and even hostile. During President Truman's presidency, for example, Senator Joseph McCarthy played on the fears of America about lesbians and gays. At this time, over 650 people working in the State Department were defined as "subversive" because they were gay or lesbian (DeCrescenzo 1984).

In 1969, a watershed event happened for gay and lesbian rights. As was common, the New York City Police Department went on assignment to harass customers at Stonewall, a gay bar in New York's Greenwich Village. On this occasion, however, they were met by angry men and women who resisted arrest. Several days of rioting brought gay men and lesbians "out of the closet." The Gay Rights movement was born that June night when those at the bar decided to fight against the oppression they had experienced. Political organizations and social service agencies developed in the aftermath of Stonewall.

The 1969 Stonewall Uprising gave rise to the Gay Movement and the development of pride in being gay or lesbian. Kochman (1997) writes, "The changing of the name homosexual—or rather the emphasis on the word *gay*—has been in the forefront of the movement to instill pride in each individual gay person; joy at who you are rather than depression and despair" (p. 6). Several social service and political organizations were established as a result of the Stonewall Uprising, including Senior Action in a Gay Environment, Inc. (SAGE), founded in 1977 in New York City to provide homebound services for lesbian and gay elders.

Another victory in gay/lesbian civil rights occurred in 1973 when the American Psychiatric Association removed homosexuality as a disease category. As a result of this paramount decision, social work also adopted more progressive views. Over the past two decades, the profession has worked to reduce homophobia and discrimination within the profession and society in general. In addition, social work continues to develop a better understanding of the importance of sexual orientation in constructing service objectives with clients (Black et al. 1999; Ryan, Bradford, & Honnold 1999).

Identity Formation

For many lesbian and gay elders, sexual orientation is not the primary reason they seek social work services. Being gay or lesbian is only one aspect of their life and is not the total sum of their identity. On the other hand, it may be incorrect to assume that because someone has been lesbian or gay for twenty, thirty, or forty years, they have resolved all their issues regarding their sexual orientation. Coming out to oneself and to others is not linear but rather a lifelong and continuous process (Herdt & Beeler 1998; Lewis 1984; Rosenfeld 1999).

How can it be that "coming out" is something that evolves over time? Demonteflores and Schultz (1978) have defined "coming out" as a developmental process through which gay and lesbian people recognize their sexual orientation and integrate it into their personal and social lives. Due to the impact of individual life-span development, couple and family life-cycle development, and homophobia and heterosexism, the process of coming out takes place over and over again for the gay and lesbian person. At various transition points in the life-span, sexual identity is reexperienced and processed.

Although numerous models of identity have been proposed, the majority of these are based upon the assumption of heterosexuality. For example, Erikson's stage model of psychosocial tasks has been questioned in relationship to development of a gay/lesbian identity (Humphreys & Quam 1998; Kropf & Greene 1994). Alternate models of identity formation have been proposed for gay men and lesbian women. Two of the most prominent are described in the following section.

Cass's Stage Model of Development

Cass (1979) proposed the first identity development model for lesbian and gay persons. This model is perhaps the most well known and has been the platform for further research on gay and lesbian identity development. Based upon this paradigm, other theorists have continued to develop and expand identity development in the gay and lesbian population.

The Stage Model identifies six stages of identity formation applicable for lesbians and gays. The model is based on two assumptions: (1) that identity formation is a developmental process and (2) that change in identity is a process that happens in the interaction between individuals and their environments. The stages include:

■ *Stage 1: Identity Confusion*—first awareness of homosexual thoughts, behavior, and feelings.
■ *Stage 2: Identity Comparison*—beginning alienation from behaviors, feelings, and thoughts of a heterosexual, while beginning to test self as a homosexual.
■ *Stage 3: Identity Tolerance*—realization of being gay or lesbian (e.g., "I probably am a homosexual").
■ *Stage 4: Identity Acceptance*—increased contacts with other homosexuals and decreased contacts with heterosexuals (e.g., family members) who may not accept identity/lifestyle.
■ *Stage 5: Identity Pride*—pride and a sense of belonging to the gay subculture.
■ *Stage 6: Identity Synthesis*—positive identity as homosexual; integration of homosexual identity with other aspects of self.

An individual may progress through each of these six steps in the development of a healthy lesbian or gay identity or stop at any given stage. "Identity foreclosure" is the situation of incomplete progression of all the stages in the model. Because of the social and political times during which the current cohort of older lesbians and gays became aware of their sexual identity, these individuals may be found in all stages of the model.

Friend's Model of Identity Development

An alternate model of identity has been proposed by Friend (1990). In discussing identity formation in lesbians and gays, Friend writes, "resistance and internalized homophobia are the end-points of a continuum of potential cognitive/behavioral responses to heterosexism" (p. 102). He further argues that each lesbian and gay person is challenged to make meaning out of the messages she or he has received about homosexuality, and that there are different ways to accomplish this task. His model describes these various images along two continua:

> One continuum represents cognitive/behavioral responses. At one end-point of this continuum is the internalization of the pervasive heterosexist ideologies. This results in the belief that homosexuality is sick and/or otherwise negative. At the other end of the continuum is a cognitive/behavioral response to heterosexism which involves challenging or questioning the validity of these negative messages. As a result, there is a reconstruction of what it means to be lesbian or gay into something positive and affirmative.
>
> Associated with this cognitive behavioral continuum is a set of corresponding affective responses. For example, if one end of the cognitive/behavioral continuum is the negative evaluation of homosexuality, the corresponding emotional response to these beliefs is internalized homophobia. Feelings of self-hatred, low self-esteem, and minimal or conditional self-acceptance may result. Associated with the other end of the cognitive/behavioral continuum (a gay or lesbian reconstructed as positive) are the feelings of increased self-acceptance, high self-esteem, personal empowerment, and self-affirmation. (1990, pp. 102–103)

This model has specific applicability to older adults who are gay or lesbian. Friend (1989, 1990) defines the three points on the continuum of identity formation. These are: the stereotypic, the passing, and the affirmative older lesbian and gay man.

STEREOTYPICAL LESBIAN AND GAY ELDERS

The common images in the literature for older lesbians and gays in this culture is negative. The older gay man is described as depressed, lonely, alienated, oversexed, increasingly effeminate with age, and lacking the support of family and friends (Berger 1982, 1996; Kelly 1977). The older lesbian is described as a loner who is heartless, without emotions, and bitter. Younger lesbians are said to find her unattractive, and she also is seen as being without friends or family. Dawson (1982) describes the people who have internalized the homophobic message:

> When today's older gays were young, they faced an unrelieved hostility toward homosexuality that was far more virulent than it is today. They were labeled "sick" by doctors, "immoral" by clergy, "unfit" by the military, and a "menace" by police and legislators. If identified as homosexual, they risked the loss of job, home, friends, and family. The need for secrecy caused an isolation which imperiled their most intimate relationships. And the greatest damage was done to those gay people who believed what society said about them, and thus lived in corrosive shame and self-loathing. (1982, p. 5)

The stereotypic older lesbians and gays have never challenged their internalized, extremely negative, heterosexist beliefs about themselves.

PASSING OLDER LESBIANS AND GAYS

A second category of older adults is those who manage identities in both homosexual and heterosexual worlds. This group tended to marry and to distance themselves from anything that could be seen as stereotypically lesbian or gay. The older homosexual carries the pain and the fear of being found out. "Passing" can lead to poor self-concept, depression, and other emotional problems, since these individuals have both a public world as a heterosexual and a private world as a lesbian woman or gay man (Berger 1996). In an early work on identity development, the cognitive dissonance theory was used to explain how "passing" behaviors lead to internalized homophobia (Festinger 1957). The older homosexual who passes engages in daily behaviors that are inconsistent with the belief that "it's OK to be homosexual." According to cognitive dissonance theory, passing will lead to the development of a belief system that says "I am bad," and hence to a poor self-concept.

AFFIRMATIVE OLDER LESBIANS AND GAYS

In the past few years, researchers have found that this group of people has deconstructed the negative images and reconstructed what it means to be lesbian or gay into something affirming and positive. They are described in the literature as psychologically well adjusted, vibrant, and growing older successfully. They have developed a comfort and acceptance of homosexuality and are able to manage the heterosexism in the culture (Berger 1982, 1996; Friend 1989; Kelly 1977, Kimmel 1977). These lesbians and gays have developed survival skills, which Kimmel (1978) calls "crisis competence." Dunker (1987) suggests that older gay men and lesbian women have had to establish coping skills to deal with the oppression and discrimination that they have experienced. Out of necessity, these men and women have had to take charge of their lives and develop autonomy. These are the skills that all older adults require in order to experience a successful aging process.

Successful Aging

Although there is little research about the number of older lesbians and gays who comprise each identity group, one theory reflects that those older lesbians and gays who fall on the affirmative end of the continuum have achieved a degree of successful aging. These individuals have learned skills to manage in a heterosexist world and will age more successfully than their heterosexual counterparts or those older lesbians and gays who have lived their lives as stereotypic or passing older people (Friend 1989, 1990). When lesbians and gays come out to themselves and others, they are confronted with the potential or real loss of family and friends. The successful management of those issues, including dealing with negative attitudes about homosexuality, may have given older lesbians and gays the opportunity to develop psychological skills in dealing with loss, which is a process that also occurs in aging.

Another aspect of their experience can also prepare gay men and lesbian women for the tasks of late adulthood. Older lesbians and gays may have experienced greater flexibility in gender role definition than their heterosexual counterparts. These opportunities can result in lesbians and gays having learned and practiced skills that many heterosexual men and women may have expected their spouses to accomplish. Many older lesbians and gays may feel more comfortable with nontraditional gender role definitions (Friend 1990).

Another area that may promote successful aging is the development of families of choice for social, emotional, and recreational support. The "family" may be comprised of friends, past and current partners, as well as families of origin and may be available to provide needed services and support to aging lesbians and gays (Almvig 1982). Heterosexual men and women, as well as social service and governmental institutions, assume that families of origin will take care of aging relatives. "Stereotypic" and "passing" older lesbians and gays may have limited supports and face some of the same emotional and financial fears as older heterosexuals without family support.

A third area important to successful aging is developing advocacy skills to deal with the legal and health care system. Friend (1990) writes, "developing an affirmative identity as a gay or lesbian person involves restructuring the meaning of homosexuality as something positive. As a result of this process, certain attitudes, skills and emotional resources are gained that function to promote successful aging. . . . These resources include: individual psychological processes, social and interpersonal dimensions and legal and political advocacy" (p. 115). Again, the experience of battling homophobia and heterosexism through life can prepare gay and lesbian elders with advocacy skills that may be used in other areas during later life.

Families and Social Support

Larry finished loading the dishwasher. These new fangled things, I don't think I'll ever get used to them, he thought. But, Rob loves gadgets and machines of all kinds, and it was at his insistence ten years ago that they put a dishwasher in their kitchen. Larry and Rob had been together for twenty-three years now. Larry was forty-seven when he finally had gone through the painful process of divorce from his wife of twenty-six years. Not an easy thing this coming to terms with oneself, he thought, as he reminisced about his younger years.

Rob had been in a fifteen-year relationship with Ric, who died at the early age of forty-two from heart disease. Rob found himself a forty-one-year-old widower. Rob was sure that his life would never be happy again, and then, when he was forty-five, he met Larry. They have been together ever since. Larry looked around the kitchen and dining room that was filled with talk and laughter. Their house has always been the gathering place for their family of friends.

One of the great myths about older gay and lesbian persons is that they live lonely and isolated lives filled with bitterness and depression (Ehrenberg 1996; Friend 1990). Such negative myths and stereotypes are associated with society's nonaffirming environment of homophobia and heterosexism, and imply that gay and lesbian elders are perhaps without family and friends. What does the social support network of gay and lesbian elders look like?

Couplehood: Creating a Family

Everyone longs for an intimate, loving, long-term relationship, and lesbian and gay men are no different. What is different is that lesbian and gay partners are forced to create their couplehood in what is a predominantly nonaffirming environment. There are no legal protections that sanction and honor their creation of a family life together. There are none of the social benefits or safety nets for the gay or lesbian couple that the married heterosexual couple may easily take for granted. McNaught (1997) has compiled a list of some legal rights inherent in heterosexual marriage and yet denied to lesbian and gay couples (pp. 60–61):

- status of next of kin for hospital visits and medical decisions where one partner is too ill to be competent
- joint insurance policies for home, auto, and health
- joint parenting; joint adoption; joint foster care, custody and visitation
- automatic inheritance of jointly owned real and personal property through the right of survivorship
- benefits such as annuities, pension plans, Social Security, and Medicare
- dissolution and divorce protections such as community property and child support

- immigration and residency for partners from other countries
- joint leases with automatic renewal rights in the event one partner dies or leaves the house or apartment
- spousal exemptions to property tax increases upon the death of one partner who is co-owner of the home
- veteran's discounts on medical care, education, and home loans
- joint filing of tax returns, joint filing of customs claims when traveling
- wrongful death benefits for a surviving partner and children
- bereavement or sick leave to care for a partner or child
- decision-making power with respect to burial or cremation for a deceased partner
- domestic violence protection orders
- crime victim's recovery benefits

The lack of legal and social protections intensifies the sense of vulnerability and powerlessness of elderly gay and lesbian couples during a crisis.

An additional dynamic that is active in the ongoing development of the gay and lesbian couple relates to the individual's own sexual identity development (McVinney 1998; Slater 1995). For example, it is not uncommon for a gay or lesbian person to have attempted to live a heterosexual life, to have married, and even to have had children before deciding to "come out." This process can happen at any age, including the sixties and seventies (Quam 1993; Rosenfeld 1999; Sitter 1997).

There have been several key studies on the development of gay and lesbian couple relationships across the life span. McWhirter and Mattison (1984) developed a stage model of gay coupling that ranges the life span of the couples from Stage One, which is characterized by high compatibility, through Stage Six, which describes four characteristics of couples who have been together more than twenty years: achieving security, shifting perspectives, restoring the partnership, and remembering. The results of working through these four characteristics include a strong sense of well-being and permanence in the relationship, reaffirmation of the relationship, and a developing sense of meaning and integration of one's life and the couple's life together. Concerns related to older age, health, finances, and the potential loss of one's partner through death are also characteristic of this final stage.

It is well documented that women comprise a greater percentage of those Americans who are sixty-five years and older. Consequently, couples made up of two women are apt to be well represented in our aging population. In her landmark work on the lesbian family life cycle, Slater (1995) derived five life cycle stages of the lesbian couple, with the first stage describing the formation of the couple and the final and fifth stage describing the tasks and issues of lesbian couples over sixty-five. Given the life span of women in general, this stage of lesbian family life can easily be twenty years or more. Key tasks and issues that are evident for the couple during stage five include: adjusting to imposed life changes, reworking of the balance of togetherness and separateness, adjustment to health related changes, and widowhood.

One common myth about gay men and lesbian women is that these older adults have no children or grandchildren. Gays and lesbians may have children (and consequently grandchildren) from a previous heterosexual marriage. In addition, gay and lesbian elders could have children through adoption and through conceptions by alternative insemination. Children and grandchildren are possible extended support for these elders if there has been ongoing acceptance and support of the elders' sexual orientation and lifestyle. However, there may be little support and possible hostility from such extended families for the gay or lesbian couples, with specific negativity aimed at the partner. Quam (1993, 1997a) documents two case examples that illustrate the vulnerabilities that lesbian elders may face:

> A 63-year-old lesbian came out to her adult daughter several years ago, but her daughter asked that the grandchildren not be told. Will this lesbian grandmother be able to count on support from family members who are not aware of her life and her sexuality? (1993, pp. 11)

> Anne was a school teacher who began living with Carrie in 1951. . . . Carrie and Anne never discussed the nature of their relationship with any family member and were very "closeted" in the ways in which they lived their lives. . . . They did have friends "of the same ilk" and they occasionally had "house parties" which were very private gatherings. . . . Two years ago Anne fell and broke her hip and her arm, requiring considerable caretaking from Carrie. . . . The hip did not heal well. . . . Anne agreed to go into the hospital for hip replacement. But, while Anne was hospitalized, Carrie had a stroke and became disabled. . . . Anne was ready to return home, but since there was no one to care for her, she was sent to a nursing home. Anne was distraught about what was happening to Carrie. A social worker was called in to talk with Carrie about her depression. The social worker, who was also a lesbian, quickly began to realize the nature of the relationship between Carrie and Anne but respected Anne's wishes to keep the information confidential. The worker contacted Carrie's family because she wanted to arrange a visit between Carrie and Anne and determine if it was possible for them to maintain a household again in the future. Carrie's sister and brother-in-law refused to allow the visit saying that Anne was always upsetting to Carrie. In fact, they had already decided that Carrie was unable to ever return home and were selling Carrie's house and all of the belongings. (1993, p. 98)

Issues of Diversity

It is very important to realize that there is a great diversity of ethnicity and culture among gay and lesbian elders. Gays and lesbians are represented in every cultural and ethnic group on earth. The influence of one's ethnicity and culture on how "family" is conceptualized and experienced is important to keep in mind when working with gay and lesbian elders.

The cultural norms and values in which one is raised has a significant impact in shaping how one lives one's life. For gays and lesbians, it may impact possible issues around identity formation and processes of coming out, internalized homophobia and shame, and degree of connection to family of origin and community in which one grew up (Baez 1996; Morales 1989). For example, Latino cultural values around machismo, the role of women, and the significance of inclusion and family of origin may create exceptional strain on gay Latinos and lesbian Latinas throughout their life-span.

A Family of Friends

Being without the assumed affirming social supports and built-in family-of-origin support, gay and lesbian couples create their own (Barranti 1998). Functioning like an extended family, gay and lesbian families create a support network of life-long friends and supportive family members that make up what Weston (1991) has called "families of choice." As with any group, there is a great deal of diversity in social support networks related to individual differences in culture, ethnicity, socioeconomic status, and religious affiliation. Perhaps the most crucial factors affecting the quality and extent of affirming social support networks for gay and lesbian persons, however, is one's level of comfort with one's sexual orientation (sexual identity development, internalized homophobia, and coming-out processes), level of acceptance of family of origin, degree of external community homophobia, and the availability and accessibility of a lesbian and gay community (Barranti 1998).

The research that has been done on the quality of gay and lesbian elders' social support networks indicates that both elderly gay men and lesbian women have more friends on the average than their heterosexual peers (Lipman 1986). This fact is understandable since older gay and lesbian persons prefer the company of other gay and lesbian persons who are like themselves. As a result, their closest friends are often other gays and lesbians (Lipman 1986; Quam 1993).

The quality and extent of support from family of origin and extended family members has been found to be related to the family's degree of acceptance. Friendship support and the creation of "families of choice" have been found to be the predominant support systems for those individuals whose families had been rejecting. In other situations, families of friends were found to function as supplemental support systems for those whose blood relatives had been accepting of their sexual orientation. Sensitivity to and recognition of the importance of the "family of choice" is critical to the provision of quality care for older gay men and lesbian women.

Living in Rural America

One of the myths that exist about gay and lesbian persons is that they live only in urban areas. However, like any other diverse group, lesbian and gays grow up in small towns and rural areas all across the United States. Some leave their rural towns in an effort to find a supportive community and never return. Others, however, return to rural areas, while some live their entire life in a rural community.

Like those who live in cities, rural gays and lesbians are faced with discrimination, prejudice, and oppression (Smith & Mancoske 1997). However, rural dwellers are apt to experience injustice more often and in more blatant ways within a rural context (Butler & Hope 1999). For example, rural communities tend to be characterized by a more conservative political climate, rely on their church as a center for the community, and engender more traditional morals (Lindhorst 1997). Finding an affirming social environment as a gay man or lesbian women and developing an affirming family of friends becomes very difficult. Hence, the possibility for experiencing isolation is very real for rural lesbian and gay persons (Lindhorst 1997; Smith 1997). The fear of being "found out" and the consequent efforts at "fitting in" create tremendous psychosocial stress, anxiety, and isolation.

Health and Social Well-Being

Marti had a rough life, so her friends thought. She always down-played her early life experience that included forced psychiatric hospitalizations by her parents when she was kicked out of college for falling in love with her best friend and losing her job in teaching after confiding in a colleague about the break-up of a ten-year relationship with a woman. Talk to a doctor about her problems! She was old, but she knew better than to talk to a shrink, no matter how bad she felt.

For the most part, gay and lesbian elders experience the same age-related health problems as their heterosexual peers. For example, lesbian and heterosexual women experience higher rates of disabling illnesses, such as osteoporosis, than do either gay or heterosexual men. While health problems may be similar, lesbian and gay elders do experience a difference in the health care they receive. Unlike heterosexual elders, gays and lesbians are confronted with the impact of homophobia and the consequent prejudices, neglect, and rejection experienced with individual health care providers and health care systems (Butler & Hope 1999; Peterson 1996; Peterson & Bricker-Jenkins 1996; Schwartz 1996). In addition, the impact of heterosexism and the assumption of heterosexuality directly affects the kind of information that is collected and omitted, thus affecting the quality of diagnosis, treatment, and aftercare provided to gay and lesbian persons (Peterson 1996). Although health problems of all elders are predominantly similar, there are two diseases that have been found to predominate among gay and lesbians person: AIDS and breast cancer.

HIV/AIDS

The AIDS epidemic has had a devastating impact on the gay men's community. AIDS has no limitation when it comes to age, sexual orientation, or gender and can be contracted by anyone at any age who is engaging in at-risk behaviors, such as unsafe sex or needle-sharing (Aronstein & Thompson 1998). AIDS has also affected some who were exposed through contaminated blood transfusions. Not only has AIDS been responsible for significant and overwhelming rates of devastating illness, but it has left many partners widowed (Scherroff 1997).

The incidence of AIDS among the older population is an issue that has received very little attention (Anderson 1998). This situation is partly due to a mistaken notion that AIDS is a sexually active gay man or bisexual man's disease and in part is due to the mistaken notion that being sexually active is a young person's domain. Bressler (1989) studied HIV-positive (HIV+) elders using a Philadelphia sample of older adults and found that AIDS is no stranger to the older population. Her review of demographic data of Philadelphia's AIDS cases indicated that 7.7 percent of those diagnosed as HIV+ were ages fifty to fifty-nine, and 3.3 percent of the cases were age sixty and older. She found that while a majority of the elders with AIDS were gay or bisexual, 25 percent of the sixty and older group who had been diagnosed as HIV+ had contracted the virus through blood transfusions.

It is important to note that the current group of elders lived a majority of their lives during a time when the need for safe sex was unknown and the need to lead clandestine lives was a necessity for survival (Linsk 1997). Many were sexually active during the years that AIDS was only first being discovered and the means of infection undetermined. They may not have been privy to safe sex practices or may not have fully understood the importance of using them in their later lives. In fact, Linsk (1997) notes that older gay men as a group have not been identified as needing HIV education and are often omitted in prevention program planning and delivery. This is a critical matter as current national statistical estimates indicate that 10 percent of newly diagnosed AIDS cases are among those fifty years old and older (Benjamin 1990; Linsk 1997). It is estimated that during the first decade of the twenty-first century, 10 percent of those infected with AIDS may be sixty years old and older (McCormick & Wood 1992).

While health care studies on gay men and lesbians indicate discrimination and neglect, the impact of being HIV+ seems to compound possible psychosocial stressors (Bressler 1989; Peterson 1996). Research with samples of HIV+ older men and women indicated that these persons experienced diminished social support and alienation, hostility from those who were fearful of AIDS, depression, severe financial issues, and dissatisfaction with their health care (Bressler 1989; Linsk 1997). Clearly, gay and lesbian elders with HIV benefit from health care and psychosocial interventions to manage health and social support needs.

Breast Cancer

Breast cancer affects one in every eight women in the United States. Research that explored lesbian specific health care issues has documented that the risk of breast cancer is significantly higher for lesbians, affecting one in every three (Rounds 1993). This higher risk of breast cancer among lesbians was found to be directly related to the lack of childbearing among a majority of the women that responded to the National Lesbian Health Care Survey (Bradford & Ryan 1988). Research on cancer has long since documented the impact that stress plays on the immune system as an additional risk factor. In addition, the health care system is unresponsive to ways that lesbians may cope with their experience, such as employing nontraditional or alternative treatments (Bricker-Jenkins 1994). The stressors of living in a nonaffirming and hostile social environment are not to be underestimated when considering risk factors that increase the incidence of breast cancer among lesbians (Stevens & Hall 1988).

Barriers to Health Care

The effect of homophobia and heterosexism on the health care of gay and lesbian persons has undoubtedly been a lifelong experience (Butler & Hope 1999). For example, lesbian women seek health care less frequently than heterosexual women because of experiences of injustice related to homophobia (Simkin 1991). The occurrence of the AIDS epidemic has perhaps highlighted the existence of homophobia and heterosexism among health care providers (Schwartz 1996). For example, research on health care provider attitudes toward homosexuality indicates that those with negative attitudes toward lesbians and gays were also unwilling to care for gay persons diagnosed with AIDS (Scherer, Wu, & Haughey 1991).

In addition to discrimination, Peterson and Bricker-Jenkins (1996) identified two other barriers to health care experienced by lesbians. While this research did not include gay men, these same barriers are more than likely experienced by them as well. In addition to discrimination, these barriers include lack of financial resources and the exclusion of family and friends. The high financial cost of health care is a national concern that impacts all citizens including gay and lesbian elders. An additional component affecting gay and lesbian couples is the inability to provide health care coverage for one another if needed. While there are a few companies who recognize domestic partnership and allow for insurance coverage of one's same-sex partner, most older gay men and lesbian women have not been allowed this benefit.

While discrimination and financial barriers are difficult lifelong issues, undoubtedly the most damaging barrier to quality health care for the gay or lesbian elder is the exclusion of his or her partner and family of friends, because this directly impacts the elder's social support system. For example, it is not uncommon for gay and lesbian persons to be denied access to partners in emergency rooms and intensive care settings. For the elderly this can be especially devastating when it comes to issues related to assisted living arrangements, long term care, nursing home residence, and hospice.

As described in the previous sections, the current cohorts of lesbian and gay elders have experienced homophobia and heterosexism that affects the ability to self-disclose their sexual orientation to others. As a consequence of such experiences, many lesbian elders do not label themselves as "lesbian" or "homosexual." They may refer to themselves as "people like us" and refer to their partners as "roommates" or "friends." Lifelong experience in negotiating daily living in homophobic environments has given many the ability to sense the lack of safety in interpersonal exchanges (Deevey 1990). Sensitivity on the part of social workers in creating an open and accepting environment is critical in breaching this barrier.

Housing and Long-Term Care Issues

Despite the fact that housing and long-term care are of significant concerns for gay and lesbian elders, the invisibility of lesbian and gay elders and the omission of this population in social services research has resulted in little data concerning housing and long term care needs of this group of elders (Connolly 1996; Wolfe 1997). Most of the known research has focused on the anticipated needs and expectations of caregiving needs of midlife lesbians and gays who are not current residents of long term care institutions or retirement communities (Hamburger 1997; Quam & Whitford 1992; Tully 1989). Results of these studies indicate that, overall, gays and lesbians expressed a preference for gay/lesbian-only retirement communities. In these segregated communities, these older adults felt that they could live free from possible discrimination and find an affirming and supportive community of peers and support staff (Hamburger 1997; Quam & Whitford 1992).

Mental Health and Addiction Issues

The review of mental health literature contains research that has been conducted using samples representing white, well-educated, middle-class and upper-class lesbians and gays who are active or networked to gay and lesbian organizations (Ehrenberg 1996). Recognizing these limitations, such research has indicated that lesbian and gay elders are healthy, happy, well adjusted, and able to negotiate the challenges of aging in successful ways (Almvig 1982; Berger 1996; Deevey 1990; Ehrenberg 1996). In fact, some researchers suggest that the process of coming out and living an open lifestyle provides the gay elder with a sense of competency to manage life challenges and crises (Kimmel 1978). However, the experience of having lived a life of secrecy may have a different impact on an adult's mental health status. Those elders who have lived a closeted life, feared homophobia and heterosexism, and experienced discrimination and prejudice may have difficulty in adjusting to the challenges of aging (Kimmel 1979).

While the research on gay and lesbian elders has found healthy and positive adjustment to aging, it has also shown an increase in alcohol and tobacco use in this population (Bradford, Ryan, & Rothblum 1994; Deevey 1990). In Bickelhaupt's (1995) review of alcoholism incidence studies of lesbian and gays, approximately 25 percent of the samples of men and women were found to be heavy users of alcohol. While these studies did not focus on elders, it can be deduced that the prevalence of alcohol problems in the gay and lesbian community may extend to elders as well.

The higher incidence rate of alcohol and drug use among gays and lesbians can be attributed to many factors, including biological, psychological, social, cultural, and political ones (Anderson 1996). The stress of living in a homophobic and unaccepting social environment cannot be underestimated as a risk factor in the use of alcohol and drugs by lesbian and gay persons. Internalized homophobia and ambivalence and/or internal conflict about one's sexual identity have also been identified as risk factors for alcohol/drug abuse and dependency (Anderson 1996; Coleman 1981/1982; Glaus 1988). This potential problem is reinforced by prevalence of the bar scene as a primary socializing place for gays and lesbians. For these reasons, it is not surprising to note that the high use of alcohol among the gay and lesbian population is related to biopsychosocial factors (Anderson 1996).

Social Work Practice Issues

Gay men and lesbians share the same concerns that all older adults have about health care, housing, transportation, meaningful leisure time activities, income, and family and friends. They also experience the same fears about loneliness, loss of autonomy, physical dependency on others, reduction in income, and apprehension of dying prematurely or alone. In addition, gays and lesbians face fears associated with their sexual orientation, such as coming out to family, friends, and service providers. They also face discrimination, lack of legal protection, lack of access to a supportive community, and lack of the opportunity to meet other gay and lesbian older adults (Kochman 1997; Quam 1997b).

Social work intervention with older gays and lesbians involves working with individuals, families, groups, communities, and organizations. Interventions may not significantly differ from working with other older population groups, but social workers need to be aware of both their own internalized homophobia and institutional homophobia and heterosexism that may affect the delivery of services. Social workers may assume a variety of roles in working with older lesbians and gays, including broker, advocate, teacher, counselor, case manager, staff developer, administrator, and change agent (Scheafor, Horejsi, & Horejsi 1997).

The social work *broker role* includes linking older lesbians and gays with appropriate services, including those that welcome and embrace homosexuals. Services for older lesbians and gays include outreach, education, and social activities. For example, SAGE (Senior Action in a Gay Environment) was founded in 1979 and is one of the largest and most comprehensive models of service delivery to lesbian and gay elders. Some other organizations around the country include Gay and Lesbian Elders in Minneapolis (GLEAM) and Gay Lesbian Outreach to Elders (GLOE) in San Francisco.

The social work *advocacy role* involves assisting individual clients in receiving services and resources, as well as trying to change policies that discriminate either because of the client's age or lifestyle. The National Gay and Lesbian Task Force and the Human Rights Campaign are two organizations that work at the federal level to end discrimination based on sexual orientation. Old Lesbians Organizing for Change (OLOC) is another advocacy organization specifically trying to create positive change for older lesbians.

The social work *educator role* may adress the needs of both client and staff. Specific programs may provide training for staff working with older gays and lesbians (Metz 1997), educating older lesbians and gays about daily living skills, teaching older gay men about safe sex, or informing older lesbians and gays about community-based services. Examples of organizations providing education include SAGE (Senior Action in a Gay Environment), GLOW (Gay and Lesbian: An Older Way), Project Rainbow: Society for Senior Gay and Lesbian, and the American Society on Aging.

In a *counselor role*, the social worker assists older clients with problem solving and decision making. With older gay and lesbian clients, specific issues may include helping a partner deal with bereavement issues when a partner dies, assisting a "closeted" gay or lesbian talk with his or her family of origin, or initiating a gay friendly support group that would allow a safe place for older lesbians and gays to reminisce about earlier times (Galassi 1991). The *case manager role* is important in helping lesbians and gays to connect with appropriate services and to monitor those services to make sure that this population does not fall through the cracks.

Social workers in more *administrative roles* can assure that appropriate programs are available for older gay men and lesbian women. As administrators, social workers maintain programs and policies serving this client group, develop new ones as the need arises, and evaluate the effectiveness of the programs and policies in responding to older lesbians and gays. Operating from an ethical mandate, the social worker functions as a change agent to identify community or agency problems, gaps or barriers in services, and homophobia within social institutions.

From a social welfare policy perspective, laws and policies need to be developed to support families of gay men and lesbian women of all ages. "Gay friendly" policies include changes in domestic partnership ordinances, recognition of same-sex relationships for insurance benefits, reduction of institutional homophobia, and protection of inheritance for surviving partners. In addition, support must be made available for older couples, especially when one partner has to be institutionalized.

Conclusion

Contradicting myths that are associated with this older population, several studies have reported that older lesbians and gays are happy, well adjusted, and report high satisfaction with their current life (Berger 1982; 1984; Kehoe 1988; Kimmel 1978; 1979; Quam & Whitford 1992). Several reasons can account for a successful aging process in this group of older adults. The acceptance of their sexual identity as a lesbian or a gay person may provide these elders with coping skills to deal more effectively with the aging process. Older lesbians and gays have developed skills in coming out and managing a social perception of being "different." In many ways, the stigma of being "old" is less severe than the label of "homosexual" earlier in their life. As a consequence, these older adults have already learned to handle a crisis in identity. In addition, lesbians and gays have often been rejected by family and have developed a family of choice to give them support and assistance. Finally, lesbians and gays exhibit greater flexibility in gender roles, which is likely to be another asset in the aging process. Without falling into typical roles of mother, father, grandmother, or grandfather, older lesbians and gays can be recognized for who they are, not the roles they fill.

While the experiences of coming out and living in a nonaffirming society have given gay and lesbian elders positive coping skills, there are significant barriers that impact gay and lesbian older adults when they are faced with the challenging events that are normally associated with aging. The very real fears of discrimination and prejudice due to homophobia and heterosexism create difficult challenges for these elders. They are vulnerable and at risk as a result of the lack of legal rights and of consequent legal protection.

Social workers are in an excellent position to provide affirming support to gay and lesbian elders. Sensitivity to and acceptance of an elderly person's sexual identity and the consequent issues he or she faces are critical to developing and providing affirming services. In addition, social workers in more macro-practice roles can promote services that are accepting and appropriate for this segment of the older population. Finally, all social workers should join in advocacy efforts to eradicate prejudice and discrimination against gay men and lesbian women of every age.

Discussion Questions

1. Why is sexual orientation an important factor in working with elders?
2. What critical historical events impacted the current cohort of gay and lesbian elders? What impact did these events have on the development of their identity? How might their experiences influence how they interact with social service providers?
3. Describe what is meant by the "invisible minority." What kinds of gay and lesbian samples are used in current research? What does this tell us and not tell us about what we know about gay and lesbian elders?
4. What barriers do lesbians and gays experience in receiving health care? As a social worker, how might you begin to advocate for gays and lesbians and their access to health care?
5. What issues of diversity are important to consider when working with gay and lesbian elders?
6. Now that you are sensitive to the impact of homophobia and heterosexism on the aging experience of lesbian and gay elders, what areas of public policy would you identify as needing change to protect the basic rights of these elders? With which area would you start?
7. As a coordinator for staff training, you realize that the staff of your agency need a series of training sessions on working with gay and lesbian elders. Design a training series for your staff. What information would you include? What goals and objectives would you identify for helping your staff become more effective and sensitive to needs of gay and lesbian elders? How would you know the training was effective?

Experiential Learning

Activity: Being Invisible

One of the primary difficulties for lesbian and gay elders is the invisibility of their sexual orientation, significant life partner, and family of choice. Has there ever been a time when you felt invisible to others or when your needs where unrecognized or invalidated? The following activity is designed to help you with gaining insight and understanding of the subjective experience of being an invisible minority.

Imagine that you and your own current significant other have been together for many years. You have always been deeply in love and maintained a nurturing and supportive relationship. Your significant other becomes extremely ill and requires emergency hospitalization.

You are not allowed in the emergency room. When he or she is transferred to intensive care, you are not allowed to visit. Your "in-laws" are called on to make critical decisions for your loved one, and you are not consulted. You make phone calls to take care of your partner's business, but the companies will not talk with you about your inquiries or take action because your name is not the name on the account and you are not "married" to the account holder.

Imagine this scenario with as much feeling and awareness as you can muster. Identify your feelings and thoughts. Share these with a discussion group.

■ How would you ask for help?
■ What risks would you consider before doing so?
■ What would you want from a social worker?
■ What kinds of policy changes would you want to see happen?

Activity: My "Family of Choice"

Our social support networks are an especially important factor that determines the quality of our well-being. In this chapter you learned that gay and lesbian persons develop an affirming social support network made up of a family of friends and accepting relatives. One way of becoming sensitive to the importance of a client's social support network is to become aware of our own and how we interact with and are dependent on our own "families of choice." Who makes up your support network? Who would you call on in time of need or in time of celebration? Who would call on you for the same?

■ On a piece of paper draw a large circle to represent your social support network, and place yourself in the middle.
■ Draw another circle outside where you are and within the boundary of the large circle. This will create two rings.
■ Within the first ring, identify those with whom you are closest and would call on first in time of need.
■ Within the second ring identify others with whom you may be close but may not call on first.
■ Outside your largest circle identify any kinds of social agencies, programs, or policies that provide you with some safety net of support for your life.
    What do you notice?

Activity: Word Match

Listed are several terms that have been used in this chapter to identify issues related to the gay and lesbian population. Match up the terms with the correct definition.

1.	Coming out	A.	A behavioral science term that describes negative attitudes, fears, hatred and/or dislike of homosexuals and results in prejudice, discrimination, and hate.
2.	Homophobia	B.	Describes someone who is not open about his or her sexual orientation with family, at work, with colleagues, or even him- or herself.

3. Heterosexism   C.   A developmental process of recognizing and integrat-
                                   ing knowledge of one's sexual orientation into personal
                                   and public life. A continual process.
4. Sexual orientation   D.   Blatant cultural and societal omission of nonheterosex-
                                   ual family life and sexual orientation.
5. Closeted   E.   Individual's sexual and affectional preference for part-
                                   ners of the same sex, opposite sex, or both sexes.

ANSWER KEY:
1. C   2: A   3: D   4: E   5:   B

Case Studies

See Appendix B for guidelines in analyzing gerontological social work practice.

Case 1: Michael and Ray

Michael and Ray were both in their early seventies. They had been in fairly good health
all of their lives and enjoyed good jobs, which gave them ample retirement on which
to live. They had a lifelong circle of friends, many with whom they shared the joys and
sorrows of their thirty-one years together. Most of Michael's family had passed away. Ray
had three nephews whom he adored and who kept in touch with Ray from the various
places in the country where they lived. One afternoon after a short walk through the
neighborhood, Ray collapsed. With help from a neighbor, an ambulance was called, and
Ray was taken to the nearby hospital. This was a day they both had dreaded and thought
they had prepared for. Once at the hospital, Ray was wheeled into the emergency room,
and as Michael went along with him he was blocked from going into the examination
room. Michael told himself that this would just be temporary. He waited anxiously in
the waiting room. After several hours the nurse let Michael know that Ray was being
placed in intensive care. Michael was not allowed to see Ray as he was not "next of
kin." Michael was devastated and knew that Ray would be wanting his comfort and support. He stood there in shock and disbelief and felt like he couldn't think clearly enough
to move. Hours must have passed before he realized that he hadn't moved from the waiting room.

Case 2: Karen and Sherrie

Karen and Sherrie first met when they were in their early twenties. That was fifty years ago.
They had led a quiet life. Karen, a high school teacher, was thought of as the school "spin-
ster," and Sherrie had retired from the gas company. They had a small circle of friends with
whom they socialized. Neither of their families knew the depth of their relationship, that
they were each other's love. Karen and Sherrie felt it was really something that they didn't
want to bring up with their family members, since they wouldn't understand. After all, they
had seen what had happened to their friends who had told others or had been discovered.
But now Karen worried. She worried so much that she couldn't sleep, and eating was not
something she was eager to do. She was losing weight and starting to have a difficult time

keeping their small two-bedroom home organized. But it was really Sherrie who was not doing well, Karen thought. Ever since Sherrie fell and broke her hip she hadn't been able to do much for herself. Karen was exhausted and finally forced herself to see her doctor, who immediately hospitalized her. Sherrie's niece in a nearby city was contacted to help care for Sherrie. Against Sherrie's wishes, she was taken to her niece's home, and plans were made for nursing home placement. Sherrie grew depressed, and Karen was desperate to do something to stop the tearing apart of her family. Karen began to insist on leaving the hospital, although she was not yet strong enough.

Annotated Bibliography

Adelman, M. (Ed.). (1986). *Long time passing: Lives of older lesbians*. Boston: Alyson Publications.

Adelman presents a remarkable collection of the reflections of twenty-two lesbian elders on their experience of the aging process. Through the autobiographic telling of their life stories, the reader is privileged to "live" life as a lesbian in the pre–World War II era through the prefeminist liberation era, gay liberation, and into the present. One of the common themes of the stories of these brave women is that the most critical factor in determining psychological well-being in lesbian elders is the degree of homophobia and heterosexism that exists in society.

Alexander, C. J. (Ed.). (1996). *Gay and lesbian mental health: A source book for practitioners*. New York: Harrington Park Press.

Eleven issues that lesbian and gay persons may experience during their lifetimes are identified, and clinical interventions are discussed. Some of the issues discussed include mental health and aging, coming out, parenting, and use of support groups.

Berger, R. M. (1996). *Gay and gray: The older homosexual man* (2nd ed.). New York: Harrington Park Press.

This book, first published in 1982, provided the first full-length study of older gay men. Findings from ten in-depth interviews are discussed which helped to break the old myths that older gay men are lonely, isolated, and oversexed. Berger finds that older gay men are well-adjusted to both their sexual orientation and to aging. The second edition includes new chapters on such topics as Friend's theory of successful gay and lesbian aging.

Cruikshank, M. (1991). Lavender and gray: A brief survey of lesbian and gay aging studies. In J. A. Lee (Ed.), *Gay midlife and maturity: Crisis opportunity, and fulfillment* (pp. 77–87). New York: Harrington Park Press.

This chapter provides an excellent chronology and review of lesbian and gay aging research and writings. The article provides evidence of a growing body of research on lesbian and gay elders that began in the 1970s and continues into the present.

Hidalgo, H., Peterson, T. L., & Woodman, N. J. (Eds.). (1985). *Lesbian and gay issues: A resource manual for social workers*. Silver Spring, MD: National Association of Social Workers.

This book provides accurate information, interventions, and resources for social workers working with the lesbian and gay population. Strategies for intervening at the intrapersonal and community level are discussed. Concerns about homophobia and heterosexism are addressed, with suggestions for staff development and continuing education programs so that workers can develop the special knowledge, skills, and attitudes necessary to work with this marginalized group.

Kehoe, M. (1988). Lesbians over 60 speak for themselves. *Journal of Homosexuality, 16.*

This ground-breaking volume details a nationwide study of 150 lesbian women over the age of sixty. It provides a thorough description of the historical context of the subjects and explores family and social relationships, sexual identity, and specific issues related to aging. Like Berger's work, Kehoe's study challenges the myths of older lesbians as bitter, isolated, and depressed with her data that indicates a well-adjusted population of lesbian elders. Methodology and questionnaires are included in the volume.

Kus, R. J. (Ed.). (1995). *Addiction and recovery in gay and lesbian persons*. New York: Harrington Park Press.

    This book is a good survey of current issues and research in the area of gay and lesbian addiction and treatment. Special treatment issues for gays and lesbians are related to homophobia, heterosexism, AIDS, dysfunctional relationship patterns, and sexual abuse. The significance of spirituality and the impact that negative religious beliefs about homosexuality have had on gay and lesbian persons is discussed.

Peterson, K. J. (Ed.). (1996). *Health care for lesbians and gay men: Confronting homophobia and heterosexism*. New York: Harrington Park Press.

    This text examines health care issues facing lesbian and gay persons from youth through old age. The impact of homophobia and heterosexism on the health care of lesbian and gay persons is discussed. Legal issues in health care for gay and lesbian people are identified. Finally, concrete suggestions for social work interventions are offered.

Quam, J. K. (Ed.). (1997). *Social services for senior gay men and lesbians*. New York: Harrington Park Press.

    This is one of the few books that specifically address issues, challenges, and needs faced by gay and lesbian elders. The first chapter provides an excellent historical overview related to the gay and lesbian elderly. Other topics include housing, community programs, staff development, and issues related to working with gay elders. Practice recommendations are made throughout the book. Case studies are provided.

Shernoff, M. (Ed.) (1996). *Human services for gay people: Clinical and community practice*. New York: Harrington Park Press.

    A wide range of human service issues with specific application to the gay and lesbian population are explored in this volume. Models of practice and interventions are presented. Such topics as mental health, needs of HIV-negative men, violence faced by lesbians and gays, chemical dependency, and spirituality issues of Latino men are addressed.

Shernoff, M. (Ed.) (1997). *Gay widowers: Life after the death of a partner*. New York: Harrington Park Press.

    Provides first person accounts of what it is like to lose a partner and to become a widower in a society that does not recognize the relationship. A diversity of experience is offered, which provides the reader with an opportunity to gain insight and understanding.

Slater, S. (1995). *The lesbian family life cycle*. New York: Free Press.

    This ground-breaking text presents the first affirming work on the life-span development of the lesbian family. Slater presents an informative discussion of the issues facing lesbian couples and the impact these have on couple formation and development. She presents five stages of a lesbian family life cycle ranging from formation to couples over sixty-five years old.

Smith, J. D. & Manscoske, R. J. (1997). *Rural gays and lesbians: Building on the strengths of communities*. New York: Harrington Park Press.

    This book offers an important contribution to social work practice and gay and lesbian studies. Rural gay and lesbian persons have traditionally been omitted and unrecognized in social work practice and research. Identifies specific and unique challenges and needs of those living in rural areas. Practice recommendations for supporting rural gay and lesbian persons are made.

General Bibliography

Berzon, B. (1988). *Permanent partners: Building gay and lesbian relationships that last*. New York: Dutton.

Berzon, B. (1992). *Positively gay: New approaches to gay and lesbian life*. Berkeley, CA: Celestial Arts.

Cass, V. C. (1979). Homosexual identity formation: A theoretical model. *Journal of Homosexuality, 4*, 219–235.

Eichberg, R. (1990). *Coming out an act of love*. New York: Plums.

Eliason, M. E. (1995). Attitudes about lesbians and gay men: A review and implications for social service training. *Journal of Gay and Lesbian Social Service, 2*(2), 73–90.

Friend, R. A. (1990). Older lesbian and gay people: A theory of successful aging. *Journal of Homosexuality, 20*, 99–118.

Herdt, G., Beeler, J., & Rawls, T. W. (1997). Life course diversity among older lesbians and gay men: A study in Chicago. *Journal of Gay, Lesbian, and Bisexual Identity, 2*(3/4), 231–245.

Humphreys, N. A. & Quam, J. K. (1998). Middle-aged and old gay, lesbian, and bisexual adults. In G. A. Appleby & J. W. Anastas (Eds.), *Not just a passing phase: Social work with gay, lesbian, and bisexual people* (pp. 245–267). New York: Columbia University Press.

Laird, J. & Green, R. J. (Eds.). (1996). *Lesbians and gays in couples and families: A handbook for therapists*. San Francisco: Jossey-Bass.

Macdonald, B. & Rich, C. (1983). *Look me in the eye: Old women, aging, and ageism*. San Francisco: Spinsters, Ink.

Mallon, G. P. (Ed.). (1998). *Foundations of Social Work practice with lesbian and gay person*. New York: Harrington Park Press.

Marcus, E. (1992). *The male couple's guide: Finding a man, making a home, building a life*. New York: Harper Perennial.

McDaniel, J. (1995). *The lesbian couples' guide: Finding the right woman and creating a life together*. New York: Harper Perennial.

McNaught, B. (1997). *Now that I am out, what do I do?* New York: St. Martin's.

Morales, E. (1989). Ethnic minority families and minority gays and lesbians. *Marriage and Family Review, 14*, 217–239.

Morrow, D. F. (1996). Heterosexism: Hidden discrimination in social work education. *Journal of Gay and Lesbian Social Services, 5*(4), 1–16.

Riley, M. W., Ory, M. G., & Zablotsky, D. (Eds.). (1989). *AIDS in an aging society: What we need to know*. New York: Springer.

Roberto, K. A. (Ed.). (1996). *Relationships between women in later life*. New York: Harrington Park Press.

Sophie, J. (1986). A critical examination of stage theories of lesbian development. *Journal of Homosexuality, 12*(2), 39–51.

Tully, C. T. (1989). Caregiving: What do midlife lesbians view as important? *Journal of Gay and Lesbian Psychotherapy, 1*(1), 87–103.

Tully, C. T. (1995). In sickness and in health: Forty years of research on lesbians. *Journal of Gay and Lesbian Social Services, 3*(1), 1–18.

Weston, K. (1991). *Families we choose: Lesbians, gays, kinship*. New York: Columbia University Press.

White, J. & Martinez, M. C. (1997). *The lesbian health book: Caring for ourselves*. Seattle, WA: Seal Press.

References

Adelman, M. (Ed.). (1986). *Long time passing: Lives of older lesbians*. Boston: Alyson Publications.

Almvig, C. (1982). *The invisible minority: Aging and lesbianism*. New York: Utica College of Syracuse University Press.

Anderson, G. (1998). Providing services to elderly people with HIV. In D. M. Aronstein & Thompson, B. J. (Eds.) *HIV and social work: A practitioner's guide* (pp. 387–480). New York: Harrington Park Press.

Anderson, S. C. (1996). Substance abuse and dependency in gay men and lesbians. In K. J. Peterson (Ed.), *Health care for lesbians and gay men: Confronting homophobia and heterosexism* (pp. 59–76). New York: Harrington Park Press.

Aronstein, D. M. & Thompson, B. J. (Eds.). (1998). *HIV and social work: A practitioner's guide*. New York: Harrington Park Press.

Baez, E. (1996). Spirituality and the gay Latino client. In M. Schernoff (Ed.), *Human services for gay people: Clinical and community practice* (pp. 69–81). New York: Harrington Park Press.

Barranti, C. C. R. (1998). Social work practice with lesbian couples. In G. P. Mallon (Ed.), *Foundations of Social Work practice with lesbian and gay persons* (pp. 183–207). New York: Harrington Park Press.

Benjamin, A. E. (1990). AIDS, aging and long-term care. *The Gerontologist, 30*(4), 564–567.

Berger, R. M. (1982). The unseen minority: Older gays and lesbians. *Social Work, 27,* 236–242.

Berger, R. M. (1984). Realities of gay and lesbian aging. *Social Work, 29,* 57–62.

Berger, R. M. (1996). *Gay and gray: The older homosexual man* (2nd ed.). New York: Harrington Park Press.

Bickelhaupt, E. E. (1995). Alcoholism and drug abuse in gay and lesbian persons: A review of incidence studies. *Journal of Gay and Lesbian Social Services, 2*(1), 5–14.

Black, B., Oles, T. P., Cramer, E. P., & Bennett, C. K. (1999). Attitudes and behaviors of social work students toward lesbian and gay clients: Can a panel presentation make a difference? *Journal of Gay and Lesbian Social Service 9*(4), 47–68.

Bradford, J. & Ryan, C. (1988). *The national lesbian health care survey.* Washington, DC: National Lesbian and Gay Health Foundation.

Bradford, J., Ryan, C., & Rothblum, E. D. (1994). National lesbian health care survey: Implications for mental health care. *Journal of Consulting and Clinical Psychology, 62,* 228–242.

Bressler, J. (1989, Fall). HIV-Infected elders: Case studies of symptomatic persons, and their medical social needs. *Generations,* 45–47.

Bricker-Jenkins, M. (1994). Feminist practice and breast cancer: "The patriarchy has claimed my right breast . . ." *Social Work in Health Care, 19,* 17–42.

Butler, S. S. & Hope, B. (1999). Health and well being for late middle-aged and old lesbians in a rural area. *Journal of Gay and Lesbian Social Service, 9*(4), 27–46.

Cass, V. C. (1979). Homosexual identity formation: A theoretical model. *Journal of Homosexuality, 4,* 219–235.

Coleman, E. (1981/1982). Developmental stages of the coming out process. *Journal of Homosexuality, 7,* 31–43.

Connolly, L. (1996). Long-term care and hospice: The special needs of older gay men and lesbians. *Journal of Gay and Lesbian Social Services, 5*(1), 77–91.

Cruikshank, M. (1991). Lavender and gray: A brief survey of lesbian and gay aging studies. In J. A. Lee (Ed.), *Gay midlife and maturity: Crisis opportunity, and fulfillment* (pp. 77–87). New York: Harrington Park Press.

Dawson, K. (1982). Serving the gay community. *SEICUS Report, 11,* 5–6.

DeCrescenzo, T. A. (1984). Homophobia: A study of the attitudes of mental health professionals toward homosexuality. In R. Shoenberg, R. S. Goldberg, & D. Shore (Eds.), *Homosexuality and Social Work* (pp. 115–137). New York: Heyworth Press.

Deevey, S. (1990). Older lesbian women: An invisible minority. *Journal of Gerontological Nursing, 16,*(5), 35–39.

Demonteflores, C. & Schultz, S. J. (1978). Coming out: Similarities and differences for lesbians and gay men. *Journal of Social Issues, 34,* 59–72.

Dunker, B. (1987). Aging lesbians: Observations and speculations. In Boston Lesbian Psychologies Collective (Ed.), *Gay and lesbian mental health: A sourcebook for practitioners* (pp. 72–82). Chicago: University of Illinois Press.

Ehrenberg, M. (1996). Aging and mental health: Issues in the gay and lesbian community. In C. J. Alexander (Ed.), *Gay and lesbian mental health: A sourcebook for practitioners* (pp. 189–209).

Festinger, L. (1957). *A theory of cognitive dissonance.* New York: Harper and Row.

Friend, R. A. (1989). Older lesbian and gay people: Responding to homophobia. *Marriage and Family Review, 14,* 241–263.

Friend, R. A. (1990). Older lesbian and gay people: A theory of successful aging. *Journal of Homosexuality, 20,* 99–118.

Galassi, F. S. (1991). A life review workshop for gay and lesbian elders. *Journal of Gerontological Social Work, 16,* 75–86.

Glaus, K. O. (1988). Alcoholism, chemical dependency, and the lesbian client. *Women and Therapy*, 8(1/2), 131–144.

Hamburger, L. (1997). The wisdom of non-heterosexually based senior housing and related services. *Journal of Gay and Lesbian Social Services*, 6(1), 11–25.

Herdt, G. & Beeler, J. (1998). Older gay men and lesbians in families. In C. J. Patterson & D'Augelli, A. (Eds.). *Lesbian, gay, and bisexual identities in families* (pp. 177–196). New York: Oxford Press.

Humphreys, N. A. & Quam, J. K. (1998). Middle-aged and old gay, lesbian, and bisexual adults. In G. A. Appleby & J. W. Anastas (Eds.), *Not just a passing phase: Social work with gay, lesbian, and bisexual people* (pp. 245–267). New York: Columbia University Press.

Jacobson, S. A. (1995). Methodological issues in research on older lesbians. *Journal of Gay and Lesbian Social Services*, 3(1), 43–56.

Jacobson, S. A. & Grossman, A. (1996). Older lesbians and gay men: Old myths, new images and future directions. In R. C. Savin-Williams & K. M. Cohen (Eds.), *Developmental, clinical and social issues among lesbians, gay men, and bisexuals*. New York: Harcourt Brace.

Kehoe, M. (1986a). Lesbians over 65: A triple invisible minority. *Journal of Homosexuality*, 12, 139–152.

Kehoe, M. (1986b). A portrait of older lesbians. *Journal of Homosexuality*, 12, 157–161.

Kehoe, M. (1988). Lesbians over 60 speak for themselves. *Journal of Homosexuality*, 16, 1–111.

Kelly, J. J. (1977). The aging male homosexual: Myth and reality. *The Gerontologist*, 17, 328–332.

Kimmel, D. C. (1977). Psychotherapy and the older gay man. *Psychotherapy: Theory, Research and Practice*, 14, 386–393.

Kimmel, D. C. (1978). Adult development and aging: A gay perspective. *Journal of Social Issues*, 34, 113–130.

Kimmel, D. C. (1979). Adjustment to aging among gay men. In B. Bergon & R. Leighton, (Eds.) *Positively gay* (pp. 146–158). San Francisco, CA: Celestial Arts.

Kochman, A. (1997). Gay and lesbian elderly: Historical overview and implications for social work practice. *Journal of Gay and Lesbian Social Services*, 6(1), 1–10.

Kropf, N. P. & Greene, R. R. (1994). Erikson's eight stages of development: Different lenses. In R. R. Greene (Ed.), *Human behavior theory: A diversity framework* (pp. 75–91). New York: Aldine De Gruyter.

Lewis, L. A. (1984). The coming out process for lesbians: Integrating a stable personality. *Social Work*, 29, 464–469.

Lindhorst, T. (1997). Lesbians and gay men in the country: Practice implications for rural social workers. *Journal of Gay and Lesbian Social Services*, 7(3), 1–11.

Linsk, N. L. (1997). Experience of older gay and bisexual men living with HIV/AIDS. *Journal of Gay, Lesbian, and Bisexual Identity*, 2(3/4), 285–308.

Lipman, A. (1986). Homosexual relationships. *Generations*, 10, 51–54.

Mallon, G. P. (Ed.). (1998). *Foundations of Social Work practice with lesbian and gay persons*. New York: Harrington Park Press.

McCormick, W. C. & Wood, R. W. (1992). Clinical decisions in the care of elderly persons with HIV. *Journal of the American Geriatric Society* 40(9), 917–921.

McNaught, B. (1997). *Now that I am out, what do I do?* New York: St. Martin's.

McVinney, L. D. (1998). Social work practice with gay male couples. In G. P. Mallon (Ed.), *Foundations of Social Work practice with gay and lesbian persons* (pp. 209–228). New York: Harrington Park Press.

McWhirter, D. P. & Mattison, A. M. (1984). *The male couple: How relationships develop*. Englewood Cliffs, NJ: Prentice-Hall.

Metz, P. (1997). Staff development for working with lesbian and gay elders. *Journal of Gay and Lesbian Social Services*, 6(1), 35–45.

Morales, E. (1989). Ethnic minority families and minority gays and lesbians. *Marriage and Family Review*, 14, 217–239.

Peterson, J. K. (1996). *Health care for lesbians and gay men: Confronting homophobia and heterosexism*. New York: Harrington Park Press.

Peterson, J. K. & Bricker-Jenkins, M. (1996). Lesbians and the health care system. *Journal of Gay and Lesbian Social Services, 5*(1), 33–47.

Quam, J. K. (1993, June/July). Gay and lesbian aging. *SEICUS Report,* 10–12.

Quam, J. K. (1997a). The story of Carrie and Ann: Long term care crisis. *Journal of Gay and Lesbian Social Services, 6*(1), 97–99.

Quam, J. K. (Ed.). (1997b). *Social services for senior gay men and lesbians.* New York: Harrington Park Press.

Quam, J. K. & Whitford, G. S. (1992). Adaptation and age-related expectations of older gay and lesbian adults. *The Geronotologist, 32,* 367–374.

Rosenfeld, D. (1999). Identity work among lesbian and gay elderly. *Journal of Aging Studies 13*(2), 121–141.

Rounds, C. S. (1993). Are lesbians a high-risk group for breast cancer? *Ms, 3*(6), 4–45.

Ryan, C. C., Bradford, J. B., & Honnold, J. A. (1999). Social workers' and counselors' understanding of lesbian needs. *Journal of Gay and Lesbian Social Service 9*(4), 1–26.

Scherer, Y., Wu., Y. W., & Haughey, B. P. (1991). AIDS and homophobia among nurses. *Journal of Homosexuality, 21*(4), 17–27.

Scheafor, B. W., Horejsi, C. R., & Horejsi, G. A. (1997). *Techniques and guidelines for social work practice* (4th ed.). Boston: Allyn and Bacon.

Shernoff, M. (1997). *Gay widowers: Life after the death of a partner.* New York: Harrington Park Press.

Schwartz, M. (1996). Gay men and the health care system. *Journal of Gay and Lesbian Social Service, 5*(1), 19–32.

Simkin, R. J. (1991). Lesbians face unique health care problems. *Canadian Medical Association Journal, 145*(12), 1620–1623.

Singer, B. L. & Deschamps, D. (1994). *Gay and lesbian stats: A pocketbook of facts and figures.* New York: New Press.

Sitter, K. (1997). Jim: Coming out at age 62. *Journal of Gay and Lesbian Social Services, 6,*(1) 101–104.

Slater, S. (1995). *The lesbian family life cycle.* New York: Free Press.

Smith, J. D. (1997). Working with larger systems: Rural lesbians and gays. *Journal of Gay and Lesbian Social Services, 7*(3), 13–21.

Smith, J. D. & Mancoske, R. J. (1997). *Rural gays and lesbians: Building on the strengths of communities.* New York: Harrington Park Press.

Stevens, P. D. & Hall, J. M. (1988). Stigma, health beliefs and experiences with health care in lesbian women. *Images, 20*(2), 69–73.

Tully, C. T. (1989). Caregiving: What do midlife lesbians view as important. *Journal of Gay and Lesbian Psychotherapy, 1*(1), 87–103.

Weston, K. (1991). *Families we choose: Lesbians, gays, kinship.* New York: Columbia University.

Wolfe, K. (1997). Help for aging gays and lesbians. *Progressive 61*(11), 14.

Zack, P. D. (1999). Invisible men: Gay at midlife. *In the Family 4*(2), 12–15.

Few people approach "old age" without acquiring medical conditions or illnesses which affect their mobility, vision, hearing, or cognitive abilities. To what degree are these medical or health changes a normal part of living? When do these changes lead to disability? The answers depend on a combination of factors including: how long we live; our heredity; how well we maintain our health; our gender, race, and/or ethnicity; where we live; and economics. Just as there are a variety of contributing factors leading to our experiences of health, illness, and disability, we may have several different responses or reactions to these experiences.

While some people acquire disabilities in old age, others age with a preexisting disability. Some individuals live with the disability and accommodate to it by "joining the disability community." For others, the diagnosis of a disability may serve as a reason for changing one's lifestyle. A third response might be to refuse to acknowledge one's disability and thus fail to take advantage of available disability-based services and technology. This chapter will provide the reader with insights of what it is like to age with a disability, what it is like to acquire a disability when older, and knowledge needed by social workers, whether as clinicians, program planners, administrators, or policy analysts, in their work with individuals with disabilities who are also older.

Definition of Disability

Depending upon the definition of disability used, estimates of the prevalence of disability range from 36 million to 50 million people in the United States (Pope & Tarlov, as cited in Hahn 1997). As cited by Asch and Mudrick (1995) the 1990 U.S. Census estimated that there were 22.4 million people age sixteen and over with a "work disability, mobility limitation, or self-care limitation (p. 753). The National Health Interview Survey (NHIS) (as cited in Asch & Mudrick 1995) reported that there were 33.8 million people with disabilities that impose "major limitations on activities or limited an important activity" (p. 753). The 1990–1991 Survey of Income and Program Participation (SIPP) (as cited by Asch & Mudrick 1995) reported that there were 50 million people with disabilities living in the United States.

The NHIS estimated that, in 1989, 13.7 percent of males had a disability, and 14.4 percent of women had a disability (Asch & Mudrick 1995). The 1990/1991 SIPP estimated that 18.7 percent of men and 20.2 percent of women had a disability (Asch & Mudrick 1995). Indicating a clear age and disability interaction, Asch and Mudrick (1995) report that of people with disabilities 36.9 percent were between the ages 65 and 69 years old, and that 39.0 percent of people with disabilities were seventy years old or older. The most common disabling conditions, diseases of the musculoskeletal system and connective tissue, of the circulatory system, of the respiratory system, and of the nervous system and sense organs commonly have an onset in mid-life or later (LaPlante 1996).

In the report of the National Organization on Disability (N.O.D.) Harris Survey on Employment of People with Disabilities (Lou Harris and Associates 1995), it was stated that by disability, "we mean: people who are deaf or with very limited hearing; who have walking problems and always use canes, crutches or a wheelchair, or people without an arm or leg; or who are blind or visually impaired; or who have serious speech problems. We also include people with mental illness or mental retardation or with a serious learning disability" (p. 1). According to the Americans with Disabilities Act of 1990 ([ADA] Pub. L. No. 101-336, 104 Stat. 327 (1990), an individual is considered to have a disability if the person: (a) has a physical or mental impairment that substantially limits one or more major life activities; (b) has a record of a physical or mental impairment; or (c) is regarded as having a physical or mental impairment that substantially limits a major life activity.

The selection of a definition of disability is more than a problem of semantics (National Institute on Disability and Rehabilitation Research [NIDRR] 1993). It is often linked to access to entitlements, policy development, cost-containment, ideology, and advocacy. Definitions of disability range from chronic medical conditions, physical or mental conditions; a functional consequence of the physical or mental condition; or limitations that occur as a consequence of lack of social or physical environmental access (Asch & Mudrick 1995). Asch and Mudrick note that despite such variance, there is general agreement that a disability can be a permanent physical or mental impairment or a chronic physical or mental health condition. It may be visible or invisible, be present at birth, or be acquired at any point during an individual's life. Disabilities vary in level of severity and need for social, physical, sensory, or environmental accommodation.

When Aging and Disability Intersect

Whenever we discuss disability and aging it is important to acknowledge the tremendous heterogeneity within these two communities. The social, political, and economic experiences of an individual with cerebral palsy may be quite different from those of an individual who acquires a spinal cord injury at age forty-five. Similarly, the experiences of an individual who is fifty-five years old may be quite different from those of an individual who is eighty-five. Within the contexts of disability and of aging, we should be aware of the impact of economics, culture, race, ethnicity, gender, and sexual orientation on the individual.

As a first approach to understanding the aging disabled person, we must consider a broader context of disability and aging. Within this broader context, it is necessary to examine the experiences of people with preexisting disabilities who age in place (Gilson & Netting 1997; Trieschmann 1987; Turk, Overeynder & Janicki 1995) in comparison to people who acquire disabilities as they age. Within the group of individuals who have preexisting (lifelong or long-term) disabilities, it is important to distinguish between the issues faced by two groups. The first group involves adults with preexisting disabilities who are experiencing an accelerated aging. This group would involve individuals with such conditions as cerebral palsy, muscular dystrophies, childhood onset diabetes, and forms of juvenile arthritis. These individuals will undergo a process of advanced loss of physical capabilities. In the second group, impairment is relatively stable, anticipating no further compromise to individuals' musculoskeletal, sensory, emotional, or cognitive systems. Disabilities with this group would include mental retardation, blindness, deafness, and corrected orthopedic conditions. As a group, individuals who acquire disabilities before middle age tend to be more homogenous in the impact of their disabilities on the socio-emotional and physical aspects of the aging process.

Many people with preexisting or long-term disabilities have experienced life with the need to develop accommodations or seek adaptations that permit and/or enhance their participation in activities such as education, work, and recreation. Examples of such adaptation are outfitting one's home with visual signal devices that replace doorbells and telephones, installing ramps for access and egress, as well as installing roll-in showers, grab bars, or elevated toilets. In education or work settings, adaptations take the form of scheduled paratransit services, attendant services to assist with eating or toileting, use of a computer with grammar check and spelling check software, or software based on the sound of one's voice, making the computer "voice activated." For the individual with a preexisting disability, interaction with health care or social service providers will have been within the context of their disability, even if indirectly. Disability will have been incorporated into the fabric of friendships, family relationships, as well as work and other community relationships. There will be an increased likelihood that the individual will have had social and friendship contacts with others who have disabilities.

Because few people grow up with a person with a disability or have intimate relationships with disabled people, acquiring a disability can be a new experience. An individual begins the experience of disability with little background or true understanding of the full range of issues involved in having a disability. The adaptations and accommodations that the individual may need will rarely have been anticipated and are often unknown. Attendant care, paratransit services, and rehabilitation technology are often outside of the experience of many nondisabled people. The individual must first know that the services exist before he or she can ask for a particular piece of technology or arrange for attendant care or paratransit services. Utilization of technology and services often depends on learning about their existence. For many, utilization will be dependent upon "accepting" or believing that disability technology and services are intended for them, thereby acknowledging that they have a disability. The identification of disability may be as overwhelming as learning about rehabilitation technology or attendant services.

While there is considerable common ground between individuals with preexisting disabilities and individuals who acquire disabilities as they age, there are also considerable differences. Data from the 1990 and 1991 Survey of Income and Program Participation, Bureau of Census (McNeil 1993) on the disability status of noninstitutional population of the U.S. provide an important profile of people with disabilities:

■ As an individual ages there is an increased likelihood of having a disability. Survey data show a disability "prevalence rate of 5.8 percent among persons less than 18 years old, 13.6 percent among persons 18 to 44 years old, 29.2 percent among persons 45 to 64 years old, 44.6 percent among persons 65 to 74 years old, 63.7 percent among persons 75 to 84 years old, and 84.2 percent among persons 85 years old and over" (p. 8).

■ 13.4 percent of males sixty-five years and older had a disability, and 20.4 percent of females age sixty-five years and over had disabilities.

■ The likelihood that the individual's disability will be severe also increases as one ages. Among individuals under eighteen years old, the likelihood that the disability was severe was 21.8 percent; among persons eighteen to forty-four years old, 38.2 percent; among persons sixty-five to seventy-four years old, 56.8 percent; among persons seventy-five to eighty four years old, 65.1 percent; and among individuals eighty-five and over, 81.2 percent.

■ Males sixty-five years of age and older made up 15.5 percent of all persons with a severe disability, and females sixty-five years and over constituted 27.7 percent of all persons with a severe disability.

■ Of persons sixty-five years old and over with a disability, 17.4 percent needed personal assistance with an activity of daily living (ADL) or an instrumental activity of daily living (IADL). Activities of daily living (ADL) include getting around inside the home, getting in or out of a bed or chair, taking a bath or shower, dressing, eating, and toileting. Instrumental activities of daily living (IADL) include going outside the home, keeping track of money and bills, doing light housework, and using the telephone (McNeil 1993).

■ Of all persons with a severe functional limitation, 56.8 percent were persons sixty-five years and over. Of all individuals needing assistance with an ADL or IADL, 57.9 percent were persons sixty-five years and older. Of all the individuals who used wheelchairs, 64.6 percent were sixty-five years and older, and 71.9 percent of all persons who used a cane, crutches, walker, or other such aid for six months or longer were sixty-five years and older.

The data on disabled people age sixty-five and over serve as a distinct profile of the needs and issues faced by older disabled persons. McNeil (1993) noted that:

■ Of persons sixty-five years old and over with a disability, 15.9 percent had difficulty seeing words and letters, 14.5 percent had difficulty hearing normal conversation, 2.5 percent had difficulty having their speech understood, 27.3 percent had difficulty lifting and carrying ten pounds, 30.6 percent had difficulty climbing stairs without resting, and 30.6 percent had difficulty walking three city blocks.

■ Of persons sixty-five years old and over with a disability, 7.7 percent had difficulty getting around inside the home, 9.5 percent had difficulty getting in or out of a bed or a chair, 9.5 percent had difficulty taking a bath or shower, 6.2 percent had difficulty dressing, 2.1 percent had difficulty eating, and 4.4 percent had difficulty using the toilet, including getting to the toilet.

■ Of persons sixty-five years old and over with a disability, 16.0 percent had difficulty going outside the home, for example, to shop or visit a doctor's office, 7.5 percent had difficulty keeping track of money and bills, 9.3 percent had difficulty preparing meals, 12.2 percent had difficulty doing light housework, such as washing dishes or sweeping a floor, and 6.5 percent had difficulty using the telephone.

■ Of both sexes, persons sixty-five years old and over with a disability, 3.7 percent had a mental or emotional disability. Of males sixty-five years and older, 2.9 percent had a mental or emotional disability, and 4.3 percent of females sixty-five and older had a mental or emotional disability.

People with disabilities, as compared to nondisabled people, are at increased risk for having lower levels of income and for living in poverty (McNeil 1997b). Of those persons who participate in means-tested assistance programs, a large proportion have disabilities. However, most people with disabilities do not receive benefits from an assistance program (McNeil 1997a). Data from the 1994–1995 Survey of Income and Program Participation (McNeil 1997a) show that among persons age sixty-five and over, the presence of a disability increases the chance of having a low (less than half the median) income. Of people sixty-five and over with no disability, 16.7 percent had a low income; of those with a nonsevere disability, 25.0 percent had a low income; and of persons with a severe disability, 35.5 percent had a low income. People with disabilities are more likely to have government health insurance coverage and less likely to have private coverage than nondisabled people.

Aging Services and Disability

In 1991, the American Association of Retired Persons (AARP) commissioned the National Senior Citizens Law Center (NSCLC) to examine Titles II and III of the ADA (National Senior Citizens Law Center [NSCLC] 1992) and their effect on the rights of older people with disabilities. "Title II prohibits discrimination on the basis of disability by state and local government programs, even when those programs receive no federal funds. Title III specifies that no person shall be subject to discrimination on the basis of disability in goods and services in any commercial facility or place of public accommodation" (NSCLC 1992, p. i). The NSCLC conducted a nationwide survey of State Units on Aging, Area Agencies on Aging, state protection and advocacy organizations, legal services programs, private attorneys, and law school clinical programs. The NSCLC found that:

■ Clients of the organizations surveyed were most likely to have physical impairments; to have their mobility impairments be the source of their greatest limitations; to more often frequent physicians' offices, stores, and senior centers than other public accommodations; and to be consumers of Departments of Social Services programs.
■ The most frequently encountered barriers included "lack of assistance for people who appear confused or who cannot understand the process, [and] inadequate physical access to offices, services, and activities" (p. ii).
■ Accommodations currently in place are most frequently found in "Departments of Social Services and senior centers, most likely to focus on physical access to facilities unlikely to include telecommunications devices" (TDD/TTY) for deaf and hard of hearing people, media available in alternative format (e.g., Braille, audiotape, disk materials), and "least likely to involve people with cognitive impairments or people who are homebound" (p. ii).

Rose (1991) has suggested that chronic health conditions pose the greatest threat to quality of life of older Americans. The impact or consequence of chronic health conditions and disability on the older persons is, in part, related to the age of onset. The experiences and perspective of the older adult who enters older age with a preexisting chronic health condition or disability may be quite different from older persons who develop a chronic health problem in their sixties. The individual who contracted a chronic disease or acquired a disability in young adulthood or earlier commonly will have made adjustments to the likelihood of the realities of reduced educational and vocational opportunities and options, "curtailed activity, and difficult psychosocial challenges" (Rose 1991, p. 93). This will also have meant that the individual, if he or she sought health care and social services, would have had the primary point of contact through the disability habilitation and rehabilitation services system (Gilson & Netting 1997). For people who age with a disability this often means that they will have as their primary reference group the disability community (Trieschmann 1987; Turk et al 1995). Individuals who acquire disabilities as they age will often choose the aging community as their primary reference group (Gilson & Netting 1997). Because it has been only relatively recently that individuals with moderate or severe disabilities lived into old age, professionals in disability habilitation and rehabilitation services have had few opportunities to work with people as they age.

If aging is a universal process, and if there is an increased likelihood that health and physical impairments will co-occur with aging, then when do "normal aging processes" lead to disability? While this may seem a relatively straightforward question, the answers are both complex and simple. On the simple side, relying on the ADA, at the point that the individual experiences a limitation in one or more major life activities, or develops a record (medical, social, economic, or other) of an impairment, or is regarded (by themselves or others) as having an impairment that substantially limits a major life activity, they have a disability. But, for many, disability is much more than that. We also know that many people who develop hearing losses, lose visual acuity, or develop arthritic conditions do not consider themselves as having a disability. Why would individuals with apparent impairments not consider themselves to have a disability or be considered by others not to have a disability?

Part of the answer can be found in descriptions of what it means to be disabled or to have a disability. Often, these descriptions are based on a social construction of the meaning of disability, the attributions that one makes toward disability, and what having a disability may mean for one's participating in the full range of benefits and opportunities in the community. This is not to take away from the clear medical demarcations of disabled/nondisabled, such as what would occur following a spinal cord injury. Rather, it is to suggest that part of what "handicaps" people are social, attitudinal, and environmental barriers to participation. Providing ramps and automatic doors makes entering and exiting buildings easier, large print luncheon and dinner menus can make ordering a meal at a restaurant possible, or having captioning regularly offered at movie theaters can make the difference between being able to socialize in the community and staying at home.

By their late sixties, most older persons experience multiple chronic health problems. The majority of limiting chronic health conditions, such as sensory impairments, arthritis, cancer, heart conditions, hypertension, and diabetes, increase in prevalence with age. It is the functional limitation rather than the disease itself that often presents the older person with the greatest worry. In terms of access to programs and services this often means that, for the individual who acquires the disability as he or she ages, health care and social services will commonly be provided through the aging network. Simon-Rusinowitz and Hofland (1993) have suggested that an example of the differing perspectives of the disability services professional and the aging services professional is the language used to refer to the service recipient. Services recipients are "referred to by gerontologists as clients or patients but by the disability community as consumers" (Simon-Rusinowitz & Hofland 1993, p. 159). In recent years, the delivery of health care services to people with disabilities has increasingly been linked to the principles of independent living, self-determination, autonomy, and empowerment (Mackelprang & Salsgiver 1996), characteristics which are the basis of the consumer perspective of disability and disability services.

Despite apparent differences between the perspectives of disability service and the aging service professionals, older persons and disabled persons share the common experiences of lack of barrier-free and affordable housing and transportation services (Gilderbloom & Rosentraub 1990). As a consequence many older people and disabled people "are prevented from participating in employment, health care, shopping, social and recreational activities, and from exercising their freedom to live independently" (Gilderbloom & Rosentraub 1990, p. 271). This common experience is related to a societal devaluation that results in excluding these individuals from major areas of community life (Racino & Heumann 1992). Racino and Heumann have suggested that "like younger disabled people, older adults—those who are disabled and those who are not—are often seen as being unable to fulfill accepted adult roles" (p. 80). When cities fail to provide sidewalks or curb cuts, it is a clear signal that people with disabilities are not valued. When an accessible mass transit and paratransist system is not in place, that is a further sign that people with disabilities as well as older people are not welcomed. Failure to provide accessible and affordable housing is yet another indication that disadvantaged families, of which a disproportionate number of people with disabilities and older persons are members, are not wanted (Gilderbloom & Rosentraub 1990). For the individual who is both older and disabled, these experiences of social devaluation are often compounded. "An older person with a disability may find him- or herself viewed as sick and therefore unable to benefit from technology and supports that could help maintain the person's life style in the community" (Racino & Heumann 1992, p. 81).

Shared common experiences of the disability community and the aging community, as well as the compounding experiences of aging and disability, suggest that professionals in disability services and aging services have much to learn from each other. There is also much that individuals with disabilities and older persons may exchange, with such interaction serving as the basis for coalition building and combined social and political advocacy. The advances in rehabilitation technology, the movement toward long-term consumer-directed health care, the emphasis on empowerment and self-determination, as well as other emerging trends in the disability community, when combined with the sophisticated organizing and advocacy activities of groups such as the AARP and the Grey Panthers, suggest a formidable force that could dramatically change the nature of service supports and delivery for older persons, persons with disabilities, and older persons with disabilities.

The following three case studies illustrate the varying experiences of the aging and disabled. Accelerated aging, aging in place, and acquiring a disability through the aging process are phenomena with similar characteristics, yet they require very different service responses.

Aging with a Disability—Accelerated Aging

Jonathan, now fifty-six years old, contracted polio at age four, which affected both legs. During his early and middle-childhood, Jonathan was involved in aggressive rehabilitation efforts, including multiple surgeries and extensive physical therapy. As a result of the hospitalizations associated with the surgeries, Jonathan spent considerable time separated from his family, and the majority of his relationships were with adult medical professionals. His involvement with other children was primarily with those also admitted to the hospitals and rehabilitation units. Jonathan's elementary education was hospital and home-based.

As a result of the lack of muscle development, Jonathan was fitted with leg braces and forearm crutches for mobility. By the time he reached his mid-thirties, he had developed problems with strain and inflammation of his shoulders, elbows, and wrists due to use, or more correctly, overuse of his forearm crutches. This excessive wear of his upper limb joints left him with few options other than becoming sedentary or beginning to use a manual wheelchair. Jonathan did purchase a wheelchair and used it intermittently. Jonathan's physical condition remained relatively stable until his mid-forties, at which time there seemed to be an unexpected (to him, at least) loss of muscle strength, general muscle fatigue, and pain in his joints and muscles. Along with these changes in his physical condition, Jonathan began to experience periods of depression. After extensive medical testing, Jonathan learned that these physiological and psychological changes were commonly associated with post-polio syndrome.

ISSUES FOR JONATHAN

Jonathan was experiencing the process of accelerated aging. Having contracted polio at age four, he experienced his life as a disabled person. Jonathan's reference group is the disability community (Gilson & Netting 1997). He grew up during a period of many social and legal changes affecting the lives of individuals with disabilities. Among the legal and civil rights changes have been the passage of the Rehabilitation Act of 1973 [Pub. L. No. 93–112, 87 Stat. 355, 394 (1973)], the Education for All Handicapped Children Act of 1975 [Pub. L. No. 94–142, 89 Stat. 773 (1975)], the Air Carrier Access Act of 1986 [Public L. No. 99–435, 100 Stat 1080 (1987)], the Fair Housing Amendments Act of 1988 [Pub. L. No. 100–430, 102, Stat. 1619 (1988)], and the ADA of 1990. Social changes have included the deinstitutionalization of many individuals with disabilities (Sullivan 1992), the emergence of the independent living (IL) movement (DeJong 1984; Heumann 1993), the development of expanded job and career opportunities for people with disabilities (Kregel & Wehman 1997), the evolution of the principles of self-determination, self-advocacy, and empowerment (Gilson 1998; Hahn 1997), and the growth of an identifiable disability community (Gilson, Tusler, & Gill 1997). These interacting experiences had a profound impact upon Jonathan in terms of how he views himself as a disabled person, his identification of needed services, the role of the service provider, and his place in the community. Because disability is a cultural as well as biological experience (Gill 1997; Linton 1998), Jonathan's experience of disability would likely have positive connotations with a recognition of the impact and consequences of discrimination and oppression.

However, Jonathan is also experiencing symptoms associated with post-polio syndrome (PPS). About 25 percent of polio survivors in the United States may be affected with PPS (National Institute of Neurological Disorders and Stroke 1997). Individuals who have consistently overused their residual muscles are at risk for progressive post-polio muscular atrophy. Post-polio syndrome may have many causes. Some of the symptoms may be the result of the natural aging of previously damaged muscles and joints. Unrelated medical conditions may lead to new symptoms and a progression of weakness. Unexplained new muscle atrophy and weakness may develop in some polio survivors. The overuse or repetitive use of weakened muscle fibers and tissues leads to musculoskeletal pain. For the polio survivor, increased pain leads to the need for increased rest, which leads to further atrophy and a possible increasing level of impairment (Maynard 1998). For Jonathan, as for many survivors of polio, this onset of new symptoms may be completely unexpected. The onset of unexpected acute symptoms related to a chronic condition may pose unique issues not only for the polio survivor but also the service provider system. It is this onset of post-polio syndrome that signals Jonathan's accelerated aging. The symptoms are increasing impairment and compromise of the biological system.

This phenomenon of accelerated aging is not limited to individuals with polio (Trieschmann 1987). Similar aging patterns are apparent in individuals with cerebral palsy (Kailes 1992; Turk et al. 1995) and other neuromuscular disabilities, such as multiple sclerosis, muscular dystrophy, and juvenile arthritis (Gilson & Netting 1997). Joints wear out because of personal decisions and professional encouragement not to use adaptive or assisted mobility equipment (for example, canes instead of crutches, crutches instead of wheelchairs, and manual wheelchairs instead of power wheelchairs). The inability to maintain proper body alignment puts excessive strain on otherwise unaffected muscles and on the skeletal system. Unfortunately, rehabilitation medicine has focused most of its attention on the management of newly acquired disabilities and acute conditions, not on aging with a long-term disability (Kailes 1992). These changes, however, go beyond those just of disability. Kailes (1992) suggests that many people with physical disabilities experience "the natural process of aging superimposed on other impairments that have imposed a range of physical, emotional, and financial" consequences on their daily lives (p. 151). As Jonathan ages, he will enter the aging services system with a clear identity as a disabled person but with increasing rehabilitation needs; Jonathan, as a consumer, will seek services from professionals who instead may view him as a client or patient.

Aging in Place

Mary is entering her early sixties with a good understanding of her experiences of depression that first occurred when she was in her twenties. She continues to take antidepressant medications, and her medication regimen is prescribed by a psychiatrist. She participates in a twice-monthly, psychiatric survivor/ex-patient support group. In addition to her mental disability, Mary has a physical disability that resulted from an automobile accident when she was thirty-five years old. As a consequence of the accident, Mary's left leg was amputated, and she was fitted with a lower leg prosthesis. For the great majority of her activities, Mary requires no additional ambulation supports other than her prosthesis. However, on occasion, Mary will use a wheelchair for mobility when long distances are involved. Mary's physical and mental disabilities are stabilized, with minimal likelihood of further impairment or an exacerbation of symptoms. However, both of her disabilities will require ongoing support from the service delivery system. As she ages, Mary will move from using the disability service system to using the aging service system as her primary provider. For several years, Mary has been considered a disability activist, serving on several disability councils and testifying before her city council as well as the state legislature on disability related policies, regulations, and laws.

Although Mary's physical disability may put added strain on her musculoskeletal system as she ages, it may not have the same accelerated impact as Jonathan's disability. This may be due to her not needing to use crutches, which put a strain on shoulder, elbow, and wrist joints, and her periodic use of a manual wheelchair when extended mobility is required. However, Mary will continue to require periodic adjustments and fittings of her prosthesis.

Unlike individuals who have a late life lower limb loss, Mary is well acquainted with a life that includes periodic visits to prothetists and physical therapists. As a result of the relatively recent advancements in weight, design, and flexibility of leg prostheses, Mary will have an increased likelihood and desire to seek out the latest advancements in adaptive equipment. Because individual prosthetic devices are designed to enhance performance in a variety of activities, including snow skiing, bike riding, running, and walking, Mary's selected recreational activities may necessitate multiple and advanced technology prostheses. This familiarity with and use of task-specific prostheses will be unexpected by aging services professionals, who themselves may lack an understanding of and familiarity with the range of capabilities of prosthetic devices.

Support of Mary and her mental disability will require treatment from a mental health system and an aging services system that Biegel, Shore, and Silverman (1989) assert lack "ongoing organizational relationships" (p. 151). They note that among the system barriers of mental health services is a "belief that older persons are not suitable candidates for 'treatment' or therapy and are therefore viewed as 'hopeless'" (p. 151). Aging services professionals tend to hold negative attitudes toward mental health problems, and mental health professionals tend to hold negative attitudes toward aging (Biegel et al. 1989). For Mary, as for many older persons, the aging services professional will need to be assertive in locating mental health treatment professionals who can accurately recognize symptoms of a mental illness and prescribe treatment based on her mental health disability. All too commonly, professionals view symptoms such as withdrawal, isolation, sadness, or periods of confusion as "signs" of the aging process and not as symptoms of a treatable mental disability.

Acquiring a Disability During the Aging Process

Although Martha had not been one for joining a gym and exercising, her job as a junior high school teacher kept her quite active. At sixty-eight years of age, Martha began to experience dramatic shifts in her sense of independence and autonomy. Her husband had recently passed away, and her closest living relative was her sister, who lived with her husband in a town ten miles away. Martha had a lifelong hearing loss that seemed to become progressively worse as she reached her early sixties. At sixty-three years of age, she decided to have her hearing evaluated by an audiologist, who fitted her with a hearing aid.

For much of her adult life, Martha considered herself to have a "weight problem." Shortly after her visit to the audiologist her physician tested her for adult onset diabetes. Diagnosed with diabetes, Martha began to follow a diet that was restricted in sugar intake, and she also began a more vigorous weight loss program. When Martha turned seventy, her circulatory problems associated with her diabetes increased in severity, leading to a decrease in mobility and independent ambulation. As a result of these limitations, she was prescribed a scooter for mobility. Additionally, Martha found herself growing tired faster and had less agility; she was less able to lift pots, pans, and dishes from her shelves or put away her groceries without resting. Following several occasions when she felt "light headed," weak to the point of not being able to rise from her chair or scooter, and after falling at the community center, Martha was hospitalized for a series of medical tests, including physical therapy and occupational therapy evaluations. Being able to return home following these evaluations was dependent upon a variety of changes and adjustments occurring in her life environment. These included, among others, making her house more accessible, and arranging door-to-door transportation (paratransist services). Someone needed to be identified who could assist Martha in both activities of daily living and accessing responsive and accessible community services and programs. When Martha and her husband purchased their home they were in their early thirties, they had not anticipated either of them having limited mobility. As a consequence, there were few accommodations in place, such as adequately wide door openings, accessible cabinets, accessible appliances, or accessible entranceways.

Martha had very little personal contact with human services, rehabilitation services, and health services professionals prior to her being evaluated for and fitted with a hearing aid at sixty-three years of age. Following her husband's death, Martha started to attend activities at the local community center for seniors. She joined in on excursions, arts and crafts classes, and other activities designed for people who are at least sixty years old. She was elected to the Board of Advisors of the local Area Agency on Aging (AAA). Joining the AAA marked a move by Martha toward increased community involvement and activism. Martha enjoyed her role as a representative and spokesperson of the aging community. Despite her hearing loss, Martha did not consider herself to be hard of hearing. Using a scooter seemed strange. The only time she saw someone using wheel mobility was when she visited friends at the hospital and people were being pushed in wheelchairs. Those people were "sick." When she was younger she had occasionally watched telethons that raised money for "handicapped" children. Now, finding herself using "one of those things," a scooter, she was not sure what to think.

Her hearing loss and her diabetes forced her to seek health care services—for her these were services designed to "treat" older persons. These professionals were the experts. They knew what she had, what caused it, and what she needed. Their views of Martha will often be in relation to her illness, disability, or impairment, conditions that need to be treated with a medical plan, with physician and nurse oversight—in other words, a "medicalization" of aging and disability. Clark (1995), in reporting the findings of McCullough, Wilson, Teasdal, Kolpakchi, and Skelly, notes that the values of many older persons may be more related to their self-identity than concerned with their physical or mental health, as may be the situation for Martha. This does not mean that Martha will not want health care services. Rather, it is that the consumer–health care professional relationship should be a partnership: "Professionals must be open to the empowerment of the elderly individual with disabilities with recognition that it is he or she who must define the appropriate means and ends of care" (Clark 1995, p. 409).

Martha, like other women, has an increased rate of activity limitation due to a health condition and is therefore at greater risk for institutionalization in long-term care facilities (Rundall 1992). Living in her own home alone and with her health conditions, Martha, like other older persons in her situation, may increasingly need in-home services such as home-delivered meals, homemaker services, and home health services (Rundall 1992). Martha's quality of life will be influenced by the degree to which her aging-based health care providers adopt a progressive view "on measures related to functional independence and autonomy" (Clark 1995, p. 403). Clark (1995) suggests that overreliance on simple individual autonomy ignores the critical contributions made to life by a sense of community (p. 403). Further, it will be essential that Martha and her health care providers reject the notion of "successful aging"—a concept that suggests that failure in growing older is signified by the onset of a chronic health condition or disability (Clark 1995). Quality of life for Martha, as for many people, will be determined by involvement and engagement in life, "not simply assuring survival and postponing institutionalization" (Clark 1995, p. 404).

Comparison of Service Needs

Jonathan presents the social worker with a variety of health and social service intervention needs. He may need the social worker to help coordinate the services that he requires, as well as new services as his needs change with the progression of his post-polio syndrome (PPS). Many of his health and social service needs will be met by existing community and disability services. However, because PPS tends to be progressive and is associated with aging, we may see the emergence of aging-oriented services based within disability services. Jonathan will require referral to, and monitoring by, a physical therapist trained to work with progressive neuromuscular disorders. If it is determined that he could benefit from an aquatic program, either swimming or aquatic exercise, Jonathan should be referred to an accessible community fitness center. As Jonathan's physical condition changes, he should be referred for periodic evaluation and review of his rehabilitation engineering and assistive technology needs. Currently, these services are most commonly found within the disability services system. As his requirements for an accessible living environment change, Jonathan would benefit from a referral to a housing specialist, an individual with an understanding of the issues of adaptive housing and universal design. Universal design is based on the principle that all new buildings or houses can be constructed to be accessible so that there would not be a need to have to remodel in order to accommodate individuals who acquire disabilities. Clearly, professionals within the aging services system have a great deal of experience in working with residential relocation. The social worker will also need to work with Jonathan to address possible socio-emotional needs. Jonathan may benefit from referral to a counselor who has expertise in both aging and disability. It will not be enough to refer him to a counselor with expertise in either aging or disability, because for Jonathan, as for many others, these issues will intersect and overlap.

Like Jonathan, Mary presents with a variety of intersecting health and social service needs. Her social worker should be prepared to assist with service identification and coordination. As for many individuals with disabilities now aging, her needs may best be met by providers from both systems. Her physical therapy and assistive technology evaluation and services may be best met through existing rehabilitation services. Because of her recreation interests, it will be important that she work closely with a recreation therapist and rehabilitation engineer. Mary's social worker should be able to assist her in securing funding support from manufacturers, athletic equipment suppliers, or other interested parties as she seeks to purchase the latest available prosthetic equipment.

Like Jonathan and Mary, Martha may benefit from an evaluation of her assistive technology needs. If it is determined that Martha's activity and participation levels could be increased and/or her life satisfaction enhanced by having adaptive equipment made specifically for her or modified for her particular needs, she will need to be referred to a rehabilitation clinic that has access to a rehabilitation engineer. Her paratransit services may be arranged through the aging services or the disability services network; however, the social worker will need to work with the paratransit services to assure that they provide Martha with maximum response to her transportation needs and not slot her into the schedule of availability.

Social Work Issues

Jonathan, Mary, and Martha share similar health- and disability-related needs, yet each of their individual diagnoses and conditions necessitate individualized responses. As part of the larger older disabled community they may require services from both rehabilitation services professionals and aging services professionals. These services, despite common or shared areas of concern, often approach aging and disability from divergent vantage points. Yet, because individuals with long-term or preexisting disabilities are entering the aging health care and social services systems, change is taking place.

The involvement of people with disabilities with the aging services system is having an impact on the conceptual and value framework that drives direct, administrative, and policy practice. One form that this impact is taking involves an examination of the principles of long-term and community care, self-determination, empowerment, and independence. "The expression 'adding life to years rather than years to life' captures the changing direction in the care of the frail elderly over the last decade" (Clark 1995, p. 402) and is reflective of changes in the conceptual and value framework of aging services. What is it that we mean by quality of life? Do consumers have the same definition as providers? (Clark 1995). What do we mean by independence? (Cohen 1992).

Quality of life and independence are more than survival and staying out of an institution. Disabled people bring to the field of aging a view of services less as compensating for physical and psychological deficits than as enhancing or limiting independence (Cohen 1992, p. 91). Quality of life and independence are also tied to the definition of the "problem to be solved," not only in a descriptive sense, but as a means of defining "the range of options available to solve it" (Clark 1995, p. 404).

Who controls or determines services, the consumer or the agency/professional? When we talk about successful aging, just what do we mean? Implied in this phrase is that aging with an illness, health condition, or disability is "unsuccessful aging" (Clark 1995) or perhaps "incompetence." Cohen (1992) suggests that many disabled elderly persons, "and perhaps even worse, the advocates, policy makers, program planners, and practitioners" (p. 94) support a model of aging services built upon "The Elderly Mystique." As adapted from Rosenfelt (1965) and Cohen (1988), this mystique is focused on older people with disabilities.

> The mystique now holds that *any* disability in old age marks the beginning not only of inevitable decline and an ignominious end, but also the end of mastery. According to this mystique, the elderly who become disabled can no longer travel as they wish, eat what they want, engage in physically demanding activities, or exercise dominion over a work space or group of people. They have no schedules they must keep, and so forth. (Cohen 1992, emphasis in original, p. 94)

If the service provider as well as the person with the disability are to move beyond this view of older disabled people, we must examine whose definition of need or problem is used. Models based upon professional control over the definition serve to exclude a partnership between the individual and the health care professional. Clark (1995) suggests that the person who controls the definition subsequently controls or defines the range of available options. The development and support of open patterns of communication are critical if social workers are to practice from a framework of empowerment and supportive self-determination. The push toward empowerment and self-determination will reinforce a necessary shift away from practices of paternalism and professional domination.

Perhaps nowhere else has the impact of consumer control been felt more than in the delivery of personal assistance services (PAS). By having control over the amount and choice of who is to deliver PAS, many individuals have moved from nursing homes or avoided admission altogether. Not only has this increased quality of life, it has also brought cost savings for public and third party insurers.

Consumer-Directed Attendant Services

A key to community living for many people with disabilities, young as well as older, is the availability of personal assistance services (PAS). Personal assistants or attendants provide services such as help with mobility needs, transferring in and out of a bed or wheelchair, bathing, dressing, grooming, toileting, preparing meals, check writing, and communication interpretation (DeJong & Wenkler 1979; Gilson & Casebolt 1997). Personal independence, dignity, and control over one's life are important values for all citizens. Being older and having a disability in no way lessens the importance of these values (Barker 1993). Providing older individuals with disabilities "the assistance of another person in tasks that individuals would normally do for themselves if they did not have a disability" (Heumann 1993, p. 253) is essential to a self-empowered and self-determined quality of life that is linked to a sense of community. The consumer-directed model of attendant care is based upon the premise that the disabled person is the expert on his or her health care and social service needs. Litvak (1990) describes a PAS model that incorporates a continuum of levels of primary consumer-managed services. The continuum reflects that:

> People vary in their desire and/or ability to be self-reliant. People with disabilities are no different when it comes to managing their personal assistants. On one end of the continuum, there are many who are both capable and willing to manage all aspects of personal assistance—the who, how and when. At the other end of the continuum, we find those who are either unable or unwilling to totally manage their own assistant. And of course there are those in between. (Litvak 1990, p. 13)

The nature and degree of the disabilities of some older people will interfere with their capability to manage their attendant. However, because older persons with a disability are commonly viewed as sick and therefore at risk of being judged incompetent (Cohen 1992), an assumption of the continuum must be consumer competence. Rather than the consumer having to prove competence to utilize consumer-directed services, health care providers need to prove incompetence in order to withdraw self-directed services.

Assistive Technology

Assistive technology (AT), devices and services that are used to increase, maintain, or improve the functional capability of individuals, help promote the independence and comfort of the older disabled person (Mann, Hurren, & Tomita 1993). Assistive technology devices are mechanical devices and instruments that are used by disabled people to communicate, see, hear, or maneuver (Cook & Hussey 1995). Examples of these devices include:

> (i) manual wheelchairs, motorized wheelchairs, motorized scooters, or other devices that enhance the mobility of an individual; (ii) hearing aids, telephone communication devices for

the deaf (TTD/TTY), assistive listening devices, visual and audible signal systems, and other aids that enhance an individual's ability to hear; and (iii) voice-synthesized computer modules, optical scanners, talking software, Braille printers, and other devices that enhance a sight-impaired individual's ability to communicate. (Senate Bill 402, 1998)

Individuals with preexisting sensory and physical disabilities are likely to know when assistive technology is needed, how to use it, and how to get it paid for. For many individuals with disabilities, assistive technology has been an essential element in enabling and enhancing their participation in education, work, recreation, and community residence. Many individuals who acquire disabilities as they age are less likely to have the same knowledge of or experience with assistive technology. Because access to AT devices and services is commonly by way of the disability services system (i.e., educational and vocational services), unless older persons have been involved with disability services, they may not be aware of the resources available to pay for them. If it is perceived that AT must be paid for out of pocket or that it is too expensive, those in need of the technology tend not to purchase it. Therefore, there is a need to seek out AT equipment loan programs, allowing individuals to try out the equipment before purchase in order to determine if it is worth the expense.

Community Housing

The independent living and supported living movement, like those committed to the right to age in place "are premised on the value of individual choice and the conviction that people have the right to intense personal assistance and other necessary services available in their own home in regular neighborhoods" (Racino & Heumann 1992, p. 83). Community living and participation depends upon accessible, available, and affordable housing. Centers for Independent Living (CIL) typically are involved in housing referral and accessibility issues. The independent living movement, of which CILs are a part, in addition to pushing for accessible housing, advocate for supportive services to truly make participation in the community and society possible. Supportive services include personal assistance (mentioned earlier) and peer support. If these services are to be universally available to people with disabilities who are growing older, policies and programs must be put in place that stop "forced choices between living at home and receiving needed support" (Racino & Heumann 1992, p. 85). For older persons with disabilities, supports that help ensure continued noninstitutional community living include access to senior centers, senior center meals, specialized transportation (paratransist), home-delivered meals, homemaker services, visiting nurses, home health aide services, and the availability of adult care programs (Rundall 1992).

One of the most significant implications for social workers in their work with people with disabilities, young and old alike, is the development of interdisciplinary relationships. Disabilities require people from various professions to interface on a regular basis. These interdisciplinary relationships may involve more "typical" interactions with professionals such as physical therapists who help the social worker better understand how the body works, but the relationships may also require that the social worker interact with the rehabilitation engineer who is involved in designing and adapting assistive technology devices (Personal communication, E.F. Netting, March 30, 1998). Work with individuals with disabilities who are also aging will be as varied as work with any other community. A key will be to both individualize the interventions and to respect the value of the individuals' involvement with disability and aging groups. The social worker well-versed in rehabilitation issues and programs will need to develop an understanding and awareness of aging processes, those that are normative or typical, those that may be unique to a type of disability, and those that may be person-specific. The gerontological social worker will need to become informed on the rapid and widespread changes that are taking place in the disability and rehabilitation fields. Changes along these lines include an appreciation of the importance that assistive technology, simple as well as high tech, can play in the lives of individuals. Additionally, more philosophical considerations include an awareness and understanding of an approach to services that is focused on community-based independent living and consumer direction of services. The social worker will partner with the individual to identify service needs and help coordinate necessary and desired health care and social care providers and options. In some instances these interventions may take the form of providing direct services such as counseling, and in others, serving as a case manager or services coordinator.

Social workers involved in working in the disability and aging field must be willing to confront the biases and prejudices that they may hold with regard to both aging and disability. Social definitions of aging and of disability often tend to be based on paternalistic attitudes and feelings of pity—pity for the assumed consequences of growing older and pity for the life experiences of disability. The development of paternalistic attitudes and practices is often linked to assumptions of lack of competence and incapability. It is also clear, largely based on pressure from people who are growing older and from disabled people, that there is a growing challenge to these assumptions. The person who enters old age without a disability may primarily identify with the aging community, whereas the disabled person may enter old age with a disability community perspective. This identification perspective may present important challenges to social work practice. As suggested by Simon-Rusinowitz and Hofland (1993), among others, gerontological social workers may approach their work with older persons with disabilities from a medical model perspective. Disabled people may enter old age firmly connected to a independent community living model. This clash of ideologies may raise profound dilemmas for social work practice.

Conclusion

It is important to recognize that much of this discussion of aging and disability has focused on physical disabilities with some mention of mental disability. There are many other issues of health care and disability associated with cognitive disabilities and dementias that are beyond the scope of this discussion. Nevertheless, if we are to ask why is it important for us to know about disability and aging, it may be useful to remember that it is likely that most of us will either have or acquire a disability as we grow older, or we will be a caregiver of one who does. We must work to prepare the system not only for older Americans but for older Americans with disabilities. As people with disabilities are increasingly empowered and know what services they want, we may need to think in terms of what the Gray Panther movement has accomplished for the aging community. No one should be surprised that, out of the strong linkages developing between aging services and disability services, there emerges a new and joint activist voice.

Discussion Questions

1. What are some of the differences in experiences of an individual with a preexisting disability who ages in place and an individual who is older and acquires a disability? What are some of the shared experiences?

2. Why would someone with a disability experience accelerated aging?
3. Why would someone with a disability be more likely to have government health insurance coverage and less likely to have private coverage than a nondisabled person?
4. What is the greatest threat to quality of life of older Americans?
5. When do normal aging processes lead to disability?
6. Why would an older person with impairments not consider herself or himself to be disabled?
7. What can the disability community teach the aging community about self-empowerment?
8. Why is the development of interdisciplinary relationships so important for social workers who work with older persons with disabilities?
9. Why would having a disability community perspective be helpful for an older individual who acquires a disability?
10. Why do social workers who work with an aging population need to know about universally designed housing and assistive technology?

Experiential Learning

Activity 1

Contact your local Area Agency on Aging (AAA) after obtaining a list of community activity programs for elderly persons, including community center settings, day program services, and nursing home services. Select three of those programs and make an appointment to visit each setting during a structured activity period. Include at least one nonresidential, nonmedical setting and at least one identified residential nursing home setting.

Following your visits to the three settings, write a brief report, with examples, that evaluates and summarizes your observations regarding the nature of the experiences. Observe the elders and think about how they experience the setting. What did you notice in terms of the amount of participant choice regarding level of involvement in the activity? Who directed the activity? Was it acceptable for some people to "just watch?" Did you identify examples of empowerment and self-determination? Who decided when to start and stop the activity? How would you feel as the resident participating in the activity? How would you feel as the professional participating in the activity?

Thinking about yourself as a social worker, how can you include your reactions, observations, and experiences into your work? What might you do differently? What might you continue to do?

Activity 2

Identify three community-based settings where elderly persons are likely to spend time or receive community living supports. Include a program such as "Meals on Wheels," and one non-organized setting, such as a local shopping mall. For the third setting select an established activity such as "bingo night," church group, or other "natural" recreational or social activity.

Contact the local shopping mall to find out if there are any days of the week that are advertised as "senior days" or stores that offer "senior citizen discounts."

Schedule a three-hour time period to go to the setting (shopping mall, restaurant, church, or other) and observe the activities and interactions of the elderly participants.

Volunteer to spend an equal amount of time as a "ride along" with the Meals on Wheels program.

Write a brief essay describing your observations and reactions to the elderly citizens. What surprised you? What did you expect? What new experiences did you have? What were the differences and similarities between the elderly people whom you met during your ride and those that you observed at the shopping mall? At the church groups?

Imagine yourself to be an elderly person at the three settings. Where would you feel the best and why? Where would you be the least comfortable and why?

Activity 3

Relying upon your instructor, a referral from you local Area Agency on Aging (AAA), a community-based program for elders, or the gerontology program at your college or university or that at a nearby college or university, contact two elders. Interview the two individuals about their life stories, particularly that part of their story that has taken place after their fifty-fifth birthday. What do they have in common with the life stories of the three individuals that you read about? What are some of the differences? What did you learn that you did not know, or had not expected? How do the lives of the individuals that you interviewed compare to the stereotypes about elders that exist in your culture? As you look forward to your life as an elder, how do you imagine your life being in comparison to the lives of the people you read about and the lives of the people you interviewed? What does this tell us about our efforts in social work?

Life Stories

Life Story 1: Senator Mary Jackson

Although the section of the meeting set aside for public comment had just ended and the Chair of the Disability Commission had just adjourned the hearing, Senator Mary Jackson continued to sit in her chair. She looked more drawn than usual, clearly weary from the contentious debate. The last three hearings had focused on a move by the state Department of Medicaid Services to establish a waiver program for consumer-directed personal assistance services. As I had been a frequent attendee at the Disability Commission hearings, Senator Jackson and I had developed a close professional relationship, one that included stopping by the capitol coffee shop for lunch and conversation following many of the hearings. It was during the course of these conversations that I grew to know more about her.

Senator Jackson, after having served in the legislature for twenty years, announced that she would retire at the end of her current term. Due to health reasons, her husband had taken an early retirement three years ago. He increasingly depended upon his wife for many of his activities of daily living, such as getting out of bed in the morning, help with his showering, and getting dressed. Senator Jackson had also experienced a similar change in her independent living skills. She had been a nurse during one of the United States peacekeeping missions following the Korean War. She always requested to serve in an active battle zone. Following a night of particularly heavy shelling and counterattack, she noticed that she seemed to miss parts of conversations and not notice when someone behind her would try to get her attention by calling out her name. She had her hearing checked, and indeed she had developed a permanent hearing loss. Though she developed compensatory skills, such as lip reading, and strategically placing herself in the midst of conversations, she decided to leave the military and return to the civilian world.

It was not long before she decided to do two things: open up a real estate office and run for office. As she had been in other parts of her life, she was successful in these endeavors. Because the legislature in her state was not a full-time legislature, she was able to devote a sufficient amount of time to both careers to be highly successful at each. Early on in her legislative career she had selected her primary legislative interest areas as aging and disability. Since there were legislative commissions for each of her areas of interest, she sought and was appointed and subsequently continually reappointed to both the Commission on Aging and the Disability Commission.

Almost five years ago, Senator Jackson started to be affected by the symptoms of glaucoma that runs in her family. She joked about having a standing appointment with her optometrist and the laser machine! Despite the best of care, her vision continued to change to the point where she could only attend night meetings and legislative sessions if she had someone to drive her to those appointments and to her home or hotel when they ended. This past year she had also experienced a significant increase in the severity of her arthritis.

Accompanying these physical and sensory changes was a continued record of outstanding legislative success. In fact, for the past four years she had led both the Senate and the House in being the chief patron of legislation that passed both houses and was signed by the governor. (She accomplished this despite being in the minority party, and having a governor of the majority party.) Her real estate company was more successful than ever. She found herself in the enviable position of working hard "not to work too hard." She was able to turn down listings and only take those that intrigued her the most.

Some of the public comments in today's hearing struck her as most curious. The supporters and the opponents of the proposed Medicaid waiver seemed to divide into clearly distinct categories. The supporters included people with disabilities, many of whom already were receiving personal assistance services, providing poignant and impassioned testimony on behalf of the principles of consumer direction and control. The opponents, however, were primarily direct service providers and directors of home health care agencies. The basic arguments put forth by the opponent group were that people who were aging should not be considered in the same group or class as younger disabled people, that elders were at greater risk for harm, and that they needed someone, usually a professional, to either help them decide or decide for them what home services they needed. An argument repeatedly presented was that for people fifty-five years of age or older there should be a regular screening to determine their capability to decide what services they should have, and whether or not they had the capacity to utilize consumer-directed services. A difference in perspectives in the testimony was the belief that people who were aging, in contrast to younger individuals needing similar services, would do better if a human service professional helped them decide what, when, how, and by whom home independent living services should be provided.

Senator Jackson stated, "If I were judged by my disability alone I would be presumed to be competent, that I would have to demonstrate incapacity before my rights to consumer-directed services would be taken away, whereas if I were judged by my age, it would be presumed that I was incompetent and needed someone else to decide the nature of my independent living services." She needed to cut our lunch short today; she had two more legislative hearings today and a community town hall tonight.

Life Story 2: Mr. Jones

At seventy-two, Mike Jones considered himself in a prime position to make the changes in his life that would give him the time to spend long weekends at his lake cabin, continue his part-time law practice, and devote time to the local Area Agency on Aging (AAA). When he went to his cabin, because of the specialized pier and dock he had recently installed, he was now able to fish for the deep water bass that he was previously only able to access if a friend took him out in a boat. Now he could fish whenever he wanted, regardless of who was around. What a great relief! He tried to limit his law practice to mostly business consultation. He had decided a few years ago that continuing as a trial lawyer, with scheduled court dates, interfered with his desire for flexibility. His law firm had always considered community participation and pro bono services an essential part of giving back to the community. Thus when one of his law partners approached him about serving on the board of directors of the AAA, how could he refuse? (That was twelve years ago!)

Mr. Jones's days in law school preceded passage of the Rehabilitation Act of 1973, and becoming partner in the firm took place long before the Americans with Disabilities Act was passed in 1990. He remembers having to make special requests to have law classes made accessible and extra time and assistance given to him for tests. He knew that because his family had a history of making large donations to his university that his opportunities were much better than many of the students in his segregated "cerebral palsy classes" in elementary school, middle school, and high school. He is also certain that he was able to get accepted into college in the first place because his family could afford to hire a tutor for him throughout his public school years. Neither his family nor he expected much from his teachers in terms of preparation for work, much less preparation for college. Mr. Jones's cerebral palsy at times made his speech difficult to understand, necessitated that he use a power wheelchair for mobility, and resulted in his needing assistance with some of his instrumental activities of daily living, such as shopping and cleaning his house. The modifications made to his "city" house and his lake cabin, as well as those to his van, enabled him to live and play where and when he wanted.

About five years ago Mr. Jones starting dating one of the other members of the board of directors. They entered the relationship with a mixture of caution and excitement. Once they started becoming more "serious," they acknowledged that ethics required that they inform the other board members of their relationship. The difficulty, of course, was figuring a way to do this that was thoughtful and dignified. They were now ready to embark on an even more consequential dimension of their relationship: marriage. Mr. Jones was not quite sure just what to tell his friends about this; after all, Martha Williams was only sixty-one years old. A more difficult area for Mr. Jones to discuss with someone was his intention to resume the sex life that had halted with the death of his first wife when he was sixty-three years old. Ms. Williams and he held several conversations about the impact of his cerebral palsy on their soon-to-be-active sex life, in much the same manner as they had discussed what impact the aging processes might have. Her husband had died twelve years ago. Both Ms. Williams and Mr. Jones had been celibate since the deaths of their partners. They also began to wonder just how his children and grandchildren and her son and his wife and children would react to the marriage, and to the other recreation, career, and community service life changes.

Life Story 3: James Morrison

Although James Morrison had a low level spinal cord injury since his accident at age five, it was not until after his fifty-fourth birthday that he began to experience significant daily mobility limitations, nearly unbearable pain, and severe balance difficulties. When he was a child he wore leg braces and "orthopedic shoes," the kind that all the other children would make jokes about. When he was thirteen he had his first follow-up spinal surgery. Over the course of his teenage, young adult, and adult years he had three other spinal cord surgeries. He resisted having them, because the risk for further spinal cord damage was great and they seldom provided long lasting pain relief. Most of his adult life he did not use crutches for mobility support; however, when he was forty-eight years old, his gait had become unsteady enough that their use became necessary not only as a mobility aid, but as a safety precaution—a means to decrease the number of falls. He had been active in recreational sports since his youth, with his true recreational love being alpine skiing. This year the outrigger poles did not seem to be able to give him enough support, necessitating that he consider using a sit-ski. It was a few summers ago that he had to stop riding his bicycle, with the past summer marking the beginning of his use of a handcycle. His increasing debilitation necessitated a parallel increase in his reliance on others for assistance in both some of his ADLs and IADLs.

Compounding the problems for Mr. Morrison was development of an intimate relationship with a wheelchair user, Shirley Hall. Ms. Hall, though having had an accident necessitating initial use of forearm crutches twenty years ago, for the past two years had started using a wheelchair for nearly 80 percent of the time, using the forearm crutches for short distances and around the house. The twenty years of crutch use had taken their toll, not only in terms of worsening arthritis in her back and shoulders, but with the exacerbation of a lower spine disorder.

As Mr. Morrison and Ms. Hall began the conversation about their future life together, the inevitability of their requiring the services of a personal care attendant became a central element of their planning. The question, for them, was not if this would be necessary, but when? Each of them brought similar physical limitations to the relationship, complicating virtually every decision that they would make. One example is the extra work that automatically occurs with decisions of travel. This includes making sure that there was extra travel time when air travel required multiple plane changes (being first on and last off an airplane can add nearly an hour to plane transfer requirements). Lodging must be in accessible settings, adding to the planning time and reducing the number and availability of settings. This reduction of lodging options is due to fewer hotel or inn rooms being retrofitted for disability access. This consequence also leads to an increase in cost because of market circumstances. These are but a few of the issues that they must face with great regularity.

As they plan for their life as a couple, their physical abilities and limitations cannot be after-thoughts; they are primary factors.

Annotated Bibliography

Aging with a disability. (1995, July/August). Special Issue. *Disability Rag & Resource, 15*(4).

Contents include: New realities, new concerns; Advocating for more than health reform; Horror stories; Misguided pride; Women with disabilities at mid-life. This magazine is essential reading for anyone interested in disabilities. Aging with a disability provides the reader with a perspective on this issue from those most directly affected, people with disabilities.

Ansello, E. F. & Eustis, N. N. (Eds.). (1992). *Aging and disabilities: Seeking common ground.* Amityville, NY: Baywood.

This edited work provides excellent information about the intersection of aging and disability. The principal focus is on aging and developmental disability. The contributors, all with outstanding insights and excellent credentials, present information and raise questions that all workers interested in this field must confront.

Gilson, S. F. & Netting, E. F. (1997). When people with pre-existing disabilities age in place: Implications for social work practice. *Health & Social Work, 22*(4), 290–298.

The focus of this article is on people with disabilities who are "aging in place." This discussion examines issues of, and needs faced by, individuals aging with preexisting physical disabilities. The authors distinguish between individuals who experience prolonged aging and those who experience accelerated aging.

Linton, S. (1998). *Claiming disability: Knowledge and identity.* New York: New York University Press.

An essential beginning point for working with people with disabilities, regardless of age, is an understanding of the meaning and experience of disability. Although written principally as a discourse on disability studies, *Claiming disability,* provides the social worker with an excellent examination and discussion of disability and what it means to be disabled.

Quinn, P. (1998). *Understanding disability: A lifespan approach.* Thousand Oaks, CA: Sage.

Written by a social worker, *Undersanding disability* details expected developmental stages and the impact of disability at each stage. The life span approach will help the social worker anticipate the issues that disabled persons may face as they age, as well as some of the issues that may be experienced when an individual acquires a disability at a distinct life stage. Disabilities discussed include: Down syndrome, visual impairment, cerebral palsy, spina bifida, and spinal cord injury.

RRTC on Aging with a Disability, Rancho Los Amigos Medical Center, Los Amigos Research & Education Institute, Inc. (LAREI), 7601 East Imperial Highway, 800 West Annex, Downey, CA 90242; (562) 401-7402 (Voice); (562) 401-7011 (Fax); (562) 803-4533 (TDD).

"This project, funded by National Institute on Disability and Rehabilitation Research, helps people who are aging with a disability by conducting a series of studies, using a sample of 1,000 people, with a variety of disabilities represented. Studies include:

1. the natural course of aging with a disability, which investigates physical, function, and psychosocial aging with a disability over time;
2. a cross-ethnic-group study, focusing on assisting family caregivers of people aging with a disability, and comparing stress, support, coping preferences, and appraisals of caregiving for people aging with a disability and evaluating the effectiveness of a structured group intervention;
3. improving community integration and adjustment, focusing on depression and how it affects community integration and demonstrates effective treatment;
4. secondary complications such as diabetes and thyroid disorders, determining if providing feedback to patients' primary physicians regarding these illnesses results in appropriate treatment, and if functional impairment is related to these illnesses;
5. bone mass, focusing on whether a regimen of exercise and vitamins improves bone density; and
6. the effectiveness of assistive technology (AT) and environmental interventions (EI) in maintaining functional independence, evaluating differences between those receiving intensive AT and EI services and those receiving standard care."

RRTC on Aging with Mental Retardation (RRTCAMR), University of Illinois-Chicago, Department of Disability and Human Development, 1640 West Roosevelt Road, Chicago, IL 60608-6904; (312) 413-1520; (312) 996-6942 (Fax); (312) 413-0453 (TDD); Web: *http://www.uic.edu/orgs/rrtcamr/*

"The Center is funded by National Institute on Disability and Rehabilitation Research. The mission of the Center is to promote the independence, productivity, community inclusion, full citizenship, and self-determination of older adults with mental retardation through a coordinated program of research, training, technical assistance, and dissemination activities. The main goal of the research is to translate the knowledge gained into practice through board-based training, technical assistance, and dissemination to persons with mental retardation, their families, service providers, administrators and policy makers, advocacy groups, and the general community. A major dissemination vehicle is the Center's Clearinghouse, web page, and its newsletters.

The RRTC Projects address six priority areas:

1. Increasing empowerment and self-advocacy through training in person-centered later life planning and leadership skills, and by providing information about the Americans with Disabilities Act (ADA)
2. Understanding how age related changes affect medical and psychosocial well-being
3. Developing service models for the needs of families from diverse cultures
4. Enhancing coping techniques for changing capabilities through in-home interventions and assistive technologies
5. Supporting individuals through life transitions including the death or incapacity of the caregiver
6. Expanding retirement, financial, health, and independent living options."

RRTC on Aging with Spinal Cord Injury, Rancho Los Amigos Medical Center, Los Amigos Research & Education Institute, Inc. (LAREI), 7601 East Imperial Highway, 800 West Annex, Downey, CA 90242-3456; (562) 401-7402 (Voice); (562) 401-7011 (Fax); (562) 401-4533 (TDD).

"Funded by the National Institute on Disability and Rehabilitation Research, this RRTC is devoted to understanding the unique problems people with spinal cord injury experience as they age.

The Rehabilitation Research and Training Center (RRTC) on Aging with Spinal Cord Injury (SCI) is devoted to understanding the unique problems people with spinal cord injury experience as they age. Topics of research include:

1. The course of aging with SCI;
2. Cardiovascular and pulmonary aspects of aging with SCI;
3. Bone loss across ethnic groups;
4. Activities of daily living;
5. Employment;
6. Depression; and
7. Formal and informal care systems for people aging with SCI.

The RRTC has several goals for education, training, dissemination, and utilization:

1. To train current and future health, allied health, and rehabilitation professionals about aging with SCI;
2. To train and develop rehabilitation research professionals in the area of aging with SCI;
3. To have health and rehabilitation professionals adopt and use knowledge and treatment regimens developed in the RRTC;
4. To disseminate information about aging with SCI to people with SCI and their families; and
5. To train graduate students and medical students in advanced knowledge and techniques from studies about aging with SCI."

Seltzer, M. M., Krauss, M. W., & Janicki, M. P. (Eds.). (1994). *Life course perspectives on adulthood and old age*. Washington, DC: American Association on Mental Retardation.

The authors provide an important focus on developmental disabilities. This book focuses on the major issues that middle-age adults not currently in the social service system, and their parents/

caretakers who are also aging, are facing. For many people, little planning has been initiated by the social services system that will help begin or pick up services and supports currently provided by families.

Skoog, I., Blennow, K., & Marcusson, J. (1996). Dementia. In J. E. Birren (Ed.), *Encyclopedia of Gerontology* (pp. 383–403). San Diego, CA: Academic Press.

This article provides an excellent generic overview of the dementias, reviewing the epidemology, diagnostic evaluation procedures, and pharmacologic treatment and care.

The Health, Wellness and Aging Disability Mailing List.

This (e-mail) mailing list will alert the reader to news items, conferences, web sites, and publications related to disability, health, wellness, and aging. To subscribe, send a message to majordomo @tripil.com with the following text in the BODY of the message (subject line is ignored): subscribe hwawd. For additional assistance, contact June Isaacson Kailes, Disability Policy Consultant at jik@pacbell.net

The National Institute on Consumer-Directed Long-Term Services. *Consumer choice news.* Washington, DC: National Council on the Aging.

This publication, the result of a partnership between The National Council on the Aging, Inc. (NCOA) and the World Institute on Disability (WID), focuses on issues associated with the development of and the provision of consumer-directed home and community based services for people. It is an important source of information on consumer-directed choice in long-term services. The address is: National Council on the Aging, Inc., 409 Third Street SW, Washington, DC 20024.

The National Senior Citizens Law Center. (1992). *Implementation of the Americans with Disabilities Act.* Washington, DC: American Associated of Retired Persons.

This study reports on an examination of Titles II and III of the Americans with Disabilities Act (ADA) on the rights of older people with disabilities. It took the form of analysis of the statute, its legislative history and implementing regulations, and identification of issues that may arise under the ADA. The National Senior Citizens Law Center also conducted a survey of State Units on Aging, Area Agencies on Aging, state protection and advocacy organizations, legal services programs, private attorneys, and law school clinical programs as part of their data collection process.

Trieschmann, R. B. (1987). *Aging with a disability.* New York: Demos.

Though dated, this examination and discussion of the issues associated with aging and disability is a classic. Trieschmann was instrumental in laying out what we might expect as we age with our disabilities, as well as what the health care workers must understand if they are to best help us meet the needs of people with disabilities as they age.

Turk, M. A., Overeynder, J. C., & Janicki, M. P. (Eds.). (1995, June). *Uncertain future: Aging and cerebral palsy—clinical concerns: A report of the workgroup on aging and cerebral palsy.* Albany: New York State Developmental Disabilities Planning Council.

One of three reports on aging and cerebral palsy. This report examines some of the physical and psychosocial aspects of aging as experienced by adults with cerebral palsy. In addition to identifying current knowledge, the report outlines questions in need of further study and highlights areas of personal or clinical concern that need further attention.

General Bibliography

Abrams, J. Z. (1998). *Judaism and disability: Portrayals in ancient texts from the Tanach through the Bavli.* Washington, DC: Gallaudet University Press.

Adler, M. (1995, February). Population estimates of disability and long-term care. *ASPE Research Notes . . . Information for Decision Makers.* [On-line]. Available: *http://aspe.os.dhhs.gov/rn/Rn11/htm*

Albrecht, G. L. & Devlieger, P. J. (1999). The disability paradox: High quality of life against all odds. *The Journal of the American Medical Association 282*(1), 977–988.

Bachelder, J. M. & Hilton, C. L. (1994). Implications of the Americans with Disabilities Act of 1990 for elderly persons. *The American Journal of Occupational Therapy 48*(1), 73–81.

Barnes, C. & Mercer, G. (Eds.). *Exploring the divide: Illness and disability.* Leeds, United Kingdom: The Disability Press.

Carlson, J. E., Ostir, G. V., Black, S. A., Markides, K. S., Rudkin, L., & Goodwin, J. S. (1999). Disability in older adults 2: Physical activity as prevention. *Behavioral Medicine* 24(4), 157–168.

Charlton, J. I. (1998). *Nothing about us without us: Disability oppression and empowerment*. Berkeley: University of California Press.

Chiriboga, D. A., Ottenbacher, K., & Haber, D. A. (1999). Disability in older adults 3: Policy implications. *Behavioral Medicine* 24(4), 171–180.

Disability Rights Advocates. (1997). *Disability watch: The status of people with disabilities in the United States*. Volcano, CA: Volcano Press.

Ellis, C. (1995). *Final negotiations: A story of love, loss, and chronic illness*. Philadelphia, PA: Temple University Press.

Gliedman, J. & Roth, W. (1980). *The unexpected minority: Handicapped children in America*. New York: Harcourt Brace Javonovich.

Gostin, L. O. & Beyer, H. A. (Eds.). *Implementing the Americans with Disabilities Act: Rights and responsibilities of all Americans*. Baltimore, MD: Paul H. Brookes.

Harris, L. (1986). The ICD survey of disabled Americans. Bringing disabled Americans into the mainstream. (Study N. 854009). New York: ICD-International Center for the Disabled.

Hevey, D. (1992). *The creatures time forgot: Photography and disability imagery*. London: Routledge.

Hockenberry, J. (1995). *Moving violations: War zones, wheelchairs, and declarations of independence*. New York: Hyperion.

Hogan, D. B., Ebly, E. M., & Fung, T. S. (1999). Disease, disability, and age in cognitively intact seniors: Results from the Canadian study of health and aging. *Journals of Gerontology: Series–A: - Biological Sciences and Medical Sciences* 54A(2), M77–782.

Ingstad, B. & Whyte, S. R. (1995). *Disability and culture*. Berkeley, CA: University of California Press.

Jamison, K. R. (1995). *An unquiet mind*. New York: Knopf.

Jankowski, K. A. (1997). *Deaf empowerment: Emergence, struggle, & rhetoric*. Washington, DC: Gallaudet University Press.

Jennings, B. (1999). A life greater than the sum of its sensations: Ethics, dementia and quality of life. *Journal of Mental Health and Aging* 5(1), 95–106.

Johnson, M. & the Editors of *The Disability Rag*. (Eds.). (1992). *People with disabilities explain it all for you: Your guide to the public accommodations requirements of the Americans with Disabilities Act*. Louisville, KY: The Avocado Press.

Keysor, J. J., Desai, T., & Mutran, E. J. (1999). Elders' preferences for care setting in short- and long-term disability scenarios. *The Gerontologist* 39(3), 334–344.

Kleege, G. (1999). *Sight unseen*. New Haven, CT: Yale University Press.

Kosciulek, J. F. (1999). Consumer direction in disability policy formulation and rehabilitation service delivery. *The Journal of Rehabilitation* 65(2), 4–9.

Kutchins, H. & Kirk, S. A. (1997). *Making us crazy: DSM: The psychiatric bible and the creation of mental disorders*. New York: Free Press.

Ladika, S. B., Jenkins, D. L., & Nickerson, P. Z. (1999). The internetwork approach to providing mental health care to older persons: The case of Oneida County. *Administration and Policy in Mental Health* 26(4), 297–302.

Lane, H., Hoffmeister, R., & Bahan, B. (1996). *A journey into the Deaf-world*. San Diego, CA: Dawn Sign.

Lawton, M. P. (1999). Quality of life in chronic illness. *Gerontology* 45(4), 181–183.

McNeil, J. M. (1993). *Americans with disabilities: 1991-92 U.S. Bureau of the Census. Current population reports, P70–33*. Washington, DC: U.S. Government Printing Office.

McNeil, J. M. (1997a). *Americans with disabilities: 1994–95*. [On-line]. Available: http://www.census.gov/hhes/www/disable.html

McNeil, J. M. (1997b). *Disability*. [On-line]. Available: http://www.census.gov/hhes/www/disable.html

Moody, H. R. (1998). *Aging: Concepts & controversies* (2nd ed.). Thousand Oaks, CA: Pine Forge.

National Organization of Disability. (1994). *N.O.D./Harris survey of Americans with disabilities*. New York: Louis Harris and Associates.

O'Shea, E. & Kennelly, B. (1996). The economics of independent living: Efficiency, equity and ethics. *International Journal of Rehabilitation Research* 19(1), 13–26.

Ostir, G. V., Carlson, J. E., Black, S. A., Rudkin, L., Goodwin, J. S., & Markides, K. S. (1999). Disability in older adults 1: Prevalence, causes, and consequences. *Behavioral Medicine* 24(4), 147–156.

Padden, C. & Humphries, T. (1998). *Deaf in America: Voices from a culture*. Cambridge, MA: Harvard University Press.

Rioux, M. H., & Bach, M. (Eds.). (1994). *Disability is not measles: New research paradigms in disability*. North York, Ontario: Roeher Institute.

Scotch, R. K. & Schriner, K. (1997). Disability as human variation: Implications for policy. *The Annals of the American Academy of Political and Social Sciences 549*, 148–159.

Shakespeare, T. (1999). The sexual politics of disabled masculinity. *Sexualtiy and Disability 17*(1), 53–64.

Shapiro, J. P. (1993). *No pity: People with disabilities forging a new civil rights movement*. New York: Times Books.

Slivinske, L. R., Fitch, V. L., & Wingerson, N. W. (1998). The effect of functional disability on service utilization: Implications for long-term care. *Health and Social Work 23*(3), 175–185.

Stone, D. (1986). *The disabled state*. Philadelphia, PA: Temple University Press.

Stuck, A. E., Walthert, J. M., Nikolaus, T., Buela, C. J., Hohmann, C., & Beck, J. C. (1999). Risk factors for functional status decline in community-living elderly people: A systematic literature review. *Social Science and Medicine* 48(4), 445–469.

The Disability Statistics Center. (On-going). *Disability Statistics Abstracts*. The Disability Statistics Center, Institute for Health and Aging, School of Nursing, University of California, San Francisco, CA. Availability: *http://www.ed.gov/offices/OSERS/NIDRR/pubs.html*

Thompson, T. (1995). *The beast: A reckoning with depression*. New York: G.P. Putnam's Sons.

References

Air Carrier Access Act of 1986, Pub. L. No. 99-435, 100 Stat 1080 (1987).

Americans with Disabilities act of 1990, Pub. L. No. 101-336, 104 Stat. 327 (1990).

Asch, A. & Mudrick, N. R. (1995). Disability. In R. L. Edwards (Ed.), *Encyclopedia of Social Work* (19th ed.). (Vol. 1, pp. 752–761). Washington, DC: NASW Press.

Barker, D. (1993). Human rights for persons with disabilities. In M. Nagler (Ed.), *Perspectives on disability* (2nd ed.) (pp. 483–494). Palo Alto, CA: Health Market Research.

Biegel, D. E., Shore, B. K., & Silverman, M. (1989). Overcoming barriers to serving the aging/mental health client: A state initiative. *Journal of Gerontological Social Work, 13,* 147–165.

Clark, P. G. (1995). Quality of life, values, and teamwork in geriatric care: Do we communicate what we mean? *Gerontologist, 35,* 402–411.

Cohen, E. S. (1988). The elderly mystique: Constraints on the autonomy of the elderly with disabilities. *Gerontologist, 28* (Suppl.) (3), 24–31.

Cohen, E. S. (1992). What is independence? In E. F. Ansello & N. N. Fustis (Eds.), *Aging and disabilities: Seeking common ground* (pp. 91–98). Amityville, NY: Baywood.

Cook, A. M. & Hussey, S. M. (1995). *Assistive technologies: Principles and practice*. St. Louis, MO: Mosby.

DeJong, G. (1984). Independent living: From social movement to analytic paradigm. In P. Marinelli & A. Dell Orto (Eds.), *The psychological and social impact of physical disability* (pp. 39–64). New York: Springer.

DeJong, G. & Wenkler, T. (1979). Attendant care as a prototype independent living services. *Archives of Physical Medicine and Rehabilitation, 60*(10) 477–482.

Education for All Handicapped Children Act of 1975, Pub. L. No. 94-142, 89 Stat. 773 (1975).

Fair Housing Amendments Act of 1988, Pub. L. No. 100-430, 102 Stat. 1619 (1988).

Gilderbloom, J. I. & Rosentraub, M. S. (1990). Creating the accessible city: Proposals for providing housing and transportation for low income, elderly and disabled people. *American Journal of Economics and Sociology, 49,*(3) 271–282.

Gill, C. (1997). Four types of integration of disability identity development. *Journal of Vocational Rehabilitation, 9,*(1) 39–46.

Gilson, S. F. (1998). Choice and self-advocacy: A consumer's perspective. In P. Wehman & J. Kregel (Eds.), *Employment and careers for people with disabilities: A consumer-driven approach* (pp. 3–23). Baltimore, MD: Paul H. Brookes.

Gilson, S. F. & Casebolt, G. J. (1997). Personal assistance services and case management. *Journal of Case Management, 6,*(1) 13–17.

Gilson, S. F. & Netting, F. E. (1997). When people with pre-existing disabilities age in place: Implications for social work practice. *Health & Social Work, 22,*(4) 290–298.

Gilson, S. F., Tusler, A., & Gill, C. (1997). Ethnographic research in disability identity: Self-determination and community. *Journal of Vocational Rehabilitation, 9,*(1) 7–17.

Hahn, H. (1997). An agenda for citizens with disabilities: Pursuing identity and empowerment. *Journal of Vocational Rehabilitation, 9,*(1) 31–37.

Heumann, J. E. (1993). Building our own boats: A personal perspective on disability. In L. O. Gostin and H. A. Beyer (Eds.), *Implementing the Americans with Disabilities Act: Rights and responsibilities of all Americans* (pp. 251-263). Baltimore, MD: Paul H. Brookes.

Kailes, J. I. (1992). Aging with a disability: Educating myself. In E. F. Ansello & N. N. Eustis (Eds.), *Aging and disabilities: Seeking common ground* (pp. 149–156). Amityville, NY: Baywood.

Kregel, J. & Wehman, P. (1997). Supported employment: A decade of employment outcomes for individuals with significant disabilities. In W. E. Kiernan & R. L. Schalock (Eds.), *Integrated employment: Current status and future directions* (pp. 31–47). Washington, DC: American Association on Mental Retardation.

LaPlante, M. P. (1996. September). Disability conditions and Impairments causing disability. *Disability Statistics Abstracts, 16.* San Francisco: Disability Statistics Rehabilitation Research and Training Center, University of California, San Francisco.

Linton, S. (1998). *Claiming disability: Knowledge and identity.* New York: New York University Press.

Litvak, S. (1990). *Final performance report: New models for the provision of personal assistance services: A research and demonstration project.* Oakland, CA: The World Institute on Disability in collaboration with Rutgers University, The Bureau of Economic Research.

Lou Harris and Associates, Inc. (1995). *The N.O.D./Harris Survey on Employment of People with Disabilities.* (Study No. 951401). New York: Author.

Mackelprang, R. W. & Salsgiver, R. O. (1996). People with disabilities and social work: Historical and contemporary issues. *Social Work, 41,*(1) 7–14.

McNeil, J. M. (1993). *Americans with disabilities: 1991–92 U.S. Bureau of the Census. Current population reports, P70-33.* Washington, DC: U.S. Government Printing Office.

McNeil, J. M. (1997a). *Americans with disabilities: 1994-95.* [On-line]. Available: http://www.census.gov/hhes/www/disable.html

McNeil, J. M. (1997b). *Disability.* [On-line]. Available: http://www.census.gov/hhes/www/disable.html

Mann, W. C., Hurren, D., & Tomita, M. (1993). Comparison of assistive device use and needs of home-based older persons with impairments. *American Journal of Occupational Therapy, 47,*(11) 980–987.

Maynard, F. M. (1998, February 25.). *The post-polio syndrome and rehabilitation.* [On-line]. Available: http://www.azstarnet.com/~rspear/rehab2.html.

National Senior Citizens Law Center. (1992). *Implementation of the Americans with Disabilities Act.* Washington, DC: American Association of Retired Persons.

National Institute on Disability and Rehabilitation Research. Office of Special Education and Rehabilitation Services. Department of Education. (1993). Bringing Research into effective Focus. *Rehab Brief, 24*(8). Washington, DC: Author.

National Institute of Neurological Disorders and Stroke. (1997). *Post-polio syndrome: Fact sheet.* [On-line]. Available: www.ninds.hih.gov/HEALINFO/DISORDER/ppolio/ppolio.

Racino, J. A. & Heumann, J. E. (1992). Building coalitions among elders, people with disabilities, and our allies. In E. F. Ansello & N. N. Eustis (Eds.), *Aging and disabilities: Seeking common ground* (pp. 79–90). Amityville, NY: Baywood.

Rehabilitation Act of 1973, Pub. Law No. 93-112, 87 Stat. 335 (1973).

Rose, J. H. (1991). A life course perspective on health threats in aging. *Journal of Gerontological Social Work, 17*(3/4), 85–97.

Rosenfelt, R. (1965). The elderly mystique. *Journal of Social Issues, 21*(3), 37–43.

Rundall, T. G. (1992). Editorial: Health services for an aging society. *Medical Care Review, 49*,(1) 3–18.

Senate Bill 402, Assistive technology device warranties act; created, General Assembly of Virginia. Chapter 67. (1998).

Simon-Rusinowitz, L., & Hofland, B. F. (1993). Adopting a disability approach to home care services for older adults. *The Gerontologist, 33*,(2) 159–167.

Sullivan, W. P. (1992). Reclaiming the community: The strengths perspective and deinstitutionalization. *Social Work, 37*(3), 204–209.

Trieschmann, R. B. (1987). *Aging with a disability.* New York: Demos.

Turk, M. A., Overeynder, J. C., & Janicki, M. P. (Eds.). (1995, June). *Uncertain future: Aging and Cerebral palsy—clinical concerns: A report of the workgroup on aging and cerebral palsy.* Albany: New York State Developmental Disabilities Planning Council.

Appendix A: Selected Internet Web Sites

Academic/Higher Education

Syracuse University Maxwell School of Citizenship and Public Affairs

www.cpr.maxwell.syr.edu

Provides information on research and publications related to aging and long-term care. Other resources include: Center for Demography and Economics of Aging; Cross-National Studies in Aging; Gerontology Education Project; Economics of Aging Interest Group; and the University Gerontology Center.

Interest Groups

Alliance for Aging Research

www.alz.org

Nonprofit bipartisan organization dedicated to promoting research on human aging and independence of older Americans. The primary mission of the organization is to advocate for greater federal involvement in scientific research that can lead to a healthy and productive old age.

American Association of People with Disabilities

http://www.aapd.com/info/

The American Association of People with Disabilities (AAPD) is an organization conceived by, advised, and managed by people with disabilities for people with disabilities. It consists of a dues-paying membership and a representational board of directors. Among other objectives, it was established to further the productivity, independence, full citizenship, and total integration of people with disabilities into all aspects of society and the natural environment.

American Association of Retired Persons (AARP)

www.aarp.org

American Association of Retired Persons is located in Washington, D.C. The AARP is the nation's leading organization for people age fifty and older. It serves their needs and interests through information and education, advocacy, and community services provided by a network of local chapters and experienced volunteers throughout the country.

American Disabled for Attendant Programs Today

http://www.adapt.org/

American Disabled for Attendant Programs Today (ADAPT) focuses on promoting services in the community instead of warehousing people with disabilities in institutions and nursing homes. Attendant services (help with things like eating, dressing, toileting, moving from wheelchair to bed) are the cornerstone to community-based services for people with severe disabilities. ADAPT is working to get 25 percent of the Medicaid long-term care funds redirected to pay for a national, mandated attendant services program.

Cornucopia of Disability Resources

http://codi.buffalo.edu/

Cornucopia of Disability Resources (CODI) serves as a community resource for consumers and professionals by providing disability information in a wide variety of areas. The information addresses university (UB), local (Buffalo & WNY), state, national, and international audiences. Submissions are welcome from these communities. Areas include education, statistics, government documents, computer access, legal, publications, bibliographic references, aging, assistive technology, universal design and announcements.

FamiliesUSA

www.familiesUSA.org

National consumer advocacy organization working for change in health and long term care systems. Issues reports to educate the public and policymakers, and also works at a grassroots-level to encourage the public to participate in the health care debate.

National Caucus and Center on Black Aged

www.ncoa.org/lcao.members/naaaa.htm

A direct service and advocacy organization on policy issues affecting low-income and minority elderly. Policy priorities include income security, employment, housing, and health care.

National Committee to Preserve Social Security and Medicare

www.spry.org

Grass-roots education and advocacy organization. A direct service and advocacy organization whose primary mission is to keep members informed on issues and bring key legislation issues to national attention. The organization focuses on: passage of long-term care legislation; removal of Social Security from the federal budget calculations; protection of Social Security cost-of-living adjustments, and improvement of Medicare reimbursement procedures.

National Council of Senior Citizens

www.nscinc.org

Advocacy organization comprised of older persons involved in legislative and political issues relevant to retirement age. Key sponsor of housing for low-income elderly and the disabled and employment. Founded in 1951, the NCSC was a key figure in the battle to enact Medicare.

National Organization on Disability

http://www.nod.org/

National Organization on Disability (NOD) promotes the full and equal participation of America's 54 million people with disabilities. NOD is the only national disability network organization concerned with all disabilities, all age groups, and all disability issues.

Older Womens' League

www.ncoa.org/lcao.members/owl.htm

The only national grass-roots organization that focuses exclusively on women as they age. OWL works to achieve economic and social equity and is active in education, advocacy, and research on the contributions of older women to society.

World Institute on Disability

http://www.wid.org/

The World Institute on Disability (WID) is a nonprofit public policy center dedicated to the promotion of independence and full inclusion in society of people with disabilities. Founded in 1983 by leaders of the Independent Living/Civil Rights Movement for people with disabilities, WID is committed to bringing policy into action.

Professional Organizations

American Geriatrics Society

www.americangeriatrics.org

Professional health care organization of health care providers with over six thousand members. The AGS has become a pivotal force in shaping attitudes, policies, and practice regarding health care for older people.

American Society on Aging

www.asa.org

Provides professional information on aging and the well-being of older people and families, and the publications *Generations* and *Aging Today*. Also notable for extensive constituent units and member interest groups.

Gerontological Society of America (GSA)

www.geron.org

Founded in 1945, the Gerontological Society of America is the largest national organization of professionals working in the field of aging, and the oldest multidisciplinary organization in the United States. Publications include monthly newsletters, refereed journals—

The Gerontologist, and *Journals of Gerontology.* Services include on-line keyword search and information about interest groups, and links to policy and practice.

National Academy on Aging

www.gsa.iog.wayne.edu/NAA/naahome.html

The National Academy on Aging provides a neutral forum to evaluate public policy implications of the longer lives and growing population of older persons in our society. Such issues include health care, long term care, and income security in an intergenerational context.

National Center for the Dissemination of Disability Research

http://www.ncddr.org/

The National Center for the Dissemination of Disability Research's (NCDDR's) purpose is to enhance the dissemination efforts of National Institute on Disability and Rehabilitation Research-funded research projects and to increase the accessibility of research outcomes for the benefit of their consumers, particularly those from minority backgrounds.

National Council on Aging

www.ncoa.org

National Council on Aging, the professional organization for Area Agencies on Aging (AAAs) responsible for Older Americans Act Programs. NCOA provides policy briefs on current Older Americans Act issues and the Leadership Council on Aging.

Society for Disability Studies

http://www.uic.edu/orgs/sds/

The Society for Disability Studies (SDS) is a nonprofit scientific and educational organization established to promote interdisciplinary research on humanistic and social scientific aspects of disability and chronic illness.

Government Sites

Congressional Budget Office

www.cbo.gov

The Congressional Budget Office (CBO) has current and projected economic and budget outlook related to government-funded programs.

Department of Health and Human Services Administration on Aging

www.aoa.dhhs.gov

Department of Health and Human Services, Administration on Aging (AoA) serves as an advocate for the elderly within the federal government and helps states develop comprehensive services systems. Provides many resources online including the Profile on Older Americans fact sheet and internet resources in aging.

Health Care Financing Administration
www.hcfa.gov
The Health Care Financing Administration is the federal agency that oversees Medicare and Medicaid.

National Institute on Aging
www.nih.gov.nia.org
The National Institute on Aging, part of the National Institutes of Health (NIH), supports healthy aging by conducting and supporting biomedical, social, and behavioral research and public education.

National Council on Disability
http://www.ncd.gov/
The National Council on Disability (NCD) is an independent federal agency making recommendations to the President and Congress on issues affecting 54 million Americans with disabilities. NCD is composed of fifteen members appointed by the President and confirmed by the U.S. Senate.

National Institute on Disability and Rehabilitation Research
http://www.ed.gov/offices/OSERS/NIDRR/
The United State Department of Education's Office of Special Education and Rehabilitation Services (OSERS), through its National Institute on Disability and Rehabilitation Research (NIDRR), conducts comprehensive and coordinated programs of research and related activities to maximize the full inclusion, social integration, employment, and independent living of disabled individuals of all ages.

National Institutes of Health
http://www.nih.gov/welcome/nihnew.html
The National Institutes of Health (NIH) mission is to uncover new knowledge that will lead to better health for everyone. The goal of NIH research is to acquire new knowledge to help prevent, detect, diagnose, and treat disease and disability, from the rarest genetic disorder to the common cold.

Office of Disability, Aging and Long-Term Care Policy
http://aspe.os.dhhs.gov/daltcp/home.htm
The Office of Disability, Aging and Long-Term Care Policy (DALTCP) is a component of the Office of the Assistant Secretary for Planning and Evaluation, within the U.S. De-

partment of Health and Human Services. The DALTCP is responsible for the development, coordination, analysis, research, and evaluation of HHS policies and programs that support the independence, health, and long-term care of persons with disabilities—children, working age adults, and older persons. The Office is also responsible for policy coordination and research to promote the economic and social well-being of the elderly.

Social Security Administration

www.ssa.gov

Social Security Administration provides publication abstracts, annual statistical supplements, and copies of the *Social Security Bulletin*.

Quasi-Government Organizations

National Association of Area Agencies on Aging

www.ncoa.org/lcao.members/nasua.htm

Represents the interests of Area Agencies on Aging under the Older Americans Act.

National Association of State Units on Aging

www.ncoa.org/lcao.members/nasua.htm

Public interest organization formed to provide specialized information and support to State Units on Aging responsible for the implementation and oversight of the Older Americans Act.

Provider Interest Groups

National Association for Home Care

www.nahc.org

Represents home care providers and works to sponsor research, influence legislation, and promote higher standards of care.

General Resource

disABILITY Information and Resources

http://www.eskimo.com/~Jlubln/disabled.html

Jim Lubin's disABILITY Information and Resources provides an extensive listing of available links to disability internet sites

Disability Social History Project

www.disabilityhistory.org

The Disability History Project is a community history project that provides an opportunity for disabled people to reclaim their history and determine how they will define themselves and their struggles. People with disabilities have an exciting and rich history that should be shared with the world. Preserving and examining the history and culture of the oppression and struggle toward freedom of people with disabilities is important to an ongoing conceptualization of a group identity and the continuation of the struggle for civil rights. This site provides an extensive listing of links to other disability projects and sources of information.

Evan Kemp Associates Disability Resources

http://www.eka.com/

Provides links for people with disabilities and chronic health conditions to resources, products, and services that promote active, healthy independent living.

General Resource

Post, J. A. (1996). Internet resources on aging: Ten top web sites. *The Gerontologist*, 36(6), 728–733.

Appendix B: Suggested Tasks in Analyzing Case Studies of Gerontological Social Work

■■■■■■■■■■■■■

DIRECTIONS	QUESTIONS TO ASK YOURSELF
Identify the important elements of the case study	What are the important facts?
	What is happening to whom?
	Is all relevant information accessible?
Specify the major issues	Who is responsible for making decisions?
	What decisions need to be determined?
	What issues and consequences need to be considered?
Evaluate constraints and resources	Which forces support and oppose which actions?
	What are the major barriers?
	Which resources are available for plans/actions?
Determine objectives and goals to be achieved	Which results are possible?
	Which are desirable?
	Which objectives are most important to whom?
Evaluate the behavior of professionals and clients	Does the social worker exhibit leadership?
	Is the client involved in the decision making?
Assess the conflicts or professional dilemmas	In what do the conflicts or dilemmas consist?
	Can conflicting plans be reconciled?
	Can dilemmas be resolved?
Identify alternative plans or programs	Are there plans, ideas, or programs that have not been identified?
	Are the alternatives mutually exclusive?
Assess the consequences of possible decisions and actions	What outcomes are likely to result from the decisions made?
	What are the short and long term consequences for the individuals and the profession?
	What unintended consequences might evolve?
Review appropriate strategies	What are the most effective ways of achieving the goals sought?
	What recommended actions seem appropriate now? In six months?

Index